LUKE

THE NIV APPLICATION COMMENTARY

From biblical text . . . to contemporary life

LUKE

THE NIV APPLICATION COMMENTARY

From biblical text . . . to contemporary life

DARRELL L. BOCK

ZondervanPublishingHouse
Grand Rapids, Michigan

A Division of HarperCollinsPublishers

The NIV Application Commentary: Luke
Copyright © 1996 by Darrell L. Bock

Requests for information should be addressed to:

 ZondervanPublishingHouse
Grand Rapids, Michigan 49530

Library of Congress Cataloging-in-Publication Data

Bock, Darrell L.
    Luke / by Darrell L. Bock.
        p. cm—(NIV application commentary).
    Includes bibliographical references and index.
    ISBN: 0-310-49330-7 (hard cover)
    1. Bible. N.T. Luke—Commentaries. I. Title. II. Series.
  BS2595.3.B57 1996
  226.4'077-dc 20
                                               95-36893
                                                   CIP

This edition printed on acid-free paper and meets the American National Standards Institute Z39.48 standard.

Edited by Verlyn D. Verbrugge

Printed in the United States of America

---

96 97 98 99 00 01 02 /❖ DC/ 10 9 8 7 6 5 4 3 2 1

Contents

NIV Application Commentary
Series Introduction

THE NIV APPLICATION COMMENTARY SERIES is unique. Most commentaries help us make the journey from the twentieth century back to the first century. They enable us to cross the barriers of time, culture, language, and geography that separate us from the biblical world. Yet they only offer a one-way ticket to the past and assume that we can somehow make the return journey on our own. Once they have explained the *original meaning* of a book or passage, these commentaries give us little or no help in exploring its *contemporary significance*. The information they offer is valuable, but the job is only half done.

Recently, a few commentaries have included some contemporary application as *one* of their goals. Yet that application is often sketchy or moralistic, and some volumes sound more like printed sermons than commentaries.

The primary goal of The NIV Application Commentary Series is to help you with the difficult but vital task of bringing an ancient message into a modern context. The series not only focuses on application as a finished product but also helps you think through the *process* of moving from the original meaning of a passage to its contemporary significance. These are commentaries, not popular expositions. They are works of reference, not devotional literature.

The format of the series is designed to achieve the goals of the series. Each passage is treated in three sections: *Original Meaning*, *Bridging Contexts*, and *Contemporary Significance*.

THIS SECTION HELPS you understand the meaning of the biblical text in its first-century context. All of the elements of traditional exegesis—in concise form—are discussed here. These include the historical, literary, and cultural context of the passage. The authors discuss matters related to grammar and syntax, and the meaning of biblical words. They also seek to explore the main ideas of the passage and how the biblical author develops those ideas.

After reading this section, you will understand the problems, questions, and concerns of the *original audience* and how the biblical author addressed those issues. This understanding is foundational to any legitimate application of the text today.

Bridging Contexts

THIS SECTION BUILDS a bridge between the world of the Bible and the world of today, between the original context and the contemporary context, by focusing on both the timely and timeless aspects of the text.

God's Word is *timely*. The authors of Scripture spoke to specific situations, problems, and questions. Paul warned the Galatians about the consequences of circumcision and the dangers of trying to be justified by law (Gal. 5:2–5). The author of Hebrews tried to convince his readers that Christ is superior to Moses, the Aaronic priests, and the Old Testament sacrifices. John urged his readers to "test the spirits" of those who taught a form of incipient Gnosticism (1 John 4:1–6). In each of these cases, the timely nature of Scripture enables us to hear God's Word in situations that were *concrete* rather than abstract.

Yet the timely nature of Scripture also creates problems. Our situations, difficulties, and questions are not always directly related to those faced by the people in the Bible. Therefore, God's word to them does not always seem relevant to us. For example, when was the last time someone urged you to be circumcised, claiming that it was a necessary part of justification? How many people today care whether Christ is superior to the Aaronic priests? And how can a "test" designed to expose incipient Gnosticism be of any value in a modern culture?

Fortunately, Scripture is not only timely but *timeless*. Just as God spoke to the original audience, so he still speaks to us through the pages of Scripture. Because we share a common humanity with the people of the Bible, we discover a *universal dimension* in the problems they faced and the solutions God gave them. The timeless nature of Scripture enables it to speak with power in every time and in every culture.

Those who fail to recognize that Scripture is both timely and timeless run into a host of problems. For example, those who are intimidated by timely books such as Hebrews or Galatians might avoid reading them because they seem meaningless today. At the other extreme, those who are convinced of the timeless nature of Scripture, but who fail to discern its timely element, may "wax eloquent" about the Melchizedekian priesthood to a sleeping congregation.

The purpose of this section, therefore, is to help you discern what is timeless in the timely pages of the New Testament—and what is not. For example, if Paul's primary concern is not circumcision (as he tells us in Gal. 5:6), what *is* he concerned about? If discussions about the Aaronic priesthood or Melchizedek seem irrelevant today, what is of abiding value in these passages? If people try to "test the spirits" today with a test designed for a specific first-century heresy, what other biblical test might be more appropriate?

Yet this section does not merely uncover that which is timeless in a passage but also helps you to see *how* it is uncovered. The author of the commentary seeks to take what is implicit in the text and make it explicit, to take a process that normally is intuitive and explain it in a logical, orderly fashion. How do we know that circumcision is not Paul's primary concern? What clues in the text or its context help us realize that Paul's real concern is at a deeper level?

Of course, those passages in which the historical distance between us and the original readers is greatest require a longer treatment. Conversely, those passages in which the historical distance is smaller or seemingly nonexistent require less attention.

One final clarification. Because this section prepares the way for discussing the contemporary significance of the passage, there is not always a sharp distinction or a clear break between this section and the one that follows. Yet when both sections are read together, you should have a strong sense of moving from the world of the Bible to the world of today.

THIS SECTION ALLOWS the biblical message to speak with as much power today as it did when it was first written. How can you apply what you learned about Jerusalem, Ephesus, or Corinth to our present-day needs in Chicago, Los Angeles, or London? How can you take a message originally spoken in Greek and Aramaic and communicate it clearly in our own language? How can you take the eternal truths originally spoken in a different time and culture and apply them to the similar-yet-different needs of our culture?

In order to achieve these goals, this section gives you help in several key areas.

First, it helps you identify contemporary situations, problems, or questions that are truly comparable to those faced by the original audience. Because contemporary situations are seldom identical to those faced in the first century, you must seek situations that are analogous if your applications are to be relevant.

Second, this section explores a variety of contexts in which the passage might be applied today. You will look at personal applications, but you will also be encouraged to think beyond private concerns to the society and culture at large.

Third, this section will alert you to any problems or difficulties you might encounter in seeking to apply the passage. And if there are several legitimate ways to apply a passage (areas in which Christians disagree), the author will bring these to your attention and help you think through the issues involved.

In seeking to achieve these goals, the contributors to this series attempt to avoid two extremes. They avoid making such specific applications that the commentary might quickly become dated. They also avoid discussing the significance of the passage in such a general way that it fails to engage contemporary life and culture.

Above all, contributors to this series have made a diligent effort not to sound moralistic or preachy. The NIV Application Commentary Series does not seek to provide ready-made sermon materials but rather tools, ideas, and insights that will help you communicate God's Word with power. If we help you to achieve that goal, then we have fulfilled the purpose for this series.

—The Editors

General Editor's Preface

WHAT DOES THE GOSPEL OF LUKE have to teach us today? Plenty.

Read the newspaper almost any day of the week, and you cannot help get the impression that our world suffers from a new intellectual virus: the problem of the many and the one. Many races, one humanity. Many species, one creation. Many nations, one world. Many rights, one truth. We can see, as plain as the nose on our face, the diversity in the world. At the same time, however, we know that diversity can too quickly turn to divisiveness and death if some reason to be unified is not found.

This problem virus, the many and the one, is by no means new. But the form in which it is attacking us seems resistant to most of the antidotes offered to date. One antidote, the move toward one world government, seems least likely to solve the problem. With the breakup of formerly huge governments such as the USSR and Yugoslavia, we seem bent on more nations, not fewer. Racial and ethnic groups seem more eager to fight for their identity (witness Cambodia and Rwanda) than to seek common ground. Can anything stop this out-of-control virus of peace-destroying tribalism?

The gospel truth that Luke describes has the best chance. How? Let me explain. As Darrell Bock shows us in this volume, Luke was concerned to show us that the whole world ran according to a single plan laid out by God. Thus, the first sections about Jesus as a baby and young child illustrate how God was already at work in Jesus' life; the stories of John the Baptist and Jesus' baptism and temptation define a call to ministry that was worked out in precise detail; Jesus' early ministry around the lake called Galilee reveal a minister of extraordinary power and authority; in his final journey to Jerusalem, Jesus met all kinds of resistance and showed us how people following God's plan are able to persevere; and the stories of Jesus' final days demonstrate with clarity how Jesus practiced a spiritual leadership that was qualitatively different from the other leaders of the day—political, economic, and religious. Luke shows us that this extraordinary life was not a happenstance coming together of random factors; it was a life breathed by God.

A life breathed by God is one that sets the pattern for everyone. It is precisely this life, the life of Jesus Christ, our Lord and Savior, that pulls the fragmented and divisive elements of the world together. Luke takes great pains to explain how this God-breathed life made the old distinction between Jew and Gentile moot. It is the life of Jesus Christ that pulls together competing visions of life and work.

And it is precisely this truth that forms the central application of Luke's Gospel for our world today. Only God, through the incarnation of Jesus Christ, can pull a fractious world together. The divisions of our day seem much more complicated than the biblical illustration of Jew and Gentile. But the principle is the same: God unites. God unites not by denying us our distinctiveness—our race, our nationality, our culture. God, after all, made us who and what we are. No, God unites by standing for something above and beyond anything we know, thus providing us with a reason to pull together even as we enjoy our unique, God-created identities.

Darrell Bock has done us a great service by bringing a lifetime of scholarly work on what Luke meant when it was written, and then by answering the question over and over again in the subsequent discussions: What does Luke mean for us today? The answer is, in one word, plenty. We can live together in peace only if we focus beyond ourselves to our sovereign God and the Son sent to save us.

—Terry Muck

Author's Preface

MY RELATIONSHIP TO THE GOSPEL OF LUKE dates back to my days as a doctoral student in Aberdeen, Scotland. Whether I have lived on the edge of the Scottish highlands, in the plains of Texas, or beside the Schwabian mountains in Southwest Germany, this Gospel has been on my heart and mind. The present work represents over fifteen years of study and is my third commentary on this Gospel.

Someone may ask, "Why write a third commentary on the same book?" This is a good question, and I continually asked myself that same question while writing this work. The answer, in the end, is simple: In this commentary I get to apply the Gospel and concentrate on its message for today. Let me explain.

My two-volume commentary published by Baker Book House is a full technical, exegetical discussion of Luke. If someone wishes to know the ins and outs of the many scholarly views about Luke, that is where to go. I had the space there to consider how Luke is like and unlike his fellow Evangelists in his presentation of Jesus, as well as the many historical issues and cultural background questions that impact the understanding of this Gospel. There also I traced which features of that message spoke to our era. This work was designed for scholars, pastors, seminarians, and others who wanted to get into the details of the Greek text and the immense discussion that surrounds it.

My commentary for InterVarsity Press went the next step. There I was asked to build on the earlier work and explain the text, but also to present a more homiletical feel and make clear how Luke relates to the present. In that book I tried to concentrate on application as well as exegesis. This was a work for pastors and laypeople that still sought to trace and explain the message but present it with relevance for today.

The present work is different still. I have been asked to cover the textual message with adequate thoroughness, but more briefly than I did for Baker and with a different focus than for InterVarsity. Half the total commentary discusses not only application for today, but also how one gets there from the message of the past. I have tried to meet that equal division of labor as much as I could. I have given attention to the rationale for application, just as most commentaries explain and defend each step in their interpretation. It was a fresh challenge I accepted as a natural final step to take with this Gospel.

Author's Preface

Any pastor or seminarian knows how the full process of interpretation taxes a whole range of skills and raises a set of distinct questions, whether one is interpreting, preaching, or simply applying the text. The present volume assumes much work in the previous two commentaries and attempts to complete the cycle. It could not have been written without the research that went into the earlier studies, but it also is by no means a mere re-presentation of them. I leave my readers to judge its success. My hope and prayer is that the study of this Gospel will lead to a closer walk with God and a better understanding of the one who fulfills God's promises.

My thanks go to Zondervan Publishing House and to Stan Gundry, Jack Kuhatschek, Verlyn Verbrugge, and Terry Muck for their kind invitation to share in their series, especially to Jack and Terry for their helpful comments on the initial draft of the commentary. Their labor has made the task enjoyable, and their counsel has been full of wisdom. I also profited greatly from suggestions made by Marianne Meye Thompson and Klyne Snodgrass. They helped me say things more precisely and spurred my thinking in several application areas. Ken MacGillivray gave a careful proofreading of a draft of this commentary.

I dedicate this volume to my family, who always asked if I would ever get finished writing on Luke! I am especially grateful to my children, Elisa, Lara, and Stephen, who gave of their time so their father could work—yes, I can play a little more basketball now. To my brother, John, and my two sisters, Darcy and Joady, I offer appreciation for enduring life with a hyperactive brother. To my in-laws, Joe and Ann Painter, I express gratitude for allowing me the joy of sharing life with their wonderful daughter, Sally, and being patient as I grew up and took on the responsibility of helping to raise some of their precious grandchildren. And finally I dedicate this work to the memory of my deceased parents, whom God saw fit to take early in my life, but who left me a legacy of love that helped me appreciate what God's love could be like.

—Darrell L. Bock
October 31, 1994

Abbreviations

AB	Anchor Bible
ACNT	Augsburg Commentary on the New Testament
AnBib	Analecta biblica
BAGD	Bauer, Arndt, Gingrich, and Danker, *A Greek-English Lexicon of the New Testament and Other Early Christian Literature*
BAR	*Biblical Archaeology Review*
BBB	Bonner biblische Beiträge
BBR	*Bulletin for Biblical Research*
BETL	Bibliotheca ephemeridum theologicarum lovaniensium
BibSac	*Bibliotheca Sacra*
BJRL	*Bulletin of the John Rylands University Library*
BNTC	Black's New Testament Commentaries
CBQ	*Catholic Biblical Quarterly*
CNTC	Cambridge New Testament Commentaries
CT	*Christianity Today*
EBC	*Expositor's Bible Commentary*
EKK	Evangelisch-katholischer Kommentar
ExpTim	*Expository Times*
FB	Forschung zur Bibel
HNT	Handbuch zum Neuen Testament
HTKNT	Herders theologischer Kommentar zum Neuen Testament
ICC	International Critical Commentary
JBL	*Journal of Biblical Literature*
JRS	*Journal of Religious Studies*
JSNT	*Journal for the Study of the New Testament*
JSNTMS	Journal for the Study of the New Testament—Monograph Series
JSNTSS	Journal for the Study of the New Testament—Supplement Series
JTS	*Journal for Theological Studies*
LCC	Library of Christian Classics
NAB	New American Bible
NASB	New American Standard Bible
NCB	New Century Bible
NIBC	New International Biblical Commentary

Abbreviations

NICNT	New International Commentary on the New Testament
NIDNTT	*New International Dictionary of New Testament Theology*
NIGTC	New International Greek Testament Commentary
NIV	New International Version
NovT	*Novum Testamentum*
NovTSup	Novum Testamentum Supplement Series
NTS	*New Testament Studies*
NTD	Das Neue Testament Deutsch
PTMS	Princeton Theological Monograph Series
PTS	Paderborner theologischen Studien
RNT	Regensburger Neues Testament
SBLDS	Society of Biblical Literature Dissertation Series
SBLMS	Society of Biblical Literature Monograph Series
SNT	Studien zum Neuen Testament
SNTIW	Studies of the New Testament and Its World
SNTSMS	Society for New Testament Studies Monograph Series
SNTU	Studien zum Neuen Testament und seiner Umwelt
TDNT	*Theological Dictionary of the New Testament*
THKNT	Theologischer Handkommentar zum Neuen Testament
TPINTC	Trinity Press International New Testament Commentaries
TS	*Theological Studies*
WBC	Word Biblical Commentary
WUNT	Wissenschaftliche Untersuchungen zum Neuen Testament
ZNW	*Zeitschrift für die neutestamentliche Wissenschaft*

Introduction to Luke

Overview: Why Read Luke?

MOST PEOPLE DO not realize that Luke is the longest Gospel—not in chapters, but in verses. In fact, Luke as an author is the largest contributor to the New Testament, if one counts verses (Luke, 2157 verses [Luke + Acts]; Paul, 2032 verses; John, 1416 verses; [1]Matthew, 1071 verses; Mark, 678 verses). The Gospel of Luke also is unique in that the story of Jesus has a sequel in the account of Acts. Thus, the work of Jesus and the church are related together through the eyes of the same human author. This means that the introductory concerns of the two volumes overlap; that is, evidence from Acts is also evidence about Luke.

Luke-Acts is about God's plan. The Gospel explains who Jesus was, what he did, why he came, and how he prepared the disciples for the role they would have in that plan. Basic questions are a part of the Gospel's story or are set up by the Gospel's story. A major concern in Acts, for example, is the relationship of Jews to Gentiles. In this context, the Gospel of Luke probes such issues as these: How did an originally Jewish movement become the basis for an offer of salvation to all? Do Gentiles really belong? If Jesus was originally the Messiah for Israel, how was it he met so much opposition that they crucified him? Even more, how could a crucified Messiah become the basis for hope for all humanity? How could an absent, slain figure be the center of God's hope? In sum, why should anyone respond to Jesus as the center of God's plan and what is it he calls us to do?

This commentary will show how virtually every unit in Luke's Gospel challenges us to respond to Jesus. Starting with categories of Jewish hope like Messiah, it reveals who Jesus is. But by allowing Jesus' ministry to reveal who he is, we come to see that he is more than a messianic figure. Luke reveals this Jesus to us gradually, a progression we tend to miss since we are nearly two thousand years on the other side of these events and are already thoroughly familiar with his message from start to finish.

Why did Jesus come? Luke tells us it was not only to die for our sin, but also to form a people of God who, renewed by his Spirit, are able to serve

---

1. The numbers for John include Revelation and the Johannine letters. These numbers may vary slightly, depending on how one assesses certain text critical problems.

him in righteousness and holiness all of their days (Luke 1:73–75). He came to declare the initial realization of God's promise, a promise made "in the Law of Moses, the Prophets and the Psalms" (Luke 24:44).

What did Jesus do? Luke explains how he revealed that the way to God is through the sinner's recognition that one must turn to God for help. The author also makes clear that the way of God is through Jesus. To show his power, Jesus preached the kingdom of God and the time of fulfillment (Luke 4:16–30; 11:14–23). He overcame nature, exorcised demons, healed from disease, and raised one from death to show he could overcome every type of enemy that opposes humanity (8:22–56). All the while he prepared his disciples for the journey of salvation by showing them that glory was reached only after suffering (9:21–27).

What does Jesus want people to do? He calls sinners to repent (Luke 5:31–32), disciples to take up their cross daily as they follow him (9:23), and witnesses to take the message of repentance for the forgiveness of sins to all the nations (24:43–49). He promises the Spirit for the task, since many will reject their message. Still, they are called to love their enemies and pray for them (6:27–35).

At the center of every step of activity in God's plan stands Jesus. He is the one who is to be trusted with revealing God's way. He is the one who calls disciples. He is the one who sends the Spirit. He is the one who brings God's forgiveness (Luke 5:12–26; 7:36–50). The gospel is open to all, because Jesus is Lord of all. When Luke states that he wishes to reassure Theophilus (1:4), it is reassurance that Jesus is the source of divine blessing and that Theophilus has every right to embrace him as the bearer of God's grace and promise.

This Gospel also explains how Jesus came to be rejected by the Jewish leadership. It tells how the message of the gospel came to include all nations in its promise (Acts fills out this theme more completely). This Gospel tells the kind of people Jesus wants his followers to be and what kind of community he wants them to possess. It describes the role of many key women in that community, the ethical call of Jesus, the importance of prayer, the attitude of joy in the midst of rejection by the world, and the importance and prominence of the Spirit. At the center of everything is the activity of a gracious God who keeps his promises, vindicates his people, and accomplishes his word. Believers love this Gospel because it not only gives them Jesus' teaching, especially in the form of parables, but it also reveals his involvement with people—especially sinners, the poor, and the rejected of society. The God of compassion shows himself fully in this Gospel. The God of the Bible shows himself the God of the world.

We are accustomed to highlighting the diversity of people in our world. Ours is a multicultural and multidimensional world in the way it sees things. The Gospel of Luke explains how God can take those many ethnic backgrounds and dimensions and mold them into a new special community. In Jesus, though we have different roots, we can come to oneness. The more we closely examine first-century people, the more we see that they are just like us. Their problems and attitudes concerning sin, money, anxiety, hope, community, rejection, vengeance, pride, humility, and God's direction mirror questions we face. Luke gives insight into how Jesus addressed such topics, and he makes clear how we can come to know God.

This latter issue puts the other topics into perspective and explains why we should listen carefully to Luke. The plan of God is often a great theological abstraction until we can see just how we fit into it. Luke's goal is to make our place in that plan clear. He invites us to see how we can have a relationship with God that is a journey of faith and a tour through life as it was meant to be lived.

The Composition of Luke's Gospel[2]

Author

NEITHER LUKE NOR Acts gives the name of its author. We must therefore examine evidence in these books and church tradition to determine authorship. Luke-Acts indicates two key facts about its author. (1) He was not an eyewitness to most of the events described, especially those in the Gospel (Luke 1:1–4). Rather, his sources were previous works that summarized the life of Jesus. (2) The author was a companion of Paul, according to the "we sections" of Acts (Acts 16:10–17; 20: 5–15; 21:1–18; 27:1–28:16). This second fact narrows the possibilities of authorship, though it also is disputed.

Some have argued that the "we sections" are either a literary device or the itinerary notes that the author simply took over without change, not the experiences of the author of Luke-Acts himself.[3] Associated with this

---

2. In this introduction, we confine ourselves to the basic features that introduce the historical setting of the third Gospel. For summaries of this work's structure and biblical theology, see D. L. Bock, "Luke, Gospel of," in *Dictionary of Jesus and the Gospels*, ed. by J. B. Green, S. McKnight, and I. H. Marshall (Downers Grove, Ill.: InterVarsity, 1992), 495–510. For a more complete treatment of the book's theology, see my "A Theology of Luke-Acts," in *A Biblical Theology of the New Testament*, ed. by R. Zuck and D. Bock (Chicago: Moody, 1994), 87–166.

3. For this position, see E. Haenchen, *The Acts of the Apostles: A Commentary* (Oxford: Basil Blackwell, 1971), 85.

discussion is the debate over whether the Paul of the New Testament letters that bear his name is really like the Paul of Luke. Some argue the writer of Acts was not a companion of Paul, since there appears to be so much difference in Luke's portrait of Paul and Paul's own view of himself.[4] If the author did not know Paul, then either he cannot be the person traditionally associated with the book, Luke, or Luke himself was not an associate of Paul.

Fitzmyer has fittingly responded to the claims about the "we sections" as a literary device by noting how arbitrarily they appear in the account. If they really were creative literary devices, why did they appear so sparsely and why are they not located in more texts? The "we sections" are more than mere inserts of notes from someone else, and their haphazard use reflects authenticity. On the matter of Paul, we must reckon with the reality of how one's self-assessment and an assessment by another person often differ. In addition, the fact that the writer of the "we sections" worked with Paul on some occasions does not mean he was a constant companion of Paul. Furthermore, on the theological portrait of Paul in Luke versus that of Paul himself, the case can be made that the two are compatible.[5] None of these considerations, of course, proves the author is Luke. But what it shows is that in Luke-Acts, the evidence points to at least a second-generation Christian who knew and occasionally worked with Paul.

The possibilities arising from the evidence within Luke-Acts does limit the possible candidates, though if one were to construct a possible list of traveling companions to Paul on the basis of his letters, it would be a long one: Mark, Aristarchus, Demas, Timothy, Titus, Silas, Epaphras, Luke, and Barnabas. It is significant that despite this plethora of such candidates, early church tradition was unanimous in identifying the author as Luke. By A.D. 200, this identification was a given. Justin Martyr (c. A.D. 160) in *Dialogues* 103.19 speaks of a memoir of Jesus written by a follower of Paul. The Muratorian Canon, written a decade or two later, names Luke the doctor. Around the same time, Irenaeus ties the Gospel to Luke and notes the "we sections." Tertullian and Eusebius also tie this book to an author with Pauline connections and note Luke's role. Given the options available, the tie to Luke is impressive evidence of the memory of the church about the third Gospel's author.

What we know about Luke suggests that he was not Jewish, though it is possible that he was a Semite, perhaps a Syrian from Antioch rather than a Greek (Col. 4:10–11). His knowledge of the Old Testament and his discus-

---

4. This case is made most forcefully by P. Vielhauer, "On the 'Paulinism' of Acts," in *Studies in Luke-Acts*, ed. by L. E. Keck and J. L. Martyn (London: S.P.C.K., 1966), 33–50.

5. F. F. Bruce, "Is the Paul of Acts the Real Paul?" *BJRL* 58 (1975/76): 282–305.

sion of God-fearers may suggest he had some previous connection to Judaism and may even have been a God-fearer. The connection of Luke to medicine comes from Colossians 4:14.

Genre

A GOSPEL IS a unique genre in the New Testament. It is the story of both a person and his ministry, though it is different from a biography in that it does not seek to tell us about a life from start to finish. Luke places great stock in the roots of the tradition he works with to present his account. Luke 1:1–4 details how the roots of the Jesus accounts rest in eyewitness testimony. Yet it would be a mistake to say Luke was a scissors-and-paste editor who just put these traditions together. A comparison of this Gospel with the other two Synoptics shows that the author arranged his presentation, sometimes on the basis of themes and sometimes through the influence of additional sources.[6] Luke also highlights how Jesus came to be understood as the risen, exalted Lord and how the Jewish rejection of Jesus took place. He outlines Jesus' teaching in a way the other Gospels do not, since several of the parables are unique to him. Jesus' concern for discipleship and one's neighbor, especially the rejected of society, stand out in his account. A gospel is both theology and history. It is written not only to instruct but also to exhort. The combination makes Luke a historian, theologian, and pastor.

Date

MANY DATE THIS book after A.D. 70, usually in the mid-eighties, based on the fact that the texts on the judgment of the nation are so specific about Jerusalem's destruction (Luke 19:41–44; 21:20–24). But the author's descriptions of this destruction simply argue that God will judge the nation for covenant unfaithfulness, along the same lines as the judgment Assyria and Babylon brought to the nation of Israel.[7] Given that prophetic background, there is no need to posit a writing after the fact.

A more likely date is some time in the sixties. The last event in Acts is dated A.D. 62; since Luke appears to be closely related to Acts, the release of the two volumes would have been fairly close to each other. This date is suggested because Paul's death is not noted in Acts, and time must be allowed for the other sources, which included either Mark or Matthew, to circulate.

---

6. My two volumes on Luke, *Luke 1:1–9:50* and *Luke 9:51–24:53* (Grand Rapids: Baker, 1994 and forthcoming) make such detailed comparisons a verse at a time and a passage at a time. Given the detail there, I am not repeating such comparisons in the current commentary.

7. C. H. Dodd, "The Fall of Jerusalem and the Abomination of Desolation," *JRS* 37 (1947): 47–54.

Audience

DISCUSSION ABOUT LUKE'S audience runs the gamut. Is he writing for a Jewish audience, given his full attention to their rejection? Is he writing for Gentiles, given the prominence of that mission in Acts? Is it a combination of the two? Part of the problem in deciding the audience is that the destination of this Gospel is not clearly known. Theophilus, to whom the Gospel is addressed in Luke 1:1–4, seems to be a socially prominent figure, but we do not know where he lived, nor are we certain of his nationality. The recipient has had some exposure to the faith, and the fact that he needs reassurance means he is likely a believer. It also seems clear from the way Luke wrote that he also knew Theophilus would not be his only reader—note the general character of many of the Gospel's exhortations. To sort out the question of whether the Gospel had a Jewish or Gentile audience in view, we must discuss the purpose of Luke's two volumes as a whole and how the Gospel fits into this purpose.

Purpose

SCHOLARS HAVE OFFERED numerous suggestions for the purpose of Luke-Acts.[8] There are elements of truth in many of these suggestions, but only a few are comprehensive enough to be possible expressions of Luke's fundamental goals. For example, Conzelmann argues that Luke was attempting to explain why Jesus has not returned yet, but little of this work discusses the Second Coming. The author spends far more time discussing the mission of the new group Jesus formed.

Several have suggested that the work is a "defense brief" of sorts, either for Christianity or for Paul as he was preparing to face his Roman date in court. The major problem with this thesis is that over three-quarters of the two volumes do not relate directly to a defense. What official would wade through some forty chapters before getting to the real point of the story? A variation of this view has Paul being defended before the Christian community. There is little doubt that a major theme of Acts is an explanation of how the gospel went out to Gentiles, with Paul being a representative of that mission. Yet this purpose does not clearly explain the function of the Gospel of Luke.

Still others have argued that Luke wants to combat Gnosticism, a major Greek philosophical movement that emerged in full force well after the time of Jesus. This approach seeks a Hellenistic setting for the Gospel. Other

---

8. For a more complete discussion as it relates to Luke, see the discussion on introduction in *Luke 1:1–9:50*.

than the problem of late date for the emergence of this movement, only portions of the resurrection account, where Jesus is portrayed as having a bodily resurrection, offer clear challenges to that philosophical approach.

Several scholars have argued a broad purpose of evangelism or a presentation of the theme of salvation. Salvation is certainly a major concern, but that theme can be expressed so broadly that it can serve as the purpose for a number of New Testament books. Efforts to specify the theme of evangelism put us a little closer to the center of Luke's effort. For example, Luke spends much time explaining how Jesus' rejection by the Jewish leadership is within God's plan. In addition, he probes how the nation of the covenant promise has been so negative toward her Messiah. This means that a theodicy in defense of God's faithfulness may well be an important part of the volumes, including a careful presentation of the nature of God's plan. When one considers Acts, it is also clear that the emerging significance of the Gentile mission and the justification for how it took place, including the fact that Gentiles did not have to become Jews to be Christians, is another major theme.

When one considers Luke alone, it is the person of Jesus and the nature of God's work through him to deliver humanity that takes center stage. Theophilus is probably a believer, who as a Gentile, a non-Jewish Semite, or a God-fearer may well be wondering what he is doing in an originally Jewish movement that has faced so much rejection from the Jews. Does he really belong, and is salvation really found in that movement? Is this what God is about? Luke reassures Theophilus that Jesus does stand at the center of God's redemptive plan by explaining how that rejection took place. He explains that the community Jesus formed must be prepared to walk a similar path.

Luke's work also was intended to benefit any Jewish Christians who might have lingering questions about Gentile involvement and the path this was taking. Jesus' suffering and rejection was not a surprise; they were designed by God. The reaction to the new community is also not a surprise. The road to vindication assumes the sort of suffering Jesus experienced. In the meantime, the disciples must witness to this redemption and respond to their rejection in love. That is why so many of the parables and so much of Jesus' teaching deals with accepting or rejecting Jesus, with the nation's role in that decision, and with the call to persevere and live in an ethically honorable manner as a representative of Jesus. Luke is a profoundly practical Gospel. His message is not only to be embraced; it is to be reflected in how we relate to others. Luke is also known as the writer who tells us much about the Holy Spirit, but this emphasis is less dominant in Luke than in Acts. Nonetheless, Jesus' ministry not only fits within God's plan, it is empowered by God's enabling

Spirit (Luke 4:16–18). The church's ministry has a similar dynamic (Luke 24:43–49; Acts 1:8).

The Structure of Luke's Gospel

MY OUTLINE OF Luke's Gospel divides it into five basic sections. Elsewhere I have given a detailed defense for these major divisions.[9] Since this commentary focuses on application and teaching, I will combine some subdivisions previously made as the units of tradition in the Gospel, in order to create larger preaching units. I have opted to combine as few texts as possible, so that Luke's basic structure and order of themes still remains evident. In this section of this introduction, I will survey the book and suggest where these themes might lead in terms of application.

The *infancy material* (1:1–2:52) is not just infancy material; it extends into Jesus' preteen years. Nonetheless, it shows the presence of divine activity from the start. Luke indicates how Jesus is superior to his forerunner, John the Baptist. He also reveals how God has revisited his people in the activities associated with the forerunner and the one who is to follow him (1:68–79). Two other crucial themes dominate: (1) God has a plan that he is executing through Jesus, and (2) God keeps his promises; thus, believers must continue to trust his word. Both Zechariah and Mary teach us about trust in God's promise. Those who do trust experience his grace and can rest in the service they give to their God.

The second unit of the Gospel (3:1–4:13) shows *John's call to prepare a people for Jesus and Jesus' qualifications to be the Promised One.* John's ministry reveals the nature of repentance in preparation for Jesus' ministry. Repentance involves turning to God by recognizing our sins and serving others. But John's main goal is to point to the One who follows. Jesus' gift will not be a representative rite, but a bestowal of the Spirit, who purges between those who are God's and those who are not. The Messiah will be known as the one who brings God's Spirit.

The *Galilean ministry section* (4:14–9:50) highlights the activity and power of Jesus. Here declaration of the fulfillment of God's promise, teaching, and miraculous work combine to ask the question, "Who is Jesus?" The answer comes in Peter's confession of Jesus as the Anointed One of God. Whether Jesus' power is exerted over nature, demons, disease, or death, he is the Promised Messiah. As such, the disciples must understand that he has also

---

9. See *Luke 1:1–9:50* and *Luke 9:51–24:53*, where literary issues of the division of the Gospel are given full treatment at the beginning of each division.

been called to suffer. They must likewise understand that there is no glory without suffering. One cannot follow Jesus without realizing that the way to glory comes through rejection. As disciples themselves participate in the world, which will reject them, they are called to love their enemies and pray for them and to serve others.

This section also explains how Jewish opposition to Jesus arises. His claims and his actions, which point to the great authority he possesses, offend many Jews theologically. For example, Jesus claims to be able to forgive sin, an act they view as blasphemous. Their reactions to Jesus' claims and to his willingness to associate with sinners explain why some challenge him. After all, one who claims to forgive sins can do so only with divine authority. Jesus' opponents can tolerate his prophetic actions and his claim to be the Promised Ruler of God who delivers his people, but when he claims prerogatives over spiritual judgment, that is going too far. Yet this is precisely this question Luke wishes to place on the table. Everything Jesus does is designed to highlight this unique point.

The *Jerusalem journey section* (9:51–19:44) is the major unit in the gospel that treats discipleship. It has two major concerns. (1) Jesus needs to train the disciples for life after he has departed. This concern becomes evident when one sees the amount of unique teaching, especially the parabolic teaching, that Luke uses in this section. (2) Luke also explains how opposition to Jesus heightens, resulting in the Jewish leadership's call for his death. In this context, Jesus also calls his disciples to persevere and remain faithful to him. He shows that Israel as a nation is facing judgment for missing the time of God's visitation. To miss God's presence is a dangerous thing.

The final section (19:45–24:53) details *Jesus' last days in Jerusalem—his destined march to trial, his death, and his resurrection.* A series of controversies in Jerusalem indicates just how different Jesus is from the official leadership. The discourse about the end times compares the coming destruction of the temple with return of the Son of Man. In his death, God's plan reveals how Jesus has suffered as an innocent person, just as he predicted earlier in his ministry—God's word is coming to fulfillment. Jesus' resurrection catches the disciples by surprise. It means that the mission of Jesus' followers will continue. The next stage in God's plan is to proclaim the realization of God's promise in the Messiah, which will be the task of faithful disciples—something the Gospel hopes to create.

Luke wrote his Gospel to reassure Theophilus of the truth of the things in which he has been instructed (1:1–4). He can be confident that Jesus is the Promised One of God, who brings forgiveness of sins and represents the inauguration of the completion of God's plan. He can also be sure that the suffering the disciples currently experience in the world is no surprise to God, since they are marching in the footsteps of the Savior. Jesus himself resides at God's side, sharing in divine authority; he is the source of all the benefits of salvation God graciously bestows on his children. Theophilus can know that the Spirit will be a source of comfort to him in the midst of his daily walk. He can look forward expectantly to the return of Jesus, when God moves decisively to vindicate his people. God will keep his promises. As Luke 7:28 teaches, the one who is the least in God's kingdom is greater than the greatest prophet of the old era. In effect, Luke says to Theophilus and to all of us, "Be reassured. If you know Jesus, you are right where you should be." In an age such as ours where people struggle for identity and worth, what better message can there be than to know that you know God and share in his promise. The treasure of Luke's Gospel comes in the nuggets of reassurance he has left to the church.

Contemporary Significance

MUCH OF THE ATTENTION in this study of Luke will move from the first-century setting of Luke to modern application of its message. Luke suits such a goal. The author's combination of action and teaching shows us a great deal about God, his plan, and the character of Jesus. To ponder this topic is of great significance, since the better we know God and the Savior, the better we can understand our calling and his purposes in our lives. Furthermore, we will be in a better position to deepen our walk of faith, since we will appreciate the character of God and his expectations of us.

Jesus' teachings about sin and forgiveness impact both our understanding of our humanity and our worth and role in creation. Luke notes that God's people do not always escape pain and are not always accepted in this life. How does one live in a world where walking with God may mean facing misunderstanding, if not outright hostility, from others? Yet the discipleship to which Jesus calls us as his followers also receives the provision of enablement through God's Spirit, who empowers us to walk in a way that is pleasing to him. Through him, we can fulfill all that God asks us to be.

In terms of its worldview, its theology, and its practical presentation of principles, this Gospel explains how we can serve God better. That is why the author examines such topics as money, anxiety, persecution, the manner in which races or genders relate to each other, prayer, joy, and praise. Such topics are just as vital today as they were when Luke wrote.

Luke also analyzes various types of people, such as those who reject God's way, those who hesitate to respond, and those who respond with varying degrees of sensitivity. The characters in this Gospel tell us much about how people respond to Jesus, as well as what values and priorities can prevent people from responding to him. These topics are rich in their potential for reflection about application.

This does not mean that application of Luke is always a straight-line journey from the past to the present. The situation of the church today is different from when Luke wrote. In his day, the church was "the new guy" on the religious block. It was a young and growing movement, seeking to establish itself. Now the church has its own history and tradition, and the movement is internationalized today in a way that could only have been a dream when Luke wrote. The inclusion of Gentiles, a fact so controversial in the early days, is now a given, while the role of Israel in the promise of God, a question central to the earlier discussion, is hardly even thought about today. Luke spends much time on this question; he points out how God is committed to giving everyone access to his promise. The church has also come to span all classes in a way that was impossible for a distinctly minority movement. At the same time, the church today has become institutionalized, to the point where the possibility of exercising power (and of abusing it) exists in ways the earliest community never faced. The call to service is often harder to exercise when power is so readily available. All these factors make application more complex.

Furthermore, some cultures, rightly or wrongly, think of themselves as Judeo-Christian in roots. This impacts how people understand Christianity, for many see themselves as born into a Christian culture or as knowing what Christianity is from the culture. Such a perspective colors how believers perceive the faith today. This possibility also impacts application.

On the other hand, we should also consider greater religious pluralism today, given the "global village" that communication makes possible. For many, the issue of a single message from God is problematic, not because one must choose between the true and the false (as most people used to believe), but because to many the only thing that matters is the sincere pursuit of God. The exclusive claims of Jesus as the unique Son of God and Savior and of God's revelation as located in Christ alone fly in the face of a worldview that sees all attempts to reach God as legitimate. Jesus challenges this cultural expectation.

What these various factors mean is that Luke is a stimulating oasis for spiritual reflection about who I am and what God wants me to do. When one adds to that the natural scriptural emphasis of belonging to a community of people who have experienced God's grace, who live in a world that does not easily embrace the things of God, and who share a unity in the community he formed to minister to that world, the issues of healthy relationships with God, with one another, and with those who are not a part of the community also come to the fore. Believers are called to live a life that looks to God, because he has poured his grace out on those who have received forgiveness and life in Jesus. Luke tells the story of how Jesus revealed that grace, died to provide it, rose to bestow it, and will return to establish its presence over all the creation. The church must show what such grace looks like in ministry, in relationships, and most of all, in a close walk with God. That new way of knowing God is the light of the gospel and the call of the church. That is what Luke's story is about. That is why reading and reflecting on this story changes lives and one's view of the definition of a life lived before God.

Outline to the Gospel of Luke

I. The Infancy Narrative (1:1–2:52)
  A. Preface: A Reassuring History (1:1–4)
  B. Announcing John the Baptist, the One Who Goes Before (1:5–25)
  C. The Announcement of the Birth of Jesus (1:26–38)
  D. Mary's Visit of Elizabeth (1:39–56)
  E. The Birth of John the Baptist and Zechariah's Song (1:57–80)
  F. The Birth of Jesus and the Heavenly Response (2:1–21)
  G. A Pious Man and a Prophetess Testify About Jesus (2:22–40)
  H. A Glimpse at Jesus' Self-Perception (2:41–52)
II. Preparation for Ministry (3:1–4:13)
  A. John the Baptist and Jesus' Baptism (3:1–22)
  B. The Genealogy of Jesus (3:23–38)
  C. The Temptations of Jesus (4:1–13)
III. The Galilean Ministry (4:14–9:50)
  A. An Overview of Galilean Ministry (4:14–44)
    1. Ministry: A Summary and in the Synagogue (4:14–30)
    2. Ministry in Capernaum (4:31–44)
  B. The Gathering of Disciples (5:1–6:16)
    1. Two Calls and Two Miracles (5:1–32)
    2. The New Era Means a New Way (5:33–6:5)
    3. Opposition and the Gathering of the Twelve (6:6–16)
  C. Jesus' Teaching (Luke 6:17–49)
  D. Movement to Faith in Christ (7:1–8:3)
    1. Jesus' Authority: From Faith to Resurrection (7:1–17)
    2. Jesus and John the Baptist (7:18–35)
    3. Exemplary Women of Faith (7:36–8:3)
  E. Faith and Questions About Jesus (8:4–9:17)
    1. The Call to Receive the Word (8:4–21)
    2. Miracle 1: The Stilling of the Storm (8:22–25)
    3. Miracle 2: Jesus Exorcises Demons in Gerasa (8:26–39)
    4. Miracles 3 and 4: A Healing and a Resuscitation from the Dead (8:40–56)
    5. Jesus' Ministry Expanded and Contemplated (9:1–9)
    6. The Feeding of the Multitude (9:10–17)

F. Confessing the Christ and Facing Up to Discipleship (9:18–50)
1. Peter's Confession and a Prediction of Suffering (9:18–22)
2. The New Way of Suffering (9:23–27)
3. Transfiguration: A Vote of Confidence and a Call to Hear (9:28–36)
4. The Disciples' Failures and Jesus' Instructions (9:37–50)
IV. The Journey to Jerusalem (9:51–19:44)
A. The Disciple's Privilege, Mission, and Commitment (9:51–10:24)
1. Discipleship in the Midst of Rejection and the Kingdom's Call (9:51–62)
2. The Mission of the Seventy-Two (10:1–24)
B. Discipleship to One's Neighbor, to Jesus, and Before God (10:25–11:13)
1. On Being a Neighbor: The Good Samaritan (10:25–37)
2. Discipleship and Jesus: Mary's Good Choice (10:38–42)
3. Discipleship and Prayer Before God (11:1–13)
C. Controversies, Corrections, and Calls to Trust (11:14–54)
1. The Meaning of Jesus' Works (11:14–23)
2. Warnings About Response (11:24–36)
3. Jesus Rebukes the Pharisees and Scribes (11:37–54)
D. Discipleship (12:1–48)
1. Fear the Lord (12:1–12)
2. The Parable of the Rich Fool (12:13–21)
3. Do Not Be Anxious (12:22–34)
4. Being Ready As Faithful Stewards (12:35–48)
E. Know the Nature of the Time (12:49–14:24)
1. Warnings About the Times for Israel (12:49–13:9)
2. A Sabbath Healing (13:10–17)
3. The Kingdom's Coming and Israel's Peril (13:18–35)
4. A Sabbath Meal Calls for Reflection (14:1–24)
F. Pure Discipleship and Counting the Cost (14:25–35)
G. Why Does God Pursue Sinners? (15:1–32)
1. The Parables of the Lost Sheep and Coin (15:1–10)
2. The Parable of the Forgiving Father and His Two Sons (15:11–32)
H. Generosity: Handling Money and Possessions (16:1–31)
1. The Parable of the Crafty Steward (16:1–13)

E. The Resurrection and Ascension of Jesus (24:1–53)
   1. Resurrection Discovered (24:1–12)
   2. The Journey on the Emmaus Road (24:13–35)
   3. Jesus' Commission, Promise, and Farewell (24:36–53)

Select Annotated
Bibliography on Luke

THE FOLLOWING IS A SELECT BIBLIOGRAPHY for Luke. It contains mostly commentaries and major Lucan monograph studies. Not all the works noted here are cited in the commentary. Of the commentaries, the most helpful for technical studies in English are those by Marshall, Nolland, and Fitzmyer. For a quicker reference, the commentaries by Tiede, C. A. Evans, Danker, Stein, and L. T. Johnson are helpful. (I will not comment on my own works and where they fit. For those, see the preface.) For major biblical theological themes in Luke, the key English studies are those of Marshall, Franklin, O'Toole, and Tannehill, and the article in Zuck-Bock.

Achtemeier, P. "The Lucan Perspective on the Miracles of Jesus: A Preliminary Sketch." Pp. 153–67 in *Perspectives on Luke-Acts*. Ed. C. H. Talbert. Edinburgh: T. & T. Clark, 1978.

Aland, K. *Synopsis Quattuor Evangelorum*. Tenth Edition. Stuttgart: Deutsche Bibelstiftung, 1978.

Arndt, W. F. *The Gospel According to St. Luke*. St. Louis: Concordia, 1956.

Bailey, K. E. *Poet and Peasant: A Literary Approach to the Parables in Luke*. Grand Rapids: Eerdmans, 1976.

Berger, K. *Formgeschichte des Neuen Testaments*. Heidelberg: Quelle & Meyer, 1984.

Blomberg, Craig. "The Law in Luke-Acts." *JSNT* 22 (1984): 53–80.

———. *Interpreting the Parables*. Downers Grove, Ill.: InterVarsity, 1990.

Bock, D. L. *Luke*. The IVP New Testament Commentary Series. Downers Grove, Ill.: InterVarsity, 1994.

———. *Luke 1:1–9:50*. Baker Exegetical New Testament Commentary. Grand Rapids: Baker, 1994.

———. *Luke 9:51–24:53*. Baker Exegetical New Testament Commentary. Grand Rapids: Baker, forthcoming.

———. *Proclamation from Prophecy and Pattern: Lucan Old Testament Christology*. JSNTSS 12. Sheffield: Sheffield Academic Press, 1987.

Bovon, F. C. *Das Evangelium nach Lukas*. EKK 3/1. Köln and NeuKirchen-Vluyn: Benzinger Verlag und Neukichener Verlag, 1989.

———. *Luke the Theologian: Thirty-three Years of Research (1950–1983)*. Trans. Ken McKinney. PTMS 12. Allison Park: Pickwick Publications, 1987.

Brawley, R. L. *Luke-Acts and the Jews: Conflict, Apology, and Conciliation*. SBLMS 33. Atlanta: Scholars Press, 1987.

Brown, R. E. *The Birth of the Messiah: A Commentary on the Infancy Narratives of Matthew and Luke*. London: Geoffrey Chapman, 1977.

————. *The Death of the Messiah: From Gethsemane to the Grave*. 2 vols. New York: Doubleday, 1994.

Brown, S. *Apostasy and Perseverance in the Theology of Luke*. AnBib 36. Rome: Pontifical Biblical Institute, 1969.

Bruce, F. F. *The Book of the Acts*. Revised edition. NICNT. Grand Rapids: Eerdmans, 1988.

————. "Is the Paul of Acts the Real Paul?" *BJRL* 58 (1975/76): 282–305.

Büchele, A. *Der Tod Jesu im Lukasevangelium*. Frankfurt am Main: J. Knecht, 1978.

Bultmann, R. *The History of the Synoptic Tradition*. Trans. J. Marsh. Revised edition. New York: Harper & Row, 1963.

Busse, U. *Die Wundern des Propheten Jesus*. FB 24. Stuttgart: Katholisches Bibelwerk, 1979.

Cadbury, H. J. "Lexical Notes on Luke-Acts: II. Recent Arguments for Medical Language." *JBL* 45 (1926): 190–206.

————. "V. Luke and the Horse-Doctors." *JBL* 52 (1933): 55–65.

————. *The Making of Luke-Acts*. 2d edition. London: S.P.C.K, 1958.

Cassidy, R. *Jesus, Politics and Society: A Study of Luke's Gospel*. Maryknoll, N.Y.: Orbis, 1978.

Chance, J. B. *Jerusalem, the Temple, and the New Age*. Macon, Ga.: Mercer Press, 1988.

Conzelmann, H. *The Theology of St. Luke*. Trans. Geoffrey Buswell. New York: Harper & Row, 1960.

Craddock, F. *Luke*. Interpretation. John Knox: Atlanta, 1991.

Creed, J. M. *The Gospel According to St. Luke*. London: MacMillan and Company, 1950.

Danker, F. *Jesus and the New Age*. Revised edition. Philadelphia: Fortress, 1988.

Dibelius, M. *Studies in the Acts of the Apostles*. Ed. H. Greeven. Trans. M. Ling. New York: Charles Scribner's Sons, 1956.

Dillon, R. J. *From Eye-Witnesses to Ministers of the Word*. AnBib 82. Rome: Pontifical Institute Press, 1978.

Dodd, C. H. "The Fall of Jerusalem and the Abomination of Desolation." *JRS* 37 (1947): 47–54.

Dupont, J. *The Salvation of the Gentiles: Essays on the Acts of the Apostles*. New York: Paulist, 1979.

Egelkraut, H. *Jesus' Mission to Jerusalem: A Redaction Critical Study of the Travel Narrative in the Gospel of Luke, 9:51–19:48.* Bern/Frankfurt: Lang, 1976.

Ellis, E. E. *The Gospel of Luke.* NCB. London: Oliphants, 1974.

Esler, P. F. *Community and Gospel in Luke-Acts.* SNTSMS 57. Cambridge: Cambridge Univ. Press, 1987.

Ernst, J. *Das Evangelium nach Lukas.* RNT. Regensburg: Pustet, 1977.

Evans, C. A. *Luke.* NIBC. Peabody, Mass.: Hendricksen, 1990.

Evans, C. F. *Saint Luke.* TPINTC. London: SCM, 1990.

Farmer, W. *The Synoptic Problem.* Revised edition. Dillsboro, N.C.: Western North Carolina Press, 1976.

Farris, S. *The Hymns of Luke's Infancy Narratives.* JSNTSS 9. Sheffield: JSOT Press, 1985.

Feiler, P. F. *Jesus the Prophet: The Lucan Portrayal of Jesus as the Prophet Like Moses.* Dissertation; Princeton: Princeton University, 1986.

Fitzmyer, J. *The Gospel According to Luke.* 2 volumes. AB 28, 28a. Garden City, N.Y.: Doubleday, 1981, 1985.

————. *Luke the Theologian: Aspects of His Teaching.* London: Geoffrey Chapman, 1989.

Fornara, C. W. *The Nature of History in Ancient Greece and Rome.* Los Angeles: Univ. of California Press, 1983.

Franklin, E. *Christ the Lord: A Study in the Purpose and Theology of Luke-Acts.* London: S.P.C.K., 1975.

Geiger, R. *Die Lukanischen Endzeitreden: Studien zur Eschatologie des Lukas-Evangeliums.* Europäische Hochschulschriften 16. Frankfurt am Main: Peter Lang, 1973.

Giblin, C. H. *The Destruction of Jerusalem According to Luke's Gospel.* AnBib 107. Rome: Biblical Institute Press, 1985.

Glöckner, R. *Die Verkündigung des Heils beim Evangelisten Lukas.* Walberberger Studien 9. Mainz: Matthias-Grünewald Verlag, 1976.

Godet, F. *A Commentary on the Gospel of St. Luke.* 2 volumes. Edinburgh: T. & T. Clark, 1870 (repr. 1975).

Goulder, M. *Luke: A New Paradigm.* JSNTSS 20. Sheffield: Sheffield Academic Press, 1989.

Grundmann, W. *Das Evangelium nach Lukas.* THNT III. Berlin: Evangelische Verlagsanstalt, 1963.

Haenchen, E. *The Acts of the Apostles: A Commentary.* Trans. B. Noble, G. Shinn, H. Anderson, and R. McL. Wilson. Oxford: Basil Blackwell, 1971.

Hemer, C. J. *The Book of Acts in the Setting of Hellenistic History.* Ed. C. Gempf. WUNT 49. Tübingen: J. C. B. Mohr, 1989.

Hendriksen, W. *Luke.* Grand Rapids: Baker, 1978.

Hengel, M. *Acts and the History of Earliest Christianity*. Trans. John Bowden. Philadelphia: Fortress, 1980.

Hobart, W. K. *The Medical Language of St. Luke*. Dublin: Hodges, Figgis, 1882.

Jeremias, J. *The Parables of Jesus*. Trans. S. H. Hooke. New York: Charles Scribner's Sons, 1972.

_____. *Die Sprache des Lukasevangeliums*. Göttingen: Vandenhoeck und Ruprecht, 1980.

Jervell, J. *Luke and the People of God*. Minneapolis: Augsburg, 1972.

Johnson, L. T. *Luke*. Sacra Pagina 3. Wilmington, Del.: Michael Glazier, 1991.

_____.*The Literary Function of Possessions in Luke-Acts*. SBLDS 39. Missoula, Mont.: Scholars Press, 1977.

Keck, L. E., and Martyn, J. L., eds. *Studies in Luke-Acts*. Nashville: Abingdon, 1966.

Klostermann, E. *Das Lukasevangelium*. HNT. Tübingen: J. C. B. Mohr, 1929 (repr. 1975).

Knox, J. *Marcion and the New Testament*. Chicago: Univ. of Chicago Press, 1942.

Kümmel, W. *Introduction to the New Testament*. 17th ed. Nashville: Abingdon, 1975.

Laurentin, R. *Struktur und Theologie der lukanischen Kindheitsgeschichte*. Stuttgart: Katholische Bibelwerk, 1967.

Leaney, A. R. C. *The Gospel According to St. Luke*. BNTC. London: Adam and Charles Black, 1966.

Liefeld, W. "Luke." Pp. 797–1059 in vol. 8, *The Expositor's Bible Commentary*. Ed. Frank C. Gaebelein. Grand Rapids: Zondervan, 1981.

Linnemann, E. *Parables of Jesus: Introduction and Exposition*. London: S.P.C.K., 1966.

Loos, H. van der. *The Miracles of Jesus*. NovTSup IX. Leiden: E. J. Brill, 1968.

Luce, H. K. *The Gospel According to St. Luke*. CGTC. Cambridge: Cambridge Univ. Press, 1933.

Maddox, R. *The Purpose of Luke-Acts*. SNTIW. Edinburgh: T. & T. Clark, 1982.

Manson, T. W. *The Sayings of Jesus*. London: SCM, 1949.

Marshall, I. H. *Commentary on Luke*. NIGTC. Grand Rapids: Eerdmans, 1978.

_____. *Luke: Historian and Theologian*. Grand Rapids: Zondervan, 1970.

Mattill, A. J., Jr. "The Jesus-Paul Parallels and the Purpose of Luke-Acts: H. H. Evans Reconsidered." *NovT* 17 (1975): 15–46.

_____. *Luke and the Last Things*. Dillsboro, N.C.: Western North Carolina Press, 1979.

Metzger, B. *A Textual Commentary on the Greek New Testament*. London: United Bible Societies, 1971.

Minear, P. *To Heal and to Reveal: The Prophetic Vocation According to Luke*. New York: Seabury, 1976.

Moessner, D. *The Lord of the Banquet*. Philadelphia: Fortress, 1989.

Neyrey, J. *The Passion According to Luke*. New York: Paulist, 1985.

Nolland, J. *Luke 1–9:20*. WBC 35a. Dallas: Word, 1990.

O'Neill, J. C. *The Theology of Acts in Its Historical Setting*. 2d ed. London: S.P.C.K., 1970.

O'Toole, R. F. *The Unity of Luke's Theology: An Analysis of Luke-Acts*. Wilmington, Del.: Michael Glazier, 1984.

Parsons, M. C. *The Departure of Jesus in Luke-Acts: The Ascension Narratives in Context*. JSNTSS 21. Sheffield: Sheffield Academic Press, 1987.

Pilgrim, W. E. *The Death of Christ in Lucan Soteriology*. Dissertation; Princeton: Princeton University, 1971.

————. *Good News to the Poor*. Minneapolis: Augsburg, 1981.

Plummer, A. *The Gospel According to St. Luke*. 5th ed. ICC. Edinburgh: T. & T. Clark, 1922.

Reicke, B. *The Roots of the Synoptic Gospels*. Philadelphia: Fortress, 1987.

Rengstorf, K. H. *Das Evangelium nach Lukas*. NTD 3. Göttingen: Vandenhoeck und Ruprecht, 1968.

Rese, M. *Alttestamentliche Motive in der Christologie des Lukas*. SNT 1. Gerd Mohn: Gütersloher, 1969.

Sanders, J. T. *The Jews in Luke-Acts*. Philadelphia: Fortress, 1987.

Schlatter, A. *Das Evangelium nach Lukas*. 2d ed. Stuttgart: Calwer Verlag, 1960.

Schmid, J. *Das Evangelium nach Lukas*. RNT. Regensberg: Pustet, 1960.

Schmidt, T. E. *Hostility to Wealth in the Synoptic Gospels*. JSNTSS 15. Sheffield: Sheffield Academic Press, 1987.

Schneider, G. *Das Evangelium nach Lukas*. ÖTKNT 3. 2 vols. Gütersloh: Gerd Mohn, 1977.

————. *Lukas, Theologe der Heilsgeschichte*. BBB 59 Königstein/Ts.-Bonn, Peter Hanstein Verlag, 1985.

Scott, B. B. *Hear Then the Parable: A Commentary on the Parables of Jesus*. Minneapolis: Fortress, 1989.

Schramm, T. *Der Markus-Stoff bei Lukas*. SNTSMS 14. Cambridge: Cambridge Univ. Press, 1971.

Schürmann, H. *Das Lukasevangelium*. HTKNT III. Erster Teil. Freiberg: Herder, 1969.

Schwiezer, E. *The Good News According to Luke*. Atlanta: John Knox, 1984.

Seecombe, D. P. *Possessions and the Poor in Luke-Acts*. SNTU, B6. Linz: Verlag F. Plöchl, 1982.

Sloan, R. B., Jr. *The Favorable Year of the Lord*. Austin: Scholars Press, 1977.

Soards, M. L. *The Passion According to Luke: The Special Material of Luke 22.* JSNTSS 14. Sheffield: Sheffield Academic Press, 1987.

Stein, R. *Luke.* NAB. Nashville: Broadman, 1992.

Strack, H., and Billerbeck, P. *Kommentar zum Neuen Testament aus Talmud und Midrasch.* 6 vols. München: C. H. Beck, 1926.

Talbert, C. H. *Literary Patterns, Theological Themes and the Genre of Luke-Acts.* SBLMS 20. Missoula, Mont.: Scholars Press, 1974.

_____, ed. *Luke-Acts: New Perspectives from the Society of Biblical Literature Seminar.* New York: Crossroad, 1984.

_____. *Luke and the Gnostics: An Examination of the Lucan Purpose.* Special Studies Series 5. Danville, Va.: Association of Baptist Professors of Religion, 1978.

_____, ed. *Perspectives on Luke-Acts.* Edinburgh: T. & T. Clark, 1978.

_____. *Reading Luke.* New York: Crossroad, 1982.

Tannehill, R. C. *The Narrative Unity of Luke-Acts: A Literary Interpretation.* Vol. 1. Foundations & Facets: NT. Philadelphia: Fortress, 1986.

Theissen, G. *The Miracle Stories of the Early Chrsitian Tradition.* Trans. F. McDonaugh. Edinburgh: T. & T. Clark, 1983.

Tiede, D. L. *Luke.* ACNT. Minneapolis: Augsburg, 1988.

_____. *Prophecy and History in Luke-Acts.* Philadelphia: Fortress, 1980.

Townsend, J. T. "The Date of Luke-Acts." Pp. 47–62 in *Luke-Acts: New Perspectives from the Society of Biblical Literature Seminar.* Ed. C. H. Talbert. New York: Crossroad, 1984.

Tuckett, C. M. *The Revival of the Griesbach Hypothesis.* SNTSMS 44. Cambridge: Cambridge Univ. Press, 1983.

Tuckett, C. M., ed. *Synoptic Studies.* JSNTSS 7. Sheffield: Sheffield Academic Press, 1984.

Turner, M. M. B. "The Sabbath, Sunday and the Law in Luke-Acts." Pp. 99–157 in *From Sabbath to Lord's Day.* Ed. D. A. Carson. Grand Rapids: Zondervan, 1982.

Tyson, J. B. *The Death of Jesus in Luke-Acts.* Columbia, S.C.: Univ. of South Carolina Press, 1986.

_____, ed. *Luke-Acts and the Jewish People.* Minneapolis: Augsburg, 1988.

Unnik, W. C. van. "The 'Book of Acts' the Confirmation of the Gospel." *NovT* 4 (1960–61): 26–59.

Untergassmair, F. G. *Kreuzweg und Kreuzigung Jesu.* PTS. München: Ferdinand Schöningh, 1980.

Vielhauer, P. "On the 'Paulinism' of Acts." Pp. 33–50 in *Studies in Luke-Acts.* Ed. L. E. Keck and J. L. Martyn. London: S.P.C.K., 1966.

Wiefel, W. *Das Evangelium nach Lukas.* THKNT 3. Berlin: Evangelische Verlaganstalt, 1988.

Wilson, S. G. *The Gentiles and the Gentile Mission in Luke-Acts.* SNTSMS 23. Cambridge: Cambridge Univ. Press, 1973.

_____. *Luke and the Law.* SNTSMS 50. Cambridge: Cambridge Univ. Press, 1983.

Zahn, T. *Das Evangelium des Lukas.* Wuppertal: R. Brockhaus Verlag, 1920 (repr. 1988).

Zmijewski, J. *Die Eschatologiereden des Lukas-Evageliums.* BBB 40. Bonn: Peter Hanstein, 1972.

Zuck, R., ed., and D. L. Bock, consulting ed. *A Biblical Theology of the New Testament.* Chicago: Moody, 1994.

Luke 1:1–4

❦

MANY HAVE UNDERTAKEN to draw up an account of the things that have been fulfilled among us, ²just as they were handed down to us by those who from the first were eyewitnesses and servants of the word. ³Therefore, since I myself have carefully investigated everything from the beginning, it seemed good also to me to write an orderly account for you, most excellent Theophilus, ⁴so that you may know the certainty of the things you have been taught.

THE OPENING SECTION of this Gospel (Luke 1:1– 2:52) introduces the ministry of Jesus against the backdrop of his superiority to John the Baptist. Since John is a great prophet, Jesus as his superior must be even greater. The narrative also points to the promised regal deliverer of the house of David (1:31–35, 67–69). Since he comes according to God's promise and word, Luke's readers can be assured that God keeps his promises. This major theme dominates the entire unit. What God says, he will do. But before turning to this infancy period and one event of Jesus' preadolescent childhood, Luke introduces his entire work with a short preface of why he wrote his Gospel.

Whether one read the great ancient Jewish works like 2 Maccabees, the Jewish historian Josephus, or the Greek historian Lucian, ancient histories usually opened with a short explanation for the work.[1] Luke's pastoral history is an "account" (v. 1) or narrative about Jesus, like others that have preceded his. It treats events of fulfillment, where God has been at work in a fresh and spectacular way to deal with the needs of humanity. He calls the previous accounts *diegesis*, which simply describes a narrative that can be oral or written. Since Luke uses the word *epecheiresan* in verse 1 (lit., "set one's hand to"), he may have written accounts in mind, while the report of the tradition in verse 2 may be oral. The oral tradition itself is rooted in those who saw and experienced what is reported.

---

1. See Lucian's, *How to Write History*, 47–48. L. Alexander, "Luke's Preface in the Context of Greek Preface Writing," *NovT* 28 (1986): 48–74. On the genre of Luke, G. E. Sterling, *Historiography and Self Definition: Josephos, Luke-Acts, and Apologetic Historiography* (NovTSup 64; Leiden: E. J. Brill, 1992).

41

The Greek in verse 2 makes it clear that the people referred to had two roles: They were "eyewitnesses" and "servants of the word." The combination of the single article ("those") and the trailing participle ("were") suggest this identification.[2] Part of the certainty one gains from Luke's account comes from these roots. The fact that this material has been "handed down" highlights its being part of a stream of tradition, something the Jews knew how to handle with care.[3] In the same way as the previous accounts came from eyewitnesses who were servants of the Word, so Luke's account has been constructed with care. He wants to join this tradition of rendering the Jesus story, adding new material and eventually providing a sequel, the book of Acts (v. 3: "therefore" is more literally "it seemed good also to me" and shows that Luke sees himself following in the line of these earlier precedents).

Luke tells us four things about his work before he tells us why he writes. (1) He has "investigated" the story. That is, he has followed it closely. He has taken a long and careful look at what he is about to tell us. (2) He went back to "the beginning." This is why he starts his story with John the Baptist, the forerunner, who points to Jesus. (3) Luke was thorough, having studied "everything." This is undoubtedly why there is so much fresh material in his account. About thirty percent of this Gospel is not found elsewhere, including several of Jesus' parables. (4) Luke worked "carefully," taking great care to develop his orderly account in a way that told the story clearly.

When Luke calls his account "orderly," he probably is not referring to temporal order. By examining the account and comparing it to other accounts, it seems clear that chronological order of events is not what he meant (cf. the relocating of the synagogue incident of Luke 4:16–30 much earlier than Mark 6:1–6). Rather, Luke is concerned to relate the account of Jesus' ministry in a logical way, including some topical arrangement.

Luke wants to reassure Theophilus, in order that he "may know the certainty of the things [he has] been taught" (v. 4). Theophilus was probably a new believer, who as a Gentile found himself in what had started out as a Jewish movement. He may have come to Christ as a God-fearer—that is, a Gentile who first came to Judaism and then to Christ. (This may explain why Luke loves God-fearers as he tells his story in Acts.) Theophilus may not be entirely at home in his new, racially mixed community, especially if he previously had allied himself to the older Jewish community. Does he really belong here? Luke is trying to show him that he does fit in and that

---

2. J. A. Fitzmyer, *The Gospel According to Luke, I–IX* (AB 28a; Garden City, N.Y.: Doubleday, 1981), 294.

3. R. Riesner, "Jesus as Teacher and Preacher," in *Jesus and the Oral Gospel Tradition*, ed. H. Wansbrough (JSNTMS 64; Sheffield: Sheffield Academic Press, 1991), 185–210.

God had brought him in by design, along with others who share the path of his journey.

INTRODUCTIONS ARE LIKE road maps—they tell us where we are headed. Even in the first century, the author of a major work often explained briefly what he was doing. For example, the author of 2 Maccabees wrote this about his work (2 Macc. 2:29–31):

> Just as the architect of a new house is responsible for the construction as a whole, while the man undertaking the ceramic painting is responsible for estimating the decorative requirements, so, I think, it is with us. To make the subject his own, to explore its by-ways, to be meticulous about details, is the business of the original historian, but the man making the adaptation must be allowed to aim at conciseness of expression and to forgo any exhaustive treatment of his subject.
>
> So now let us begin our narrative, without adding any more to what has been said above; there would be no sense in expanding the preface to the history and curtailing the history itself.

An ancient preface like this one informs the reader of the author's intentions. Histories in the ancient world had three functions: to entertain, to instruct, and to set forth in a concise, often summarized, form the case the historian wished to make. Usually the topic was about the people to whom he belonged. For example, in *Jewish War*, Josephus defended the Jews before Rome by explaining that only a fringe group, the Zealots, was responsible for the chaos of the war that led to Jerusalem's fall in A.D. 70. Thus, Luke explains the roots of a new movement, which he calls "the Way," by detailing the story of its founder and the tie he has to God's long-promised redemption. This is a story with a long heritage and an open ending, since the story of the Way is still being written.

Luke's preface tells us that his story is rooted in sources and his careful work. His goal, to reassure, means that he wants to solidify the understanding of those inside the movement that God is at work. Such solidification in a multicultural context like ours today is still necessary, even though we are no longer dealing with a new movement but one rich in history and heritage. The issue now is not, "Does the Way have a right to exist and should Gentiles be included?" but, "Is its claim of exclusivity for Jesus something that can be sustained in a world of instant communication and of multiple religious presence?" We sometimes forget that pluralism was also present in the ancient world. So Luke's address of Jesus' uniqueness comes from a context not unlike our own. Our multicultural awareness might be greater today because of satellites and television, but our need for God and for a true revelation of him is just as necessary today. In that sense, Luke's claims are as timely now as they were in his day.

One other key point is raised by this introduction. Luke makes clear his qualifications to present the story by stressing his carefulness and thoroughness. He underscores the credibility of what he has done, so that his work can be trusted. We may not write a gospel about Jesus, but we too must be sensitive to the fact that telling the gospel story means we must have credibility. Integrity is what produces authority, because all other authority is short-lived and temporary. Our strength comes when our message and our lives match. From the moment we meet people and they come to know we are committed to Jesus, until we actually share our message with them, the trustworthiness and ability to assure rests on the conjunction that exists between what we claim and what we do. To state it negatively, if there is no walk to match the talk, then all we will do is sow seed that will bear thorns of rejection. Part of the power in Jesus' story was the coherent mix he brought to his story. Everyone did not accept it, but they did recognize that something was different about him.

There are two additional points of contact between the original story and our world. (1) When we read any written document, we need to know what type of an account it is. Is it a mystery novel, a comedy, fiction, non-fiction?[4] Knowing the type helps us to understand what is being said. This preface indicates both what we are reading and why it was written. The ancients, just like us moderns, knew the difference between history and fiction.[5] A check of historians like Lucian, Josephus, and Thucydides[6] indicate how well they knew their task (e.g., Lucian, *How to Write History*, 39–40). The Gospel of Luke is narrative history. Although the author chooses, summarizes, and arranges how to present the events recorded, the account is an attempt to chronicle what happened nonetheless. Just as a horror film will have eerie music in the background to identify the nature of the scene, so this preface tells us what kind of story we are reading—an authentic portrait of Jesus. We cannot ask this book to do more than it intends. In other words, we cannot expect it to reveal questions about the exact order of events or what precisely was said. Some arrangement is topical, and some of the dia-

---

4. On hermeneutics and genre, R. Stein, *Playing by the Rules: A Basic Guide to Interpreting the Bible* (Grand Rapids: Baker, 1994). To know the genre is to know how to read the text. Luke is writing theological narrative history.

5. Fitzmyer, *The Gospel According to Luke, I–IX*, 16.

6. C. W. Fornara, *The Nature of History in Ancient Greece and Rome* (Berkeley: Univ. of California Press, 1983).

logue is condensed in summarized presentation. When this occurs, we will try to note and explain how one can see that this might be the case. But, be assured, Luke wrote history, not fiction or myth.

(2) The background of Theophilus illumines our Gospel. Many people entering the church walk into a new world. The "church" society often has its own theological language, its initially strange customs, and its traditions of worship and interaction. At the start, the fit may seem awkward. To become a Christian in Bible times required a cultural shift, just as it does now. People today need to be reassured that the change in their life is for the best. They live in a world that often regards Christianity as a man-made religion, as a perversion of Judaism, as one of many ways to God, or as one cultural expression of religion. Luke argues that Christianity is unique, in that God worked in Christ for those who trust him. Luke reassures his Christian readers that they belong in relationship with God in this new community, the church. What God did in Jesus, he did for those who have come into this community, as well as for others like them who recognize they must come to God on his terms, not their own.

 THE THREE POINTS of application from the preface are linked to the two strands of contact we already noted. (1) Luke tells us of God's acts in history *through Jesus*. This main character is not a Savior made up in the image of a person's imagination. After all, who on his or her own would create a Savior who makes us all responsible for our sin and then chooses to pay the penalty for that sin by offering himself? Who would design a regal Messiah who is born in a stable and never wears a crown or sits in a palace? Who would make a hero out of a figure who was rejected by his own? This history cannot be concocted fiction. It is grounded in real events of an extraordinary figure with an extraordinary story. The unusual nature of the story is a testimony to its authenticity. Its reality is the basis for the assurance Luke wishes to give his readers. God has been working through the One he has sent to show us the way (Luke 1:78–79). In doing so, he has shown himself to be a God who cares about our character and our honesty before him. He also cares enough to be sure that provision was made for us.

(2) God wants us to sense that we fit into his community. He wants us to see that the Jesus story is not only about him, but about us—God reaching out with both power and humility to lift us up and bring us into his presence. God takes people who are "outside" his care and makes them "insiders," involved and related to the God of the universe. This is good news indeed. The entire story reassures us that God does what he promises.

Thus the preface not only indicates we are dealing with history and his story, but also with our own. We can rest in the comfort of knowing that what God plans and reveals will come to pass. His promise to save us is a commitment to deliver us completely from sin and its devastation, a process that begins when we trust Christ and is completed when we share in glory forever in a sinless new heaven and new earth.

(3) We can trust the Gospel as we read it. Unlike some, even in the scholarly community, who argue that the Gospels are filled with much fabrication, Luke, as a solid ancient historian, records the real Jesus for us and reveals the heart of God in doing so.[7] He may not have used footnotes as we do today, nor did he have a tape recorder to record Jesus' speeches, but he lived in a community that passed on tradition with care and was sensitive to telling the story accurately in a summarized form. He worked under God's direction, carefully passing on a tradition from those who saw what they preached (v. 2). We can read Luke with full confidence that God is introducing us to Jesus. God reveals himself in the Word so that we may know our real need and story. As John Calvin says,

> Just as old or bleary-eyed men and those weak with vision, if you thrust before them a most beautiful volume, even if they recognize it to be some sort of writing, yet scarcely construe two words, but with the aid of spectacles will begin to read distinctly; so Scripture, gathering up the otherwise confused knowledge of God in our minds, having dispersed our dullness, clearly shows us the true God. This, therefore, is a special gift, where God, to instruct the church, not merely uses mute teachers but also opens up his own most hallowed lips.

Later in the same section he adds, "God, the Artificer of the Universe, is made manifest to us in Scripture, and that what we ought to think of him is set forth there, lest we see some uncertain deity by devious paths."[8] Calvin is able to say this to us, because Luke has made clear that he did his work carefully and that God's promises are true.

---

7. For example, the recent work by the Jesus Seminar, *The Five Gospels* (ed. R. Funk and R. W. Hoover [New York: Macmillan, 1993]) argues that over fifty percent of the teaching attributed to Jesus has no historical contact with him at all! The fifth gospel is the extrabiblical *Gospel of Thomas*. They received much attention in late 1993 with their color coding of the sayings of Jesus: red = from Jesus; pink = a paraphrase of Jesus; gray = not Jesus' words but may go back to him; and black = not from Jesus at all. For an incisive evaluation of this excessively skeptical approach to the Gospels, see *Jesus under Fire: Modern Scholarship Reinvents the Historical Jesus*, ed. J. P. Moreland and M. Wilkens (Grand Rapids: Zondervan, 1995).

8. Both citations are from John Calvin, *Institutes of the Christian Religion*, 1.4.1.

Luke 1:5–25

IN THE TIME of Herod king of Judea there was a priest
named Zechariah, who belonged to the priestly division of
Abijah; his wife Elizabeth was also a descendant of Aaron.
⁶Both of them were upright in the sight of God, observing all
the Lord's commandments and regulations blamelessly. ⁷But
they had no children, because Elizabeth was barren; and they
were both well along in years.

⁸Once when Zechariah's division was on duty and he was
serving as priest before God, ⁹he was chosen by lot, according
to the custom of the priesthood, to go into the temple of the
Lord and burn incense. ¹⁰And when the time for the burning
of incense came, all the assembled worshipers were praying
outside.

¹¹Then an angel of the Lord appeared to him, standing at
the right side of the altar of incense. ¹²When Zechariah saw
him, he was startled and was gripped with fear. ¹³But the angel
said to him: "Do not be afraid, Zechariah; your prayer has
been heard. Your wife Elizabeth will bear you a son, and you
are to give him the name John. ¹⁴He will be a joy and delight
to you, and many will rejoice because of his birth, ¹⁵for he will
be great in the sight of the Lord. He is never to take wine or
other fermented drink, and he will be filled with the Holy
Spirit even from birth. ¹⁶Many of the people of Israel will he
bring back to the Lord their God. ¹⁷And he will go on before
the Lord, in the spirit and power of Elijah, to turn the hearts
of the fathers to their children and the disobedient to the wisdom of the righteous—to make ready a people prepared for
the Lord."

¹⁸Zechariah asked the angel, "How can I be sure of this? I
am an old man and my wife is well along in years."

¹⁹The angel answered, "I am Gabriel. I stand in the presence of God, and I have been sent to speak to you and to tell
you this good news. ²⁰And now you will be silent and not able
to speak until the day this happens, because you did not
believe my words, which will come true at their proper time."

²¹Meanwhile, the people were waiting for Zechariah and
wondering why he stayed so long in the temple. ²²When he
came out, he could not speak to them. They realized he had

seen a vision in the temple, for he kept making signs to them but remained unable to speak.

²³When his time of service was completed, he returned home. ²⁴After this his wife Elizabeth became pregnant and for five months remained in seclusion. ²⁵"The Lord has done this for me," she said. "In these days he has shown his favor and taken away my disgrace among the people."

LUKE BEGINS HIS story by placing it in an established historical setting—the reign of Herod the Great (37–4 B.C.). The NIV's language "in the time" is a smooth rendering for the Greek "in those days," which is adapted from the scriptural language of the Greek Old Testament, the LXX (Judg. 13:2; Judith 1:1; Tobit 1:2).[1] Herod had done much building up of the nation, receiving his commission from Mark Antony in 40 B.C. and returning to Judea to rule in 37 B.C. When the angel appears to Zechariah (Luke 1:11), we are near the end of his reign (5–4 B.C.).

The announcement of the birth of John the Baptist has three aspects to it: the revelation that God has a plan to direct the affairs of humanity and restore his relationship to it, the outline of the career of John himself, and the interplay of the living drama of disappointment in the lives of righteous people, as these "blameless" servants of God had lived with the reality and frustration of being childless. All three themes are central to the original message.

In his goodness, God picks an important moment in the career of Zechariah to make his divine move. As a priest he served at the temple for two one-week periods a year.[2] He was a member of one of twenty-four divisions in the first-century priesthood (Josephus, *Life* 1 § 2; *Antiquities* 7.14.7 §§ 363–67), one of approximately 18,000 priests.[3] More specifically, he was a member of the eighth order, Abijah (1 Chron. 24:10). A priest only officiated at the sacrifice once in his life, having been selected by lot (*m. Tamid* 5:2–6:3). The setting is one of two times for daily prayer set aside at the temple (9 A.M. or 3 P.M.); it is the time of the "perpetual offering" (Ex. 29:38–42). The angel appears as Zechariah places the incense on the altar (Luke 1:11).

---

1. The more detailed story of this Jewish surrogate ruler is told in the ancient works of Tacitus (*Histories*, 5.9.3) and Josephus (*Antiquities*, 14.14.4–5 §§ 383–86; 14.15.1 §469; 17.8.1–3 §§ 191–99).

2. I. H. Marshall, *Commentary on Luke* (NIGTC; Grand Rapids: Eerdmans, 1978), 52.

3. H. Strack and P. Billerbeck, *Kommentar zum Neuen Testament aus Talmud und Midrasch* (München: C. H. Beck, 1926), 2:71–75.

At this high moment, God begins to work in a fresh way to redeem humankind by revealing his sending of the forerunner of the One who would take sin away from the world. How appropriate to pick a moment of worship and a time when people recognized their need for cleansing from sin!

The initial encounter produces terror in Zechariah, though that is not uncommon when one senses that God or an agent of his is present (Ex. 15:16; Judg. 6:22–23; Isa. 6:5; Dan. 8:16–17). After comforting Zechariah, the angel announces why he has come. His name, Gabriel (v. 19; cf. Dan. 8:15–16; 9:21; Tobit 12:15; 1 Enoch 40:9), probably means "God is my hero," though Luke makes nothing of the name.[4]

God's plan in the Old Testament had Israel at its hub. She would be the "model people" through whom God would show his grace (Gen. 12:1–3). Luke continues to use language and imagery drawn from the Old Testament as he tells the story of Zechariah and John the Baptist. The birth of this child is similar to other births to formerly barren wives or other announcements of the birth of a special child (Gen. 16:10–11; 17:15–17; 18:10–15; 25:23; Judg. 13:3–21). Telling the story in this manner indicates that God has renewed his work among his people. His plan is once again being taken up in a direct and active way. The story of John the Baptist and of the One who follows him is a resumption of the sacred story of God's activity.

John has a special place in that plan. This prophet will live an ascetic lifestyle, like the special people of God who took vows to show their devotion to God. He may drink no strong drink. Since most in that culture, including the righteous, did drink some wine, this command indicates John's special level of dedication to God (cf. Eph. 5:17–18; cf. Deut. 14:26; 29:6 [29:5 MT]; Prov. 20:1; 23:20–21, 29–35; 31:6). This is likely not a Nazirite vow, however, since there is no mention of not cutting his hair. Gabriel notes that this prophet will have the responsibility to "go on before the Lord, in the spirit and power of Elijah" (Luke 1:17) and will "bring back [the people of Israel] to the Lord their God" (v. 16).

The angel is alluding here to Malachi 3:1 and 4:5 [MT 3:24] (cf. Sirach 48:1). Going before the Lord describes John as a prophet of the period of restoration of the promise. His preparation for the Lord refers to God's powerful coming through his agent, Jesus (Luke 3:15–18). God is the subject because Jesus has not even been mentioned yet. "To turn hearts" and "make ready a people" reflects John's call for repentance as he turns the nation's attention back to God and to righteousness ("turning" is a standard Old Testament metaphor for repentance; cf. Deut. 30:2; Hos. 3:5; 7:10).[5] "A people

---

4. Fitzmyer, *The Gospel According to Luke, I-IX*, 328.
5. Bertram, "ἐπιστρέφω," *TDNT*, 7:727.

prepared for the Lord" recalls Isaiah 40:3. For God to lead his people effectively, they must be ready to respond to him. To get them ready for the new era was John's call; he proclaimed reconciliation within families as sons and fathers are turned to one another.

The third element in this passage is the personal story of Zechariah and Elizabeth. These righteous people have lived with deep disappointment, never having the child they longed for—what Elizabeth even calls a "disgrace" (v. 25). The personal story is clearly drawn by the personal description at the start of the passage. Both husband and wife are "upright" people (v. 6; cf. Deut. 6:25; 24:13; Ps. 106:31),[6] and their situation is thus not the result of personal sin. Sometimes righteous people do have disappointments in life. The two in this story have prayed about their situation (that seems to be one aspect of their prayer being answered, v. 13), when the angel announces the coming of a child. This promised child answers two prayers at the same time: for a child in the house of Zechariah, and for God to work redemption in the nation. God is often able to work simultaneously personally and corporately.

But Zechariah and Elizabeth represent two different kinds of righteous people. Zechariah raises doubts about the angel's message, for the prospective parents are now beyond normal childbearing age (v. 18). Sometimes even good people have doubts about God's promise. The angel tells Zechariah in effect, "Just be quiet for awhile and watch God work." So a sign of silence is given until God performs his word. Zechariah becomes temporarily mute until these things come to pass.[7] This sign is a pointer to the major lesson of this passage: *God will bring his promise to pass*. He will perform his word. Zechariah must listen to God and trust that he will do what he has promised. When Zechariah departs and is unable to give the customary blessing (*m. Tamid* 7:2; cf. Num. 6:24—26), the crowd knows something unusual has taken place. Verse 22 adds a note of drama to the account.

Elizabeth pictures the righteous saint who takes her burden to God and rejoices when that burden is lifted. Such action by God is treated as gracious, since God "has shown his favor" (v. 25; cf. Gen. 21:6; 30:23, where praise is offered for the provision of a child). God did not owe her this response. Yet Elizabeth does not react as a victim who has been bitter at God for her lack of a child. In fact, she seems to have accepted this fate and served God faithfully anyway. Thus, when the burden is removed, she rejoices as the object of God's personal concern.

---

6. J. Nolland, *Luke* 1:1—9:20 (WBC 35a; Dallas: Word, 1989), 26.

7. That he is deaf as well is indicated by the signing they do to him in v. 62.

Bridging Contexts

A FUNDAMENTAL QUESTION about applying biblical narrative must be raised with this first narrative. How does one take material from the unique
culture of the first century, which involves unique
events in the plan of God, and study them for current understanding about
what God would have us do? The answer comes at three levels. (1) We can
study the *character of God.* These texts reveal God at work, and we can see how
God approaches people, whether they are among the faithful or not.

(2) We can study the *characters in the narratives.* They describe real historical people, but they also represent certain kinds of people who find themselves in a variety of positions. We see ourselves in them or in other people
we know. In this way Scripture instructs us. We learn lessons from how they
respond and whether they respond well or poorly. In this process of application, we must be careful where texts are like and unlike our own world. I
will attempt to make clear in this commentary where links to the present are
clean, where they are implied, and where they should not be made and why.

(3) A special point to consider are *attitudes* that the text draws us toward
or away from possessing. Luke may describe a character's state of mind, or
he will summarize at the end of a unit the mood that closes the event. The
attitudes may come in a monologue, a dialogue of the characters, or their
direct address of God. We must also pay attention to whether a character is
portrayed as reliable or has doubts raised about his or her credibility. Part of
this reading requires us to have some understanding of the perspectives and
responses that fit the first-century setting, since cultures differ from one
another in expectation. I will therefore highlight cultural expectations by
citing extrabiblical evidence from the cultural and/or religious milieu of the
first century, to get a clue as to how people viewed certain situations.[8] Such
sources do not possess inspired authority, but they do reveal how people in
Bible times lived and saw things. All of these observations are part of reading narrative and understanding history carefully, so that an ancient text's message can be discerned.

To tell the story of salvation as it occurred in the past is to tell the basis
of what God does with humanity today. So the plan of God and the role John

---

8. In some cases I will cite material from later Judaism, either from the Mishnah (the written record of the oral law recorded, in c. A.D. 170), the Talmud (the official rabbinic commentary of the Mishnah from the fifth century A.D.), or the Targums and Midrashim (the
rabbinic translations and commentaries on Scripture of the same period). Though these texts
are later than the period in question and thus cannot be said to have a direct link to first-
century culture, they often reflect the kind of mood that existed in Judaism, a religious culture of rich history and tradition that often changed slowly as to its religious sensibilities.

the Baptist plays are indications of the detail God took in reaching out to save humanity. He did not just send a Savior; he sent someone to point the way to him. God often leaves indicators that he is at work, if we just keep our eyes and hearts open for them. Rarely does he just show up. In addition, the Savior did not come just to make us right with God and to give us forgiveness; he called people to be prepared to receive his coming. He wants us to embrace a new way of life, not as the basis of salvation, but in response to his goodness. Repentance, the turning of a heart to be open to him, is the door through which grace is offered and faith planted.

The story of John and Zechariah is timeless. Its fundamental facts serve as the historical foundation and bedrock of our faith. The biblical God is not a creation of human imagination. Rather, his story reflects real divine involvement with the flesh and blood affairs of people. There were no surprises when God sent John; he had designed everything. The unchanging God relates to us in the same way today, in terms of our attitudes and character. We ourselves learn how to relate to God, even in the midst of deep personal disappointment. We may, of course, ask God questions about his actions that are difficult for us to understand, as several of the psalmists do in their laments. But we must also be ready for the answer he gives. While our visits from God may not be as dramatic as Zechariah's, it is just as personal. Often the best lessons come to us through our interaction with God in terms of real life situations, when we experience things that drive us to him and to his promises.

One of the keys to narrative, as I noted above, is to recognize that a story's characters represent certain types of people. In Zechariah and Elizabeth, we see not just historical figures but representative personalities, and we can identify with their attitudes. We can sympathize with Elizabeth's plight of childlessness. But she also is an example in how she responds. Despite her personal disappointment, she faithfully serves God. And even when the situation is reversed, she does not forget God, but rejoices in what he has done to renew her.

From righteous Zechariah we also learn something about walking with God. This Gospel is full of such exemplary characters. Those who teach by example (or counterexample) and those who learn from their experiences to listen to and trust God. How John the Baptist's role belongs in this type of teaching through characterization is something we discuss below.

Both Zechariah and Elizabeth are at the heart of the bridge between the past and the present. Our pain may not be the absence of a child, but there are a myriad of things that can bring disappointment in life. Yet one thing neither Zechariah nor Elizabeth succumbed to was bitterness, even though Elizabeth felt "disgrace." Maybe that is one reason God called them upright and blameless. But good people need to learn to rely even more on God. Sometimes the answer to their disappointment is not clear. Whether it be the loss of a child to premature death, a financial collapse, dealing with a child who falls into calamity or serious sin, or an unfortunate accident, the hard times are not always self-explanatory. God never guarantees that life will come without pain and disappointment. The central issue is how we handle it. Bitterness will yield the fruit of anger and frustration, sapping the joy from life. Trust and dependence will cause us to find fulfillment in ways we would not even have considered otherwise. For example, how many childless couples have made a life out of ministering to other children, either through service in the church or adopting a child who no longer had parents who cared? Sometimes a roadblock is not a dead end, but a fresh turn in the road.

We should also note that what had been a long-term void in this couple's life was part of God's sovereign plan, where he stepped in late in the game to change the direction of past disappointments. The blessing was sweeter once it came, because when the child arrived, he was not taken for granted. The child clearly was what all children are—a gift from God. The seemingly random falling of the lot to Zechariah was actually designed to set the stage for this fresh entry of God into this couple's life and into the nation's life as well. Sometimes God's timing, though different from ours, is infinitely wiser.

THE APPLICATION OF this text in terms of God's plan is basic. It will be a refrain through the entire Gospel. Are we prepared for God and do we respond to his work through the One he sent to lead us to him? John will point the way. Do we take the path of sensing our need for God and of responding to the One who offers forgiveness to us? Are we humble before God, taking the path he calls us to, or do we opt to go our own way?

John is someone whose dedication to God is expressed even in his lifestyle. That lifestyle, as reported to Zechariah, shows how totally focused John must be as he represents God. Filled with the Spirit from birth, he will testify to Jesus even by kicking in his mother's womb (Luke 1:44). The presence of the Spirit in Luke is often accompanied by a powerful testimony. Those who are directed by God in the Spirit do not render testimony to God in the privacy of their own home, as the many Spirit-filled characters in the book of Acts will also show. If we have the Spirit, God will be manifest in both our words and deeds.

Yet different ways for doing this exist (cf. Luke 7:24—35). John's greatness is not found in his choice of lifestyle, but in the fact that in understanding his calling, he pursues it fully and carries out God's will faithfully. John's style will be different from that of Jesus. God does not make all people to minister in the same way. That diversity allows different types of ministry to impact different kinds of people. We should not make everyone minister in the same way and with the same style. The test of ministry is not its external appearances; instead, it is found in much less visible ways. As a servant of God, John became a catalyst who encouraged others to live before God in a way that honored the Creator. Not everyone responded to him, so success need not be measured by numbers. John's mission to be a source of stimulating others to find God is something we all can seek to follow.

The turning of the fathers and sons to each other and to God (v. 17) shows how important reconciliation within the family is.[9] Colossians 3:21 states clearly how the father's approach to his child can help form or deform a child's self-image. Yet what is needed is not merely a reconciled relationship between father and child, but a spiritual relationship secured by a strong bond uniting them to God. In this way both are turned, so that "the disobedient [are turned] to the wisdom of the righteous" (v. 17). One need only read all the wise words of the father to his son in Proverbs to sense how crucial a three-way relationship between parent, child, and God is.

We can also apply the lessons that Zechariah and Elizabeth teach us. We must not presume upon God by either always seeing struggles in life as evidence of the presence of sin or by calling on God to bless us with everything we desire. Elizabeth teaches us to take our sense of grief over our disappointments to God, and to be sure to take our rejoicing to him as well.

Elizabeth's dilemma is different from modern expectations in one important way. She would not have had the type of concerns modern people do about self-fulfillment through her bearing a child. In the ancient world, particularly given the hazards of having children, the issue is more related to expectation of having heirs and building a family that can share in its responsibilities. In the Old Testament, this is shown by customs like Levirate marriage, where the concern is to provide an heir for a man who dies childless. Children gave a woman her place in the community (see Prov. 31). The sense of disgrace in being childless had to do with these more communal concerns. Still, the disappointment was real (cf. Elizabeth's remarks in vv. 24–25). Though her pain and subsequent relief were rooted in different concerns from those of today, they were just as decisively met by what God graciously did.

---

9. Two excellent works on the role of the man, especially in terms of family, are both written by Steve Farrar: *Point Man* (Sisters, Ore.: Multnomah, 1990) and *Standing Tall* (Sisters, Ore.: Multnomah, 1994). Luke 1:5–25 reveals how one of the outworkings of a good relationship with God is the potential to reconcile family members to each other.

Zechariah teaches us that God occasionally instructs saints through difficult times.[10] Sometimes underestimating God is as dangerous as rebelling against him. Our sin may not be a matter of doing overt wrong but of being hesitant to pursue righteousness and to trust fully in the Lord. Once God speaks, we should respond. People often pursue relationships or actions they know are wrong, often with a sense of having been a victim, as if that justifies their turning away from God. But we can also do the same thing using more subtlety, with a type of lukewarmness that says, "I am happy with where I am spiritually, so I will not pursue God as in former days." Such a "cruise control" approach risks a slow spiritual decline. One senses that Zechariah needed a fresh lesson of faith to avoid such a slow motion spiritual fall.

The fact that Zechariah doubted the angel's word meant he was already at risk. What God promises, he will perform—only he will do it in his time and sometimes in surprising ways. When the time of fulfillment comes, we realize that his timing was better than ours. Perhaps we sometimes wish we could be in the boardroom of heaven, telling God how to make his plans. This passage calls us to see that his plan has its own design and timing. The Creator of the universe knows what he is doing.

Finally, God is gracious in seemingly mysterious ways. Sometimes we are deprived of something because God has better things awaiting us down the road. When we wait patiently on the Lord, he often gives us more than we imagined possible. Zechariah and Elizabeth wanted a child; what they got was a prophet. God's ways are set to his clock, and they are often filled with things that cause us to wonder as we rejoice at his surprises.

---

10. Philip Yancey, *Where Is God When It Hurts?* (Grand Rapids: Zondervan, 1990), is an excellent discussion of this question of pain and the Christian.

Luke 1:26-38

IN THE SIXTH month, God sent the angel Gabriel to Nazareth, a town in Galilee, 27to a virgin pledged to be married to a man named Joseph, a descendant of David. The virgin's name was Mary. 28The angel went to her and said, "Greetings, you who are highly favored! The Lord is with you."

29Mary was greatly troubled at his words and wondered what kind of greeting this might be. 30But the angel said to her, "Do not be afraid, Mary, you have found favor with God. 31You will be with child and give birth to a son, and you are to give him the name Jesus. 32He will be great and will be called the Son of the Most High. The Lord God will give him the throne of his father David, 33and he will reign over the house of Jacob forever; his kingdom will never end."

34"How will this be," Mary asked the angel, "since I am a virgin?"

35The angel answered, "The Holy Spirit will come upon you, and the power of the Most High will overshadow you. So the holy one to be born will be called the Son of God. 36Even Elizabeth your relative is going to have a child in her old age, and she who was said to be barren is in her sixth month. 37For nothing is impossible with God."

38"I am the Lord's servant," Mary answered. "May it be to me as you have said." Then the angel left her.

Original Meaning

THE ANNOUNCEMENT TO Mary parallels the announcement to Zechariah, but the differences are also significant. Whereas the first announcement takes place in the temple in the center of Israelite culture, this one takes place in an obscure Galilean village much to the north of the capital. The humble nature of the announcement parallels the humble nature of Jesus' birth and ministry. Whereas the announcement about John involves a man, the one about Jesus involves a woman. This is significant because it reflects the gender diversity of such birth announcements or inquiries about births in the Old Testament (e.g., Abraham, Rebekah, the wife of Manoah). In addition, the perspective differs from Matthew, who tells Joseph's story (Matt. 1:18–25). Everything about the birth echoes the later words of Paul, that Jesus' life reflected the humility of "emptying himself" as he took on humanity (Phil. 2:5–11).

The announcement in Nazareth shows that Mary came from humble, agrarian roots. Galilee was not a respected region. It was hardly the expected locale for one sent from God (John 7:41). Gabriel, the same angel who spoke to Zechariah, brings the divine message. Luke identifies Mary as a virgin, engaged to Joseph; that is, she was pledged to him sometime in the previous year. A Jewish betrothal involved two steps: the formal engagement including a contract and exchange of a bridal price, and then about a year later, a wedding (Deut. 22:23; *m. Ketub.* 4:4–5).[1] Mary's age is not given, but in this culture she could be as young as twelve. It is Joseph who is tied to the house of David in this text.[2]

Mary is "highly favored" (v. 28), receiving God's grace on the basis of his sovereign action. One can always rejoice when God chooses to show his presence through his grace. Thus the Lord is with her (v. 28). Her initial fear is calmed when the angel explains the reason for his presence. She has "found favor" (v. 30)—a second indication that she is the object of God's grace.

Mary is then told of the greatness of the child to come in a manner that recalls the birth announcements of the Old Testament (Gen. 16:11; Judg. 13:5; Isa. 7:14). Jesus' greatness is superior to John's: Whereas John is "great in the sight of the Lord" (v. 15), Jesus is simply "great" (v. 32). As with John, Israel is at the center of the story, since Jesus will be a king on the throne of David his father.

This promise involves the sonship promise of the Old Testament spoken about a son of David, that God would be his father (2 Sam. 7:6–16). As Son of the Most High, Jesus takes on a special relationship to God as the representative of divine promise on earth. Once his kingdom is established, it will never end. The one who always was king will set up a kingdom where the presence of his authority and the benefits of salvation are distributed to those who ally themselves to him (Luke 1:67–79). This child will be both "Son of the Most High" (v. 32) and "the Son of God" (v. 35). Luke will spend much of his Gospel explaining what these titles mean; for now they describe a regal figure chosen by God, whose human origins reside in a supernatural

---

1. Fitzmyer, *The Gospel According to Luke, I–IX*, 343.

2. This is the most natural reading of the Greek word order (see *TDNT*, 4:238, n. 29). A connection between Jesus and the Davidic house through Joseph is not problematic, since Jesus would be the perceived son of Joseph, even though he was virginally conceived. Human inheritance would come to him through that connection. Precedent for nonbiological ancestry exists in levirate marriage (Deut. 25:5–10).

conception. Luke chooses to present his understanding of Jesus gradually, building the reader's awareness one step at a time. He starts with categories the reader understands, like king, regal Son of God, and Messiah. But the birth suggests and the rest of the Gospel will make clear that more than a regal king is present. The drama of how this portrait is built is sometimes lost on us who know the whole story, but to Luke's initial readers, the steps in the story were necessary to explain and reassure that Jesus was all God revealed him to be.

The special child is a beneficiary of a unique birth, since Mary is a virgin (v. 27). Mary understandably wonders how a child can be promised to her, since she is sexually inexperienced. God's special creative work through the Holy Spirit will cooperate in the realization of this child's arrival, so that the child will be known as holy and Son of God. Though Luke does not allude to Isaiah 7:14 as Matthew 1:23 does, the picture of this Old Testament passage is evoked by the setting.[3]

All of these details reaffirm why, at the start of this passage, Mary is called "highly favored" (v. 28) and one who has "found favor" (v. 30). She is honored by God not because of her own merit or because she has done anything, but simply because she is the chosen vessel for this demonstration of God's grace. God even gives a sign that these events are taking place. The angel reveals that her old relative will bear a child too, and he reminds her that "nothing is impossible with God." As with Zechariah, this remark indicates that God can and will perform his word. His promise can be trusted.

Mary's response reveals her character. "Let it be to me as you have said" (v. 38). This was no simple matter. She is being asked to bear a child as a virgin without being married. In standing up for God and his power, she will probably become the object of much doubt and ridicule. But Mary knows she is God's servant, so she will allow God to work through her as he wills. He can place her in whatever difficult circumstances he desires, for she knows that God is with her.

Again Luke has not only explained how the plan of God is advanced by telling the details of the birth announcement, he also has revealed the character of those surrounding the birth of these two great men of God. All the figures involved are examples of spirituality as they respond to what God is

---

3. It is debated whether or not Isaiah 7:14 plays a major role in Luke's portrayal. He certainly is less explicit in any allusion to the passage than Matthew, who cites the text (Matt. 1:21–23). The issue here is not whether Luke sees a virgin birth, since the dialogue with the angel makes clear that that is what Luke sees. Rather, the question is whether Luke noted the tie to the Old Testament. Nothing in the description clearly makes the connection, though nothing excludes it either.

doing among them. In the midst of the cosmic story, there are human stories. The narrative wants the reader to sense both levels of the story.

THE BRIDGES IN this text parallel the previous section. We have the unique details of God's plan, involving a unique birth and a unique child. These details are timeless, setting in motion the redeeming acts of God. Luke reveals the depth of Jesus' uniqueness one step at a time. His unusual birth at the start prepares us for more that is unusual about Jesus.

The child is introduced in terms all the readers can understand, as a king for Israel. The origin and humble setting for the birth of such a stellar regal figure should already alert us to the fact that God often works in strange ways. There will be surprises with Jesus. God's plan, though outlined in Scripture, cannot be prepackaged for delivery. To see God work, one must listen for him to reveal how he does it. Most of us, had we designed the plan, would have made great pomp and circumstance out of the arrival of the king. But the fact that his birth was like any other common birth says a lot about the great lengths God goes to in order to identify with the most humble people of the world. God may be the God of the universe, but he is no elitist.

The character of Mary is also worthy of study. Even though the events that take place with her are unique, her attitudes are held up within the narrative as exemplary and worthy of praise. These textual clues help us focus on central elements in the story. Thus, for example, the words of 1:45 in the next section present Mary as an example in terms of her response to all these events. The fact that the hymn she offers is generic in describing the kind of person, like her, whom God blesses reinforces reading the text this way.

Mary reflects the person whom God unexpectedly chooses to use. She brings no outstanding credentials to the task and lives on the edge of the nation. She brings nothing on her résumé other than her availability and willingness to serve. But those characteristics are the most basic ones anyone can offer God. So he puts her to use in his plan, taking her through a process for which she has had no training or preparation. He simply promises to be with her in the journey, and she responds by being willing to go on the ride. The angel, faithful in his task, wants Mary to know just how favored she is. With God's grace behind her, Mary knows that she can do what God asks. The text's description of her as a virgin reveals that she had grown up with a sense of personal responsibility and integrity.

Contemporary Significance

THE HUMBLE SETTING of Jesus' birth not only reveals the nature of God's plan, it also reveals the character of God's heart. God loves those who are humble in spirit. Even his Son, as the King of Israel, the Promised One of all time, is born of a humble, country maiden. This example of God's unpretentiousness is an attitude that we as his children should possess. We might expect great things from God and anticipate that he will work through the great in society. But God shows his greatness by working with anyone on the street who is willing to be used by him. Spiritual greatness is not a matter of social class, monetary clout, or degreed background; it is a function of the heart. God's approach stands in contrast to the type of credentials our world looks for and honors. Externals count for little with him; other issues matter much more. God can do great things through those who entrust the journey with him to his care. That means when God leads, the saint must simply reply, "May it be according to your will."

This passage suggests four other important lessons: (1) the certainty that God will perform his promise, since nothing is impossible with him, (2) Mary's example as one chosen to serve God, an example that extends even beyond the willingness to be used to trust God to take us beyond our limitations, (3) the significance of the Virgin Birth of our Savior, and (4) the importance of sexual faithfulness throughout our lives.

The entire infancy narrative stresses God's completing his promises, for every short-term promise he made comes to pass exactly as spoken. We can trust God to perform his promises. He will do it at his own time and in his own way, but it will come to pass. If God has such integrity, we as his children should imitate that character and be true to our word. In a culture where lies are often seen merely as "half truths," this revelation of character is important.

On the other hand, Mary reflects the proper response of anyone who has been called by God with no credentials other than availability and a responsive heart. She is the Lord's servant, and so are we, if we know him. God's servants have the right attitude and perspective to accomplish great things for him if they say: "Use me as you will. I will not refrain from serving because I do not feel qualified or usable." Behind the availability to service is an attitude that trusts God for direction and enablement. God has called all believers to minister to the body (Eph. 4:7–16), and he does not call us to a task he will not prepare us to perform.

With God's call comes a need to be responsive to his leading. Submitting to God's will means realizing how that road is best traveled. Service is generally given low ratings in our world; we prefer to have other people serve us. This perspective tends to make us focus on ourselves and, in fact, often subverts one of the activities that can bring the most satisfaction. If God has created us to be his servants and "vice regents" on the earth, as Genesis 1 suggests by saying we are created in God's image to subdue the earth, then when we simply serve ourselves, we lose an important part of who we are to be.

Furthermore, with God there is no need to have an inferiority complex about how he may use us and what we bring to the task. More than being willing to go where God will take us is realizing that he can help us overcome whatever limitations we bring to the effort. In faithfulness there is spiritual strength. Luke wants us not only to see Mary as the humble mother of Jesus, but also as an example of faith. Just as Elizabeth pictured the one who rejoices in being used of God, so also Mary paints a portrait of going wherever God leads, knowing that he will supply whatever is lacking.

The fact of the Virgin Birth also underscores that God is our Creator, and his creative power is capable of making life out of nothing merely through his overshadowing presence. If anything expresses the sovereignty of God, it is his ability to create life. I do not know if there has been any more powerful moment in my life than when my children were born. To cuddle a newborn and recognize that nine months of biological miracle produced this tender, new life that must be nurtured and cared for stresses just how precious life is and how powerful God's creative skill is.

The importance of the Virgin Birth is illustrated by an article I noticed recently in one of our metropolitan newspapers.[4] Our culture has a strong temptation to deny the uniqueness of Jesus. The article in question noted the claim of some scholars in the Jesus Seminar that the Virgin Birth did not really take place and that Bethlehem might not be Jesus' birthplace. Such claims are not new. The birth is only noted in Matthew and Luke, but that is because John starts with Jesus as the preexistent Word and Mark has no infancy material at all. These are mere literary choices by the human authors of the Bible. The Virgin Birth is significant because it shows special divine involvement with Jesus from the start. It also reasserts the fundamental power of God to reshape life. As John's Gospel puts it, the Word became flesh. Such supernatural activity marks Jesus out as unique from the start.[5] A person's response to the truth of such an event also suggests their worldview about God and his ability to act in the world. The difference in worldview

---

4. Jim Jones, "The Gospel Truth?" *Fort Worth Star-Telegram* (Dec. 16, 1994), front page of Metropolitan section.

5. For a classic work on the Virgin Birth, see J. Gresham Machen, *The Virgin Birth* (Grand Rapids: Baker, 1965 reprint).

involves a picture of God as a spectator in the creation in contrast to a view of deity that sees him as a creative participant with us in life.

Though Jesus' life is unique and has a unique origin, every life is precious, a testimony to God's amazing creative power. Even the anticipation of the arrival of such a life is special and should not be trivialized. Conception, because it is precious, should be treated with respect. I suspect this is why God values sexual faithfulness and virginity. Those who keep themselves pure until the proper time set a table of faithfulness not only for the partner they share life with, but also for the precious child they will have steward-ship over after the birth. New life is so precious we owe the child such fore-thought. Unfortunately, often we are shortsighted, so that the child is put at risk, whether before birth through the threat of abortion or after birth through the trauma of divorce created through unfaithfulness.

Luke 1:39–56

A T THAT TIME Mary got ready and hurried to a town in the hill country of Judea, ⁴⁰where she entered Zechariah's home and greeted Elizabeth. ⁴¹When Elizabeth heard Mary's greeting, the baby leaped in her womb, and Elizabeth was filled with the Holy Spirit. ⁴²In a loud voice she exclaimed: "Blessed are you among women, and blessed is the child you will bear! ⁴³But why am I so favored, that the mother of my Lord should come to me? ⁴⁴As soon as the sound of your greeting reached my ears, the baby in my womb leaped for joy. ⁴⁵Blessed is she who has believed that what the Lord has said to her will be accomplished!"

⁴⁶And Mary said:

> "My soul glorifies the Lord
> ⁴⁷   and my spirit rejoices in God my Savior,
> ⁴⁸for he has been mindful
>   of the humble state of his servant.
>   From now on all generations will call me blessed,
> ⁴⁹   for the Mighty One has done great things for me—
>   holy is his name.
> ⁵⁰His mercy extends to those who fear him,
>   from generation to generation.
> ⁵¹He has performed mighty deeds with his arm;
>   he has scattered those who are proud in their inmost
>   thoughts.
> ⁵²He has brought down rulers from their thrones
>   but has lifted up the humble.
> ⁵³He has filled the hungry with good things
>   but has sent the rich away empty.
> ⁵⁴He has helped his servant Israel,
>   remembering to be merciful
> ⁵⁵to Abraham and his descendants forever,
>   even as he said to our fathers."

⁵⁶Mary stayed with Elizabeth for about three months and then returned home.

THIS PASSAGE CONTAINS two parts. First is the meeting between Mary and Elizabeth, which takes place in the hill country of Judea, somewhere outside of Jerusalem, a three-day journey of some eighty to one hundred miles from Nazareth. The meeting demonstrates Mary's obedience, since it reflects her desire to observe the sign the angel had told her about in verse 36. Mary "hurries" to obey where God is taking her. The event possesses little significance on the surface, but for Luke, it is a major literary bridge, since the two major characters of the account meet symbolically through their mothers. John the Baptist starts "pointing to" Jesus even from the womb, just as 1:15–17 had predicted. The second part of this section is Mary's hymn—the *Magnificat*, a name that reflects the Latin wording of the hymn's beginning. Mary pours out her soul, rejoicing as she shares in these events.

The meeting between the childbearers recalls Genesis 25:22–26, although this passage contrasts significantly with the earlier one. Whereas Jacob and Esau battled for supremacy within a single womb, John rejoices at the superior role Jesus possesses by leaping in Elizabeth's womb (Luke 1:41, 44).[1] The remark about the Spirit's filling Elizabeth is crucial, for it indicates that her remarks and emotions are directed by God.[2] In an enticing omission, the text never tells us how Elizabeth knew Mary was expecting this child. This adds to the mystery of the event.

The humility reflected here by John's mother in feeling honored just to be in the presence of the child is expressed more fully by her son in John 3:30: "He must become greater; I must become less." It is expressed in a way that recalls 2 Samuel 6:9 and 24:21. Peace reigns among those who serve God as each understands his or her place in God's plan.

The note of joy in the passage echoes a theme already sounded by the previous events. The sense of privilege and favor at being used by God finds fresh expression here. Elizabeth knows God does not owe her such a central role, yet she is amazed at God's involvement with her. In asking "Why am I so favored?"(v. 43), she understands that she is but a humble beneficiary of God's grace.

Alongside her amazement is the lesson of Mary's blessing. As verse 45 says,

---

1. The idea of children reacting to events from the womb is known in Judaism. The later *Targum to Psalm* 68:27 calls on the fetus in the womb to praise God, while *Odes to Solomon* 28:2 speaks of a child leaping in the womb. The precedent for such hope is Genesis 25:22. In the *Palestinian Talmud*, the fetuses present at the Exodus were said to react at the parting of the sea.

2. Friedrich, "προφήτης," *TDNT*, 6:835.

"Blessed is she who has believed that what the Lord has said to her will be accomplished!" This is the first beatitude in this Gospel.[3] A major theme of the first two chapters of Luke is that God does what he says. Rich is the blessing that comes to those who share in and believe in that truth. When God steps into our lives, we should rejoice and trust that he will do as he has promised.

We should not miss the significance of the testimony about these children that comes through this grateful mother-to-be. Three points are central: (1) Mary's child is especially blessed, being at the center of God's fresh activity; (2) there is amazement in being any part of these astounding events; and (3) joy and blessing come to those who believe that God does what he says.

Mary's hymn, a thanksgiving psalm, comes in two parts. That it is a praise psalm is indicated by "my soul magnifies the Lord and my spirit rejoices in God my Savior" (vv. 46b–47), similar to Hannah's praise to God (1 Sam. 2:1; cf. Ps. 35:9). Luke 1:46–49 gives Mary's personal praise for her specific situation, while the rest of the hymn praises God's activity in more general terms. A shift of tenses from present (v. 46b) to past (vv. 47–48a) to future (v. 48b) shows the broadening scope of her basis for praise. The idea that all generations will praise her (v. 48b) leads to the idea of how God treats other "God-fearers" (vv. 49–53). This mention of "those who fear [God]" may especially open up this psalm to Luke's audience, which likely included former Gentile "God-fearers." Though Israel is clearly in view in the psalm (vv. 54–55), the implication of the general praise in verse 50 opens up the possibility that others outside the nation may also be blessed.

The hymn echoes language from the Old Testament as Mary rejoices in the saving action of God on her behalf (Pss. 34:3; 69:30).[4] Despite this woman's "humble state" (2 Kings 14:26; Pss. 9:11–14; 25:16–18), God has acted on her behalf in great things that manifest his holiness. Thus, Mary rejoices in the Mighty One (Deut. 10:21; 34:11; Pss. 44:4–8; 89:8–10; 111:2, 9; Zeph. 3:17). She rejoices in his favor, exercised as her Savior (Ps. 25:5–6; Isa. 12:2; Mic. 7:7). The God who sits in heaven has shown concern to his lowly servant. In the midst of all he does in creation, she has been noticed. She will testify to God's care for her, just as he cares for others.

When Mary says that she rejoices (*egalliasen*), she uses the same term that appears in 1:14. In other words, this is the first fulfillment of the promises made about the significance of John the Baptist. Even though Mary has in view the events associated with the bearing of Jesus, those events are not

---

3. A. Plummer, *Luke* (ICC; Edinburgh: T. & T. Clark, 1896), 30.
4. For a chart covering the Old Testament background of the hymn, see ibid., 30–31.

detached from her contact with Elizabeth and John. By this word association, Luke fills the account with an air of fulfillment from its earliest moments.

Mary will be honored "from now on" by all generations, not because she is special, but because she is the model and representative of what it is to experience God's grace and mercy (v. 50).[5] Luke loves to note how events tied to God's activity change everything "from now on" (Luke 5:10; 12:52; 22:18, 69; Acts 18:6).[6]

Mary's feelings are clear. God owes her nothing, while she has received everything from him. But her story illustrates how God treats others, so she goes on to indicate that her story could be repeated a thousand times over. God's "mercy" extends to those who fear him (v. 50). This mercy is his loyal love, what the Old Testament calls God's *hesed*. This love is faithful and gracious (Ps. 103:2–6, 8–11, 13, 17).[7] If one wants to see mercy defined, God's rescue of the humble and his bringing down of the proud show how he cares for those who trust him (Deut. 4:34; Pss. 44:3; 68:1; 89:10, 13; 107:9; 118:15; 146:7; 147:6). Love, mercy, and loyalty are key interconnected attributes of God. God will rescue those who turn to him and are in need. The hungry are blessed, while the rich go away empty (cf. this theme in 1 Sam. 2:5; Job 15:29; Jer. 17:11). The idea of the removal of rulers is also found in the Old Testament (1 Sam. 2:7; Job 5:11; 12:19).[8] God's mercy eventually expresses itself in power, redemption, and justice. This is how he has helped Israel, the special nation of his love and "his servant," as he remembers mercy to Abraham and his descendants (Isa. 41:8–9; 42:1–2, 21; 45:4; 48:20; 49:3). This historical reference recalls God's covenant commitments to his people made through Abraham, Isaac, and Jacob. Once again Luke emphasizes how God keeps his word. As this Gospel continues, the commitments to those who fear God will stretch beyond Israel's boundaries.

The tenses of the verbs in verses 51–55 are aorist, a fact that has raised much discussion about what is intended.[9] Is Mary referring to past events? Are these gnomic aorists (that is, referring to what God habitually does throughout time)? Or are they prophetic aorists, with the promises so certain in the text that they are expressed vividly as already being in place? This latter sense best fits the forward-looking introduction to these verses (v. 49). Though what is said here is true of God in all time, his actual vindication of the poor comes, with full certainty, in the future.

---

5. Fitzmyer, *The Gospel According to Luke, I–IX*, 367.
6. Stählin, "νῦν," *TDNT*, 4:1111, 1113.
7. Marshall, *Commentary on Luke*, 83.
8. Plummer, *Luke*, 33.
9. Marshall, *Commentary on Luke*, 83–84.

These texts should not be read merely as a sociological commitment by God to the poor. The lead line into the general refrain makes it clear that "those who fear [God]" are the blessed (v. 50). The poor are the "pious poor," or those whom the Old Testament often calls the *anawim* (Pss. 9:11–12, 17–20; 10:1–4; 12:1–5; 18:25–29). They recognize their need and are thus less reluctant to turn to God. Mary expresses hope for Israel's vindication before her enemies. God will deliver this and more through Jesus. Those who turn to God can expect him to show his love and justice on their behalf in a time he deems appropriate. God does so because he "remembers" his promises (Luke 1:54).

TWO KEYS UNLOCK these texts: (1) the representative roles Elizabeth and Mary possess as picturing two qualities of believers, and (2) the realization that Mary's hymn is a story not only about herself but about all those who fear God and are the objects of his mercy and grace.

Mary and Elizabeth picture the believer's amazement in sharing in the blessings of God. Elizabeth's humility stands out as she senses that she does not even deserve to be where she finds herself. She praises Mary (and those like her) who believe that God will do what he says. This generalizing of the lesson is why the blessing of verse 45 is stated in general terms of how God works rather than with specific reference to Mary. The intent is to broaden the application beyond this one event.

Humility is the natural product of reflection about who God is. In the ancient world, relationship with God was not a casual affair, as if God were a friendly neighbor. Rather, it was seen as an honor, and it called for a deep sense of respect, much like a person might respond to hosting a famous dignitary. After all, he is the Creator, who is responsible for our being a part of his creation. So much awe was reserved for God in Judaism that they discussed in detail how he should be approached in worship at the temple, even giving the precise route the priests should take in approaching him.[10] The point is not that we should replicate such detail or go back to the Law, but we should note how much care and consideration was given to approaching God. Like Moses who had to shed his shoes in Exodus 4, we should appreciate the honor of what it means to know God. Both Mary and Elizabeth

---

10. Such detail is spelled out in the Jewish recording of oral tradition found in the *Mishnah*. In the tractate *Tamid*, the details of the daily worship are presented a step at a time, even giving the direction one must go around the altar as the offering is given.

communicate the sense of respect that reflects the fear of the Lord as the beginning of knowledge (Prov. 1:7).

As Mary's hymn moves from her situation to how God treats certain groups in general, her message becomes not just her own, but that of millions of others. They can enter into her praise, for they know what rejection by the world is, what being humble before God is, and maybe even what being poor is. The awareness that God is addressing the pious poor should not allow us to ignore the sociological element in the description. Often it is the poor who are most sensitive to God and recognize their need for him. Mary's song reveals God's character and attributes not as abstract expressions of holiness, mercy, and saving power, but in concrete relationship to people and in the detailed working of their lives. God's attributes are meant not only to be understood and worshiped, but they are to be experienced as well, seen in the everyday affairs of life. So those who appear to be powerful in the world are often impotent before God, while those who seem to be hopeless and helpless are under God's watchful eye.

There is another cultural side note that stands behind this text. It can be summarized by Mary's dilemma and the old expression, "Good girls don't." In ancient culture, virginity was an honored state, a badge of self-control and moral faithfulness. Mary would appear to many to have conceived a child out of wedlock. Her explanation of a divine conception would be hard to swallow (cf. Matt. 1:18–25). Her own question about lack of sexual experience in Luke 1:34 also indicates her own awareness of her faithfulness in this regard. Our culture unfortunately accepts sexual experience before wedlock as almost a given. Thus it is hard to appreciate the walk of faith Mary is asked to take here. In the midst of it all, however, what overwhelms her is not the "risk" of appearance, with its potential risk to her reputation, but the joy of serving and being involved with God. We too should have moral integrity and be quick to serve God, even at great risk to our reputation. This stands in contrast to seeking a misdirected self-fulfillment that not only dishonors our moral integrity before God, but also risks adding tension to our relationship to a future spouse.

Contemporary Significance

LUKE AIMS AT the heart with these texts. Believers must take God at his word and be amazed at his involvement with the details of their lives. God owes us nothing; we who have trusted Christ owe him everything. As the child leaped in Elizabeth's womb, so should our hearts leap in our breasts when we consider the many blessings of God that we experience. God does what he says, and he has said much on behalf of the believer. The key is to expect a reversal of fortune and a deliverance in the future. Whatever our lot in this sinful and fallen world now, those who fear God can expect vindication.

Also reflected in the hymn is a theology of status. Social standing is not a matter of the size of the balance in a checkbook or the address at which we live. We tend to view the rich and famous as blessed and powerful, as somehow favored by the divine. Yet this text makes it clear that God honors the humble and poor. He sees them, while we often ignore them. This has much to say about the value of every person. The address that matters to God is not a number on a street or bank account, but the stamp on a human heart. Many ministries go unsung that are committed to ministering in such contexts. It takes hard work. Often it involves breaking down years of skepticism and distrust. Such ministries lack the glamour of hanging out with the big hitters, but they please God.

Recently *Christianity Today* ran a story about Kathy Dudley, an Anglo-American woman with everything society could offer, spending her time ministering to the poorest of the poor in the inner city of Dallas. She sought to minister hope to kids who often had no parents and lived with the daily threat they might be assaulted or killed. In the midst of such urban terror, she tried to play a song of God's love and care. That kind of ministry reflects the values of this hymn. It paints a picture that replicates Jesus' own ministry, which singled out the poor for special attention (Luke 4:18–21; 7:22–23).[11]

It is important to be sensitive to the perspective of others as we minister and develop a Christian mind. Note the following poignant description of the current situation by William Pannell:

> The resources of my brethren—and a few sisters—are formidable in both human and economic terms. Influence among them and channeled through them is even more impressive. Some of them can pick up the phone and reach whoever is in the White House, and I suspect they can get a former President off his horse long enough to talk. With all the stored-up influence and IOU's these people have going for them, it would have been possible that they could have predicted an urban explosion in some major city. After all, the rumblings were there; a big one was as predictable as anything from a seismic center at Cal Tech.

---

11. Often one of the obstacles to effective ministry in the inner city is that we do not understand how minorities feel about their plight. An excellent work outlining that clearly and forthrightly is William Pannell, *The Coming Race Wars? A Cry for Reconciliation* (Grand Rapids: Zondervan, 1993). On a more international scale, one can note John Stott, *Involvement: Being a Responsible Christian in a Non-Christian Society*, vol. 1 (Old Tappan, N.J.: Revell, 1984).

But there were no warnings, no urgings to prepare, no emergency units available to the churches in the event of an explosion. Conferences were still being held. Pastors from mega-congregations were still convening in mountain settings to harangue seminaries for being irrelevant and to plan strategies for getting bigger and better. No black pastors were present at these gatherings, of course, even though their churches were "mega" before church-growth experts coined the phrase. The city was not on the agenda of those who attended the conferences, perhaps because their churches are not in cities. . . .

Though I am thankful for the help many evangelicals provide to ease the pain, the end point of my pondering on contemporary evangelicalism is disappointment. I expected more because, like their politically conservative counterparts, they said they have more to give. They were supposed to know more of the answers because they had learned to ask better questions after the debacle of a spent liberalism. I expected more because there has come to be an acceptance of the notion that conservative theology automatically translates into conservative politics and social agendas that sound impressive. By now, I thought, my evangelical colleagues would have put it together better, would have come up with a marriage of their theology and their political ideology, laid it alongside the heartbreak of the city, and carved out some outposts of the Kingdom there.

Those outposts are there. But their leaders won't be invited to the latest gatherings of the evangelical club. Those outposts are lead by a new breed, and they have yet to be discovered. That may not be a bad thing, either.[12]

Pannell is probably correct that our priorities are often geared to more "romantic" ministry needs. To face such realities, we need a "Christian mind," as John Stott defines it:

"The renewed mind." "The mind of Christ." "The Christian mind." Harry Blamires popularised this third expression in his book of that title, which since its publication in 1963 has had widespread influence. By a "Christian mind" he is referring not to a mind occupied with specifically "religious" topics, but to a mind which can think about even the most "secular" topics "Christianly," that is, from a Christian perspective. It is not the mind of a schizoid Christian who "hops in and out of his Christian mentality as the topic of conversation

---

12. Pannell, *The Coming Race Wars?* 38–39. I cite this section in detail so that the pain and mood of the remarks are clear.

changes from the Bible to the day's newspaper." No, the Christian mind, he writes, is "a mind trained, informed, equipped to handle data of secular controversy within a framework of reference which is constructed of Christian presuppositions."[13]

Only thinking Christianly will help us minister as Kathy Dudley does.

Those who know God and his grace can well echo Mary's song. We do not have the honor of giving birth to the Savior of the world, but we do have the blessing of becoming one of his children. The promises God makes to his humble and poor children, revealed by Mary in her hymn of praise, are promises in which we share. No deed is more powerful or heroic than rescuing humanity from sin. No act is more gracious than God's extension of mercy through his powerful, faithful, compassionate hand. The message of this text involves a call to rejoice that God is active and involved in the affairs of his children. As the well-known Christian song says, echoing this hymn, God works on behalf of those who fear him "from generation to generation."

There is no doubt that God expects the church to show compassion to the poor, because they are in a unique position to appreciate that they must be dependent on God. One of the delusions of wealth, power, and status is that we think we might be in control of life. Another illusion is that we are somehow better than others. God disdains the proud and that type of wedding to the trappings of the world (James 4:6–10). In our materialistic Western culture, where most of us are wealthy by world standards, it is easy to become blind to how materialistic we are and what we think we must have. This text reminds us that God values the heart, not what we possess.

On the other hand, this text is not a political manifesto that simply says the poor are right and so one can fight and even take up weapons for them. This text has often been used as the basis of a theology of liberation because of the passage's strong support to the poor. Such theologies have even defended taking up arms on behalf of the poor. But the vindication God supplies does not come through the barrel of a gun, but through a heart turned to God. The blessed are not the poor, but the pious poor. The difference is significant, because God does not fight with bullets but with changed souls.[14] Nevertheless, the church ignores the poor and their plight to its peril. Since God is clearly targeting the poor, so should the church. Inner-city ministry and active outreach programs that are after the heartbeat of God will find themselves ministering and communicating God's love to the poor.

---

13. Stott, *Involvement*, 1:58.

14. For a balanced evaluation of liberation theology, see Emilio Nuñez, *Liberation Theology* (Chicago: Moody, 1985).

Finally, let us note what causes Mary to be grateful. In an age where we expect so much as a matter of personal or human rights, we develop an attitude that much is owed us. How we can give or serve, or how much honor there is in doing so, is not high on our priority list. We even risk treating God more as if he were a friend or neighbor to be joked with or negotiated with, rather than as the Almighty Creator. Mary understands the difference and recognizes the honor given her to have God actively involved in her life. The sense of privilege, lacking any hint of merit, spills over into a waterfall of praise and gratitude—praise that is refreshing for its passion and sense of wonder.

Luke 1:57–80

WHEN IT WAS time for Elizabeth to have her baby, she gave birth to a son. ⁵⁸Her neighbors and relatives heard that the Lord had shown her great mercy, and they shared her joy.

⁵⁹On the eighth day they came to circumcise the child, and they were going to name him after his father Zechariah, ⁶⁰but his mother spoke up and said, "No! He is to be called John."

⁶¹They said to her, "There is no one among your relatives who has that name."

⁶²Then they made signs to his father, to find out what he would like to name the child. ⁶³He asked for a writing tablet, and to everyone's astonishment he wrote, "His name is John." ⁶⁴Immediately his mouth was opened and his tongue was loosed, and he began to speak, praising God. ⁶⁵The neighbors were all filled with awe, and throughout the hill country of Judea people were talking about all these things. ⁶⁶ Everyone who heard this wondered about it, asking, "What then is this child going to be?" For the Lord's hand was with him.

⁶⁷His father Zechariah was filled with the Holy Spirit and prophesied:

⁶⁸"Praise be to the Lord, the God of Israel,
    because he has come and has redeemed his people.
⁶⁹He has raised up a horn of salvation for us
    in the house of his servant David
⁷⁰(as he said through his holy prophets of long ago),
⁷¹salvation from our enemies
    and from the hand of all who hate us—
⁷²to show mercy to our fathers
    and to remember his holy covenant,
⁷³   the oath he swore to our father Abraham:
⁷⁴to rescue us from the hand of our enemies,
    and to enable us to serve him without fear
⁷⁵   in holiness and righteousness before him all our days.
⁷⁶And you, my child, will be called a prophet of the Most
        High;
    for you will go on before the Lord to prepare the way
        for him,

⁷⁷ to give his people the knowledge of salvation
   through the forgiveness of their sins,
⁷⁸ because of the tender mercy of our God,
   by which the rising sun will come to us from heaven
⁷⁹ to shine on those living in darkness
   and in the shadow of death,
to guide our feet into the path of peace."

⁸⁰And the child grew and became strong in spirit; and he lived in the desert until he appeared publicly to Israel.

WHEN GOD ACTS, we should listen. Zechariah has learned this lesson. When the birth of John was announced to him, he could not believe it, so the Lord gave him a sign for reflection: He would be unable to speak until all was fulfilled. Then he would know that God does what he says. The present passage shows the outcome of Zechariah's reflection. As a righteous man, he has learned from his mistake. Through the pain of the discipline, he emerges a stronger man of God. Those who are arrogant, thinking they know it all, have no need for God or for instruction. Zechariah is not an arrogant man.

In the midst of great joy and the recognition that God has been merciful to this priestly family, the time has come for the circumcision and naming of the child. Events like this are filled with custom. Tradition dictated that the child should receive a family name, honoring a parent, a grandparent, or some other relative (1 Macc. 1:1–2; Jub. 11:15; Josephus, *Life* 15).[1] Perhaps given Zechariah's recent debilitating condition, the crowd expects the child to be named Zechariah Junior.[2] But Elizabeth gives her son the name "John," sending shock waves of surprise through the crowd. The neighbors are so convinced an error had been made, since the name has no family precedent, that they ask the father through sign language (v. 62). Apparently Zechariah can neither hear nor speak. On a wood tablet probably covered with wax, Zechariah writes the name the angel had given him for the child (v. 13).[3] Zechariah knows he must follow those instructions, so he announces the child's name as "John."

---

1. E. Earle Ellis, *The Gospel of Luke* (London: Nelson, 1966), 78. Often the naming of a child took place earlier, at birth (Gen. 4:1; 25:25–26).

2. The imperfect in verse 59 is conative: The crowd "was wishing to name him" Zechariah.

3. Frederick Danker, *Jesus and the New Age* (Philadelphia: Fortress, 1988), 46.

Immediately his tongue is freed, and he speaks in praise to God. The long silence has allowed him to reflect on what God called for him to do, and he is now prepared to do it. Zechariah has learned that even righteous men have something to learn from God.

The event also indicates that the unusual sequence of events surrounding John points to the unusual nature of this child. The question of verse 66, "What then is this child going to be?" is a way of getting Luke's readers to pause and reflect on this special child. In some ways we lose the sense of drama today, because the story is so well known. To Luke's readers, the whole sequence would have raised interest, since these events take surprising turns. The sequence involving Zechariah opens up the drama of the Gospel to suggest the story is just getting interesting. Stay tuned, Luke implies, there is more explanation to come of just how special this child and the one to follow him is.

With his lips freed to speak, Zechariah now praises God for what he is doing. This second hymn is known as the *Benedictus* (again, the opening word of the Latin translation of this passage). Whereas Mary's hymn spoke in personal and general terms, this hymn of praise anticipates and overviews the careers of the two children whom divine destiny has brought together. Though John is the child born, Zechariah's hymn focuses on the person to whom John will point—the One promised long ago who would be sent to rescue and bless those who turn to him. Like Mary's hymn, this thanksgiving psalm is filled with Old Testament imagery and declares how the strong one from the house of David will be a light of rescue and guidance for his people. Luke introduces it as a response to the Spirit's filling of Zechariah. As is often the case in Luke, the Spirit leads to bold testimony and praise (cf. 1:41).

The psalm's main theme appears in verses 68–70, while its elaboration is the remainder of the psalm. The Lord God of Israel has once again acted on behalf of his people by visiting them and redeeming them (v. 68). As 2:26–32 makes clear, God's visitation comes with the Messiah's visitation.[4] God "has raised up a horn" in the house of David (v. 69), through which the visit comes. Zechariah's remarks here serve as a literary elaboration of 1:31–35. The image of the horn points to the strength of the one to come, since the metaphor looks back to the strong horns of an ox that can defeat opponents (Deut. 33:17). It represents an image of war (1 Sam. 2:10; 2 Sam. 22:3). An image of battle is invoked, and the Son of David is the powerful one in the midst of the conflict. The appeal to David's house makes it clear that God is

---

4. The theme of God's visit (*episkeptomai*) is important in Judaism as well as in the Old Testament; Wisdom 3:7; Psalms of Solomon 3:11; 10:4; Genesis 50: 24–25; Exodus 3:16; 4:31; 13:19; 30:12; Isaiah 23:17; Psalm 80:14; see Nolland, *Luke 1:1–9:20* (Dallas: Word, 1989), 86.

doing what the prophets promised long ago.[5] Zechariah anticipates messianic redemption and thanks God for it.

So what does Zechariah look forward to? He anticipates rescue from Israel's enemies and from the hands of all who hate God's people (v. 71). He foresees God showing mercy—that loyal love (*hesed*) that Mary spoke of—to the fathers, as God remembers his covenant promises and performs them through the one he sends (v. 72). Connecting "mercy" and "covenant" is not unusual, given Old Testament precedent (Deut. 7:9; 1 Kings 8:23). God's mercy is not a matter of mere words; it expresses itself in concrete action. So Zechariah describes what God will do in line with his promises. These oaths reach back to the early days of the nation and to Abraham (v. 73). The mention of Abraham looks back to God's first promise to Israel (Gen. 12:1–3).

What Zechariah desires most is to be rescued from his enemies so that he can serve God his whole life without fear and in righteousness and holiness (vv. 74–75). Here is the pious person's creed: "I want to serve you with my whole life, O Lord; enable me to do so and vindicate me in my pursuit." Zechariah is thrilled that the powerful Promised One has the authority to overcome such opposition and to provide the opportunity for such undistracted service. The term for service, *latreuo*, is used exclusively in the New Testament of service given to God or the gods (Luke 2:37; 4:8; Rom. 1:25).[6]

A national focus on concerns for Israel is clear in the hymn's introduction, where the God of Israel receives praise (Gen. 9:26; 1 Sam. 25:32; 1 Kings 1:48; Pss. 41:13; 89:52). The text from 1 Kings is significant, since there Solomon, another Son of David, is in view. The hymn's verbs contain more prophetic aorists,[7] since it is clear that Zechariah's remarks anticipate what Jesus and John will do.

Zechariah speaks as a righteous Jew here. He longs for the nation's vindication, possibly from Rome and the forces that direct her. In Luke's story, however, the scope of the hymn's hope may even be broader. He will show how the Promised One from David's house has power that extends beyond the political forces that sit over Israel (8:22–56). God has "raised up" (cf. Deut. 18:15, 18; Judg. 3:9, 15; 1 Sam. 2:35; 2 Sam. 23:1) this significant figure onto the world's stage. The Son of David (God's "servant"; v. 69) will become a servant himself (cf. Phil. 2:7). He will take on the cosmic forces that oppress humanity and bring pain and suffering into the world. When liberation comes through his ministry, sin and Satan will lead the enemy lines

---

5. For more on the hermeneutics of this passage's teaching, see Darrell L. Bock, "The Son of David and the Saints' Task: The Hermeneutics of Initial Fulfillment," *BibSac* 150 (1993): 440–57.

6. Strathmann, "λατρεύω," *TDNT*, 4:62–63.

7. See the comments on the prophetic aorist in the discussion of Luke 1:51–55.

(Luke 4:16–30; 11:14–23). That is why when Zechariah turns to compare the career of his son John with the child to come, it is the spiritual issues of their ministry that dominate.

Zechariah indicates that his own son will be a prophet for the Most High God, preparing a people for this coming visit of the Lord by telling them about "salvation through the forgiveness of sins" (vv. 76–77). He will go "before the Lord,"[8] preparing the way (cf. 1:17). Of course, the way of God is inseparably linked to what he will do through his Messiah. The message about salvation and the forgiveness of sins, which John preaches, will be like the commission Jesus gives to the church in 24:43–47, except that at that later commission, events will have filled in details that are only vague here.[9] God's tender mercy is at work in this plan. This portrait of John as forerunner and prophet, a bridge between the old era and the new, is reinforced in 7:26–35.

God will not only work through John. He will send "the rising sun" (v. 79; lit., "the morning star"), a likely allusion to Numbers 24:17 and Isaiah 11:1–10.[10] The king, seen as light, shows the spiritual dimension of his rule and indicates that he not only comes as a political figure, but also as a spiritual one. The image of light is important to Luke (Luke 2:32; Acts 13:49; 26:17–20). Once it is introduced in the Messiah, it is not withdrawn. So the Son, who serves as a bright morning light, comes from heaven and shines on those in darkness and death, guiding them into the path of peace. Significantly Zechariah puts himself among those in darkness. As a spiritual man, he knows that the only way to walk righteously is to follow the path God sets. Zechariah knows that the Messiah is coming. He will be powerful; but more than that, he will be light.

Bridging Contexts

APPLYING THE MESSAGE of hymns or psalms can be tricky. We all sense as we read a text like this one that our experience is not quite that of the psalmist and that his concerns are not quite ours. Zechariah, for example, has worries about Rome, which we no longer have!

---

8. On the debate whether God or Jesus is meant by "Lord" here, see Fitzmyer, *Luke I–IX*, 385–86, and Danker, *Jesus and the New Age*, 49. Danker has the better case here in terms of this literary context in seeing God in view. But it is important to remember how linked God is to his work through Jesus in this text.

9. On forgiveness of sins, see Colin Brown, "Redemption," *NIDNTT*, 3:212.

10. On the "rising star," see Raymond Brown, *The Birth of the Messiah* (Garden City, N.Y.: Doubleday, 1977), 373–74. The allusion to *anatole*, which is a reference "to that which springs up," may conceal a double entendre—a reference to the morning sun and to the branch, since the term is also used that way in the Greek Old Testament (Isa. 11:1–10; Jer. 23:5; Zech. 6:12).

The lesson from such a passage is not grounded in the fact that we replicate the psalmist's experience in terms of its details, but that we share in the spiritual tension or hope of faith into which experience has placed him. The hymn asks us to enter in by identifying with the psalmist's attempt to come to grips with his circumstances, much like we have to come to grips with the circumstances God puts into our lives. Thus the attitudes of faith, trust, hope, joy, sorrow, and sometimes the honesty with which a problem is faced often instruct us.

As with the previous portions of this introductory section of Luke, the interpretive bridge comes through the character representation of Zechariah and the teaching of his hymn. Zechariah portrays the reflections of a mature and pious man who still has much to learn about trusting God. Here is a spiritual man who knows that one never coasts on the basis of past spirituality. God revealed to him through the sign of silence that the time to talk had passed. It was time to listen silently to God. During the months of Elizabeth's pregnancy, while God's promise was slowly coming to pass, Zechariah was learning that God brings his promise to fruition in his own timing and in his own way. He has learned his lesson, and his obedience becomes public, resulting in praise to God.

Thus, in terms of the narrative, Zechariah speaks as a more mature man now, one who has just been taught much by God during the silent reflection God gave him. He speaks from his experience now with a credibility that asks for our reflection. One of the major lessons is that even if all his neighbors do not understand why Zechariah does not do things the way they have been done, he will walk where God tells him to walk. The pressure of custom will not become a reason to disobey God.

This lesson is an important one. Peer pressure and the attitudes of the world can often make us act in ways that differ from where God would take us. Whether in values, entertainment, or the way we do business, the world's ways are not God's ways. To hear God and not the customs of the world is important. But there is a more subtle form of following peer pressure, when custom becomes confused with commandment in the church. I have heard about churches fighting over the color of the new carpet, the nature of the music in the praise service, the age of hymns, the use of drama, and other things that can only be classified as neutral in themselves. Yet sometimes we exalt taste and custom to the level of a revelation from Mount Sinai. Zechariah's moment of reflection and resistance to the path of popular custom show that he will follow God's direct leading over "the way this is normally done."

The hymn is a grand overview of God's bringing his larger promise of salvation and deliverance to pass. Bridging it into the present involves restating how timeless the events tied to Jesus are and highlighting the manifestation of God's attributes that are evident in these events. Here two great promises of God—one to Abraham (v. 73) and one to David (vv. 69–70)—are alluded to as being realized in the events surrounding these two newborns. The hope for the saints is rescue and redemption, which enable them to serve God without distraction, for their enemies stand vanquished in the power of the promised king. But the Messiah of power is also the king of spiritual light. He now guides the path of those who follow him. The superhighway he has built is named peace. That is the path he pursues as he takes others who follow him out of the shadow of death.

BESIDES THE OVERVIEW and description of the careers of John and Jesus that serve as the content base for this text's teaching, several key attitudes are central to the application of this text. The lesson that pious Zechariah learns is important, especially to those who have a rich spiritual heritage. He is a man of lifelong faith who still needed to grow. It is all too easy to view one's spiritual life as something that can be mastered rather than something to be maintained.

Often we are tempted, on the basis of past experience, to put our spiritual well-being on cruise control and rest on the laurels of a tradition of activity. I love seeing a saint in his seventies who has known the Lord for decades but who still wants to know him better and more deeply. What an encouragement such a person is to me as a younger saint, for I know that, Lord willing, there are many years of the walk still ahead. How thrilling it is to know that some see their walk with God as a challenge and that the thrill of divine involvement in life has not waned, even though the years have moved on. It causes one to desire to keep on keeping on. Zechariah reveals that even good men can get better and learn to walk in deeper trust with God. That simple lesson comes to the fore in his naming his child John even though others want to name him something else. God has taught him in the quiet moments of the time between the announcement of the birth and the child's arrival that his sovereign will must be done and his mercy, though sometimes working in surprising ways, must be followed.

We have our Zechariahs today—those who seek to serve God with fullness of heart as they realize that one has much yet to learn from God, even after years of walking with him. An interesting work to ponder comes from the pen of Henri Nouwen.[11] His autobiography relates a fascinating journey

---

11. Henri J. M. Nouwen, *In the Name of Jesus: Reflections on Christian Leadership* (New York: Crossroads, 1994). Citation below is from pp. 71–72.

from teaching pastoral psychology and theology at Notre Dame, Yale, and Harvard for twenty years to burnout. From there he undertook a ministry in the home of the mentally challenged. There he learned that "service" given even to those whom the world does not see taught him as much as or more than his learning in seminary. Sometimes God is able to teach us in the midst of surprising circumstances. Ministry is not power and prestige, but humble service and trust. Those who seek God's deliverance and pursue it in holiness and service sometimes find themselves in places they never imagined ministering and in ways they never contemplated. Here is his own testimony:

> Let me summarize. My movement from Harvard to L'Arche made me aware in a new way how much my own thinking about Christian leadership had been affected by the desire to be relevant, the desire for popularity, and the desire for power. Too often I looked at being relevant, popular, and powerful as ingredients of an effective ministry. The truth, however, is that these are not vocations but temptations. Jesus asks, "Do you love me?" Jesus sends us out to be shepherds, and Jesus promises a life in which we increasingly have to stretch out our hands and be led to places where we would rather not go. He asks us to move from a concern for relevance to a life of prayer, from worries about popularity to communal and mutual ministry, and from a leadership built on power to a leadership in which we critically discern where God is leading us and our people.
>
> The people of L'Arche are showing me new ways. I am a slow learner. Old patterns that have proved quite effective are not easy to give up. But as I think about the Christian leader of the next century, I do believe that those from whom I least expected to learn are showing me the way. I hope and pray that what I am learning in my new life is something that is not just good for me to learn, but something that helps you, as well, to catch a glimpse of the Christian leader of the future.

Though our God is awesome and powerful, he uses that power in surprising ways. He sends a king who leads initially not with a sword, but with his word. He rescues not through a bloody war, but with a new way. He leads not just with might, but with light—his teaching and life. When we think of a promised king, we think of a palace and knights, the king's army arrayed to defend his people. Jesus' kingship does not seclude itself in a palace, nor does he have a round table. This king walked among his people and lived as they did. He was baptized by the one pointing the way to him, because life is not a function of power as the world tends to think, but is a reflection of character and light.

If one asks why this king, sent by God, rules by being like the morning sun, it is because the way of life and the path to peace is not a matter of coercion or the controlling use of power. It is a matter of character. Why else would the forerunner, preparing the way for God, address forgiveness of sin? Why else would the king who leads people out of darkness and death's shadow be compared to a light? Why else would a journey metaphor, the path of peace, be the picture of what it means to be redeemed? Though entry into it takes but a moment, salvation is not a momentary affair. It is a lifelong journey of the heart, a journey guided by one's allegiance to the Morning Star, who not only goes before us but shows us that the way to reflect God is to refract his character in ever-growing ways.

In other words, the question remains before us: How do we define life? Is it in power and in the ability to "take control," or is it in following the one who is in control? The text leaves no doubt that we should follow the one who is the source of light. The only road to righteousness and peace, even for a righteous man like Zechariah, is to be prepared to see the light and follow it. The text raises the question and answers it with notes of praise. See the morning star, Jesus, and follow the light in the way of peace. What precisely that pathway involves is the rest of this Gospel's story, for which this hymn serves as a guiding introduction. In a real sense, the application of this text is found in the entirety of this Gospel's message.

Luke 2:1–21

IN THOSE DAYS Caesar Augustus issued a decree that a census should be taken of the entire Roman world. ²(This was the first census that took place while Quirinius was governor of Syria.) ³And everyone went to his own town to register.

⁴So Joseph also went up from the town of Nazareth in Galilee to Judea, to Bethlehem the town of David, because he belonged to the house and line of David. ⁵He went there to register with Mary, who was pledged to be married to him and was expecting a child. ⁶While they were there, the time came for the baby to be born, ⁷and she gave birth to her firstborn, a son. She wrapped him in cloths and placed him in a manger, because there was no room for them in the inn.

⁸And there were shepherds living out in the fields nearby, keeping watch over their flocks at night. ⁹An angel of the Lord appeared to them, and the glory of the Lord shone around them, and they were terrified. ¹⁰But the angel said to them, "Do not be afraid. I bring you good news of great joy that will be for all the people. ¹¹Today in the town of David a Savior has been born to you; he is Christ the Lord. ¹²This will be a sign to you: You will find a baby wrapped in cloths and lying in a manger."

¹³Suddenly a great company of the heavenly host appeared with the angel, praising God and saying,

¹⁴"Glory to God in the highest,
   and on earth peace to men on whom his favor rests."

¹⁵When the angels had left them and gone into heaven, the shepherds said to one another, "Let's go to Bethlehem and see this thing that has happened, which the Lord has told us about."

¹⁶ So they hurried off and found Mary and Joseph, and the baby, who was lying in the manger. ¹⁷When they had seen him, they spread the word concerning what had been told them about this child, ¹⁸and all who heard it were amazed at what the shepherds said to them. ¹⁹But Mary treasured up all these things and pondered them in her heart. ²⁰The shepherds returned, glorifying and praising God for all the things they had heard and seen, which were just as they had been told.

²¹On the eighth day, when it was time to circumcise him, he was named Jesus, the name the angel had given him before he had been conceived.

Original Meaning

IN THE ANCIENT world, if anyone had asked if there was a more important person than Caesar, the emperor and ruler of the vast Roman empire, the answer surely would have been no. Yet it is the birth of a little boy in a rural Judean village that causes the angels to launch into praise. The circumstances of Jesus' birth are so basic and humble in origin that it is hard to appreciate just who it is that is born here. Most regal figures are born with great ceremony and celebration. But Jesus' birth is as average as it comes. His birthplace is determined in part by the need to fill out a census—probably a means to register for paying taxes.[1] The journeying of everyone "to his own town to register" appears to be a sensitive decision by the Romans that allowed the Jews to follow their own custom of going to one's ancestral home.[2] So Joseph and Mary go to Bethlehem, a place identified as "the town of David," because of Joseph's lineage in the family. Mary, who did not have to go, goes anyway, possibly because Joseph wants to be present at the birth of her child, soon to happen.

The birth takes place in humble circumstances, for the child is born in either a stable or a cave.[3] The wrapping of his fragile limbs in cloths was common in the ancient world to keep them protected and in place. They are in this strange birthing room, "because there was no room for them at the inn." Though modern renditions dramatize a search for a room, the text tells the story with exceptional brevity. Such inns would have been either the second story of a house that housed animals below or a one-story building with a

---

1. The issue of the timing of this census is one of the most heavily debated chronological-historical issues in this Gospel. The mention of Quirinius and a first census while he was governor of Syria in v. 2 is a major problem, since he is known to have produced a census in A.D. 6 (Josephus, *Antiquities* 17.13.2 §§ 34–44; 17.13.5 § 354; 18.1.1 §§ 1–10), about ten years after the placement of Jesus' birth during the time of King Herod, who died in 4 B.C. (see Luke 1:5). Some are convinced there is an error here (e.g., R. Brown, *The Birth of the Messiah*, 547–56). In a detailed excursus, I have defended the historicity of the remark elsewhere (see Darrell L. Bock, *Luke* [Baker Exegetical Commentary of the New Testament; Grand Rapids: Baker, 1994], excursus 2, "The Census of Quirinius in the Time of Herod the Great").

2. Brown, *The Birth of the Messiah*, 549, allows for this possibility. Other Jewish customs the Romans allowed were a tax exemption every seventh year and Sabbath observance.

3. Demonstrated by his being laid in a manger, an animal's feeding trough. About the Greek word for manger (*phatne*), see Hengel, "φάτνη," *TDNT*, 9:53–54.

stable next to it. Since no such locale has a vacancy, the couple finds shelter where they can. Jesus therefore enters the world in as mundane a way as possible. His first hours of human existence are spent in a manger. The agent of God lives without pretense.

The testimony to Jesus' birth from the angelic host to shepherds is significant in scope. Creation has no more mysterious and exalted beings than angels, who represent the testimony of the heavens to what is occurring. Moreover, there are no more "normal Joes" in ancient culture than shepherds. They represent the lowly and humble who respond to God's message, for their vocation is seen positively in Scripture (Matt. 18:12; Mark 6:34; Luke 15:4; John 10; Eph. 4:11; Heb. 13:2; 1 Peter 2:25). Thus, heaven meets and greets the average person through the angelic announcement to these pastoral figures. Jesus' birth is more than a family affair.[4] The announcement of "good news of great joy that will be for all the people" (v. 10) indicates that God desires to speak to every person about the coming of Jesus, since all humanity is impacted by his coming.

The announcement by an unnamed angel is the third such announcement in the infancy material (see Luke 1:5–25, 26–38). The narrative follows a standard form: appearance (v. 9a), fear (v. 9b), a "do not be afraid" remark (vv. 10–11), and the announcement of a verifying sign (v. 12). The angel informs the shepherds of what God is doing through Jesus. The glory of God's presence surrounds the heavenly witness, adding drama to the scene. Like the fear that gripped earlier participants (1:12, 29), the visible presence of heavenly authority makes the shepherds nervous.

After calming the shepherds' fears, the angel declares what God is doing. Humanity has nothing to fear when God moves in grace. The text refers to the announcement as "good news," using the verbal form of the word from which we get the term *gospel*.[5] The term is not culturally insignificant, since the birth of the emperor Augustus was announced with a report of "good news" and the arrival of a "savior."[6] Luke's remarks intend a similar declaration of this baby's greatness. This is why all people can be filled with joy. Jesus may be lying in an animal trough, but heaven is present at his birth.

The titles the angel uses for the newborn child are significant. "Savior" (*soter*) reflects the call of Jesus to deliver his people, as Mary's and Zechariah's hymns had declared (cf. 1:46–55, 67–79). This term is rich in Old Testament roots, especially as a figure for divine deliverance (Deut. 20:4; Josh. 22:22;

---

4. R. Tannehill, *The Narrative Unity of Luke-Acts: A Literary Interpretation*, vol. 1 (Philadelphia: Fortress, 1986), 38.

5. Friedrich, εὐαγγελίζομαι," *TDNT*, 2:710.

6. Marshall, *Commentary on Luke*, 109.

Pss. 24:5; 25:5; Isa. 25:9). In Greek culture, all types of figures were called *saviors*, from doctors and rulers to philosophers.[7] "Christ" (from the Greek word for "Anointed One") is indicative of his role as the promised Messiah. "Messiah" (Hebrew for "Anointed One") is a rare term in the Old Testament. Psalm 2:2 is the main technical regal use, and Luke's use looks back to Luke 1:27, 31–35, 68–72, 79; 2:4.[8] What about "Lord"? Of the three titles, this one is left unexplained in this context. One could well argue that the rest of this Gospel and the book of Acts serve to explain the nature of Jesus' authority and lordship, as well as the extent of the exercise of his power in overcoming sin and the forces of evil.

The angelic revelation of a sign implies that the angel wanted the shepherds to go and see the child for themselves. They will recognize the child when they see a newborn baby in the town of David "wrapped in cloths and lying in a manger." As with all prophetic declarations of a sign, a visible physical reality confirms the announcement. This is the third sign in the infancy material (1:19–20, 36).

As if the announcement were not enough, the heavenly choir strikes up in praise to God, giving him honor for what is taking place. The angels' refrain serves as a commentary on the flow of events. Glory should be given to God in the most exalted of ways, while on earth one should see that this child means peace for those "on whom his favor rests." The picture of being a person of God's favor was a Jewish way of saying that someone was numbered among God's chosen people, much like the "God-fearers" of 1:50–53. This remark makes it clear that salvation and its fullness are not automatic for everyone. Only those who respond to God's grace and follow the path lit by the rising sun will experience the peace into which that path leads (1:78–79). Jesus comes for all, but not all respond to and benefit from his coming.

The shepherds decide to take a look at what God is doing. They find the child in the manger, just as the angel has said. Once again God is shown to keep his word. The shepherds share their story with those present. They respond with obedience and cannot contain themselves from testifying to what God has done in making Jesus' presence evident to them. Luke's reader is supposed to identify with their response to God's first revelation of this birth to the human race.

As is often the case when God's work is reported, those who hear their testimony are amazed (cf. 1:21, 63; 2:33), while Mary simply ponders it all. The event closes with the shepherds' returning to their flocks and giving

---

7. Foerster and Fohrer, "σωτήρ," *TDNT*, 7:103–21.

8. On the term *anointed one*, see M. De Jonge, "The Use of the Word 'Anointed' in the Time of Jesus," *NovT* 8 (1965–66): 132–48.

glory and praise to God, for things were just as he said. God will perform his word. This is the final note that Jesus' birth should bring.[9]

Jesus is circumcised as any eight-day-old Jewish boy would be (Gen. 17:11—12; Lev. 12:3) and is officially given his name, "Jesus." His parents reflect the characteristics of those who follow God's law and obey him (cf. 1:31). Jesus' family roots are steeped in Jewish piety and faithfulness.

HOW DO WE learn from Scripture? One way is through reading the text and seeing how its assessment of people and what is important contrasts with the ways we make such assessments today. Such instruction tends to emerge in the major themes of a passage, not in its minor details of description. In other words, sometimes the portrait of Scripture screams out in its contrast to the way we do things. It asks whether something in our life or value structure needs reflection and revision. The present passage is such a text. The arrival of the incarnated Son of God is a study in contrast between how God did it and how we might have done it.

Thus, the key bridge to our context is gained from reflecting on the contrasts of this text. In Luke 1, the angel announced that Mary's child would be a king of an everlasting kingdom. Zechariah noted that the Coming One would be like the rising sun, who provides light to guide our feet in the way of peace. Yet the birth of the Christ child is so simple and is located in as average a village as one can have. This is no normal setting for the birth of a king; Jesus' birth is almost a story of the "rags of royalty." When his parents wrap Jesus in cloths to keep his limbs straight and lay him in the manger, the humble emptying of the Christ has begun (Phil. 2:5—11). Importance is not a matter of one's environment or the supposed status that things bring. Rather, importance is a function of one's role in God's work. Jesus is important not because of the setting of his birth, but because of who he is before God. For one moment, the center of God's activity resides in an animal trough. The dignity of this event comes from the person lying at the center. Sometimes God's work goes on quietly in hidden locales.

Another significant note is the sense of community and involvement God gives to this event. Though in one sense this is a private moment for Mary and Joseph, in another it involves others, such as shepherds and angels. God is not a God of isolation. He seeks to involve himself with creation. The birth of the Son of God involves the response of all the parts of creation, from those who tend sheep to those who watch over them from heaven.

---

9. This conceptual combination is frequent in the Old Testament (Josh. 7:19; 1 Chron. 16:35; Pss. 66:2; 106:47).

Noteworthy too is the choice of shepherds to be among the first to hear about the new child and see him. Some commentators argue that the shepherds symbolize God's meeting the despised, but this negative reputation for shepherds is later than the first-century Judaism.[10] The biblical shepherd imagery is mostly positive, and the association of shepherds with these events adds an image of everyday living to the scene. God is involved not just with the special or the great, but with all people. His announcement of the child's arrival to everyday folk shows his commitment to the mass of humanity. Those "on whom God's favor rests" include those whose claim to fame may be nothing more than that they wake up each day and pursue a living in service to God.

The notes of praise that have filled the opening chapters continue in this section. The need to praise God is universal, no matter what era we belong to. The notes of praise underline the importance of verbal praise to God. These heavenly notes lift up the soul and open us up to be receptive to God. Praise given to God benefits those who offer that praise by refreshing their souls.

Another key issue is the presence of the supernatural in the story. Such detail is hard for many in the modern world to swallow. But the modern world has a strange love-hate relationship with the supernatural. Many dive into astrology, believing in forces at work behind the stars, but they pause at angels. They deny the existence of these unseen forces, but only until a crisis comes and they cry out to them out of their helplessness. They challenge the existence of the God of the Bible, but rush headlong into bookstores to discover the latest about the spirits at work in nature or devour the most recent New Age craze. Does such schizophrenia make sense?

The discussion of angels in Scripture (or demons, for that matter) is like heaven pushing back the curtains on a world behind the scenes. When Paul says in Ephesians 6:12 that our struggle is not against flesh and blood, but against principalities and powers, we learn something about invisible but real forces with which we must deal blindly unless we walk in the faith. We must realize that not every spiritual force in the world is a good one that roots us in our relationship to God, as these angels in Luke 2 (see Eph. 2:2!). Hebrews 1:14 tells us that good angels are ministering spirits who serve God. We cannot see them, but they do labor on our behalf, and in that we can rejoice.

Now, one should not be preoccupied with the angels' existence, nor with the existence of Satan and his demons. Rather, as Ephesians 6:10—18 argues,

---

10. This is, for example, the interpretation of William Hendriksen, *The Gospel According to Luke* (Grand Rapids: Baker, 1978), 149. The evidence for this Jewish view of shepherds is late, involving the *Talmud* and the *Midrash to the Psalms*, texts produced centuries later.

we should stand faithful with our armor on, walking with God to resist whatever obstacles such hostile forces might raise against us. As we walk with God, we possess ample resources to resist the devil.

THE BIRTH OF Jesus is a lesson in God's faithfulness, but it also reveals God's heart and character. For God identifies with the human race, and this birth reflects such identification. The most humble birth for the most exalted figure ever born shows that the key values of life are found in the life itself, not in the accouterments that come with life.

The note of humility surrounding this birth of Jesus issues a major challenge to our culture, where braggadocio and self-promoting public relations are often a way of life. Such tensions can hit us at a personal or corporate level. I choose a corporate example, because personal applications, involving competition and jealousy, seem more obvious. As a theological school we are told that in order to "sell" ourselves to our potential constituency, we must have a "niche," something that says we are unique. We have to demonstrate to people why they would want to study with us. Churches can face similar situations. But how does such a quest meet the humility test? Scripture tells us we are all special and that we all have a niche in the body. Competition is something God abhors. Institutions—colleges, theological schools, churches, etc.—should present themselves as servants, as partners with many other agencies that also serve God. Some students God calls to study with us; others he will call elsewhere. Humility means essentially faithfully serving God with integrity in ministry. One can pursue excellence without hoping to run others into the ground. Ministries do need serious affirmation, but we must avoid the temptation to shout about our presence. If credit comes, let God and others bring it. If we are doing a solid job of presenting and reflecting truth, let others note it. Trumpets are best left in the hands of angels, not ourselves.

The birth of Jesus also shows that greatness is not a function of the size of one's bank account or one's social résumé. Status does not make the person, for God recognizes the quality of the inner person. In Jesus, of course, that was a given, but God also makes a point about status by the way he introduces Jesus into the world. The Incarnation displays divine values by how the most powerful person ever born entered the world, in total simplicity and humility. Simplicity has a divine power all its own. God shows his greatness walking with us as we are where we are, not in elitist isolation and insulation, which is often the way the powerful live in the world. We learn to see things the way God does if we do not pay attention to addresses, clothes, bank accounts, or résumés, but consider who honors God (James 2:1–5).

In a real sense, the story of Jesus is our story, told to us and for us just as if we had been among the angels on that night near Bethlehem. What the angels announced to the shepherds that night is announced on behalf of all humanity. Their journey to see these things should be every person's journey to see what God is up to in Jesus. When people see that everything happened according to what God had told the shepherds, they and we should sense that God does what he says. Their sense of amazement should be matched by our own. The best way we show our amazement is with the response of a grateful, faithful walk that has ample donations of praise.

Perhaps after almost two thousand years of publicity about Jesus, the church takes the amazing involvement of God with us for granted. The world certainly rarely takes the time to really look and see what Jesus is all about. Usually it never gets past the story about the baby Jesus. Is that the church's fault for failing to engage the world? Is the world too busy to stop and notice or too distracted by other appeals? Is it both? If the world does stop and look, it often sees Jesus as one teacher among many. But the teaching of the heavenly host rules out such a limiting view of Jesus. He is the Savior, who is Christ the Lord. He is no longer in a crib and no longer confined to a manger. He is now seated at the right hand of God, aware of what we do and say (Luke 22:69). Who the baby Jesus was is nothing compared to who he is. His birth and the testimony surrounding it tells us he was a special child. But his life, ministry, and resurrection secure the fact that he is unique. No wonder Mary pondered all these things in her heart, as even we should today. But she has seen nothing yet, and neither have we. God has only just begun to reveal his story of his involvement with us through Jesus.

The response of the shepherds and Mary involves both praise and obedience. Mary's obedience extends to her naming of the child. When God spoke, Mary listened. The testimony to her obedience is short, but telling. Similarly, the announcement of the sign leads the shepherds not only to follow where God has led them, but also to share what God has shown them when they arrive to see God's word come to pass. So also we should follow where God leads and with grace testify to his direction in our lives. When God guides us through trial, a vocational crossroads, or a decision involving a mate, our future, or our children, we should be prepared to speak about how he has impacted our lives. Often we share this with fellow friends in the church, but a word to anyone who might listen should not be shunned.

The variety of reactions to the birth of Jesus noted here should not surprise us. People respond to him differently. Some are amazed, but do not engage him at any deeper level. Others offer praise, while others ponder what Jesus means. There is no doubt that in this passage Mary and the shepherds are the central exemplary characters, reflecting the testimony and obedience that should characterize saints.

All of the figures in this story received a new revelation of who God is and what he is about. But we should never take God for granted, nor should praise become formal and routine. What an honor it is to know God and see him active in our lives. To regain the flame, we must turn to him and honestly admit where we are and ask him to open our cloudy eyes. Sometimes just the reflection that comes from the Christmas season or reflecting on Jesus' story can renew our sense of relationship to God. The King, the Son of David, the Lord, the Savior, was sent from heaven to identify with us, walk with us, die for us, be raised for us, and to relate to us—that is the story of Jesus, a story worthy of praise and worthy to be told. No wonder the famous and beloved blind believer and hymn writer, Fanny Crosby, wrote:

> To God be the glory great things He hath done!
> So loved He the world that He gave us His son,
> who yielded His life an atonement for sin
> and opened the Lifegate that all may go in.

Here is the testimony of a woman who knew pain and yet saw God in her darkness. That is why the earth should hear his voice in our testimony to his love. That is why the world should see our testimony in a life that honors him. That is why we of all people should rejoice at the story of his coming.

The reason for our rejoicing starts with Jesus in the story of his birth, but it does not stop there. He is involved in our lives even now. By the Spirit his presence continues to express itself in us. In his care we see his hand working for us. Sometimes he works to reshape us, and the reworking means pain. But it is always done with an eye to our care. Now instead of our looking on his meekness as he is laid as a babe in a manger, he looks on our weakness as he cares for us as the Great Shepherd. The story of Jesus' birth does not end with him wrapped in swaddling clothes. Often the beauty of the Christmas story gets treated as if it were the whole story about Jesus—God showing himself in the birth of a special child. But this story is only the beginning of God's new work. That labor has continued century after century in fresh generations of believers who have shared in the blessing of relationship he provides. As believers we belong to a great train of witnesses spanning the ages, who have lifted their voices and offered their souls in gratitude for what this birth meant. One day in heaven, face to face with men and women of every generation and nation, we will offer thanks before him. There is nothing wrong with getting a little practice now!

Luke 2:22–40

❦

WHEN THE TIME of their purification according to the Law of Moses had been completed, Joseph and Mary took him to Jerusalem to present him to the Lord ²³(as it is written in the Law of the Lord, "Every firstborn male is to be consecrated to the Lord"), ²⁴and to offer a sacrifice in keeping with what is said in the Law of the Lord: "a pair of doves or two young pigeons."

²⁵Now there was a man in Jerusalem called Simeon, who was righteous and devout. He was waiting for the consolation of Israel, and the Holy Spirit was upon him. ²⁶It had been revealed to him by the Holy Spirit that he would not die before he had seen the Lord's Christ. ²⁷Moved by the Spirit, he went into the temple courts. When the parents brought in the child Jesus to do for him what the custom of the Law required, ²⁸Simeon took him in his arms and praised God, saying:

> ²⁹"Sovereign Lord, as you have promised,
>   you now dismiss your servant in peace.
> ³⁰For my eyes have seen your salvation,
> ³¹   which you have prepared in the sight of all people,
> ³²a light for revelation to the Gentiles
>   and for glory to your people Israel."

³³The child's father and mother marveled at what was said about him. ³⁴Then Simeon blessed them and said to Mary, his mother: "This child is destined to cause the falling and rising of many in Israel, and to be a sign that will be spoken against, ³⁵so that the thoughts of many hearts will be revealed. And a sword will pierce your own soul too."

³⁶There was also a prophetess, Anna, the daughter of Phanuel, of the tribe of Asher. She was very old; she had lived with her husband seven years after her marriage, ³⁷and then was a widow until she was eighty-four. She never left the temple but worshiped night and day, fasting and praying. ³⁸Coming up to them at that very moment, she gave thanks to God and spoke about the child to all who were looking forward to the redemption of Jerusalem.

³⁹When Joseph and Mary had done everything required by
the Law of the Lord, they returned to Galilee to their own town
of Nazareth. ⁴⁰And the child grew and became strong; he was
filled with wisdom, and the grace of God was upon him.

JESUS WAS BORN to parents who kept the laws of
Judaism. In these two scenes, they engage in the
prescribed rites of purification after the birth of
a child and travel to Jerusalem to present Jesus to
the Lord. Such acts of piety show that Jesus has roots in pious faith. The point
is significant because of Jesus' later conflict with the Jewish religious leadership. Does he challenge them because he was raised in a home that did not
honor the faith? Obviously not. Jesus came from a family that sought to
honor God.

The journey of Jesus' parents to the temple in Luke 2:22–24 combines
three separate ceremonies as recorded in God's law: the purification of a
woman forty days after the birth of a child (Lev. 12:2–4, 6), the presentation
of the firstborn to God (Ex. 13:2, 12, 16; 34:19; Num. 18:15–16), and the
dedication of the firstborn into the Lord's service (1 Sam. 1–2).[1] Though
this dedication to service is like many others that took place in Israel for
centuries, this one is unique because of the call of this child.

The rite of purification involved the offering of a burnt sacrifice and sin
offering. The mention of turtledoves indicates that Joseph and Mary uti-
lized the offering of the poor, though middle classes also made such sacrifices.[2] The text refers to "their" sacrifice, which seems odd at first glance in
that a purification offering would normally be Mary's alone. However, seeing that Joseph undoubtedly helped in Mary's delivery at the distant town,
he was also rendered unclean and needed to make a sacrifice for himself (*m.
Niddah* 5.1; 2.5; 1.3–5). Another possibility is that Luke is alluding in verse
22 to all the sacrifices involved in the three ceremonies and that those offerings, some hers and others theirs, are combined. All these sacrifices indicate
how seriously Judaism took approaching God in worship and how prepared
a heart and soul one should have as they address God.

As Joseph and Mary proceed, they meet a pious old man, Simeon, either
in the court of the Gentiles or the court of women (since Mary is present).
We are not told Simeon's vocation; all we know is that he is "righteous and
devout" (v. 25). Among the "righteous" (*dikaios*) of the Old Testament were
Job (Job 1:1) and many of the prophets. The word "devout" (*eulabes*) was used

---

1. Reicke, "παρίστημι," *TDNT*, 5:841, esp. n. 14.
2. Plummer, *Luke*, 65; C. Brown, "Bird," *NIDNTT*, 1:172.

in Greek culture of statesmen (Plato, *Statesman*, 311b); Philo used this word to describe Abraham (Philo, *Who is the Heir?* 6 § 22). Whereas the shepherds symbolized the average person on the street, Simeon represents the testimony of a wise elder who has walked with God. Part of his wisdom is seen in that he is looking for the hope of the nation, the consummation of God's promise—"the consolation of Israel" (v. 25). Saints in touch with God's heart often await expectantly the completion of God's promises. This revered saint is led to see what the arrival of this child means.

Simeon, like Zechariah and Mary, is expectant that God will deliver Israel. He has not given up believing that God will complete his promise, and his living in light of that hope brings perspective to the present. The Spirit, the source of all revelation and testimony, has told him that before he passes away, he will see "the Lord's Christ." Therefore, when the child Jesus arrives, he is there and is led by God to offer a note of praise (known as the *Nunc Dimittis*, a name that comes from the Latin beginning to the hymn). In that song, which includes some prediction, not all the notes are happy, for the career of the Lord's Christ, though glorious, is not absent of trial and disappointment. The locale of Simeon's prophecy, the temple, is significant for Jewish readers, for this prophet is testifying to Jesus in the midst of the nation's most sacred locale. Simeon begins by saying that God can take him now, for he has fulfilled his call of seeing the child who is the Christ. Once again, Luke has emphasized how God has performed his word.

This child is the salvation of God and represents the public display of God's concern for people (vv. 30–31). Jesus is light, a theme already noted in 1:78–79 and one that remains in Luke's mind as late as Acts 26:22–23. Simeon's remarks recall Isaiah 60:1–3, where the light of salvation comes with revelation and glory as the result. Jesus serves two constituencies with his salvation, Israel and the Gentiles, but each in a slightly different way. He is light for all, but is "revelation to the Gentiles" and "glory to your people Israel."[3] He is a "revelation" to Gentiles, for they will be brought into blessing through his ministry in a way they could have hardly imagined before his coming (cf. also John 1:3–9). Jesus is "glory" to Israel, for through him they will perform their service of ministry to the world. All eyes will be drawn to Israel through what her Messiah achieves. He is the magnet that makes her great. When the promises of God come, they come through the Promised One of Israel.

As the parents marvel at the note of praise, the more somber notes of promise are revealed. Everything is not roses in Israel, for Jesus' coming will

---

3. On the syntax of this line, where "light" is the general point applied for all, while "revelation" is for Gentiles and "glory" for Israel are parallel to one another, see Fitzmyer, *Luke*, 428.

yield the rising and falling of many in the nation. This imagery is from Isaiah 8:14–15 and 28:13–16, texts often used in the New Testament to describe reactions to Jesus (Luke 20:17–18; Rom. 9:33; 1 Peter 2:6–8). Jesus will split the nation in two.[4] Some will see him as someone to be opposed ("a sign to be spoken against"). But his ministry reveals where the thoughts of one's heart are. As the salvation of God and the expression of God's will, the reaction to him reveals one's reaction to God.

The opposition he produces will be a source of pain to Mary, whom Simeon addresses with this parenthetical remark in verse 35a. The mother's pain will emerge from the intense rejection the child will experience and from his priorities in ministry. Nothing can be done to avoid it. In a sense, the initial fulfillment of this remark comes in the next event, where Jesus' commitment to do the Father's work causes him to stay at the temple, and his parents have to journey back to Jerusalem, causing them pain. That is but the start, however, since the cross will cause Mary to suffer even more.

The second prophetic witness in this section of Luke is Anna. She is merely introduced and her career summarized. In all likelihood, she is over a hundred years old, having served God faithfully with worship, prayer, and fasting for years.[5] Sometimes our most productive years in spiritual service for God come after our most productive years of earthly toil. She has given herself full-time to a ministry of intercession. Like Simeon, she hopes for "the redemption of Jerusalem" (v. 38; Isa. 40:1; 49:13; 51:3; 57:18; 61:2) and tells others that the baby Jesus is a reason for praising and thanking God (Isa. 40:9; 52:9; 63:4). While her words are not recorded in Luke, her testimony makes everyone aware that God is doing something special in this child. Those who are faithful to God will hear her report and share in her praise.

Mary and Joseph return home after these days of worship and set about raising their child, who grows strong.

Bridging Contexts

THIS TEXT WITH its discussion of legal practices and prophecies raises questions about how we can apply texts that discuss practices we no longer engage in or are responsible to keep. The issues of temple worship no longer occupy us as Christians, neither does the formal keeping of the ceremonial aspects of the law. Nonetheless, these texts

---

4. Danker, *Jesus and the New Age*, 68.

5. On the question whether she was a widow for eighty-four years or was eighty-four years of age, see Marshall, *Commentary on Luke*, 123–24. It seems more likely her widowhood is in view here. Remember that in the first century, young women were married at around thirteen. This makes her around one hundred and five.

still have value in revealing how faithful people responded to the responsibilities God gave them at the time they lived. Thus, while certain practices may no longer be with us, attitudes that are a part of those practices may well be instructive as we take on the responsibilities God gives us today. It is these that we will note as we move through this passage.

We also do not have the type of special revelation about God's plan of salvation that Simeon and Anna present to Jesus' parents. The closest equivalent we have is Scripture itself, especially the New Testament, which details how Jesus is the hub of that plan. We can, however, learn from how they carry out their role, since they function as credible witnesses to the role God has called them to have.

As with the earlier units of the infancy section, many key bridges emerge from this narrative's exemplary characters. The faithful attitude of obedience and worship from Jesus' parents reveals a concern that attests to Jesus' earthly roots. From his earliest days, the child was associated with the center of Jewish faith at the temple. The predictions given by Simeon about Jesus' life do emerge later in Luke's writings, for the career of our Lord did lead to "light . . . to the Gentiles" and "glory to . . . Israel." Moreover, the nation was painfully divided over him.

Simeon also exemplifies how one can define life in terms of faithfully following God and serving him with joy and surrender. When his duty is done, he is ready to be with the Lord. Anna pictures the constancy of faith, revealing that even late in life God can use one in ministry. The story of John the Baptist and Jesus involves people of all ages; even the elderly have a place in the story. It is never too late to be ministered to by God, nor is it too late to minister for him. The testimony of these witnesses adds to the collage of heavenly and earthly voices that have spoken up for Jesus.

One other bridge that often is ignored is the note about piety and sacrifices. Since the New Testament does not require sacrifices of those who worship God as the Old Testament did, we tend to move past such verses quickly. But there is something fundamental in the issue of uncleanness and sacrifices that should not be missed as we think about drawing close to God. To approach God properly, we must be prepared in spirit and body to draw near to him (John 4:24). One of the provisions Jesus makes for us through his death is the permanent cleansing that allows us boldly to approach God's throne (Heb. 10:19–25). Yet the caution and sense of sacredness suggested in these verses about approaching God should not be lost, even though we no longer offer animal sacrifices.

This passage offers a whole perspective on life and on contentment. Here are two people near the end of their life, still serving God full steam ahead. Contentment is not a matter of age or energy level, neither is it a function of accumulation. It is defined by an openness to serve God and to share him with others. Such a perspective calls for serious reflection.

BESIDES THE EXAMPLES of faithfulness and constancy of service, one can see how Christian ministry requires constancy and an awareness of its demands. In praising Jesus, Simeon does not fail to note that the Messiah's course will be hard. The same can be said for the Messiah's followers. Ministering in a world hostile to God can mean becoming the objects of hostility and ridicule. If Jesus faces division and rejection, those who follow him can expect the same. Yet notes of praise and amazement never leave the story, for despite everything, Jesus triumphs. This note of triumph in the face of pressure makes for a significant emotional mix in this text. Even in the midst of hostility one can thank God (Acts 4:24–31).

A clear theological point dominates the application. To see Jesus is to see God's salvation. To see Jesus is to see God's light and revelation. What Luke says here, John's Gospel says this way: "In the beginning was the Word, and the Word was with God, and the Word was God." To see Jesus is to see God and his way revealed. Jesus is no longer visibly around so that we can look him in the face, but he is in the world in his body, the place where he is pouring himself to express his fullness (Eph. 1:23). This means that in a real sense we become little incarnations of Jesus. Just how true this is can be seen by the role Barnabas and Paul attribute to themselves in Acts 13:47, where they take on the role of the servant of God as light, a role Jesus already had. Of course, we do not possess all the perfections that Jesus had, but our testimony to Jesus should be such that the hope he represents can be seen in us. In our opportunities to serve, people are given a chance to see Jesus. In Matthew 25:40, 44–45, for example, Jesus notes that service to those in need is service to Jesus. That is, if he were still here, Jesus would be ministering to the type of people mentioned in these verses. But now we minister in his place and on his behalf. What an honor it is for us to be used for his glory!

Simeon's sense of identification with doing God's will and then surrendering to the timing of his own death shows just how committed he is to God's timing. His attitude is paralleled by Paul in Philippians 1:21–26. Here is a servant who seeks only to do what God has called him to do. The timing of his life and death are in God's hands.

Furthermore, having seen Jesus and knowing him, Simeon is at peace. Everything else in his life pales in comparison. He has met Jesus, and the details of the rest of his life's résumé are irrelevant. Again, Paul gives a similar testimony in Philippians 3:1–12. For him, everything else he has done in life as an accomplished, successful Pharisee is like garbage compared to knowing Jesus and serving him. One's walk with God and faithful service to him are what define everything else about life. Such service can take on various forms, for not everyone who serves God can be a preacher or serve in full-time ministry in a local church. Like Simeon, some may be called to a special task of testimony or encouragement. Others may be called to be the one point of testimony where they work or at their children's school.

Simeon knows that he can be content with his life, since he has had the honor of witnessing God's salvation. This attitude is important because it puts the other events and traumas of life into perspective. If this can be how Simeon feels, knowing that death is approaching, how should we feel when many of us have much of life still ahead of us?

Simeon's attitude stands in marked contrast to much that takes place in our culture. *McCall's* magazine of January, 1995, ran a short article on New Year's resolutions entitled "Ten Little Health Resolutions (With Big Payoffs)." Now health and exercise are important and should be appreciated, but what was interesting was a look at the top four resolutions we make, according to a Gallup poll: (1) improve personal finances, (2) stop smoking, (3) lose weight, and (4) get more exercise. If our resolutions reflect our concerns and where we want to improve ourselves to have a sense of contentment, these preferences do not reflect high goals. Except perhaps for personal finances, neither family nor God makes any appearance. We tend to define contentment in a privatized way about how our personal lives are going. Since we set goals that have nothing to do with relationships, many of us find ourselves lonely and discontent, for God has created us to relate to him and to others. One of the effects of a culture that elevates individual rights and personal focus as ours does is that we lose sight of how we can gain contentment by interacting with God and others.

Where are the goals that relate to pursuing God or knowing him better? Why do resolutions for the most part deal with external matters? Is the soul so unimportant? If exercise is valuable for physical well-being, should we starve our inner being? If contentment is based on externals that slowly wither away, will we not set ourselves up for disappointment if we focus on such goals? Simeon suggests a better way. To know God is best. That means that we can transcend circumstances, because to know him means to "have learned, in whatever state I am, to be content" (Phil. 4:11). Simeon can be content even as he faces death, knowing that he has been carrying out the Lord's call. His goal is knowing God, with whom he will have a relationship forever. Contentment means knowing the source of life who can help us see even beyond our death.

We should also note in Luke 1 and 2 how God uses a wide range of people and a vast array of social backgrounds to testify to Jesus: people in a rural setting and people in the city, male and female, a young betrothed couple and a pair of senior citizen saints—all share in the joy of his coming. Jesus comes for all humanity to unite all humanity.

Finally, the age of Simeon and Anna reminds us that "retirement" years may be a misnomer for believers. Many elderly people are freed up by retirement to pursue ministry in a way they could not give full energy to when they were employed. I am reminded of a group of senior citizens in our church, a group whom we affectionately call "the gray beards." One of them has taken on the responsibility of editing the church paper after years of helping edit the high school paper where he taught. For years God had prepared him to have a ministry of communication to our body. Another couple have dedicated themselves to various projects at a sister church of ours in the inner city, whether it means tutoring kids of different ethnic origin who lack parental involvement or just helping with various building projects at the church. A woman with severe arthritis cannot do much but pray regularly for the body. She may be one of our strongest members who is doing more than many. Finding contentment doing God's will is a goal that can be reached as we creatively reflect on how we can best minister for him.

Luke 2:41–52

EVERY YEAR HIS parents went to Jerusalem for the Feast of the Passover. ⁴²When he was twelve years old, they went up to the Feast, according to the custom. ⁴³After the Feast was over, while his parents were returning home, the boy Jesus stayed behind in Jerusalem, but they were unaware of it. ⁴⁴Thinking he was in their company, they traveled on for a day. Then they began looking for him among their relatives and friends. ⁴⁵When they did not find him, they went back to Jerusalem to look for him. ⁴⁶After three days they found him in the temple courts, sitting among the teachers, listening to them and asking them questions. ⁴⁷Everyone who heard him was amazed at his understanding and his answers. ⁴⁸When his parents saw him, they were astonished. His mother said to him, "Son, why have you treated us like this? Your father and I have been anxiously searching for you."

⁴⁹"Why were you searching for me?" he asked. "Didn't you know I had to be in my Father's house?" ⁵⁰ But they did not understand what he was saying to them.

⁵¹Then he went down to Nazareth with them and was obedient to them. But his mother treasured all these things in her heart. ⁵²And Jesus grew in wisdom and stature, and in favor with God and men.

Original Meaning

TECHNICALLY THIS EVENT is not an infancy story, since Jesus is twelve years old, one year away from accountability as a Jewish boy.[1] But in literary terms, since the close of the passage in verse 52 parallels that in verse 40, this unit is a part of the introduction to Jesus. This account is his initial testimony to himself, a fitting close to a section where various people have been speaking about him.

The annual trip for the Passover was one of the highlights of the Jewish year, one of three annual festivals that were celebrated in the capital (Ex.

---

1. Jewish boys became responsible for their actions at thirteen (*m. Niddah* 5.6; *m. Megillah* 4.6). At the age of twelve the instruction of boys became more intensive in preparation of the recognition of adulthood (*m. 'Abot* 5.21). The Bar Mitzvah of modern times, however, postdates the time of Jesus by five hundred years (Fitzmyer, *Luke,* 440).

23:14–17; 34:22–23; Deut. 16:16; Tabernacles and Pentecost were the other two). Most families that lived some distance from Jerusalem, such as Jesus' parents, went to only one feast a year. Passover fell in the Jewish month of Nisan (late March and early April). The feast celebrated the birth of Israel's freedom at the Exodus (Ex. 12). Men were required to attend, but women were not (*m. Hagigah* 1.1), so Mary's going shows the depth of the family's piety. The trip from Nazareth normally took three days. People traveled in caravans for protection. We do not know if men and women and children were separated during the journey.

On this particular occasion, Jesus remains behind in Jerusalem. Only after a day's travel do his parents discover he is not with the group, for they do not find him with relatives. They undoubtedly assumed Jesus was somewhere in the throng, though the text itself does not explain how he could go unmissed for a day. By the time they find their son, he has been missing for three days—one day out with the caravan, another day back, and one day looking for him. They discover Jesus among the teachers in the temple, listening to them, asking questions, and giving reply. In that day, it was not unusual for students to gather at the feet of the rabbis to discuss theology, often in a question-and-answer discussion format.[2] Even at this young age Jesus has amazing knowledge of the things of God. In fact, those listening to him are astonished at his understanding, a reaction that will occur later to Jesus' miraculous work (8:56). Already early in life Jesus values the pursuit of comprehending God, as he increases "in wisdom and stature" (2:52). His approach to knowing God and seeking understanding pictures how we should pursue the same, even at a young age.

Any parent reading this account understands what happens next. Jesus' parents are overwhelmed by what has taken place and move to recover their son. A frustrated mother asks her budding adolescent how he could have behaved this way, leaving his parents with a major anxiety attack (*odynomenoi*, v. 48). This term refers to deep mental anguish and pain (16:24–25; Acts 20:38).

Jesus' reply is just as direct: "I must be about the ... of my Father" (lit. trans.). This elliptical saying has been variously understood. The NIV's rendering about being "in my Father's house," is the preferred way to render this idiom.[3] Jesus' point is that his career must be about instruction on the way

---

2. C. Schneider, "κάθημαι," *TDNT*, 3:443.

3. There are two main options for this cryptic text. (1) "I must be about my Father's business." Jesus' point is that he must do God's will. (2) "I must be in my Father's house." Jesus must be involved with the instruction of divine things that is associated with the temple. For a discussion of these options and other views, Brown, *The Birth of Messiah*, 475–77; Fitzmyer, *Luke*, 443–44. The second view is preferred (Gen. 41:51; Esth. 7:9; Job 18:19).

of God, for the temple was not only a place of worship, but was also a place of teaching. Jesus has a call to instruct the nation. Though he is twelve now, a day is coming when this will be his priority.

The reference to his Father is also crucial, since it infers an intimate personal relationship to God that drives him (cf. 10:21–22). Early on Jesus understands that he is called to do his Father's work. By saying "I had to be," Jesus begins to undertake such a path, a route that one day will mean he will go his own way. Luke loves to mark key sayings with *dei* ("it is necessary") to show the presence of the fulfillment of God's plan (4:4; 9:22; 13:33; 17:25; 19:5; 22:37; 24:7, 26, 44). Here is the high point of the infancy narrative, as Jesus explains his call in his own words. In the meantime, he is obedient to his parents.

All Mary can do is ponder such events in her heart, something Luke's reader is to do also. We should recall that Jesus makes it clear that those who know God have, in a sense, two families—the biological one in which God has placed them and the spiritual one they have because they know him.

Bridging Contexts

THIS PORTRAIT OF Jesus reflects his own self-understanding. Here is a case where dialogue reveals the main point of a passage. Like many texts in the Gospels, this is called a pronouncement account, where the key to the passage is found in a decisive pronouncement near the end of the story.

What was true of Jesus during his New Testament ministry in terms of pursuing God's call is true of him today. He is still about the things of his Father, seated at God's right hand in heaven, interceding for us, and watching over us. His unique call and relationship to God reveal why his ministry was so special. His special access to God means that Jesus is not merely a prophet or great teacher, but the one who proclaims and brings the way of God. As the Son, he is more than an ethicist or a venerated religious figure. He is unique. At times his ways are unusual, but that is but a sign of his authority.

But Jesus' ministry also has its proper timing, so Jesus will wait to launch what he is destined to do. He is not impatient about starting his ministry and will wait until the time is right. He must, of course, wait for the forerunner before beginning his own task. Thus, the next chapter in Luke records the ministry of John the Baptist some seventeen years later. Jesus does not seek to run ahead of God or drag his feet behind his timing; rather, he seeks only to do what God calls him to do, when God calls him to do it. The best timing is God's timing. We too must be about God's will, seeking his timing.

Jesus' attitudes about his walk with God, his call to serve him, and his pursuit of intimacy with him are not a product of his unique sonship with God. They picture how all of us should prioritize our lives before God. Sometimes we have to make choices that others do not understand, for God has called us to set priorities that differ from people who go through life without any reference to him. Granted that Jesus was a unique person with unique gifts, yet the way he lived his life and pursued God faithfully reflects how we should seek God's face. Time spent before him "in the temple" or at his feet "in the Word" or using our hands "in ministry" may not be understood by people with a different set of priorities. Sometimes our choices will be difficult, as we are perhaps not where others would like us be. Tensions between secular commitments to our job and making time available for ministry may lead some to misunderstand why we do what we do. This comes with the territory of a walk with God. God calls us, like Jesus, to be active and prepare ourselves for service with others.

IN A REAL sense the reader is in a similar dilemma as the one Jesus' parents faced. Who is Jesus, and is his authority such that even the most basic human relationships, like the parent-child relationship, are transcended? We can identify with Joseph and Mary's response to Jesus in this incident. Yet the issue he raises in his reply is that the unique call he possesses and the unique relationship to God he has makes his parents' indirect rebuke of him irrelevant. Jesus transcends normal categories of evaluation. At least that is the realization Luke sets before the reader. As with many texts in this Gospel, the basic question is: What do you think of Jesus' authority? Will you respond or reject his claims? Our relationship to God is determined by this response, since this unique One is so closely related to him.

There is another key implication here. The world tells us to treat Jesus as one great religious figure among many in history. Luke does not give us that option. Rather, as the unique Son, Jesus has exclusive rights to reveal the way of God, and one either accepts or rejects that revelation. If Jesus says he is the way (John 14:6), then either he is or he is not; there are no other options. C. S. Lewis is known for allowing only three options about Jesus: Liar, Lunatic, or Lord. In fact, the discussion really boils down to two: Either he is the Son or he is not. Jesus does not leave the world the option of merely ranking him among the religious greats of history. He is either much more or much less. Luke's Gospel is committed to showing he is much more.

Many contemporary portraits of Jesus view him too much as a modern man, concerned about individual freedom or self-fulfillment. I am reminded of the film *The Last Temptation of Jesus*, which caused such a furor a few years ago because it tried to portray Jesus in strictly human terms. The problem, however, was not the attempt to wrestle with Jesus' humanity, but the assumption that he shared struggles of personal actualization like those many talk shows discuss today. This cheapened the depth of the human dimension to Jesus. Jesus displayed a humanity that resisted the temptation to selfishness that often plagues humanity, an approach to life that takes far more discipline than simply giving in to self. Jesus was unique not only in his divinity but also in his humanity, namely, in his ability to focus on and carry out God's will in his life.

Sometimes Jesus did things that were surprising, which did not fit the custom of the time. Yet in his authority he had the right to do things differently. Jesus' departure as a twelve-year-old to discuss divine things in the temple was a problem for his parents and for the culture of that day. But sometimes Jesus leads us into seeing God do surprising things in the context of the culture—not by rewriting moral values, but by calling us to creativity in issues of style and approach to God's Word.

Sometimes God has us consider initially surprising things as we pursue service to him. For this reason, efforts to create times of worship in church that are seeker-friendly need not be rejected, if the church decides as a community that she is going to use her time together for evangelism as well as nurture. The thing to watch in such a move is that the church ministry does not become so seeker-friendly that nurture of believers is ignored. There may also be times when legitimate discussion may center on the style and tone of worship, the music in the service, or what kinds of ministries we might engage in. Sometimes a fresh way of doing ministry is not a matter of right and wrong but of determining clearly what kind of ministry we will have. On other occasions, other probing questions may need our attention. Are perhaps some ministries better supported through offering aid to existing parachurch ministries, rather than reduplicating an existing ministry?

Sometimes the church needs to be "unleashed" to see its ministry extending not to what takes place within its walls, but through what its members do outside its walls.[4] Luke 2:42–52 is the first of several units where Jesus

---

4. One of the more well-known churches in the 1980s was Bear Creek in the Denver area, which developed a church philosophy it called "the church unleashed." Their point was that ministry is as much what happens away from the church home as what happens within its walls. So they sought to encourage all ministry involvements of its members, whether the local body received direct benefit or exercised any oversight role. Their attitude was if the ministry was meaningful and the goals biblical, then Bear Creek would cheer them on and say, Amen! The church needs more communities like that who seek to work for the body of Christ as a whole and do not require their people "to stay at home."

"stretches the envelope" of common practice to reveal that God is at work in a fresh way. Jesus must teach the things of God, and so must the church. Such teaching should be creative in whom it approaches and how it is given. Jesus is in the temple here, but later he will be among those who need to hear the Word and will share it with them. His call to be in the temple is a recognition that he will be in the public square, sharing the Word with all people, since the temple was one of the most public locales of ancient Judaism. One of the dangers for the church is that in her commitment to being God's people, she isolates her teaching to inside the walls of the church.

The church must be "envelope stretching" in its efforts to preach the Word. In our church community, for example, one men's fellowship group, seeking to minister to others in the body, held a "maintenance ministry" for widows and single mothers in the church. They changed the oil in their cars, looked them over, and offered to do any heavy moving work that needed to be done. Needless to say, this unusual ministry of help was well received. Other fellowship groups in our community have undertaken to minister in some of the food shelters in the city. Our church does not try to tell small groups how they should operate by giving them only one program to follow. One must be in the house of God to get the strength and resources for mission, but one need not stay there to perform it.

In moving from Jesus to us, the text also suggests another common tension: the choice between community and family tensions. Prioritizing God, family, and ministry is not always easy. I remember a discussion with a great Latin American saint who shared that when he was in seminary years ago, he lived in one country while his wife was at home in another country. As they were expecting a child, this student faced a dilemma. The seminary had an attendance requirement, but the student wanted to go home to be with his wife and celebrate the arrival of the new child and rejoice at what God was doing in his family. He asked a professor if he could cut class to do this. The professor felt that he owed God the time of his class first and family second; thus, the professor refused the cut. In response, the student said that he would go to be with his wife and accept any consequences, for he felt God wanted him to honor his wife and family; preparation for ministry could face this short hiccup. Though I never found out if the school penalized him (he later became president of that school!), he did say that our institutions are more sensitive to helping students balance ministry and family now.

On the other hand, sometimes we feel guilty if we sense a closeness with believers that does not match what we have with our families, but we need not feel this way. It is only natural in relationships where we share the deepest level of commonality by sharing the same God that we feel a kinship of the soul that we might not have with biological kin. Luke 12:51–53 suggests that a sense of estrangement from family who do not share our faith commitments may result from coming to Jesus. The pangs of of Jesus' priorities are what Mary and Joseph felt here. It is not unlike the pain some parents feel when children choose to serve God on the mission field or opt to go into ministry instead of into a "real profession." Sometimes the pain is a helpful reminder that our top priority is to serve God. Sometimes parents may need to let go of their children, because the children are faithfully serving God.

One final application emerges from Jesus' stop at the temple. Sometimes we think adolescents are beyond useful spiritual reflection, having entered a twilight zone from which they hopefully will emerge in their twenties. I once heard this definition of a teenager: "At fourteen years old, one minute they think you are the greatest father on earth, and the next minute they seriously wonder why God created you! At sixteen, they make a decision, and the choice is not encouraging." We sometimes treat Jesus as an exception, because he was the Son of God. But Jesus took on humanity to show us how to live and walk with God. Here is a twelve-year-old seeking to know God better. We sometimes underestimate what our children are capable of reflecting on, if encouraged.

When we went to Germany for the first time, my seven- and eight-year-old absorbed German far faster than either my wife or I did. Sometimes it was embarrassing but necessary to hand them the phone so they could translate for us. Teenage years are not necessarily lost years decreed to be spent in exile on Gilligan's Island. Our children should be encouraged to develop spiritually, whether through their involvement in church or in discussion of topics that matter with their parents and others. Jesus could sit with the rabbis; maybe our children can as well, if we will be sensitive to the potential they have and relate to them at a level to which they can respond.

Luke 3:1–22

I N THE FIFTEENTH year of the reign of Tiberius Caesar—
when Pontius Pilate was governor of Judea, Herod tetrarch
of Galilee, his brother Philip tetrarch of Iturea and Tra-
conitis, and Lysanias tetrarch of Abilene—²during the high
priesthood of Annas and Caiaphas, the word of God came to
John son of Zechariah in the desert. ³ He went into all the
country around the Jordan, preaching a baptism of repentance
for the forgiveness of sins. ⁴As is written in the book of the
words of Isaiah the prophet:

> "A voice of one calling in the desert,
> 'Prepare the way for the Lord,
>   make straight paths for him.
> ⁵ Every valley shall be filled in,
>   every mountain and hill made low.
> The crooked roads shall become straight,
>   the rough ways smooth.
> ⁶ And all mankind will see God's salvation.'"

⁷John said to the crowds coming out to be baptized by
him, "You brood of vipers! Who warned you to flee from the
coming wrath? ⁸Produce fruit in keeping with repentance. And
do not begin to say to yourselves, 'We have Abraham as our
father.' For I tell you that out of these stones God can raise up
children for Abraham. ⁹The ax is already at the root of the
trees, and every tree that does not produce good fruit will be
cut down and thrown into the fire."

¹⁰"What should we do then?" the crowd asked.

¹¹John answered, "The man with two tunics should share
with him who has none, and the one who has food should do
the same."

¹²Tax collectors also came to be baptized. "Teacher," they
asked, "what should we do?"

¹³"Don't collect any more than you are required to," he told
them.

¹⁴ Then some soldiers asked him, "And what should we do?"
He replied, "Don't extort money and don't accuse people
falsely—be content with your pay."

¹⁵The people were waiting expectantly and were all wondering in their hearts if John might possibly be the Christ.¹⁶John answered them all, "I baptize you with water. But one more powerful than I will come, the thongs of whose sandals I am not worthy to untie. He will baptize you with the Holy Spirit and with fire. ¹⁷His winnowing fork is in his hand to clear his threshing floor and to gather the wheat into his barn, but he will burn up the chaff with unquenchable fire." ¹⁸And with many other words John exhorted the people and preached the good news to them.

¹⁹But when John rebuked Herod the tetrarch because of Herodias, his brother's wife, and all the other evil things he had done, ²⁰Herod added this to them all: He locked John up in prison.

²¹When all the people were being baptized, Jesus was baptized too. And as he was praying, heaven was opened. ²²and the Holy Spirit descended on him in bodily form like a dove. And a voice came from heaven: "You are my Son, whom I love; with you I am well pleased."

Original Meaning

THE SECOND MAJOR unit of the gospel extends from Luke 3:1–4:13 and shows how John pointed the way to Jesus (3:1–20), how Jesus was baptized (3:21–22), how Jesus' roots stretch back through David and Abraham to Adam (3:23–38), and how Jesus resisted succumbing to Satan's temptations (4:1–13). The entire unit demonstrates how Jesus is qualified to represent both humanity and the nation of Israel as her Messiah.

Unlike the other Synoptic Gospels, which tend to intersperse their reports about John the Baptist throughout their works, Luke opts to tell most of the story about John's ministry and arrest here, except for a brief exchange in 7:18–22. By doing so, once the story of John is dealt with, Jesus permanently holds the center stage. Luke shares the temptation account with Matthew, but opts to place the genealogy between the baptism and the temptation. In this way he makes two points: (1) Jesus as the representative of humanity is tested by Satan as to whether he is God's Son, and (2) the nature of Jesus' roots relate him to all people, since Luke takes the list back through Adam, while Matthew stops with Abraham. Luke also has a different order to the temptations, saving the temple scene for last, probably because Jerusalem plays a major role in the central portion of the Gospel

(9:51–19:44). These differences show Luke wants to place some of his own distinct emphases on his portrait of Jesus.[1]

The flow of the unit is straightforward. The ethical exhortations that set the stage for Jesus' ministry appear in John the Baptist's remarks. A certain type of heart is needed to respond to the gospel, which is why John calls for repentance. The divine voice identifies Jesus at his baptism in what is probably a private experience, marking out his call to be the Messiah-Servant. Jesus' lineage also fits messianic expectation. The Son shows his moral qualifications by relying on God and his word, rather than, like Adam, reaching for power that Satan tempts him to make. What Adam as son of God was not, Jesus is. So he is ready to minister on behalf of all humanity.

Much of the material in 3:1–22 is unique to Luke. Only Luke details John's teaching (3:10–14), and only he extends the citation of Isaiah to include more of Isaiah 40:4–5. Only Luke mentions John's imprisonment this early in the account, and only he places the ministry of John in its larger historical frame. The rest of the account has parallels in Matthew 3:7–17; Mark 1:2–11; and John 1:29–34.

This subunit begins by placing Jesus in the context of world history (3:1–2) and biblical promise (3:4–6). The linking verse is the brief description of John's ministry. According to Isaiah 40, God will deliver his people and give them the comfort of salvation. When the Gospel writers point to this text, they inform us that John's ministry means God is at work again to save his people. God is approaching us, so that creation should unfurl itself like a giant red carpet with pomp and honor to note his arrival. Among the evidences of such a carpet is a contrite heart (Isa. 57:14–17).

Luke places John in history, working from the most distant figure to the more proximate. John's ministry emerges in A.D. 28–29, Tiberius' fifteenth year.[2] Though Caesar had great power, his rule was felt in Palestine only through those who administered on his behalf—the prefect, Pontius Pilate, and the appointed Jewish ruler, Herod, one of three tetrarchs from Herod the

---

1. This study will not fully analyze such differences, though it will discuss major points as they emerge. For detailed analyses of them, see Darrell L. Bock, *Luke*, vols. 1–2 (Grand Rapids: Baker, 1994 and forthcoming). This more technical commentary assesses the literary and historical significance of these differences for Luke.

2. There is discussion about how the fifteen years are counted. Was it from coregency in A.D. 11 or from Augustus's death or the Senate's voting Tiberias into office in A.D. 14? Was the accession year excluded, so A.D. 12 or 15 starts the reckoning? And which calendar was used (Roman, Jewish, Syrian, or Egyptian)? The issues here are complex, but it seems most likely that Luke refers to an accession year, which starts the count of fifteen years. This put us in A.D. 28–29 (H. Hoehner, *Chronological Aspects of the Life of Christ* [Grand Rapids: Zondervan, 1977], 29–44).

Great's sons. Pilate was responsible for keeping the peace and collecting taxes (Josephus, *Jewish War* 2.9.2 §§ 169–77). Herod also kept an eye on the region, giving an air of Jewish self-government, though his family held political power through Rome's kindness since 63 B.C. Herod's brother Philip served as tetrarch in a neighboring region. We know little about Lysanias outside of this reference.

The Jewish religious authority was held by the house of Annas. He had been high priest from A.D. 6–15, and his sons and other relatives held the office in an almost unbroken chain for years afterward (Josephus, *Antiquities* 18.2.1–2 §§ 26–35). Caiaphas was Annas's son-in-law. Power in Palestine was often a family affair. Respect for Annas is indicated by the fact he kept the title "high priest" even though he was no longer functioning in the office. John began his ministry in this complex setting: political Rome, political Israel, and religious Israel all had a stake in the affairs of the region (cf. Josephus, *Antiquities* 18.5.2 §§ 115–18).

Luke portrays John's ministry as a call to repentance. The ethical thrust of Luke's Gospel begins here. Ministering in the desert in fulfillment of the pattern of salvation indicated by Isaiah, John preaches "a baptism of repentance for the forgiveness of sins." His ministry in the Jordan River region is designed to get people ready for the arrival of God's salvation by having hearts open to respond to the coming Messiah (1:15–17, 76–77). That is why in citing Isaiah, Luke mentions the leveling of obstacles in the way of God's arrival. If the creation bows to God's coming, certainly human hearts should as well.

The rite of baptism is unprecedented. Judaism knew of repeated baptisms for temporary cleansing, but this was a call to prepare for the arrival of salvation, a one-time baptism in honor of the arrival of the eschatological era of salvation.[3] Interestingly, like John's call for repentance, Jesus will later see his mission as saving sinners (5:31–32; 19:10), and his disciples will carry a similar message as they share the gospel (Luke 24:43–47).

John preaches in the manner of the Old Testament prophets, seeking for a "turning" of the heart. Though the Greek word for "repentance" (*metanoia*) means "a change of mind," the concept of repentance has Old Testament roots in the idea of turning to God (1 Kings 8:47; 2 Kings 23:25; Ps. 78:34; Isa. 6:10; Ezek. 3:19; Amos 4:6, 8; cf. Jesus' comments in Luke 24:43–47, where the Old Testament and repentance are linked). To be prepared for God's salvation, one's heart must be opened to his message. Any doubt that

---

3. Fitzmyer, *Luke*, 460; H. Schürmann, *Das Lukasevangelium. 1 Teil. Kommentar zu Kap. 1,1– 9,50* (HTKNT 3; Freiburg: Herder, 1969), 154–57; Nolland, *Luke 1:1–9:20*, 141; esp. R. Webb, *John the Baptizer and Prophet: A Socio-Historical Study* (JSNTMS 62; Sheffield: Sheffield Academic Press, 1991), 214–16, 254–348.

this is John's thrust can be seen in his exposition of repentance in Luke 3:10–14, where it is defined not as an abstract act of the mind, but as something that expresses itself in action. John is a sentry keeping watch over God's plan and blowing a trumpet to announce preparation for the Messiah's arrival. When it comes, all humanity will see the salvation of God (v. 6).

The possibility of salvation also implies the approach of judgment. Thus, opportunity will become tragedy if one does not respond. John warns the people as he prepares them by mentioning the ax lying at the root of the tree. Relying on ancestry and heritage will not commend one before God. Salvation is not by family inheritance but by faith, by turning in trust to the living God.

John forthrightly warns the crowds about not relying on their genealogies or a professional connection in order to guarantee them blessing.[4] Luke 3:7–9 stresses that judgment is near, while 3:10–14 explains how one should react. What is interesting about the combination is that awareness of our accountability to God should make us more sensitive to how we treat others. For John the ethical dimension of life is fed by our sensitivity to our horizontal relationship with God.

John compares the crowd to snakes fleeing a fire in the desert. When the heat comes up, the snakes crawl out of their holes. Snakes often represent God's enemies (Matt. 12:34; 23:33; cf. Isa. 14:29; 59:5; Jer. 45:22). He portrays the people as sensing that "fire" is near and feeling the need to flee. Still, they should pay attention to the real possibility of wrath, the day of God's judgment. The imagery recalls Day of the Lord concepts (Isa. 13:9; 30:23; Mal. 3:2). As John proclaims the approaching salvation, the good news has a flip side—the threat of judgment for failing to respond to God.

In effect, John is asking if they understand what his baptism is really about and what is at stake. So he issues an ethical call in common Old Testament style. The people are to produce fruit worthy of repentance. If one turns to God, one's life should look different. The New Testament loves to emphasize such "doing" (Luke 6:43–45; 13:6–9; 1 Cor. 9:23; Col. 3:17; James 1:19–25; 3:12–18). To turn to God means being prepared to serve others.

There is a danger in facing this choice, in that one can rely on lineage to get himself or herself in. John's audience may have assumed that because they were Jews, having Abraham as their father, they were guaranteed salvation as part of the elect family of God. John describes such thinking as

---

4. Interestingly, the parallel in Matt. 3:7 identifies the audience as the Sadducees and Pharisees. Apparently John spoke to all, but his remarks were particularly of value for the leadership.

deadly. Jews were proud of their heritage (cf. 4 Ezra 6:56–58; Josephus, *Antiquities* 3.5.3 §§ 87–88), but John warns that such a heritage means nothing to an individual who does not personally turn to God.[5] God is able to make his children out of objects of creation, such as stones. Since Abraham is a "rock" from which his children are cut (Isa. 51:1–2), John is saying that God can create a fresh batch of people. He has the creative power to bring to him those who are not a part of the elect nation.

Judgment is primed for those who do not respond. In fact, the ax is sitting at the tree's root, ready to cut down those trees that lack fruit. Those trees, once felled, will be sent to the fire (cf. Ps. 74:5–6; Jer. 2:21–22; 11:16; Ezek. 15:6–7; Hos. 10:1–2). John uses the imagery of the Old Testament to prepare people for the new era.

The crowd understands the message and asks what they can do to avoid the wrath to come. The repetition of the word "do" or "produce" (*poieo*; vv. 8, 10, 12, 14) shows the link between John's remarks and the crowd's response. The crowd knows that the important issue is not getting baptized but responding to God with a certain kind of heart and life.

John tells the crowd to be generous, giving a tunic to one who needs it and food to those who lack it. The hated tax collectors also respond.[6] These people operated in a sort of pyramid scheme, since the collection of taxes was put out for bids and commissions were built into the collection. The fact that "tax collectors" are often paired with "sinners" in the New Testament shows how much disdain Jewish society had for them. John tells them to collect only what is required. Finally, the soldiers, who kept the peace and wielded great power, are told not to use that force to extort money or accuse people falsely, but to be content with their wages.[7] This last point is important, because financial pressure could lead to extortion, given that the soldier earned only a basic wage. The word for "to extort" (*diaseio*) is particularly descriptive, since it means "to shake violently."

John preaches personal preparation, but he also points to Jesus (3:15–17). When the issue is raised whether John might be the Messiah, he denies the speculation and explains how they may know that the Christ has come. There is in fact so much difference between the two that John feels he is not worthy to do the most menial of tasks that a slave might do, to untie the

---

5. Tannehill, *The Narrative Unity of Luke-Acts*, 50–145.

6. Donahue, "Tax Collectors and Sinners," *CBQ* 33 (1971): 39–61, details how tax collection worked and how hated these Jewish men were for working for Rome. Taxes in the ancient world covered 20–30% of one's income.

7. On soldiers, see Marshall, *Commentary on Luke*, 143; Heiland, "ὀψώνιον," *TDNT*, 5:592; Josephus, *Antiquities* 17.8.3 §§ 198–99.

thong of the coming stronger one's sandal.[8] The way that they will know when the Christ has come is to compare their baptisms. John baptizes with water, but the Christ will bring the baptism of the Spirit.

Baptism with Spirit and fire represents a presence and a purging that divides (Isa. 4:4–5).[9] The Spirit's coming is often linked in the Old Testament to the era of the end times (Isa. 32:15; 44:3; Ezek. 36:25–27; Joel 2:28–32). That presence and purging are in view is made clear by verse 17, where the "winnowing fork" is said to be ready to clear the threshing floor. The harvesting image refers to a wooden fork that lifted beaten grain in the air, so that the wind could drive away the light chaff and the grain fall to the floor to be gathered (Prov. 20:28; Jer 15:7; Isa. 34:8–10). The Spirit's baptism will gather some, while others will be left to the wind (cf. also Luke 12:49–53; 17:29–30).

Luke notes that there is much more to John's teaching as he exhorts the people with the "good news" (v. 18). It is interesting how Luke juxtaposes good news and judgment, a combination we seldom put together today. The text is honest about God's judgment and the vindication of justice it represents. That is why judgment can be good news. Where there is judgment, there is the offer of mercy.

John's message reaches the upper echelon of society, and no one escapes his penetrating call to repent. He takes Herod to task for his marriage to Herodias, both of whom left marriages to marry each other. In addition, Herodias had been married to Herod's half-brother, a relationship that by Jewish law prevented Herodias from being Herod's wife (Lev. 18:16; 20:21).[10] But this is only one moral issue John tackles. Herod responds to this with the typical reaction of a hardened sinner—by striking back and locking John in prison. Given the choice of repenting or denying sin, the ruler tries to remove the source of accountability. Luke moves up the account of this jailing, so that when he turns to Jesus, he can tell the story of that ministry uninterrupted.[11]

As we turn to consider Jesus' baptism, few moments are as important as when heaven speaks (in this event and in the Transfiguration). This event has

---

8. So menial was this task that a Jewish slave was exhorted not to perform it (*Mekilta de Rabbi Ishmael* on Ex. 21:2).

9. J. D. G. Dunn, *Baptism in the Holy Spirit* (London: SCM, 1970).

10. On Herod, see Hoehner, *Herod Antipas: A Contemporary of Jesus Christ* (Cambridge: Cambridge Univ. Press, 1972).

11. Luke has clearly arranged this remark for literary reasons, because the next event has John baptizing Jesus, an event that clearly precedes John's arrest. The parallels to the arrest are Matt. 14:3–5 and Mark 6:17–20.

three significant points. (1) Jesus is identified with the ministry of John.[12] Though Matthew 3:13–17 brings this out more explicitly, Jesus accepts baptism so that he can identify with John's message.[13] When Jesus submits to this washing, he is declaring that John's message is true and that people must get prepared to receive salvation.

(2) In a note unique to Luke, Jesus is praying when the Spirit descends like a dove on him. Luke loves to mention how Jesus bathes his life in prayer (6:12; 9:18, 29; 11:1; 22:41). This divine endorsement comes in the midst of a sweet communion between the Father and the Son.

(3) Something often missed in this account is that this is probably a private experience of Jesus. The voice speaks directly to him; Luke does not record any reaction or response from the crowd, as in other cases when such events occur more publicly (e.g., Acts 9). Mark and Luke both have the voice speaking directly to Jesus (using "you"), while Matthew summarizes the significance of the remark by saying, "This is my beloved Son." John's Gospel notes only that the Baptist saw the dove descend.

More important is the "anointing" that takes place (cf. Luke 4:16–18). The Spirit descends like a dove on Jesus. The symbolism of the dove is difficult to ascertain. The Spirit is associated with the presence of God in his creative work and in the presence of his grace (Gen. 1:2; 8:8–12).[14]

The most important feature of the text is the endorsement itself: God identifies Jesus as his Son as he anoints him for ministry. This event confirms the call of Jesus and names his function. The remark about "my Son, whom I love; with you I am well pleased" weaves together three Old Testament allusions.[15] (1) Jesus is identified in Psalm 2:7 as the messianic Son. As we noted in Luke 1:31–35, the title "Son" in Judaism refers to the Son of God. The roots of the title go back to the Davidic covenant, where God agreed to treat David's descendants as a father does a son (2 Sam. 7:7–16). In Psalm 2, the psalmist explains the importance of the sovereignty of the Son even in the midst of opposition and rejection. So when God uses this title here in Luke, he is marking out Jesus as the sovereign king.

(2) The next allusion comes from Isaiah 42:1, a Servant passage (Matt. 12:18). The identity of the "Servant" in the Old Testament is debated. Is he

---

12. Commentary on the significance of John's ministry appears in Luke 7:26–35; Acts 10:37–38; 13:23–25.

13. More like Luke is the other parallel from Mark 1:9–11. Telling the event from the Baptist's perspective is John 1:29–34. Matthew and Mark note that Jesus came to John from Galilee.

14. For summaries of the options, Marshall, *Commentary on Luke*, 153–54.

15. D. Bock, *Proclamation From Prophecy and Pattern: Lucan Old Testament Christology* (JSNTMS 12; (Sheffield: JSOT Press, 1987), 100–105.

a messianic or prophetic figure? Isaiah's portrait of the Servant gives him many prophetic qualities, and the use of a conceptually parallel text from Isaiah 61:1—2 in Luke 4:16—30 also shows these more prophetic qualities. Later in the Servant songs, the unique, more messianic, suffering qualities of the Servant emerge, but it appears that by calling Jesus the one "with [whom] I am well pleased," the voice alludes to Jesus' prophetic quality, combining the recognition of his authority with the presence in him of revelatory truth.

(3) Whether a third allusion appears in "whom I love" is debated. Some cite background in Genesis 22:12, 16 and see the reference as a description of Jesus as God's only Son.[16] This is possible, but to work the allusion to mean Son must take on two senses at once: one appealing to regal imagery, the other to Isaac typology. Another more likely option is to see an allusion to Isaiah 41:8, where the ideas of a chosen Servant and a beloved Person line up. The stress here is on the chosen nature of the Son's position and on his special relationship to God.

This event "coronates" Jesus' ministry, not by making him what he was not before, but by recognizing that now the beloved Son will launch out into actively exercising the authority he possesses.

MOST OF THIS section in Luke deals with the ministry of John the Baptist. Included in that ministry is the baptism of Jesus. We will bridge the contexts of these two units separately.

John the Baptist's Ministry

JOHN HAS A unique ministry, since there is only one forerunner to prepare us for the Christ; yet his ministry reflects the Old Testament prophets in general. This point of connection helps us bridge the contexts. Old Testament prophecy, though addressed to the covenant people of Israel, reflects the ethical values of God. So such texts are profitable for correction, reproof, and instruction in righteousness (2 Tim. 3:16—17). Beyond that, we today also have a ministry that presents Christ in light of what he has done. The kind of preparation John calls for ("repentance") is like the message Jesus calls his disciples to take to the world (Luke 24:47). So this passage reveals the kind of heart God desires.

This passage also shows an apparent mix between secular history and sacred history. In a sense, we cannot distinguish the two, since God is

---

16. For example, W. R. Stegner, *Narrative Theology in Early Jewish Christianity* (Louisville: Westminster/John Knox Press, 1989), 15—31.

involved in all history. We tend to divide the secular and the sacred today. The prophet John is as concerned to announce the coming of Jesus as he is to discuss Herod. His prophetic role is to address sin or blessing wherever it surfaces. There is a danger today, as evangelicals reenter the political arena, that they will confuse party and church, making politics the answer for something that requires more than a majority of votes or the raw and clever exercise of political power. We risk becoming selective in our engagement of sin by attacking the laziness of those who abuse welfare, while ignoring the real inequities that cause people to grow up in poverty or in the midst of horrific violence. Materialism and self-indulgence, Herod's sins, are equally as spiritually damaging as laziness. Passing legislation without the moral fiber to appreciate why such laws are present is only a Band-Aid for true reformation of character.

Many of the concepts in this passage represent fundamental theological responses to the revelation of God—for example, repentance in the face of judgment and not relying on heritage as the basis for entry into blessing. In fact, the description of those who rest on their ancestral laurels as snakes shows just how much God dislikes such presumption. He only honors the genuine pursuit of forgiveness.

Thus one should be careful in reading a passage like this and in assuming a kind of permanent genealogical inoculation from the consequences of sin. Granted, when we trust Christ, we receive forgiveness from all our sin, but that does not mean we are given license to do whatever we wish. God hates sin, whether we commit it as believers or unbelievers. Sin still needs to be brought before him in sincere confession with contrition. The Old Testament pictures such acknowledgment in preparation of Jesus' work in the sin offering. If he died for sins committed before we come to him, he has also paid just as dearly for the sins we commit afterward.

In a real sense, this passage applies to another group, which I call the "tweeners." "Tweeners" are people who see themselves as "in" relationship with God, but who in fact are not really in communion with him, because they have not trusted him. They look in, but really are out; thus, they are located "between" their claim and the reality in a way someone who openly rejects God is not. Many of the Jews John addresses see themselves as "in" with God because of ancestry or some sense of association with him. John stresses that relationship with God is not predicated on a claim of association, but on a heart turned consciously to him seeking forgiveness. That means that some whom John addresses, even though they see themselves as "in," may in fact be "out." One of the most fundamental truths of the Christian life is the awareness that our salvation in Christ is not because of any inherent right we have.

No human can make such a claim against God (Rom. 3:9–19; Eph. 2:8–10). The truth is that we are his only because we know we need his grace so he can make us into the people God has designed us to be. Only he can help us deal with our inherited sin. Forgiveness and righteousness, to be manifest in this life, must come by the grace of God, and the gift of new life he gives to those who turn to Christ with a heart that is aware of their need. Success in the Christian life continues to recognize that without him and his grace, we are prone to sin. Thus John's message, even though it warns outsiders and tweeners, also reminds us that the life we possess from God is ours by his grace, whose richness we continue to draw from to sustain us. As we draw on that grace, God will bring forth from us fruit worthy of repentance. The grace of God exists so that we might turn to him and become people "eager to do what is good," as Paul writes in Titus 2:11–14. Such fruit is evidence that God's grace is active in our life.

The fundamental ethical value of treating others well also has timeless value. Such treatment of others grows out of our appreciation of God and his creation. John's warnings are directed toward a world and toward people in it. Where authority is wielded with such unchecked power that the possibility of abuse is almost a given. Luke 3:10–14 contains John's call to the tax collector or soldier not to abuse power. To apply such texts in many third-world settings is to require a radical redefinition of the use of powers. To the third world, abuse of power often comes visibly and automatically with the wielding of power. Of course, other abuses of authority or business practices are possible that are more subtle than extortion or excess surcharges. First-world abuse often takes the form of asking people to do more than is healthy for their families in light of the requirements of the business. First-world abuse may be not honoring a workman with wages that reflect his contribution, while people at the top take in more than they deserve. First-world abuse in the church constantly takes advantage of well-meaning volunteers without even once stopping to thank them genuinely or offer some type of concrete recognition for their labor. First-world abuse at societal levels may leave those without money with little voice, while those who have resources can lobby the rich and powerful. If John condemns the practices recorded here for the Roman world, he also condemns the more subtle forms of abuse of position.

The idea that all are accountable for the moral quality of their walk should not be missed in this passage. Herod may have seen himself as above God's moral law, but John does not see it that way. Regardless of what authority Herod can yield against the prophet, God still holds him responsible for his own moral decisions.

John's faithfulness as a prophet shows an ability to address issues of sin and judgment directly. Even though it is risky and unpopular, John knows what the moral call of God asks of him. He also knows where to leave the responsibility of judgment. The ax is not his to yield; the prophet can only point to God, who will eventually swing the blade.

Jesus' Baptism

JESUS' BAPTISM HAS two major points of contact into the present. (1) That baptism endorses John's ministry. Everything said about John in Luke 3:1–20 is confirmed when Jesus steps forward to receive his baptism. But it is not the rite that makes it important, but what the rite represents. Everything that is true about preparing for the arrival of God's salvation in Jesus in the first century in terms of heart response is true today. To come to Jesus one must seek forgiveness of sins.

(2) Jesus comes fully approved by the Father. He has sovereign authority as the promised Son over the blessings of salvation. He is a prophetic figure who reveals the way of God. He is chosen for the task and is a unique object of God's love. All of this transcends the picture of Jesus that our culture presents.

God's method of communication at Jesus' baptism differs from the way he normally speaks to us. We seldom if ever hear God speak in an audible voice from heaven. Instead, the presence of the Spirit within us directs us, especially as we seek God's direction in prayer and in consultation with the Scriptures. In addition, God may speak to us through the words of other believers who care about us. That is why community, where the communion of the Spirit among the saints occurs, is so important.

AS WITH BRIDGING Contexts, most of this section in Luke deals with the ministry of John the Baptist. But included in that ministry is the baptism of Jesus. We will apply these two units separately.

John the Baptist's Ministry

JOHN ILLUSTRATES HOW the proclaimer of the Word should perform his task. The preacher must bear good news as well as news that exposes sin. Some preachers in the past tended to emphasize sin so much that one wondered where grace might be found. Today our problem is the opposite: being able to confront people with their accountability and culpability before God. A preacher of God's message must be balanced in delivering both messages. Forgiveness cannot occur except where one realizes responsibility for sin and repents of it.

Recognizing that we are accountable to God can be either suffocating or liberating. It suffocates us when we insist on continuing to sin, deepening our culpability. It liberates when we turn to God for forgiveness and experience the blessing of being forgiven. The dynamics of this for the believer are just as important, in that the forgiveness obtained at the cross when we come to Jesus covers all sin. Although those who have received forgiveness are not judged eternally when they continue to sin, they still suffer the consequences that sin inevitably brings. On the other hand, seeking forgiveness means that we can claim the reality of the forgiveness Jesus has made available once for all.

Forgiveness has another corollary. When we are forgiven after turning to God, such forgiveness should yield a transformed character as a response to the grace of God. John assumes that repentance will have a fruit. Jesus will say later in this Gospel that one who is forgiven much loves the Lord much (7:47). The depth of our sense of forgiveness serves as the drive for our sense of need for transformation. When we realize what sin costs us and what it cost God, we are better prepared to turn from it.

If one asks what a transformed life looks like, the simple answer here involves treating people with generosity in meeting their needs and in refusing to abuse authority (3:10–14). In other words, a transformed life transforms our ways of relating to others. People are not to be ignored, used, or abused. God honors those who honor others. That is why in the Lord's Prayer we pray to have our sins forgiven as we forgive others. The forgiven person is to become a forgiving person. The delivered person is to be a delivering person. As the Father has shown his goodwill to us, so we should show it to others.

Another important note in this text is the idea that cultural connections do not assure salvation. Being born in a "Christian country," growing up in a "Christian home," going to a "Christian church," and living a moral "Christian life" mean nothing, if we have not personally responded to the offer of forgiveness found by coming to Jesus. No baptism, no amount of church attendance, and no history of Christ in the family can substitute for a personal turning to Jesus with an awareness that he provides forgiveness for our sin. There is no greater application of the forerunner's message than to turn to the Stronger One he pointed to as bringing the salvation of God. To trust Jesus for forgiveness is to apply this text in its most ultimate form.

It is the importance of Jesus' coming as a divider in the midst of humanity that makes response so imperative. He is much greater than any prophet; he is not just a moralist as our culture tends to portray him. As the bearer of the Spirit who divides wheat from chaff, everyone clearly has a stake in Jesus' coming. No one can escape responding to him. He owns the winnowing fork, and all of us will be tossed into the air and assessed for how well we have responded to him.

The rebuke of Herod drives the point home even more. Even those of the highest social class and those who wield the highest degree of secular power are subject to his moral claim on their lives. The powerful sometimes feel most immune from accountability to God and can develop a false sense of independence. John's rebuke indicates that although he cannot force Herod to repent, Herod is responsible to God for his conduct. No one is above God's standard. When it comes to him, all play on a level field.

Herod's response yields another lesson. Sometimes sinners respond with hostility when sin is called sin. Herod tried to stop the presence of a human conscience by locking John up. However, nothing Herod does can change his accountability.

John's faithfulness leads to a final observation. Sometimes doing God's will is not popular; it may involve personal risk. John speaks up and has to suffer the consequences of his public stand. He describes what sin is and calls people to account before God for it, but he also shows the way out of its sinister grip. The church today needs to do the same. We need to share honestly what the cross cost God, because sin is costly to humanity. We also need to be clear that we personally are not immune from the confession of sin we call for others to make. Jesus does not save perfect, but forgiven, people—folks whose sin takes many forms but to whom the same forgiveness is offered because of the greatness of the source of that forgiveness. A warning without the gospel is as imbalanced as the gospel without an awareness of culpability for sin. The church's message must be balanced between sin and forgiveness. The bridge over the chasm of sin is the recognition that with repentance comes forgiveness. Understanding the depth of God's goodness engenders the faith that saves.

Jesus' Baptism

THE FACT THAT Jesus' baptism occurs framed by prayer should not be missed. If the beloved Son communes with God through prayer as he pursues his direction in life, how much more should we! Regular time in prayer is a lifeline in our relationship to God. Failure to pray is like trying to go through marriage without talking to your spouse. It becomes almost impossible to be on the same page as one faces the challenges of life. So Scripture urges us to pray without ceasing (cf. Luke 18:1; 1 Thess. 5:17).

The primary application of this text comes in its Christology. Many in our culture respect Jesus, regarding him as a religious teacher of great significance and even placing him among the top religious teachers of all time.

Others even acknowledge him as a prophet, giving him a seat in a rather limited club of divine revealers. But as high as these notes of respect are, they pale in comparison to the biblical portrait. Luke shows that Jesus is not like anyone who came before him or anyone since. The Hall of Religious Fame into which he is placed has only one portrait in it—his. There have been other great teachers, prophets, and kings, but there is only one who has combined all of those roles as God's Son.

The significance of that reality is that when one comes to Jesus, one is not approaching one truth among many. Religion is not like a line in a cafeteria, where one has a choice of what meal to eat. The message of Jesus is unique. The road to the Father comes through him (John 14:6; Acts 4:12). Nor is religious faith in the world like a vast interstate highway system where many roads lead to God. Jesus is available to all humanity, so the offer he makes is not an exclusive one. But in order to know the Father, one must know the Son. That message may cut against the grain of our current cultural pluralism, but it does reflect that Jesus is unique: "You are my Son, whom I love; with you I am well pleased." With a divine endorsement like that, we must listen to him.

Unfortunately, even some evangelicals today are questioning just how exclusive and necessary the recognition of faith in Jesus is. They claim that we must be "open to God" and argue for the possibility that God saves some outside of Jesus on the basis of Jesus' work.[17] Yet such an emphasis makes no sense of the kind of appeals Paul made to Jews, who knew Yahweh and were as sincere about their beliefs as they could be (Rom. 9:33–10:4). If those who have not heard can be saved without Jesus, why share the gospel with them and put them at risk? The unique Son of God had a unique mission. He is the way, the truth, and the life; no one comes to the Father except through him (John 14:6). Such fundamental biblical truth cannot be revised, no matter how hard it is for our pluralistic worldview to swallow. In an earlier essay, I summarized the issue this way:

> Ignorance and "God-fearing devotion" in themselves provide no hope that one can enter God's presence outside Jesus, as the New Testament shows. Devotion to God must be according to knowledge. In other words, one must believe in the righteousness that come from God through faith in Jesus. Perhaps Acts 17:30–31 (RSV) says it best: "The times of ignorance God overlooked, but now he commands all

---

17. For a look at this debate, see William V. Crockett and James G. Sigountos, ed., *Through No Fault of Their Own? The Fate of Those Who Have Not Heard* (Grand Rapids: Baker, 1991); Ramesh P. Richard, *The Population of Heaven* (Chicago: Moody, 1994); Roger Olson, "Has God Been Held Hostage by Philosophy?" *CT* 39 (January 9, 1995), which is one of several reviews in that issue on the most recent discussion.

men everywhere to repent, because he has fixed a day on which he will judge the world in righteousness by a man whom he has appointed, and of this he has given assurance to all men by raising him from the dead." To know God one must know the appointed one. In short, to be a part of the kingdom, one must know the King.[18]

---

18. Darrell Bock, "Athenians Who Have Never Heard," in Crockett and Sigountos, *Through No Fault of Their Own?* 124.

Luke 3:23–38

❧

NOW JESUS HIMSELF WAS about thirty years old when he began his ministry. He was the son, so it was thought, of Joseph,

the son of Heli, ²⁴ the son of Matthat,
the son of Levi, the son of Melki,
the son of Jannai, the son of Joseph,
²⁵ the son of Mattathias, the son of Amos,
the son of Nahum, the son of Esli,
the son of Naggai, ²⁶the son of Maath,
the son of Mattathias, the son of Semein,
the son of Josech, the son of Joda,
²⁷ the son of Joanan, the son of Rhesa,
the son of Zerubbabel, the son of Shealtiel,
the son of Neri, ²⁸the son of Melki,
the son of Addi, the son of Cosam,
the son of Elmadam, the son of Er,
²⁹ the son of Joshua, the son of Eliezer,
the son of Jorim, the son of Matthat,
the son of Levi, ³⁰the son of Simeon,
the son of Judah, the son of Joseph,
the son of Jonam, the son of Eliakim,
³¹ the son of Melea, the son of Menna,
the son of Mattatha, the son of Nathan,
the son of David, ³²the son of Jesse,
the son of Obed, the son of Boaz,
the son of Salmon, the son of Nahshon,
³³ the son of Amminadab, the son of Ram,
the son of Hezron, the son of Perez,
the son of Judah, ³⁴the son of Jacob,
the son of Isaac, the son of Abraham,
the son of Terah, the son of Nahor,
³⁵ the son of Serug, the son of Reu,
the son of Peleg, the son of Eber,
the son of Shelah, ³⁶the son of Cainan,
the son of Arphaxad, the son of Shem,
the son of Noah, the son of Lamech,

[37] the son of Methuselah, the son of Enoch,
the son of Jared, the son of Mahalalel,
the son of Kenan, [38] the son of Enosh,
the son of Seth, the son of Adam,
the son of God.

KEEPING RECORDS OF ancestry was popular in Judaism. One need only read Genesis 4–5; 10; or 1 Chronicles 1–9 to see how important tracing one's lineage was in Jewish thinking.[1] The Greeks also loved to trace their roots (Diogenes Laertius, *Life of Plato* 3.1–2; Plutarch, *Parallel Lives*, Alexander 2.1).[2] Thus, when Luke records Jesus' ancestors, the readers would have appreciated what he was doing.

Ancestry can be revealing. In the case of Jesus, this is especially so. Several features stand out about Luke's genealogy in comparison to Matthew 1:1–17. (1) Luke puts his genealogy in a different place than Matthew. Matthew opens the book with his list, while Luke places it between Jesus' baptism as Son and the temptations that test him. Luke is answering the question: Is Jesus qualified to be God's promised Son? (2) Luke's list goes in an opposite order from Matthew's—going from the present to the past. (3) Luke's list goes farther than Matthew's. Matthew stops with Abraham, while Luke goes all the way back to Adam. With this touch, Luke indicates that Jesus' story is humanity's story.

(4) There are also some differences in the listing, the explanation for which is not entirely certain. Matthew traces Jesus through Solomon, while Luke passes through Nathan. Jesus' grandfather in Matthew is named Jacob, but in Luke he is Heli.[3] Some think these differences cannot be reconciled, while others believe they can be. Some argue that Luke supplies Mary's line, while Matthew has Joseph's, since Luke tells the story from Mary's perspective. The problem with this approach is that a line based on Mary would be unprecedented, especially when no other single woman appears in the line. Others suggest Joseph's line is being traced in two different ways: Matthew gives the natural line, while Luke has the royal line. Others make the same distinction but argue it goes the other way. Still others make the distinction

---

1. Josephus notes the importance of lineage for Jews in *Life* §§ 3–6; *Against Apion* 1.7 §§ 30–36.

2. L. T. Johnson, *Luke* (Sacra Pagina 3; Collegeville, Minn.: Liturgical Press, 1991), 72.

3. R. H. Stein, *Luke* (The New American Commentary; Nashville: Broadman, 1992), 141.

between the physical line and the legal line, noting the presence of some levirate marriages in the list (Deut. 25:5—10), especially at the grandfather level. Nolland suggests that perhaps Eli (=Heli) lacked sons and adopted Joseph, so that Luke's list reflects an adoption.[4] Luke's line may also be a legal one because of the curse of Jeconiah (Jer. 22:30), for Matthew mentions him and Luke does not. There is no way to establish the superiority of one of these options over the other, except to note that a reconciliation between the lists is possible in a variety of ways.

The overall intention of Luke's list is clear. He wants to show Jesus' connection to David, to Abraham, and to Adam. Each connection allows a point to be made about who Jesus is and whom he is qualified to serve. The connection to David establishes his rights as regal heir; Jesus can be king of Israel.[5] "Son of God" in this sense involves the right to rule as the Promised One, the Son of David (1:31—35; cf. 2 Sam. 7:6—16). The connection to Abraham links Jesus to the national promise and hope. The connection to Adam allows Luke to argue that Jesus represents all humanity. So in Jesus God has carefully designed affairs so that as Son Jesus can realize both the hope of the Old Testament and the hope of creation.

As Luke introduces his genealogy, he gives the age of Jesus at the start of his ministry as being about thirty (3:23). He also notes that Jesus was "thought" to be the son of Joseph, reaffirming his earlier assertions about the miraculous birth through Mary. Despite this qualification, legal paternity was still the source of ancient ancestry, so it is likely the line is Joseph's. It is this distinction that makes Luke's line a "legal" line.

Bridging Contexts

LUKE'S GENEALOGY CLEARLY serves an authenticating role for Jesus' right to serve God as mediator for humanity. Since the ancestry is unique and applies only to him, there is not much bridging that needs to occur. We need only to reflect on this passage that shows the richness of background in Jesus' family.

The fact that this list of ancestry extends to Adam makes a fundamental point. The promised king of Israel is also the head of the human race. God's promise to Israel becomes our promise in Christ. Gentiles have been grafted

---

4. Nolland, *Luke 1:1—9:20*, 170—72.

5. Some argue that Luke's choice of Nathan as son of David indicates a prophetic, not a regal, concern; so M. Johnson, *The Purpose of Biblical Genealogies* (SNTSMS 8; Cambridge: Cambridge Univ. Press, 1988), 234—52. But Fitzmyer (*Luke*, 497) rightly contends that this alternative requires that Nathan son of David equals Nathan the prophet, an identification that cannot be established. So a prophetic emphasis is unlikely. If one were to argue for the Nathan line, it still would have to be through a regal emphasis.

into blessing alongside Jews who believe in Jesus. Anyone who trusts Jesus becomes a child of Abraham (Rom. 4; 11; Gal. 3:26—29) and shares in this line of promise. This list of names spanning the centuries declares that God is about something special, even unique, in his creation. Association with Jesus and the promise is an opportunity to blessing that God took centuries to prepare.

It is important to appreciate the uniqueness of this list. We all have genealogies, but none of them qualifies us to be God's chosen Son. We receive our role in God's family through him. In a sense the only genealogy that counts for us is the one that connects us to Jesus, for his work makes our biological roots less relevant. He makes his children out of Jews and Gentiles, males and females, blacks and whites, Croats and Serbs (Gal. 3:29).

WHAT GENEALOGIES LIKE this show is that no person is an island unto himself or herself. We come into the world reflecting a heritage and representing someone. Jesus is no exception. His family is full of significant historical figures besides David, Abraham, and Adam: for example, Zerubbabel, Jesse, Boaz, Judah, Jacob, Isaac, Shem, Noah, and Enoch. In this list are some who walked closely with God and some whose walk was uneven. In a sense, Jesus represents them, much as he does us. In the list is also a variety of humanity. Some of the people are well-known Old Testament people who made a great mark; others are known to us only in this listing. Jesus represents both the well-known and the unknown of the world.

Churches mirror this truth. Some who function in the Christian community receive much public attention; others are barely known. Yet God knows them all and honors all faithfulness, no matter how much public acclaim such faithfulness receives when it is done. One of the great examples of such truth is to hear the testimony of great saints, only to realize that God got their attention through a grandparent, relative, or friend the world never knew. God's work often takes mysterious twists and turns.

Finally, Jesus' roots go back to Adam, the figure through whom all of us are connected to one another. In a day when ethnic diversity and hatred are raised to almost religious levels, we do well to reflect that even in our diversity humanity is one. In his provision for humanity, Jesus represents all of us. It is easy to let our nationality, race, or social status blind us to this fundamental truth. As human beings we not only share a planet, we share a relationship to each other. Transcending that is the fact that Jesus, as Son, offers an opportunity to any of us to share in God's rich blessing.

Jesus came to reconcile us to each other (Eph. 2:11–22), and he is in a unique position to accomplish that goal. God's plan of salvation indicates that he did not want to be a tribal god of only one people or of only one region. He came for everyone.

Luke 4:1–13

J ESUS, FULL OF the Holy Spirit, returned from the Jordan
and was led by the Spirit in the desert, ²where for forty
days he was tempted by the devil. He ate nothing during
those days, and at the end of them he was hungry.

³The devil said to him, "If you are the Son of God, tell this
stone to become bread."

⁴Jesus answered, "It is written: 'Man does not live on bread
alone.'"

⁵The devil led him up to a high place and showed him in an
instant all the kingdoms of the world. ⁶And he said to him, "I
will give you all their authority and splendor, for it has been
given to me, and I can give it to anyone I want to. ⁷So if you
worship me, it will all be yours."

⁸Jesus answered, "It is written: 'Worship the Lord your God
and serve him only.'"

⁹The devil led him to Jerusalem and had him stand on the
highest point of the temple. "If you are the Son of God," he
said, "throw yourself down from here. ¹⁰For it is written:

'"He will command his angels concerning you
to guard you carefully;
¹¹ they will lift you up in their hands,
so that you will not strike your foot against a stone.'"

¹²Jesus answered, "It says: 'Do not put the Lord your God
to the test.'"

¹³When the devil had finished all this tempting, he left him
until an opportune time.

Original Meaning

BEFORE BEGINNING HIS ministry, Jesus faces off
with Satan after being led by the Spirit into the
desert.[1] Luke makes such leading clear by noting
both that Jesus was "full of the Holy Spirit" and
that he was "led by the Spirit in the desert." What occurs here, therefore, takes

---

1. This event has two parallels. Mark 1:12–13 only briefly summarizes this event.
Matthew 4:1–13 is parallel except that the order of the temptations differs, with Luke's third
temptation being Matthew's second. Most likely Luke has altered the order so that Jerusalem

place under God's direction. Also important to the event's background is the fact that it takes place after forty days of fasting. Forty is a significant number in the Bible (Gen 7:4; Lev. 12:1—4; Num. 14:33; Deut. 25:3; Ezek. 4:6; on fasting, see Ex. 34:28; Deut 9:9; 1 Kings 19:8).[2] Such fasting probably involved minimum drink only. The remark is significant, since Jesus' testing takes place in an environment opposite to the one Adam faced.

The comparison to Adam is suggested by "the son of Adam, the son of God" conclusion to the preceding genealogy (3:38). The cosmic confrontation of Jesus with Satan recalls that earlier encounter, which had such dire consequences for humanity. Another major biblical event surfacing in this passage is the Exodus, for Jesus uses the book of Deuteronomy to reply to each satanic temptation.

Jesus' successful encounter with the devil reveals how thoroughly dedicated he is to God's will and call. Jesus will take only the road God asks him to follow. He will not take any shortcuts. He knows that a successful walk with God only goes where the Father leads.

The event is built around three distinct temptations. Two of them specifically make Jesus' Sonship the issue (vv. 3, 9). They argue in vivid terms, using a conditional clause in which the word "if" (*ei*) presents the condition as if it were so, though Satan has more sinister motives. Satan tempts Jesus to act in a way that supports his Sonship. Of course, his goal behind these temptations is the exact opposite: luring Jesus to act independently of the Father and thus creating a rebellious Sonship. In each case, Jesus uses Scripture to counter Satan's attempt.

The first temptation questions God's provision and care. Satan's premise is that Jesus' Sonship must mean that God does not want him to starve in the desert, so the mighty Son should simply turn stone into bread and meet his basic needs under his own power. But Jesus understands that the request is not a challenge to be strong, but to be independent. Such independence is weakness and leads to failure. Jesus' reply comes from Deuteronomy 8:3b, arguing that life is run by more than food. In fact, in the priority of things, life is not defined by bread at all. Instead, life is defined by doing God's will and depending on his leading. In the Deuteronomy citation, the next line refers to living by every word that proceeds from the mouth of the Lord. To follow God is to live.

---

is the climactic temptation since Jerusalem is so important to Luke's story. The absence of clear temporal markers in Luke supports this conclusion, as well as the lack of any note of Satan's dismissal. For other possible explanations, see C. Kimball, *Jesus' Exposition of the Old Testament in Luke's Gospel* (JSNTMS 94; Sheffield: Sheffield Academic Press, 1994), 81, n. 8.

2. Marshall, *Commentary on Luke*, 169.

The second temptation is an invitation to worship Satan and abandon loyalty to the Father, a direct challenge to the first commandment (Ex. 20:3). Satan allows Jesus to see all the kingdoms in the world and promises him authority over all of them if he will only worship him.[3] The proposal is of an alliance between the Son and Satan. The temptation is not only to join Satan, but for Jesus to excuse himself from all that lies ahead in his ministry. He can leave behind the rejection and suffering for quick access to power.

Though Satan possesses great authority (John 12:31; 14:30; 16:11; 2 Cor. 4:4; Eph. 2:2), he really cannot grant this wish. The proposal is a delusion and a lie, as are all of Satan's attempts to get us off track. Jesus' reply makes it clear he knows which way is true. Going Satan's way is not the way to gain power, but to lose it. There is no quick and easy road to messianic glory or to spiritual survival in a hostile world. Jesus opts to receive from the Father what is the Father's to give. Therefore, Jesus replies with Deuteronomy 6:13. Only one Being is worthy of worship—the Lord God. This text comes from a portion of a passage that follows the *Shema* (Deut. 6:4–9), which a Jew recited daily. That verse notes one other important reality, that with worship comes service. True service means remaining allied to God.

The third temptation, like the second, involves a vision-like experience. Jesus is taken to the temple in Jerusalem—probably on the Royal Porch on the temple's southeast corner, which looms over a cliff and the Kidron Valley some 450 feet below.[4] Josephus mentions that just looking over the edge made people dizzy (*Antiquities* 15.11.5 §§ 411–12). To cast oneself down from such a height and survive would take divine intervention. The location of the temple probably underscores the idea of God's presence to help. There is no indication that this temptation occurred as a public act.[5] Rather, it seems to have been a type of creative enactment of a "potential" situation.

Satan adds to his enticement by quoting Scripture himself, citing Psalm 91:11–12, a text that promises God's protection for his own. The premise is, "If God protects his own and you are his Son, then you can jump and not worry; you can run over the edge and not be crushed." He suggests such wonder-working protection will enhance Jesus' unique dependence on God as he flings himself into his caring arms. Furthermore, surely God will not let his own suffer pain.

As spiritual as this sounds, Jesus recognizes the remark as a presumptuous test of God's care. God has not asked Jesus to engage in such a test, and

---

3. The Greek is particularly striking here. Literally, the word order reads, *"To you* I will give all this authority and their glory." In other words, the request is put in self-indulgent terms.

4. Plummer, *Luke,* 113.

5. B. Gerhardsson, *The Testing of God's Son* (Lund: Gleerup, 1966), 56–58.

the action artificially creates a need for God to act. Since it puts God in a "show me" position, the action is really a private test of God and a sign of a lack of faith. These kinds of tests God's children are not to pursue. So Jesus replies with Deuteronomy 6:16, a text that rebuked Israel for testing God in places like Massah (Ex. 17:1–7). Jesus will not test God or characterize his ministry with a flashy display engaged in for selfish purposes. Jesus' messianic ministry will not be a traveling road show of the miraculous.

Having failed three times, Satan departs for a while. His departure is not a long one, since confrontation with demons resurfaces in 4:31–44. Through it all, Jesus emerges as a loyal Son. He has shown the qualities that make him a worthy and exemplary Son.

Bridging Contexts

THE TEXT REVEALS both how Satan tempts and how Jesus resists. As noted above, in each case Satan uses a selfish tactic in justifying the action he wants Jesus to take: "Surely you should feed yourself, Jesus"; "Surely the Father wants you to have authority, so just give me your allegiance"; "Surely God will protect his Son, so why not try him out?" Such independence from God is the essence of spiritual defection and desertion. It recalls the original temptations in Genesis 3:1, 5: "Did God really say...?" and, "God knows that when you eat of it ... you will be like God."

While Jesus' temptations are unique, the satanic challenges to loyalty are not. Satan may not replicate the same temptations with us, especially since we are not the unique Son of God, but he does use the same key issue, namely, a challenge to faithfulness. He tries to subvert our walk with God by offering shortcuts to spirituality—which are really dead ends. In response, we must rely on God and, in some cases, walk the hard road with him. Anything we do independent of the Lord expresses a lack of connection to him. Just as Jesus shows loyalty as the Son, we must show loyalty as God's children.

Jesus' knowledge of God's Word is a bridge. Here is a means by which we come to understand God's will and direction. Loyalty to him involves loyalty to the Word, and such loyalty is paramount. God uses tests in our lives to show us where we stand before him. Jesus' temptations shows he stands solidly with God. Our temptations should be resisted in such a way that we reveal a similar character.

A final key issue emerges in how Jesus handles these temptations. He does not think or rationalize his way out of God's will. He could easily have said that God would not want his own Son to starve, to suffer rejection, or to die. Furthermore, the kingdom was going to belong to him anyway, so what did it matter how it came into his hands? But Jesus avoids this kind of end-justifies-the-means thinking as he responds to these undermining proposals of Satan. We must be careful that the shortcuts that often become possible in life do not in fact reflect rationalization to avoid God's will.

THE FIRST APPLICATION emerging from this event is about temptation itself. Tests in life are not bad; in fact, they can be divinely sent (James 1:2–4). The main issue is my response to a test. Do I respond in a way that looks to God to guide me through it? Do I trust him, or do I put him to the test? How do I respond to personal struggles in my life? Do I get angry? Do I seek to reassert my control (even when I know I cannot control events!)? Or do I rest in faith, look for God's hand, and ask him what I should learn from what I am going through? Though I personally wish I could say that I always do the latter, I know I do not, but that should certainly be my goal. If I am to grow spiritually, I can expect trial. If I am to grow spiritually, I need to look to God in the midst of it.

Such trust can extend to provision. Though Satan tested Jesus about the most basic of needs, bread, we sometimes desire to "feed ourselves" with things we feel are basic to life. But those "basic things" frequently involve a larger home, more gadgets, the finest appliances, the most expensive clothes, and a host of other material possessions to say that we have arrived. Yet life is not defined materially; rather, it is defined relationally and spiritually in terms of knowing God and serving him in the context of his will. Sometimes giving resources to the accomplishment of ministry may mean giving up personal material pleasures.

The pursuit of material goals can become a driving force in our lives. But where does God's Word and leading stand? Will Satan succeed in testing us to take bread that God is not asking us to eat, while we ignore the most basic meal of all, his will? Sometimes God provides marvelously in the midst of a sacrifice made for his will. Seeking to have less materially may mean having much more.

Another way we show lack of trust is to grab for power that is not ours or to take power in a way it is not intended to be received. Satan tempts us to slip into idolatry as directly as he did here with Jesus, using subtle substitutes. Perhaps we worship our work, our status, our possessions, our family, or other unsuitable items that stand in the way of knowing God. Maybe he asks us to take the easy path of "growth" without suffering or facing rejection in our stand for Jesus or for divine values. Sometimes opting for comfort means selling our soul to the prince of this world. Of course, God desires to give us rich blessing, even to share in the benefits of his authority, but to worship Satan and to take his path to get there is to lose whatever access to blessing we may possess.

The implications of such a power grab extend into how we exercise authority in the home, how we conduct our businesses, and how we relate to others. The best authority is one exercised not under threat but because of earned respect. The most genuine authority is not that which is seized, but that which is received from the God who honors faithfulness.

A final way we tend to show a lack of trust in God is to try to force him to act on our behalf. In the test we often set up, we want to see if he is for us or against us. This type of spiritual wagering does not involve leaping from tall buildings, but in walking into events where we say in effect, "If you care for me God, then this situation will turn out this way." In effect, we test the "emergency broadcast system" of God's presence and presume on how he should react. This kind of testing is an attempt to control God, not follow his leading. We are setting ourselves up for disappointment, since it may be in our best interest for events to go in a different direction than we desire.

Another way we can sense a problem here is by blaming God whenever suffering occurs, at least indirectly. We may feel that he has abandoned us, when, in fact, he may be getting our attention, revealing a better way to us, or asking us to meet him in the midst of the adversity. I am reminded of how Elisabeth Elliot must have felt when she lost her husband, Jim, to murder and martyrdom by Latin American Indians in the mid-1950s.[6] Yet she turned her disappointing experience into an opportunity to listen to God in the midst of uncertainty, only to find a fresh ministry of depth in her testimony about how God cared for her in the midst of such disappointment. She did not abandon God or test him, but accepted the uncharted journey he called her to take. Of course, that journey was uncharted only for her, not for the God who walked with her down that road. As Jesus turned down Satan and consciously chose to follow God down the hard road of his ministry, so too we must be prepared to walk into events under his leading, even where the outcome is not clear.

---

6. See her book *Through Gates of Splendor* (New York: Harper & Row, 1957).

Luke 4:14–30

JESUS RETURNED TO Galilee in the power of the Spirit, and news about him spread through the whole countryside. [15]He taught in their synagogues, and everyone praised him.

[16]He went to Nazareth, where he had been brought up, and on the Sabbath day he went into the synagogue, as was his custom. And he stood up to read. [17]The scroll of the prophet Isaiah was handed to him. Unrolling it, he found the place where it is written:

[18] "The Spirit of the Lord is on me,
because he has anointed me
to preach good news to the poor.
He has sent me to proclaim freedom for the prisoners
and recovery of sight for the blind,
to release the oppressed,
[19]   to proclaim the year of the Lord's favor."

[20]Then he rolled up the scroll, gave it back to the attendant and sat down. The eyes of everyone in the synagogue were fastened on him, [21]and he began by saying to them, "Today this scripture is fulfilled in your hearing."

[22]All spoke well of him and were amazed at the gracious words that came from his lips. "Isn't this Joseph's son?" they asked.

[23]Jesus said to them, "Surely you will quote this proverb to me: 'Physician, heal yourself! Do here in your hometown what we have heard that you did in Capernaum.'"

[24]"I tell you the truth," he continued, "no prophet is accepted in his hometown. [25]I assure you that there were many widows in Israel in Elijah's time, when the sky was shut for three and a half years and there was a severe famine throughout the land. [26]Yet Elijah was not sent to any of them, but to a widow in Zarephath in the region of Sidon. [27]And there were many in Israel with leprosy in the time of Elisha the prophet, yet not one of them was cleansed—only Naaman the Syrian."

²⁸All the people in the synagogue were furious when they heard this. ²⁹They got up, drove him out of the town, and took him to the brow of the hill on which the town was built, in order to throw him down the cliff. ³⁰But he walked right through the crowd and went on his way.

THE NEXT LARGE section of Luke's Gospel (4:14–9:50) describes Jesus' ministry. It is dominated by teaching and miracles. Throughout the section the main question is, "Who is Jesus?" Various answers surface, such as teacher and prophet. These offices only begin to tell the story, for Jesus is much more than these titles suggest. The key reply comes from Peter in 9:18–20: Jesus is "the Christ of God." He develops what this messianic role means in the verses that follow this confession. Strong opposition will rise up against Jesus and his followers, and he will be rejected as Messiah. In the midst of such opposition, Jesus begins to instruct the disciples that they must love differently than sinners do, for they must love their enemies.

Luke 4:14–44 summarizes Jesus' powerful teaching and healing ministry. After noting in 4:14–15 how that ministry is drawing attention, Luke gives an exemplary day in the synagogue, where Jesus declares himself and his ministry to be the fulfillment of promise (4:16–30). Then follows a series of miracles that show his ability to cast out demons and heal (4:31–44). Those in Capernaum want him to stay, but his call requires that others hear about the kingdom of God as well. The unit shows the extent of Jesus' claims and authority.

Luke 4:14–15 (cf. Matt. 4:13–17; Mark 1:14–15) introduces and summarizes the general character of Jesus' ministry during its early Galilean stage. Since Galilee is Jesus' home, it is not surprising that his ministry begins there. Exposure to Jesus in Galilee will be a requirement for apostolic selection (Acts 1:21–22), so this period is foundational for building up a base of disciples.

As with his temptations, Jesus is under the guidance of the Spirit. Luke loves to note how Jesus is responsive to God's leading. As he ministers, his fame spreads.[1] In the ancient world, these reports went by word of mouth. It is debated whether the reference to the power of the Spirit also alludes to Jesus' miraculous activity.[2] However, Luke makes it clear when Jesus' miracles

---

1. The Greek word for "news" (*pheme*) is the word from which we get the English word "fame." In Greek this refers to news passing through the public.
2. Argued by Nolland, *Luke 1:1–9:20*, 187.

are in focus (5:17; 6:19; 8:46). What catches people's interest is his teaching, so much so that they "praise" him. This word (*doxazo*) is normally reserved for praise to God.[3]

Luke goes on to illustrates his point (4:16–30). When Jesus preaches in the synagogue in Nazareth, the people are impressed with him, though not necessarily persuaded. In this important passage, we get a glimpse of how Jesus preaches in the synagogues and what he has to say about himself and his activities. Unlike the Sermon on the Plain (6:20–48), where the topic is the ethics of the disciple, Jesus here describes his mission.

This account of Jesus' teaching ministry should be paired with Luke 4:31–44, which highlights his ministry of miracles. Jesus combines word and event. His message of love is supported by his ministry of compassion. Luke has transferred the synagogue event here from its location in Matthew 13:53–58 and Mark 6:1–6a.[4] He details the nature of the exchange in the synagogue of Nazareth, so that we know much more about this scene than we do from the other Synoptics; this indicates its importance and representative character. This event becomes a snapshot of what Jesus' entire Galilean ministry will be like: People will be amazed at his teaching and claims, but they will not flock to him.

The message of freedom in this passage is so distinct that it has become a central text for a theological movement known as "liberation theology."[5] This theology teaches that Jesus sides with the poor. In its more radical forms it advocates the use of any and all means of disruption to help those in power yield their oppressive grip on social structures so that the poor are no longer trapped in their social status. It sees a strong political message and overtone to Jesus' message. Only a careful assessment of the passage itself can answer whether and in what way such emphases are present.

According to his custom, Jesus is in the synagogue on the Sabbath, a presence that reflects his respect for the worship of God. To appreciate what happens here, one must understand the synagogue service order. Our knowledge of such a service comes from ancient Jewish sources such as the *Mishnah*, the Jewish codification of their oral law.[6] To have a service, ten men

---

3. Schürmann, *Das Lukasevangelium*, 223. Note also Luke 2:13, 20, 28; 7:16.

4. Marshall, *Commentary on Luke*, 177–80; D. Hill, "The Rejection of Jesus at Nazareth," *NovT* 13 (1971): 161–68; C. J. Schrenk, "The Nazareth Pericope: Luke 4,16–30 in Recent Study," in *L'évangile de Luc*, ed. F. Neirynck (BETL 32; Leuven: Leuven Univ. Press, 1989), 397–471.

5. For a careful assessment of this movement, see E. Nuñez, *Liberation Theology*, trans. P. Sywalka (Chicago: Moody, 1985).

6. The *Mishnah* was compiled in c. A.D. 170, but many of its customs, especially the practices associated with worship in the synagogue, probably reflect older practices, since

must be present. The congregation recites the *Shema*, the confession recorded in Deuteronomy 6:4–9. Then they share in prayer—some of them set prayers, such as the *Tephillah* (also called the *Shemoneh Esreh* and the Eighteen Benedictions). Then comes a reading from God's Law, the *Torah*, followed by a reading of the Prophets. These texts are read in Hebrew and translated into Aramaic, the dominant language of the region. Then follows an exposition that usually ties the readings together, and the service closes with a benediction.

Presumably Jesus speaks during the exposition section of this service. This may explain a peculiarity in his citation, for he not only cites Isaiah 61:1–2, but mixes into it an allusion to Isaiah 58:6.[7] The mixture may well represent a summary of a larger reading or set of remarks.

The text begins by certifying that the Spirit is on the speaker. In the context of Isaiah, the remarks foresee a prophetic figure who declares the arrival of divine salvation for the nation. The passage is not explicitly a Servant Song, but many of the themes of the Servant Songs are present. Since Jesus speaks of himself as fulfilling this text, he is the one to whom the text applies (v. 21). Insofar as the text speaks explicitly of being anointed by the Spirit, this anointing looks back to the bestowal of the Spirit on Jesus at his baptism by John (3:21–22).

Jesus' task involves a message, and that message has an audience: the poor. It cannot be denied that "poor" here refers to those who live in a socially and economically limited environment. But according to the use of this term in the Old Testament and in Luke, that is not all that is intended here. The Old Testament background points to the *anawim*, the "pious poor," the afflicted (2 Sam. 22:28; Pss. 14:6; 22:24; 25:16; 34:6; 40:17; 69:29; Amos 8:4; Isa. 3:14–15).[8] These are the humble whom God will exalt (Luke 1:51–53) and who like the prophets suffer for being open to God (6:20–23; cf. the description in 1 Cor. 1:26–29; James 2:5). They are open to God and his way since they are frequently the first to recognize how much they need God.

To such spiritually open folks, Jesus proclaims release, recovery of sight, and freedom from oppression. The background to this imagery is the Year of Jubilee, in which all debts were declared null (Lev. 25:8–17). Just as the Year of Jubilee initiated a new start, so Jesus proclaims a new start through his offer of divine deliverance. He both proclaims that release and accom-

---

religious liturgy tends to be slow to change. The synagogue services are described in *Megillah* 3–4 and *Berakoth* 2.

7. There are a few minor variations in these citations from both the Hebrew Old Testament and the Greek Old Testament, but they do not influence the basic sense of the passage; for details see Bock, *Proclamation from Prophecy and Pattern*, 106–7.

8. Bammel, "πτωχός," *TDNT*, 6:888.

plishes it. His setting free of the blind probably alludes to both his miraculous work of the physically blind and his spiritual work of salvation, since Jesus brings light to those in darkness (see Luke 1:78–79).

The idea that Jesus actually brings liberty rather than merely proclaiming it alludes to Isaiah 58:6. Jesus actually uses this text in a contrastive way from its original setting. In Isaiah 58, God is making a complaint against the nation of Israel for not living out her calling in proper Sabbath worship. She has failed to be a source of liberty for those who are oppressed. The rebuke and call are especially clear in 58:13–14. Jesus will therefore do what Israel has failed to do: He will bring about the salvation of God and free those who suffer from the oppression that is a part of life (cf. also Luke 11:14–23, 31–32; 18:38–39; 19:37–38). This is why Jesus can speak of the arrival of "the year of the Lord's favor," the phrase that explicitly alludes to the release that came in the Jubilee Year.[9]

In sum, Jesus makes three points here: (1) He is anointed by the Spirit to perform a specific ministry; (2) he is a prophetic figure who declares the arrival of the new era; and (3) he will actually bring about the release that he proclaims. The combination means that Jesus functions as both prophet and Messiah.[10] This combination is important, because the following verses compare Jesus to the prophets Elijah and Elisha, but his anointing recalls his messianic function.

Jesus concludes his remarks by telling his audience that they are seeing the fulfillment of these words of Isaiah. Now every Jew will know that Isaiah 61 was associated with the decisive end-time salvation of God, which Jesus will introduce. That program is going to come in phases, as will be made clear in the rest of Luke, but here Jesus notes that the fulfillment has started.

The crowd reacts with marvel at the words of grace spoken by Jesus and are overwhelmed by the content of his message. But assessment must follow. The issue of Jesus' pedigree raises questions in their minds. This is Joseph's son, so how can such a humble figure possibly be all the things declared by Isaiah. They cannot fit Jesus' ancestry with his claims.[11] Despite their amazement, they are skeptical.

Jesus responds with three points. (1) He cites a proverb expressing a request that one should do his work in his own backyard to prove his claims.

---

9. On this theme, R. B. Sloan, *The Favorable Year of the Lord* (Austin: Scholars Press, 1977).

10. There is much debate whether Luke 4 stresses Jesus' prophetic or his regal, messianic role. Actually, both are involved. Within Luke 4 and its illustrations, the stress is on Jesus as prophet. But in light of the baptism and the nature of Jesus' anointing, the portrait includes the messianic emphasis.

11. The Greek in verse 22 expects a positive answer to the question about Jesus' roots going back to Joseph.

The call for the physician to heal himself is a demand that Jesus do the works he has done elsewhere and show himself approved.[12] The townsfolk want him to show his stuff. There is another possible implication in their choice of this proverb. It may suggest that though Jesus presents himself as one who can heal, they ironically believe he is sick in some sense. Something is not quite right with his claim of fulfillment. Something about Jesus needs treatment, unless he can prove otherwise.

(2) Jesus notes how a prophet is without honor in his own land. Jesus knows that many of Israel's prophets in the Old Testament were not well received—a theme Luke notes elsewhere (11:49–52; 13:32–35; 20:10–12; Acts 7:51–53). God's message often meets with rejection.

(3) Jesus then gets specific. He singles out the period of Elijah and Elisha, one of the lowest, most apostate periods of the nation's history (1 Kings 17–18; 2 Kings 5:1–14). He reminds the people that during that time, the prophets did no work in the nation but they did heal a couple of Gentiles! This remark is strong for two reasons: (a) It compares the current era to one of the least spiritual periods in Israel's history, and (b) it suggests that Gentiles, who were intensely disliked among the Jews, were more worthy of ministry than they were. Jesus is warning his audience that their reaction recalls some of the lowest years in Israel's past. A choice surrounds Jesus, and to choose wrongly is to lose opportunity for blessing. In that sense Jesus' message is like John the Baptist's warning. The opportunity for blessing holds out an equal opportunity for judgment, if the wrong choice is made.

Jesus' remark angers the crowd, and they want to remove him and cast him over the cliff—possibly an allusion to their perception that he is a false prophet worthy of complete rejection (Deut. 13:5–6). Instead Jesus walks away. The opportunity for blessing has become a moment when paradise is lost.

Bridging Contexts

THIS SECTION BEGINS with a glimpse of the importance of teaching for Jesus' ministry. To be responsive to God, one must know what he desires and how he sees issues. Thus teaching from God is a central component to his ministry. What makes Jesus' teaching stand out is the authority with which it is delivered, as this Gospel will make clear.

---

12. This verse is why many suspect the event has been moved forward in Luke. Jesus has not been to Capernaum (see Luke 4:31–44), yet he has apparently already done works there.

When one turns to the scene of Jesus' preaching in the synagogue, it becomes evident that his mission is unique. The note of fulfillment he raises has at its base the message of release. Virtually every aspect of Jesus' message and ministry has relevance to us. For example, when Paul and Barnabas preach in Acts 13, they call themselves "light" (Acts 13:47), using the same image that is applied to Jesus here. Their message parallels his message, and their call is an outgrowth of his. Jesus can therefore say to those who hear the gospel preached: To hear them is to hear me.

The kind of reaction Jesus gets shows that he does not fit our expectations about where the origins of God's decisive agent ought to be. Some people never get past Jesus' background. Would the God of the universe manifest his glorious message in someone of such humble roots? The answer in part comes in Jesus' own message. He preaches to the pious poor, so that in reaching out to them, he is someone who can identify with them. The picture of a grand, regal, and elite Messiah is what most expected. The fact that Jesus is merely Joseph's son is too much for them. As the complaint in John 1:46 puts it, "Can anything good come from [Nazareth]?" As we already noted in the infancy material, God sometimes surprises us by the way he works and how he chooses to reveal himself.

The nature of Jesus' criticism and the crowd's reaction to it are also significant. Jesus warns that failure to respond positively to him risks making the doubting generation equal to the worst days in Israel's history. Those thus criticized and warned respond with anger. Both the warning and the response are elements we need to hear today.

Some may ask whether the presence of a synagogue audience and the use of Isaiah mean that Jesus' remarks are uniquely aimed at Israel. In one sense, Jesus is inviting this specific audience to participate as a faithful "remnant" in God's plan. Later, Jesus will explain how those who refuse the invitation lose out on something that is offered to others (14:15–24). The party will not be delayed or put off; instead, the invitation to celebrate is extended to others. What is offered here is still part of the promise Jesus offers to all, both to those inside and those outside the nation of Israel (Eph. 2:11–22).

IT IS IMPORTANT to appreciate how central good teaching is to ministry. In an era when feelings and interpersonal relationships are high on the agenda, it is wise to reflect on why Jesus spent so much time instructing people. One of the fundamental biblical assumptions is that human cultures distort reality. Our minds need reshaping and renewing, so that our feelings and reactions will be more like what God desires

(Rom. 12:1–2).[13] In a provocative summary, Walsh and Middleton have analyzed our culture's total commitment to science, technology, and economics this way:

> We are living in the "last days" under the economy of the unholy trinity. The promised land is just around the corner, and we are in the final stage of secular "redemptive history." Just as God the Father sent the Son to effect our salvation, and the Holy Spirit now dwells with us to apply that salvation to our lives in the here and now, so it is in the redemptive history of secularism. The absolutization of science in the Renaissance fathered a tremendous technology which brings salvation, and the blessing and presence of these humanistic deities are today mediated to us through the economistic consumer society in which we live and move and have our being. The high god, scientism, in its omniscience conceived a divine plan and sent the son of technical mastery to subdue nature for our benefit. Divine reason took on flesh in the scientific-technological conquest of the natural world.
>
> When the disciples of the new religion gathered at the industrial revolution, the spirit of capitalism was outpoured. And now in these last days we are filled with this spirit and empowered to do mighty acts of production and consumption, looking for and hastening the day when the invisible hand will cause the blessings of the economistic age to trickle down to all nations. And in that day everyone, great and small, will have prosperity. From the beginning of time never has such a day been; wealth will cover the earth, and weeping and toil will be no more.

In the words of Canadian songwriter Bruce Cockburn, our modern prophets have offered us

> something for nothing, new lamps for old,
>
> and the streets will be platinum, never mind gold.

But as Cockburn continues,

> Well, hey, pass it on.
>
> *Misplaced your faith* and the candy man's gone.

How the vision is shattered! The age of unlimited economic expansion is coming to an abrupt close. We are coming up against the lim-

---

13. For a solid yet popular analysis of how our culture does this, see James Sire, *Chris Christman Goes to College* (Downers Grove, Ill.: InterVarsity, 1993), and *The Universe Next Door*, 2d ed. (Downers Grove, Ill.: InterVarsity, 1988). Sire carefully analyzes the different "isms" that exist at a philosophical level in our culture and assesses them from a Christian point of view. Sire covers the "isms" of individualism, pluralism, relativism, and privatization on pp. 20–27.

its of creation itself. God's covenantal curses are raining on our heads for our idolatrous disobedience. The secular gods have not delivered. When a culture's gods fail, the time is ripe for serious world view reconsideration.[14]

It takes careful cultural discernment to know how to respond to the subtleties our culture feeds us.

Since Jesus' ministry was built around his teaching and since he showed that God's will was not what the religious culture was delivering, then how careful should we be to make sure that our communities are well instructed and grounded in God's truth! Such instruction means careful pastoral preparation of messages, including giving the pastor enough time to do it as well as developing training institutions that focus on substance. Encouragement should be given to underwrite students who seek to train for ministry, not by seeing how quickly they can complete their training, but how deeply grounded they will be when they emerge to enter ministry. A colleague of mine has asked how may of us would be proud and comforted to hear from a heart surgeon before we are wheeled into the operating theater that he got his degree in a year or two! How much more for those who minister to the soul! If teaching is central to effective ministry of the church, then solid training should be at the top of the list. Is it any accident Jesus trained his disciples for over three years to prepare them for their role as apostles?

It is not merely a matter of teaching doctrine and facts, but also of relating that teaching to life and putting flesh and blood on it. I often tell my students that the ministry is as much exhortation and encouragement as pure teaching. We speak to hearts, not just minds. But there must be content to send to the heart, or else we are ministering with nothing more than what a person can get in the lifestyles section of the bookstore or what they can receive from their neighborhood counselors.

The major application emerging from the scene where Jesus preaches in the synagogue involves the nature of his mission. The church's call is but an extension of Jesus' mission. The fulfillment he proclaims is part of the fulfillment that the church proclaims. Values reflected in this mission should be reflected in the church's outreach. For example, the church should engage in its preaching and evangelistic task with an understanding that the gospel message is more suited to those who are poor and already live in a dependent context. Independent, well-to-do people often have a false sense of security about life, as if it is really within their control. Our culture tells

---

14. Brian J. Walsh and J. Richard Middleton, *The Transforming Vision: Shaping a Christian World View* (Downers Grove, Ill.: InterVarsity, 1984), 139–40.

people to take control of their own lives—as if they can grab life by the reins and steer their own way. The poor, however, live under no such delusions and are usually better prepared to turn toward God.

Despite this potential openness of the poor and the suitability of the gospel for them, ministry groups often target the wealthy. Ministry in the inner city or in less visible locales are often hard to launch and sustain. The church, of course, is called to offer the gospel to all people, so ministry to these other social groupings is not wrong. But the text does raise the question of whether more effort should be made to minister to those groups for whom the gospel may be an easier fit.

We ought also to raise the question about how best to reveal our concern and compassion for those in need. Sometimes in saying, "God loves you and has a plan for your life," an act of compassion illustrates our claim more than any opening evangelistic line. True, the gospel is not primarily a commitment to change society but hearts. Yet when hearts are changed, compassion emerges and society is changed. Expressing concern for people can become a powerful tool in evangelism. Jesus communicated this sense of redemption to notorious sinners and those who stood in dire need. His relating to people's pain had much to do with it. The people not only heard his message of repentance, forgiveness, release, and fulfillment of promise, but they also saw his compassion and care.

Another major application of this passage centers on the nature of salvation. The one metaphor that dominates Jesus' declaration of fulfillment here is *release*. The picture of Jubilee, which foresees a total release from all enemies and debt, wonderfully describes the essence of salvation. The books are wiped clean; all legal obligations are removed through the grace Jesus provides. In addition, there is a new way of seeing, so that life from the old perspective is now appreciated as darkness and blindness. One needs only to look at Jesus' compassionate ministry through miracles to see the sense of release that so many experienced from what he did. These miracles, as we shall argue shortly, are an audio-visual of deeper realities that are at the center of his work.

According to this passage, the church must care about the oppressed. There is much discussion today about how our culture fails to take responsibility for its actions, becoming instead a culture of victims in which everyone else is blamed for my problems but there is no recognition of the sin and responsibility I bear for the present situation. Whether it be bad parents, the other gender, a poor environment growing up, or some other outside constraint, our culture says I am who I am because of outside forces.

Such a cultural reading reflects blindness. For while it recognizes the pervasive presence of sin in the world, it ignores my own personal contribution to that mix. Sin is in every house but my own. Such a distorted view of reality cannot help us deal with what is really wrong in our world, since the one person each of us has most access to is our own individual soul. Yet Jesus focuses less on how to change societal structures and more on how to change the individual. Structures cannot change until the people who operate them are changed. The world of "I want" ends up crushing others who get in the way. With an honesty about sin and a compassion for others comes the possibility of reversing the oppression that reigns in the world.

Part of the liberty of the gospel is coming to the Father with the recognition that he supplies what we really need to release us from perspectives in life that chain us down and cause us to mistreat others. This is why in other texts where Jesus describes his mission, he makes it clear that he focuses on calling sinners to repentance and on finding the lost (5:31–32; 19:10). The way to start fixing what is wrong in the world is to start with fixing ourselves. Only then will we have the eyes to see how we contribute to the problems that sometimes make the world a painful place of broken relationships.

As the church calls people to take a serious look at themselves, patterning itself after Jesus in his comparison of the current generation to the spiritually empty days of Elijah and Elisha, the church must also understand that many will not respond with joy to the mirror held up to their faces. Sometimes rejection is an indication of success, not failure. This is because the gospel does not tickle the ears of its hearers with compliments. It can be hard to look into a truly reflective mirror and see what is there.

The church has a difficult task. On the one hand, to discuss redemption and release we must mention sin. On the other hand, the offer of the gospel is ultimately positive, so that the goal is not a message of doom but of hope. Granted there is a choice at stake, but the offer is made to anyone who will enter. God has an open door for any heart that is open. The risk of the church is that we will become selective in our choice of sins or set a decidedly negative tone as we risk becoming defensive in the face of a hostile culture. Abortion or homosexuality are bad, but somehow divorce, greed, covetousness, mental cruelty, or abuse of power are tolerable. To have credibility in identifying sin, the list cannot be selective or prioritized in such a way that some sins are less dangerous or more dignified than others.

Though Jesus outlines his mission here, the application emerges when we reflect on the entirety of his career that mirrors the values of his divinely-commissioned ministry. I always am left wondering when I consider Jesus' ministry as a whole that although he challenged all sin, he tended to be clearer about the more subtle sins we tend to downplay. These ideas and applications reflect what it means to gain liberty and adopt a new perspective that the gospel calls us to possess.

One final note emerges. Sometimes blessing surfaces in surprising places. When Elijah and Elisha began their ministry, they would have been dumbfounded had someone told them that their major miracles would involve a widowed Gentile and a leprous Syrian, neither of whom were in their target audience. In other words, this passage warns us against being able to figure God out. Jesus' reference to Elijah and Elisha illustrates that some of those whom God blesses (Gentiles) were not among those one would have expected him to bless (Israel), given the nature of the promise at the start. We must remain open to God's turning our ministries in directions we do not anticipate. Sometimes a closed door in one field is an open door to another opportunity.

Such changes can take various forms. I know of many people with opportunities to minister who say, "I don't have any experience at that!" In the process they may be turning away from something fresh God may do. Note that when God did open up the gospel to Gentiles in Acts, he had to convince the church that this new direction was possible (Acts 10–11). He had to reveal and support that revelation with his continued direction. Only as the church allows itself to be so led in reaching out to people—not by changing the essence of the message but by thinking through the various ways God can reach those is need—will the church penetrate the various groups of lost people he calls us to reach.

Luke 4:31–44

THEN HE WENT down to Capernaum, a town in Galilee, and on the Sabbath began to teach the people. ³²They were amazed at his teaching, because his message had authority.

³³In the synagogue there was a man possessed by a demon, an evil spirit. He cried out at the top of his voice, ³⁴"Ha! What do you want with us, Jesus of Nazareth? Have you come to destroy us? I know who you are—the Holy One of God!"

³⁵"Be quiet!" Jesus said sternly. "Come out of him!" Then the demon threw the man down before them all and came out without injuring him.

³⁶All the people were amazed and said to each other, "What is this teaching? With authority and power he gives orders to evil spirits and they come out!" ³⁷And the news about him spread throughout the surrounding area.

³⁸Jesus left the synagogue and went to the home of Simon. Now Simon's mother-in-law was suffering from a high fever, and they asked Jesus to help her. ³⁹So he bent over her and rebuked the fever, and it left her. She got up at once and began to wait on them.

⁴⁰When the sun was setting, the people brought to Jesus all who had various kinds of sickness, and laying his hands on each one, he healed them. ⁴¹Moreover, demons came out of many people, shouting, "You are the Son of God!" But he rebuked them and would not allow them to speak, because they knew he was the Christ.

⁴²At daybreak Jesus went out to a solitary place. The people were looking for him and when they came to where he was, they tried to keep him from leaving them. ⁴³ But he said, "I must preach the good news of the kingdom of God to the other towns also, because that is why I was sent." ⁴⁴And he kept on preaching in the synagogues of Judea.

THIS UNIT SUMMARIZES several distinct events that take place in Capernaum, the ancient city where Jesus sets up his base for operation. This city was located on the northwest shore of the Sea of Galilee, some 680 feet below sea level. It was a major Jewish center in the region, with trade centering in fishing and agriculture (Josephus, *Life* 72 § 403; *Jewish War* 3.10.8 § 519).[1]

The unit in Luke divides clearly: an introduction (4:31–32), an exorcism (4:33–37), the healing of Simon's mother-in-law (4:38–39), another encounter with a demon (4:40–41), and a closing mission statement (4:42–44). Three miracle accounts dominate this description of Jesus' activity. His ministry reflects the compassion he came to reveal.

Luke introduces here two of his five examples of Jesus' performing miracles on the Sabbath (see 4:31–37, 38–39; 6:6–11; 13:10–17; 14:1–6). He has declared the fulfillment of God's promise at a synagogue in Nazareth on the Sabbath. Now he shows the presence of such fulfillment. Like Mark 1:21–39, Luke is working with a series of events that serve as a snapshot of the activities that accompany Jesus' ministry. Mark tends to focus on the miracles themselves, while Luke balances his portrait between teaching, exorcism, and healing. For Luke words and deeds belong together.

There is variety in Jesus' ministry. He deals with individuals and crowds; he heals men and women; he teaches and exercises authority. His miracles may not surprise us since we are so familiar with these accounts of Jesus' work. Yet one should not lose sight that in the ancient world such action, though perhaps more accepted in that culture, was still rare and produced marvel and surprise.

As important as miracles are as events in the life of Jesus, they also serve as visual indications of deeper realities. Perhaps the clearest example of this is 5:1–11, where a catch of fish becomes the basis for Jesus' call to "catch men." All Jesus' miracles in some way reflect a visual representation of some significant spiritual reality—often the depth of the cosmic struggle associated with his ministry. Since his work represents the powerful arrival of the force of righteousness into God's world, is it any wonder that Jesus must go in hand-to-hand combat with the forces of evil? In a real sense, the miracles pull back a veil on the cosmic forces at work within creation.

The major feature of the initial summary of Jesus' ministry in verses 31–32 is the recognition of the authority inherent in his teaching. If the rabbinic works of a few centuries after Jesus' time are any indication, most rabbinic

---

1. Marshall, *Commentary on Luke*, 191.

arguments took on an anthological approach to teaching, where each rabbi's opinion on a matter was set out in a kind of listing and where truth was often a matter of establishing a precedent for an idea. Jesus does *not* teach this way. He declares God's will directly, even keeping his direct use of Scripture to a few limited situations. The crowds recognize his distinct approach to teaching and are astonished by it.

The first miracle of this Gospel is an exorcism. The major opponent in Jesus' ministry consists of the spiritual forces of evil. Demons are noted twenty-three times in this Gospel, with fourteen of those references occurring between here and 9:50 in the Galilean ministry section. Judaism believed that in the messianic times demonic power would be crushed.[2] Jesus has already met with Satan; now he is facing off against Satan's cohorts.

In the synagogue, a man is possessed by "an unclean spirit of evil" (lit. trans.), an intentional stacking up of descriptions showing just how serious the situation is. Luke distinguishes demon possession from physical illness, as does the rest of the New Testament (Matt. 4:24; Luke 4:40–41; 7:21; 9:1; 13:32)—though on occasion the concepts overlap (cf. Luke 8:29; 9:39; 11:14–20; 13:11, 16, where the symptoms of the presence of a demon look like illness). A distinguishing feature of demon possession is erratic behavior or severe physical distortion (Mark 5:1–20; Luke 8:29; 9:39, 42; 11:14; 13:10–17).

Jesus' presence makes the demon nervous, and it cries out through the man, asking him what he is planning to do. Will he destroy it? In Greek the question in verse 34 is an idiomatic way of asking, "Why do you want to bother us?"[3] The remark is revealing, since it indicates both the inherent authority Jesus possesses and the demon's awareness of that power. In addition, the demon makes a confession: Jesus is "the Holy One of God" (cf. 1:31–35). It recognizes him as uniquely set apart for service to God. The title recalls figures like Aaron (Ps. 106:16), Samson (Judg. 13:7), and Elisha (2 Kings 4:9).

Jesus rebukes the evil spirit, and immediately the man is restored. He also silences it. Apparently Jesus wants nothing to do with demonic confession of him in public. It is not clear why, except that perhaps Judaism expected the Messiah to be proclaimed in limited ways and the title itself may produce expectations that Jesus will have to correct.[4] Even the demon's attempt to

---

2. *Testament of Zebulon* 9:8; *Assumption [Testament] of Moses* 10:1. For the Jewish view of demons, see Josephus, *Jewish Wars* 7.6.3. § 185; *1 Enoch* 19:1; *Jubilees* 10:5; *Testament of Benjamin* 5:2; Foerster, "δαίμων," *TDNT*, 2:8–9.

3. Danker, *Jesus and the New Age*, 111; Seesemann calls it "a defensive formula," "οἶδα," *TDNT*, 5:117–18.

4. R. Longenecker, *The Christology of Early Jewish Christianity* (London: SCM, 1970), 71–74; R. H. Stein, *Luke*, 163.

harm the man by throwing him to the ground fails to have results. The destructive tendencies of evil are overcome by the authority that Jesus possesses to deliver humanity from the clutches of the demons.

The amazing event and its lesson are not lost on the crowd, who immediately begin asking the basic question: "What is this teaching?" The people recognize that demonic forces have been subdued by his word. Jesus has both authority and power. Luke's reader is left pondering the question the crowd has raised. News of the event spreads throughout the region.

The next healing is less dramatic but just as significant. Jesus encounters Peter's mother-in-law at Peter's home, sick with a high fever. If this house were typical of ancient Palestinian homes, she would be in a single-room house. Jesus acts against another distinct threat to life. As he has just done with the demon, so now with disease. He rebukes the illness, and the woman is restored to life and begins serving them. This remark not only testifies to her recovery; it also reflects her gratitude.

Word spreads quickly, and Jesus finds himself dealing with people who come to him with all kinds of maladies. Healings continue without interruption. There is no unevenness in his ministry. His authority flows constantly. In addition, demons are exorcized regularly. They confess Jesus to be the Son of God, meaning that they recognize him as the Christ. The Anointed One is showing the evidence of his unique calling. As he has done earlier, he silences any attempts at demonic confession.

Jesus on occasion withdraws for a private time of prayer, but the people look for him. Those in Capernaum want him to stay, but Jesus' mission is not provincially limited. Jesus has been called to preach the kingdom of God elsewhere, so he must go where he is sent. This means that Jesus must preach in other synagogues throughout the land. His message of "the kingdom of God" is like the message he preached at Nazareth (4:16–21)—a word of release and fulfillment. Luke does not specify or define what the kingdom is here. The message of release in Luke 4 suggest its nature as a place of deliverance, where the forces of evil can be overcome. Other texts will develop the idea more clearly.

Bridging Contexts

A DOMINANT ISSUE in the bridging of contexts is the presence in Jesus' ministry of miracles. This introduces a particularly controversial discussion, for two approaches to the existence of miracles exist today within the church, not to mention the skepticism that exists about miracles outside the church.

We begin with the view of miracles outside the church. Ever since the Enlightenment, many have rejected the reality of miracles. Such rejection assumes either an absence of deity or a noninvolvement by him in creation. The basic issue, therefore, centers on whether God exists and, if he does, whether he acts in the world.[5] At the center of this dispute is the resurrection of Jesus. Christianity declares a living Savior who had been crucified. For that to be true, resurrection must be a reality—a view that argues miracles do occur, at least to the extent of bringing a dead person back to life. Those who deny miracles must explain how the early church came into existence and defended the teaching of a risen Lord fifty-two days after his death, even with the sacrifice of their own lives. Something must have turned their thinking around. Arguing that they fabricated the doctrine fails, because it cannot explain why the disciples were willing to die for something they knew to be a lie. One can attempt to argue for delusion, but that also must argue for multiple delusion, since many disciples risked their lives on their belief.

Behind the discussion on miracles stands a worldview question about God's existence and activity. If God exists, should we expect him to be entirely disengaged from his creation? Is he really to be seen as a spectator, watching the creation and eating his popcorn as he enjoys the show? It is hardly a given that the presence of God in the creation means the absence of evidence of his powerful work. Experience often testifies otherwise, for most communities can speak of events where someone has been spared in what can only be explained as divine intervention.

Turning to views within the church, some argue that while God still occasionally performs miracles today, there is no *gift of miracles* in the church—that is, no one performs miracles as Jesus or his apostles did. This position is known as cessationism. Others argue that the gift of miracles still functions today, so that one can have a ministry like that of Jesus.[6] The debate is complex and has often been raised to heavily polemical levels.

---

5. Perhaps the best known contemporary defense of miracles is the work by C. S. Lewis's *Miracles* (New York: Macmillan, 1947). For a Catholic statement on miracles not conceding the principle of analogy (like today, so yesterday—so no miracles yesterday), see J. P. Meier, *A Marginal Jew*, vol. 2 (New York: Doubleday, 1994), 528–29 and n. 24. Another key work is C. Brown, *Miracles and the Critical Mind* (Grand Rapids: Eerdmans, 1984).

6. The classic work arguing for the cessation of such gifts is B. B. Warfield, *Counterfeit Miracles* (London: Banner of Truth, 1972; repr. of 1918 ed.). More recently is the cessationist argument by T. Edger, *Miraculous Gifts: Are They for Today?* (Neptune, N.J.: Loizeaux Brothers, 1983). A work arguing for such gifts is Jack Deere, *Surprised by the Power of the Spirit* (Grand Rapids: Zondervan, 1993). Deere interacts directly with Warfield, but works hard to try to explain why gifts today are not as frequently and consistently displayed as in the time of the apostles. More mediating is D. A. Carson, *Showing the Spirit: A Theological Exposition of 1 Corinthians 12–14* (Grand Rapids: Baker, 1987).

It might be helpful to note first what both sides agree on. Both affirm the possibility of God's miraculous intervention when he sovereignly chooses to act. In other words, the discussion is not between God's performing miracles or not. Rather, the disagreement is whether God gives specific people the consistent ability to heal and desires ministries to focus on healing. Those who argue God does not work though the gift of miracles today believe that gifts of healing were given for a limited period to introduce the arrival of the new era (e.g., see Heb. 2:3–4, which treats the attestation work of the Spirit as something in the past). They also note how Jesus deemphasized his own miraculous work, for fear that people would focus on the signs rather than on him (Matt. 12:38–42; Luke 11:29). Those who do see the gifts functioning today argue for a ministry in a manner analogous to that of Jesus.

My own cautious approach is that the gift of miracles does not function today. We do not see either the variety or rates of healing evidenced in Jesus' ministry to treat contemporary examples as analogous. One proponent, for example, has acknowledged that the rate of success in contemporary requests for healing is about two percent. This is a significantly different ratio from what Jesus or the disciples appeared to yield. Such a percentage looks more like an example of God's sovereign activity than a residing gift, where successful response would come more frequently. In other words, though God does still heal, I do not expect the consistency of the healing aspect of Jesus' ministry to be replicated today. I would treat the issue of exorcism in a similar way. Such limitations on healing do not evidence a lack of trust on how God works, since his sovereign right to heal is still affirmed. What it questions is whether God continues to give gifts of healing to individuals through whom people are healed.

A main bridge into the present is the character and goal of ministry. Jesus' actions show a commitment to service and compassion, even in the midst of confrontation. The miracles reveal where the real battle for humanity lies and how Jesus has authority to overcome such obstacles. When Jesus acts to exorcize demons and to cure disease, both cosmic forces and diseases become subject to his will. That Jesus possesses such total authority should grip us and cause us to reflect that he is capable of delivering on his promises to save. It also implies his ability to guide us in such a way that such forces can never totally overtake us. Hostile forces may try to destroy us, but he has the capability of helping us resist. The obstacles of life that threaten us as human beings are not so great or powerful that Jesus cannot overcome them. In fact, it is the exact reverse.

IT IS IMPORTANT first of all to note that Jesus receives authentication through the work he performs as the unique, set-apart One from God. The best commentary on these events is Acts 10:38–42.

Another key application emerges as an implication of Jesus' type of ministry. Many missionary organizations and churches in recent history have organized benevolent ministries and hospitals as expressions of the type of compassionate service Jesus performs here. Such a connection is justified. What the healings and exorcisms show is God's power and concern for humanity. The church should show no less compassion today. When we deal with the ravages of disease or show concern to those who are hurting, we are reflecting the kind of love God has for people who live in a fallen world.

Another application emerges in the area of counseling. We can minister to people's souls by helping them wrestle with the presence of sin and the Fall in their lives through a biblically-centered counseling approach that seeks to understand who people are and why they are hurting. This is not to argue that mental health and exorcism are the same, for they are not. But it is to suggest that the type of compassion that engaged in exorcism is similar to the type of compassion needed for one to minister to a hurting soul afflicted by a mental disturbance.

What is needed is good counseling—counseling that integrates the truth of Scripture about the character of sin and fallenness in our world and environment with the study and analysis of the symptoms and causes of our struggles. To ignore either aspect, so that personal responsibility for our condition is avoided or a person is always made to feel the blame, is a mistake. Our school has begun an effort to bring together theologians and counselors to address this combination in a healthy effort to integrate and talk about both sides of this equation. Too often counselors are left on their own, and theologians are unaware of the various factors that reflect sinful roots and play into a person who is emotionally at risk.

In Jesus' ministry we see the exercise of whatever resources he had to aid those who were afflicted by the forces that attack humanity and debilitate it. Though the form of such ministry today might differ, the compassion that motivates such service does not.

Luke 5:1–32

ONE DAY AS Jesus was standing by the Lake of Genesaret, with the people crowding around him and listening to the word of God, ²he saw at the water's edge two boats, left there by the fishermen, who were washing their nets. ³He got into one of the boats, the one belonging to Simon, and asked him to put out a little from shore. Then he sat down and taught the people from the boat.

⁴When he had finished speaking, he said to Simon, "Put out into deep water, and let down the nets for a catch."

⁵Simon answered, "Master, we've worked hard all night and haven't caught anything. But because you say so, I will let down the nets."

⁶When they had done so, they caught such a large number of fish that their nets began to break. ⁷So they signaled their partners in the other boat to come and help them, and they came and filled both boats so full that they began to sink.

⁸When Simon Peter saw this, he fell at Jesus' knees and said, "Go away from me, Lord; I am a sinful man!" ⁹For he and all his companions were astonished at the catch of fish they had taken, ¹⁰and so were James and John, the sons of Zebedee, Simon's partners.

Then Jesus said to Simon, "Don't be afraid; from now on you will catch men." ¹¹So they pulled their boats up on shore, left everything and followed him.

¹²While Jesus was in one of the towns, a man came along who was covered with leprosy. When he saw Jesus, he fell with his face to the ground and begged him, "Lord, if you are willing, you can make me clean."

¹³Jesus reached out his hand and touched the man. "I am willing," he said. "Be clean!" And immediately the leprosy left him.

¹⁴Then Jesus ordered him, "Don't tell anyone, but go, show yourself to the priest and offer the sacrifices that Moses commanded for your cleansing, as a testimony to them."

¹⁵Yet the news about him spread all the more, so that crowds of people came to hear him and to be healed of their sicknesses. ¹⁶But Jesus often withdrew to lonely places and prayed.

¹⁷One day as he was teaching, Pharisees and teachers of the law, who had come from every village of Galilee and from Judea and Jerusalem, were sitting there. And the power of the Lord was present for him to heal the sick. ¹⁸Some men came carrying a paralytic on a mat and tried to take him into the house to lay him before Jesus. ¹⁹When they could not find a way to do this because of the crowd, they went up on the roof and lowered him on his mat through the tiles into the middle of the crowd, right in front of Jesus.

²⁰When Jesus saw their faith, he said, "Friend, your sins are forgiven."

²¹The Pharisees and the teachers of the law began thinking to themselves, "Who is this fellow who speaks blasphemy? Who can forgive sins but God alone?"

²²Jesus knew what they were thinking and asked, "Why are you thinking these things in your hearts? ²³Which is easier: to say, 'Your sins are forgiven,' or to say, 'Get up and walk'? ²⁴But that you may know that the Son of Man has authority on earth to forgive sins. . . ." He said to the paralyzed man, "I tell you, get up, take your mat and go home." ²⁵Immediately he stood up in front of them, took what he had been lying on and went home praising God. ²⁶Everyone was amazed and gave praise to God. They were filled with awe and said, "We have seen remarkable things today."

²⁷After this, Jesus went out and saw a tax collector by the name of Levi sitting at his tax booth. "Follow me," Jesus said to him, ²⁸and Levi got up, left everything and followed him.

²⁹Then Levi held a great banquet for Jesus at his house, and a large crowd of tax collectors and others were eating with them. ³⁰But the Pharisees and the teachers of the law who belonged to their sect complained to his disciples, "Why do you eat and drink with tax collectors and 'sinners'?"

³¹Jesus answered them, "It is not the healthy who need a doctor, but the sick. ³²I have not come to call the righteous, but sinners to repentance."

Original Meaning

THIS LARGE LUCAN unit describes Jesus' gathering together a band of followers, the disciples (meaning "learners"), whom he will train. They come from various vocations of life: fishermen, tax collectors, political zealots, and ordinary folk. In these "call scenes," Jesus takes sinners and transforms them into instruments for God's use.[1] Jesus also continues to exercise his authority, particularly in forgiving sins and doing good on the Sabbath—actions that raise opposition to his ministry.

Call of the First Disciples

THE FIRST CALL scene is Luke 5:1–11. Sometimes service for Jesus starts out rather innocently. Just ask Peter. In a text that is probably a distinct event from Matthew 4:18–22 and Mark 1:16–20, Jesus issues a call to Peter and some of his companions for their future in ministry.[2]

The entire episode is both surprising and revealing. The crowds are pressing around Jesus at the Sea of Gennesaret (Sea of Galilee). On the shore are some fishermen, cleaning their nets. To avoid the crush, Jesus decides to get on Simon's boat and pushes out from the shore a little so that he can address the crowds. Jesus' teaching has become popular. If this were an average ancient fishing boat, it would have been twenty to thirty feet long.[3]

After teaching, Jesus tells Peter to head out and go fishing. Note the irony. Here is a carpenter's son and itinerant preacher telling a fishermen it is time to fish! Conditions were certainly not right for fishing, as Peter notes. Not only is it still daylight, since Jesus has just finished preaching, but the previous night has been a waste. Nevertheless at Jesus' word, Peter agrees to cast the nets. This indicates potential in Peter, for he responds to Jesus' leading.

The effort is successful, almost too much so. The boat overflows with fish and begins to sink. Peter calls out to James and John for help. The nets are breaking, and fish are spilling out everywhere. In the rush, something profound dawns on Peter. What has taken place is no accident; only an agent of God could have produced such a catch in the middle of the day.

Knocked off his task of saving his boat and collecting his fish, Peter bows before Jesus. In words full of respect and awe, he asks Jesus to depart. The premise behind this remark is that a man of God surely would want to have nothing to do with an everyday sinner. Peter does not feel worthy of Jesus' blessing or of making such an acquaintance. He believes that God works

---

1. Call scenes appear in 5:1–11, 27–39; 6:12–16.

2. This passage's relationship to the calls in Matthew and Mark is not entirely clear. The Lucan event seems to be a distinct and confirmatory event, since the activity of the fishermen differs slightly (washing versus mending nets), the nets described are possibly different (Luke refers to deep sea nets, Mark to shallow fishing nets), and Andrew is not mentioned here. Luke's greater detail does indicate why a disciple felt Jesus' call was compelling.

3. Stein, *Luke*, 169; S. Wachsmann, "The Galilee Boat—2,000-Year-Old Hull Recovered Intact," *BAR* 14 (1988): 18–33.

with and uses only the pious. It is too dangerous to be a sinner and to be in God's presence.

What Peter does not realize is that admitting one's inability and sin is the best prerequisite for service, since then one can depend on God. Peter's confession becomes his résumé for service. Humility is the elevator to spiritual greatness. So Jesus replies by telling Peter not to fear. It is one thing to be a sinner and deny it. It is another to know who you are before God and humbly bow before him.

Thereupon Jesus notes that Peter will start catching men. Jesus does two things with this remark. (1) He issues a call to Peter to enter into the process of gathering people and rescuing them from the danger of a fallen world. Unlike fish, which are caught to be flayed and devoured, Peter will catch people and bring them into life. Boats and nets will no longer be his tools; instead, God's word will. Jesus reverses a normally negative figure and makes it into a positive one, just as he is transforming Peter's role of service. For Jesus, only sinners who know they are sinners in need of help can enter his service. Rather than being unworthy, Peter is ready to serve with him.

(2) The miraculous catch indicates how miracles are pictures or metaphors of spiritual realities. The miraculous catch of fish produces the metaphorical call to catch people. Jesus' prophetic leading and insight powerfully illustrate his call, indicating graphically the mission Peter has before him.

The disciples respond to Jesus' call by leaving all and following him. That was the last time they spent the day just as fishermen. Jesus changes people's priorities. A call to ministry transcends their previous vocation.

Two Healing Miracles

AFTER THIS INITIAL call, Luke relates two miracles that present further details about Jesus' authority (5:12–26) and compassion. By working with a leper and a paralytic, he shows how he can cleanse physical ailments as well as restore people to a walk with God. Both miracle stories illustrate the redemptive goals of Jesus' work, reinforcing his teaching. This section also records the first organized opposition of Jesus' leadership, which centers on Jesus' claim to forgive sin. Since only God can make such claims, the question of Jesus' authority becomes more central to the flow of events in this Gospel. Furthermore, just as the miracles in 4:31–44 set up Peter's response in 5:1–11, so these miracles serve as a backdrop to the call to Levi in 5:27–32.[4] Jesus' ministry opens people up to be responsive to him. Finally, Jesus' ministry

---

4. C. Talbert, *Reading Luke: A Literary and Theological Commentary on the Third Gospel* (New York: Crossroad, 1982), 63. The parallels to these healings are Matthew 8:1–4 and Mark 1:40–45 (for the leper) and Matthew 9:1–8 and Mark 2:1–12 (for the paralytic).

here also illustrates the nature of the times, since Judaism believed that healing would accompany the messianic days.[5]

Luke introduces the first healing by mentioning that Jesus is "in one of the towns." He is venturing to other parts of Galilee, as he said he must do (4:43–44). A man full of leprosy approaches him. The term *lepra* can refer to a wide array of diseases.[6] It produces lesions or other swollen areas on the skin. Sometimes it attacks the nervous system. It includes not only Hansen's disease, but psoriasis, lupus, ringworm, and favus. The Old Testament gave specific instructions about identifying its presence and how to declare someone clean who had recovered from the condition (Lev. 13–14). To have the disease meant ostracism (Lev. 13:45–46; 2 Kings 7:3), for anyone with this condition had to announce it to others by shouting, "Unclean! Unclean!" Having this disease led to social isolation, not unlike what some AIDS victims experience today. Jesus' ministry to a leper therefore reveals his attention to the outcasts of society, demonstrating that such people can have access to God's blessing.

The man approaches Jesus with humility, bowing before him. His request raises the question of Jesus' willingness to heal, not his capability.[7] In fact, the leper assumes Jesus can do it. Perhaps he feels beyond the reach of God's mercy, so he expresses himself timidly. The very fact that he has approached and addressed Jesus at all has taken great courage.

Jesus responds to the leper's request by declaring his willingness and announcing that he is cleansed. Jesus also touches him, showing the tender touch of compassion and acceptance to a man who could not be touched by others (cf. Lev. 14:46; cf. *Mishnah, Nega'im* 3:1; 11:1; 12:1; 13:6–12), and he is restored whole immediately. The picture of redemption should not be missed. Those who turn to Jesus for cleansing receive it from him because he willingly gives it.

Jesus tells the man to go to the priest and not say anything to anyone. Understandably, the man must follow the legal requirements of Leviticus 14, but why the command to silence is given is not clear. Perhaps Jesus does not want anything said until the requirements before the priest are met, and he wants to discourage undue attention to his miraculous work (Luke 4:35, 41; 8:56; see also Matt. 9:30; 12:16; Mark 1:34; 3:12; 5:43; 7:36; 8:26).[8] According to the law, this testimony before the priest will take a week. The

---

5. Schürmann, *Das Lukasevangelium*, 276; Jubilees 23:26–30; 1 Enoch 5:8–9; 96:3; 2 Esdras 7:123; 2 Baruch 29:7.

6. Michaelis, "λέπρα," *TDNT*, 4:233–34.

7. Luke uses a third class Greek condition at the end of verse 12 to express the man's uncertainty as to whether Jesus might act.

8. Marshall, *Commentary on Luke*, 209; Plummer, *Luke*, 149–50.

ritual pictured the cleansing and removal of sin, so even the follow-up program for the leper reinforces the message of what Jesus has done. The fact that the testimony is for the priests is not surprising, given their need to understand what Jesus represents.

But despite Jesus' efforts to control the news, reports go out anyway, spreading throughout the land. Though Jesus is in Galilee, news spreads as far south as Judea and Jerusalem. These reports explain why the Jewish leadership is present at the next event.

Luke bridges the two miracle stories and the hectic pace Jesus is leading by noting that he stops for prayer (5:16). In the quietness that comes privately after a rapid rush of events comes the solace and gaining of perspective that keeps Jesus close to God. Luke regularly notes such commitments to prayer (3:21; 6:12; 9:18, 28–29; 11:1; 23:46).[9]

The next healing is that of a paralytic man (5:17–26). Mark 2:1 tells us this miracle took place in Capernaum. Pharisees and teachers of the law (better known as scribes) have joined the crowd. The Pharisees were one of four religious parties in Judaism (Sadducees, Zealots, and Essenes are the others). They were a nonpriestly, lay separatist movement that tried to stay faithful to the Mosaic Law. They developed many traditions and oral rulings to establish how the Law should be applied in their generation. Such judgments were made by the trained scribes who were a part of the sect.[10] These leaders are now watching Jesus.

The Lord has power to heal (v. 17b). This small narrative note prepares Luke's readers for what is coming. As Jesus is teaching, a group of men try to bring a paralyzed man to him for healing, but the crowd is too large. Therefore, they go on the roof, either by a ladder or built-in steps that allowed access to the top of an ancient house.[11] Working their way through the tiles, they lower the man before Jesus. Getting a hole in the roof would have involved working through a muddy layer above the roof beams.[12]

Jesus sees "their faith," a remark that is easy to move past. Faith in this text must mean the visible expression of faith, not a mere attitude, since Jesus sees it in the actions of the men. As a result, Jesus acts, giving the man much more than he was seeking. He declares his sins to be forgiven.

A chain reaction follows. The Pharisees and scribes begin to think about the theological implications of what Jesus just said. They know that only

---

9. A. Leaney, *A Commentary on the Gospel According to St. Luke* (New York: Harper, 1958), 124.

10. Marshall, *Commentary on Luke*, 212; Fitzmyer, *Luke*, 581.

11. S. Safrai, *The Jewish People in the First Century*, sec. 1, vol. 2 (Philadelphia: Fortress, 1976), 730–32.

12. Plummer, *Luke*, 153.

God forgives sin; so to claim to do what God does is blasphemy, a slander against God.[13]

Whenever Luke reports what someone is thinking, instruction from Jesus usually follows. Jesus asks the Pharisees to ponder a question that is really a dilemma. Is it easier to declare sins are forgiven or tell a paralytic to get up and walk? Logic tells us is that it is easier to say one's sins are forgiven, since that cannot be seen; but in fact that is more difficult, since one must have the authority to do that. Then Jesus links the two issues together. He acts so that the audience can know the Son of Man has authority to forgive sins.[14] He tells the man to walk. He enables the hard thing—having the paralyzed man get up and walk—in order to show the even harder thing—the power to forgive sin.

The man gets up and walks away. If God heals only those who are free from sin and if he does not manifest himself through those who make false claims, then why did this man get up? That is the question his walking away poses for the audience. The success of the miracle has narrowed the options. The crowd praises God and recognizes that they have seen wonderful and amazing things through Jesus.

This event reveals one further picture. The ability of the paralyzed man to resume his walk of life is a picture of what Jesus does when he saves. His message is a liberating one.

The Calling of Levi

LUKE 5:27—32 ONCE again reveals a pattern in Jesus' ministry: He reaches out to those on the edge of society. In 5:12—26 it was to those suffering from physical limitations. Now it is to those who are perceived as social outcasts. Jesus calls a despised tax collector, an act that produces a reaction from the religious officials. In Luke 3:10—14, we considered how tax collectors were viewed in Jewish culture—as defectors from Israel and notorious sinners.

---

13. No Jewish text extant today shows a person forgiving sin. One text is disputed— *The Prayer of Nabonidus* from Qumran (4QprNab 1.4). However, this text should not be interpreted to mean that the exorcist mentioned in the text forgave sin. See D. Bock, "The Son of Man in Luke 5:24," *BBR* 1 (1991): 109—21, esp. 117, n. 26.

14. A later Jewish text in the Talmud, *Nedarim* 41a reads, "No one gets up from his sick bed until all his sins are forgiven." The "Son of Man" title is debated and involves a series of complex questions. At this early point in Jesus' ministry, the term is simply a way for Jesus to refer to himself. It is Jesus' favorite title for himself, probably because it refers to a human figure who possesses supernatural authority. Later he will reveal that the imagery comes from Daniel 7:13—14. For more on the Son of Man title, see Bock, *Luke 1:1—9:50*, excursus 6. The Son of Man image in Daniel describes a human figure who bears authority from God and who rides the clouds as God does.

The question faced here is whether Jesus and his disciples should practice a type of separatism like that of the Pharisees. This is a consistent issue of contention in Luke (15:1–32; 18:9–14; 19:1–10; also Matt. 20:13–16).[15] What Levi represents is the successful outcome of a call to repentance summarized in the passage's commentary (5:31–32).[16]

Sometime after the healing of the paralytic, Jesus goes out and spots a tax collector at his toll booth, whose job is to collect the surcharge as people travel from city to city. Jesus initiates the entire encounter, a significant point since his taking the initiative with such people is controversial. He calls Levi to "follow" him, a frequent call of Jesus (9:23, 59; 18:22; cf. 5:10–11). In effect, Jesus is asking him to become a disciple. Just as sinners can enter into an intimate relationship with God (5:10–11), so can tax collectors. In other words, *anyone* who responds to Jesus can receive a blessing. Levi responds to the invitation, leaving his vocation and financial security behind to follow Jesus.

Levi then throws Jesus "a great banquet," a feast.[17] Invited to the table are Levi's circle of notorious friends, "tax collectors and others," whom the Pharisees call sinners in verse 30. Levi has now turned his resources over to reveal his new relationship with Jesus to his friends. He points them to this different type of religious leader, one who seeks out those who have been separated from God.

The associations Jesus makes causes other religious figures to raise questions. They take their complaints to the disciples. The Greek term *egongyzon* ("complained") is a graphic, even emotive term, where one can hear the complaints even in the sounds of the word.[18] The complaint is direct and clear: "Why do you eat and drink with tax collectors and 'sinners'?" In ancient culture, to sit at the table communicated an acceptance, thus frequently subjecting Jesus to a charge (5:33; 7:33–34). The Pharisees, on the other hand, avoided sinners in order to avoid the suggestion that they endorsed the sinner. The two perspectives cannot be more opposite. The Pharisees prefer a level of quarantine from sinners; Jesus prefers to aim for recovery of the

---

15. Fitzmyer, *Luke*, 589; Michel, " τελώνης," *TDNT*, 8:105. Fitzmyer details how the Pharisees viewed such associations with contempt.

16. The parallel to this text includes Matthew 9:9–13 and Mark 2:13–17. The tax collector in Matthew is named Matthew. This has raised a question whether this is the same event. Most equate the two figures, since the accounts are so agreed in the details and since of the Twelve, only Matthew-Levi is a tax collector. Double names are also common in this culture; Acts 1:23; 4:36; 12:25; 13:9; Josephus, *Antiquities* 18.2.2 § 35.

17. On the term "banquet," see Gen. 21:8; 26:30; Est. 1:3; Luke 14:13; Grundmann, "δοχή," *TDNT*, 2:54.

18. The Greek version of the Old Testament also used this word to describe Israel's complaints in the desert (Ex. 15:24; 16:7–8; Num. 14:2, 26–35; 16:11).

sinner. His action suggests that the separationism the Pharisees advocate does not honor God.

Jesus then gives the theological and missiological rationale for his actions. The image he uses is fundamental in pointing out the issues. Jesus notes that a healthy person does not seek a physician; the sick do. So Jesus' mission is not to call the healthy but the sick "to repentance." The picture of a doctor is a well-known ancient metaphor (2 Chron. 16:12; Isa. 3:7; Jer. 8:22; Sir. 10:10; 38:1–15).[19]

The image is strong. When I go to the doctor, I know several things: I am sick, I need help, and I cannot help myself. In other words, Jesus' call goes out to those who realize they need help. To seek out sinners is to go to people who recognize they are not all they can be. But Jesus does not go to offer placebos. Rather, he calls them to repent. As we saw in 3:7–14, repentance means a change of direction, a turning that manifests itself in a difference. So Jesus calls on those who are not well to get better by coming into the grace God offers them. If they desire to know God, the Lord will not reject them, but will begin the process that will make them well.

Jesus reaches out to sinners because he sees the potential for their being renewed through God's grace. Jesus knows such change does not happen when those who seek sinners isolate themselves. His mission is to regain the lost by going to them, as he does here with Levi.

Bridging Contexts

THE RESPONSES TO Jesus in this text lie at the heart of its teaching. We begin with Peter's response to the call of the Lord to cast his nets. Though humble in character, he misunderstands how God works with those who understand their failings and turn to him. He feels that as a sinner he has no chance with God. Jesus shows him that this sense of being less than God and less than holy is precisely what God can work with. The important thing is what happens after one experiences a sense of helplessness upon confronting God. Jesus cannot have a disciple, a "learner," until one realizes there is much to learn!

The call and mission of Peter are no different from the call and mission of the church or of the individuals within the church. Peter is the representative disciple here, much more than he is one of the twelve. Though the call is issued to Peter, all those present leave their boats (v. 11). This literary shift from "you will catch men" to "they . . . left everything" shows that the call is not unique.

---

19. Schrenk, "δίκαιος," *TDNT*, 2:189; Priesker, "μισθός," *TDNT*, 4:717.

The response of leaving everything, however, implies another question. Must all disciples leave their vocations to serve Jesus? How is the call to believers like and unlike this call to Peter? The answer to that question emerges in the history of the church. As the New Testament letters show, not everyone is called into full-time ministry. In fact, Paul kept right on working as a tentmaker as he ministered. The important element is that the call to walk with Jesus takes on a priority, so that we are prepared to be whatever or wherever God calls us to be. For some, like the healed Gerasene demoniac, it means staying home to testify to Jesus (8:38–39). For others it means traveling with Jesus. For some, it may mean the mission field; for others, it may mean the mission field at their daily job or in a parachurch ministry. The mission is "catching men." Sometimes one's work is the best place to find the fish, while church is not.

The import of Peter's three responses during the catch reflect emotions that span the centuries: casting out his net, bowing before Jesus, and leaving all to follow him. Peter shows the way to fruitful response to Jesus' call and presence. We should consider his responses carefully. The idea of a fisherman taking instructions on fishing from a teacher of religion would be humorous, if the surprising results did not end up so overwhelming. Especially insightful is to probe why Peter felt he was a sinner when the catch came in. Was it because, although he cast the nets, he did so with a lack of faith that a catch would really come? It is hard to be sure, but to Peter's credit, he did follow the Lord's direction. We should be willing to follow the Lord's leading, even if it looks on the surface as if we will have a difficult, unfruitful task.

The text also reveals Jesus' special insight and gifts. He understands and controls the mission he will launch. He does not need people who will direct him but people who will serve him. In addition, he is capable of directing them on how they can best serve him. If he can direct the disciples, he certainly is able to direct us through his Spirit as we depend on him (Eph. 6:18–20).

The fishing metaphor is an appropriate one for evangelism. Catching fish is by no means automatic, as Peter's outing the night before showed. Much preparation is needed in going out for the catch, and much labor is required, especially in the ancient world where fishermen worked with large nets. Often the kind of fishing Peter engaged in took teamwork. It is no accident that our Lord chose this metaphor to describe the task.

Regarding the two miracles in Luke 5:12–26, we have already argued (4:31–44) that performing miracles as a function of a gifted ministry is not to be sought today. Yet the compassion expressed here through these miracles does provide a meaningful bridge. Jesus heals outsiders and commends the faith of those whom he heals. That is, Jesus ministers to a wide segment of the population, including those ostracized by society at large. In addition, though Jesus does not explain why he acts to forgive the paralytic's sin, the text reveals that the faith expressed by those who approached Jesus led him to act. This text is the first of several that will highlight the importance of faith. Faith here is not mere intellectual trust or a mere attitude; it expresses itself in the intent to get near to Jesus.

A major concern of the miracles is the question of Jesus' identity. What is significant is the way Jesus boxes in the options. He argues that the miracle shows he has the authority to forgive sin. The opponents insist that only God can forgive sin. If the man gets up and his sin is truly forgiven, then what does that make Jesus? The options are limited here and in 11:14—23. God is dishonored when someone claims to do something in his name they cannot do, but what if God vindicates their claim?

Issues of healing were important in the first century, because the ability to care for the sick was limited, given a lack of quality medical care such as we have today. Serious cases often appealed for the help of a prophet like Jesus. Interestingly, the care of doctors was discussed in Judaism. Was it an affront to faith to seek the care of doctors? The ancient Jewish book of Sirach 38:1—4 reads as follows:

> Honor physicians for their services, for the Lord created them; for their gift of healing comes from the Most High, and they are rewarded by the king. The skill of physicians makes them distinguished, and in the presence of the great they are admired. The Lord created medicines out of the earth, and the sensible will not despise them. (NRSV)

Yet later in the same chapter the text (vv. 9—15) brings in spiritual issues:

> My child, when you are ill, do not delay, but pray to the Lord, and he will heal you. Give up faults and direct your hands rightly, and cleanse your heart from all sin. Offer a sweet smelling sacrifice, and a memorial portion of choice flour, and pour oil on your offering, as much as you can afford. Then give the physician his place, for the Lord created him; do not let him leave you, for you need him. There may come a time when recovery lies in the hands of physicians, for they too pray to the Lord that he grants them success in diagnosis and in healing, for the sake of preserving life. He who sins against his Maker, will be defiant toward the physician. (NRSV)

Thus in Judaism, it appears as if sin and medical treatment were mixed together. Healing came from the Lord, but a major agent in bringing it was a doctor. When healing took place more directly and instantly, then a prophet was present. Given this background, it is not surprising that Jesus is regarded as a prophet and that the issue of the paralytic raises the topic of sin.

Mortality is a product of fallenness, both in the biblical view and in Judaism, and disease may relate to sin. Today we tend to leave sin out of the health equation, seeing it primarily as a matter of chemicals or biology. While John 9 warns us against always making a sin-health equation, sometimes we are not well because we have lived unwisely. Pushing ourselves hard, the presence of guilt, and escaping to substances are symptoms of deeper questions that lead us to ill health. Still the release from some conditions, like this healing of Jesus, comes only by the grace and sovereign work of God.

The call of Levi in 5:27–32 has one of the most direct bridges of any text in Luke's Gospel. As Jesus' mission was evangelism, so is that of the church. As Jesus possessed a message of salvation and healing for sinners in restoring their relationship to God, so does the church. It is crucial that the church come to see the importance of reaching out to others and initiating that contact. We can learn from how Jesus handled sinners, how sinners reacted to Jesus, and how the Jewish leadership reacted to both.

Concern for appropriate separation is important, but texts like Ephesians 5:7–14 help to sort out how proper separation works. We must separate ourselves from the "deeds of darkness," from the acts of sin, but we must not isolate ourselves from sinners. The function of light is to shine in the midst of darkness. Jesus himself had table fellowship with sinners, an important method of relating in ancient culture. In fact, the Pharisees later complained about these relationships (15:1–2).

The text also teaches us about humility. One danger of piety is the danger of separatism. An excessive form of separatism, such as the Pharisees called for, can kill mission. That is why Jesus responds to the Jewish leadership as he does. Certainly no one cares more about a life of righteousness and moral integrity as our Lord does, but he refuses to get into a type of "appearance of evil" that prevents him from relating to sinners in contexts where such associations do not produce moral compromise. In fact, Jesus takes the initiative in seeking out sinners and calling them to God. In a similar manner, we should be proactive in pursuing the lost.

Contemporary Significance

THE MAJOR APPLICATION in the miracle of the catch of fish centers around Jesus' instructions and Peter's responses. In the midst of teaching many, Jesus calls a few people to more focused service. Peter is one example of such a call. Everyone has a ministry, and all are equal before God, but some are called to serve him directly. Peter has the three necessary qualities Jesus is looking for. He is willing to go where Jesus leads, he is humble, and he is fully committed.

(1) In his willingness to cast out the nets, Peter responds solely on the basis of Jesus' word (v. 5). His professional training told him that there was no chance for a successful catch, but Peter apparently knew enough about Jesus that the latter's insight might just exceed his own. This willingness to follow where Jesus leads may occasionally go against the grain of culture, custom, or common wisdom. Sometimes God takes us in surprising places in surprising ways to stretch us.

Several year ago I took a sabbatical leave in Germany. No one worried about me or my wife, but the standard question was, "What will you do about the kids?" Behind their question was the view that no one should take children of eight, seven, and five years and throw them into a fresh culture so early in their education, even if God calls us there for a time. Our position was different. God had called us to Germany, in part to experience Germany. So we did not look for an English-speaking school. We trusted that God would care for us in a new context. I make this point not to say that everyone who travels overseas should make such a cultural commitment, but to say we felt God was directing us in this decision.

It was amazing how God provided. At the little elementary school in a town of five thousand people where we lived, there was a second language class, so my children attended school not only with German children, but also with children from eight other countries—all learning German starting from the same place. We came during a time when refugees were flooding in from Eastern Europe. These classes were a new venture for this community. My middle daughter walked into a class that had a child from a bilingual family— the mother was from England and the father from Germany. Her teacher was the only one that our children had who did not know any English! But God provided a built-in translator, an eight-year-old bilingual child, who could get things started until my daughter could make it on her own. My older daughter, on the other hand, had to fend for herself. God did not provide in the same way for each child, yet he cared for both of them. In sum, God cared for us in different ways, as we went where he led, fully committed (well, mostly so) to trusting him. As a result of the experience, which was not easy but which taught us much about faith, my children have developed a fascination for people of different cultural backgrounds, something that will benefit them as they serve God in the future.

(2) Peter's humility is also exemplary. God could use Peter because he knew that he needed God, not the other way around. Some people in ministry give the impression God would really be struggling if it were not for them. But as Eliza's song to Professor Higgins in *My Fair Lady* goes, "The world will still be there without you." Peter understood that as a sinner he brought nothing to the table except what God was able to direct. That did

not make Peter insignificant, but his strength came from knowing his weakness and letting God direct the work. Paul expresses a similar attitude in Philippians 2:1–11, where he cites the Lord as exemplifying a humility that was willing to serve.

(3) Peter is willing to leave everything to follow Jesus. I know many seminarians who have given up what on the surface seems a lot in order to go into the ministry. Some have left lucrative business careers, others have sold their homes to finance their training, and still others have traveled thousands of miles to be better equipped when they step into the pulpit. In each case, their priority is to serve God and answer his call faithfully. When the fishermen leave their nets to become disciples, they embark on a three-year intensive internship program, with God directing them and supplying their needs. I often wonder what advice Peter would have received if, as a businessman and marine entrepreneur, he had had a personal financial accountant. Would his CPA have been pleased to see his boats on the shore?

Peter understood that there is no greater call than to cast nets for Jesus and minister to those who find their way into the saving net of the gospel. When he first encountered God's power, he thought Jesus must leave, because the teacher was in the midst of sinners. Jesus taught Peter that sinners who turn to God are the people God can use the most. So Peter simply followed Jesus.

The most significant lesson from the cleansing of the leper story is that even outsiders can experience God's healing grace. The church is called by this example to reach out to those on the fringes of society. Leprosy in its time was seen as reflecting the presence of sin, so reaching out to sinners is pictured here. I often cringe when I see how many in the church react to those who have AIDS (the closest parallel to leprosy today), as if they are beyond God's potential reach. The argument that AIDS victims are often engaged in serious sin is no excuse; Jesus came to save people from sin, any sin, no matter how serious. So the ministry of compassion he reveals here should be matched by the church's efforts with those that most of society have given up on. It is interesting how mission agencies in remote areas of the world accept this principle as a basis for their initial outreach, while we ignore it at home.

The leper's healing pictures Jesus making someone clean from sin. We tend to treat a leper as something ugly, but excuse our own sin as something that is a given. This text warns us not to take any sin lightly, for it makes us unclean. God took sin so seriously that he gave his own Son to purify us from its stain. Even if we stand on the other side of forgiveness, having been cleansed by Jesus' work, we should meditate on what this text implies about sin and Jesus' readiness to forgive anyone who comes to him with the attitude, "If you are willing, you can make me clean."

Jesus' sojourn for prayer is an important note at this point in his ministry.

He teaches us how important it is to commune with God, especially when we tend to ignore him because things are so busy. Sometimes the best thing we can do in the midst of the rush of life is to slow down and listen to God. We err seriously if we argue that we do not have time, for what we need under pressure is God's presence and calming involvement in our lives.

The healing of the paralytic reveals that faith expresses itself in diligent trust. That is what the paralytic's friends show and what Jesus commends. This faith is active, going to great lengths to seek Jesus' presence. Such faith catches Jesus' eye and touches God's heart.

The challenge of the Pharisees reveals an emerging point in this Gospel. One senses that they have come to "check Jesus out." That certainly becomes their attitude. They risk closing themselves off from the revelation of God through Jesus by making judgments about him too quickly. Though we do not get their reaction in this text, subsequent texts indicate that they do not take to heart what happens in this healing. It even seems as if their mind has been made up beforehand. That is what hardness of heart can do. It may make us hasty in our judgment about what God is doing.

The notes of praise and wonder in verses 25—26 recall similar notes in the infancy narratives. God's work is surprising, and we should rejoice to share in it, even if getting there is sometimes hard and obstacle-ridden.

Several applications emerge from Jesus' encounter with Levi in verses 27—32. Note Levi's response in both following Jesus and hosting a banquet for him. Here is a sinner whose life takes a total turn because of Jesus and who cannot wait to share Jesus with the friends of his former circle. Frequently for a new Christian, evangelism is strongest in the first two years after conversion. Then the change of one's circle of friends cuts off further opportunity. Jesus, though he never lived in that former circle, extends himself toward others in such a way that they do hear his message. Perhaps in becoming overly sensitive about how association with the world might corrupt the righteous, we isolate ourselves as the pious Pharisees did and lose the opportunity of seeing someone's life turn around, as Levi's did.

Jesus' initiative is also revealing. He seeks sinners, keeping his eye out for them and making reaching out to them a priority. I have been in enough churches to know that Christians often avoid sinners. Rather than seek them out, we run from them, often filled with fear about what issues they might bring up or what types of situations we might find ourselves in. Evangelism is a countercultural exercise that will produce its awkward moments.[20] Some-

---

20. A helpful work on this topic that is balanced and full of wisdom is Joseph C. Aldrich, *Life-Style Evangelism: Crossing Traditional Boundaries to Reach the Unbelieving World* (Portland: Multnomah, 1981).

times language or jokes are not in the best taste. Topics of discussion may get uncomfortable. Favorite activities of the lost may result in invitations to be involved in things that may need to be graciously refused. Still, many opportunities can be pursued that are not awkward. This is why I admire many parachurch ministries that reach out to the lost, whether to high school kids through Young Life or to college kids through Campus Crusade and Navigators or to business people through Search ministries. These organizations do a great job in taking the initiative to reach out and develop relationships with the lost. For evangelism to be effective, the unsaved must be reached, since they are not looking to come into the church!

Many today debate the value of seeker-friendly services, but one thing can be said for the movement. It has made the entire church more sensitive to being creative about evangelism and the need to seize the initiative in reaching out to the lost. This effort thinks through how to build bridges to the lost and to develop interests that can become opportunities for evangelism. The goal of such ministries moves closer to the desire God has for all of us to function as those who point the way to the Great Physician. A few churches targeted to such audiences benefits the body at large and helps to fulfill the Great Commission.

The attitude of the Pharisees, in contrast, is censured in this text. They are so concerned with appearance that people are crushed or ignored in the process. Purity at the expense of serving people is not purity; it is isolationism—and sin. Jesus is against such an approach to engaging the world. Though the Pharisees have a piety, it is a destructive piety that ignores the needs of people.

Finally, our mission involves preaching a call of repentance to sinners. We must be careful not to only reach out to the attractive, to those who seem pretty well, but also to the ostracized and rejected, as Jesus does with Levi. Some of the most unsung ministries work in the dark shadows of the inner city among the unseen. But whomever we seek to reach, we must offer the hope of the call of the gospel. To give such a call involves humility in two forms. (1) The person issuing the call is reminded of how God's grace is an act of surgical care extended to the believer; the one who shares Jesus knows what it means to be where the lost person is. This should create a sense of empathy and humility as we seek to encourage others to find the Lord.

(2) But humility is also required in the responder, since to come to God for spiritual healing means to recognize one's need and inability to heal oneself. The world's call to take control of our lives is diametrically opposed to the call of God, which says to give God control over the direction and restoration of our lives. Often when we seek to take matters in our own hands, we compound our problems, because such a grasping for control

reflects selfish motives. In turn, these motives mean we are uncaring and insensitive to others. When God gives his saving grace to us and begins to work in our lives, he wants to make us more service-oriented and giving to others. Control is no longer our concern; loving others is. Levi's response to Jesus shows such a change of direction. The banquet he gives Jesus is not just an expression of thanks, but a recognition that since God gives graciously, so should we (Eph. 4:30–5:2).

Luke 5:33–6:5

THEY SAID TO him, "John's disciples often fast and pray, and so do the disciples of the Pharisees, but yours go on eating and drinking."

34Jesus answered, "Can you make the guests of the bridegroom fast while he is with them? 35But the time will come when the bridegroom will be taken from them; in those days they will fast."

36He told them this parable: "No one tears a patch from a new garment and sews it on an old one. If he does, he will have torn the new garment, and the patch from the new will not match the old. 37And no one pours new wine into old wineskins. If he does, the new wine will burst the skins, the wine will run out and the wineskins will be ruined. 38No, new wine must be poured into new wineskins. 39And no one after drinking old wine wants the new, for he says, 'The old is better.'"

6:1One Sabbath Jesus was going through the grainfields, and his disciples began to pick some heads of grain, rub them in their hands and eat the kernels. 2Some of the Pharisees asked, "Why are you doing what is unlawful on the Sabbath?"

3Jesus answered them, "Have you never read what David did when he and his companions were hungry? 4He entered the house of God, and taking the consecrated bread, he ate what is lawful only for priests to eat. And he also gave some to his companions." 5Then Jesus said to them, "The Son of Man is Lord of the Sabbath."

Original Meaning

LUKE DESCRIBES A series of controversies in 5:33–6:11 that explain the kind of opposition Jesus' ministry receives. The initial controversy concerns fasting, while the next two deal with the Sabbath. In each case, Jesus' authority is expressed or implied, either because of who he is or because it reflects the new era he brings. After these controversies the Jewish leadership begins to discuss what they might do to Jesus, showing a solidification in the opposition.

Jesus does things differently from customary practice. Luke 5:33–39 discusses one example: his disciples do not fast.[1] Fasting in Judaism was a major rite of piety. Highly regarded as an act of worship, it took place at major events, like the Day of Atonement (Lev. 16:29, 31). A four-day fast accompanied a commemoration of the fall of Jerusalem (Zech. 7:3, 5; 8:19). Fasts usually involved penitence, mourning, or a plea for deliverance. Pharisees fasted twice a week (Luke 8:12).[2] Usually fasting was a one-day affair. However, a fast could run three days or even three weeks (Est. 4:16; Dan. 10:2–3). In the Judaism of Jesus' time, fasting was regarded as a virtue (Testament of Joseph 3:4–5; 1 Enoch 108:7–9). The failure of Jesus' disciples to fast could be read as reflecting a lack of respect for God, a severe absence of piety.

Luke's account assumes that those who ask Jesus about fasting are the same as those who grumbled about his associations in 5:30. Given the Jewish respect for fasting, why do his disciples not fast? Jesus not only explains why he does not fast, he also explains the deep significance of the refusal. The picture he uses is a wedding—a symbol often used to describe God's relationship with his people (Isa. 54:5–6; 62:4–5; Jer. 2:2; Ezek. 16).[3] Since the groom is now present and the wedding is taking place, there is no need to mourn or seek deliverance. But in the future, the groom will be taken from them; then fasting will be appropriate. Here is the first hint of Jesus' approaching suffering. It is no accident that Jesus makes this point as the opposition is arising. When the groom is gone, then God's people will long for the completion of redemption (Rom. 8:17–30; 1 Cor. 15:20–28). Though no law is given about how often to fast, then it will be appropriate again.[4]

Jesus has not only answered the question; he develops his reply in three pictures, each using "no one" to make the point (vv. 36, 37, 39). A new era with new perspectives has arrived. (1) The time Jesus brings is like a new piece of cloth. One does not take such cloth and sew it onto an old garment. That is not a good use of what is new. Jesus knows that if one makes such a mismatch, the new cloth will shrink on washing while the old cloth will not, resulting in a tear and rendering both fabrics useless. Jesus' point is simple: One cannot mix what Jesus brings with the old ways without creating a destructive mix. His new way needs new ways of doing things.

(2) Jesus' era is also like wineskins in that were usually made from sheepskin or goatskin. The neck of the animal became the neck of the wineskin.

---

1. The parallels to this text are Matthew 9:14–17 and Mark 2:18–22. Mark's placement in his Gospel parallels Luke's. Matthew places it later in a more topically oriented section of his Gospel.

2. Behm, "νῆστις," *TDNT*, 4:928–29.

3. For this image in Judaism, see Jeremias, "νύμφη," *TDNT*, 4:1101–3.

4. Danker, *Jesus and the New Age*, 128.

Once the hide was stripped of hair and cured, it could be used to store wine. New wine put in old wineskins is another tragic error in judgment no one makes. Since the new wine is still fermenting, the old wineskin cannot expand with the fermentation. Its age and brittle quality causes it to rip, and the wine is lost. The story is told with a "what a waste" feeling. The point again is that the new era will bring new ways, which must therefore have new containers. Jesus is more than a reformer of Judaism; he has come to refashion it into something fresh.

(3) The last picture looks at how traditional Jews may have viewed the changes Jesus was bringing. Jesus uses a common proverb.[5] Those who like old wine do not try the new, for their minds are already made up: "The old is good." So Jesus expects many not to respond to his new way. They are comfortable with life and piety as it is. Jesus' remark is both a description and a warning. John the Baptist came to tell the people that a new era and change was coming, but Jesus knows that some do not want change.

Luke moves immediately into the next event, the plucking of grain on the Sabbath (6:1–5). On a particular Sabbath the disciples are moving through a grain field.[6] As they go, they pluck grain from the stalks in the field, rubbing them with their hands to get to the grain. The action on the surface seems innocent enough. The taking of grain itself is not a problem, since in Israel a portion of the field was to be left for those in need (Deut. 23:25). But it is the Sabbath, the holy day of rest. Jewish tradition specified what one could and could not do on the Sabbath. The *Mishnah* (an ancient Jewish rule book), contained instructions about Sabbath practice. *Shabbath* 7:2 gives a list of thirty-nine prohibited activities known as the "forty less one."[7] The Jews were aware of how particular these customs were, since they said that "the rules about the Sabbath . . . are as mountains hanging by a hair, for Scripture is scanty and the rules many." (*Mishnah, Hagigah* 1:8). According to that list, the disciples have multiple violations: They are guilty of reaping, threshing, winnowing, and preparing food.

Some Pharisees just happen to be keeping an eye on Jesus' disciples. The text does not tell us why, but the fact that they know what the disciples are doing shows how carefully the disciples are being watched. They ask them, "Why are you doing what is unlawful on the Sabbath?" The question is specific, since it uses the legal term *exestin*, which refers to what is legally allowed.

---

5. Marshall, *Commentary on Luke*, 228; cf., Sirach 9:10; *Mishnah, Aboth* 4:20.

6. The parallels to this passage are Matthew 12:1–8 and Mark 2:23–28. Luke has the event in a sequence that resembles Mark. Matthew's distinct positioning comes in a section where he is working more topically in summarizing Jesus' ministry.

7. Lohse, "σάββατον," *TDNT*, 7:12–13.

In the Jewish view, they should have prepared a meal ahead of time to be ready for the Sabbath.

Jesus defends the actions of his colleagues by citing the Scripture. He begins with the challenging remark, "Have you never read. . . ?" Jesus knows the Pharisees have read 1 Samuel 21:1–7 and 22:8–9, but he argues they have misunderstood it. So his reply begins with an implied rebuke. In that passage, David gathers showbread from the tabernacle so that he and his men can eat it—a clear violation of the law.[8] Jesus explicitly notes that they did what was not lawful (again using the legal term *exestin*). They ate "the consecrated bread" ("the bread of the Presence," Ex. 25:30) that the law said was only for priests. Since David was not disciplined by the high priest at the time, the Old Testament suggests that what he did was appropriate. Jesus' reply has the Pharisees in a dilemma. In effect, if they condemn him on this issue, they criticize David as well.[9]

The point of Jesus' reply simply makes a comparison between David and himself. The thrust of his point has been defended in two ways. Either Jesus is arguing that God's law never intended to exclude people from meeting basic needs like eating, so that David becomes an example of what the law really intended, or Jesus is arguing that in certain situations of need, the law can be superseded. The text itself is not clear which of these options is behind Jesus' remark. However, it is no accident that this text follows the previous text on the new way Jesus brings, because this event shows a different approach to Sabbath issues than the traditions of the Jewish leadership. New wine is going into new wineskins.

But Jesus is not done. He adds a note about his authority, arguing that the Son of Man is Lord of the Sabbath. This argument goes one step further than the parallel with David. The fact that Jesus is Son of Man, that he is the commissioned agent of God, means that he has the right to regulate what takes place on the Sabbath. This remark underlines his unique position. His actions are not the issue; his authority is. He rules over the application of one of the Ten Commandments. The question for all to ponder becomes: "Does Jesus reveal God's way and have authority over it, or does he not?" The statement at the end of the passage implies Luke's reader should carefully consider the response.

---

8. That David is at the tabernacle is suggested by the remark in 1 Sam. 21:7 that he was detained before the Lord. That he fed more than himself is suggested by the request for five loaves of bread.

9. Danker, *Jesus and the New Age*, 131.

Bridging Contexts

JESUS HERE DISCUSSES a change of administrative eras in the plan of God. A new dispensation is dawning, in which things will be done differently, though Jesus does not develop exactly how that will work here. The New Testament letters make it clear that the dynamic of the presence of the Spirit has brought major changes in how God works with us (2 Cor. 3–4; Heb. 8–10). Faith is still what saves and God still looks for faithfulness, but some of the regulations of worship have changed with the coming of Jesus. Thus, we do not come to church with sacrifices, nor do we worry about clean and unclean foods. Circumcision is no longer an issue for male believers. Gone are the long rules of details about how to worship, like those that run page after page in the *Mishnah*, though at the time of Jesus and the early church, they were heavily discussed and debated (see Mark 7:1–22; Acts 10–11 for clean and unclean foods; Acts 15 for circumcision).

Jesus' way is revolutionary in the dynamic it calls for from God's people—so revolutionary that we are tempted to slip back into a mode of approaching God through rules and regulations, as if spirituality is a matter of activities that can be separated from issues of the heart. The bridge into the present discussed in this passage is one of the most basic spiritual bridges that the Bible gives us. Jesus is bringing about the new era in which we now share. He is opening a door that is the entry way to God. The new way means the end of the old way. Christianity has its roots in Israel and in Jewish expectation, but old things have passed away and new things have come.

In the early church, this new way took on a focused character that should still be present in our communities. There was less concern with the externals of relating to God and more serious concern with nurturing the condition of the heart and the treatment of others, both in the community and outside of it. The privatized form of religion that our culture promotes can be slow to recognize how Jesus' presence should impact the way we relate to others. We sometimes assess our spiritual life in terms of our feelings about God or the number of activities we are involved in completing, rather than in assessing the quality of our relationships with others or the quality of our private time with him.

God wants to be worshiped and praised, but a major way to make that happen is in the edifying activity of the church. Sections like Romans 12–16 and Ephesians 4–6 show how Paul's applications majored on character, not on ritual (cf. also 1 Peter, with its call to live holy lives in an alien land). Christ's words here warn us that it is what is inside that counts. External activity is not the issue, nor is merely going through certain religious exercises or attending so many services. God longs for a heart that celebrates his presence by responding to him and caring for others.

The Pharisees picture how resistant we can be to things being done in a different way under God. Jesus' presence demands that we reflect on how he is leading us to manifest our piety. Ritual for sheer ritual's sake receives no commendation from our Lord. His disciples could have continued fasting as a show of pietism, but Jesus wants them to reflect on the special time his presence indicates. There will be a time for fasting again after he departs, but a fast is the last thing to do in the period of the arrival of the new era.

Two issues are central in considering how to apply the plucking grain passage. (1) Jesus' authority over something as fundamental as the Jewish Sabbath law indicates just how central a role he has in God's plan. The law was the central regulating force for life in Israel for centuries. Jesus now claims that he has the right to exercise authority over it. This is a significant claim, since Yahweh himself had been responsible for setting up the law.

(2) As to the function of the law, though the text is not clear on exactly what logic is presupposed by Jesus' reply in terms of the law's scope, Jesus' application reveals that the law is not to be applied in a casuistic manner, where every exception to the letter of the law is automatically a violation. There is no doubt that David's men did something that was prohibited. While we may not know exactly what Jesus means here by this example, his point is still that what appeared on the surface as a violation was not one in the case of David or the disciples.

The passage, then, tells us something about how the law functions in the new era. The simple theological answer is that the law has passed away. But Jesus' handling of such issues suggests a more fundamental answer as one sees what the law intended to accomplish. As later conflicts over the Sabbath will show, compassion is always to be available to people. A rigorous application of specific laws is not always correct, for they were not intended to prevent people from having a meal or from saving a person in need. The Sabbath law was to free humankind up to rest and enjoy God, not to shackle them from serving others or prevent basic needs from being met.

But neither is this an invitation to license. License is not caring about the law at all and arguing one can do anything one wants. Jesus is arguing that the law seeks to encourage righteousness and healthy involvement with people, not the creation of a host of rules. Jesus makes the point while also pointing to his authority, so that it is clear his insight on the law explains how it was designed to function.

THE CHRISTIAN IS "between eras." We share in the benefits that Jesus brings, yet we still await his full redemption. Jesus no longer tells us to fast regularly on fixed days set by the law, but acts of worship in anticipation of his future coming and our full redemption are commendable. The bridegroom has been taken from us, and we long for his return. Not only can we celebrate this reality through fasting, but it is recalled whenever we share in the Lord's table—an affirmation not only of our relationship to Jesus but also of our belonging to the same confession with one another (1 Cor. 11:23–26). All of this makes us aware that though we share in the initial benefits of the new era, we have not experienced all God has for us, and life on this earth is but a preliminary stage in what God is doing.

The passage also warns against syncretism between Christianity and any other religion. If syncretism were possible, one would think that Judaism would be the best candidate. Judaism was older, worshiped the same God, shared the same hope in the Messiah, and prayed for the same deliverance. Jesus makes it clear that although he is the fulfillment of promise, the new way he brings is not to be mixed with the old. The old ways of worship and sacrifice are no longer necessary and the old signs of piety are no longer required. One may engage in them, as Jewish Christians did in the New Testament and still do today, but not on the basis of a moral necessity. If Christianity cannot be mixed with Judaism, its closest cousin, then certainly it cannot be mixed with anything else available in the world's cafeteria of religions. To do so will destroy both.

We also learn how people resist change, even change directed by God. Most people are content with the way things are. The Jewish leadership was content with religious life under the law, so Jesus' challenges to their religiosity were viewed as threats. Content in the limitations of the old system, they did not even consider the new era. Christians can fall into such ruts of ritual contentment today as well, assuming the way they worship is the way everyone must worship. This kind of a problem is more subtle than the Pharisees' outright challenge of Jesus, for what may be a good and meaningful practice in one context may not need to be replicated by others in exactly the same way. Music styles or certain church practices are elevated to the level of necessity, rather than seen as means to an end.

I am reminded, for example, of exhortations that quiet times should always come first thing in the morning. The result has been that some people, who had fulfilling quiet times later in the day, felt guilty because they did not "get up with God first thing in the morning." The timing of the act of worship became more important than having a time of worship and making a positive spiritual experience of that time. We must be careful not to make a law of that which Scripture does not command.

Rejection can take place in many forms. While some resist because they are hostile to what Jesus is doing, others resist because they are content with life as it is. We should be sensitive to the difference as we seek to share Jesus. It is hard to convince a person who is content that he or she is not; these are often the hardest people to reach. The best that can be done is to hold out the hope that life can be even better. But if the old wine seems good, often such people are not interested even in a sip of the new. Their security and identity are so clearly tied to other things that they will not even think of trying the new way God can bring to them. There are times when we must accept that is where some people are.

The primary application emerging from the disciples' plucking of grain, as with so many texts in this section of Luke, centers around the authority of Jesus. In the end the correctness or error of what Jesus does with his disciples rests on his claims. Does he have authority as the Son of Man, so that his analysis of the Old Testament and the present situation are authoritative over the law? If so, who then is Jesus? This is the fundamental question within this text. The Pharisees do not believe Jesus has the authority to say what he is teaching. Today people still challenge Jesus' authority. But if he is the interpreter of the law, he must be heard, for he reveals the way to God.

There is also an application about the law. God never intended for the law to be followed in such a way that basic needs like eating a meal are denied as a matter of regulation. It was never supposed to be applied so harshly. The relationship of the law to the Christian in this new era is still a debated matter.[10] Even the present text is not clear on exactly how the argument is

---

10. For a full discussion of the options, noting five distinct views, see *The Law, the Gospel, and the Modern Christian*, by G. Bahnsen, W. Kaiser, D. Moo, W. Strickland, and W. VanGemeren (Grand Rapids: Zondervan, 1992). According to these views, the Law can be seen as (1) "the perfection of righteousness in Christ Jesus," (2) "still fully applicable," (3) "God's guidance for the promotion of holiness," (4) "replaced with the law and gospel of Christ," and (5) "is fulfilled in the Law of Christ." All views argue that in one sense or another, Christ is the representation of what the law intended, but they disagree on how that is to be done and which parts of the law can be carried over into application today. Theonomy applies more of the law for today than any other approach. Others either explain how the demands of the law can be met internally through the Spirit, so that it still has merit, or they argue that it is illustrative of the kind of righteousness God demands, that its moral demands still need to be met, or that the law of love in Christ becomes that which fulfills what the law called for. The issue of the law is complex and cannot be solved here. The New Testament values the Old Testament as instructive (2 Tim. 3:15–17), while making it clear that the era of the Spirit has changed the way it is to be seen (2 Cor. 3–4; Heb. 7–10).

made. But whatever approach is taken, it is clear that the disciples did not violate the moral requirements of God by their meal.

One gets a sense of how things have changed when one considers how the issue of circumcision for Gentiles was handled by the early church. Here a central command about identification as the people of God is not applied to those who have entered into the Christian faith. Granted, this example is not one of basic need, but it does show how God reexamined the function of the law in the new era, where some formerly central laws ceased to have any role. What became the central mark for the Christian was not circumcision, but the indwelling Spirit (Acts 15:1–21). That indwelling was seen as equivalent to physical circumcision because it involved circumcision of the heart (Phil. 3:1–3). In other words, this change indicates that the new era approaches matters of the law in a fresh way. Jesus has the authority to explain and justify the shift of emphasis.

Luke 6:6–16

O N ANOTHER SABBATH he went into the synagogue and was teaching, and a man was there whose right hand was shriveled. ⁷The Pharisees and the teachers of the law were looking for a reason to accuse Jesus, so they watched him closely to see if he would heal on the Sabbath. ⁸But Jesus knew what they were thinking and said to the man with the shriveled hand, "Get up and stand in front of everyone." So he got up and stood there.

⁹Then Jesus said to them, "I ask you, which is lawful on the Sabbath: to do good or to do evil, to save life or to destroy it?"

¹⁰He looked around at them all, and then said to the man, "Stretch out your hand." He did so, and his hand was completely restored. ¹¹But they were furious and began to discuss with one another what they might do to Jesus.

¹²One of those days Jesus went out to a mountainside to pray, and spent the night praying to God. ¹³When morning came, he called his disciples to him and chose twelve of them, whom he also designated apostles: ¹⁴Simon (whom he named Peter), his brother Andrew, James, John, Philip, Bartholomew, ¹⁵Matthew, Thomas, James son of Alphaeus, Simon who was called the Zealot, ¹⁶Judas son of James, and Judas Iscariot, who became a traitor.

Original Meaning

THE INCIDENT IN verses 6–11 is the third in a series of controversies involving Jesus. Again this activity occurs on the Sabbath.[1] While teaching in a synagogue, Jesus sees a person in need, a man with a shriveled right hand, and takes the initiative to heal him. Such an injury would prevent the man from pursuing a vocation. In other words, while not in mortal danger, the man is limited in what he can do.

The scribes and Pharisees watch Jesus. The Greek word for "watched" means "to spy on" or "to watch out of the corner of one's eye" (cf. Ps. 36:12

---

1. The parallels to this text are Matthew 12:9–14 and Mark 3:1–6. The question of Matthew's later placement of this event is similar to what happened with the parallels of Luke 6:1–5.

LXX).[2] They want to level a charge against Jesus. This attitude is emerging out of what is becoming a growing opposition. In the Jewish view, a person who is not in mortal danger can wait to be healed.[3]

Jesus raises a fundamental question before doing anything, for he knows the Pharisees' thoughts. He tells the man to come and stand before him and then asks, "Which is lawful on the Sabbath: to do good or to do evil, to save life or destroy it?" The question has an ironic edge, because Jesus is looking at the Sabbath from a relational angle. In fact, the way he pursues the question almost suggests that a failure to act here would be doing evil. The leadership, on the other hand, is plotting evil.

The action becomes a test. Will God allow the healing to take place? Will he vindicate Jesus and reveal the answer to Jesus' question? Jesus looks at everyone and then acts. He asks the man to stretch out his hand, and the man is able to respond, indicating that healing has occurred. But rather than rejoicing at his restoration, the leadership becomes angry at Jesus' success. The word for "anger" is a strong term, describing irrational anger, even pathological rage.[4] A turning point has come. The authorities must do something to stop Jesus, and they begin their plan. Refusing to accept the evidence Jesus has laid before them, they reveal hardness of heart and cast their vote against Jesus.

Rising opposition means that Jesus must organize his followers. His selection of the twelve (vv. 12–16) is preparation for the missions to come (9:1–6; 10:1–12), as well as an anticipation of his future departure through death.[5] At the top of this organized group of disciples stand these twelve men. All but Judas Iscariot will come to have a central role in the development of the early church.

The setting of Jesus' selection is no accident. He spends the entire previous night in prayer. Thus his selection is set in a context of communion with God. This is the only place in the New Testament where an all-night vigil is noted. Jesus selects twelve men. The number is designed to suggest a parallel to Israel (cf. 22:29–30; Matt. 19:28). Only Luke calls the group "apostles" as he lists their names. That title indicates their role as commissioned representatives of Jesus on behalf of the kingdom message.[6]

---

2. Reisenfeld, "παρτηρέω," *TDNT*, 8:147.

3. *Mishnah, Yoma* 8:6.

4. Behm, "ἄνοια," *TDNT*, 4:963.

5. The parallels to this passage are Matthew 10:1–4 and Mark 3:13–19. Again Mark and Luke are close in their relative placement of this event. Matthew holds his listing until the discussion of the mission of the Twelve.

6. Fitzmyer, *Luke*, 617; Marshall, *Commentary on Luke*, 238–39.

Three facts dominate the list, along with its parallels: (1) Peter is always first; (2) the first four are Peter, Andrew, James, and John (though sometimes in different order); and (3) there are three groups of four, with Peter, Philip, and James son of Alphaeus leading each group.[7]

Peter is a key figure. He often speaks for the disciples and takes a key role in the group. His brother, Andrew, is hardly discussed outside the lists. The sons of Zebedee, James and John, complete the initial group and the sequence of four fishermen. In the second group, Philip is mentioned separately only a few times in John. Bartholomew may well be the same person as Nathaniel in John 1:45, since many Jews had two prominent names.[8] Matthew is probably Levi, the tax collector.[9] Thomas is the disciple who will have to be convinced of Jesus' resurrection (John 20:24–29). In the third group, we know very little about James of Alphaeus. Simon the Zealot was a political nationalist before meeting Jesus.[10] He would have hated someone like Matthew, who as a tax collector represented the despised Roman state. Judas, not Iscariot, may be Thaddaeus of other lists. Judas Iscariot will become infamous through his betrayal of Jesus. This diverse group of twelve men of the street forms the leadership base for Jesus.

Bridging Contexts

THIS PASSAGE AGAIN reveals the will of God by exploring what can be done on the Sabbath. Though the question of Jewish law is no longer a concern for the church, the issue of how others are treated, even on the day of rest, is. Jesus shows that God does not intend us to ignore acting with love and mercy whenever the opportunity to do so exists. Here is the "law of love" at work.

Christians still discuss how a day like the Sabbath (our Sunday) should be treated. Different traditions have different emphases.[11] Some, arguing from the continuing validity of the Ten Commandments, see the day of rest principle as still in effect. This view has been called a "sabbatarian" position and has roots in Augustine and Thomas Aquinas. The result is a lifestyle on

---

7. Plummer, *Luke*, 172.

8. Plummer, *Luke*, 173.

9. See discussion of Levi in Luke 5:27–32.

10. Though the formal Zealot party that led to the fall of Jerusalem in A.D. 70 probably did not yet exist, the nationalist tendencies that became associated with that later movement are probably reflected in Simon's nickname.

11. For a comprehensive study of this question, see D. A. Carson, ed., *From Sabbath to Lord's Day: A Biblical, Historical, and Theological Investigation* (Grand Rapids: Zondervan, 1982), esp. the closing essay by A. T. Lincoln (pp. 343–412).

Sunday that purposely restricts activity and the scope of leisure so that the day can be given over for rest and the Lord. Other traditions argue that Christ is the end of the law, that the Sabbath principle is nowhere reaffirmed in the New Testament, and that all days are holy (cf. Rom. 14:5–8). Such traditions are less specific about what can and cannot be done on Sunday. I tend to think in the latter terms, because of reasons summarized in the second century by Justin Martyr in *Dialogues* 12:3:

> The new law requires you to keep perpetual sabbath, and you, because you are idle for one day, suppose you are pious. … The Lord God does not take pleasure in such observances; if there is any perjured person or thief among you, let him cease to be so; if any adulterer, let him repent; then he has kept the sweet and true sabbath of God.

The values found in this quotation reflect those of Jesus here. Observance has no value, and neither does debate over the day if the attitudes of service and faithfulness are not pursued in everyday life. Psalm 118:24 says it best, as we consider any day to be the Lord's: "This is the day the LORD has made; let us rejoice and be glad in it."

God vindicates Jesus through this healing, which itself pictures God's deliverance. Here is more evidence that God is behind Jesus. Had God rejected what Jesus was doing, he could have shut the door and prevented the healing. Jesus' claims take on more significance because God is acting through him. It is this combination of word and deed that forms a powerful testimony for Jesus.

The passage focuses on the opposition to Jesus. Despite all the signs of God's favor surrounding Jesus' activity, the Jewish leadership gets more hostile. Jesus in effect charges the Pharisees with legalism—that is, overapplying the law to such an extent that people are crushed or ignored. The sovereignty of a rigid rule becomes a yoke too great to bear (cf. Acts 15:10). Even today sometimes, in our efforts to defend the law, we break it. I remember stories in my seminary days of a particular church fighting fiercely over the order of service as each side staunchly defended a certain sequence of hymns, announcements, and message. Though this may be an outrageous example, each of us have been guilty of more subtle forms of insisting that our way was the only way to do something. All too often when we discuss issues of form or style, we concentrate on legalism rather than matters involving explicit moral choices or correct theology. We must learn toleration and deference in such "neutral" topics, for each side is responsible before God for their actions and for pursuing a clear conscience before him (Rom. 14–15).

Jesus' choosing of the Twelve reflects a unique, diverse group. He did not select a homogenous club. There were fishermen, tax collectors, a staunchly political person, and a few others whose identities are left undeveloped. These are everyday sorts of people, showing the grass-roots character of Jesus' ministry. What a contrast to the selection of leadership we tend to make in our culture, where money, status, and power bring a person to the leadership table. There is something to be said for choosing a leadership mix that is sensitive to the key issues of character and integrity over status. How many churches have been damaged because the leadership is selected from people who do not have spiritual qualifications, but qualify for the Fortune 500 in terms of lifestyle, values, and use of power?

THIS PASSAGE DEMONSTRATES the priority that showing mercy has in the mind of God. He is compassionate and wants us to help others whenever possible. Even a day of rest, like the Sabbath, is no reason to opt out of doing good. Jesus goes out of his way to show his opponents that this is how God desires others to be treated. He dedicated himself to serving others, especially others in need. One even notes an urgency in Jesus that help ought to be offered as soon as possible. Though this particular healing could have waited until after the Sabbath, sparing Jesus the leadership's reaction, he acted at the first opportunity. Our rapid response should match his as well.

The major emphasis in the passage is the rising opposition to Jesus and its cold, irrational nature. Such a reaction to Jesus parallels opposition today and should not surprise believers, for it gives evidence of a sinful reaction to the mercy of God. The Jewish leadership ignored the restoration of the man's hand, because all they could see was a Sabbath violation. Sometimes those who reject Jesus respond as if the pursuit of a morally sensitive and serving lifestyle represents the presence of a criminal element. This is the world turned morally upside down. I know, for example, of believers ministering in the "darker" side of town, who dress and present themselves with a style that is not out of place in such contexts. They do not engage in the activities of the people they seek to reach, but simply love them enough to make an effort to reach out to them by identifying with their dress, their style of music, and so forth. Sometimes such people are judged as sinners hanging out with sinners—a charge not unlike the one Jesus heard! But we should consider the evidence of compassion that accompanies such a ministry, motivated by a sincere and righteous desire to serve God.

Jesus met such opposition by simply continuing to minister with love to those who needed compassion. Here we see his heart in contrast to a heart that does not respond to the moral call of God to serve at all times. Paul calls this the "law of Christ" (1 Cor. 9:21) and James the "royal law" (James 2:8). Even if facing strong opposition, those who walk with Jesus are called to a ministry of service and love.

When we turn to the selection of the twelve disciples, Jesus consciously selected a diverse group of people, presumably to keep his ministry team balanced. Their central bond was Jesus. The new community he builds today is just as varied, and we should rejoice in that diversity. Jesus does not expect all of us to be the same. Our differences should not prevent a unity from forming among this nucleus, as Jesus bonds us together.

The inclusion of a Judas in the group also has its lesson. Not everyone remains a team player, and defection can come from the innermost ranks. Close association with Jesus does not necessarily reveal the real condition of the heart. Though John calls Judas "a devil" (John 6:70–71), for years he was viewed as one of Jesus' closest associates. Unfaithfulness and denial eventually shows itself, but for a significant period of time it is hard to tell where Judas really is.

A final question emerges from this selection. How do we choose our leadership? What criteria do we use? Does character count for much? Do we consider those who have a good reputation outside the community as well as within (1 Tim. 3:7)? Is someone selected to our board simply because of his or her connections and the networking that person can help us do? Is someone chosen because he or she can give a lot financially? Jesus was looking for a few good men and chose them in the hopes of building their character to the point where they could lead the church he left behind.

That goal makes another key point about leadership. The best leader is one who so prepares his community for the future that when he departs, he is barely missed, since solid leadership is left behind. That principle warns us against a strong one-person show, which often sows the seeds for later destruction. The best leadership is frequently seen not in what happens while the person is still around, but by what develops after he or she has left. If the Twelve as a group are measured by this standard of leadership, then Jesus' choice for successors was a strategic one, since this group came to shake and shape the world.

Luke 6:17–49

HE WENT DOWN with them and stood on a level place. A large crowd of his disciples was there and a great number of people from all over Judea, from Jerusalem, and from the coast of Tyre and Sidon, ¹⁸who had come to hear him and to be healed of their diseases. Those troubled by evil spirits were cured, ¹⁹and the people all tried to touch him, because power was coming from him and healing them all.

²⁰Looking at his disciples, he said:

> "Blessed are you who are poor,
>> for yours is the kingdom of God.
> ²¹Blessed are you who hunger now,
>> for you will be satisfied.
> Blessed are you who weep now,
>> for you will laugh.
> ²²Blessed are you when men hate you,
>> when they exclude you and insult you
>> and reject your name as evil,
>>> because of the Son of Man.

²³"Rejoice in that day and leap for joy, because great is your reward in heaven. For that is how their fathers treated the prophets.

> ²⁴"But woe to you who are rich,
>> for you have already received your comfort.
> ²⁵Woe to you who are well fed now,
>> for you will go hungry.
> Woe to you who laugh now,
>> for you will mourn and weep.
> ²⁶Woe to you when all men speak well of you,
>> for that is how their fathers treated the false prophets.

²⁷"But I tell you who hear me: Love your enemies, do good to those who hate you, ²⁸bless those who curse you, pray for those who mistreat you. ²⁹If someone strikes you on one cheek, turn to him the other also. If someone takes your cloak, do not stop him from taking your tunic. ³⁰Give to

everyone who asks you, and if anyone takes what belongs to you, do not demand it back. ³¹Do to others as you would have them do to you.

³²"If you love those who love you, what credit is that to you? Even 'sinners' love those who love them. ³³And if you do good to those who are good to you, what credit is that to you? Even 'sinners' do that. ³⁴And if you lend to those from whom you expect repayment, what credit is that to you? Even 'sinners' lend to 'sinners,' expecting to be repaid in full. ³⁵But love your enemies, do good to them, and lend to them without expecting to get anything back. Then your reward will be great, and you will be sons of the Most High, because he is kind to the ungrateful and wicked. ³⁶Be merciful, just as your Father is merciful.

³⁷ "Do not judge, and you will not be judged. Do not condemn, and you will not be condemned. Forgive, and you will be forgiven. ³⁸Give, and it will be given to you. A good measure, pressed down, shaken together and running over, will be poured into your lap. For with the measure you use, it will be measured to you."

³⁹He also told them this parable: "Can a blind man lead a blind man? Will they not both fall into a pit? ⁴⁰A student is not above his teacher, but everyone who is fully trained will be like his teacher.

⁴¹"Why do you look at the speck of sawdust in your brother's eye and pay no attention to the plank in your own eye? ⁴²How can you say to your brother, 'Brother, let me take the speck out of your eye,' when you yourself fail to see the plank in your own eye? You hypocrite, first take the plank out of your eye, and then you will see clearly to remove the speck from your brother's eye.

⁴³"No good tree bears bad fruit, nor does a bad tree bear good fruit. ⁴⁴Each tree is recognized by its own fruit. People do not pick figs from thornbushes, or grapes from briers. ⁴⁵The good man brings good things out of the good stored up in his heart, and the evil man brings evil things out of the evil stored up in his heart. For out of the overflow of his heart his mouth speaks.

⁴⁶"Why do you call me, 'Lord, Lord,' and do not do what I say? ⁴⁷I will show you what he is like who comes to me and hears my words and puts them into practice. ⁴⁸He is like a

man building a house, who dug down deep and laid the foundation on rock. When a flood came, the torrent struck that house but could not shake it, because it was well built. ⁴⁹But the one who hears my words and does not put them into practice is like a man who built a house on the ground without a foundation. The moment the torrent struck that house, it collapsed and its destruction was complete."

Original Meaning

IF LUKE 4:16–30 summarizes the note of fulfillment in Jesus' teaching, this discourse highlights the ethical expectations he has of his followers. The Sermon on the Plain is Luke's equivalent to Matthew's Sermon on the Mount. Luke presents this sermon without the legal elements that Matthew treated, probably because of his Gentile audience.[1] The fact that Luke can summarize for Gentiles what Jesus originally delivered to a Jewish audience shows how timeless and fundamental the Evangelist saw this ethic as being for the Christian community. This view holds true whether the sermon is an anthology of Jesus' remarks or reflects a single occasion. The fact of conceptual parallels to Matthew shows that what Jesus taught must still be taken seriously by Jesus' disciples today, even if some of the particular legal examples recorded in Matthew are omitted because of their lack of direct relevance.[2]

The unit begins with a summary introduction to Jesus' teaching ministry (vv. 17–19), the fourth such summary to appear in Luke (cf. 4:14–15, 31–32, 40–41). Following that is the actual sermon (6:20–49), whose major

---

1. The question of the relationship between this sermon and the Sermon on the Mount is complex. I regard this sermon as Luke's summary of the sermon Matthew records. For details, comparisons, and a discussion of the ethical-theological role of the Sermon on the Mount and Plain, see D. Bock, *Luke 1:1–9:50*, excursus 7: "The Sermon on the Plain in Luke." Also covered in detail there is whether the sermon represents a single occasion or an anthology of Jesus' ethical teaching. Either option is possible, though I prefer to see a specific event. I think it less likely that Luke used Matthew. Raher, he seems aware of a tradition about the sermon like that found in Matthew.

2. To make such a point may seem odd, but some expressions of dispensational theology in the first half of this century argued that the Sermon on the Mount addressed issues of the future kingdom and thus were not directly relevant for today. Many evangelicals still think this is the dominant position held within this tradition, but they are mistaken. For a discussion of this issue from a dispensational point of view and a short history of dispensational interpretation, see C. Blaising and D. Bock, ed., *Dispensationalism, Israel, and the Church: A Search for Definition* (Grand Rapids, Zondervan, 1992), esp. the article by John Martin, "Christ, the Fulfillment of the Law in the Sermon on the Mount," 248–63.

theme is a call to exceptional love in light of the offer of God's gracious blessing. Jesus outlines what he desires of his followers, especially as they relate to those outside the community, including those who oppose them.

Jesus ministers here to three groups: apostles, "a large crowd of his disciples," and "a great number of people." He preaches "on a level place." The locale may be a level area in the midst of a more mountainous region (Isa. 13:2; Jer. 21:13).[3] The people gather for two reasons: to listen to Jesus' teaching and to be healed by him. Teaching and compassionate service combine to touch the people. Jesus' message of God's kindness is supported by his actions. The healings involve both sicknesses and exorcisms. The power that proceeds from Jesus indicates the authority with which he works.

The sermon itself divides into three parts: the prophetic blessings and woes (vv. 20–26), an exposition about exceptional love, mercy, and a hesitation to judge (vv. 27–38), and remarks about righteousness, fruit, and wise building (vv. 39–49).

Call of Blessings and Woes. The sermon begins with a prophetic call— an invitation and warning to those listening to him. The first part declares God's grace of blessing to those who identify with him. In contrast, the woes, unique to Luke's Gospel, show God's displeasure on those who oppose the blessing Jesus gives and who persecute his disciples as a result.

God commits himself to his disciples in the present age and will bless them richly in the future. The four descriptions of the righteous in verses 20–22 should not be seen as separate groups, but as elements of one portrait describing those for whom God has compassion.[4] The blessings of God's promised rule belong to such as these.

The "poor" are discussed first. This term recalls Jesus' remarks in 4:16– 20. As with that passage, the poor are the pious poor, who are blessed because they have a position in the kingdom of God, the delivering rule of his presence. These poor are the special objects of Jesus' ministry, as Luke repeatedly mentions (1:52–53; 4:16–20; 7:22; 14:13, 21). The roots of this idea appear in Psalms and in prophets like Isaiah (Pss. 25:9; 34:2; Isa. 42:1– 18; 61:1).[5] Jesus preaches and ministers to all the poor as a means of finding

---

3. This explanation means that there is no problem with identifying this event and Matthew's sermon as the same.

4. To say the poor are Jesus' special concern is not to say he excludes the rich, since Zacchaeus is blessed in Luke 19:1–10. But there is a consistent note that Jesus pays special attention to this group. This text should not be spiritualized, so that the poor cease to be a point of focus. Jesus chooses this description of his audience on purpose. Too often we ignore the sociological element in this description, even though it also has a religious element.

5. Guelich, *The Sermon on the Mount* (Waco, Tex.: Word, 1982), 67–72.

the responsive and pious among them who will receive God's grace. Such people understand that they must depend on God, because life is beyond their control.

Those that hunger now are promised satisfaction in the future. Hunger is a result of religious persecution and harsh treatment by people of power who take advantage of others. Hunger is one of the consequences of poverty (cf. Isa. 32:6–7; 58:6–7, 9–10; Ezek. 18:7, 16). These people may be deficient in material goods, but they have turned to God for care, and he will care for them and satisfy them. The blessing they will receive transcends any lack they have now.

Those who are poor and hungry are also sad because of the strain of life, but there will come a time when they will laugh. God sees their tears, and their tears will become smiles. Disappointment and pain will turn into joy. Weeping as a picture of those who suffer unjustly is also an Old Testament theme (Pss. 126:5–6; 137:1; Isa. 40:1–2). Those who weep have paid the price of painful rejection for lining up with God.[6]

The last unit is the key remark of the blessing sequence, because it shows the religious dimensions of those who are blessed. These people suffer hatred, insult, rejection, and exclusion from the Jewish community. That community gives them an "evil name," because they have come to the Son of Man, that is, to Jesus. These remarks clearly presuppose a life that has faced religious persecution, and the four descriptions depict an escalating negative reaction to their association with Jesus. Religious convictions were not a private matter in ancient times, similar to many countries outside the West today. A choice for Jesus meant the loss of family fellowship, dismissal from the synagogue, and removal from social contact. To be tossed from the synagogue meant being viewed as an unclean person. Yet despite such circumstances, the disciples should rejoice, for God sees them and will bless them. They have ancestors, the great prophets of old, who were treated similarly. The call to "rejoice" is the one command among the blessings; everything else is promise. God's grace will help them overcome their suffering for their faith.

The four woes match and contrast the four blessings, revealing Jesus' displeasure with people who are uncaring about those around them and who refuse to be sensitive to God. As with the blessings, the four descriptions are not four distinct groups but four related descriptions of one kind of person. The prophetic woes are utterances of pity and pain for those who will face misfortune or judgment.[7]

---

6. Rengstorf, "γελάω," *TDNT*, 1:660; "κλαίω," 3:722–23.
7. Danker, *Jesus and the New Age*, 142.

The "rich" are singled out because they often take advantage of the poor (James 2:1–7; 5:1–6). The remark is, of course, a generalization, since some rich do respond to the Gospel. But the warning is serious, for wealth can create a sense of independence that results in distance from God and callousness toward others (1 Tim. 6:6–18).[8] The "comfort" is their wealth, which they cannot take with them.

The next woe is against those "who are well fed now." In a classic case of reversal, they will be hungry on the Judgment Day—a warning that recalls the Old Testament (Isa. 5:22; 6:13; Amos 8:11).[9] Those who ignore God and place their hopes solely on the good life here have little comfort for the future. Those who "laugh now" will someday mourn and weep (cf. Isa. 65:14); they are too enthralled with the pursuit of life to care about anything else.

The final woe reveals the spiritual depravity of these people. They are spoken well of by others, just like the false prophets of old. They have settled for an approach to life that does not challenge them to live any differently. They wrongly see themselves as unaccountable to God.

This series of four woes shows the serious spiritual condition of these people, who think they are on top of the world. As the sequence of blessings and woes reveal, appearances can be deceiving.

Call to Love and Mercy. With the word of encouraging invitation and warning in place, Jesus turns to address the disciple's ethical character and call (vv. 27–38). Fundamental to ethics is love—not a love like the world's, but a unique love that endures. These exhortations are expressed with reference to enemies in verses 27–28, from a human perspective in verse 31, and as a divine standard in verse 35. Two sets of illustrations support the exhortation (vv. 29–30, 32–34). Love evidences mercy, just like the Father (v. 36), so that the result is a hesitation to judge and a readiness to forgive (v. 37). The concept has rich Old Testament roots (Pss. 86:15; 103:4; 112:4).

Four exhortations in verses 27 and 28 make the key point. The special objects of love are one's enemies. The love Jesus commands is not an abstract love tucked away in the person's inner recesses, but a love that demonstrates itself in concrete action. The disciple should do good to those who hate them, bless those who curse them, and pray for those who abuse them. The exhortations expect action, not just a private expression to God. In the context of rejection, Jesus calls for extraordinary trust in God. Disciples should reflect such love constantly.

Lest there be any doubt that Jesus calls his followers to active, visible

---

8. W. E. Pilgrim, *Good News to the Poor* (Minneapolis: Augsburg, 1981) is an excellent book on this topic.

9. Plummer, *Luke*, 182.

love for their enemies, four illustrations guarantee that this is his focus. Turning the cheek pictures a person slapped on the cheek in rejection. The action involves an insult that may well be associated with removal from the synagogue.[10] Numerous examples of this kind of use of violence appear in Acts (18:17; 21:32; 23:2). Yet the early church consistently turned the other cheek by continuing to share the gospel with those who rejected them. They have never fought back in kind, but attempted to overcome evil with good.

The second illustration continues the picture of being vulnerable. Those who take the outer garment should also be allowed to have the undershirt. Jesus' point here is not to stand on a street corner and allow oneself to be robbed, but that ministry in the context of rejection, which includes economic isolation, requires being vulnerable again and again. Missionary work can expose one to danger, but that should not stop us from making multiple efforts to win people.[11]

The disciple should also be compassionate and generous and should thus give to the needy. The giving of alms to the poor was an important part of Jewish piety. Jesus' words here fit into that background,[12] as do numerous Old Testament texts (Deut. 15:7–8; Ps. 37:21, 26; Prov. 19:17; 21:26b). Such compassion represents a fundamental expression of love.

The final illustration involves retribution for wrong done. Jesus does not want a disciple to seek to get back what has been taken from him. This exhortation involves amazing restraint. Paul seems to be aware of this in his remarks in 1 Corinthians 6:1–8.[13] It is better to be defrauded than to bring reproach on Jesus' name. Those who strike against the disciples should be treated differently by the disciples.

All of these exhortations assume that the disciple understands that God is watching over him or her. Any vindication should be left in his hands. The greatest vindication of all is to transform the enemy into a friend of God through the example of love. Saul is perhaps the most prominent biblical example. A supporter of Stephen's stoning, he was transformed by God in answer to Stephen's prayer that those who were stoning him should be forgiven (Acts 7, esp. v. 60; 9:1–19).

The exhortation is repeated, only now a human standard of expectation serves as the basis for the ethical call (v. 31). This remark, known as "the Golden Rule," is often seen as one of the pinnacle points in Jesus' ethical

---

10. 1 Esdras 4:30; Stählin, "τύπτω," *TDNT*, 8:263, nn. 23–24.

11. Ellis, *Luke*, 114–15.

12. Guelich, *The Sermon on the Mount*, 223.

13. See also 1 Peter 2:21–24.

teaching, though it reflects a common ethical theme in the culture.[14] Jesus states no ulterior motive here. The essence of love is a sensitivity to the needs of others, deferring to how they prefer to be treated. Such love takes great sensitivity and a spirit that desires to hear what others have to say. It is another way of showing respect for others.

Jesus drives home the point with a series of questions (vv. 32–34), radicalizing the positive exhortations of verses 29–30. The fundamental point is that if we love only those who are kind to us, that takes no special effort (2 Clement 13:4). Even sinners love that way. The call of the disciple is to a greater love, a distinct love, a love that is unique in the world.

This love even involves using our resources to meet the needs of others. We should not lend in such a way as to expect a return. Jesus is drawing on Old Testament principles here (Ex. 22:25; Lev. 25:35–37; Deut. 15:7–11): As the year of release from debt approached, one was not to become more hesitant to lend because that year was approaching. One was not to be tight-fisted or hardhearted, but openhanded to the needy. Failure to respond meant that the one needing the money could cry out to God against the lender. So Jesus argues in kind: No one should give a loan simply because he or she expects to ask for a loan in return some day in the future.[15] Rather, one should simply be generous and seek to meet human needs. To lend in any other way is to lend as a sinner lends.

Jesus then restates the exhortation: Love your enemies, do good, lend while expecting nothing back, and expect a reward from the God who lives in heaven (v. 35). Jesus' disciples should love with an exceptional love, a love so different that the world can see it. Such love is rewarded because it marks out the presence of the children of God, who reflect the character of God. God himself is kind to the ungrateful and selfish. To be his child is to reveal the Father's character (cf. Ps. 112:4–5).

In other words, the standard of the disciple's behavior is the merciful character of God (v. 36). Again Jesus echoes Old Testament descriptions of God (Ex. 34:6; Isa. 63:15; Jonah 4:2). To be his child is not only to be brought into a relationship where God has forgiven us; it is the beginning of a process of reflecting God's gracious, merciful, and forgiving character to the world. As we do so, we live out our call to be like him, to reflect his image. "Moral likeness proves parentage."[16]

---

14. D. Bock, *Luke 1:1–9:50*, on Luke 6:31. In the discussion of this text, eleven cultural parallels are cited. Among the most accessible are Sirach 31:15; Tobit 4:15; 2 Enoch 61:7. However, it should be noted that Jesus' version is the most emphatically stated form.

15. Marshall, *Commentary on Luke*, 263.

16. Plummer, *Luke*, 189.

Also in imitation of God, the disciple should be slow to judge (v. 37).[17] Love for one's enemy does not fix a view of him in stone. Moreover, the measure we use toward others is the measure God will use toward us. If we do not judge, he will not judge us. If we do not condemn, he will not condemn us. If we give, he will give to us in "good measure." The picture of the good measure pressed down draws on what happened in the ancient marketplace, where a seller placed grain in a container. Then he shook the container to get the grain to level out so that he could put more grain in the measure. That is how God measures for the generous and those who give. In fact, he gives so that the cup runs over. This abundant measure God pours into the "lap" or fold of one's ancient garment. God honors a compassionate spirit. Jesus reveals the contrast to this attitude in the Pharisee of 18:11–14, whose pride led him to judge others just by looking.[18]

Call to Righteousness, Fruit, and Wise Building. Jesus begins the final unit with a warning that calls disciples to pay attention to which teachers they follow. A blind leader will only lead someone into a pit. The question, "Can a blind man lead a blind man?" expects a negative answer in the Greek. The second question, "Will they not both fall into the pit?" expects a yes answer. Jesus' point is that the disciple is like the teacher, so if the teacher is blind, the student will be blind too. Blindness is a common figure for spiritual blindness (Ps. 25:5; 86:11; 119:35);[19] thus, Jesus is warning here about religious leadership. One should follow the right teacher and not apply too much authority to one's self. In the context of this discourse, only one such teacher exists—Jesus. A disciple should not try to go beyond him.

Jesus continues to attack a critical spirit, like that of the Pharisees, by mentioning the quickness with which we are hypocritically aware of a little fault in someone else but ignore the log in our own eye.[20] According to Jesus, it takes nerve to talk to a fellow human being about his or her little faults while pretending we have none of our own. Jesus does not absolve us of community accountability, however. The way to deal with it is by paying attention to our own faults first and dealing fully with them before turning our attention to the treatment of the little faults of others (cf. Gal. 6:1–5).

From accountability, Jesus take up the issue of character (vv. 43–45).

---

17. Judaism shared this view in some of its literature. *Mishnah 'Abot* 1:6 reads, "When you judge, incline the balance in his favor"; *Sota* 1:7 reads, "With the measure a man measures, it will be measured to him again."

18. Ellis, *Luke*, 116.

19. Michaelis, "ὁδηγός, ὁδηγέω," *TDNT*, 5:100.

20. The reference to the beam refers to a large beam of a building that is actually bigger than our two by four planks! A hypocrite in Greek was a "play actor," someone who was different in behavior than in character; Danker, *Luke*, p. 154.

How can one know the character of a person? Jesus says to check the fruit. A good tree bears good fruit, not bad, and vice versa; every tree is known by its fruit. A bad tree cannot yield good fruit, nor a good tree bad fruit. The agricultural illustrations, drawn from Palestinian everyday life, depict people. Good people produce good deeds from a good heart, while evil people sprout evil deeds from a destructive heart. Jesus highlights speech here. "Out of the abundance of [one's] heart [one's] mouth speaks." James makes similar remarks (James 3:1–12). The tongue is a litmus test of the soul, and the product of one's life is a litmus test of the heart. Each one should examine one's own self in this regard, not others.

Finally, Jesus returns to the issue of his authority (vv. 46–49). Any disciple who respects Jesus should do what he says. How can one call him "Lord" and not do what he says? That is hypocrisy. This is one of several texts that highlight hearing and doing. To drive the point home, Jesus closes his sermon with a parable. To hear Jesus and do what he says is like building a home with a solid foundation. Such a home can stand up against the floods of life. Even when the surging waters beat against the house, it stands, because it is well built. In contrast, the person who does not follow what Jesus says becomes a tragic figure. That home is built without a foundation. When the problems of life rise and tensions flood, they sweep the house away. The roots of Jesus' imagery here comes from Ezekiel 13:10–16. If we recall the Mississippi floods of 1993, we can sense the devastating portrait Jesus paints.

It is therefore foolish to build a house without a foundation. Likewise, it is foolish not to listen to Jesus. We should hear his invitation to enter God's grace and experience the assurance God offers. We should follow his call to love in a way that differs from the world, be merciful and gracious to others, work on our own faults rather than those of others, and follow the words of Jesus. As a teacher of light, he will not allow his followers to end up in the pit. For Luke there is but one who is worthy of being followed: His name is Jesus.

Bridging Contexts

REGARDING VERSES 17–19, Jesus' ministry involved both preaching and meeting the needs of people. He did not presume on his audience with words only; he showed compassion through caring as well. The church's ministry today ought likewise to reach out with hands of compassion.

A major key to determining the importance of this version of Jesus' sermon is to compare it with its parallel, the Sermon on the Mount. Matthew has 137 verses, Luke 30. Luke omits the portions that treat legal issues of concern to Matthew's Jewish audience. The comparison is significant, since it indicates that Luke presented the core of Jesus' sermon to his Gentile audience. This fact means that the ethical core of the sermon is intended for all Jesus' followers, up to the present time.

Call to Blessings and Woes. The blessings and woes reflect fundamental ethical values of God and his grace towards those who align themselves with him at great cost. God knows those who are his and who stand up for him. Jesus offers blessings, a theme that is popular today. We like to consider how God will welcome us. But what about his threatened judgment? Many, trying to make Jesus more palatable in a modern multicultural setting, argue that the themes of judgment have been added to the portrait of Jesus by some editor. The recently well-publicized Jesus Seminar takes such a position on most of the texts where Jesus discusses judgment. Yet such claims are inconsistent with the recognition that Jesus preached like a prophet of old. Which of the prophets of Israel called to righteousness without also warning of judgment? We must not tone down hard texts like the ones that warn the rich and popular that God notes their lack of attention to him through their lack of attention to others.

Call to Love and Mercy. It is difficult for many to bridge from the issues of persecution raised in this sermon into many present-day cultural contexts. However, we must never forget that there are parts of the world today, like areas of the Middle East, Asia, and Africa, where persecution and the risk of losing one's life for Christ are real. In addition, in much of the Western world persecution is subtle, being more indirect and less physical in style. Believers may not be beaten up, but perhaps on a college campus they are maligned for not being "with it" or being "strange" or being a "prude" because of certain ethical standards. Perhaps our business practices, reflecting a commitment to integrity, will be seen as not playing for the team and will cost us. But whatever we are asked to bear because of our faith commitments, we should continue to love, serve, and show mercy to those who oppose us.

Another debatable issue in understanding this text and bridging it into our world is the force of the figures of speech. Is Jesus speaking in hyperbole here when he refers to saints being taken advantage of in the context of religious persecution? Hyperbole is not, of course, an unusual rhetorical style for a prophetic declaration. Its recognition allows one to focus on the central and concrete application behind the rhetorically presented image. How then does one know when hyperbole is present? There are at least two keys to identifying this figure of speech: (1) Does the strict, literal application of the remark lead to an absurd result, and (2) do examples of application in the early church illustrate more concretely the intended application?

Let's see how this applies. (1) When, for example, Jesus suggests that the one who takes a disciple's cloak be allowed to take his tunic too, it seems clear that Jesus is not arguing a disciple should willingly be stripped literally down to their skin and go about naked! The point has to do with the risk taken in being totally exposed, even to the point of being totally taken advantage of. (2) We can note that even though Paul continually exposed himself to great danger for the sake of the gospel, there were occasions when the church sent him away from a dangerous area for his own protection (e.g., Acts 16:40; 17:10, 13–14). Thus, sometimes it was prudent to protect oneself from persecution by moving a ministry elsewhere. On the other hand, Stephen forgave his enemies who were putting him to death, just as Jesus had done on the cross (Acts 7:60). Sometimes God calls us to give even our lives.

We live in a world that is often hostile to the gospel today, so we share the ancient context with the disciples who turned to Jesus. Our suffering may or may not take the same form as it did in the time of Jesus, depending on where we live, but the call to love others with an exceptional love remains. God promises that those who respond with mercy will receive much from God's hand—maybe not those things the world sees as valuable, but real blessings that come from God's hand. To the one who pardons comes pardon; to the one who gives come gifts from God's hand.

Call to Righteousness, Fruit, and Wise Building. The warning about following Jesus and not anyone else (v. 39) reflects a fundamental value of the church. Jesus is the center of the faith. The apostles he commissioned are called to reveal his way. Thus the importance of following the right teacher is important. One must hear Jesus, for he is the unique hub of the Christian faith, the mediator of our relationship to God. That claim is the offense of the gospel, which makes sharing Christ difficult in a world that compares religion to a vast interstate highway system where all roads lead to God. Jesus did not present himself as one of many ways, but as *the* way. In fact, it is this section of the parallel Sermon on the Mount that led me, as an unbeliever, to consider the Lord's claims more seriously. After reading it, I clearly felt that Jesus did not merely teach a way of wisdom, but the way to knowing God. The challenge to build wisely by responding to Jesus is what led me to him years ago.

There is also a great need for fruitfulness today in one's testimony for Christ. All too often the lost refuse to listen to the claims of Jesus because they know Christians who are hypocrites. When such a charge is raised, there is some value in pointing out that Christians are not perfect, just forgiven sinners—but that will only go so far. The church needs people who know God and walk with him in such a way that the roots of their relationship to God shine forth as light. Fruitfulness makes that clear.

In sum, this sermon is a timeless ethical outline of how believers should manifest the gracious character of the Father as his children. Mercy, love, and grace should dominate our character, even if it requires great personal risk.

THE SUMMARY SECTION (vv. 17–19) yields important applications, for it describes the varied elements in Jesus' ministry. Any ministry worth its salt should reflect compassion and not just be a ministry of words. Jesus showed how God cares for the people he loves. If God loves those to whom the church preaches, then certainly his servants should show that love. These verses also underscore the authority of Jesus. The people knew he had access to divine power. Mary could see that Jesus mediated God's power and forgiveness. What he did for sin on the cross, Jesus pictured in his healing ministry.

Call to Blessings and Woes. The blessings and woes possess two central points. (1) God is aware of what we are going through, and he promises to vindicate the faithful. We who belong to the kingdom can rest assured that our Lord will grant us the blessing of eternal restoration and reward. To start here is fundamental, because the ethics of Jesus call for sacrifice and patience. To love in a way that is unlike the world risks being misunderstood. Only those who rest in God's care and have assurance of his blessing can endure that hard path. These blessings, then, encourage us to remain strong before the world in the midst of weakness. We do not need to seek vindication for ourselves, we can turn the cheek, and we can be generous to those who will not be generous back. Acceptance comes from the Father, whom we seek to imitate. As a result, acceptance from others matters less.

(2) The blessings and woes also reflect God's values. Whom does he honor? He responds to the poor, the hungry, those who mourn, and those who are rejected. These categories reveal a major audience to whom he offers the hope of the gospel. However, they are also social descriptions of the condition of those who are blessed. I was personally insensitive to this aspect of the text until I began to minister periodically in Guatemala. It was there I began to ask serious questions about American values such as materialism and to consider the issue of being sensitive to the poor. In the Western world, such questions also scream out for consideration in some of our troubled urban centers. God cares for people such as these—not only to save their souls, but to bring them into a community that evidences God's care for them in terms of life's basic needs.

It is appropriate to ask: Why does God single out the poor and suffering and issue such stark warnings to the wealthy? Surely God is affirming the dignity of people whom the world treats as trash. If God cares for such as these, should his church not do the same? It will not do to run to Matthew and emasculate Luke's words of verse 20. The point Matthew makes about "poor in spirit" (Matt. 5:3) is a true one, but so is the note that Luke raises. God has designed the kingdom for the poor, like those to whom Jesus preached. It was our Lord who invited them in to be a part of what God was doing. God extends the hope of his blessing to the poor.

Such texts make me pause when I think of ministries aimed at the powerful or wealthy. Not that I believe such ministries are wrong, since God loves all people, but the question still remains: Why does God single out those in need? If the church possesses a call to reach out in compassion, love, and service to those in need, what better audience to evidence such a gift than the poor? Disciples should be sensitive to those to whom Jesus showed sensitivity. In fact, 1 Corinthians 1:26–31 makes a point out of this contrast in looking at the make-up of the church in Corinth. A commitment to reach those whom the world forgets highlights that every person is significant to God, even if the world views them as insignificant.

This suggests that the church be more involved than it is in ministries that reflect this priority. Such an emphasis does not represent an acceptance of a social gospel, since the social gospel is devoid of the redemptive message that is so central to God's saving work. What it does represent is the recognition that God seeks to redeem the total person and to create a community interested in all dimensions of life for those who are saved. There are evangelicals in other parts of the world who have much to teach us here. We should listen to them more humbly and carefully.[21]

Call to Love and Mercy. To exemplify love in a hostile world is difficult. It takes a supernatural perspective and a change of thinking. The world is used to dealing with people either on the basis of power, utility, or equal exchange. The idea of simple service and unconditional love are not in vogue. When Jesus calls us to love our enemies, I have a hard time seeing that love in the way we communicate with those who possess different values from our own. We must hold to our convictions while communicating a sensitive, loving concern. The world may misunderstand us, but that does not allow us to be insensitive or to harbor misunderstanding towards them.

Love, doing good, blessing, and praying for those who are our enemies also assumes another reality, that we are in relational contact with the outside

---

21. An example of such work is *Crisis and Hope in Latin America: An Evangelical Perspective*, by Emilio A. Nuñez and William D. Taylor (Pasadena, Calif.: William Carey, 1995). This work evidences a concern to understand the culture in which Latin Americans minister as well as deal with the life-and-death issues they must face daily.

world. The ability to be struck on the cheek means we are in striking distance and have risked making the effort to have contact. The fortress mentality that sometimes invades the church is a form of retreat, as well as a denial of what Jesus calls for from disciples in this sermon. It is an abandonment of the very relational ground that can turn a Saul into a Paul. To give to those who beg means we know where they can be found. To love as we wish to be loved means acknowledging the dignity of other people as made in the image of God. To love in a way that does not reflect some personal payback is to offer the world a different kind of love that is not based on what the self receives but on what we can give. It is to love in a way different from sinners.

Sadly, often we cannot love so selflessly even within the community of God, much less to our enemies. By failing to love, we fail to reveal the loving and merciful character of God. Perhaps one reason evangelism fails is because people cannot see the grace of God evidenced in the church's relationship to herself. To accomplish such an outreach and evidence such love means to depend totally on the Father, who will reward those who reflect his character to a needy but hostile world.

The connection between God's blessing and our ability to love should not be missed. Because of his blessing to us and our appreciation for him, we are able to love others. Because he gave, we can give. Because we know the joy of receiving from him, we are motivated to give to others. The actions Jesus calls for in his sermon apply to others what he has already applied to us. The deeper our understanding and appreciation of what God has done, the better prepared we will be to reflect his character to others.

Other attitudes also need to be developed. The Lord notes that overflowing blessing comes to those who are slow to condemn and quick to forgive. A censorious spirit is not open to love, since it is constantly evaluating everyone and everything around it. Judgment against another person is to be left in God's hands, and his judgment will be correct (cf. Rom. 12:17–21). This does not mean that the community lacks accountability, for Jesus addresses that question in verses 41–42. It does mean that people have a tendency to be hard on others while being lax on themselves. God's revealing how he transforms us is what should drive us, not a joy in finding others at fault. As forgiven people who rest in the reconciliation God's kindness brings, we should be quick to reflect such kindness to others.

Call to Righteousness, Fruit, and Wise Building. The ethical reversal Jesus calls for means we should be careful which teachers we follow. Many who teach about character are committed to developing character in a self-focused way, in a way that is effective in getting what we want or in a way that takes the easiest path possible. Such an agenda drove the Pharisees to try to control how others behaved. Zealous as they were, they were blind.

Trying to build ethical character while staying self-focused is the essence of blindness. We should choose our models carefully, following those who themselves are clear about following him. Only one teacher is worthy of being followed—Jesus himself.

If there is to be accountability, it must start with ourselves. We often are aware of little faults in others, such as our children or our spouses, while we ignore our own great faults. Jesus calls such priorities hypocrisy. He calls his disciples to self-accountability. Those who do the best job of restoring others in their walk are those who can restore themselves. That means being able to receive rebuke and honestly going before the Lord so that our beam may be removed. Only then are we ready to consider how to help a fellow believer remove the speck from his or her eye.

Jesus' ethical priorities also indicate that we are what we produce, especially when it comes to what we say. The mouth is a litmus test of who we are spiritually. If we evaluated the character and tone of our daily speech, would it register like acid on litmus paper or yield the sweet presence of a person secure in God's care? As James testifies, we need to learn how to control the tongue (James 3:1—12). Only the mature can do so.

In the end, the issue of our loyalty as disciples comes down to responding to Jesus in terms of what we do. His rebuke to those who call him "Lord, Lord," but ignore what he says, indicates just how seriously he takes concrete response. In fact, a biblical text or an exhortation from Jesus is not really understood until it is applied. The disciple who responds to Jesus and does what he calls for is able to stand up to the harsh realities of life in a fallen world. The disciple who learns to see and act in the world as Jesus calls the disciple to do is able to face the floods, that is, the disappointments and injuries that life often brings. In contrast, to ignore his teaching is to be set up to suffer a tragic loss. As sad as it is to lose one's home in a flood, it is sadder still for one's life to be swept away because the call and advice of God was ignored. So Jesus' sermon's final word to the disciple is: "Apply yourself to apply my teaching; it is wisdom that stands up when things get tough."

The sermon's remarks about knowing a tree by its fruit raises one of the more tricky pastoral issues in the passage. Can I read a person's spiritual position by the product I see in his or her life? After all, lots of "good" people have a host of good works but may not know God. On the other hand, some who claim to be Christians struggle to live in a way that honors God.

Three points need to be made about the sermon's imagery of fruit and how we handle such a question. (1) Jesus' remarks here are not designed to examine individual moments in life but the pattern of a career-long walk with God. This point is significant because everyone sins or perhaps even goes through a period of sin. Such people may deeply regret their failure afterwards, yet it can make them wonder if their "fruit" makes it impossible to say they know God. I received an e-mail recently from a counselor who asked me how to deal with three different teenagers who had the same problem. They were convinced that some sin they had committed was so severe it severed their relationship to Jesus to an unrecoverable level, even though they regretted it. The overapplication of a text like this with reference to a particular sin can do great damage particularly to someone who sensitively reacts to his or her spiritual failure.

(2) The text indicates that although fruit may not be a certain indicator, it can be a suggestive one. Paul was so concerned about the lack of Corinthian fruit that after a long period of time, he asked them to examine themselves to see if they were in the faith (2 Cor. 13:5). What raised the question for Paul was the incongruity between their walk and their claim to have a regenerated heart. But note how Paul raises the question. He does not state he knows the answer, looking in from the outside; rather, he raises the issue for their own reflection. There are significant pastoral lessons about how to proceed with the "difficult" cases here. Some believers do live "like mere men," not because it is commendable or acceptable, but because they turn away from God for a time (1 Cor. 3:1–3). Such cases need to be challenged, but we must be careful not to ignore what Jesus warns in this sermon about judging as we seek to address someone in such a condition.

(3) Scripture does seem clear that regenerated people do bear some sort of fruit. Total absence of fruit, particularly love, does raise the question about the presence of regeneration and faith (Rom. 8:1–16; James 2:14–26; 1 John 3:1–9). We are not here confusing salvation by faith with salvation by works. We are not saying that works save. Salvation is by faith through grace, but that grace bestows a changed heart that accepts God as Father and responds at least to some degree to his presence. If the seed of new faith is present, it will sprout, though to varying degrees in different people. Jesus is instructing his followers to grow in him, to listen to him. Those who do will not have to worry about looking for fruit; they will be producing it by his grace.

Luke 7:1–17

WHEN JESUS HAD FINISHED saying all this in the hearing of the people, he entered Capernaum. ²There a centurion's servant, whom his master valued highly, was sick and about to die. ³The centurion heard of Jesus and sent some elders of the Jews to him, asking him to come and heal his servant. ⁴When they came to Jesus, they pleaded earnestly with him, "This man deserves to have you do this, ⁵because he loves our nation and has built our synagogue." ⁶So Jesus went with them.

He was not far from the house when the centurion sent friends to say to him: "Lord, don't trouble yourself, for I do not deserve to have you come under my roof. ⁷That is why I did not even consider myself worthy to come to you. But say the word, and my servant will be healed. ⁸For I myself am a man under authority, with soldiers under me. I tell this one, 'Go,' and he goes; and that one, 'Come,' and he comes. I say to my servant, 'Do this,' and he does it."

⁹When Jesus heard this, he was amazed at him, and turning to the crowd following him, he said, "I tell you, I have not found such great faith even in Israel." ¹⁰Then the men who had been sent returned to the house and found the servant well.

¹¹Soon afterward, Jesus went to a town called Nain, and his disciples and a large crowd went along with him. ¹²As he approached the town gate, a dead person was being carried out—the only son of his mother, and she was a widow. And a large crowd from the town was with her. ¹³When the Lord saw her, his heart went out to her and he said, "Don't cry."

¹⁴Then he went up and touched the coffin, and those carrying it stood still. He said, "Young man, I say to you, get up!" ¹⁵The dead man sat up and began to talk, and Jesus gave him back to his mother.

¹⁶They were all filled with awe and praised God. "A great prophet has appeared among us," they said. "God has come to help his people." ¹⁷This news about Jesus spread throughout Judea and the surrounding country.

THE ISSUES IN Luke 7:1–8:3 surround the call to faith and questions about the identity of Jesus. He heals, but in doing so he forgives sin and raises someone from the dead, so that people wonder who he is. The populace anticipates a prophetic office, but Jesus' actions suggest more. Jesus' identity raises the issue of a proper response to him. Faith is a central feature in the stories of the centurion and the sinful woman. While the relationship between John the Baptist and Jesus shows that the divine calendar has reached a turning point, Jesus does the work of the era of fulfillment.

The healing of the centurion's servant in 7:1–10 is another of Jesus' miracles that reveal spiritual realities. What makes this story different is that the major figure is a Gentile, a centurion, even though he never shows up in the passage.[1] The major topic of the healing is faith in light of Jesus' authority. A second theme of Luke's also emerges: Jews and Gentiles can get along with and respect one another. The unity of Jew and Gentile in Christ is emphasized more explicitly in the book of Acts and in Paul's letter to the Ephesians (Eph. 2:11–22).

Jesus is now in Capernaum, one of the few specific notes of locale in the Gospel. The same pattern of word and deed that we saw in 4:16–44 appears here. Jesus speaks about his authority in 6:20–49 and then demonstrates it in 7:1–17. The centurion,[2] who as a military man would be among the wealthy in the society, has come to appreciate what Jesus has been doing. Though we do not know his national background, we do know he is not Jewish. Perhaps he is a potential proselyte or, more likely, a soldier who follows the Roman custom of respecting religion as a socially healthy force in the empire.[3]

This centurion has a slave near death. He sends a delegation of Jewish elders to ask Jesus to heal this man. These are probably Jewish civil leaders, not synagogue leaders.[4] The emissaries not only bring the man's request, but

---

1. Luke has several scenes where the major figure does not speak directly: see 7:36–50 (the sinful woman), 10:38–42 (Mary), and 16:19–31(Lazarus). The parallel to this story is Matthew 8:5–13. In all likelihood, Matthew has telescoped this event, since he has the centurion address Jesus directly. But in ancient culture a commissioned person speaking for someone is like speaking to the person directly, so that Matthew, condensing the account, merely simplifies the account. What Luke's more detailed edition allows him to show is that cooperation between Jew and Gentile is possible.

2. A centurion could be a mercenary soldier or a soldier who helped collect taxes; cf. Fitzmyer, *Luke*, 651.

3. Josephus, *Antiquities* 16.6.2 §§ 162–65; 19.6.3 §§ 300–301.

4. Marshall, *Commentary on Luke*, 280.

they also lobby for him, arguing that he is worthy of aid. He has contributed to the building of the local synagogue. Such acts of generosity are not without ancient precedent.[5] He loves Israel, which may mean he has shown respect for the nation. The question raised here is significant at two levels: Will Jesus minister to someone from outside of Israel, and will he minister to a wealthy man?

Jesus turns to go to the man's house when a second delegation arrives. They report the response of the centurion in the first person, indicating that they are speaking for him. His message declares his own unworthiness in having Jesus enter his home. He does not want to trouble the teacher, but only wishes him to heal his slave. He understands Jesus' authority and knows that if he just issues the order, the healing will occur. To drive the point home, he illustrates his understanding by appealing to his own role as a man in authority. All he needs to do is issue an order, and it is obeyed.

These remarks amaze Jesus, insofar as a Gentile has such faith. In fact, this Gentile has faith that is more perceptive and sensitive than anything Jesus has seen in Israel. What impresses him is both the centurion's humility and his understanding of Jesus' power (the ability to heal from a distance). One can argue that the essence of faith is humility: the recognition of the uniqueness of God's power and our unworthiness before it, while trusting in God's care. In a closing note, the text affirms that the healing takes place, just as the centurion has anticipated. The power of Jesus and the presence of faith form a powerful combination.

From the raising of a widow's only son in 7:11–17 emerge two basic questions about Jesus: What kind of understanding does the Israelite public have of him, and why do they think of him this way? The resuscitation of the boy requires Jesus' compassionate involvement with this widow, but it also suggests the Old Testament ministries of Elijah and Elisha (1 Kings 17:17–24; 2 Kings 4:8–37).[6] This connection helps us see why the public responded as they did.

The event starts simply enough in the little village of Nain. We do not know for certain the location of this town, but it is probably three miles west of Endor and twenty miles southwest of Capernaum.[7] As Jesus passes by the town, he encounters a funeral involving a widow, who has lost her only son. This detail is important, because in that culture a widow without children was alone and in need of protection. The Old Testament portrays widows and

---

5. Fitzmyer, *Luke*, 652.

6. C. A. Evans and J. A. Sanders, *Luke and Scripture: The Function of Sacred Tradition in Luke-Acts* (Minneapolis: Fortress, 1993), 223–24.

7. Marshall, *Commentary on Luke*, 284.

orphans as among the most helpless of people and uses the figure of mourning over the death of an only son as a sign of a painful loss (Jer. 6:26; Amos 8:10; Zech. 12:10). The death probably took place that very day, since the Jews usually buried immediately.[8] The body rested on a burial plank, not a closed coffin, though it would have been wrapped in cloth. Mourners followed the plank as the community shared the grief of the widow.[9]

Jesus stops the procession just outside the city and touches the burial plank. That touch renders him unclean (Num. 19:11), but it also expresses his compassionate concern. Jesus simply tells the corpse to arise, a cruel remark unless he has the power to bring it to pass. The dead man—or better, formerly dead man—sits up. In contrast to Elijah, who stretched over a corpse three times (1 Kings 17:21), and Elisha, who touched a child with a staff laid over him (2 Kings 4:31, 34–35), Jesus simply utters a word. With his work done, Jesus hands the lad over to his mother in language that parallels 1 Kings 17:23. Jesus has restored the previously broken relationship between mother and son with renewed life.

The crowd concludes that Jesus is "a great prophet." No doubt the biblical parallels are what produce this conclusion. They have respect for him, though in the context of the entire story of Jesus, Luke will show that granting Jesus prophetic status is not enough. The crowd also realizes that God is visiting the people, for these kinds of miracles are not everyday affairs. The ancients often recognized that unusual events signaled God was in their midst. The crowd here sees a connection between God and Jesus. So the report spreads far and wide throughout Judea and the countryside.

Bridging Contexts

THE MIRACLE OF the healing of the centurion's slave is less a miracle story and more a character study. The bulk of the event treats the understanding of the centurion. He is the central character, and we should concentrate on what is said about him. He is an exemplary character, even though he is an ethnic outsider and is undoubtedly among the wealthy. He represents the universality of the gospel. Here also is a soldier with compassion, reflecting the type of person John the Baptist described in 3:14. Culturally, this man occupies three positions that could make him unresponsive, yet his eyes and ears have been open to respond. Jesus is able to say things about him that he cannot say of anyone in the nation of Israel. Thus any applications from this text must come from considering his character.

---

8. *Mishnah, Sanhedrin* 6:5; 23:4–5; cf. Acts 5:1–11.
9. *Mishnah, Megillah* 4:3.

One other feature of this centurion text is crucial—the various combinations that are represented in Jesus' encounter with him. We have the crossing of ethnic boundaries as a Gentile soldier meets a Jewish teacher and prophet. We have the crossing of social boundaries as the soldier, who has means enough to contribute to a synagogue, meets a prophet who ministers most often among the poor. We have the crossing of believing community boundaries, as Jesus, the one who brings the way of salvation to God, ministers to one interested in supporting religious ideals but one who has not yet made a personal decision.

All of the above elements cross over into our world. Jesus does not refuse the man because he is of a different race. Do we have such exclusionary clauses in our ministries? Jesus does not worry about class. Do we make such distinctions in targeting those to whom we will minister? Neither does Jesus argue for a type of separationism that says the centurion is not among God's people, so he cannot receive ministry. Sometimes we underestimate the power of the testimony of the gospel to cross ethnic, social, or even lines of belief. Sometimes the way a person is drawn to God is through the indication that God can cross such boundaries to touch and change a heart.

Moreover, although Jesus is socially in the less valued position as far as the world is concerned, what he has to offer makes him the one with more to offer than the one he helps. Sometimes we let external factors affect how we see things. For example, when interacting with Christians from other cultures, we may assume those in the "superior" cultural, technological, or educational position have more to offer. Such biases are subtle, but all too real. Yet the very circumstances more socially humble believers have lived in frequently make them more sensitive to a whole array of issues that we are slow to understand.

Two personal situations are relevant, one in Latin America and the other in Eastern Europe after the fall of communism. I have traveled there with believers, only to be enlightened with how they understand poverty, suffering, persecution, and other circumstances where people have lived under severe limitations that I can hardly begin to understand. I found myself sitting at their feet, learning from their reflection on what the Lord taught them through those experiences and from their reflection on Scripture, and asking them questions about how one can best share Jesus in such circumstances. Other believers who have been to these parts of the world have told me of similar experiences. I have found a similar situation in watching some of my brothers and sisters in Christ minister in the inner city. It is not always the case that the teacher comes from a higher social station or has a higher degree!

The miracle of the resuscitation in Nain reveals much about Jesus' compassion and the extent of his authority. We may often feel concern for another's pain or suffering, but what do we do to meet it? Sometimes the first step is awkward, since we wrestle with how our effort to reach out may be received, or we wonder if by bringing up the painful topic, we will only make the pain worse. But sometimes the most effective ministry occurs in a small act of compassion, not in an attempt to solve the pain. Jesus did more here than we are able to do, but the way in which he acted is important. The touch on the coffin showed his willingness to identify with the situation and not back away from it. Perhaps the best we can do is offer a compassionate shoulder or a listening ear. But this kind of "touch" often reaches below the skin and meets the pain of a hurting heart.

As we have already seen, Jesus' miracles are audiovisuals of great truths, and no truth is more fundamental than his authority to reverse death. What was the most tragic of moments, the loss of an only child, Jesus turns into a reunion. The story connects with the sense of tragedy one feels at death and shows how Jesus has the power to reverse its presence. Our ministry of gospel should offer the hope that in Jesus death can be overcome.

The final point of connection is the crowd's speculation over the significance of Jesus. He is such a crucial figure in social history that every person must decide where he fits. The crowd expresses its opinion, and so must we. But I wonder if the crowd struggles with different things than we do. This ancient crowd does not struggle with the issue of Jesus' miracle; they are there and see it. What they struggle to understand is his great authority. Today, the battle over understanding Jesus is more comprehensive, since we are distant from the witnesses of his ministry. We may accept he was a great religious teacher and may give him the respect of a prophet. But the reality of his miracles, especially one as dramatic as this, is often questioned.

The great claims Jesus made about who he is are doubted today. Distance from Jesus allows a kind of fog to set in. Many people comment on Jesus without knowing what Scripture teaches about him. Others challenge its portrayal of him. But if Scripture does not help us understand Jesus accurately, then how can we know anything about him? His works and words go together, and so does the portrait that Scripture gives. Though people today cannot see him as those in Nain did, they must see him in us or hear him in the testimony of Scripture.

THE FIRST POINT of application regarding the centurion is that he, even as an outsider, had developed a good reputation with people from other backgrounds. One is reminded of the exhortation about elders in the church that they are to have the respect of those outside the community of faith (1 Tim. 3:7). This man achieved this reputation because he showed respect to the Jews and their customs. His support of the synagogue, even though he was not yet a believer, shows someone sensitive to the attitudes of others. The Jews, in turn, were responsive to him, indicating how mutual respect is one means of overcoming cultural and ethnic barriers. Luke is pointing out here that Jews and Gentiles can respect one another if each side makes the necessary effort, especially when each group is open to God's way.

I am reminded of how missionaries respond to entering a foreign field or how one might approach a multicultural environment. The natural response is to honor one's own cultural customs and keep to one's own circle. Missionaries sometimes do this by associating primarily with fellow missionaries. But in a multicultural context, this is a form of isolation. One ministers less effectively to people of a different background and slows the process of learning to love, respect, and understand them unless one makes a concerted effort to enter into their world and attempts to appreciate their culture. In our country, as we become more diverse, Christians will need to develop cultural sensitivity if we hope to share the gospel in all the possible contexts. The Bible communicates a respect for "God-fearers" like Cornelius (Acts 10) and this centurion. With such openness we can build new bridges for the gospel where we might have formerly isolated ourselves through fear or ignorance.

Another application is that a position of power and wealth can be used in ways that do not use people but serve them. Here is a man of wealth who used his resources and power to the benefit of those around him. Here is a man of wealth who seemed open to the worship of God.

A look at two sets of statistics about giving in this country is appalling. The average person in this country gives less than five percent of his income to charity or other causes, though we consume over twenty percent of the earth's resources. One wonders if percentages in the church are any different. By the world's standards, most Christians in this country are wealthy. But do we use our privileged position for ourselves or for others, especially those in the household of faith? The Jews argued the centurion was worthy of Jesus' attention. Part of the reason was his exemplary generosity and openness towards the people of God to whom Jesus came to minister. Should we who know him be any different?

The central lesson of the centurion story is the nature of the man's faith. His humility had allowed others to honor him as a worthy man, but standing before the presence of God's messenger, he understood that God owed him nothing. He did not even feel worthy of being visited by God's agent. Yet he also understood God's authority to heal and his compassion. He believed Jesus could heal by a simple sovereign word even at a physical distance—a situation that applies even more today in light of Jesus' presence in heaven. And he knew that Jesus cared enough to do so. Such faith and humility in approaching God's power are what amaze Jesus. This passage calls us to possess a similar faith. God owes us nothing, yet he extends his compassion to us. God honors us with his grace, not because we deserve it, but because he cares (1 John 4:9–10).

In the story of the resuscitation of the widow's son we see the powerful reversal of death. Jesus deals here with the most fundamental obstacle we will ever face. If death were the end, then there would be no hope in this life or after (1 Cor 15:12–19). The judgment of God would make no sense, nor would his claim to restore and redeem us. Thus this miracle testifies to a central aspect of Christian hope. Its touching image reminds us that renewal and reunion are not an impossible dream. God promises to restore to life those who know his touch. In Jesus God takes the initiative to accomplish this renewal.

I recall a funeral I attended of one of my former professors. When I was a student, our school had celebrated the fiftieth anniversary of his coming to faith in Jesus. On that occasion he spoke of his hope in Jesus, planted in his heart in the 1920s when he was a young man. At the funeral, as speaker after speaker rejoiced at the ministry of his life and in his now being present with the Lord, I reflected on the great hope of overcoming death that we as Christians have, a hope this miracle pictures so vividly.

Even as I write, a six-year-old girl lies dying of leukemia in the hospital, just having lapsed out of a remission that looked so encouraging. Our church community, along with many others in our city, had interceded before the Lord for over eighteen months to spare her. On the one hand, I ask, "Why, Lord, are you taking her so young and so slowly? Why this pain, especially for her parents?" On the other hand, this text reminds me that ultimately God has control over bringing new life out of death and that one day, perhaps soon, should she not recover, this little girl will be free from her pain and present with the Lord.

What this dual reflection about these two dear believers tells me is that whether a saint dies old, after years of testimony, or dies tragically at a young age, the hope of what the miracle of the widow's son pictures is still vibrantly alive. Death is not the end for those who know him. It involves a transfer into a level of life not known on this earth. While this miracle reminds us of our frailty and mortality, it also shouts out to us about God's power to raise and transform. No wonder the crowd who saw this miracle was filled with awe. We should be too, as we contemplate his creative power and compassion.

Luke 7:18–35

JOHN'S DISCIPLES TOLD him about all these things. Calling two of them, [19]he sent them to the Lord to ask, "Are you the one who was to come, or should we expect someone else?"

[20]When the men came to Jesus, they said, "John the Baptist sent us to you to ask, 'Are you the one who was to come, or should we expect someone else?'"

[21]At that very time Jesus cured many who had diseases, sicknesses and evil spirits, and gave sight to many who were blind. [22] So he replied to the messengers, "Go back and report to John what you have seen and heard: The blind receive sight, the lame walk, those who have leprosy are cured, the deaf hear, the dead are raised, and the good news is preached to the poor. [23]Blessed is the man who does not fall away on account of me."

[24]After John's messengers left, Jesus began to speak to the crowd about John: "What did you go out into the desert to see? A reed swayed by the wind? [25]If not, what did you go out to see? A man dressed in fine clothes? No, those who wear expensive clothes and indulge in luxury are in palaces. [26]But what did you go out to see? A prophet? Yes, I tell you, and more than a prophet. [27]This is the one about whom it is written:

> "'I will send my messenger ahead of you,
>   who will prepare your way before you.'

[28]I tell you, among those born of women there is no one greater than John; yet the one who is least in the kingdom of God is greater than he."

[29](All the people, even the tax collectors, when they heard Jesus' words, acknowledged that God's way was right, because they had been baptized by John. [30]But the Pharisees and experts in the law rejected God's purpose for themselves, because they had not been baptized by John.)

[31] "To what, then, can I compare the people of this generation? What are they like? [32]They are like children sitting in the marketplace and calling out to each other:

"'We played the flute for you,
and you did not dance;
we sang a dirge,
and you did not cry.'

³³For John the Baptist came neither eating bread nor drinking wine, and you say, 'He has a demon.' ³⁴The Son of Man came eating and drinking, and you say, 'Here is a glutton and a drunkard, a friend of tax collectors and "sinners."' ³⁵But wisdom is proved right by all her children."

THIS PASSAGE HAS three subunits: John's question to Jesus (vv. 18–23), Jesus' view of John (vv. 24–30), and Jesus' parable of rebuke (vv. 31–35). John's question in verse 19 is significant because it signals that even Jesus' forerunner is struggling to understand the nature of Jesus' ministry. Jesus is not the type of agent John was expecting, so he sends emisaries to Jesus just to make sure.[1] Jesus' reassurance of John makes the latter a figure like Theophilus (1:4). John's question is also significant because it follows immediately the crowd's recognition that Jesus is a great prophet. When the Baptist asks if Jesus is the "one who was to come," the question intimates the inadequacy of the popular perception of Jesus. Popular perceptions are often wrong. In the case of Jesus, they are also short of the mark.

John's question emerges because his disciples report to him what Jesus is doing. The word of his miracles gives encouragement that Jesus is a significant figure, but something still does not fit right. Where is the powerful sovereign judge John predicted (3:7–9)? From prison, John sends two of his followers to ask Jesus if he really is the one to come. The use of two messengers will certify that the reply comes back faithfully to John (Deut. 19:15).[2]

The question John asks shocks some students of the Scripture, who cannot accept the fact that John doubts Jesus.[3] His question is specific. He does not wonder whether Jesus has been sent from God; he simply wants confirmation that his ministry is the promised ministry of deliverance. Even the best of God's servants need reassurance from time to time. The reference to "the stronger one who was to come" recalls John's own words in 3:15–16. So John is asking if Jesus is the Messiah.

---

1. The parallel to this unit is Matthew 11:2–19.

2. Danker, *Jesus and the New Age*, 163.

3. So, for example, W. F. Arndt, *Luke* (St. Louis: Concordia, 1956), 209, who argues John is only seeking to reassure his disciples.

The envoys ask the question in the same words John gave them. Jesus' reply is not direct, but calls for an inference. Before recording the reply, Luke interjects a reminder about the scope of Jesus' ministry; it has involved healings, exorcisms, and even sight given to the blind.[4] Jesus' ministry "graced" many with restoration. The envoys are simply to report what they have seen, using a collage of Old Testament phrases from Isaiah (Isa. 35:5–6; 26:19; 29:18–19; 61:1), all of which refer to the coming period of decisive deliverance. Jesus' ministry signals fulfillment of these prophecies. The reply closes with a beatitude that calls for faith. Blessing belongs to the person who is not offended by Jesus. His style of ministry might not be with the powerful flair of position and status the world expects, but he has been sent from God nonetheless.

Jesus then raises the question about John for the crowd. He notes that people did not journey to see reeds in the desert or fine clothes when they went to see John. The reference to reeds is either an allusion to the scenery at the location of John's ministry or a figurative, ironic reference to John as a spineless man. Either is possible, but since the next statement about fine clothes should be taken literally, the reference to reeds is also likely literal. People did not go to see John because of the scenery at the Jordan River or for a fashion statement! They came for another reason: to see a prophet.

In fact, John was more than a prophet. At the time of his birth he was the greatest man yet born, since he represented the end of an era and pointed to the dawn of a new era of realization in God's plan. The words of Scripture in verse 27 from Malachi 3:1 point to his forerunner role. Like Elijah boldly preaching to the nation, John declared God's will to the people and helped prepare them for that new era. The imagery of John's going before the people[5] also recalls the language of Exodus, where the Shekinah guided and directed the people in the desert (Ex. 23:20). God was pointing the way in this forerunner, a witness to the approaching realization of promise.

Yet John's greatness is nothing compared to those who participate in the new era's blessings and benefits. Jesus' remark in verse 28 is one of the greatest affirmations of the believer's status in Scripture. To belong to the kingdom is a great privilege. John is the bridge between the two eras, but those who follow where the Baptist points come into a closer, more intimate relationship

---

4. The two terms for disease in the verse suggest an escalation from simple maladies to more debilitating illness.

5. One can argue that the second person reference in the Malachi 3:1 quote is an indirect allusion to Jesus. If so, then it means that John goes before Jesus. But the context of these verses highlights the people's response, and the theme reflects what Luke 1:17 taught. So a reference to going before the people is more likely.

to God that transcends even the best the old age offered. That is how great Jesus' work is in this new era.

In an aside, Luke again notes the varying responses to John, setting up the parable that follows. The people and tax collectors are acknowledging God's work and responding to John's baptism, but the leadership remain hesitant. They do not recognize their need to repent and so reject God's counsel. The reversal of where one expects piety to reside signals another surprise in the events of fulfillment.

Jesus therefore warns the current generation of religious leaders about their response to John. He does so through a parable, as he often does when discussing the kingdom or God's plan (Matt. 13:24; 18:23; 22:2; 25:1; Luke 13:8). He compares them to an ancient game of children at play.[6] One can call this comparison "the parable of the brats." But are there two bickering groups or just one group of upset children? And who are the complainers— God's messengers or the Jewish rejecters? The second question is easier than the first, since Jesus is clearly comparing the complaining children to this generation, that is, to the Jewish objectors (Luke 7:33–34). The parable is told from their perspective. They are the children who are seated and refuse to play, complaining that John and Jesus do not dance to their tune. Whether they play a light tune on the flute or a funeral dirge, these two men do not follow the Jewish leadership's desires. They charge John with being demonic and Jesus with gluttony and questionable friendships. Jesus' open effort to reach sinners and represents a repudiation of the leadership's more separatist approach (5:31–32; 15:1–32).

Those who respond, wisdom's children, are contrasted with those who do not, like the comparison in verses 29–30.[7] Jesus' associations and John's call have registered with some. The presence of the restored vindicates God's way, revealing his wisdom. The divine attempt to reach out to sinners means that they should not be ignored but pursued. The rebuke through the parable is another way to say that the leadership is hardhearted in its rejection of God's way.

Bridging Contexts

THE MAJOR FEATURES of this passage are the details it gives on Jesus' and John's ministries, the nature of John's reaction to Jesus, and the importance of the new era. Though John and Jesus are unique figures in the plan of God, some characteristics in their ministries are fun-

---

6. Marshall, *Commentary on Luke*, 300; Nolland, *Luke 1:1–9:20*, 344.

7. On the figure of wisdom's children, see Sirach 4:11; Proverbs 8:32–33; Nolland, *Luke 1:1–9:20*, 346.

damental to any outreach effort. In fact, one of the fascinating aspects of this passage is the different styles used to accomplish the same goal: bringing sinners to God. The fundamental issue in evangelism is not in the style or form of evangelism, but in the commitment to lead people to God. John, the ascetic withdrawn in the desert, and Jesus, the "gluttonous" friend of tax collectors and sinners, are both accomplishing God's will. We should major not on style, but on having substance in our ministries.

Issues of style are still with us today. For years I was exposed to Young Life, beginning when I was an unsaved teenager. Young Life was about the only religious meeting I could tolerate. The singing was fun, the skits were always a laugh, and the speaker always put the message at a level I could relate to, in which I was forced to think about what was being said. I know that for some, this laid-back, teenage style of evangelistic outreach receives disdain as lacking substance. But it was a perfect place for my saved friends to bring me as an unsaved person. I am not sure where I would be today if a ministry like Young Life had not existed.

As an adult who serves in the church, I find myself every now and then reminding myself of what it was like to be a teenager, especially when I see present-day youth ministries doing things that might strike me as odd. My own past experience has taught me to be more patient about what I see and not to mix style and substance. This does not mean that sometimes these efforts cannot go too far, but it does warn me that sometimes my adult views are matters of taste versus real substantive objections as to what is taking place. Many youth leaders know what it is to be accused of lowering standards to minister. Most of them need to be given a break as they try to reach out to kids who need relationships built with them as a means of considering a walk with God.

Another key point of tone here is that Jesus' lack of messianic flash does not mean his ministry lacks authenticity. John raises questions because his preconceived scheme of how things should work comes up short. Jesus impresses people not through claims and pomp, but through substantive ministry. It is not "what is up front" that counts, but what is in the heart. Style tells us little compared to substance.

We need to be careful not to confuse our expectations with the variety of styles God uses in ministry to reach a wide array of different types of people. Sometimes God is doing something powerful, but we miss it because of our expectations of what he should do and how. John anticipated Jesus would take an instant road to glory. When he did not, John had questions. How often do we fall into the same trap? We sometimes expect God to do something a certain way, and when he does not, we think that he has failed. Such expectations may cover a variety of things—from God's helping to make a certain business situation successful, to God's promising to heal us from a debilitating condition, to our expectation that the Christian life will be free of hardship. Any of the preconditions for how God must work may work against us when he chooses to build character by taking us down a harder road.

Furthermore, we sometimes also place the same kind of expectations on those who minister to us. If they do not take us down a path of comfort or encouragement, then we conclude God is not working through them. Sometimes the truth needs to be told that life with God is not always the road to prosperity. God can and does bless through hardship. Will we hear such a message if it comes from the Lord? Can we see God in the midst of events that go a different way from what we had hoped or would have designed if we had been at the planning table with God?

With the message of reality that Jesus gives John about the surprisingly difficult and humble nature of his ministry also comes an exhortation that is almost too much to fathom. To be a saint in this era is to have a spiritual advantage that the saints of old would have loved to have had (cf. 10:23–24). Our resting in the grace of Jesus' forgiveness, now obtained once for all, and our permanent access to God through the Spirit are benefits the old era lacked. Even as we await the rest of what God will do, we tend to underestimate or underappreciate what he has already done. John the Baptist has nothing over us when it comes to access to God's grace. Hard as it is to believe, we are in a greater position than he was when he was ministering as a forerunner to Jesus.

THE MAJOR ISSUES of this text are John's relationship to Jesus and questions about ministry style and response. At a theological level, the subordination of John to Jesus is most obvious. What is surprising is the subordination of the prophet John to any who belong to the kingdom (v. 28). That is to say, a distinct break in God's plan of salvation came with Jesus' arrival (16:16). The blessing of those in the kingdom is greater than anything a prophet of the old era could bring to the table.

This observation is significant, because often we feel that the prophets of old had all the advantages. We think how great it would have been to be with Moses, Isaiah, or John the Baptist. How wonderful to see God "really" work. But this passage indicates that anyone who truly knows Jesus has greater blessings. Those Old Testament prophets would love to experience what we as believers have (1 Peter 1:10–22). It is easy to take our blessings for granted. The resources we have are so great. Just think, we have the Spirit of God within us and within our communities. We possess a forgiveness that is complete because of Jesus' finished work on the cross. They are greater than the more temporary, individualized bestowals of the old era. Paul underscores that the ministry of the current era has a new and greater depth than that of the past (2 Cor. 3–4). God has given the church all the gifts we need to be effective in ministry, provided everyone does his or her part (Rom. 12; 1 Cor. 12; Eph. 4:7–16).

Jesus' ministry is one of substance, not mere claims. Even when John asked him directly about his identity, Jesus' only response was to point to his works. The Savior refused to trumpet his claims far and wide. In an era where advertising often calls on us to boast our accomplishments and our record of service, Jesus presents a different perspective. Claims are a dime a dozen, but in-depth ministry speaks volumes. Jesus simply let John deduce who he was on the basis of his works. They indicate that Jesus is the Messiah promised in the Old Testament. Our ministries should have similar substance that points the way to its origin.

Jesus is again the central issue for Luke. All the other applications are irrelevant if one has not responded to him. As Jesus told John, "Blessed is the man who does not fall away on account of me."

The value of John's struggle should not be missed. Here is a man of God needing reassurance that Jesus is truly the one he anticipated. We sometimes think that the great saints never doubted. In doing so, we deny that they were normal human beings. The Scripture is honest and open about such struggles and doubts, just as the Christian community today should be. The way to deal with them is to express them, as John did. However, with the expression of doubt should be an open and receptive ear prepared to hear the answer. The difference between healthy doubt and destructive doubt is not the uttering of uncertainty but the response that follows it. The laments of the Psalter teach us that saints can be brutally honest on how they feel about God, but they also teach us that after they share their complaint with the Lord, they humbly await his reply. Disappointment often calls us to a deeper, less self-focused walk with God.[8]

The response to tax collectors and sinners also suggests that we can anticipate being surprised at who might respond to the gospel. In fact, some of those we might least expect will respond. This is why we can never anticipate whom God might bring to himself through us. We must be ready to share the gospel with anyone, even with those who at first may seem impossible cases.

---

8. For a thoughtful study of this issue, see Philip Yancey, *Disappointment with God* (Grand Rapids: Zondervan, 1992).

The differences in style also contribute to this emphasis. One of my best friends and I came to the Lord in very different ways. I was brought to the Lord in a low-key evangelistic style over a five-year period. My friend did not hear the gospel until he was in college and came to the Lord within a few weeks of hearing the gospel for the first time. He was impacted by a confrontational style of evangelism that had turned me off. We often laugh at the different means God used to bring us to himself. I needed a long, slow process; he needed to be whacked by a two-by-four! The differences in John's and Jesus' style remind us that different people are reached in different ways.

We also learn something here about those who reject Jesus. The parable of the brats indicates how superficially pious people sometimes want God to approach them on their own terms. They want God to respond to their music, rather than follow God's tune. People are often uncomfortable responding to God's call that they must come to him, recognizing their need for his grace and forgiveness. Do we ask God to serve us? Or do we serve him? The passage ultimately makes it clear that Jesus is the only way. The blessing of being greater than a prophet comes only from following his call to enter into God's grace and to dance to the music of the divine musician.

NOW ONE OF the Pharisees invited Jesus to have dinner with him, so he went to the Pharisee's house and reclined at the table. ³⁷When a woman who had lived a sinful life in that town learned that Jesus was eating at the Pharisee's house, she brought an alabaster jar of perfume, ³⁸and as she stood behind him at his feet weeping, she began to wet his feet with her tears. Then she wiped them with her hair, kissed them and poured perfume on them.

³⁹When the Pharisee who had invited him saw this, he said to himself, "If this man were a prophet, he would know who is touching him and what kind of woman she is—that she is a sinner."

⁴⁰Jesus answered him, "Simon, I have something to tell you."

"Tell me, teacher," he said.

⁴¹"Two men owed money to a certain moneylender. One owed him five hundred denarii, and the other fifty. ⁴²Neither of them had the money to pay him back, so he canceled the debts of both. Now which of them will love him more?"

⁴³Simon replied, "I suppose the one who had the bigger debt canceled."

"You have judged correctly," Jesus said.

⁴⁴Then he turned toward the woman and said to Simon, "Do you see this woman? I came into your house. You did not give me any water for my feet, but she wet my feet with her tears and wiped them with her hair. ⁴⁵You did not give me a kiss, but this woman, from the time I entered, has not stopped kissing my feet. ⁴⁶You did not put oil on my head, but she has poured perfume on my feet. ⁴⁷Therefore, I tell you, her many sins have been forgiven—for she loved much. But he who has been forgiven little loves little."

⁴⁸Then Jesus said to her, "Your sins are forgiven."

⁴⁹The other guests began to say among themselves, "Who is this who even forgives sins?"

⁵⁰Jesus said to the woman, "Your faith has saved you; go in peace."

8:1 After this, Jesus traveled about from one town and village to another, proclaiming the good news of the kingdom of

God. The Twelve were with him, [2]and also some women who had been cured of evil spirits and diseases: Mary (called Magdalene) from whom seven demons had come out; [3] Joanna the wife of Cuza, the manager of Herod's household; Susanna; and many others. These women were helping to support them out of their own means.

SINNERS RESPONDED TO John, and they also responded to Jesus. The reasons for their response become clear in this passage, where Jesus' approach to sinners makes a striking contrast to that of the Pharisees. This passage is also the first of two that commend the faith response of women to Jesus. Thus, the issue of faith continues to take center stage in Luke's account.

The central themes of this account are linked to the main characters.[1] The woman illustrates the gratitude, boldness, and humility of faith. The Pharisee pictures separatism confronted by Jesus. Jesus explains why sinners should be pursued with his message. He also reveals how forgiveness possesses transforming power.

Jesus is asked to dinner and accepts the invitation. Even though the Pharisees oppose him, he accepts the opportunity to visit with some of them. As was common in the ancient world, the guests recline on cushions beside the table. Since Jesus is a public figure, the door to this meal likely remains open, so that interested people can enter, sit on the edge of the room, and hear the discussion. The rebuke in verse 39 is not because the woman has come to the meal, but because she did not stay on the sidelines.

The woman says nothing in this narrative, but her actions produce a wide range of discussion.[2] Her sin is not identified. Perhaps she is a prostitute or has engaged in some other promiscuity to gain her reputation. But she boldly enters into the room and anoints Jesus' feet with a jar of expensive perfume. That act reflects great sacrifice, for such perfume was very costly. If she used nard, for example, the cost would be about 300 denarii a pound, an average person's annual wage! Such perfume, like myrrh, was used for burial or to purify priests (Ex. 30:25–30).[3] The presence of this

---

1. This passage is unique to Luke. Though some equate it with Matthew 26:6–13; Mark 14:3–9; John 12:1–8, it really is a distinct account. In these other passages, the woman is not a notorious sinner, nor is the host a Pharisee.

2. The name of this woman is never given. She is not Mary Magdalene, who is introduced in the next event. Efforts to tie the two together are late.

3. See also Josephus, *Antiquities* 3.8.6 § 205; 19.9.1 § 358.

perfume indicates that the woman treats Jesus as an important visitor. Moved by the moment, she weeps as she anoints Jesus and kisses his feet. The action reflects her humility.

But the action is shocking to Jesus' host. Taken aback, the Pharisee begins to think to himself that Jesus must not be a prophet to allow such a woman to come into contact with him. The text uses a "contrary to fact" second class conditional clause to present the Pharisee's remark, so that the leader clearly doubts Jesus' prophetic credentials. Ironically, Jesus reads his mind and tells a parable that explains his actions.

The parable pictures two debtors: one with a fifty denarii debt and the other with a five hundred denarii debt (a two-month's debt versus a twenty-month debt for a basic wage earner). The debt collector discovers that neither of them can pay. Yet unlike most collectors, who would turn up the heat, he forgives each debt. Now, Jesus asks, who would love the collector more? Simon gives an astute reply: the one who has been forgiven more. Here is the heart of Jesus' relational ethic. Unlike the Pharisee, who can only dwell on the sinner's past record, Jesus prefers to see the potential that love and forgiveness possess for changing a person's heart. So he points out how the woman cared for him in a way his host has not. He mentions the washing of his feet, the greeting she gave in kissing his feet, and the anointing of his feet with perfume. None of these actions were required by the host, but the fact that the woman has engaged in them shows that she has taken extra steps to greet him.[4]

But there is a reason for her love—her many sins now stand forgiven (v. 47). The one who is forgiven little, on the other hand, loves little. To understand Jesus' point, the parable and his remarks must be put together. According to the parable, the basis of love is a previously extended forgiveness that produces a response of love. So Jesus indicates that the woman's actions reflect her experience of forgiveness from him. The Lord's declaration to her of forgiveness of sins serves to confirm what the parable has already indicated. There also is an implied warning from Jesus to the Pharisee, who probably sees himself as a "little sinner": "Your love may not be great, because you have not appreciated the depth of forgiveness God has made available to you. Instead, you judge this woman in order to gain a good feeling about yourself." Jesus challenges such a way of looking at sin.

Jesus' words of forgiveness are also significant. Earlier the Pharisee raised the question whether Jesus is a prophet (7:30; cf. also 7:16). But here he is forgiving sins, an act limited to God, as the Pharisees well know (v. 49). As in 5:24, this action gets the attention of the theological experts. They know

---

4. Marshall, *Commentary on Luke*, 311–12.

that Jesus is appropriating to himself the ultimate level of authority. But that does not stop Jesus, who turns to the woman in the midst of the objections and tells her to go in peace because her faith has saved her.

This final comment is significant, since up to this point the issue has been the presence of love. Jesus' remark reveals a crucial theological sequence: first an offer of forgiveness from God, then the faith that saves. Such faith evidences itself in the acts of love that she has performed for Jesus. Such is the fundamental cycle of relationship that exists between God and a believer. The possibility of establishing a healthy relationship with a sinner is why Jesus pursues and relates to sinners. He does not take the Pharisee's more distant and critical attitude. The potential for divine transformation through forgiveness and faith compels Christ to reach out to sinners and engage them relationally (5:31–32; 15:1–31; 18:9–14).

In 8:1–3, unique to Luke, the Evangelist notes the work of three women of faith. As Jesus ministers, he draws followers who come from a wide variety of backgrounds. Mary Magdalene serves after having seven demons exorcised by Jesus. Joanna, as the wife of Herod's steward Cuza, gives evidence that Jesus' message has reached even into the palace. When these and other women come to faith, they immediately give of their resources to enable Jesus' ministry to continue. This note is important, since the passage makes clear that those contributing to Jesus' ministry span both gender diversity and the social scale. The pattern of grace received and ministry pursued emerges in the exemplary response of these women. Their ministry comes at two levels: personal involvement and the contribution of resources. Both levels of involvement are important to effective ministry.

THE CONTRASTING ATTITUDES apparent in the text reveal a fundamental paradigm for relating to the world. The Pharisee, in his desire for purity, separates himself from fellowship with sinners. He keeps a woman like the one who approaches Jesus at great distance, thereby making it clear that her lifestyle is not endorsed. Jesus talks and preaches about sin, but he does not isolate himself from sinners. He understands that in order for light to shine in darkness, the light must engage the darkness.

This contrast is a timeless one in terms of how to view the ministry the church has in the world. The world has always had sinners in it, even notorious ones. In teaching this passage—one of my favorites in Luke—I am tempted to ask: "What if a contemporary figure like Madonna, a woman with an established reputation as a sinner, came to the Lord, how would we respond if she, in effect, came and sat at the Lord's feet?"[5] That is the hard question this text asks. Do we see sinners for who they have been or for what God can make of them? If the church believes that it has something to offer, then the church should show concern and the potential of relating in a new way to God, as Jesus did.

The theological principles at work here extend into our era. God's fundamental way of transforming people is through his offer of grace and forgiveness. Without the opportunity to restore a broken relationship, the way back to God is blocked. Some people desire to start over again, but are not assured it can be done. Jesus shows through the example of the notorious sinner that no hole is too deep for the reach of God's delivering, compassionate hand. This means that as we meet people whose lives are radically out of touch with God, we must be patient, realizing that without God we should not expect anything different from them. The gospel offers them not only what they need but also supplies what is lacking. We sometimes want to put the cart before the horse and make the cleanup of life take place first, whereas God promises that by his grace he will establish the relationship that cleans up a person's life. Only as long as we keep the possibility of God's activity in our minds will we be in a position to relate more sensitively to those who need God. It is important to recall where we were before he gave us his grace that is the ground of our transformation. It is he who makes us different, and not we ourselves. That is precisely why all of us need to come to him.

In sum, the proper way to study this passage is through the perspective of each character in the story. The Pharisee reveals how not to approach the question of sinners. Jesus rejects that perspective. The woman pictures a sinner who responds in faith boldly in an exemplary way. She represents the hope that sinners, even notorious ones, can find God. Jesus supplies the commentary, both relationally and theologically, to what has taken place.

The fundamental pattern of ministry in respone to grace is the prominent theme of 8:1–3. Those who enter the community are not spectators to ministry. Rather, they use their gifts and resources in service to Jesus. Whether delivered from the power of demons or sent from the courts of the kings, these women give to make effective ministry possible. Part of their ministry is to minister to others who minister, a key role in any community. Texts like this, affirming the role of women in a first-century culture where they were either seen as property or relegated to an almost invisible role, are significant in showing that women play a major role in contributing to the ministry of the church.

---

5. For an imaginative way in which Jesus might engage Madonna and other modern celebrities, see Lee Strobel, *What Would Jesus Say?* (Grand Rapids: Zondervan, 1994).

The view of women today differs significantly from the first century. Many women are as educated and qualified for various roles as men, and many serve with distinction in various capacities. In light of the more traditional distinctions the church has made between the role of men and women, this text has produced much questioning about whether women can do everything in the church, including senior pastoring and eldering—offices the New Testament had limited to men. In the midst of the debate about the role of women, we should never lose sight of one thing, that we are all called to serve the Lord by serving one another. One of the great regrets in the current discussion on the role of women is that the discussion has centered on power, fueled more by cultural standards than biblical standards of service. Even those texts that affirm the headship of the male do so as a way to point to service, not to the callous exercise of raw power (e.g., Eph. 5:23–33). More attention to these themes might lessen the battles on other matters.[6]

THE APPLICATIONS OF Jesus' teaching are open-ended. Fundamentally, believers must remain open to relationships with those outside the faith. The separation that the Pharisee desired should be rejected out of hand. In fact, a question to ponder is why those outside the faith, like tax collectors and sinners, were so drawn to Jesus. What did they sense from him that made his message of interest to them? Should not the church, while upholding God's truth and character, be equally open to outsiders?

---

6. For a defense of a more traditional understanding of the role of women, see John Piper and Wayne Grudem, *Recovering Biblical Manhood and Womanhood: A Response to Evangelical Feminism* (Wheaton, Ill.: Crossway, 1991), and Stephen B. Clark, *Man and Woman in Christ: An Examination of Roles of Men and Women in Light of Scripture and the Social Sciences* (Ann Arbor: Servant Books, 1980). For a more egalitarian approach, arguing for women in every role of church life, see Gretchen Gaebelein Hull, *Equal to Serve* (Old Tappan, N.J.: Revell, 1987), and Craig Keener, *Paul, Women, and Wives: Marriage and Women's Ministry in the Letters of Paul* (Peabody, Mass: Hendricksen, 1992). I remain personally more persuaded that Paul's appeal to creation looks at roles distinguished in terms of head and helpmeet as a part of God's initial design and is not a reflection of cultural limitations placed on him as a result of living in a patriarchal first-century culture (esp. 1 Cor. 11:7–9; 1 Tim. 2:11–15). Despite holding to a more traditional approach, I am grateful that evangelical feminism has caused all of us to look harder at the issue of women's roles and has led to a consideration and affirmation of women's ministry, even if I share concerns that some steps have gone too far. Those who hold to a more traditional view have tended to overuse power metaphors in the discussion. Two excellent practical works on being a woman and pursuing ministry are Vickie Kraft, *The Influential Woman* (Dallas: Word, 1992), and Mary Farrer, *Choices: For Women Who Long to Discover Life's Best* (Sisters, Ore.: Multnomah, 1994).

In our era, there is much debate about "user-friendly" churches that openly seek outsiders. Important questions surface, such as whether the church should minister primarily to the saints and whether truth will have to be watered down when outsiders are let in. There are dangers here that need serious reflection.[7] But we must look at Jesus' own teaching style and consider how he carried out his mission. He used illustrations from commerce and agriculture, plugging into the very activities of life that all people, including unbelievers, experienced. We will be hard pressed to see Jesus engaging the public in technical theological jargon.

This is not to say that the church should not seek to minister to the saints or that teaching deep theological truth is not a part of the church's call. I would not have given my life to such training if I did not think God has called the church to have such training. But we should not be harsh on those who feel called to target those who have not yet come to faith. The church needs more workers in the fields.[8] To harvest grain one must not only plant but also work in the fields. Jesus' attitude encourages such openness in reaching out with hope to those whose past might suggest they are beyond God's reach. Strobel summarizes the importance of staying in touch this way:

> Part of your hesitation in proceeding might stem from your own uncertainties about Unchurched Harry and Mary. You may wonder whether you really understand them well enough to know how to lovingly, tactfully, and powerfully bring them the Gospel. After all, it may have been quite a while since you've lived a secular lifestyle—if you've ever lived one at all.

> You may have found that since you've become a Christian, your unbelieving friends have drifted away as you've become increasingly involved in the social network of the church. It has been said that within two years of becoming a Christian, the average person has already lost the significant relationships he once had with people outside the faith. Without frequent heart-to-heart conversations with unchurched people, it's easy to forget how they think. . . .

> Frankly . . . some of my best friends are, in reality, hell-bound pagans, and I am impassioned about wanting to see them transformed by the same amazing grace that radically redirected my trajectory of my own life.[9]

---

7. See the warnings in Os Guinness, *Dining with the Devil: The Modern Church Movement Flirts With Modernity* (Grand Rapids: Baker, 1993).

8. For an instructive and practical work on understanding how the lost think, see Lee Strobel, *Inside the Mind of Unchurched Harry and Mary* (Grand Rapids: Zondervan, 1993).

9. Ibid., 15.

It is important to love the lost, not in their lostness, but for the hope that amazing grace might come their way.

The sinful woman in 7:36–50 illustrates some basic truths about faith and love. In terms of faith, she demonstrates an ability to overcome barriers, such as the popular perceptions about her. As a woman, even to contemplate publicly drawing near to Jesus was a risk, because women did not do such things in that culture. The fact that she was a sinner only heightened the risk, since a religious figure like Jesus might reject her. Yet her gratitude and humility were so great that drawing near to Jesus was all she cared about. She counted the cost and reckoned that Jesus would respond to her humble approach towards him. Her faith was honored. One wonders how many of us today would be so bold as to come forward and identify with Jesus in the face of known public rejection of our approaching him.

The woman expressed herself not by a loud voice but by quiet action. She speaks no words in this story, yet her actions of devotion to Jesus speak volumes. Her testimony stands on its own merit. Some perhaps misunderstood and even doubted it, but God sees her heart and declares her clean. The church needs less noise in its testimony and more heartfelt devotion and service.

Regarding the Pharisee's response, how many believing communities are guilty of thinking about sinners and relating to them as the Pharisee did? It is so easy to wall people off subtly from God and give the impression they are beyond God's reach, rather than trying sincerely to bring them into the sphere of God's forgiveness. In the public debate on the great moral issues of today, the church cannot risk being right while making its case in a wrong way by using the same politics of power and pressure that the world wages. Such an attitude will not yield the fruit of forgiveness, especially if the opportunity of forgiveness and the tone of divine love that led Christ to die for sinners never surface as the church communicates its message. In pursuing moral values in our communities, we must never lose the ability to communicate the most important value of all—the love of God expressed in the offer of forgiveness. Crusading for righteousness without compassion for the sinner forgets that we all started out at the same place, in need of divine forgiveness. Our gratitude to God should translate into offering the same compassion to others he has given to us (6:27–36).

It is Jesus, not us, who has the right to forgive sin. He is the one who calls the heart to change. We as believers serve and point to him. Any righteousness we possess comes because he has worked in our lives. We have not earned it, but received it because of his grace. We are all in the position of the woman at Jesus' feet. We must never forget that truth, so we can show to others the way to his feet.

Finally, the story of the sinful woman teaches a crucial lesson about depth of love for God. The greater our sense that God has dealt with us in mercy, the greater love we will have for him in return. If our love for God is cold, it may well be because we have come to think he owes it to us, not that he paid our debt. The gospel is like a banker walking up to us when we cannot pay our mortgage; rather than foreclosing, he writes a check that pays off the debt. If you met a banker like that, you would always be grateful to him and tell your friends about him. God is that spiritual banker, who has paid our debt of sin through Jesus. The deeper we realize that he has dealt with us out of mercy in the midst of our disobedience, the greater will be our response of love. It is dangerous to see ourselves as "little sinners" as the Pharisee did. Rather, we should see ourselves as unworthy objects of God's rich grace, as the woman did.[10]

Luke 8:1–3 highlights three women for special mention who ministered with their resources. In dealing with ministry and resources, we can champion two equally dangerous imbalances. (1) We can look at ministry as simply a matter of throwing money at a need. But ministry without heart, even well-financed ministry, is not ministry in God's eyes. A ministry can possess the best equipment, the finest quality of buildings, and the largest mailing list, and still not be doing God's work with quality if people do not remain more important. Excellence defined by standards of appearance is not excellence in God's eyes. I have seen organizations lose effectiveness in their testimony because they developed a reputation for caring more about programs and buildings than people. I have also been in ministries, especially in the poorer countries of the world, where the buildings and facilities leave much to be desired, but heart is in the ministry so that people are cared for as a matter of priority. Throwing money at a ministry and paying others to do the church's work while making it look nice is not ministry in God's sight.

(2) The opposite error is to argue that resources do not matter and are best left undiscussed. This passage, Jesus' discussion of the widow's mite in 21:1–4, and Paul's discussions of resources (see 1 Cor. 16:1–4; 2 Cor. 8–9; 1 Tim. 6) show that money is an important aspect of ministerial stewardship for the believer. I am amazed at how many churches have received pastors from the same school for years but do not have that seminary on their supporting budget. These schools prepare the next generation of ministers, and the local church is the major beneficiary of such ministry. In denominations there is usually a formal way to provide for such institutions, but in independent circles such recognition and accountability often go ignored. The minister is

---

10. For a good discussion of the issue of self-worth, pride, and humility, see Joseph M. Stowell, *Perilous Pursuits* (Chicago: Moody, 1994).

worthy of his wage, and so are those institutions that serve the church. Those who receive grace should render grace in return (1 Cor. 9:11). Furthermore, too often a subtle attitude exists towards those in the ministry: I can expect the best for my family, but my pastor must live in a way that leaves him totally dependent on God. This subtle double standard is not biblical. All of us should be generous, and if the Old Testament is any guide, those who minister in the temple should be well provided for, so they can concentrate on the task of ministry. One of the reasons Jesus and the Twelve were so effective in their ministry was because disciples like these women stood totally behind their ministries.

Luke 8:4–21

W HILE A LARGE crowd was gathering and people were coming to Jesus from town after town, he told this parable: ⁵"A farmer went out to sow his seed. As he was scattering the seed, some fell along the path; it was trampled on, and the birds of the air ate it up. ⁶Some fell on rock, and when it came up, the plants withered because they had no moisture. ⁷Other seed fell among thorns, which grew up with it and choked the plants. ⁸Still other seed fell on good soil. It came up and yielded a crop, a hundred times more than was sown."

When he said this, he called out, "He who has ears to hear, let him hear."

⁹His disciples asked him what this parable meant. ¹⁰He said, "The knowledge of the secrets of the kingdom of God has been given to you, but to others I speak in parables, so that,

"'though seeing, they may not see;
though hearing, they may not understand.'

¹¹"This is the meaning of the parable: The seed is the word of God. ¹²Those along the path are the ones who hear, and then the devil comes and takes away the word from their hearts, so that they may not believe and be saved. ¹³Those on the rock are the ones who receive the word with joy when they hear it, but they have no root. They believe for a while, but in the time of testing they fall away. ¹⁴The seed that fell among thorns stands for those who hear, but as they go on their way they are choked by life's worries, riches and pleasures, and they do not mature. ¹⁵But the seed on good soil stands for those with a noble and good heart, who hear the word, retain it, and by persevering produce a crop.

¹⁶"No one lights a lamp and hides it in a jar or puts it under a bed. Instead, he puts it on a stand, so that those who come in can see the light. ¹⁷For there is nothing hidden that will not be disclosed, and nothing concealed that will not be known or brought out into the open. ¹⁸Therefore consider carefully how

you listen. Whoever has will be given more; whoever does not have, even what he thinks he has will be taken from him."

¹⁹Now Jesus' mother and brothers came to see him, but they were not able to get near him because of the crowd. ²⁰Someone told him, "Your mother and brothers are standing outside, wanting to see you."

²¹He replied, "My mother and brothers are those who hear God's word and put it into practice."

LUKE 8:4—9:17 CONSIDERS what faith looks like by calling on disciples to cling to the Word of God (8:4—21). The parable of the soils commends only the ground that holds to the Word with patience. Jesus goes on to declare his family to be those who obey God's Word, a message he describes simply as light that will not be covered. A series of miracles follows in 8:22—56, which show Jesus' power over nature, demons, disease, and death and serve as a comprehensive survey of his authority. Then in 9:1—17, Jesus begins to show his Twelve how they will share in his ministry through their mission and the feeding of the five thousand. Questions about Jesus surface as the disciples (8:25) and Herod (9:7—9) wrestle with who he is. This entire unit sets up a major turning point in the Gospel, Peter's confession in 9:18—20.

As Jesus gathers disciples and gains opposition, the question about how people respond to his message surfaces. The parable of the soils (8:4—15) is the one kingdom parable Luke chooses to narrate at this point. Unlike Mark 4 and Matthew 13, where entire chapters are devoted to kingdom teaching via parables, Luke concentrates on the one theme of faith both here and in the two short passages that follow (8:16—21). There are many obstacles to faith, and yet responding with faith and obedience is crucial to responding to God. As the parable explains, just because Jesus is God's chosen agent does not mean people respond to him automatically. Diversity of response exists, though not because of a variation in his teaching. It is all a matter of the soil, the heart of the hearer.

Jesus relates the parable to "a large crowd." In Luke the mention of a large crowd often means that a warning about not getting carried away about the response follows (cf. 12:1—2). The parable of the soils is the story about much seed that gets sown, but only a small portion of which bears fruit. The imagery draws on standard Palestinian farming practices. Sowing took place from late October to early December. The sower carried a bag of grain, usually slung over his shoulder. He tossed the seed in rows. It is debated whether the seed was sown and then the land was plowed or vice versa, but it makes no difference to the parable.[1]

Jesus specifies four different types of soil on which the seed falls: the road, the rock, thorns and thistles, and good soil. The seed on the road not only has no chance to become embedded in the ground and draw nutrients from the soil, but it is also trampled upon. The rocky soil, at least in Palestine, is hard to spot, since in the hill country, much topsoil is set thinly over a limestone rock base. Weeds are also plentiful, with some able to grow up to six feet in height. The parable also speaks of a hundredfold yield, which is not bad in a culture that expected a seven to tenfold yield (although in Babylon claims of three hundredfold yields were made).[2] All these natural factors of everyday farming add life to Jesus' imagery. Anyone who worked in the field or walked by them would know the hazards of sowing seed.

Jesus tells the parable without explanation and then calls on his audience to hear what is said in it (v. 8b). Luke notes such calls to hear elsewhere (9:44; 14:35). The disciples then ask Jesus why he speaks in parables without comments. His answer reveals a twofold role. (1) The disciples have the benefit of parabolic instruction, because they are receiving the revelation of the mysteries of the kingdom. The concept of mystery (*mysterion*) is a key New Testament idea. In the Old Testament it described a revelation of God that becomes more clearly revealed. It can refer to new revelation or to clarifying something already revealed. For example, Daniel, by interpreting dreams and other signs, revealed divine mysteries. Thus the term *mystery* describes making a divine revelation clear. The disciples receive parables as a revelatory gift of God's grace. (2) To outsiders, the presence of parables is a form of judgment, a revelation concealed that prevents understanding. Jesus cites Isaiah 6:9–10 here, in which the prophet spoke judgment on a people who showed signs of being obstinate.

The major topic of Jesus' parables is the kingdom of God, another key New Testament concept. The kingdom refers to the manifestation of God's promised rule. When John the Baptist announced that it had come near (Matt. 3:2; Mark 1:14–15), he was proclaiming the approach of the rule of God through the Messiah as promised in the Old Testament. In Jesus' ministry, this era has arrived (Luke 4:16–30; 7:28; 11:19–20; 16:16; 17:20–21), though in the New Testament it arrives in phases. Jesus prepares for its coming through his ministry and by his work on the cross, which enables the new covenant promise of forgiveness of sins to be put into place and allows the disciples to begin preaching its offer to all (22:20; 24:43–47). The sign of the

---

1. Fitzmyer, *Luke I–IX*, 703.
2. Nolland, *Luke 1:1–9:20*, 371–72.

coming of the kingdom is the arrival of the Spirit (Luke 3:15–17; Acts 2:16–36). But there is more to the kingdom than spiritual blessing, for Jesus will someday exercise authority over the entire earth in the future manifestation of the kingdom (Acts 3:14–23). His preaching has to do with this promised kingdom program, since as Messiah he was and is the king of the kingdom. The parables deal with life in the kingdom both now and in the era to come.

Thus, Jesus explains to his disciples that the seed is the Word of God, that is, the revelatory message about the kingdom that goes out into the world as Jesus, the sower, tosses the seed. The focus of the parable is on the soils, not the seed, since the seed gets four different reactions. The seed on the road never has a chance, since Satan comes and picks up whatever has not already been trampled. In such cases, people have no chance to hear, believe, and be saved. The seed on the rock starts out well, as a type of short-lived faith that allows germination of the seed. Yet there is no deep root, and when pressures come, these people fall away. The seed among the thorns fights with other things in the ground for nutrients, and the thorns choke them. This describes life's worries, riches, and pleasures, a life wherein spiritual issues are not a priority. The successful seed is that which finds good soil. This grain lands on a good and true heart, which hears the message, retains it, and has the patience to hold fast to it.

Fruit is never a matter of an overnight exercise. It takes nurturing. Thus, Jesus' teaching does not look at the reaction to God's Word in a single moment but over a period of time, which may be why the planting analogy is used. It takes time to bear fruit, just as it takes time for weeds to choke the seed or for the lack of root in a plant to become evident. Jesus' point deals with how response to the Word is a product of a process. Only one soil meets the goal for which the seed was planted, the fourth soil.

This observation raises a question of interpretation that unfortunately often becomes the main focus of this parable: Which soil represents "saved" people? Clearly those represented by the first soil are not saved, while the fourth are clearly among the redeemed. The debate stems from the second and third soils, especially since Luke notes that those pictured by the second soil have faith, at least for a time. The difficulty comes in their being said to "fall away" (v. 13) and in the recognition that only one soil actually bears fruit. I contend that the parable is deliberately ambiguous here.

I must, however, make one additional observation. The situation of the second and third soils is seen as tragic, since the goal of sowing has not been reached. There is no comfort for those who are described as these soils. Rather, their situation is lamentable. This point is important, because one of the effects of stating confidently that the second and third soils are saved is that it offers comfort for those who fall into those descriptions. The parable in literary terms offers no such comfort. To "fall away" in the context of the parable is to fall away from God's Word and to reach the point where faith is no longer present. Faith that appears a short time is not faith, since other New Testament texts suggests that genuine faith never lets go of Jesus (John 15:1–6; Col. 1:21–23; 2 John 9). Though the text's portrait is not explicit on this question since it is treating another issue, the literary thrust of the image of the second soil questions its healthy status. The same can be said for the third, where faith is not mentioned.

Luke 8:16–18 calls people to respond to the light because of the dire consequences of not doing so. Jesus' message is portrayed as light. He notes that one does not light a lamp to hide it, but to make its light available by placing it on a lampstand. The function of light is to make visible that which was previously hidden in darkness. So it will be with Jesus' message. Everything that is hid will be made known, and all secrets will be brought to light. One must therefore listen with care, since we are all accountable. There is much at stake, for whoever has, in terms of responding to revelation, will get more. On the other hand, those who do not have because they refuse to respond will lose what they seemed to have, ending up with nothing.

Luke 8:19–21 also highlights the importance of responding to God's Word. Jesus' family wants to see him, but the crowds make it difficult for them to get to him. When Jesus is told they are seeking him, he replies with a proverbial-style remark that indicates where his family can be found. Jesus' family consists of those who hear the Word of God and do it. This emphasis on hearing and doing is common (6:47–49; James 1:22–25). The remark reinforces both Luke 8:14–15 and the picture of his message as light in 8:16–18.

Bridging Contexts

THE WORD OF the kingdom is still preached today, and the continuum of reactions is still with us. Thus this parable still has much truth about the various factors that impact our response to God's Word. The distractions of life still plague growth to fruitfulness, and persecution, though taking various forms, is still prevalent. Life still sends us trial in terms of testing circumstances, vocational demands, the need to support a family, the call to spend time with our children and to meet the other obligations of life, and the sometimes strain of staying healthy. Our society still tempts us in terms of our values and ethical judgments. Ephesians 5:15 calls us to watch carefully how we walk, for the days are full of evil. As we face the twenty-first century, it does not take much imagination for us to realize there are opportunities to sin at every step in life.

The sower today is no longer Jesus, at least not in the same sense as when he preached. Rather, now he works through representatives who preach the Word in his name. But Satan still hovers over the world, looking to snatch seed before it ever takes root. In other words, all the dimensions of this text still apply. Only the forms of the various factors that cause us to ignore his Word have changed.

When we approach this text, we tend to present it as a one-moment response: "As you hear this message today, which soil are you?" But the question is more comprehensive: "As you look at your spiritual walk up to today, which soil are you?" The parable looks at a career of response, as is clear when one considers that the good soil brings up various levels of fruit. The assessment is built on moments, to be sure, but it requires a life of response to consider what one's soul looks like relative to a slowly developing crop. A plant does not sprout forth overnight, nor does the harvest of the heart.

The role of Satan in a text like this is hard for a modern audience. Since he is unseen, he tends to be forgotten. Yet it is clear that Scripture attributes the failure of the Word to penetrate some hearts as a part of his work. On the other hand, some are overly sensitive to the presence of Satan. It is true, of course, that some forces in our culture are diabolical. Is it any accident that some of our most violent and notorious rock groups court satanic symbolism? Might not some obsessions represent a grip on the soul that can only be reversed with an equally radical liberation through divine forces? God's presence and power are able to overcome the forces of Satan. The prince of darkness is not so strong that Jesus cannot handle what the devil throws at us. But it is important to note that only one of the obstacles to successful response to God's Word is Satan. Our response to the Word and the circumstances of life make up two of the soils. Ignoring Satan underestimates him, but giving him too much press exaggerates his power. We should be careful not to give Satan more credit than he deserves.

Personal trauma, the fear of rejection, or the influences of the pursuit of a life of comfort often play a dominating role in our lives. If most people were honestly asked to consider how much of their time and energy are spent coping with these issues, most of us would agree they consume the majority of our energies. Yet too often we accept their impact on us as an unavoidable given. It is easy to see why Jesus names the things he does that get in the way of our bearing fruit. Nonetheless, a life dominated by these concerns is not headed for spiritual fruitfulness. A little booklet entitled "The Tyranny of the Urgent" was popular when I was in college. It argued that often our lives are driven by that which throws itself into our lives and demands our attention and fixing. Meanwhile the nurture of the soul and the pursuit of long-range spiritual development and ministry gets second place.

If we are not careful, those concerns are eliminated from the agenda altogether. Jesus' warning in the parable is one we must still hear today. The only use of God's Word that bears fruit is one that clings to it with patient steadfastness and a solid heart—a heart that says the most urgent task is to walk through life with all of its traumas clinging tightly to God's hand and his Word.

Luke 8:16–18 deals with the fundamental need to respond to God's teaching. To refuse the light is to end up in darkness. God holds us accountable for how we respond to his Word. So the warning Jesus makes here is serious, especially given the possibility of being left with nothing. Despite the tendency of our culture to treat all religious words as words from God, or at least words from man about God, a passage like this warns that distinctions should be made. Divine promise is fulfilled in Jesus alone. It is his message that is light. As arrogant as that sounds, it is reassuring to know that God has spoken clearly and authoritatively through Jesus. This claim needs to be taken seriously.

In 8:19–21 Jesus' remarks underscore the permanent importance of responding to the Word concretely, not just with intellectual understanding. The Bible contends that those who want to walk with God need to have their thinking refashioned along biblical lines. We do not by instinct know how to respond to life (Eph. 4:17–24). Jesus graphically pushes the point here of the necessity of hearing and doing the Word. Those to whom he feels closest are those who do God's will. The family of Jesus knows the importance of responding to God's word as mediated by the one God sent.

MANY THINGS CAN get in the way of responding to Jesus. Some people never seem interested—they are like the first soil. Or if they do show some interest in God's Word, only the most bizarre elements speak to them. It is hard to reach people in whom the seed has never taken root.

Others are initially drawn to God's Word, but as the difficulty of being a Christian in a world that often does not understand devotion to Christ becomes clear, their interest wanes and they drop out of sight. Identity with Christ never sinks in. These are like the second soil—people on the fringe of the church, who never seem to get with the program though they may have had some exposure to it. Some may have never been saved. They were initially attracted to the church, but their subsequent departure reflects where their heart was all along. It is tragic to be so close and yet so far. Only God knows the true heart condition of people who respond like this.

4 Still others flirt with a Christian walk, but life is either too tempting or too demanding for them to respond in a way that draws them to Jesus. The world we live in probably has more such distractions than it did during the days of Jesus. It is fair to say that most of us struggle not to let the affairs of life and the tyranny of the daily demands of life overwhelm us. The difference between soil three and soil four people seems to be the condition of the heart. A healthy heart clings to God's Word; it beats fast for him and responds to him. A damaged heart has trouble seeing him over the distraction and attraction of other things. It does take constant listening and clinging to the Word to be fruitful. To respond to God is not a matter of spiritual cruise control, where things happen automatically in instinctive response to the things of God. It takes conscious effort to focus on God and his ways so that we become consistently fruitful.

Jesus wants his disciples to understand this truth. Fruitfulness takes patience, just as it does for a farmer who sows seed. When seed is sown, he does not know the quality or condition of the ground on which it falls. It is the same seed, but not the same soil. As we labor to sow the seed of the kingdom, we must remember that different responses are inevitable. We must also be clear to discuss the many pitfalls to fruitfulness. Whether riches, fame, success, desire to be accepted, the pursuit of pleasure or comfort, or fear of letting God have control, the road to fruitfulness is packed with black holes that can swallow up any progress toward spiritual vibrancy.[3] As Jesus said, "He who has ears to hear let him hear."

In Luke 8:16–18, Jesus' teaching emphasizes paying serious attention to God's teaching. In a contemporary context where worship has a prominent place and feelings are so important culturally, the tendency is not to take God's message as seriously. Yet God holds us accountable for his Word, and it is crucial that teaching the Word and hearing it well be paramount. That same responsibility falls on unbelievers. It is easy as adults to think we are only accountable to ourselves, but Jesus warns that such a view is a major delusion. All of us are accountable to God, especially for how we respond to his revelation. He has put that revelation on a lampstand where it is visible. So we all need to pay attention to what his truth reveals about where we are and what we are doing. That often involves a call to change how we are responding to God and to look for fresh areas in our lives where God can work.

There is another implication from this section. If Jesus teaches light and we are his representatives today, then we are called both to teach and to

---

3. Perhaps no one has addressed this as effectively in our time as J. I. Packer. His works *Knowing God* (Downers Grove, Ill.: InterVarsity, 1973) and *Hot Tub Religion* (Wheaton: Tyndale, 1987) are positive and negative examinations of these themes.

reflect light (Jesus says as much to his disciples in Matt. 5:12–14). To be light means we must be filled with light (Luke 11:33–36). The parable of the soils tells us this happens through patient study and application of the seed of God's Word. This is why teaching that challenges us to live differently and biblically is so essential. Some churches, in hopes of not offending its audience, have stopped discussing sin as a topic—an amazing situation in light of the fact that even secular magazines in our time are asking the question, "What Ever Happened to Sin?"[4] If a pastor is not preaching biblically about what life looks like when one is pursuing righteousness, then we as church members are not being prepared to walk a life of light. To grow, our ways need exposure to the light, so we can better reflect who he wants us to be. True growth means transformation and change. Maturity dos not come by standing pat. Such transformation comes from careful study of God's Word and through the thoughtful comments and criticisms of others. The goal of God's shining light is to make us light, so we can shine for him.

The application of 8:19–21 is simple enough: Do not just listen to God's Word or study it, but apply it. The walk of faith does not involve a knowledge of the intricacies of theological debate. It involves engaging life with an incarnation of the character of God as revealed in his teaching. God's will for us is that we be so responsive to him that we reflect his character. This is being conformed to the image of Christ, which is the believer's mission.

Also instructive is Jesus' sense of priority in one's commitment to follow God. That may mean the pain of separation from family. The hardest part about my ministry is the travel it calls for so often. It means weekends away from my wife and children, missing activities they wish I could attend. To hear the Word means to love my wife and to raise my children in the nurture and admonition of the Lord, as well as to carry out my calling. Balancing the two is not always easy. Wisdom tells me that I should not make judgments in this area by myself, since I personally find it hard to assess from within. Thus, my spouse has a rather free hand to discuss this area with me. This tension between calling and family requires a constant assessment of what honors God most. It also means, at least ideally, that when I am available to my family, that I am truly available to them. I mention this because I believe most working people, male or female, struggle with such tensions. I use two tests as I face these difficult choices. (1) Is God leading me into this involvement? (2) Does my wife sense that this is God's direction as well? Only as my wife and I work together to seek God's will can God give us the strength to pursue the demands of his calling.

---

4. In its February 6, 1995 issue, *Newsweek* magazine presented a study on shame, our culture, and the issue of guilt. One of the sidebar articles in that issue had this title (p. 23).

◆

ONE DAY JESUS SAID TO his disciples, "Let's go over to the other side of the lake." So they got into a boat and set out. ²³As they sailed, he fell asleep. A squall came down on the lake, so that the boat was being swamped, and they were in great danger.

²⁴The disciples went and woke him, saying, "Master, Master, we're going to drown!"

He got up and rebuked the wind and the raging waters; the storm subsided, and all was calm. ²⁵"Where is your faith?" he asked his disciples.

In fear and amazement they asked one another, "Who is this? He commands even the winds and the water, and they obey him."

Original Meaning

THE SECOND NATURE miracle in Luke's Gospel develops his Christological concerns.¹ Note especially the closing query: "Who is this?" There is irony in this Christological disclosure, since professional fishermen turn to a teacher of God's truth for rescue on the seas. The irony of their desperation and its resolution reveals that Jesus is no ordinary teacher.

The event's setting involves a crossing of the Sea of Galilee. This sea is located some seven hundred feet below sea level and has hills surrounding it. The eastern side has a particularly steep set of hills. It is not unusual for a cold wind to shoot through the gaps and collide with warm air over the lake in a weather pattern that any meteorologist would recognize as dangerous.

As Jesus rests, such a weather cycle occurs. Before the disciples have time to react, a whirlwind emerges, and they find themselves at risk in the boat. Waves sweep over the edge and threaten to capsize them. Sensing the danger, the disciples cry out to Jesus of their pending doom. Can he do anything? Jesus turns and rebukes the wind, and immediately there is calm. Then he asks them a crucial question, "Where is your faith?" Do they not trust God to see

---

1. Luke 5:1–11 was the first nature miracle, and it served as the basis for a call to discipleship. This text has parallels in Matthew 8:23–25 and Mark 4:35–41. This cluster of four miracles in Luke 8:22–56 parallels Mark 4:35–5:43. Coming after the section highlighting God's Word in 8:4–21, we again get a pattern of word and deed (cf. 4:16–44).

them and care for their best interest? The dialogue stops here, so that the event can be an object of reflection.

Luke goes on to record the disciples' reactions: fear and amazement. They ask a central question: "Who is this? He commands even the winds and the water, and they obey him." The question is crucial because the Old Testament makes it clear who has authority over nature: God does (Pss. 104:3; 107:23–30; cf. also Wis. 14:3–5). Although other biblical stories have major figures imploring God or describe God's people experiencing protection from the presence of severe weather, Jesus works directly here.[2] Luke purposefully wants the question of Jesus' identity and uniqueness to be kept before his reader. The disciples are beginning to appreciate just how unique he is.

THE MAJOR FOCUS in this passage comes in the disciple's struggle of faith and in their discussion on Jesus' authority. We too can have the same desperate feeling they did. Especially in the midst of events beyond our control, we often feel that God is somehow not aware or not watching—that he is asleep at the wheel and needs rousing to care for us. Jesus asks the disciples to reflect on God's care. They do not need to panic; rather, they need to understand that God does care for them and is watching over them.

The disciples need to be made aware that their teacher has authority that extends into the operation of the cosmos (cf. Paul's words in Col. 1:15–20). The sovereignty of Jesus makes him far more than a prophet or ethicist. Confessing Jesus as Lord means that he is in control of nature with all its power. In our world where nature is often personified as its own cosmic force with an independent identity, the reminder of who really is the force behind creation is important.

In bridging contexts, our sense of helplessness need not be limited to finding ourselves at risk in settings of nature. The storms of today can arrive in a rush of circumstances beyond our control. The point of connection is not in the precise situation the disciples face in the boat, but in the feelings of helplessness they have about where Jesus has led them. Events in our lives sometimes leave us feeling at risk, whether it be in a job situation that calls us to take a stand, in the severe illness of a loved one, in an unexpected

---

2. One can think of Jonah (Jonah 1) or Paul (Acts 27:8–44). In Judaism, 2 Maccabees 9:8 relates Antiochus Epiphanes IV's claim to be able to calm the sea. Jewish tradition knows of a couple of examples where God was invoked through prayer and calm emerged (see Bock, *Luke 1:1–9:50*, 757).

tragedy, or in the breakdown of a relationship. Any of these can be a storm in which we doubt God's goodness. We may feel God has left us to fend for ourselves.

A modern, frank biographical sketch of such a restless journey comes from Dr. Larry Crabb.[3] He tells the painful story of losing his brother suddenly in a plane crash on March 3, 1991. He chronicles the stages of his reaction as he discovers a new depth in his relationship with God. He notes five steps in his walk with God: I need you; I hate you; I hate me; I will survive; here's how I will survive. Before light comes in the journey, darkness is usually there. At the foundation is trusting in God and not doubting him. God has never promised our lives would be empty of pain, disappointment, or storms. Anyone who tells you otherwise is not teaching about a true walk with God. What God does promise are resources to journey through the raging waters. Like the disciples who cry out in 8:22–25 and like Larry Crabb, stillness comes after the fierce storm.

THIS PASSAGE IS a call for a deeper, trusting faith, even in the midst of circumstances beyond our control. There is no telling how often some of the disciples, as former fishermen, had been on the lake in the midst of a storm. Yet it was clear that they were powerless to deal with such forces. Though their faith was weak, they did the right thing in turning to Jesus for help. Only their cry that they were perishing was in error. Had they understood God's care, they would have realized that divine care never takes a break, even when it leads into rough waters. Jesus' call for faith is also a call to reassurance that God is aware of whatever storms we are going through and is watching over us.

One of the great hymns of the faith was written in response to such a storm. In the nineteenth century, Horatio G. Spafford lost his four daughters when an ocean liner sank in the Atlantic; only his wife survived, sending a cable to her husband: "Saved alone."[4] Here was a storm that seemingly overwhelmed him. But what did this saint write as he contemplated what had happened? The first stanza tells us much, as does the chorus to this well-known hymn.

When peace, like a river, attendeth my way,
    When sorrows like sea billows roll—

---

3. Larry Crabb, *Finding God* (Grand Rapids: Zondervan, 1993).

4. See William J. Reynolds, *Companion to Baptist Hymnal* (Nashville: Broadman, 1976), 241–42.

Whatever my lot, Thou hast taught me to say,
It is well, it is well with my soul.

Parishioners are usually unaware of the dire circumstances under which these words were written. Here is one man who learned to trust God in the midst of the storm.

The second question in the text deals with further reflection on the identity of Jesus. Luke tells the story of Jesus from the earth up. He starts with a portrait of Jesus as teacher, prophet, and king before he develops Jesus' more transcendent qualities. Such an approach allows Luke's readers to grow a step at a time in their appreciation of who this person is. Our rush to preach the exalted Jesus and our knowledge of the rest of the story often causes us to lose sight of how gradually Luke tells his story. Nonetheless, this text is crucial in building a bridge towards a more heavenly understanding of our Savior. Those in our world who wish to relegate Jesus to the status of sage or teacher fail to reckon with texts such as this one. The disciples, as they lived with Jesus and saw him work, came to understand that they were not following an ordinary rabbi. Luke has the disciples ask here, "Who is this?" and the rest of his Gospel shows the answer to this question.

That answer is a central issue of life: He is the unique Son of God. Here is a Savior with the power to deliver and bring life out of death. I am reminded of Ephesians 1:15–23, where Paul prays especially that the Ephesian believers will come to understand that the power at work in us is like that which raised Jesus from the dead and set him over every force in the creation, both in this age and in the age to come. The One who has such power is able to deliver us, if he chooses, from whatever we face. All he asks is that we trust him as we go on the way. He also is able to deliver us ultimately from anything that overwhelms us in this life, a power that is perhaps the most crucial of all. The disciples are just beginning to come to grips with such power in the One they have walked with for nearly three years. We also must sit at his feet for some time before we really begin to comprehend how great Jesus is and how far his deliverance reaches.

Luke 8:26–39

❧

THEY SAILED TO the region of the Gerasenes, which is across the lake from Galilee. ²⁷When Jesus stepped ashore, he was met by a demon-possessed man from the town. For a long time this man had not worn clothes or lived in a house, but had lived in the tombs. ²⁸When he saw Jesus, he cried out and fell at his feet, shouting at the top of his voice, "What do you want with me, Jesus, Son of the Most High God? I beg you, don't torture me!" ²⁹For Jesus had commanded the evil spirit to come out of the man. Many times it had seized him, and though he was chained hand and foot and kept under guard, he had broken his chains and had been driven by the demon into solitary places.

³⁰Jesus asked him, "What is your name?"

"Legion," he replied, because many demons had gone into him. ³¹And they begged him repeatedly not to order them to go into the Abyss.

³²A large herd of pigs was feeding there on the hillside. The demons begged Jesus to let them go into them, and he gave them permission. ³³When the demons came out of the man, they went into the pigs, and the herd rushed down the steep bank into the lake and was drowned.

³⁴When those tending the pigs saw what had happened, they ran off and reported this in the town and countryside, ³⁵and the people went out to see what had happened. When they came to Jesus, they found the man from whom the demons had gone out, sitting at Jesus' feet, dressed and in his right mind; and they were afraid. ³⁶Those who had seen it told the people how the demon-possessed man had been cured. ³⁷Then all the people of the region of the Gerasenes asked Jesus to leave them, because they were overcome with fear. So he got into the boat and left.

³⁸The man from whom the demons had gone out begged to go with him, but Jesus sent him away, saying, ³⁹"Return home and tell how much God has done for you." So the man went away and told all over town how much Jesus had done for him.

Original Meaning

JESUS HAS ALREADY performed exorcisms in this Gospel (4:31–36, 40–41; 6:18; 8:2), so why does Luke narrate yet another exorcism here? This one has unique characteristics that make it worthy of mention. (1) It is the first exorcism that occurs in Gentile territory, since Gerasa is located east of the Jordan.[1] It shows how Jesus' ministry is expanding in scope. (2) This exorcism involves multiple possession, so it is a more intense encounter than previous ones. (3) This account deals more fully with an array of responses to Jesus' miracles, from the request of the locals for Jesus to depart to the transformation of the demon-possessed man into a witness for the Lord. (4) This miracle continues the sequence of four miracles in 8:22–56, where each one represents a different sphere of activity (nature to demons to disease to death). (5) Finally, this miracle is the only one where earthly creatures other than humans are involved. The pigs serve an important function, since their destruction pictures the kind of devastation inherent in demonic activity. Though demons themselves are unseen, the effect of their presence in the pigs illustrates just how dangerous they can be.

The account proceeds in a standard order for a miracle: setting, plea, exorcism, effect, reaction, and close.[2] The detailed description of the demoniac shows the destructive power of the demons, for the man has totally withdrawn from society, living unclothed in tombs. We are told how he has been seized many times and bound with ropes, chains, or both. But he shattered them and could not be restrained.

The man falls before Jesus as the demons confess him to be the "Son of the Most High God," and he asks Jesus not to torment him. The demon's name is Legion, indicating that a whole battle division of demons inhabit the man. In the Roman world, *legion* referred to a company of thousands of soldiers.[3] In other words, Jesus is engaging in a major battle here. He is outnumbered, but not overmatched.

The demons ask to be sent into a herd of pigs rather than into the abyss.[4]

---

1. The exact location of Gerasa is debated. Some place it on the east side of the Sea of Galilee, while other have it located in the Decapolis region east of the Jordan, twenty miles south of the Sea. Another complicating factor is that Matthew and Mark describe the exorcism as taking place at Gadara, another city of the Decapolis, five miles southeast of the Sea. Probably a reference to a countryside location has produced different local references to give the event a general locale.

2. The parallels are Matthew 8:28–34 and Mark 5:1–20. Mark's account is by far the more detailed, while Matthew is the most concise, as is often his custom.

3. Preisker, "λεγιών," *TDNT*, 4:68.

4. The abyss probably refers to the abode of the dead and a place of judgment; see Jeremias, "ἄβυσσος," *TDNT*, 1:9–10.

This request has produced much speculation, none of which is answered by the text. What the incident involving the pigs does indicate is the real impact of demonic presence and influence, namely, the destruction of life. At Jesus' command, the demons depart to enter the pigs. Their possession of them throws the herd into a panic that causes them to run over the edge of a steep bank and into the water, where they drown. The demons' effort to continue their presence in the area apparently fails.

Word spreads fast as those tending the pigs flee into the city and country to report what has happened. Most amazing of all, when many people go out to the area, they see the new character that now inhabits the formerly possessed man. He is seated calmly at the feet of Jesus, restored, clothed, and of sound mind. Jesus has rescued him from life among the tombs and brought him into the real world again. The scene is a picture of new life.

The local people do not care for Jesus' work, however. Luke does not tell us exactly why they ask him to leave other than their fear, but Mark 5:16 makes it clear that Jesus has had a negative economic impact on the region. They do not want to lose more livestock. Their fear has turned into rejection and a desire to have nothing more to do with the presence of divine authority.

The healed man wants to join Jesus' traveling group of disciples, but Jesus has another calling in mind. Someone must be left behind to share what God has done in the area. That is the man's task. He does that and more, preaching and proclaiming what Jesus has done for him. Those whose lives are most radically transformed often end up being the strongest witnesses for Jesus.

THIS MIRACLE MAKES a wonderful collage of responses to Jesus, whether one considers the demons, the locals, or the man who benefits from Jesus' work. The demons recognize Jesus' power, but that does not stop them from trying to raise havoc with those around them. Even an army that knows it is losing a war can try to inflict as much damage as possible before going down. The locals see the power of Jesus and want little to do with it. They are too afraid of God's power and presence. The healed man indicates how helpless one can be without Jesus, especially when one is shackled and stripped of sanity by forces more powerful than one's own. But his turnaround indicates the startling contrast that emerges when one is freed from such enslavement. This miracle is not only about exorcism; it is especially about the liberation of a soul.

As we have noted in other sections, miracles are audiovisuals of spiritual activity. The swine incident indicates vividly, even tragically, how deadly the forces of evil are. The presence of evil and the demonic should not be taken lightly. Jesus probably performs this incident to demonstrate in a painful manner how the presence of evil results in death. This reminds us how presence of sin in the human race required his own death as payment.

Though we rarely deal with overt cases of demon-possession, that fact should not stop us from realizing the impact the demonic has on us daily. It is not entirely clear why demon-possession is so rare in the Western world. Those who work in other cultures where the demonic is more openly accepted speak openly about its presence and see more cases of demon-possession than we do. Do we underestimate its presence? Or does Satan have less need to manifest himself openly in a culture that denies his existence? I suspect a combination is at work. The Scripture makes it clear that a fallen world is still influenced by the presence of sin and Satan, and will be until the Lord's return finishes what this healing represents (Rom. 8:18–39).

Thus the bridge into our context is the constant presence and threat of demonic influences in our world. It is not hard to spot its symptoms. Demons may not possess the soul as vividly as this example, but they do cause people to do destructive things and retain a power that is almost overwhelming. People in the grip of excessive drink, debilitating drugs, or destructive lust reflect a world where destructive indulgence inflicts not only pain on those possessed by such addictions, but also on others around them. Though the forces in view here are chemical or psychological, there can be little doubt that they are the remnants of a fallen world that Satan exploits (cf. Eph. 4:17–19). With this scriptural insight, it may be that Satan is much more active than we give him credit for today.

OUR WORLD PLAYS with spiritual forces rather than taking them seriously. Attraction to the devil and the demonic has recently taken on an avant-garde air. Some of the music that permeates our culture is loaded with innuendo and suggestion about the spirit world. One senses that those who engage in this practice are having fun and trying to be cute. It is a way of expressing rebellion. But there is a serious side to this reality. I remember my shock when one of my relatives told me of going to a family home that was awaiting sale and finding that in the basement some people had obviously made it a temporary home, including some type of animal sacrifice. The news media occasionally inform us of accounts of violence, injury, and death in groups that engage in demonic ritual. The exorcism in Luke 8 is but one picture of the dangerous character of such activity. Encounter with demons is not a neutral undertaking.

One must be careful not to overreact, however. Some people see a demon behind every bush, while our culture, being enlightened, often makes the opposite error of dismissing such talk as reflecting a primitive worldview. Both approaches are a victory for the dark side. One never fights against what one does not believe is there. On the other hand, to be preoccupied with the demonic can produce a type of fixation that does not reflect spiritual balance and can deflect taking spiritual accountability. "The devil made me do it" can turn sinners into victims who have no control over whom they decide to ally themselves to. Jesus' power over such forces should deliver us from any tendency to attribute too much to demonic power (Eph. 1:15–23).

Texts about demons are difficult for many modern people because they ask us to deal in categories that do not involve seeing or hearing. But when we see the horrific destructive character of our culture and how terribly we can treat one another, it is hard not to recognize the presence of diabolical evil in our world. It takes more than our own efforts to reverse its presence. That reality, too, is portrayed in this event. Our efforts are as successful as the attempts by the locals to chain this demoniac in order to restrain him. The power of Jesus is needed.

I am reminded of a close friend who grew up on drugs, was alienated from his family, had dropped out of school several times, and was sent to a psychiatrist for treatment. Nothing helped. Then he was led to the Lord. His life was cleaned up and his demeanor changed. His relationship to his family was restored. His psychiatrist was amazed, as were his parents. If you ask him what did it, he will tell you it was not religion, though that was the more culturally neutral term many of his unchurched relatives used. Neither was it "growing up," another popular secular answer. It was Jesus, pure and simple. The grace of God gave him a new heart. He would tell you Satan had a solid grip on him until he came face to face with Jesus. He identifies with this story in Luke 8, for Jesus delivered him from the depths that were leading him to self-destruction.

A significant human quality appears in this text. The people who ask Jesus to leave their region recognize his power, but are afraid to be too close to him. Many fear divine accountability, preferring to be left on their own and to fend for themselves. They regard Christianity as a crutch, but I wonder if in fact there is a failure to recognize where real weakness resides. The locals were so concerned with their own affairs that they could not appreciate the deliverance that had taken place before their eyes. Perhaps the biggest tragedy of all is to see God at work and pretend nothing has really happened.

The delivered man gives us a final point of application. Not everyone is called to a ministry of traveling to share Jesus. That is, not everyone is called to a mission field far from home. Sometimes Jesus wants those who have experienced his goodness to tell those in their own hometown about him. Some are called to go; others are called to stay. This newly healed and transformed man did not need to raise support to find his mission field; he simply needed to start sharing—which, in fact, he did. He could not tell the story of God's work in his life without discussing Jesus.

Luke 8:40-56

Now when Jesus returned, a crowd welcomed him, for they were all expecting him. 41Then a man named Jairus, a ruler of the synagogue, came and fell at Jesus' feet, pleading with him to come to his house 42because his only daughter, a girl of about twelve, was dying.

As Jesus was on his way, the crowds almost crushed him. 43And a woman was there who had been subject to bleeding for twelve years, but no one could heal her. 44She came up behind him and touched the edge of his cloak, and immediately her bleeding stopped.

45"Who touched me?" Jesus asked.

When they all denied it, Peter said, "Master, the people are crowding and pressing against you."

46But Jesus said, "Someone touched me; I know that power has gone out from me."

47Then the woman, seeing that she could not go unnoticed, came trembling and fell at his feet. In the presence of all the people, she told why she had touched him and how she had been instantly healed. 48Then he said to her, "Daughter, your faith has healed you. Go in peace."

49While Jesus was still speaking, someone came from the house of Jairus, the synagogue ruler. "Your daughter is dead," he said. "Don't bother the teacher any more."

50Hearing this, Jesus said to Jairus, "Don't be afraid; just believe, and she will be healed."

51When he arrived at the house of Jairus, he did not let anyone go in with him except Peter, John and James, and the child's father and mother. 52Meanwhile, all the people were wailing and mourning for her. "Stop wailing," Jesus said. "She is not dead but asleep."

53They laughed at him, knowing that she was dead. 54But he took her by the hand and said, "My child, get up!" 55Her spirit returned, and at once she stood up. Then Jesus told them to give her something to eat. 56 Her parents were astonished, but he ordered them not to tell anyone what had happened.

Original
Meaning

THE LAST MIRACLE in the Luke 8 sequence is the only intertwined miracle in the Gospels.[1] In one brief succession of events Jesus deals with both disease and death. These two miracles are related in detail so that the drama of the combination can be fully evident. As with the other miracles, the emphasis is on the authority of Jesus. However, the combination also raises another theme, faith. Both the woman and Jairus reflect different aspects of growing in faith.

The opening scene is rather poignant. Jesus finds himself in the midst of a crowd, which has been expectantly waiting for him. Among them stands a synagogue ruler, Jairus—a man in charge of arranging the service and the progress of worship.[2] Everyone knows him. As Jesus approaches, the leader falls before Jesus and asks him to come to his house where his only daughter, a twelve-year-old, is near death. We are not told the nature of her malady, only that there is not much time.[3] To rescue her requires quick action.

Jesus starts heading for his house, but along the way, another person also needs Jesus. A woman, who has suffered from a flow of blood for twelve years wants Jesus to heal her. This condition is not only frustrating; it also renders her constantly ceremonially unclean, isolating her from Jewish religious life. Even physicians have failed to help her. Understandably, she does not want a public spectacle; all she wants is to touch Jesus, an act she hopes will bring healing. Getting herself into position, she touches him as he walks by, and immediately she is healed. This is not an act of magic, since no incantations or potions are involved.[4] She simply believes that Jesus possesses great power.

There is no obvious need for what happens next to take place, but Jesus' next action puts Jairus in an awkward position. Jesus stops to find out what has just happened. He turns to the vast throng of the pressing crowd and asks, "Who touched me?" Needless to say, Peter is shocked. How can Jesus ask such a question in the press of a crowd where all are trying to get in contact with Jesus? Jesus persists. He is conscious of the fact that power has proceeded from him. The touch he asks about is not just a physical touch but a touch that pleaded for help and found it. The silent faith of the woman needs exposure.

---

1. The parallels to this passage are Matthew 9:18–26 and Mark 5:21–43.

2. Schrage, "ἀρχισυνάγωγος," *TDNT*, 7:847.

3. In Matthew's version, which is condensed, the time sequence is collapsed and the daughter is already presented as having passed away. Matthew often shortens his accounts in this way.

4. Arndt, *Luke*, 256.

The woman realizes that Jesus knows what she has done. She is no longer hidden. So with great fear, she comes forward, revealing the reasonableness of Jesus' seemingly strange question. She falls before him and relates her story. Jesus commends her, noting that her faith has saved her. This remark is significant, because sometimes this woman is maligned for her "behind the back" approach to Jesus. But there is nothing in Jesus' treatment of her that indicates rebuke. What the woman needs is reassurance and confidence that her actions need not remain secretive. As one commentator puts it, her "smoldering wick" of faith needs fanning into a flame.[5] Given the opportunity, she summons up her courage and gives her testimony to her now enhanced faith.

One can only imagine the desperate frustration Jairus feels as this delay, orchestrated by Jesus' question, proceeds. Then things get worse. Someone from Jairus's house appears to tell him it is too late and that Jesus need not be troubled. His daughter has just passed away. I suspect with this announcement that pain, disappointment, and anger flooded Jairus's soul. But Jesus relates words of comfort to the synagogue ruler, telling him not to fear but to believe. Whereas the woman's faith needed bolstering because it was shy, Jairus's faith needs to be calmed, persistent, and trusting.

When Jesus gets to the house, he allows only the family, Peter, John, and James to enter in the room where the corpse is lying. Outside, the mourners have gathered. They are only called after it is clear that death has taken place.[6] In the midst of community sorrow, Jesus calls on them to stop, for the girl "is not dead but asleep." The agent of God will move to reveal the extent of his power over forces that reveal the mortality of humanity.

The crowd laughs. Surely one cannot resuscitate someone from the dead. We often regard the ancients as gullible, but the reaction here shows they can be as empirically based as most moderns. What Jesus proposes is ludicrous, unless.... Once inside, he grasps the girl's hand and tells her to get up. There are no potions or incantations, no appeals to outside powers. There is only the touching hand of Jesus. The girl sits up, her spirit revived within her. Someone immediately gives her food. Her parents are amazed. The call to faith that Jesus made to Jairus has now received its answer.

The account closes with Jesus's instruction to say nothing about what had happened. This is an odd command, for obviously by the girl's walking the streets again, everyone will know what Jesus has done. Jesus' point seems to be that he does not want undue attention brought to what he has done. To broadcast this healing far and wide will turn him into a wonder-worker, with all the public attention focused on that ministry. Jesus wants the atten-

---

5. Liefeld, "Luke," in *The Expositor's Bible Commentary*, 8:916.
6. Stählin, "κοπετός," *TDNT* 3:844–45; Rengstorf, "κλαίω," *TDNT*, 3:724–25.

tion elsewhere, on his central teaching, and will have nothing to do with the promotion of actions that place the emphasis in the wrong place (see 4:41; 5:14). The miracles point to more fundamental realities. Jesus wants to major on the major issues.

AS WITH ALL the miracles, a fundamental point that crosses into our era is linked to the authority of Jesus. His power over disease and death shows his sovereignty over life itself, not just in terms of physical life, but in terms of life in all of its facets. This sovereignty is fundamental to the Christian hope, since life after death represents a basic characteristic of the Christian's expectation. The raising of Jairus's daughter, which called for great faith, reminds us of the faith we must have in God's power to bring us to him after we die. Standing at the center of that meeting, waiting to lift us up if we turn to him, is Jesus.

There are also fundamental lessons about faith and God's timing in this passage. We have already noted how different aspects of faith are illustrated by the woman and by Jairus. She was asked to bring her faith out of its shell; he was called on to have a faith that hangs in there. Both characteristics are important qualities of faith. What is even more enlightening is the juxtaposition of the two. Certainly as Jairus watched his daughter's life slip away while Jesus dealt with a more minor problem that was not an emergency, he must have experienced a high level of frustration. We often struggle to understand God's timing. In fact, much of faith is related to accepting God's timing for events.

IT IS OFTEN the case that what we think God ought to do right now, God chooses to act on later, while what we would put off, he chooses to handle right away. In a sense the juxtaposition of these two miracles is an exercise in time management, where everything is turned upside down. The critical life-and-death situation must wait for a healing and testimony that could have been done under less testing circumstances. Part of the faith that Jairus is called to exercise not only needed to believe that God could deal with his recently deceased daughter, but also had to rest in the trauma that the seeming delay had created. Ultimately, trusting in God's care means accepting his timing for events.

There have often been times in my life when I wish I had a seat in the council of heaven to make my case for the superiority of a timing of events that I would have preferred but that God had not delivered. What is amazing is how often, upon reflection and given the perspective of a longer range of events, the sequence God brought to pass in my life made much better sense than what I would have lobbied for.

The testimony of the previously timid woman is also instructive. She is asked to testify to an embarrassing situation and how God healed it. Not only was it unusual for a woman to speak in public in this culture, but the nature of her problem made it even more difficult. Yet when Jesus called for her to step forward, she spoke. The text is clear that she "came trembling" as she did so. It can be frightening to speak up for the Lord sometimes, but this woman found the strength by God's grace to overcome her fears and to tell the story of what Jesus had done for her. A timid faith can become a testifying faith. God longs for us to share how he has been good to us.

The most fundamental lesson in this passage is the combination of characteristics tied to faith. Faith should seize the initiative to act in dependence on God and speak about him, yet sometimes it must be patient. In one sense faith is full speed ahead, while in another it is waiting on the Lord. Our lives require a vibrant faith applied to the affairs of life, but it also requires a patient waiting on the Lord, for the Father does know best.

Luke 9:1–9

JESUS HAD CALLED the Twelve together, he gave them power and authority to drive out all demons and to cure diseases, ² and he sent them out to preach the kingdom of God and to heal the sick. ³He told them: "Take nothing for the journey—no staff, no bag, no bread, no money, no extra tunic. ⁴Whatever house you enter, stay there until you leave that town. ⁵If people do not welcome you, shake the dust off your feet when you leave their town, as a testimony against them." ⁶So they set out and went from village to village, preaching the gospel and healing people everywhere.

⁷Now Herod the tetrarch heard about all that was going on. And he was perplexed, because some were saying that John had been raised from the dead, ⁸others that Elijah had appeared, and still others that one of the prophets of long ago had come back to life. ⁹But Herod said, "I beheaded John. Who, then, is this I hear such things about?" And he tried to see him.

Original Meaning

JESUS INTENDS TO get the message of the arrival of kingdom hope spread across the nation of Israel.[1] To accomplish this, he commissions the Twelve to minister for him in the towns and villages of the nation. He sends them out with the same authority that he has exercised, including the power to heal and to exorcise.[2] They are to preach the kingdom and heal the sick. This combination reflects Jesus' ministry of word and deed, linking the proclamation of hope for the promised arrival of God's rule with the demonstration of compassion. The disciples must minister in such a way that their concern to serve people where they are hurting is never in doubt.

The disciples are not to act like other practitioners of religion in their culture, who expected to be paid for their labors and went begging house to

---

1. For more details on the kingdom hope, see discussion on Luke 10:1–24.

2. Conceptual parallels to this account are Matthew 10:1–14 and Mark 6:6b–13, though the Matthean text is really part of a larger mission that is paralleled in Luke 10:1–24.

house to get provisions.[3] Jesus calls on them to trust God. They must travel light, taking nothing extra for their journey, not even two tunics.[4] They are to stay in one place, not go from house to house. Ministry should not burden those who are ministered to; rather, it should serve them. Wherever they are welcome, they should stay and minister; if they are not welcome, they must leave, shaking the dust from their feet to indicate God's rejection for rejecting his messengers.[5] The disciples leave on this mission, preaching the good news and healing.

A linkage in this passage should not be missed. In verse 2 the disciples are to "preach the kingdom of God," while in verse 6 they "preach the gospel." In other words, the gospel announces the arrival of blessing through Jesus in conjunction with the kingdom of God. The deeds of healing make evident the rule of God (8:22–56; 11:14–23). God has the power to deliver humanity from forces hostile to us, as Luke has just recorded in the four preceding miracles. In these acts, God's power and concern have been put on public display.

Luke 9:7–9 continues to ask a basic question in this Gospel, "Who is Jesus?"[6] This time it surfaces in Herod's court. The ruler wants to see Jesus because he has heard about him. What interests Herod are Jesus' miracles (23:8); he wants to see the show. Speculation on who can produce such works center on a few options: (1) Jesus is a prophet; (2) he has taken up the cause of John the Baptist, so he may be seen as John "resurrected"; (3) perhaps he is an eschatological prophet like Elijah, announcing the approach of the end. Herod's perplexity indicates how even in the highest social circles people struggled to understand Jesus. Most opinions limited Jesus to prophetic categories, as the healing at Nain indicated (7:16; 9:19). His healing activity and challenge to walk with God remind many of the prophets of old. But the offer of the kingdom means that more is being offered by his ministry.

---

3. Danker, *Jesus and the New Age*, 190. This became such a problem later in the church that *Didache* 11–12 give detailed instructions about how to deal with traveling missionaries. It can still be a problem today to know if someone who consistently speaks of the need for money truly represents the church.

4. The difference in wording between the various parallels about whether there are instructions about taking a staff may be resolved in recognizing that Jesus speaks of traveling light, so that no extra provisions are required. Although one Gospel speaks of not taking a staff (Matt. 10:9–10) while the other does allow it (Mark 6:8–9), each may be communicating the idea that one does not need to take an extra staff, since one must travel light.

5. According to the Jewish background of this action, such shaking reflected the removal of uncleanness from their feet as they said "good riddance" to those who lived in pagan contexts; Liefeld, "Luke," 8:919.

6. The parallels to this passage are Matthew 14:1–2 and Mark 6:14–16.

THE TWO FUNDAMENTAL prongs of ministry evident in this passage cross the temporal boundaries between our era and that of the text. Preaching God's Word and performing deeds of compassionate service complement each another. To teach that God loves sinners means evidencing that compassion in the ability to meet human needs. When the disciples get no response, they must leave and announce that rejection means the approach of judgment.

The call to travel light raises questions about how we minister today. One should be careful not to equate the type of itinerant ministry in these brief mission excursions with more permanent missionary efforts today. We may think that missionaries should take the most spartan approach to ministry, but this is hardly appropriate for those who go to reside in an area. Traveling lightly is more appropriate for someone who comes into an area for a short ministry campaign. Those called by God to live in an area for some time, however, must set up shop in a way that allows them to minister fully and be good hosts and neighbors to those around them. A minister and a missionary are both worthy of their hire.

The kind of speculation we see about Jesus in Herod's house in 9:7–9 is not unlike speculation today, except that contemporary speculation tends not to give Jesus as much inherent respect as even ancient opinions did. The activity of Jesus was primarily seen as work of a prophetic nature, because of his healing and his challenge to repent. Our distance from these events and our inherent pluralism cause many today to place Jesus among the great religious teachers of all time, while questioning his miraculous power. Such a category does not offend religious sensibilities today and is culturally safe. Yet this category is inadequate as far as Luke is concerned, and he uses his entire Gospel to explain why. The claims of Jesus are not one among many. He brings a unique time of fulfillment to God's plan of salvation that calls for decision.

ONE OF THE great dangers of the church is that because of fear, we have lost our desire to minister in concrete action as we seek to share God's word. Much evangelism today can be characterized as guerrilla strikes, where we venture in for a quick moment of sharing before returning home to our safe environment. When Jesus sent out his disciples, they were to trust in God's care and become directly engaged with those to whom they were ministering. That is why they had to look for a home to stay in. They did not use guerrilla tactics of dogging the enemy and being in and out of sight, but used an infiltration strategy, where their presence would be obvious.

Evangelism requires engagement. It often requires serving people as well as preaching to them. Telling unbelievers that God cares should be reinforced by evidences of such caring. Though the service of the disciples involved miraculous activity to demonstrate God's power in the new era, that aspect does not mean that miraculous ministry is called for today in order to give testimony to the gospel. The key to the disciples' activity was the combination of compassion and message, and that is what should be displayed on a mission field as the gospel is preached in word and deed. God can and may act in a sovereign display of power, but usually our ministry of evangelism requires a more mundane approach, but one that is just as meaningful. Concentrating on a ministry of miracles, as some power evangelism groups do, puts the emphasis in the wrong place.[7] This mission of the twelve introduces the kingdom. Our call now is to reflect its presence in service.

Most churches have lost this phase of evangelism, seeking only to share on the run. As excellent as many evangelism seminars are, they often lack a concrete ministry dimension. The goal is simply to get through a tract or a questionnaire. These approaches are not wrong, but they allow churches to create ministries that are self-focused on the church's own growth and needs. What is needed are more engagement-oriented programs, where the church "travels light" and engages the community with service, not just words. Such outreach-intensive ministries are the hardest to produce and sustain because they require a great deal of labor to make them effective. Nonetheless, such ministries have the potential of speaking the gospel more clearly than words alone do. Acts of caring reinforce the claim that God cares, putting flesh and blood on the claim.

Regarding the Herod passage, religious issues are not a matter of a majority poll and vote. People love to speculate on what is taking place, even in religious spheres, but that does not make their judgment correct. All the options considered in Herod's palace came up short in explaining who Jesus was. Respect for Jesus today, even regarding him as a prophetic figure, does not go far enough. We must accept his claim to bring God's way. Islam and other world religions do respect Jesus as a man of God, but they deny his claims to bring us to God. If Jesus' teaching is considered good, can his most

---

7. For more discussion on the role of miracles today, see the discussion in Luke 4:31–44, where we discussed the power evangelism movement associated with the ministries introduced by John Wimber and Peter Wagner.

basic claim be ignored? Can we honor Jesus and reject his unique claim to be the Promised One who brings forgiveness (24:47)?

Herod appears interested in Jesus only as a matter of curiosity. He longs to see him, but only because he has heard so much about him. This is not the best way to approach Jesus. His ministry is not a matter of popular, sociological inquiry, as if he were a figure in *People* magazine. Rather, one should take seriously the claim that he has been sent from God as the Messiah and that he shows us the way to God (9:18–20). Herod pictures a figure who almost tragically trivializes Jesus and his ministry.

Luke 9:10–17

WHEN THE APOSTLES returned, they reported to Jesus what they had done. Then he took them with him and they withdrew by themselves to a town called Bethsaida, ¹¹but the crowds learned about it and followed him. He welcomed them and spoke to them about the kingdom of God, and healed those who needed healing.

¹²Late in the afternoon the Twelve came to him and said, "Send the crowd away so they can go to the surrounding villages and countryside and find food and lodging, because we are in a remote place here."

¹³He replied, "You give them something to eat."

They answered, "We have only five loaves of bread and two fish—unless we go and buy food for all this crowd." ¹⁴(About five thousand men were there.)

But he said to his disciples, "Have them sit down in groups of about fifty each." ¹⁵The disciples did so, and everybody sat down. ¹⁶Taking the five loaves and the two fish and looking up to heaven, he gave thanks and broke them. Then he gave them to the disciples to set before the people. ¹⁷They all ate and were satisfied, and the disciples picked up twelve basketfuls of broken pieces that were left over.

Original Meaning

LUKE NOW RECORDS the only miracle that is in all four Gospels: the feeding of the five thousand (Matt. 14:13–21; Mark 6:32–44; John 6:1–15). This miracle of provision obviously indicates how Jesus meets needs. But there is a second key to the miracle, in that this provision comes through the disciples. Jesus has just commissioned them to share the kingdom message (9:1–6). They need to be aware of what they can do through Christ. Jesus shows them that they have access to his authority through his enablement.

Two other images impact this event. The provision of food is conceptually similar to two key Old Testament events, God's provision of quail and Elisha's provision of barley bread (Num. 11; 2 Kings 4:42–44).[1] The pic-

---

1. Marshall, *Commentary on Luke*, 357.

ture of table fellowship also evokes images of the messianic banquet, where God's people enjoy fellowship provided by the gracious provision of the Messiah.

The miracle has a rich tapestry of fundamental themes that weave through Jesus' ministry: compassion, control over creation, and the ability to make provisions for life. In a sense, this is a cameo portrait of God's grace and the offer of his presence at a table where he provides for his children.

The disciples have returned from their mission and report to Jesus on all they have done. No details are given, though their report about a later mission is surely similar (10:17). That this report is the setting for the miracle is no accident. Luke is indicating the importance Jesus gives to the concept that he will minister through his servants. They will do great things through his enabling power.

The disciples withdraw with Jesus to Bethsaida, a city located on the west coast of the Sea of Galilee. As always, a crowd follows them. Again Jesus preaches the kingdom and heals the multitudes. But the day is winding down and the sun is setting. The disciples, who always keep the practical questions in front of them, begin to wonder where and how they will feed the crowd of five thousand men. Surely it is time to call it a day. The crowd should be dismissed to find food and lodging.

Jesus surprises his disciples by telling them to provide the food. The food accountants in the group take inventory: five loaves and two fish. It is impossible to feed five thousand with this small amount. Procuring sufficient provision for this crowd will be a logistical nightmare, even for twelve men. Surely Jesus should reconsider!

He does. He tells them to group the crowd into units of fifty. Then taking the five loaves and two fish, he invokes the blessing of God. He breaks the bread and hands the food to the disciples to distribute. Through their connection to Jesus, the disciples provide enough food for all present, with twelve baskets left over. No details of how the multiplication of loaves and fish takes place are given. Rather, Luke stresses the provision itself. Like Israel in the desert or the time of Elisha the prophet, Jesus has a ministry that can meet our most fundamental needs. Moreover, the disciples can do all things necessary for ministry through the Christ who enables them. In a sense Jesus is preparing to pass the torch of ministry to them. So lessons are present, both for those who receive the provision and those through whom Jesus provides it.

THE DYNAMICS OF successful ministry are timeless. Disciples can make provision through the enablement Jesus provides. His call to serve and provide for others out of compassion requires we think not of ourselves, but how we can reach others. Such a ministry goes counter to the way people normally operate, where self-provision is often the order of the day. The ministry of the church involves a call to minister through him and for him. Though we may discuss things today other than the procurement of a meal, the dynamic in place is the same. To minister outside of the provision Jesus provides is not real ministry. On the other hand, relying on him means that one is in touch with the One who can provide all that is necessary for effective ministry.

The disciples need to see that they can accomplish things they never dreamed of doing through their association with Jesus. Only the limits of their vision will prevent them from moving forward in ministry. On this day, they are part of something they have never contemplated doing before. They will never be the same again, because the course of instruction Jesus begins with them here teaches them the important lessons they need for effective ministry. It may take them a while to get the point, as it often does us. But they eventually come to see and draw upon the full effect of Jesus' power.

"WE HAVE NEVER done that before" or "We could never do that" are the two great killer phrases in the ministry. They sually appear because of practical concerns or because of the traditional way things have been done. In the process, great ideas can get squashed. The disciples, though not entirely surprisingly, lack vision for the new way Jesus wishes to provide for the crowd. Yet his presence changes the equation of what is possible. This miracle shows that ministers in touch with Jesus can make provision in surprising ways. Creatively relying on him brings the Twelve to new frontiers of ministry. He is able to direct them and lead them into seeing that through him comes spiritual sustenance.

The commentary of Jesus on this event in John 6 indicates how he is "the bread of life," the source of spiritual provision and direction. In Acts 3–4, the church has learned the lesson that to be effective in ministry, they must draw on what Jesus provides; throughout Acts, the church continues to learn creatively about the possibility of ministry through reliance on Jesus.

There is no one way to reach people. The ministry of provision takes many forms. But one dynamic is a constant: To be effective, the one who leads in setting out the provision must be Jesus. Whether one ministers through visiting someone in the hospital, providing meals for a family who are not able to provide for themselves, or simply being available to listen to someone's emotional trauma, those who seek to provide what Jesus offers bring a picture of God's compassion to those they serve.

There is another note in this event. The simple scene of reclining together in fellowship paints a picture of the community that Jesus seeks to provide. As the food was distributed and the meal provided, there was a sense that Jesus had ministered to all of them, since there was more than enough food provided for all those present. This setting is a statement against privatized religion, where my only concern is what God is doing with me. Jesus teaches us to minister to the multitudes and gather them together as a community. Later on, Jesus urges unity on his disciples in his call to show the world how they love one another (John 13:34–35). Our personal agendas should be left at the door when we are in the presence of the Lord.

Jesus later instituted the Lord's table to make the same point. The meal of fellowship we enjoy at Jesus' feet means we are all seated at the same table. We should minister with the awareness that the table is his and the food he has provided is his. That is why 1 Corinthians 10:16–17 and 11:23–27 emphasize the importance of unity at the table, for we all partake of one loaf and cup and we make a joint proclamation of our allegiance to Jesus.

Luke 9:18–22

ONCE WHEN JESUS was praying in private and his disciples were with him, he asked them, "Who do the crowds say I am?"

[19]They replied, "Some say John the Baptist; others say Elijah; and still others, that one of the prophets of long ago has come back to life."

[20]"But what about you?" he asked. "Who do you say I am?"

Peter answered, "The Christ of God."

[21]Jesus strictly warned them not to tell this to anyone.

[22]And he said, "The Son of Man must suffer many things and be rejected by the elders, chief priests and teachers of the law, and he must be killed and on the third day be raised to life."

Original Meaning

THE GOSPEL OF Luke comes to a major turning point in 9:18–22 as Peter confesses Jesus as the Christ. It opens the door for a full discussion of discipleship in 9:23–50. The recognition of Jesus as the Christ is fundamental to responding to Jesus, but it must be supplemented by an explanation of his messianic activity. Jesus will indeed have a period of glorious rule when he returns to earth to exercise his authority visibly. Then he will judge the unrighteous and vindicate those who are his. But before the glory comes suffering, and his disciples will walk the same road. Thus, after Peter's confession, Jesus has to teach the disciples about the Messiah. They must "listen to him" (v. 35) to understand God's plan. To minister effectively they must change their views. Their instincts alone will not be an adequate guide to negotiate their way through the road of discipleship that calls one to suffer and serve, not just to rule.

Luke has been considering the question of who Jesus is in several passages (4:14–30; 7:16; 8:25; 9:7–9). Now the disciples provide a reply that yields a positive response from Jesus.[1] Peter knows that Jesus is more than a prophet. They have been with him and know that he is not a mere teacher of God's Word or one of many agents of God; he is the promised deliverer sent by God.

---

1. The parallels to this text are Matthew 16:13–23 and Mark 8:27–33. The account is rendered with some variation, but the fundamental point of each text is the same: a confession of Jesus' messiahship.

The confession emerges gradually. Jesus first asks about popular perceptions of who he is. The answer that comes matches the speculation of 9:7–9. The crowd believes that Jesus is a prophet of some kind or the reappearance of John the Baptist. In contrast, Peter confesses Jesus as the Messiah. The importance of the difference should not be missed. He sees Jesus as God's Promised Ruler, though this category is short of a full confession of deity. More time with Jesus and more reflection on the significance of his resurrection will produce that deeper understanding of Jesus and his messianic function.

Peter's confession can lead to misunderstanding about what is ahead for Jesus, so Jesus immediately moves to correct that possibility. The disciples anticipate a direct route to glory. They believe power and privilege are the destiny of those associated with him. But they have much to learn about the road the Messiah travels. He predicts the suffering of the Son of Man in rejection, death, and resurrection. These things "must" happen; Luke uses the Greek word *dei* to indicate that God's design is involved in the call to suffer. This is the first Son of Man saying in Luke that refers to suffering.

The Old Testament background to the necessity of such suffering has been much discussed.[2] Some argue that this prediction looks too much like prophecy after the fact and that Jesus did not in fact make a prediction like this. But this underestimates the availability from the Old Testament of themes related to suffering, vindication, and victory. A combination of Old Testament teachings clearly make that association: the imagery of the suffering servant (Isa. 52:13–53:12) and the idea of the suffering of the righteous in the Psalter (Pss. 16; 22; 31; 69; 118). Both these themes teach that suffering precedes glory. It is this surprising route to glory that has caused Jesus to call for silence about the earlier confessions of him as Messiah, for the Messiah was seen as a triumphant figure who did not suffer at all. The disciples must have God's true plan explained to them before they can share it with others.

Despite the need for more instruction, Peter's confession is a crucial turning point. In recognizing Jesus as the Promised One of God, he sees that Jesus is unique. Such a building block is fundamental to understanding God's plan of redemption and its accomplishment through Jesus. Whereas "prophet" was a category that left Jesus short, "Messiah" is one that places him as the promised deliverer from God. That is why in Matthew's version of this confession, Jesus notes that "on this rock"—that is, on the confession and on people like Peter who see it—the church will be built (Matt. 16:18). To be a Christian is to understand this unique role of Jesus. There is no one else like

---

2. Nolland, *Luke 9:21–18:34*, 468–74.

him in the plan of God. He is the only foundation that can be laid to build the house of God (1 Cor. 3:11).

THE SIGNIFICANCE OF this prediction has implications for the believer's route to blessing. Jesus walks a path that his disciples are called to follow, though such suffering may well take a different form in the first century. At that time, families separated over religious issues, and isolation resulted. Some cultures today still witness such consequences for trusting Jesus; but in cultures where religious tolerance reigns, the suffering is more subtle. Believers may not be understood, for example, when they value family over a promotion in their job. They may not be understood when they desire to travel to faraway lands to minister the gospel to others rather than pursue a "normal vocation." Even one's immediate family may not understand decisions like these (see 9:57–62). Disciples are called to reflect distinct values in the choices they make in life or the values they carry.

Individual choice is not the highest value on life's board, so that the right to life for the unborn does matter, or one may turn down a job promotion if it does not enhance the possibility of being effective in serving God. Those tough choices may lead to misunderstanding. Such suffering may not be the type of physical persecution Jesus alludes to here, but it is a form of rejection that emerges because one has walked a different road for God. So though martyrdom is less likely in some parts of the world, suffering is still a reality for many who seek to engage the world with their commitment to Jesus.

THE FUNDAMENTAL SIGNIFICANCE in this text is its recognition about who Christ is. There is no greater tragedy or error of judgment in life than to underestimate him. To miss the one who possesses the gift of life is to miss life itself. To understand him as the Christ without understanding who the Messiah really is leaves us short in understanding Jesus. That is why, in 20:41–44, Jesus asks why David called the Messiah "Lord" rather than "Son." There is a hierarchy in the plan of God, and Jesus stands at the top of it, ministering for God on our behalf from the right hand of the Father. The disciples do not understand that about Jesus at this time, though subsequent events will make it clear.

Many contemporary portraits of Jesus fall short of understanding who Jesus is. Some attempt to accept him as a religious teacher, a member of the religious Hall of Fame, but do not see him as unique. This approach to Jesus is popular in our culture, since it is a tolerant stance that does not foist his uniqueness on anyone. Unfortunately, it is also a view that denies one of the most fundamental claims of the great teacher, namely, that he uniquely represented the fulfillment of all God's promises and uniquely showed the way to him. Whether one takes the Synoptic portrait of Jesus as the fulfillment of Isaiah's promise in Isaiah 61:1–2 or the Johannine portrait that he is "the way and the truth and the life" (John 14:6), the point is that Jesus is not merely a prophet, as many in his day perceived him; he is much more. Our culture's attempt to relativize one of Jesus' fundamental claims is not consistent with regarding him as the great teacher. How can one respect Jesus' religious greatness as a teacher and then reject or relativize his most fundamental claim to be the unique Son of God? One cannot have it both ways. Either Jesus was unique in fulfilling the promise of God, or else his claims were a distortion of truth—hardly a standard for a religious teacher of note.

Other more subtle contemporary attempts to relativize Jesus' claim have recently appeared among some who study the New Testament. They attempt to drive a wedge between what Jesus taught and what the Gospels portray him as teaching. The claim is that the Christ of faith does not equal the Jesus of history. Differences in the Gospel portraits are highlighted as giving evidence of the church's expansion of the teaching about Jesus. In this way, Jesus' exalted claims are seen as utterances of the early church, with the most extravagant ones put into his mouth by the Evangelists. Those who promote this position hope to reclaim a culturally palatable Jesus by showing that his uniqueness was the product of devoted followers who made more of him than he did of himself.[3] But such criticism fails to explain how Jesus could be crucified and how the disciples gave their own lives for such a belief. It also underestimates how tradition could communicate in summary form Jesus' life and teaching. It refuses to recognize the possibility that the Gospel writers, in telling their story, could each have had access to fresh facts about Jesus. It also does not recognize that the Evangelists not only quoted but also often summarized the thrust of Jesus' teaching with some variety of expression. They did so without distorting the fundamental portrait of who he was and what he did. This highly critical approach to Jesus is a modern form of attempting to treat Jesus as a prophet and not as the Promised One of God, thus falling short of Peter's confession. A Jesus who is merely a prophet reduces the Christian faith to one ethic among many, something it never

---

3. This approach to Jesus has been critiqued thoroughly in *Jesus Under Fire: Modern Scholarship Reinvents the Historical Jesus*, ed. M. Wilkins and J. P. Moreland (Grand Rapids: Zondervan, 1994).

claims to be. Peter's confession is crucial because in it he is claiming that Jesus uniquely bears the hope of God's promise.

This passage also makes clear that blessing does not always come through a path of prosperity. Spirituality often requires great cost and pain (see 9:23–27), and one must be prepared to face the same sort of reaction Jesus faced. Much of Luke 9–19 is dedicated to describing exactly what this path may involve; here we have only the first hints of what is coming. Some parts of the world have an inherently better understanding of this part of the walk with Christ than what exists in the Western world. One of the advantages of being at a seminary with students from around the world is hearing the differing conditions believers must live in as they confess Jesus. It is not unusual to hear about those who lost promotions or jobs or were forced to work on Sunday simply because people found out they were believers. Some faced prison for their beliefs. In some contexts, confessing Jesus literally meant suffering. For those of us who live in a society where sharing Jesus is not outlawed, such testimonies should encourage us to be bold.

Luke 9:23–27

THEN HE SAID to them all: "If anyone would come after me, he must deny himself and take up his cross daily and follow me. ²⁴For whoever wants to save his life will lose it, but whoever loses his life for me will save it. ²⁵What good is it for a man to gain the whole world, and yet lose or forfeit his very self? ²⁶If anyone is ashamed of me and my words, the Son of Man will be ashamed of him when he comes in his glory and in the glory of the Father and of the holy angels. ²⁷I tell you the truth, some who are standing here will not taste death before they see the kingdom of God."

Original Meaning

CROSS-BEARING IS A powerful ancient image.[1] Rejection stood at the center of that image, as well as accountability to the state.[2] The cross-bearer had committed a severe crime and needed elimination. Criminals bore their own crosses as they journeyed to their death. Thus for a Christian to bear a cross is to be prepared to face rejection and death, even as one remains accountable to God for the path one walks. It means that one has died to the world, separated from its values and lifestyle (Gal. 6:14).

Luke 9:23 has an interesting sequence of tenses. All three verbs are imperatives, but the call to "deny [one]self" and "take up [one's] cross"[3] are in Greek aorist tenses, while the call to "follow [Jesus]" is in the present. This means that discipleship involves the fundamental commitment of self-denial and bearing one's cross, while the call to follow Jesus is constant, growing out of the base commitments. Discipleship therefore requires a basic shift of orientation as we align ourselves with God's will through a humble renunciation of our own agenda. To deny ourselves in the context of cross-bearing means that the world may "kill" us for walking outside its

---

1. The parallels to this passage are Matthew 16:24–28 and Mark 8:34–9:1. The passages occupy the same relative position in each of the Synoptic Gospels. On crucifixion, see M. Hengel, *Crucifixion in the Ancient World and the Folly of the Message of the Cross* (Philadelphia: Fortress, 1977).

2. J. Schneider, "σταυρός," *TDNT*, 7:578–79; Fitzmyer, *Luke 1-IX*, 787; Marshall, *Commentary on Luke*, 373.

3. Only Luke adds the word "daily" to the idea of taking up one's cross.

paths, but we are ready to do so, because God has called us to walk a different way.

Verse 24 summarizes the point nicely. If you try to save your life by preserving yourself from the opposition of the world and/or by accommodating yourself to the world, what results is loss of real life. On the other hand, if you are willing to lose your life for the sake of the things of God, then what you save is real life. In the ancient world, choosing for Jesus meant certain opposition from people in the world. That opposition might express itself in the type of scorn Jesus saw, the type of ridicule the early church faced, beatings such as Paul experienced, or even death such as Stephen faced. The Christian faith was new and, in its Jewish context, was a threat to well-established traditions. If someone desired popularity and acceptance, he or she did not accept Christ. But the cost of popular acclaim was great, since the choice meant forfeiting the opportunity of salvation. Only those willing to line up with God and face popular rejection would respond to the gospel and enter into life. Thus, from the beginning, the choice of Jesus had built into it a sense of going a different way.

Jesus' rhetorical question in verse 25 drives the point home. "To gain the whole world" means that all the provision, power, and property the world can provide is available to us—like our idiom "to have the world by the tail." To Jesus, it makes no sense to live this way, for it makes one a loser at real life. What is described here as a proverb was earlier a temptation for Jesus. In 4:5–8, he faced a choice between walking on the path God called him to take or accepting the kingdoms of the world by bowing before Satan. Jesus knew, of course, that the choice was not a real one, for Satan could not give him what God could. Thus, Jesus calls on disciples here to follow the example he has already established. To gain the world at the expense of one's soul is a bad investment and a losing proposition.

What will such sacrifice gain? Jesus uses a negative picture to answer the question. Those ashamed or afraid to confess the Son of Man (i.e., Jesus) will face his rejection when he returns with all of heaven's glory. They will get what they have chosen: separation from him. Jesus portrays himself as the judge at the end of time, a theme Luke develops elsewhere (Acts 10:40–43; 17:30–31). Our Lord will not accept any who have asked him not to be a part of their life. But the picture is a tragic one, for when he reappears, his position and privilege will be obvious to all. To be excluded will be a public affair; facing eternity without God and knowing it is the most tragic of all positions in life. On the other hand, by implication, those who ally themselves to Jesus will experience the kingdom of God.

Jesus concludes his remarks with a note that some present with him will not taste death until they experience the kingdom of God. This remark appears to have two points of reference. (1) Some of the Twelve will journey with Jesus to the mountain and experience the Transfiguration (9:28–36), where they will receive a glimpse or preview of Jesus' coming glory. They will "see" the kingdom of God to come. (2) The reference may well anticipate as well the type of blessing that descends on the church at Pentecost, since there the power of the risen Jesus manifests itself in the distribution of the Spirit (Acts 2:14–39). With the Spirit the promise of the messianic blessing commences, and God begins to express his presence and rule from within his people (Luke 3:15–17; 24:49; Acts 1:5–8). Thus, Jesus notes that with the hard road of discipleship comes association with the rich blessing of being a part of God's kingdom.

THESE TEXTS ARE hard for us to reflect on today, because cross-bearing in the ancient sense of walking to one's death rarely happens for most Christians today. Discipleship does not come with the almost automatic sense of cost it carried then. A decision for Jesus does not bring automatic rejection today. If anything, we suffer from an opposite issue. It is possible to operate in such a closed Christian circle that one lacks all contact with the outside world and thus misses the rejection of the world that this passage assumes will be present. One can experience a type of institutionalized Christianity that assumes one is born a believer or that stays so cloistered to protect one's moral identity that one never really engages those in the world. Such a Christianity will never face the discipleship tensions Jesus describes here. But such a protected kind of discipleship is not what Jesus asks his followers to understake when he calls them to bear their cross daily. Jesus assumes those who are his will indeed represent him in the world. He also knows the world will react. Yet even those who do undertake his mission faithfully today often do not face persecution that early Christians endured.

But to note that faith today often does not involve persecution does not mean that discipleship is without cost or ceases to exist. The world is just as potent and powerfully present today as it was then. The call for us to walk differently from the walk of the world is just as essential an attribute of discipleship today as it was then. A walk of integrity, purity, faithfulness, and humble service should be just as evident today as it was in Jesus' day. If we are too comfortable in the world and if no one can tell our lives are different, it may be because we have not taken the full journey of discipleship Christ calls us to take. That does not mean that we should blow a trumpet to draw attention to our different way of living. It should emerge naturally, like lights shining in darkness.

The road of service is not a road to self-fulfillment as proclaimed by the world. It involves a type of self-denial where the spiritual and basic needs of others are rigorously pursued. In a world where individual rights have almost inviolate status, such selflessness cuts against the grain. Bearing one's cross means denying one's own agenda, seeking to serve God and follow him, so that one also serves others as a believer gives testimony to God's compassion for all of us. That is never popular in a world that exalts one's right to self-actualization.

OUR WALK WITH God is not something that takes place on "automatic pilot." For many, Christianity is merely a guaranteed ticket to heaven. But Jesus never envisioned the faith as a "one-stop" experience. This section on following Jesus makes clear just how demanding discipleship is. It requires a whole new way of thinking and of orienting oneself to life. The path of following Jesus requires spiritual labor, the bearing of a cross daily. Jesus underscores the fact that to carry a cross one must deny the self. Agendas change when one comes after Jesus, since he has already marked out the path.

Denying oneself means different things in different contexts. To a parent, it means not just seeking one's own desires, but serving the child in their best interests in terms of the investment of time and energy. To a spouse, it means not just asking what can be done for you, but considering how one can be of help to his or her partner. To a neighbor, it means considering how one can be of service and show concern in the affairs of life. To a colleague at work, it may mean not seeing how you can advance the responsibilities you have to undertake, but how you can be of service to them. Most importantly to God, it means seeking his will and spending time before him so he can lead and guide you in the way you should go. Discipleship means being a learner, a follower. It means that our attention is turned to how we can follow Jesus, not how we can make him follow us.

This means that we are seeking his kingdom, not our own. Materialism and the pursuit of power, independence, and security are probably the biggest obstacles to spiritual advancement. Everything in our culture from commercials to our education pushes us in the direction of advancing our standing of living for more comfort. To pick up a cross means walking against the grain of cultural values, so that our own expectations and needs take a back seat to God's call. Some things we may have seen as ours by natural right may need to be renounced because they represent a subtle form of idolatry. The Spirit guides us into seeing things differently than we did before. Bearing a cross may mean leaving behind dreams created for us long ago by a citizenship we have now left behind.

So discipleship requires a renewal of the mind (Rom. 12:1–2) and a commitment of the heart to that renewal. It will mean intense involvement with God's Word and with other believers who are dedicated to growing in their faith. A disciple is never stagnant and never has the spiritual life in a mode where God cannot challenge him or her to a deeper walk. As Jesus has noted, it is an offering of the self in service to the Son of Man.

Finally, Jesus saved us for discipleship. His goal was to make a people eager to be his people (Titus 2:11–14). The idea of a ticket to heaven was never his goal; that is at best a byproduct. Having eternal life is a great blessing because it means we know God and will enjoy his presence forever (John 17:3). Living forever would be useless if he were not there to be a part of it. But there is more to salvation than heaven. He saved us to change us, to make us different in the world than we were before we came to know him. That is why the spiritual person is called to follow him where he leads. In his leading, he transforms us to be more like him. So discipleship is a full-time job, not a weekend hobby. As a lifestyle and commitment, it never takes a holiday. That is why Jesus says we should bear our cross daily.

Luke 9:28–36

ABOUT EIGHT DAYS after Jesus said this, he took Peter, John and James with him and went up onto a mountain to pray. ²⁹As he was praying, the appearance of his face changed, and his clothes became as bright as a flash of lightning. ³⁰Two men, Moses and Elijah, ³¹appeared in glorious splendor, talking with Jesus. They spoke about his departure, which he was about to bring to fulfillment at Jerusalem.³²Peter and his companions were very sleepy, but when they became fully awake, they saw his glory and the two men standing with him. ³³As the men were leaving Jesus, Peter said to him, "Master, it is good for us to be here. Let us put up three shelters— one for you, one for Moses and one for Elijah." (He did not know what he was saying.)

³⁴While he was speaking, a cloud appeared and enveloped them, and they were afraid as they entered the cloud. ³⁵A voice came from the cloud, saying, "This is my Son, whom I have chosen; listen to him." ³⁶When the voice had spoken, they found that Jesus was alone. The disciples kept this to themselves, and told no one at that time what they had seen.

Original Meaning

THIS UNIQUE EVENT of the Transfiguration is one of only two places that "heaven" speaks directly about Jesus. The voice that tells the disciples to hear Jesus recalls an earlier heavenly endorsement at his baptism (3:21–22). The additional presence of Moses and Elijah also adds a note of uniqueness. No other event in the Gospels involves the presence of luminaries of the past. The visible glorification of Jesus is also unique. Even in his resurrection appearances he is not described as bearing the brilliance he does here.[1]

Jesus has just told the disciples that following him will involve a radical change of perspective. The life of the disciple is different from that of the world or even from that which the world expects God's people to have. But much instruction lies ahead for the disciples. Thus this scene emphasizes

---

1. The parallels to this event are Matthew 17:1–9 and Mark 9:2–10, where the event occupies a similar locale.

the need to hear Jesus. The rest of the events in this chapter indicate that the disciples' initial instincts about how to respond to certain events are wrong. They will need to listen carefully to correct their ways.

Jesus opts to go to a mountain to pray and takes Peter, John, and James with him. The specific mountain is not named, but suggested candidates include Mount Hermon near Caesarea Philippi, Mount Tabor in Southern Galilee, and Mount Meron, northwest of the Sea of Galilee. Tabor has the strongest support in the tradition.[2] The mountain's not being named suggests the exact locale is not significant, though Jesus' being in northern Palestine indicates that his central ministry takes place outside of Jerusalem, outside the beaten path.

During his time of prayer Jesus is transformed into a glorious figure with a brilliance like lightning. His glory recalls the description of Moses on the mountain in Exodus 34:29–34. Jesus is not alone, since he is joined by Moses and Elijah. Their presence has spawned much discussion. Why are these two present? Do they represent themselves or stand for a larger group?[3] Though these are two great saints, it is hard to believe their selection has only personal meaning for them. They represent two key periods in Israel's history. Like the figures Abraham, Isaac, or Jacob, when Moses and Elijah are mentioned, a string of associations surfaces. Moses typifies the type of prophetic office Jesus will occupy, especially since the voice from heaven will allude to Deuteronomy 18:15 (cf. v. 35). Elijah represents the prophet of the eschaton (cf. Mal 4:5), so he pictures a commitment to the arrival of the age of fulfillment. These two Old Testament witnesses highlight that Jesus represents a realization of Old Testament hope, since the two figures also span both the early and late periods of Old Testament history.

Moses and Elijah are discussing Jesus' "departure" (Gk. *exodos*). Luke is the only Gospel to note this topic of conversation. The "exodus" alludes to the journey Jesus is taking, with its turning point being his death in Jerusalem. Much of Luke's Gospel from here through chapter 19 concerns preparation of the disciples for ministry in light of his departure.

The disciples are napping but wake up to find the discussion in process (v. 32). Peter, in his excitement, asks Jesus if three booths should be built— an allusion to the Feast of Tabernacles, which looked forward to the arrival of the end times through recalling God's provision for the nation in the desert (Ex. 23:16; 34:22; Lev. 23:34; Deut. 16:13).[4] Peter correctly under-

---

2. Arndt, *Luke*, 262; Fitzmyer, *Luke I–IX*, 798.

3. For the many suggestions, see Jeremias, "Ἠλείας," *TDNT*, 2:938–39; Danker, *Jesus and the New Age*, 199; Marshall, *Commentary on Luke*, 384.

4. Marshall, *Commentary on Luke*, 386; Michaelis, "σκηνή," *TDNT*, 7:370; see also the *Mishnah, Sukka* 3:9; 4:5.

stands that Moses and Elijah represent hope and fulfillment, but he wants three booths in a way that ranks the three figures equally. Luke signals that Peter speaks with ignorance, for he does not know what he is saying (v. 33b).

Before a reply can be given, a cloud envelops the three and offers commentary. The presence of the cloud recalls the Shekinah presence of God in the Exodus. The disciples are filled with fear, but need only listen as the voice commends his Son, the chosen one, who must be heard. These remarks work like a political endorsement—only this time the endorsement is from God himself. The use of the first person "my Son" indicates who is speaking. The saying virtually parallels what was said at Jesus' baptism. There, too, the Son whom God loves was mentioned, but there is one addition and one change. (1) The description "whom I have chosen" elaborates on the "whom I love" in the baptism scene. It highlights the fact that God's choice of Jesus is conscious and makes him unique. He is the elect one, called to be the deliverer and a prophetic figure like Moses, who revealed God's way in the Law and consolidated a people he led into a new existence.

(2) The addition of "listen to him" marks out the disciples' responsibility. They must pay attention to what Jesus is saying, for they have much to learn. This phrase comes from Deuteronomy 18:15, marking Jesus out as a prophet like Moses. As he guides and directs God's people, he will form them into a newly constituted community. There is no need for three booths; they need only listen to one voice—that of Jesus.

After the endorsement only Jesus is left. The event is so startling that the disciples say nothing about it for some time. They are best silent until they understand it. No doubt the implications of it will take a while to develop. Second Peter 1:16–18 provides a later reflective commentary on this event. It is not unusual for startling events to be accompanied with a period of silence (Dan. 10:15). Some events need reflection before there can be adequate commentary.

THIS EVENT REMINDS us of the glory Jesus will possess. He has just spoken of the glorious return of the Son of Man (vv. 26–27). Now he is revealed as that figure in a sneak preview of what God's plan has in store for him. But before glory must be the "exodus" of suffering.

As with many texts in Luke, the major feature of this passage is its Christological teaching, that Jesus is the messianic chosen one who functions like Moses and Elijah. Many great Old Testament figures walk the pages of divine history, but none are more illustrious than Moses or Elijah. Yet in the face of the presence of Jesus, they are mere witnesses. In the Hall of Fame that is made up of the great figures of the Bible, no one occupies a space alongside Jesus; he is unique.

The call to hear Jesus is also timeless. What he says about discipleship and ministry here, the church needs to hear today. This is especially true of the values the church should have as it ministers (cf. 6:20–49 and chs. 9–19, which function as a commentary on "listen to him"). The ethical requirements for successful ministry never change. The disciples must understand that following him means going a different way from the world. Expediency is not the road to travel; integrity is. Ministry does not involve material gain; it is a call to serve others.

THE FUNDAMENTAL APPLICATION of this passage highlights the uniqueness of Jesus. Even though in the sense of resurrection and renewal Jesus is "the firstborn among many brothers" (Rom. 8:29), he is also the unique Son of God, the Son of David who will soon be revealed in power through his resurrection (Rom. 1:2–4). No one brings the package to the table of God's promise that he does. The surprising nature of this claim is lost on us two thousand years later, because the church's public relations within the community have been very effective. But the claim of Jesus' superiority to Moses was revolutionary at the time.

In an ironic way, however, the unique claim about Jesus is just as revolutionary today. In our pluralistic culture, we long for spiritual examples, and like Peter we want as many booths to be built in a row as possible. Our culture desires to assemble a religious hall of honor from as many religious traditions as possible, all in honor of our commitment to religious toleration. But Jesus does not ask for a booth alongside the others. The heavenly voice notes that he transcends all cultures and is called to minister to all humanity as God's chosen servant. He is the ultimate multicultural figure, calling everyone to himself in the ultimate equal opportunity call. The world does not need the clash of competing religious figures and examples. It needs a Savior for all humanity. The Transfiguration is a divine declaration that such a unique figure exists, and the world should listen to him. Any devaluation of Jesus distorts who he is.

The event also gives insight to these privileged disciples about where God's plan is headed. Jesus is not just a meek Galilean teacher, nor should he be seen as someone who merely calls on us to love one another, perhaps the most popular current image of Jesus. He is not the equal of Moses, Mohammed, or Joseph Smith. These current popular perceptions of Jesus are a major distortion of who he is. He is the glorified and chosen one of God, who one day will manifest himself with all the glory that the mountain scene revealed.

One thinks here of Revelation 4–5 and its glorious portrayal of the heavenly throne room, where God sits in glory with the "Lamb," who is worthy to reveal God's plan in the sealed scrolls. No wonder so much of the church is driven by the desire to worship this unique figure. No wonder God calls us to worship, as a reminder of just how unique he is and how honored we are to share in the blessings of his hand. No wonder the disciples who experienced this event left the scene silent for a long time about what had taken place. No wonder in church we often sing, "Worthy is the Lamb who was slain to receive power and honor and dominion." Such hymns do not emerge from thin air; they reflect the heartbeat of a community who understands the Lord whom they serve. To fathom the Transfiguration requires something other than words; it takes a new heart.

A new heart leads us to sit at Jesus' feet, ready to learn and listen. In our era, where feelings are so important, it is difficult to stress the importance of carefully laid out religious instruction. What is in view here is not the pedantic memorization of religious facts or the ability to indicate where something is in Scripture, but a reflective interaction with Scripture and one's walk with God. This dynamic between God's Word and life enables the believer to interact wisely with the culture and people God brings into his or her life.

Our walk with God requires a different way of assessing the world and expects a distinct perspective on moral values. It means that spouses treat each other with mutual respect and that issues of power dissolve in the face of mutual love and concern. It means a word given is an act performed. It means that a powerful and beautiful gift like sexuality is not cheapened by being paraded to all bidders, but is kept like a precious treasure, to use as God intended in a context of love and commitment. It means that life and the preservation of life are to be honored. It means at a social level that injustice aimed to those who do not have power and risk being dehumanized is exposed and addressed. It means that theology and a moral perspective from the Scripture are paramount, no matter what ideology or political party might be challenged in the process. It means that ethical decisions, including those related to medicine, are thought through, and the expedient choice is not all there is.[5]

---

5. For two key works touching on different areas of these questions, see Os Guinness, *The American Hour: A Time of Reckoning and the Once and Future Role of Faith* (New York: Free Press, 1993); John S. Feinberg and Paul D. Feinberg, *Ethics for a Brave New World* (Wheaton: Crossway, 1993).

These distinct perspectives do not emerge from instinct, nor are they developed overnight. The disciples required several years of twenty-four-hour-a-day life instruction from the Lord to grow in the understanding of God's call. Today's church needs a similar saturation of exposure to the voice of God. Disciples who desire to know God will not only seek to give him worship but will sit at his feet constantly listening to his voice.

Os Guinness, in analyzing our culture of secularism, notes the dead end it creates in contrast to a view infused by the living God:

> Americans with a purely secular view of life have too much to live with, too little to live for. Everything is permitted and nothing is important. But once growth and prosperity cease to be their reason for existence, they are bound to ask questions about the purpose and meaning of their lives: Whence? Whither? Why? And to such questions secularism has no answers that have yet proved widely satisfying in practice. Few of the great thinkers of the twentieth century have remained loyal to secular humanism. Secularism in its sophisticated form rarely flourishes outside intellectual centers where the mind is the organizing center of life. In its more "popular" Marxist form, it is keeling over arthritically. The very emptiness of our secular age is its deepest spiritual significance.
>
> It is even conceivable that our generation is standing on the threshold of a rebound of historic proportions. The collapse of the great counterreligious ideologies—Freudianism's failure to recodify the private world and Marxism's to recodify the public—clears the greatest obstacle to this possibility. Philosophical denials of faith have become affirmations that need denying. Social permissions have become constrictions from which we need liberating. Secular iconoclasms have become idols that need debunking. Moral inversions have become blind orthodoxies against which we need new heresies. Critical deconstruction has become destructiveness against which the need is to build and rebuild. Even secular humanism turns out to be, not the bogey its enemies fear, but an oxymoron its supporters regret—for secularism does not produce humanism; humanism requires, not secularism, but supernaturalism.[6]

This is why turning to God and allowing him and his values to direct life is not only crucial to a healthy existence but essential in serving others well.

---

6. Guinness, *The American Hour*, 398.

Luke 9:37–50

THE NEXT DAY, when they came down from the mountain, a large crowd met him. 38A man in the crowd called out, "Teacher, I beg you to look at my son, for he is my only child. 39A spirit seizes him and he suddenly screams; it throws him into convulsions so that he foams at the mouth. It scarcely ever leaves him and is destroying him. 40I begged your disciples to drive it out, but they could not."

41"O unbelieving and perverse generation," Jesus replied, "how long shall I stay with you and put up with you? Bring your son here."

42Even while the boy was coming, the demon threw him to the ground in a convulsion. But Jesus rebuked the evil spirit, healed the boy and gave him back to his father. 43And they were all amazed at the greatness of God.

While everyone was marveling at all that Jesus did, he said to his disciples, 44"Listen carefully to what I am about to tell you: The Son of Man is going to be betrayed into the hands of men." 45But they did not understand what this meant. It was hidden from them, so that they did not grasp it, and they were afraid to ask him about it.

46An argument started among the disciples as to which of them would be the greatest. 47Jesus, knowing their thoughts, took a little child and had him stand beside him. 48Then he said to them, "Whoever welcomes this little child in my name welcomes me; and whoever welcomes me welcomes the one who sent me. For he who is least among you all—he is the greatest."

49"Master," said John, "we saw a man driving out demons in your name and we tried to stop him, because he is not one of us."

50"Do not stop him," Jesus said, "for whoever is not against you is for you."

THE DISCIPLES STILL have much to learn from Jesus. Nothing makes this more evident than the failure of nine disciples to heal a demon-possessed boy while Peter, James, and John are on the mountain with a transfigured Jesus, hearing God's voice. Their impotence in working by their own means surfaces vividly here.[1] This is also the first of a series of passages, extending to 9:56, where the disciples need serious correction. As the voice in the cloud said, disciples must listen to Jesus.

Jesus encounters a man who has an only child in desperate straits.[2] He is possessed by an evil spirit that causes convulsions and leaves him bruised. Many see epilepsy here, especially since Matthew 17:15 says the boy "has seizures," which describes the disease by its effect. This condition was viewed with great fear in Judaism.[3]

Jesus' reply to the man's request for healing indicates that something is wrong, for he describes the current generation as "unbelieving and perverse." A portion of humanity is walking a crooked path, forcing God to bear with them (Isa. 46:4). The spirit suddenly casts the boy down, and Jesus issues a command for it to come out. The rebuke works. Not only does the demon depart, but the boy is left unharmed. Jesus' protection is total. The crowd is left to ponder God's majesty (1:49) and power, which can overcome terrifying conditions.

In the midst of the crowd's marveling, Jesus must remind his followers that such admiration is short-lived. He then makes a second prediction of his coming passion,[4] reiterating the coming betrayal of the Son of Man. Only Luke notes that the disciples do not understand Jesus' meaning, because the meaning has been hidden from them. Neither do they have the nerve to ask him about it. The fact that they fear asking shows that they do understand his words. What they do not understand is how betrayal can happen to a figure whom they have just confessed as Messiah. How can such a popular person of God's choice suffer? Can God's work be rejected? Yet, as Jesus has just noted, the generation of humanity can be crooked and blind.

The text is also vague on who has "hidden" the truth from them (v. 45). Is it God in the context of his plan of salvation? Or is Satan at work? In God's sovereignty, whatever is needed for them to hurdle this lack of understanding is not yet in place; though by the end of the Gospel, the blinders will be removed. God certainly is most active in that removal, as the Emmaus scene in 24:13–35 shows.

---

1. This text has parallels in Matthew 17:14–21 and Mark 9:14–29. This is also the last of thirteen miracles Luke describes in the Galilean section of his Gospel.

2. This recalls the only son of the widow of Nain in 7:11–17 and the only daughter of Jairus in 8:40–56.

3. H. van der Loos, *The Miracles of Jesus*, 401–5. It was seen as particularly difficult to cure. Some Jews attributed this disease to Balaam and Saul (Num. 24:4; 1 Sam. 19:24).

4. The parallels are Matthew 17:22–23 and Mark 9:30–32.

Two brief incidents close Luke's report on the Galilean ministry.[5] In the first, the disciples are haggling over who has the greatest position in the disciples' Hall of Fame. Jesus knows of their petty dispute, so he takes a child and points out to them the value of receiving such a child (who is culturally viewed as powerless and irrelevant). The one who receives this child also receives the one who sent him. Stature is not a matter of popular perception, but of simply being human. Even a normally disregarded child has stature. To make the least the greatest is to make all great. There are no unimportant people.

Second, neither is ministry a copyrighted monopoly. The disciples have seen someone casting out demons in Jesus' name. Since this person is not one of the elite, they have tried to stop him. Jesus tells the disciples that they are wrong. Whoever is not against them is on their side. Ministry should not be limited to a select few. Unlike the Marines, who want a few good men, Jesus wants all to serve and encourages all to do so. His remark that "whoever is not against you is for you" reflects proverbial wisdom in Jewish culture,[6] such as the attitude of Moses toward Eldad and Medad (Num. 11:26–30). Moses was glad others were being led by the Lord to do his work. Ministry should not be not limited to one group, one denomination, or one theological tradition. All who serve the Lord faithfully deserve our support.

LESSONS FOR MINISTRY about dependence, faith, rejection, the value of humanness, and elitism in ministry are fundamental themes of a walk with God, and each is taught in this section. Though the issues today may not be the ability to perform an exorcism, the need to trust God and be confident that evil can be overcome is as great today as ever. Whenever evil is defeated, we can admire the greatness of God. Dependence and faith stand up to the spiritual opposition that comes in life. It does so by drawing on the powerful resources God provides to meet the cosmic forces of darkness face to face. Ephesians 6:10–18 turns such a battle into a developed image of the armor of God, which symbolizes ethical righteousness, integrity, unity, the Spirit, God's Word, and prayer. Through such resources we can be faithful in the battle. The current discussion of spiritual disciplines attempts to renew the church's focus on such issues.[7]

---

5. The parallels to the first incident are Matthew 18:1–5 and Mark 9:33–37. The parallel to the second incident is Mark 9:49–50.

6. Fitzmyer, *Luke I–IX*, 821.

7. R. Kent Hughes, *Disciplines of a Godly Man* (Wheaton: Crossway, 1991); Stuart and Jill Briscoe, *Life, Liberty, and the Pursuit of Holiness* (Wheaton: Scripture Press, 1993).

But more than merely standing and marveling at God's word of power, we must stand up for him. Some people will not like that. Thus, just as Jesus was handed over in rejection, so his followers can expect the same. Sometimes traveling that difficult road does not make sense to us, and we cannot see why God does things the way he does. But just as the disciples learn that they must trust God's plan for Jesus, so we can learn to trust his path for us. Sometimes the path of rejection turns the corner in a surprising way, in the same way as the cross turned into resurrection.

Though we may think that ancient people are different from us, a look at the tendency of the disciples to compete and to try to build an elite ministry shows just how like us they are. Our own culture loves to compete and loves to restrict access to ministry. Jesus makes it clear that such an emphasis distorts the call of God. All are important, and ministry is open to all who embrace Christ. We must see people as God sees them and respond to them accordingly. As Jesus approaches his rejection, he knows that the complex reality of future ministry requires that the disciples appreciate the need for many laborers in the field.

SIN IS A powerful force in our lives. Satan is a strong adversary, and the opponents of righteousness in the world are formidable. When Jesus rebukes the "unbelieving and perverse generation," he is declaring war on attitudes that refuse to consider the destructiveness of evil and how it blinds us from the will of God.

But sometimes the power of the forces of evil is exaggerated, and we see ourselves as lacking resources needed to combat the damage they can do. We too quickly excuse our sin with phrases such as "The devil made me do it" or "I am just human." Feeling helpless in evil's hand, we emerge battered and bruised in the Christian life, just like the epileptic boy. Jesus is against righteous wimps who think Satan and evil are unbeatable Goliaths. Greater is the One in us than he who is in the world. That is what this miracle is designed to reveal. Jesus calls for a faith that is certain that righteousness is stronger than evil. No sin should go undefeated, nor should Satan be given more credit than he is due.

With all the resources available in Christ, there is no reason for sin to prevail, for our humanness to lead to failure, nor for demonic forces to remain in control (Eph. 1:15–23). When we fail, it is because we have not used what God has made available. To fail to draw on such resources is spiritual neglect, like trying to use a bicycle to go across the country when a jet plane is available. When the crowd at this exorcism marveled at the majesty of God, it was because his superior power became so evident.

God does not hoard his resources; he dispenses them. To draw on them is to experience the reality of exorcising the presence of evil without being bruised. This may mean nothing more than going resolutely in the direction God is leading, even if it means risk and uncertainty. It also involves applying the spiritual gifts he makes available and walking in the light he bestows. We can also draw encouragement from other saints who share our task.

One of the times we struggle in our Christian walk is when God takes us on a journey using a path marked "unknown." Jesus is here taking his disciples on such a journey when he notes his upcoming suffering (v. 44). They listen to his words and have questions. They have no idea where he is taking them or why, but they are afraid to ask. Disciples are often required to take unknown paths. Sometimes God gives us a ministry assignment within the church that on the surface makes no sense, and yet after time we see that he uses it to teach us new things. I have often heard as an elder that some person did not feel called to teach youth, only to find that after the assignment was accepted, he or she was left with the feeling, "Why have I not done this before?" We may feel unprepared and untrained, but God is saying, "Just trust me for the direction I am taking you." He takes us to our destination and wants us to trust him that walking with him does not always mean we understand him. He has his reasons, though it may be that the only result we discover is that we know him better.

The disciples continue to walk with Jesus, even though they have questions. This is the essence of faith. If faith were safe, would it be faith? I recall hearing about the inaugural speech of Richard Mouw of Fuller Seminary, where he spoke about being a "restless Christian." The phrase seems like an oxymoron, but, in fact, it is not. The Christian is in process, under renovation by God, discovering with each day just how much refashioning God is committed to performing in the Christian's life.

We feel tension living in the world while being citizens of heaven. We feel tension in wanting to be righteous and holy, while recognizing that we are not yet in glorified bodies and purified from sin. We live as aliens in a strange land, at least if we are sensitive to our call. Faith walks knowing that his hands are beneath our feet. Faith risks going down a path not because we always understand why life has turned in this direction, but because he has said, "Turn here." The disciples are called to make such a journey as Jesus prepares them for Jerusalem. Even in their fear to ask him about his rejection, they follow him. Even though it is difficult, they do not lack faith (cf. 22:28–30).

Regarding each disciple's desire to be the greatest, we often like to make distinctions, such as between the lovely and the unlovely, between gifted and the problem people, between important people and the rest of humanity.

To think this way is a travesty on the image of God in every person to think this way. While there are dangers in using the word "humanist," insofar as it frequently means relativist, one can argue that the Bible calls on Christians to be the most humanist of all. After all, what gives more dignity to a human than to say he or she is fashioned in God's image and is designed to be God's vicegerent on earth? What connects us to the cosmos in a more significant way than to be connected to its Creator and Sustainer? What gives more value to every human life than to see in every person a merit they possess inherently because they have been made by the God of the universe? Even Paul told a pagan audience that we are all God's children (Acts 17:24–28). Jesus detested the kind of competition and merit rating to which the disciples seem committed.

By highlighting the value of a child, Jesus raises everyone's stature. If the lowly are to be welcomed in Jesus' name, all are to be welcomed. We are all important to our Lord. If he died for our sin, then he has elevated the potential stature of every person who serves him, since forgiveness and full restoration are grounded in faith in him. To welcome a child is to welcome Jesus, which in turn is to welcome the God who sent them both. When the least is the greatest, all are great and the search for greatness becomes unnecessary.

Finally, a disease that plagues ministry is the belief that we are indispensable, that only we can perform it. But ministry is not a franchise with an exclusive license. The disciples must learn that in order to blanket the world, many laborers are needed, and Jesus enlists many into the ranks of ministry. Efforts to elevate some ministries over others or some areas of service as more important than others deny the variety that is the beauty of the body of Christ. When Paul discusses this topic in 1 Corinthians 12, he refers to giving greater honor to the less honorable parts, so that all may sense the acceptance of their role in the body (1 Cor. 12:21–26). Jesus wants his disciples to appreciate the right others have to minister. No one performs in the church as a lone ranger. The one who is not against us is for us; and we need all the allies we can use.

Luke 9:51–62

A S THE TIME approached for him to be taken up to heaven, Jesus resolutely set out for Jerusalem. ⁵²And he sent messengers on ahead, who went into a Samaritan village to get things ready for him; ⁵³but the people there did not welcome him, because he was heading for Jerusalem. ⁵⁴When the disciples James and John saw this, they asked, "Lord, do you want us to call fire down from heaven to destroy them?" ⁵⁵But Jesus turned and rebuked them, ⁵⁶and they went to another village.

⁵⁷As they were walking along the road, a man said to him, "I will follow you wherever you go."

⁵⁸Jesus replied, "Foxes have holes and birds of the air have nests, but the Son of Man has no place to lay his head."

⁵⁹He said to another man, "Follow me."

But the man replied, "Lord, first let me go and bury my father."

⁶⁰Jesus said to him, "Let the dead bury their own dead, but you go and proclaim the kingdom of God."

⁶¹Still another said, "I will follow you, Lord; but first let me go back and say good-by to my family."

⁶²Jesus replied, "No one who puts his hand to the plow and looks back is fit for service in the kingdom of God."

Original Meaning

THE KEY CENTRAL section of Luke's Gospel (9:51–19:44) shows how Jesus experiences rejection and prepares his disciples for his departure. Two topics dominate the unit. (1) Luke carefully traces the opposition to Jesus that grows and the deep hostility that emerges from the Jewish leadership. Much in chapters 9–14 painfully recounts this schism. (2) An extensive teaching on discipleship dominates this section, especially in chapters 14–19. Jesus stresses the total commitment that effective discipleship demands, the generous use of resources, dependence on God, and love for sinners. Where miracles dominated the previous section, parables and teaching are the key narrative elements in this section. At its end, Jesus enters Jerusalem weeping, because Israel has missed the visitation of her Messiah. Yet God's plan and kingdom march on to bless those who do turn to Jesus.

This initial unit of this section (9:51–10:24) highlights failure followed by success. The disciples fail to respond appropriately to their rejection (9:51–56), while prospective followers have much to learn about commitment (9:57–62). But the mission of 10:1–24 is a complete success, exposing the disciples to the joys and privileges of ministry. Their ministry is not a time of judgment but of invitation. An invitation refused leaves one accountable to God, but the offer of hope and forgiveness dominates the disciple's message. It is a special period in which kings and prophets longed to participate. Ministry is a great honor, but knowing God is the greatest privilege of all.

This section opens with the remark that Jesus sets his face to go to Jerusalem. The idiom "to set one's face" is an Old Testament expression for "to resolve" (Gen. 31:21; Jer. 21:10; 44:12).[1] He embarks on this journey as the days draw near for him to be received up. The journey is not a straight line trip, however, for in 10:38–42 Jesus is in Bethany near Jerusalem, in the south (cf. John 12:1), while later in Luke 17:11, he is traveling between Samaria and Galilee, in the north. Luke describes a journey of destiny, which has as its destination Israel's capital. So Jerusalem is a city of fate and destiny, where God's plan and the rejection of the prophet are realized (13:31–35). Luke highlights these themes through the journey motif in a way the other Gospels do not.

The journey starts with Jesus' expanding his ministry into Samaritan territory. To Jews, this ethnic group was traitors, a collection of half-breeds. The name came from the capital of the separatist northern kingdom of Israel, Samaria, in a rule founded by Omri (1 Kings 16:21–24). The Samaritans intermarried with the pagan nations and were thus seen as unfaithful to the nation of Israel.[2] The fact that Jesus reaches out to them indicates his desire to broaden his ministry.

As was the pattern in the earlier mission of the Twelve (Luke 9:1–6), Jesus sends messengers ahead to prepare the way for him. But what both they and he meet is rejection. Luke clearly states the reason is because Jesus is "heading for Jerusalem." In other words, as far as Luke is concerned, rejection of Jesus will extend beyond Jerusalem.

The disciples are not pleased with the lack of response in Samaria and ask Jesus if fiery judgment should be called down from heaven, as Elijah did in 2 Kings 1. Surely to reject the coming of God deserves instant eradication and vengeance. But Jesus rebukes them. Why? Luke does not record the

---

1. Lohse, "πρόσωπον κτλ.," *TDNT*, 6:776, n. 45.

2. For first-century descriptions of the hostility, see Josephus, *Jewish War* 2.12.3 §§ 232–33; *Antiquities* 20.6.1 §§ 118–23. Earlier discussion includes Sirach 50:25–26 and *Jubilees* 30:5–6, 23. Interestingly, this is the only passage in Luke where the Samaritans are portrayed in a negative light.

words Jesus uses. The company just moves on, and no execution of judgment comes. Obviously, now is not the time for judgment. Rather, it is a time to offer grace and to warn about accountability. The emphasis here is similar to Luke 4:16–19, where the citation of Isaiah 61:1–2 leaves out the reference to vengeance. Jesus' silence is not alone, for heaven is also silent to the disciples' desire for judgment.

Discipleship is not a casual affair to Jesus, as 9:57–62 certify. In a series of three encounters, Jesus shows the high priority he places on discipleship.[3] It is no accident that this text follows a passage that centered on rejection. Part of what makes discipleship so demanding is the fact that some type of rejection is a given for the believer. Discipleship takes focused commitment. Luke makes it clear that the task of kingdom preaching is the point of urgency, since two of the three calls mention the kingdom of God (on the kingdom, see 10:1–24; 11:14–23; 17:20–21).

The central term in this section is "follow" (vv. 57, 59, 61). Like the threefold call of Elisha, the text makes this central point repeatedly, but with one key difference: What involved a threefold call to a single figure in the Old Testament is a single call to three different figures in the New Testament (2 Kings 2:1–6).[4] The three cases here involve two where the disciple initiates the encounter (the first and the third) and one where Jesus does. But the point in each case is the same: In life, discipleship must come first.

The first exchange begins with a confident statement by a man that he will follow Jesus wherever he goes. This remark requires reflection, so Jesus warns the man precisely what that will require. The man probably has in view the example of students following a rabbi, where they learned from the teacher. Following a rabbi meant nothing other than walking behind him, and it also suggested the student's submission to the teacher. But to follow Jesus means a different form of discipleship. It is more like following a prophet.[5] The prophet was an itinerant teacher, not part of an established community. He had an uncertain existence and lived on the donations of those who responded to the ministry.

---

3. The parallel to this text is Matthew 8:18–22, which describes the first two of these incidents. The third exchange is unique to Luke. Matthew places this event after a summary text where Jesus heals many and before the stilling of the storm and the Gerasene healings. Thus the call to discipleship is sandwiched between a period of intense miraculous ministry. Disciples can trust in the power of God. Luke has the event after the failure in Samaria and before the larger mission, in a context of rejection. Matthew notes that one of the characters in the account is a scribe. Luke, as is his pattern, leaves the identities indefinite. One final difference is that Luke highlights the kingdom in the second and third replies, a detail Matthew lacks. So Luke's version is more explicit about kingdom urgency.

4. L. Johnson, *Luke*, 162.

5. M. Hengel, *The Charismatic Leader and His Followers* (New York: Crossroad, 1981).

To follow Jesus, therefore, is to follow a prophet who calls one to faithfulness to God. The priority is to turn one's attention to the presence and arrival of God's kingdom. It requires viewing this journey with total dedication, especially since the Son of Man will not have a home. Unlike foxes and birds, which have holes and nests, the Son of Man has no home. He is an alien sojourning for a time in a foreign land. Rejection will be a given, and finding a home may be difficult. Jesus is preparing his prospective follower for those times that lie ahead.

In the second case, a prospective follower wishes to bury his father before joining the group. The request seems reasonable, since burying a family member was a priority in Judaism (1 Kings 19:19–21).[6] In fact, Jesus' request would strike a Jewish ear as almost outrageous. But what was tolerated in the old era needs to be left behind in the more urgent new era. Strikingly, Jesus says to the man, "Let the dead bury their own dead." The seemingly harsh reply is rhetorical, but it makes the point that discipleship and one's commitment to the kingdom take priority even over family considerations. This saying is similar to other texts from Jesus that speak of hating mother and father—which means that if a choice is to be made, God must have first place. Taking care of funeral rites for a family member is a lower priority. Instead, this man must go and proclaim the gospel. More important than caring for the dead is preaching the offer of life. Disciples must move forward to share that need, not memorialize what is past.

A similar request surfaces in the third encounter. Here a man wants to tell his family farewell (cf. Elisha in 1 Kings 19:19–20). Again Jesus issues what on the surface seems a harsh warning: Those who look back are not fit for the kingdom. Jesus' remarks have Old Testament precedent. Lot's wife preferred Sodom and looked back. The Israelites longed for Egypt and complained because God brought them deliverance and a journey through the desert. Those who cling to life on earth as it is are not ready for the reformation that salvation brings. Jesus saves not just to grant us a place in heaven but to transform us here and now into new people, separated from the world (2 Cor. 5:17; Gal. 2:20; 6:14; Titus 2:11–14). The disciple cannot hang onto the old life and be prepared for the rigors of discipleship. Jesus wants to make this truth clear from the start. Salvation is not a road paved with ease, for true spirituality takes discipline.

The picture of looking back while plowing is apt, since in Palestine the terrain is rugged. To look back while plowing was asking to make mistakes in preparing the field. The task required a focused eye on what lay ahead. So

---

6. See Sirach 38:16; Tobit 4:3–4; 12:12.

discipleship demands attention to the rough road before us. To look back risks being knocked off course.

Bridging Contexts

CLEARLY THERE IS rejection of the gospel today as there was in Jesus' day. Such rejection is hard to take. But Jesus' refusal to execute judgment is a consistent pattern for ministry. As mentioned in the first section, now is not the time for judgment. Jesus is here highlighting that the current era of his ministry is the period of opportunity and invitation. Jesus does speak openly of judgment, but it will occur in the era to come, when the Son of Man returns to show his authority (9:26; 12:8—10; 17:26—37; 21:25). Note also 2 Peter 3:9, which explains the Lord's delaying judgment as an expression of his love and patience. The opportunity to respond to the offer of the gospel remains open until judgment comes.

This perspective indicates how the church should handle rejection. Since God will exercise justice at some future time, vindication is not called for now. As long as the era of grace continues, the church should continue to minister and offer her message of hope. To be a servant of the gospel is not to highlight judgment or long for execution, but to seek to save lives as long as God allows.

Luke 9:57—62 highlights the fundamental commitment that goes into being a disciple (cf. 9:23—27). The priority of discipleship is the same yesterday, today, and tomorrow: developing one's relationship to God. In order to avoid the errors that our instinct supplies to us, we must treat developing discipleship as a priority, understanding that the world will not comprehend when we go in a different direction from certain cultural expectations.

More subtle may be the way in which our own believing communities ask us to accommodate ourselves to the expectations of the world or even the Christian world around us. We may be asked not to make that prophetic challenge that asks our people to live differently, because it might not be affirming to our self-esteem or might create a reaction. Sometimes biblical examination asks us to take a long, hard look in the mirror and to make changes. Jesus' directness and the shocking quality of his remarks here show just how seriously he takes the call to discipleship. The path to following Jesus is not a part-time job; it is a perpetual assignment. Since discipleship involves responding to people as well as to God, there is no moment when we are not "on call." Those who wish to pursue spirituality as a hobby will not discover its blessing. Jesus makes that truth clear by showing that even the highest commitments to family come in second place. We may be asked to go minister in places where our families may not be near. We may be asked to take risks for the sake of the gospel that no "sane" person might take. We may have to stand up for integrity in situations that might cost us dearly.

Contemporary Significance

THE CHURCH MUST deal with the world's rejection. The world often sees our commitment to Jesus as a blind, arrogant exclusivism, when in reality it represents an invitation to share in the rich blessings of God. How should the church respond to such hostility? Many people in the world react strongly against the church's concern for the moral character of our culture and see it as a dogmatic attempt to control other people. That reading could not be more wrong. In warning against immoral behavior, the church is warning against that which is ultimately self-destructive not only to the individual who engages in it, but also to the society at large.

But how do we respond to such rejection? The disciples respond to the Samaritans with natural instinct: "Let's wipe those foolish people off of the face of the earth." But the way of Jesus is not the way of power exercised capriciously. What he calls for is continued outreach and ministry. To hold back is not an indication there will be no judgment. As 10:13–15 and 11:37–52 show, he is capable of issuing serious warnings about the consequences of rejecting him. Nevertheless, the goal of the church is continued ministry as the message of the gospel continues to be shared and as the church reaches out to others in word and deed.

When I think of this text and Jesus' rebuke, I consider how angry many Christians appear at the world as they address it. It is not unusual today to see an angry Christian face on television, expressing some form of condemnation on our society at large. Truth, justice, and the divine way are lifted up as a banner, and those who walk differently are left to hear only the words of judgment. Some have even resorted to brute force or violence to try and stop sin. Is that our only option?

When Jesus enters Jerusalem anticipating her rejection (19:41–44), he is not angry. Instead, he weeps for her. That does not mean that some things did not anger him (cf. his cleansing of the temple). But his anger was directed at a religious hypocrisy that blocked access to God. Those whom society regarded as the most excluded often received a surprising handling by Jesus, like the woman caught in adultery (John 7:53–8:11). When Jesus was on the cross with the pain of nails in his hands and feet as evidence of national rejection, he was not angry with his enemies; he interceded for them. When Stephen was being stoned by the Jews for standing up for Jesus, he too was not angry with them; he prayed for their forgiveness. There will come a time when judgment is called for, when God's righteous anger will be shown to hard hearts; but in the current era, the call of the church is to love and continue to intercede for those who reject the gospel. That does not mean that confrontation is excluded, but there is a way to confront that also holds out the invitation that forgiveness is obtainable with a change of heart. As with Saul, the keeper of the cloaks at Stephen's execution, a little forgiveness may sow a seed that the Lord can reap.

What kind of servant does Jesus desire, according to 9:57–62? What type of service does he expect? Several analogies surface. In the military, as the soldier trains for service, he or she is often required to leave home for a long time. Whether in boot camp or on call somewhere in the world, there is no time to stop and bury the dead or have contact with the family. Like a commitment to serve one's nation, discipleship is a call to serve God. Personal agendas end up suspended in the face of national realities. Jesus says the call of discipleship is like that.

Less significant but just as illustrative is a training camp in sports. During that time the players are pulled away from family and friends as they forge a unit together. Two strenuous workouts a day show just how dedicated the athletes must be to getting into shape. Nothing may get in the way of that preparation for a new season. Discipleship is the same as this, but with one difference. Here the camp is the church, and training camp never ceases. Disciples must always stay in shape. If camp goes well, friends and family share in the preparation.

Another analogy might be marriage. Until I am married, I am subject to my parents. But the establishment of a new home leads to a new set of relationships that have priority. To do justice to my new family requires an all-consuming availability. Discipleship is like that. My relationship to God becomes the defining priority against which all else is seen.

There may well be one significant difference between discipleship in Jesus' era and discipleship today after two thousand years of church history. In Jesus' time, those who came to him often had to leave family because of their decision. Jewish rejection was so strong that to decide for Jesus meant deciding against one's family. Today many grow up in Christian homes where a decision to follow Jesus is honored. To be a disciple means to share in training with loved ones. Fitness requires that all of us give ourselves fully to the task. To face it with others who walk the same road is an encouragement. This is why some of the most effective discipleship happens in small groups. It is no accident that Jesus formed the Twelve and other groups of disciples who shared the task with him. Discipleship may be a calling out of the world, but it was never intended to be an exercise in solitary assignment.

But as disciples in the world, we had better be prepared. God may call us to a place where comfort is uncertain, for the Son of Man has no lay to place his head. Because of the uncertainty, one cannot let the daily worries of this life overcome the demands of being a disciple, since the dead are to bury the dead. Discipleship has an urgency to it that should have first place. And once we go, we should not look back. God does not issue his call for a season, but for a lifetime. Service for the kingdom begins at the moment we receive Jesus and continues until the Father calls us home. What does this look like? In detail, it is different for each person. Some are called to serve where they grew up; others are called to journey thousands of miles away. Some live in hardship and lose their life for the faith, like Peter who died for the faith, while others live a long life, like John who apparently died of old age. What is the same for all is the call that discipleship should have priority over everything else.

Luke 10:1–24

AFTER THIS THE Lord appointed seventy-two others and sent them two by two ahead of him to every town and place where he was about to go. ²He told them, "The harvest is plentiful, but the workers are few. Ask the Lord of the harvest, therefore, to send out workers into his harvest field. ³Go! I am sending you out like lambs among wolves. ⁴Do not take a purse or bag or sandals; and do not greet anyone on the road.

⁵"When you enter a house, first say, 'Peace to this house.' ⁶If a man of peace is there, your peace will rest on him; if not, it will return to you. ⁷Stay in that house, eating and drinking whatever they give you, for the worker deserves his wages. Do not move around from house to house.

⁸"When you enter a town and are welcomed, eat what is set before you. ⁹Heal the sick who are there and tell them, 'The kingdom of God is near you.' ¹⁰But when you enter a town and are not welcomed, go into its streets and say, ¹¹'Even the dust of your town that sticks to our feet we wipe off against you. Yet be sure of this: The kingdom of God is near.' ¹²I tell you, it will be more bearable on that day for Sodom than for that town.

¹³"Woe to you, Korazin! Woe to you, Bethsaida! For if the miracles that were performed in you had been performed in Tyre and Sidon, they would have repented long ago, sitting in sackcloth and ashes. ¹⁴But it will be more bearable for Tyre and Sidon at the judgment than for you. ¹⁵And you, Capernaum, will you be lifted up to the skies? No, you will go down to the depths.

¹⁶"He who listens to you listens to me; he who rejects you rejects me; but he who rejects me rejects him who sent me."

¹⁷The seventy-two returned with joy and said, "Lord, even the demons submit to us in your name."

¹⁸He replied, "I saw Satan fall like lightning from heaven. ¹⁹I have given you authority to trample on snakes and scorpions and to overcome all the power of the enemy; nothing will harm you. ²⁰However, do not rejoice that the spirits submit to you, but rejoice that your names are written in heaven."

²¹At that time Jesus, full of joy through the Holy Spirit, said, "I praise you, Father, Lord of heaven and earth, because you have hidden these things from the wise and learned, and revealed them to little children. Yes, Father, for this was your good pleasure.

²²"All things have been committed to me by my Father. No one knows who the Son is except the Father, and no one knows who the Father is except the Son and those to whom the Son chooses to reveal him."

²³Then he turned to his disciples and said privately, "Blessed are the eyes that see what you see. ²⁴For I tell you that many prophets and kings wanted to see what you see but did not see it, and to hear what you hear but did not hear it."

AS LUKE 9:49–50 showed, ministry involves more than the Twelve. Jesus sends out another mission, this time involving seventy-two.¹ The Twelve may have been a part of this mission (cf. 22:35), even though they are not counted among this number, for "seventy-two others" are in view here.

Jesus sends them out in pairs. What they do is only a start, since they are to pray for more workers for the harvest. Using agricultural imagery for a spiritual harvest was common in Judaism (see Isa. 27:11–12; Hos. 6:11; Joel 3:13; also Luke 10: 10–16; John 4:31–38; Rom. 11:16–24; 1 Cor. 3:6–7).² With conversion comes the responsibility to join the task of sharing the good news. The fact that these workers emerge as a result of intercession stresses that God is the sovereign source of such blessing. He is Lord of the harvest, he leads the mission, and he is responsible for "sending out" workers into the field. Missions is not a matter of marketing but of the Lord's directing his people to share faithfully the grace they have experienced.

---

1. This passage has numerous parallel points of contact in the Synoptics: Matthew 9:37–10:16 is like Luke 10:1–12; Luke 10:13–15 is like Matthew 11:20–24; Luke 11:17–20 does not have a parallel; and Luke 10:21–24 is like Matthew 11:25–27 and 13:16–17. The Matthean parallels only mention the Twelve. In Luke the mission of the seventy-two have the same principles as the mission of the Twelve. Another issue in the passage is whether seventy or seventy-two are sent. This problem involves a difference in the Greek manuscript tradition of Luke. Either number could be correct, but slightly better manuscript evidence favors the choice of seventy-two.

2. In nonbiblical literature, see 1QS 8:5–6; CD 1:7; 1QH 8:4–11; *Odes of Solomon* 38:17–21.

Such ministry is not easy, for the workers are "like lambs among wolves." There is danger and hostile rejection on all sides (cf. 9:51–56). In Judaism, wolves often represented those who consume their enemy.[3] Despite the danger, the disciples must go forth to perform their calling.

Such danger requires the workers to travel light. The instructions are similar to 9:1–6, yet they more detail is present here. They should not carry a purse, bag, or sandals. They should not stop to salute anyone on the road, for their mission is urgent. They must not be concerned with the normal affairs of life as other people are; ministry is their priority. They are also to rest in the knowledge that God will provide for them, since "the worker deserves his wages."

When they arrive in a town, they must stay in one place, not running from house to house. They are to offer a blessing of peace to those who host them, an invocation of God's good will.[4] If some refuse to welcome them, then the blessing will recede from that house (Matt. 25:31–46). As guests, the disciples are to eat what is set before them as God's provisions for them. Their main responsibility is to heal the sick and declare the arrival of God's kingdom.

The mention of God's kingdom is central, because these disciples reflect the approach of the new era Jesus brings. God's ruling power in deliverance is coming. The expression in verses 9 and 11 about the "kingdom of God [coming] near" has been the subject of much scholarly discussion. Does it mean that the kingdom approaches but stops short of arrival? Or is the approach a way of announcing its arrival? The key to the answer is not in the Greek idea of *drawing near* in verse 11, but in the combination of the preposition with the concept of drawing near: to come *upon* you in verse 9, as it also appears in a parallel saying to this one in 11:20. That later text is a commentary on Jesus' activity that explains the import of his ministry. It is a reaffirmation of what Jesus says in 10:9. Jesus' activity is not just approaching; it has come "upon you." This idiom also appears in Daniel 4:24, 28 in the Greek Old Testament translation tied to Theodotion, where the idea is clearly arrival. The preposition addresses locale and clearly speaks of more than proximity.

Verses 17–18 confirm this understanding by picturing the mission's ministry as evidence of Satan's fall.[5] To announce the kingdom is not to say that everything associated with Jesus' authority is now manifest, for he also taught

---

3. Psalms of Solomon 8:23, 30 refer to the nations as wolves who devour Israel.
4. *Mishnah, 'Aboth* 4:15.
5. Note also 11:14–23, where Jesus' ministry evidences the defeat of Satan before a stronger foe.

that there are things he will do when he returns. But the rule of God through Jesus has begun. The power to deliver from Satan's power has started to work itself out in history and among humanity. The deeds of ministry support that claim by showing that evil forces and the presence of death cannot resist Jesus' authority.

If the disciples are rejected, then they must shake the dust from their feet and move on. This act declares a separation between God and the rejecting city, exposing their accountability to him for their decision (Luke 9:5; Acts 13:51; 19:6). To reject such a gracious invitation is dangerous, as Luke 10:13—15 reveals. Even Tyre and Sidon, two Gentile cities with reputations for evil, will come out better in the judgment than the Galilean cities of Korazin, Bethsaida, and Capernaum. This kind of threatening woe has Old Testament precedent (Isa. 23; Jer. 25:22; 47:4; Ezek. 26:3–28:24; Joel 3:4–8; Amos 1:9–10). The current era is so great, in other words, that even the most evil cities among the Gentiles would have responded to what Jesus is offering by repenting in sackcloth and ashes (1 Kings 20:31–32; 2 Kings 19:1; 1 Chron. 21:16; Joel 1:13; Amos 8:10). The destiny for rejection is "the depths" (the Greek word transliterates *Hades*). In other words, the risk of rejection is eternal.

What is not often appreciated is the unbreakable link Jesus places between himself and his messengers. They are commissioned in such a way that they represent him. For people to hear them is to hear Jesus; for people to reject them is to reject Jesus. People cannot separate Jesus from those who bear his message, and this link extends beyond the Twelve to all who faithfully preach his message. This type of linkage is not unlike the authority we give to an ambassador today. The ambassador represents his country, and what he says the government says.

The mission is a success, since the disciples return filled with excitement at the power they possess. In Jesus' name, even demons have submitted to them! Such power was exciting to contemplate.

Jesus responds by picturing the fall of Satan. Satan's descent from above, his loss of power, is evident from what has been taking place. The allusion is to imagery from Isaiah 14:12. Judaism associated Satan's end with the Messiah.[6] Jesus has given the seventy-two authority to overcome all types of evil power and representations. Later, in Luke 11:20–23, Jesus describes his own activity as pointing to the presence of a stronger one than Satan who plunders Satan's domain. Given such power, nothing can harm them—a truth Jesus expresses strongly with the Greek emphatic particles *ou me*. Yet such power is not the true ground for their rejoicing. That is, the submission of

---

6. *1 Enoch* 55:1; *Jubilees* 23:29; *Testament of Simeon* 6:6; *Testament of Judah* 23:3.

evil spirits to them is nothing compared to the fact that they are registered among the saved in the Book of Life. Here is the real cause for joy. In fact, it is cause for continuous joy, as Jesus uses a present imperative (*chairete*) to make the point. The Book of Life refers to the great census of God where the blessed will be named.[7] True and eternal life with the everlasting God is the essence of blessing.

To underscore the point Jesus intercedes with a note of praise to God. God's sovereignty sends such blessings to "little children" rather than to the wise and learned. Those of simple faith, not those who rest in their own wisdom, have come to see the blessing of God (1 Cor. 1:25–31). He honors those who in simplicity rely on him.

But there is another fundamental link that holds the chain together. The authority of the Father is placed in the Son. In turn, it is the Son who reveals the Father to others. Those who come to God have the Son as the source of such revelation. As Jesus said in the Gospel of John, "I am the way and the truth and the life. No one comes to the Father except through me" (John 14:6). There is a chain of revelation that extends from God through the Son to those who respond and bear the Son's message. That is why this mission was so important and why knowing him is so crucial.

There is a blessing of divine approval in sharing in the task of the Son. So Jesus concludes with a beatitude for those who see what the seventy-two have seen. King and prophets longed to experience what they are experiencing, but they did not get this special honor (1 Peter 1:10–12). As great as the eras of Moses, David, and Isaiah were, they are nothing compared to those who have seen the Messiah.

Bridging Contexts

THIS MISSION IS unique, given the direct involvement with Jesus and the type of authority the seventy-two possess to declare the arrival of the kingdom. Yet in 22:35–38, Jesus alters some of the instructions given here. Rather than relying on the kindness of others, disciples of the future will need to be better prepared for rejection and will have to rely more directly on their own resources. It is true that as things became more hostile in the first century, people had to be more careful. This distinction suggests different approaches are required by different preaching environments. When the environment is open and free, then we may rely on the kindness of others. But when the environment is closed and hostile, we

---

7. See Exodus 32:32; Psalm 69:28; Isaiah 4:3; Daniel 7:10; 12:1; Philippians 4:3; Revelation 3:5; 20:12, 15; 21:27.

must walk circumspectly. In our time, the difference is more easily seen in the difference in ministry style required in the more open Western states versus ministry in Muslim areas or certain parts of Asia. More hostile contexts require more care in meeting. There is one point that Jesus makes here that is repeated in 1 Timothy 5:18: The minister still deserves his wage.

God remains sovereign over the missionary task, and the world still needs more workers for the harvest. In a world of several billion, even several million Christians are not enough to reach everyone. Resources must be used wisely. Does every Christian tradition need its own missionary agency in a region, or might more cooperative efforts allow a pooling and more effective use of resources? Is the best goal always to send more foreign missionaries into a region, or should resources be expended to develop more local leadership? We must be wise in how we use the workers God gives for the task.

Special wisdom is needed as we seek to reach the unreached and those exposed to the gospel. Workers faithful to the basic message of Jesus are needed in parts of the world where the God of Abraham, Isaac, and Jacob is not well known, but also where he is so well known that he has been dismissed as irrelevant. Yet they must share that message with a sensitivity to the unique culture in which they serve. That is, they must understand that culture so they can communicate the gospel clearly in a way that ministers to people's needs. The message form and ministry style of one who serves in a Latin American barrio will surely differ from the one who ministers in a major urban center to business leaders.

The principles of traveling light and with urgency are timeless. The gospel must never burden those who are served by it. One also has to watch out for the subtlety of watering down the message in order to earn a wage. We may never deny the uniqueness of the message, and the church must avoid the temptation of receiving funds because the message has been made culturally acceptable. When resources drive the message, the message is usually lost. This danger can exist for churches, missionary organizations, seminaries, or parachurch ministries. The message of one's need for Christ must remain paramount. The church should support its various ministries strongly enough that survival does not dictate policy.

What is at stake is the destiny of every person who hears the gospel. There is no room for the suggestion that one does not need the forgiveness Jesus offers or that somehow sin is passé. That is why Jesus tells his messengers to make clear that God's blessing rejection is at stake. That is also why Jesus issues woes to those Galilean cities that reject the message. The gospel does not involve a casual, private religious expression of opinion that is one option among many. It is the revelation of God. Many in our era doubt if God speaks at all, compounding both the problem of their responding to the message. In addition, preaching that Jesus is the only way means that the Evangelist risks being misunderstood as intolerant, dogmatic, or seeking to control others. But these obstacles do not remove from us the responsibility of declaring in love and with tears what is at stake in the choices called for by God.

A cosmic battle is in place with the gospel. That battle is being waged yet today, though the question of victory was decided on Calvary's cross. What we see in the seventy-two are the first moments of triumph, much like D-Day was for the allies during World War II. The war lasted long after that battle, but the outcome was essentially decided in those first few days. Our ministry for Christ plays out that cosmic struggle, and we rejoice and share Jesus because in him rests the truth that allows one's name to be found in the Book of Life.

Think of the blessing of sharing in the harvest. We belong to a two-thousand-year-old heritage of ministry. We contribute to a battle to reverse the presence of evil in the world. We partake in a relationship with the Lord of heaven and earth. We experience the blessing of forgiveness that only he offers—a blessing that comes to those who see Jesus. Two thousand years may have passed, but the greatness and uniqueness of that blessing never fades.

THE APPLICATIONS OF this text are myriad. Christian ministry continues to need workers. Such work should not be undertaken by lone rangers. There is a sense of sharing, accountability, and protection for integrity in the fact that the seventy-two traveled in pairs. Such shared ministry prevents a dictatorial approach in ministry and helps to assure the veracity of the participants. There is wisdom in ministry that does not go it alone.

Mission must still be built through dependence on God. Such dependence starts with prayer and ends with a sense of joy in being a part of such a grand, long-standing mission. When I travel to Europe, there is something almost mystical about attending a university that was founded in the 1400s or seeing a location where the Lord has been worshiped regularly since A.D. 750. But the Christian mission depicted in Luke 10 makes all of those endeavors look young. Since the time of Jesus God has been calling workers to work the fields, always planted with emerging life that needs harvesting for him.

Through prayer, wise effort, and the strength to face rejection, each generation looks to God's direction to supply workers to the task of evangelism.

As rich as the history of the faith is, what is preached is what makes the task so precious. The call to share in God's blessing is the greatest vocation one can possess. Every believing community needs to highlight and teach its people to join in the task. Some will go great distances; others will share with friends and neighbors. But all are called to do something. Jesus did not leave the ministry only to the Twelve. Neither today are pastors the only ones called to share God's blessings with others.

Interestingly, Jesus says little about method, nor does he give his followers a developed message. Their ministry is to minister to needs, to reveal God's power, and to share where it has come from. Many are intimidated to share Jesus because they feel they do not know what to say. Jesus sends the seventy-two and tells them simply to give of themselves and point to the presence of God. Sometimes we make evangelism more difficult than it needs to be.

There should be no doubt, however, that eternal life and death are the issue when it comes to Jesus. Our era has made it to easy to pass off religious opinion as if we were choosing flavors at an ice cream store. God is not so cold as to allow such important matters to be left to human whim. In offering his Son, he has put the true life to death, so that men and women can experience life. In death the true life has removed any obstacle that may stand in the way of relationship with God. Strange as it may seem, the world often accuses God of narrowness for opening the way so wide through his Son. What seems as a narrow way in Jesus is in fact a door that opens up to a vast field of blessing. Jesus will speak of his message as the narrow door in 13:24. Disciples know that the key is not the width of the door but where it leads.

What God asks of each person is to recognize before God that he or she has not lived in a way that honors God and should therefore embrace the forgiveness and relationship he longs to provide through Jesus. God shows evidence of his good faith by providing all we need to share in such blessing. All we need to do is turn in good faith and embrace the gift he has provided. The gospel is so simple in this basic element of turning to God for forgiveness in Christ that it is too hard for many to comprehend, much less accept. Yet it is this very simplicity that caused Jesus to compare those who see and embrace it to little children. The ways of God are not to be figured out when it comes to the gospel. For what Jesus offers are things that prophets and kings longed to experience. Those who know Jesus reside in a palace whose walls will never become a museum.

Luke 10:25–37

O N ONE OCCASION an expert in the law stood up to test Jesus. "Teacher," he asked, "what must I do to inherit eternal life?"

26"What is written in the Law?" he replied. "How do you read it?"

27He answered: "'Love the Lord your God with all your heart and with all your soul and with all your strength and with all your mind'; and, 'Love your neighbor as yourself.'"

28"You have answered correctly," Jesus replied. "Do this and you will live."

29But he wanted to justify himself, so he asked Jesus, "And who is my neighbor?"

30In reply Jesus said: "A man was going down from Jerusalem to Jericho, when he fell into the hands of robbers. They stripped him of his clothes, beat him and went away, leaving him half dead. 31A priest happened to be going down the same road, and when he saw the man, he passed by on the other side. 32So too, a Levite, when he came to the place and saw him, passed by on the other side. 33But a Samaritan, as he traveled, came where the man was; and when he saw him, he took pity on him. 34He went to him and bandaged his wounds, pouring on oil and wine. Then he put the man on his own donkey, took him to an inn and took care of him. 35The next day he took out two silver coins and gave them to the innkeeper. 'Look after him,' he said, 'and when I return, I will reimburse you for any extra expense you may have.'

36 "Which of these three do you think was a neighbor to the man who fell into the hands of robbers?"

37The expert in the law replied, "The one who had mercy on him."

Jesus told him, "Go and do likewise."

Original Meaning

DISCIPLESHIP IS ONE of Luke's most important themes. Luke 10:25–11:13 focuses on this issue by highlighting relationships at three fundamental levels: with one's neighbor (10:25–37), with Jesus (10:38–42), and before God through prayer (11:1–13). The close juxtaposition of these relationships suggests the vertical-horizontal aspects of spirituality that Paul highlighted in texts like Philemon 6 and Colossians 1:3–5. Ethics is not a matter of abstract reflection on certain situations; it is a reflection of character that combines listening to God with sensitive service to people.

Luke 10:25–37 wonderfully illustrates Jesus' capacity for turning an abstract theological discussion into a discourse on real life issues. His encounter with this lawyer reveals how he does not allow distinctions to be made when it comes to the treatment of people. There are no easy escapes for failing to serve and be a neighbor.[1]

The incident begins innocently enough. Knowing that the Old Testament alludes to the "eternal inheritance" one can possess (Ps. 36:18 LXX; Dan. 12:2), a lawyer, an expert in Jewish tradition, asks Jesus what he must do to inherit eternal life. What must he do to share in the resurrection of the righteous? When future blessing comes, how can he know he will receive it?

Jesus responds with a question of his own. He turns to the Law, asking the lawyer what he sees it saying. The scribe replies with a part of the *Shema* from Deuteronomy 6:5, that portion of the Law that a Jew recited daily and that calls on the nation to love God fully. He also cites the portion of Leviticus 19:18 that calls for the love of one's neighbor. This combination was known as the "great commandment."[2]

Jesus commends the answer by noting that if the lawyer meets these demands, he will live. This reply has been interpreted as being based on a "law" premise, one that is no longer true in this era. Such a view short-circuits Jesus' point. He is not giving a dispensationally limited commendation; he is asserting the fundamental ethical call of God: to love him and respond to others in light of that love. Coming in the literary context of 10:21–24, this response means that those who love God will hear Jesus, come to him, respond to him, and receive his benefits. As Jesus makes clear later, such people will receive not only forgiveness but God's Spirit, who enables believers to become a different kind of person (Luke 24:47, 49; Acts 2:38). Love for God that comes to a person responding as a child to God means that the call of God will be heard. So Jesus rightly says, "Do this and you will live."

---

1. The parallels to this passage are debated. The parable is unique to Luke, but its introduction looks like Matthew 22:34–40 and Mark 12:28–34. Matthew and Mark are clearly parallel, but connection to Luke is less certain. The Lucan event appears to be a separate incident covering a similar theme. See R. Stein, *Luke*, 314–15, esp. n. 39.

2. G. Schenk, "δόξα," *TDNT*, 2:249–50. The answer has parallels in Judaism: *Testament Issachar* 5:1–2 refers to loving the Lord and one's neighbor, while the *Testament of Dan* 5:3 refers to loving God and one another.

The lawyer reads the reply as not answering the question specifically enough. "What is the scope of this call to love the neighbor? Is everyone a neighbor and have I fulfilled it?" Luke tell us that the lawyer wants "to justify himself." So he asks Jesus, "Who is my neighbor?" Does the lawyer seek to limit the scope so as to be able to say he has fulfilled the command? There is a cultural background to this query. An ancient Jewish book of wisdom, Sirach 12:1–4, tells its readers to not help a sinner. Thus, the lawyer's question is really an attempt to create a distinction, arguing that some people are neighbors and others are not, and that one's responsibility is only to love God's people. The suggestion that some people are "non-neighbors" is what Jesus responds to in his story.

Jesus picks a Samaritan as the highlight of the story because such a person is a "non-neighbor" in the lawyer's eyes. Jesus' story lacks the power today it had then, for we lack the cultural assumptions that made it such a shocking story. The expectations in the account are that the priest and Levite are the good guys, who could be expected to help the wounded traveler; but a Samaritan as a half-breed and renegade would be the last person from whom one could expect compassion (on Jewish views of Samaritans, see comments on 9:51–56).

Another cultural detail is important. Jesus picks the treacherous road from Jericho to Jerusalem as the cite of the incident. This seventeen-mile journey was well known for its danger. The cultural equivalent today might be a trip through parts of the inner city in the middle of the night. This road was hazardous, as the man who falls among robbers finds out. Thieves took advantage of the caves that lined the road as it wound through the desert,[3] jumping travelers as they passed through. So this man is stripped of his clothing, beaten, and robbed. He is left for dead, cast off at the side of the road.

Two opportunities for aid appear next. But both the priest and the Levite, pious though they may be, pass by on the other side of the road to avoid serving this man in desperate need. In each case as these "righteous" men happen down the path, the wounded man could have thought, "Surely help is here now." But in each case there is disappointment, for they pass by the misery lying in their way. Why do they pass by? Perhaps they fear being rendered unclean from touching what looks like a dead corpse (Lev. 21:1–3; Num. 5:2; 19:2–13; Ezek. 44:25–27), though the oral law allowed for exceptions involving priests where no family was present (*Mishnah, Nazir* 6:5; 7:1). But the text makes no mention of any motive, and it is best not to speculate.

Next comes a Samaritan. This is surprising, since one might expect a Jewish layperson to appear here, not this "half-breed." But the Samaritan has

---

3. W. Michaelis, "λῃστής," *TDNT*, 4:257–59, 261.

pity on the wounded traveler. Jesus details in a series of verbs just how active this man is in ministering to his newly discovered needy neighbor: he goes to him; bandages him, pours oil and wine on his wounds; puts him on his donkey, carries him to the inn, and takes care of him, even to the point of leaving enough money behind to make sure the man has two weeks lodging to recover. In addition, he tells the innkeeper to keep a running tab, so that when he returns he can pay for any cost overruns. Here is a ministry that underwrites the victim's recovery from start to finish. No wonder scholars call this parable an "example story," for that is precisely what the Samaritan is.

Jesus then asks a simple question: "Which of the three . . . was a neighbor to the man who fell into the hands of robbers?" The scribe cannot bring himself to identify the man by his race. The idea of a good Samaritan was an oxymoron to a Jew. So he says, "The one who had mercy on him." Jesus tells the man to "go and do likewise."

The point is obvious. The lawyer wants to know if he can be a neighbor to a select, elite few. Jesus tells him through the Samaritan's example, "Let the neighbor be you." Rather than worrying if someone else is a neighbor, Jesus' call is to be a neighbor to those who have need. By reversing the perspective Jesus changes both the question and the answer. He makes the call no longer one of assessing other people, but of being a certain kind of person in one's activity.

One additional point emerges. By making the Samaritan the example, Jesus points out that neighbors may come in surprising places. The lawyer's attempt to limit his neighbors may actually be limiting where his fellowship might come from. Those who run people through a sieve limit their capacity for meaningful friendships.

THE MAJOR CONTEXTUAL bridge in this story is easy to cross, since the ethical call to be a responsive neighbor to those in need is a basic element of discipleship with its call to love God and one's neighbor.

The aspect of this text that is much discussed is Jesus' reply to the question about inheriting eternal life. Why does he not point more directly to himself in answer to that question? We argued above that the reply is just as biblical as anything Jesus would say today. To love God is to respond to him at every level. Jesus has just noted in the previous section that responding to him means responding to the kingdom message he has sent through his servants. At an ethical level, that translates into the type of loving concern the

Samaritan shows. For Jesus the issue of responding with love is an outgrowth of what God provides when people turn to him in love.

Jesus' answer has a concrete quality that he consistently displays in his teaching. As he has said earlier, his family consists of those who hear and do what he says (8:19–21). He does not discuss here, however, the provision of the Holy Spirit, who enables such love to be expressed. Note how in Paul's letter to the Galatians, the fruit of the Spirit is expressed in relational terms (Gal. 5:22–23). Those who have life, get that life through the Spirit Jesus provides. Those who come to God in love receive the benefit of his love through the gracious provision of the Spirit (see Luke 24:49; Acts 1:8; 1 Cor. 12:13).

Another practical issue is the personal, compassionate meeting of basic needs, not the mere throwing of money at a problem in the hopes it will fix itself. The Samaritan not only provides resources but personally undertakes to make sure that others who become a part of the process are aware that he wants the victim brought back to health. Care is left in the hands of those who will responsibly compete the task.

HOW CAN ONE be a neighbor? It takes eyes and ears to be a neighbor, as well as a compassionate heart. The one major difference between the priest and Levite on the one hand and the Samaritan on the other is not what they see and hear, but what they do with what they see and hear. Only the Samaritan takes pity. Only he has a heart. Neighbors are people with a heart that does more than pump blood. It sees, feels, and serves.

One often hears that the task of dealing with pain in the world is so vast that we do not know where to begin or how we can even hope to make a dent in what needs to be done. Such thinking can become an excuse for inaction. If I cannot know where to begin, I will not even start to help, because if I do, I will be overwhelmed. A better attitude is to pitch in where one feels a sense and ability to help. Maybe I cannot help everywhere, but I can help somewhere and try to do a meaningful work of service. Being a neighbor does not require meeting every need of which I become aware, but of becoming one piece of a large puzzle that helps meaningfully in a specific context.

A church community should seek to provide a whole avenue of ministries in this regard. Churches in the inner city or in the suburbs have a unique opportunity for public ministry with kids in local schools who need tutoring or foster parenting. Our church has been involved, as a suburban church, with one of the poorest areas in Dallas, where women in our church have tutored children of differing ethnic background who lack basic skills. Such a ministry is an equivalent of binding the wounded on our streets. Children who lack parental examples and support find them in the care and concern of the church. The church should give itself to creatively thinking through how ministries can occur.

Another example of ministry in our body involves the recent launching of a mother's day out, so that young mothers can get the "sanity" break they sometimes need as parents. Other people in our church have felt called to be foster parents for days, weeks, or months while a child is being placed for adoption. Others have opted to serve that role for an orphaned teenager or runaway looking to reenter society. Such ministries are usually sacrificial, but they are extraordinary examples of trying to be a neighbor. And of course, sometimes being a neighbor means just being there when a painful situation emerges with a neighbor. Neighborliness comes in all shapes and sizes. It is limited only by our failure to see, feel, and respond.

Luke 10:38–42

᭟

AS JESUS AND his disciples were on their way, he came to a village where a woman named Martha opened her home to him. ³⁹She had a sister called Mary, who sat at the Lord's feet listening to what he said. ⁴⁰But Martha was distracted by all the preparations that had to be made. She came to him and asked, "Lord, don't you care that my sister has left me to do the work by myself? Tell her to help me!"

⁴¹"Martha, Martha," the Lord answered, "you are worried and upset about many things, ⁴²but only one thing is needed. Mary has chosen what is better, and it will not be taken away from her."

Original Meaning

THIS SHORT PASSAGE is unique to Luke and gains its significance from the prioritizing that Jesus indicates in the tension raised by Mary's lack of aid to Martha. The story can be considered from two angles. One involves the perspective of Martha, who is clearly upset at the lack of help Mary provides in offering Jesus a meal. Anyone who has seen sibling rivalry can appreciate the tone of her challenge to Jesus, "Lord, don't you care that my sister has left me to do all the work. . . ?" The way the question is asked in Greek makes it clear that Martha anticipates a positive answer to her question. She expects Jesus to come to her aid. Martha is performing a worthy task, but she is consumed with what others are doing. Jesus does not criticize her for what she is doing but for being concerned about others' activities.

From the standpoint of Mary emerges the example of someone willing to sit at Jesus' feet and fellowship with him as his disciple. There is something tranquil in what Mary does. Often in the hustle and bustle of life, we need to pause for a moment of reflection before the Lord. Jesus' emotion-filled reply to Martha, speaking her name twice, indicates just how appropriate it is for this sister to sit before him. She has chosen a needful thing, a good thing, that will meet with her reward for time well spent with him. Discipleship sometimes requires that tasks be suspended while fellowship is maintained.

THIS TEXT IS significant both for where it falls in Luke's argument and for the example Luke uses to make a point about discipleship. It comes in a series of three passages, each of which treats a different key aspect of our relationship to God: how we relate to neighbors (10:25–37), how we engage in dialogue with God (11:1–13), and how we view one another and our time with the Lord (10:38–42). The example Jesus raises to prominence is someone who does not say a word—the devoted Mary sitting at his feet. Her silent testimony makes a deep impression, representing a good choice. The fact that a woman can be portrayed in such a positive light, as one worthy to sit at the Master's feet, is also significant in a first-century culture where women were often deemed unworthy of receiving instruction. Grace knows no boundaries of gender. The openness of the Lord to cross gender and social barriers is instructive for us, for often such barriers become obstacles to potential ministry. The Lord was willing to teach all, and so should we. Instruction in the things of the Lord should be open to all.

This passage is also a key discipleship text—not in the comparison between Martha and Mary's tasks, but in how Martha has wrongly judged Mary's inaction and worries too much about what others are doing. The text has two distinct emphases: Martha's consumption with assessing others as she performs what she is called to do, and Mary's wisdom in seeking some time at the feet of Jesus. Both qualities, one negative and the other positive, are at the heart of discipleship.

AS WE NOTED, this text is not just about the role or status of women, but about discipleship. Yet the fact that Jesus pictures women as disciples shows that they are treated with respect as people and as full disciples. In a culture that tended to regard women as little more than children, this is a significant step by itself. Luke has several accounts that highlight the value of women to the cause of Jesus (see ch. 1 and 8:1–3). Today the gender battle is often fought in a different way, as opportunities open up for women that were unthinkable in the first century. Men and women are almost at war. This is most unfortunate, for Jesus foresaw a time when men and women would both contribute to the cause of Christ, working together rather than fighting for power. When service is elevated to its proper place in discipleship, then battles over power become less relevant. Thus Mary's sitting at the feet of Jesus portrays a person willing to learn from him, while Martha's busyness pictures someone serving him. Disciples need to do both.

In other words, discipleship is a balanced combination of two things: service and reflection. Mary shows the importance of reflecting on what Jesus teaches. Today that translates into time in the Word and in the church's instructing of disciples about their role in the world. It may involve moments of silence before God in prayer, listening for his voice. It is a great temptation to serve at the expense of being fed spiritually. That is what Jesus' remark to Martha means. Some activities can wait. There is a time to work and a time to listen.

Unfortunately, often when things get busy, the first thing to go is time with the Lord. The elders with whom I serve in a local church have made a pledge to one another to be leaders of prayer. This has meant a commitment to meet each Tuesday morning together for breakfast from 6:30 A.M. to 8:00 A.M. to pray for the needs of our church as noted in the weekly prayer requests collected at our service. As I calculate it, we spend about three times the amount of time together praying or getting prepared to pray as we do in tackling church business directly in group discussion. But even the way I have put this is misleading, for when we pray, we are doing the work of leadership for the church. Before activity can be meaningful and done with sensitivity, it should be bathed in prayer. I suspect many of us could use a little more Mary and a little less Martha in our lives.

Part of Martha's problem was that she worried too much about what others were doing. In asking Jesus to enter into her complaint, she assumed that her evaluation of Mary's choice of priorities was right. Jesus' refusal to endorse Martha shows that although she was doing valuable work, she should worry less about Mary's choices. We often spend too much time evaluating the walk of others and too little time being self-critical about our own actions for Jesus. Think of how more effective the church would be if we gave half the energy to assessing our own walk than we often do to assessing the walk of others. A community suffocates when all its energy is spent being an assessment agency for one another. What is really crucial for an effective community is for each member to take individual responsibility for his or her own walk and to allow the community to minister in a positive and encouraging way to each other. That does not mean ignoring sin in the midst of the community, but it does mean being slow to make assessments in areas that have nothing to do with sin. Martha crossed this line. The Lord refused to hear her complaint. Mary needed to be honored for her choice.

Luke 11:1-13

O NE DAY JESUS WAS PRAYING in a certain place. When he finished, one of his disciples said to him, "Lord, teach us to pray, just as John taught his disciples." ²He said to them, "When you pray, say:

"'Father,
hallowed be your name,
your kingdom come.
³ Give us each day our daily bread.
⁴ Forgive us our sins,
    for we also forgive everyone who sins against us.
And lead us not into temptation.'"

⁵Then he said to them, "Suppose one of you has a friend, and he goes to him at midnight and says, 'Friend, lend me three loaves of bread, ⁶because a friend of mine on a journey has come to me, and I have nothing to set before him.'

⁷"Then the one inside answers, 'Don't bother me. The door is already locked, and my children are with me in bed. I can't get up and give you anything.' ⁸I tell you, though he will not get up and give him the bread because he is his friend, yet because of the man's boldness he will get up and give him as much as he needs.

⁹"So I say to you: Ask and it will be given to you; seek and you will find; knock and the door will be opened to you. ¹⁰For everyone who asks receives; he who seeks finds; and to him who knocks, the door will be opened.

¹¹"Which of you fathers, if your son asks for a fish, will give him a snake instead? ¹²Or if he asks for an egg, will give him a scorpion? ¹³If you then, though you are evil, know how to give good gifts to your children, how much more will your Father in heaven give the Holy Spirit to those who ask him!"

Original
Meaning

AGAIN, LUKE'S POSITIONING of material is distinct from its counterpart. The Lord's Prayer appears in Matthew's large summary sermon, the Sermon on the Mount, while Luke's version appears in the midst of teaching concluding a sequence of key texts about properly relating to God. This text also precedes the dispute about the origin of Jesus' authority. In other words, Jesus instructs the disciples about the nature of their walk in the context of being challenged about the nature of his ministry. A walk with God is the best way to be prepared to face such pressure.

This passage has three parts: the Lord's Prayer (vv. 1–4), a brief parable urging bold persistence in prayer (vv. 5–8); and a two-part exhortation to pray (vv. 9–13).[1] This discussion of prayer also completes a three-step discussion on discipleship extending back to 10:25; here the topic becomes relationship to God. The discourse is opened by a request from the disciples about prayer. The request to be taught prayer like John the Baptist's community indicates the disciples are becoming an identifiable community.[2] Thus this unit also testifies to the growth of the disciples' self-identity.

The request for instruction about prayer leads Jesus to teach them a version of what has become known as the Lord's Prayer. The prayer's name is only half the story. It is called the Lord's Prayer since it comes from the Lord, but it is really the disciples' prayer, expressing their common needs and sense of togetherness. Here is a community dependent on God and united in prayer before him for even the most basic needs of life. Disciples in touch with God take nothing for granted from him.

So the prayer opens with an address of the "Father." Though this term is not the intimate "Daddy" that some have argued the Aramaic word *Abba* signifies, it does indicate the approach to God as a caring father figure.[3] Disciples are called to childlike trust, not to a shallow childish intimacy. Real intimacy with God is built not on feelings, nor on what the Father can do for me, but on an appreciation of the true nature of the believer's relationship to God. They turn to him for protection and care. Though God is a unique and great figure, he is not unapproachable. Jesus' stress on God's proximity and the access believers have with him for his provision and care make his view of God deeply personal in emphasis (Eph. 2:17–18).

---

1. The parallels to this passage are scattered throughout the Synoptics and raise difficult questions whether the overlap represents the same event or are merely conceptual parallels. Luke 11:1–4 is similar to Matthew 6:9–13, but Luke's version is shorter than Matthew's and comes in a distinct context. Luke 11:5–8 represents material unique to Luke, while Luke 11:9–13 is conceptually similar to Matthew 7:7–11, though in a different setting. Many speak of genuine parallels here, but I prefer to see distinct teaching events covering similar themes.

2. Apparently John's community had a distinct prayer. The Jews also had a well-known community prayer known as the *Eighteen Benedictions*. Such prayers gave a community a sense of shared identity. Though many traditions today look down on liturgy, there is community value in sharing a form of intercession as a body.

3. J. Barr, "Abba Isn't Daddy," *JTS* ns 39 (1988): 28–47.

Finally, Jesus wants his disciples to pray as a group, using a "you all" to make the point ("you pray" in v. 2 is plural). This is a prayer the entire community shares and prays as a body. The practice of "praying as the Lord taught us to pray" as an introduction to repeating the Lord's Prayer together has good precedent here.

Access that develops close relationship need not destroy respect. So the first address to the Father is the statement that his name be "hallowed," that is, kept holy (Ps. 111:9; Isa. 5:16; 29:23; Ezek. 20:41; 28:22, 25; 38:23; 1 Peter 3:15). God is unique and set apart in character. As we pray to him, we recognize that we are not communicating among peers. Rather, we come humbly before a being who is unequaled in the universe. Whatever awe we give to anyone in a prominent position on earth is nothing compared with the respect owed to God. Thus the opening remark sets a proper tone for our spirit as we begin.

Next is the request for his kingdom to come. We pray that God's just rule be totally manifest on the earth. In the first century, saints longed for God to show the fullness of his power and to vindicate the saints (cf. Zechariah's prayer in 1:67–75). We live in a fallen and distorted creation. The saints often suffer at its hands, but they know that one day God will reveal himself in power and rule in glory. This request longs for that hope. Life is lived more effectively when one appreciates where history is headed. In the context of eternity, our temporal requests make more sense.

We also recognize that our most basic needs come from God. So the third remark contains a request for God to provide food for each succeeding day. The meaning of the word "daily" is disputed. Does it refer to this day's food, or is it a reference to providing the food for the next day?[4] Since the term is a unique Greek term, it is hard to be sure, but the meaning is the same either way. The expectation and recognition is that God is our provider, down to the food that sustains us each day. If the earth did not provide food, where would our nourishment and sustenance come from? The disciple acknowledges God's care at this basic level (12:22–31).

The disciple also seeks forgiveness of sin, but does so recognizing that he or she must give in return what is asked for. Thus, not only is the request made that our "sins" be forgiven, but that we are ready to forgive others who are indebted to us (Matt. 18:23–25; Luke 7:41–43).[5] It is wrong to ask from God what we are not willing to give to others. Judaism also recognized this

---

4. For the options and discussion, see Foerster, "ἐπιούσιος," *TDNT*, 2:592–95.

5. See NIV text note here. Cf. Fitzmyer, *The Gospel According to Luke X–XXIV* (AB 28A; Garden City, N.J.: Doubleday, 1985), 906. Qumran also used the metaphor of debt for sin (4QMess at 2:17).

connection: "Forgive your neighbor the wrong he has done, and then your sins will be pardoned when you pray" (Sirach 28:2). We are to model what we ask for.

The final request is for spiritual protection. This petition is often misunderstood. Why should we ask God not to "lead us ... into temptation"? Surely he has our best interests at heart and does not desire that we be tempted, right? The request really reflects a fundamental recognition about ourselves. If we are to be protected from temptation, we must lean on God to protect us.[6] This sentence has the force of "do not cause us not to succumb to temptation."[7] Integrity is a result of recognizing that without God's leading we would lead ourselves straight into sin. Thus this request also reflects a depth of spiritual sensitivity, since it understands just how prone to sin we are, if we do not seek God's face.

The prayer as a whole reflects a disciple's total reliance on God and his care. Whether it be in the circumstances that lead to his control of history, the provision of basic needs like food, or spiritual protection, the disciple knows that God's presence is an absolute necessity. That recognition is at the heart of this prayer. Thus the prayer bonds the disciple to God, recognizing that the affairs of life are often a matter in which we either walk alone or walk with our hand in his hand. The disciples' prayer acknowledges that our hand needs to be in his hand.

So how should one approach prayer? Jesus has told us what to pray, but how should we come to the throne of grace? Since God is holy and the Creator of the universe, should he perhaps be approached rarely and only in moments of dire need? Such thinking is dead wrong. We should pray with a spirit of dependence and humility, looking for God's gracious provision. Jesus therefore goes on to present a parable that emphasizes that God is approachable, gracious, generous, and ready to hear our requests.

To understand this parable, we must appreciate certain aspects of first-century cultural expectation. (1) Food was not as readily available as it is today; the era of twenty-four hour convenience stores is new. Bread was baked each day to meet daily needs. (2) The culture held hospitality in high regard, almost as a duty. A visitor was to be welcomed and cared for, regardless of the hour of his arrival. Here, then, we have a dilemma: a late evening guest, but no food. What would the host do? Also behind the story stands the real-

---

6. The Jews shared this view. The Talmud, *Berakoth* 60b, reads, "Bring me not into the power of sin, nor into the power of guilt, nor into the power of temptation." The Talmud was written later than the time of Jesus, but it shows a recognition that the way to avoid sin is to depend on God.

7. Marshall, *Commentary on Luke*, 462.

ity that most ancient homes had only one room. To approach a neighbor meant risking waking the family. How bold would the host be?[8]

Jesus poses the dilemma and then asks, "Which of you would have the nerve to go wake up his friend (and possibly his family as well!) in the middle of the night to ask for bread?" The request for three loaves would meet the need, provided his neighbor still had some leftovers from the day. The answer shows the tension. He replies that he cannot be bothered, since the children are in bed and he is unwilling to risk rousing them! Anyone who has put children to bed understands how the neighbor feels. In fact, the natural quality of the reply is part of the charm of this parable.

Jesus then comes to his main point. The neighbor does respond, not because he is a friend but because the petitioner has "boldness" (*anaideian*). This Greek term is difficult to render in English. It combines two qualities: boldness and shamelessness. This man has nerve to make such a request. In recognition of his boldness, the neighbor honors the request (cf. Heb. 10:19–22).[9]

The qualification of these requests as applying to basic spiritual needs comes from the concluding verses of the unit (vv. 9–10), where Jesus issues a call to "ask," "seek," and "knock." The promise of an open door lies before the disciple, who need not be too shy to ask. Then Jesus gives another illustration. If a child asks for a basic meal, fish, or eggs, will the father give him something dangerous instead, like a snake or scorpion? What father would do that? None. So Jesus concludes, "If you then, though you are evil, know how to give good gifts to your children, how much more will your Father in heaven give the Holy Spirit to those who ask him!"

Luke's point differs from Matthew's use of this imagery. Matthew speaks of God's giving good things, a broader category of divine favor. But Luke focuses on the more narrow concern of spiritual enablement. Some see Luke's request fulfilled in Acts 2 and limit it to the new era of the kingdom, but it is probably broader than this, since the entire spiritual walk is in view. We may draw on the Spirit's resources at any point in our walk, not just at its start. The Father delights in giving the basic spiritual provisions that the disciple needs to negotiate his or her way through life. If one needs strength or insight from God, he will provide it if we but ask.

---

8. There is some debate about how the parable works, since in Greek the syntax of vv. 5–8 is difficult. Some see the point of the parable as comparing the neighbor and God. God, like the neighbor, will respond to avoid shame, that is, to preserve his honor. But this reading breaks the contextual focus on the petitioner, which is Jesus' point all the way to v. 13. God does not need to be prodded to save his honor. Therefore, the perspective of v. 8 is that of the petitioner, as "his" friend and "his" boldness show. Thus the point is not about God but about the petitioner's focus on the Lord.

9. The parable in Luke 18:1–8 adds the idea that prayer should be persistent.

For Luke the Spirit is the one who gives enablement (Acts 1:8). Thus the dependence expressed in this disciples' prayer should also lead them to trust God fully, including the right to approach him boldly for spiritual insight. Even basic relationships such as those we have with neighbors and children illustrate the point. We can seek a neighbor's aid in moments of need, or a child might seek help from a parent. Surely the most intimate of relationships, our need for God, works in the context of similar care, where we can rest in the knowledge that he cares for us and hears us.

BASIC SPIRITUAL CHARACTERISTICS are present here. The importance of dependence and prayer for every believer's walk is central. In order to build a bridge from an ancient prayer that is set forth as a model, we need to reflect on both the requests and the attitudes present in them.

Prayer links us with God in the right way and puts us in dialogue with him. Not praying is a little like walking up to the marriage altar, saying one's vows to the spouse, and then going mute as the relationship moves from day to day. There can be no development of a deeper connection without time for table talk. In fact, without such basic contact, the relationship not only fails to go forward; it goes backward. That is certainly a reason why Jesus and Luke put so much stock in prayer.

A less appreciated dimension of the Lord's Prayer is its corporate thrust. This is not my individual prayer, but one that is shared as a community, uttered as if it were one prayer spoken with one voice. In other words, the disciples pray for the same things as a part of a large family. This sense of community is developed only in limited terms in our day. Believers do not sense, nor do churches often promote, our sense of connectedness to each other. We need reminding that we share the same basic spiritual goals and have the same needs. Applications to the Lord's Prayer usually speak in terms of me or mine, rarely us and ours. We may have some community within congregations, on rare occasions across some denominational lines, but here Jesus approaches the entire believing community as if it is a unit (see John 17).

A major foundation for Christian unity is the ability to pray together. The prayer groups Joe Aldrich formed in the northwestern part of the United States and which have spread to other portions of the country are a step in the right direction. The affirmation that comes when large groups of believers affirm each other in prayer for spiritual goals, as has taken place recently with Promise Keepers, can only bring a smile to God and must cause his heart to rejoice as this unified intercession reaches his ears.

The Lord's Prayer not only asks us to pray together but to forgive one another. If our willingness to forgive is part of what God responds to in our prayers, then a key to unity is the ability to forgive, so that relationships are not shattered by the fractures that sin is so capable of generating. The tragedy of the church is that as a community built on the principle of reconciliation established at the cost of Christ's shed blood, it is often unable to demonstrate even a drop of compassion to those both within and outside her walls.

Prayer is a timeless element of spirituality. A look at the Psalms shows just how long such intercession, some of it filled with great honesty and pain, has been a part of the community's walk with God. We all need to walk and talk with God. We tend to look to him in our moments of need and dependence; but if we are wise, we will recognize that we always are in need of him. He is fully aware of and sensitive to our requests. He wants us to pray constantly and to intercede for one another. God expects boldness from his children when it comes to such spiritual requests. But it is also important to see that the asking in the passage is not open-ended (i.e., ask for anything you want). God does not promise to give us whatever we desire; only what we need.

BESIDES THE ISSUE of community that stands behind this prayer, there are several other important points. One of the most fundamental is the sense of intimacy the prayer assumes believers possess with God. This intimacy is not a matter of feelings, but is grounded in the presence of a solid, established relationship. It is not a matter of sensing closeness, but of understanding and appreciating our need for dependence and trust. This point gets harder to make in a world where many people grow up with human fathers whom they either never knew, never were close to, or never got along with. It is hard to trust a Father we do not physically see when the one we had is absent, distant, or cruel.

But God is not a cosmic grouch. He loves and cares for us, desiring what is best for us. He shows the extent of his commitment to us in the sacrifice of Jesus (Rom. 8:30–39). Nothing can separate us from a close connection with him but ourselves and our failure to accept the care, provision, and access that comes from his hands. A relationship takes more than words claiming his presence; it must be nurtured through time and effort. That is why prayer is so crucial to the Christian walk. If Jesus took the time to teach us how to pray and urged us to do so with boldness, then our calling is to make time for it.

The pursuit of spiritual discipline is receiving renewed attention today. This is only right. Our world is so hectic that often all we think we have time for is a quick "check in" with the Father above. In fact, however, the more hectic the pace, the more we need him. In Jesus' life, Luke notes him praying in the moments when things were getting the most hectic. He prayed when he was baptized, before he chose the Twelve, after Peter's confession at the Transfiguration as he prepared to face Jerusalem, and when he was in the Garden, even as the guards approached to take him prisoner—not to mention on the cross itself. When events surrounded him, Jesus circled the wagons around the courts of God. The disciples must have sensed this, because this is one of the few places where they make a specific request to be taught something. The application is simple: Make time to see his face.

Another point emerges in the juxtaposition of intimacy with respect for God's uniqueness. God is not a "buddy," he is both Father and Lord. The petitioner who recognizes his uniqueness appreciates the privilege of entering his presence. Kneeling before the God of the universe requires humility. In our culture, where respect for elders often has reversed itself into a worshiping of youth, it is important to appreciate that a relationship with God is not a peer relationship. He sits enthroned in the heavens above. Thus, humility is fundamental to the ways of discipleship. The requests in the community prayer evidence this perspective. From daily food to spiritual forgiveness to spiritual protection, the disciple looks to God. There is no moment that can spare dependence on him.

God desires prayer that is bold, even shameless, in its approach to him. It is not shameless in the sense of coming to God for all the wants that we have. But it is brash and bold in making use of the access he gives us to seek his face and call on him to develop us spiritually. He desires prayer with nerve. Our requests can be set before his table. The response, of course, is up to God, but the Lord desires we share our heart with him and come with an intense desire to knock at heaven's door. The reason we can be bold emerges in the more subtle argument of the parable: If a human being responds affirmatively to the earthly request of his neighbor, surely a gracious God will respond to our requests about basic spiritual needs. This implicit idea in verses 5–10 emerges explicitly in verses 10–13.

We are to come to the Father, knowing that his arms are open for us. I had the gift of a father who loved me. I knew what it meant to be able to walk into his room, his office, the living room, or wherever he was, and know that if I had a crucial need, he had an ear that was leaning in my direction and a heart that was open to my pain. The great lesson of a good father is that it gave me a glimpse of the heavenly Father I now have, even in the absence of my human father. I knew what it was to receive fish or eggs when

I asked for them, just as I know now what it is to receive spiritual strength for basic spiritual needs from my Father in heaven. We can be bold because he cares. We can seek his face because he is there, waiting to hear and embrace our spiritual needs.

Luke 11:14–23

JESUS WAS DRIVING out a demon that was mute. When the demon left, the man who had been mute spoke, and the crowd was amazed. ¹⁵But some of them said, "By Beelzebub, the prince of demons, he is driving out demons." ¹⁶Others tested him by asking for a sign from heaven.

¹⁷Jesus knew their thoughts and said to them: "Any kingdom divided against itself will be ruined, and a house divided against itself will fall. ¹⁸If Satan is divided against himself, how can his kingdom stand? I say this because you claim that I drive out demons by Beelzebub. ¹⁹Now if I drive out demons by Beelzebub, by whom do your followers drive them out? So then, they will be your judges. ²⁰But if I drive out demons by the finger of God, then the kingdom of God has come to you.

²¹"When a strong man, fully armed, guards his own house, his possessions are safe. ²²But when someone stronger attacks and overpowers him, he takes away the armor in which the man trusted and divides up the spoils.

²³"He who is not with me is against me, and he who does not gather with me, scatters."

Original Meaning

LUKE 11:14–54 SHOWS the widening rift between Jesus and the Jewish religious leadership, who for Luke represents a major factor, along with the political leadership, on where the nation stands on Jesus (13:31–35; 19:41–44). Thinking his miraculous power comes from Satan, they debate the source with Jesus (11:14–23). But Jesus claims to be stronger than Satan, defeating him in these hand-to-hand battles. He goes on to warn the people not to miss the moment of blessing and end up in a state worse than before, since blessing comes from obeying God's Word (11:24–29). The only sign given to this generation is the message of Jesus, which is like the wisdom of Solomon and the call of Jonah to repent (11:30–32). Our Lord wants the people to pay attention to what spiritual advice they take in, since it determines the character of their heart (11:33–36).

This unit ends with Jesus' strongest rebuke of the Pharisees and scribes in this Gospel, which show just how off-course the Jewish leadership is. Their path is destructive. The way of piety, which they perceive to abide with them, is found nowhere near them. They are leading others to death (11:37–54). These six woes are an indirect call to repent. Instead, the Jewish religious leadership resolves to deal severely with Jesus. They cannot allow him to go unchecked, and they begin to plan what they might do. Jesus draws ever nearer to his destiny in Jerusalem.

To understand the significance of Jesus' miraculous work, especially his exorcisms, one must understand 11:14–23. The miracle, told in a single verse (v. 14), reflects one of the most significant kinds of activity in Jesus' ministry.[1] Its importance emerges when one compares it to how the Evangelists present other miracles. Most of them are told with vividness and detail, while reactions to them are only briefly summarized. Here the situation is the opposite, in that the reaction and commentary dominate the account. In other words, this account summarizes the public debate over Jesus' miraculous work and carries an explanatory significance for all his miracles. They depict the comprehensive power he has over the forces of evil. As a result, his power over creation is secure.[2]

The issue here is Jesus' authority. When he exorcises a demon that is the source of a man's being mute, the discussion begins about the unusual character of Jesus' ministry. Two approaches emerge. (1) Some assign his work to Beelzebub. This name, probably originally referring to a pagan god, was applied to Satan, designating him as "Lord of the Flies."[3] This derisive name indicated a lack of respect for this powerful figure. To some, therefore, Jesus' power is demonic. (2) Others prefer to sit on the fence and wait for something more from Jesus. The request for a sign from heaven is vague, given the many acts Jesus has already done. Apparently some type of visible sign involving activity in the heavens is in view.

This questioning prevents making a commitment to Jesus, while admitting that there is something happening that requires reflection. Perhaps their testing of Jesus (v. 16) falls in line with what the Old Testament instructed God's people to do with prophets (Deut. 13:1–5). Given all that he has already done, which should be sufficient to identify him, Jesus responds only to the claim that he is connected to Satan. As for signs, Jesus will shortly make it clear that only the sign of his preaching is his message (12:29–32).

---

1. The parallels to this passage are Matthew 12:22–30 and Mark 3:22–27. It is placed earlier in Mark than in Luke or Matthew, but that may be because Mark 2:1–3:6 is more topically arranged, displaying a series of successive controversies.

2. That Satan is connected to a wider set of debilitating conditions than exorcisms is seen in a text like 13:10–17, which, though portrayed as a healing (v. 14), is also linked with Satan's activity (v. 16).

3. Fitzmyer, *Luke X-XXIV*, 920–21.

Jesus knows the speculation about him and addresses it. He rejects the connection to Satan on a simple premise. If Satan's goal is to destroy and Jesus is reversing the effects of destruction by healing, then how can one tie Jesus' work to the archdemon? That would mean a house divided and a kingdom ready to fall. Satan's kingdom cannot stand if Jesus is driving out the demons by this power.[4]

Jesus adds one more point to his assessment, that he does not act alone. Others are also driving out demons. The meaning of this point is disputed. Is Jesus pointing to all Jewish exorcists here, asking how they manage to do their work?[5] This meaning seems unlikely. Would Jesus really hold out the possibility that Jewish exorcists will help in the final judgment (as the end of v. 19 says)? Jesus could hardly be acknowledging that God works through Jewish exorcists in a community needing reform. More likely, the allusion in *hoi huioi humon* (lit., "your sons") is to Jesus' disciples, who are also Jewish but who do their work through Jesus' commission.[6] His point is that there is more than one figure in the movement that shows this authority. Divine endorsement extends to those he has commissioned. They will serve as the judges of the Jewish leadership one day, if the latter do not change their mind about who Jesus is.

If the satanic connection is out, then what remains? Jesus next issues one of the most crucial statements of his ministry: "But if I drive out demons by the finger of God, then the kingdom of God has come to you." Jesus outlines two possibilities for explaining what is taking place. Either he works by satanic power or through divine connections. There is no third option, no neutral ground. His use of the phrase "the finger of God"—which occurs in the biblical account of the Exodus (Ex. 8:19), another great moment of divine activity—shows that God is directly involved in history through Jesus with the powerful touch of his grace.

The point about God's kingdom coming is also significant. What is at stake in Jesus' ministry is a cosmic battle displaying the right to rule. Like a great war, the combatants are facing off with everything at stake. The promise of the kingdom is one of the great promises of the Old Testament. God's promised agent will rule as the vicegerent of God, restoring the presence of righteousness on the earth. Jesus' exorcisms signal its arrival. Some argue that arrival is not in view here, but merely the approach of the kingdom.

---

4. Luke presents this remark vividly in Greek using a first class condition. The vividness says in effect, "If this is really the case, then think what that really means."

5. Rengstorf, "μαθητής," *TDNT*, 4:443.

6. The NIV "your followers" takes the view that Jesus is alluding to Jewish exorcists. As I have suggested, this reading makes less sense than seeing a reference to Jesus' disciples.

But this ignores the force of the following parable, which pictures Satan's house as overrun and defeated, with the spoils of the victory being shared with those on the winner's side.[7] The language of arrival is also indicated by the phrase translated "has come to you," which looks to arrival, not approach.[8]

Jesus claims that his miracles are audiovisuals of the presence of God's victorious rule. They indicate that the great promised vicegerent has come. He is not saying that everything promised in association with that kingdom has come, only that the kingdom itself has arrived. Read in line with other New Testament texts, the passage argues that the process of establishing its presence has begun.[9] Jesus' work is a divine painting etched by the finger of God and pointing to the one through whom the forces in heaven manifest themselves on earth. He is exhibiting his authority over Satan, establishing the earth as a place where righteousness can and does triumph over destruction. Redemption comes through him. All that remains is for people to choose for him.

Jesus then summarizes his main point with a parable. A strong man occupies a house and guards his possessions. They are safe until someone stronger attacks him, overrunning his home.[10] When the stronger one comes, the armor of the original man is stripped away and the spoils are divided among the victors. Jesus claims his miracle portrays such a victory. He has superior strength over Satan. That also implies that Jesus does not work with Satan, but against him. The forces that plague human beings are overcome in Jesus. That is why to oppose Jesus is to be against him and be the source of scattering (v. 23). Jesus stresses by this closing remark just how crucial the decision about him is. There are only two sides, and the choice of allies in this cosmic battle is crucial.

---

7. Cf. Ephesians 4:7–10, which uses the same imagery in a context where victory is clearly tied to the Jesus' resurrection-ascension.

8. W. Kümmel, *Promise and Fulfillment: The Eschatological Message of Jesus* (London: SCM, 1961), esp., 107; K. Schmidt, "βασιλεύς" and "βασιλεία," *TDNT*, 1:566–76 and 580–89. For the idiom see, Daniel 4:24, 28 (in Greek Theodotion text). The key is the presence of the preposition *epi* with the verb *ephthasen*. See above on 10:9.

9. Many texts treat these themes. Two key passages that look to what the future will bring with the rule of Jesus are Acts 3:18–20 and Revelation 20–22. For a discussion of these themes in more detail, see D. Bock, "The Reign of the Lord Christ," in *Dispensationalism, Israel, and the Church: A Search for Definition*, ed. by C. Blaising and D. Bock (Grand Rapids: Zondervan, 1992), 37–67.

10. The imagery is not unusual. In Judaism, *Testament of Levi* 18:12 looked to a day when Beliar (another name for Satan) would be bound and power to tread over evil spirits would be given to the children of the promised great priest. Though the New Testament does not refer to such a distinct high priestly figure who is different from the Messiah, the concept that the promise includes victory over Satan is similar.

WITH MIRACLES AS a window to God's support and presence, Jesus explains what his ministry is all about. This passage is like pulling back the curtains on the divine perspective of Jesus' ministry. As such, the Christology it teaches is timeless, for Jesus' battle with Satan is the greatest spiritual battle of all time. Jesus establishes his position as the stronger man who overcomes the power of the evil one. His ministry was the key turning point in this battle. Though skirmishes are still being fought and the complete victory still awaits us, the victory described here is part of a fundamental perspective Jesus wants both his disciples and opponents to appreciate. The theme of his victory as pictured in his miracles speaks to every age about his matchless authority.

Jesus' work is different from Satan's labors. Whereas the devil destroys, the deliverer rescues. Whereas Satan debilitates life, Jesus enhances it. Whereas Satan cripples, Jesus liberates. Jesus shows how his work exalts life. That activity defines his service, picturing how disciples should walk in a way that seeks to encourage others to experience life in its fullness.

The decision Jesus calls for in this text is another feature that is true for every generation. His life and ministry were so unusual that one must assess its roots. The distance between the present and the past has allowed some to claim that Jesus did not really perform these wonders or give this type of evidence of his unique relationship to God. They attempt to relegate Jesus to the level of other greats of religion. But the opponents living in Jesus' time did not have the luxury of such a claim. They could not deny he had performed deeds of unusual power. The Jewish records we possess that allude to Jesus report the unusual nature of his deeds and try to explain them, not deny them. The corridors of time may dim the reality of his majestic works to an extent that some do deny he did them, but that is not a rational option. If it were, his opponents would have taken that road long ago. Those who opposed Jesus took the only logical option left to them in light of the evidence of his supernatural power: They claimed it was rooted in a diabolical force. Jesus knew the argument and dealt with it here.

AN UNDERSTANDING OF the miracle in this section as a window into the supernatural battle between Jesus and Satan has much to say both about making a decision as to who Jesus is and about the evidentiary function of miracles. Jesus' explanation helps us appreciate the supportive role of miracles and explains why he did not focus his ministry too greatly on them. They are but a portrait of more fundamental realities, namely, God's good will to restore creation and triumph over evil.

This text also has significant applications on the nature of the kingdom of God and the meaning of Jesus' victory as pictured here. Christ's rule is designed to establish the presence of righteousness on the earth through the formation of a people who reflect his character before others (Matt. 5:14–16; Titus 2:11–14). Though his kingdom will be powerfully visible one day when he returns, Jesus has gathered around himself a community of redeemed people who demonstrate the transformation and real life his victory paved the way for. That transformation is why Paul defines the gospel as the "power of God" in Romans 1:16–17. He then goes on in that great letter to describe how humanity has been delivered from the depths of sin and bondage (so also 2 Cor. 3–4, which speaks of the new covenant of the Spirit). This new community is to be a people who evidence reconciliation, the union of Jew and Gentile into a new body (Eph. 2:11–22), absent of the malice that comes from the presence of sin and from following the "ruler of the kingdom of the air" (2:2). Christ calls the church to show that it can be otherwise. Early glimpses of what this new type of community is like appear in Acts as believers shared with each other, even to the extent of raising money to meet needs across racial and geographical lines.

This discussion may seem rather abstract, but it is not. Paul's letters demonstrate that God's presence can reverse the presence of satanic forces pictured in this Lucan passage. In fact, the apostle built a theology of community around this truth. Placed in the kingdom of his beloved Son and rescued from the forces of darkness (Col. 1:12–14), we have been given all the spiritual equipment we need to become the people he calls us to be. No authority is greater than Christ's, to whom we have access (Eph. 1:15–23). The power he gives (the spoils he distributes!) includes the enablement to live as reconciled people in a community that evidences love and reconciliation in the context of renewed relationship.

The victory Jesus describes in Luke 11 clears the road of any claim that obstacles exist that cannot be overcome in the church community. If failure occurs, it is not because enablement has not been provided, but because we fail to make use of the victory Jesus provides. This does not mean we are perfect in this life, for glorification awaits us in the kingdom's future. But it does suggest a rich array of resources exist to help us overcome the forces that otherwise overpower us. It also suggests that failure to grow spiritually is our fault, since God has provided a rich reservoir of enablement through his Spirit.

In other words, this passage becomes the basis of Jesus' "Declaration of Dependence." Unlike some nations and people who pride themselves on being totally free and independent, Jesus' community sees its identity in having been rescued by him and thus permanently aligned to him. This declaration brings with it great privileges, for now the potential exists to live righteously as we walk with and respond to God's Spirit. In dependence on him, we can be the new community he calls us to be. The kingdom of God is not an abstraction; it is a community where God's presence and rule so dominate our existence that we honor him in all we do and where righteousness manifests itself in the face of a hostile world (Gal. 2:20; 5:22–26; 6:14–16). To belong to the kingdom and draw on its resources is to stand firm before Satan (Eph. 6:10–18). But this kingdom does not come and go, though our tendency to draw from it can waver if we fail to draw on its resources. To share in his kingdom is to share in the benefits that give us new life, not just in heaven but now.

Such theological background means that the fundamental application of this text is to reaffirm and pursue our identity with the stronger one who overran Satan. To decide that Jesus has been sent from God is to decide that "in him is life." If his coming means the finger of God has come with evidence of his guiding rule, then our call is to follow where he points.

Luke 11:24-36

WHEN AN EVIL spirit comes out of a man, it goes through arid places seeking rest and does not find it. Then it says, 'I will return to the house I left.' 25When it arrives, it finds the house swept clean and put in order. 26Then it goes and takes seven other spirits more wicked than itself, and they go in and live there. And the final condition of that man is worse than the first."

27As Jesus was saying these things, a woman in the crowd called out, "Blessed is the mother who gave you birth and nursed you."

28He replied, "Blessed rather are those who hear the word of God and obey it."

29As the crowds increased, Jesus said, "This is a wicked generation. It asks for a miraculous sign, but none will be given it except the sign of Jonah. 30For as Jonah was a sign to the Ninevites, so also will the Son of Man be to this genera-tion. 31The Queen of the South will rise at the judgment with the men of this generation and condemn them; for she came from the ends of the earth to listen to Solomon's wisdom, and now one greater than Solomon is here. 32The men of Nineveh will stand up at the judgment with this generation and con-demn it; for they repented at the preaching of Jonah, and now one greater than Jonah is here.

33"No one lights a lamp and puts it in a place where it will be hidden, or under a bowl. Instead he puts it on its stand, so that those who come in may see the light. 34Your eye is the lamp of your body. When your eyes are good, your whole body also is full of light. But when they are bad, your body also is full of darkness. 35See to it, then, that the light within you is not darkness. 36Therefore, if your whole body is full of light, and no part of it dark, it will be completely lighted, as when the light of a lamp shines on you."

Original Meaning

THE MINISTRY OF Jesus requires choices, the most basic choices in life. This section underscores that point with a series of exhortations indicating just how crucial the choice is.[1] The point is made by illustration (vv. 24—26), beatitude (vv. 27—28), warning (vv. 29—32), and exhortation (vv. 33—34). Each text is a call to respond faithfully to the revelation Jesus brings.

The first remark (vv. 24—26) reports of an exorcism where the demon departs a house, but nothing is put in the house to replace it. The house is clean but still left empty. So the demon decides to return and brings with him seven other spirits more wicked than himself.[2] They reenter the house, making the situation far worse than it was before the exorcism. The passage is about spiritual response. If God's grace frees someone from the presence of evil temporarily, or at least offers to do so, and then a refusal to respond comes. A dangerous situation emerges. The "house" is left clean, and the door remains open for those forces to return more determined than ever to live there. The end result is then worse than the first. Revelation missed becomes a one step closer to being left in evil hands. Refusing to respond to God's grace is not a matter of being neutral, but of remaining in destructive hands.

Next comes a short exchange that concludes with a beatitude (vv. 27—28). The possibility of falling into a worse state causes someone to change the subject and offer praise for those who cared for Jesus. The woman's blessing of Jesus' mother attempts to honor his family. It was not unusual to honor a mother in that culture by the accomplishments of her sons (Gen. 49:25; Prov. 23:24—25).[3] But Jesus transforms the remark into another opportunity to declare where real blessing in life resides—in those who hear and obey God's Word. Like the previous illustration, Jesus is focusing on the cruciality of receiving that Word. Richness and fullness of life are not a matter of biological or social origin, but relating well to the Lord of the universe (cf. 8:19—21).

---

1. One of the passages in this unit, Luke 11:27—28, is unique to Luke. Luke 11:24—26 is paralleled by Matthew 12:43—45. Luke 11:29—32 is like Matthew 12:38—42 and Mark 8:11—12, though Luke's version is closer to Matthew, where Jonah is mentioned. Luke 11:33 is similar to Matthew 5:15 (in the Sermon on the Mount) and Mark 4:21 (in the discourse on the kingdom); the remark is proverbial enough to be appropriate to each of these settings. The same is true of the parallel to Luke 11:34—36 in Matthew 6:22—23.

2. The idea of a demon seeking a place to live also occurs in Judaism: Tobit 8:3; Baruch 4:35.

3. F. Hauck, "μακάριος," *TDNT*, 4:369.

Jesus then turns to history as he issues a warning about the endless pursuit of signs (vv. 29–32). By introducing the remark with an address to "a wicked generation," Jesus makes it clear that such a continual quest, especially in light of what has already been done, is sinful. It is an excuse to refuse to face what Jesus is doing. Our Lord insists that no sign will come beside what Jonah and Solomon have provided. The comparison between the Son of Man and Jonah is not about Jonah's three days in the belly of the fish. Rather, verse 32 makes it clear that Jonah's preaching is the issue here (Jonah 3:6–10). The sign is therefore the call to repent.

Reinforcing that Jesus' teaching is the main issue is the picture of the Queen of the South, who visited Solomon to hear about his wisdom (1 Kings 10:1–13; 2 Chron. 9:1–12).[4] She came from Southern Arabia to hear his teaching. Now someone greater than both Jonah and Solomon stands before them, and his teaching offers what they longed to see. In other words, Jesus' miracles and signs point to the more important issue—his teaching. In fact, this Queen and the men of Nineveh will stand at the judgment to testify against this generation for what they are missing in Jesus. Their testimony will condemn them. The remark is a warning. To refuse Jesus is to face rejection in judgment and the condemnation of previous generations who understand the unique opportunity that Jesus' preaching provides.

Finally, Jesus uses the image of light to make his point more strongly (vv. 33–34). He compares his teaching to "a lamp," which in the ancient world was a candle or some type of oil lamp. One does not go to the effort of lighting a lamp in order to place it where its light is covered. It goes on a lampstand, where it can give light. Thus, Jesus' teaching is light made available for all to see. What he says is not designed to be concealed, since God intends Jesus to reveal God's promises.

But light not only has to be lit; it has to be received by the eye. The juxtaposition of this image with the previous one suggests the need to draw on the light Jesus provides. So Jesus compares the eye to a lamp—a substitution figure of speech known as metonymy, where the means of reception (eye) is associated with that which is received (light). The eye is a lamp in the sense that it is a doorkeeper (cf. 2 Baruch 18:1–2 [Syriac] for use of this imagery). What the eye lets into the mind makes up the person. When such eyes are good, letting in light, then the person is full of light and reflects light in life. But if the eyes are bad, letting nothing good come in, then the body is a dark place, since our inclinations unled by divine revelation take us in destructive directions. Of course, what is let in is a reflection of where our heart is. Jesus, therefore, calls for people to be full of light. They are to

---

4. See also Josephus, *Antiquities* 8.6.5–6 §§ 165–75.

respond to the light of God's Word by receiving it. To take in light is to shine from the inside.

Such light imagery is frequent in the New Testament (Luke 1:78–79; 2:32; John 1:4; 3:19–21; 9:39–42; Acts 26:18; 2 Cor. 6:14–15; Eph. 5:14–15; 1 John 1:6–10). As a fundamental image, it indicates that without God's presence, only darkness presides. There is no automatic "inner light" as far as Jesus is concerned. So we must be careful what goes into our soul through the door (the eye). The Great Physician recommends that the intake be filled with light.

 THIS PASSAGE HIGHLIGHTS our need to respond to Jesus. One crucial issue today must be addressed, if we are to speak to our world. When Jesus taught, people assumed both the reality of revelation from God and absolute truths; the issue was merely pursuing and finding them. Today, however, many deny absolute truth even exists. In our culture, particularly in its more philosophical form, the most one can claim is that truth is perspectival. It is true that recognizing perspective in viewing a topic need not lead to relativism. But often the claim today is that all perspectives are relative, functioning as strictly human constructions. Truth for me is only where I see it, and it fits only within a self-constructed system of reality. No one has the corner on truth to the point where he or she can dictate it to others. Any other view is ruled out as dogmatism or a quest for power.

This position needs to be addressed at two levels. (1) The claim of absolute authority for this relative view is itself an absolute claim that cannot be made, if absolute statements are not tenable. The attempt to rule a discussion of absolutes out of bounds by definition trips over its own assumptions. Unfortunately, many do not understand the subtlety of this logical contradiction.

(2) A more substantive reply starts with the assumption of the objector. If truth is an experience to be appreciated and if it operates within a given perception of reality, then that is exactly what Jesus offers for our consideration. Here Jesus offers a perspective on reality that includes God, wrestles with claims of transcendent truth, and asserts responsibility and accountability for the choices made. This latter point is especially important, for it is often missed in the debate over whether absolute truth exists. Jesus does not compel a decision for his model. He simply notes that the one who rejects what he has on offer is responsible for that decision. One may reject the light he offers, even though that rejection may cost dearly. Theology, as

the church has presented it, is not just a matter of truth, but just as importantly, a matter of accountability and responsibility. This is why Jesus calls his teaching "light." It illumines and shows the way. The refusal to walk in its path means one is free to negotiate life in the darkness with all the rights, privileges, and obstacles that such darkness sets in the way.

One additional proviso is raised in this text. Someday we will see God, and he will ask us what we have done with his light. Witnesses from the ages will testify to our response. That is accountability. In the modern era, the way to share the light is to highlight such accountability. Truth, in terms of experience, is a choice; but with choice there is profound responsibility. Watch closely and choose wisely.

I am reminded of Shakespeare's remark, "All the world's a stage and we are merely players in it." Though he used it to speak of our roles in a life designed by destiny, there is another way to see the figure. Our view of truth and our choices are on public view, part of a cosmic broadcast about who we are. Our actions and choices reveal our character and values. The idea that our choices about truth are private is a bold distortion. So Jesus claims his teaching is light. The bridge to our context is that claim, as is our responsibility to respond.

THE APPLICATION OF Jesus' claim to reveal light and of his call to be careful how we respond to God's presence and revelation is to take seriously the claim that he offers light. In our society, responsibility for truth has been abandoned to the black hole of shifting public perception. The church may never again function in a world where objective truth is seen as a given. So we must think through representing our message in light of the abandonment of a belief that such truth exists. The life raft to get to the human heart lost in this sea of relativity is not merely to refight the battle for objective truth, but simply to affirm the immense responsibility of living in a universe where one is responsible for one's choices. In fact, this second approach may be more fruitful in personal evangelism, for it makes clear that our choices come at great risk.

In terms of experience and perception, life often is a constructed reality. We have to make judgments about what life is and how it works. We must choose the sources and influences that form how we see life. The issue is whether it is well constructed. The challenge of the church of our age is to have people see that there is no escape from responsibility for reflecting over ultimate questions. In the future, God will ascertain the fate of every person's decision. The church's role is to set forth its message in the public square and make clear what is at stake.

There is another crucial application here. No religious discussion is a private affair. One's decision made about religion is privately made and considered, but the consequences are decidedly public, since character and morals are often the product of our religious choices. Our culture's commitment to relegate religious discussion to the sidelines of life represents one of the great abdications of intellectual and spiritual well-being in the history of humanity. To pursue every other avenue of life with diligence and energy while ignoring the soul is to produce people whose lives may be full of activity, but whose souls are empty shells, houses waiting to be filled with something. Hollow people often live shallow lives. If any discussion should fill the public square, it is that of religion. The possibility of the existence of light means that discussion about where it can be found should proceed with vigor for everyone.

Luke 11:37–54

❦

WHEN JESUS HAD FINISHED speaking, a Pharisee invited him to eat with him; so he went in and reclined at the table. ³⁸But the Pharisee, noticing that Jesus did not first wash before the meal, was surprised.

³⁹Then the Lord said to him, "Now then, you Pharisees clean the outside of the cup and dish, but inside you are full of greed and wickedness. ⁴⁰You foolish people! Did not the one who made the outside make the inside also? ⁴¹But give what is inside the dish to the poor, and everything will be clean for you.

⁴²"Woe to you Pharisees, because you give God a tenth of your mint, rue and all other kinds of garden herbs, but you neglect justice and the love of God. You should have practiced the latter without leaving the former undone.

⁴³"Woe to you Pharisees, because you love the most important seats in the synagogues and greetings in the marketplaces.

⁴⁴"Woe to you, because you are like unmarked graves, which men walk over without knowing it."

⁴⁵One of the experts in the law answered him, "Teacher, when you say these things, you insult us also."

⁴⁶Jesus replied, "And you experts in the law, woe to you, because you load people down with burdens they can hardly carry, and you yourselves will not lift one finger to help them.

⁴⁷"Woe to you, because you build tombs for the prophets, and it was your forefathers who killed them. ⁴⁸So you testify that you approve of what your forefathers did; they killed the prophets, and you build their tombs. ⁴⁹Because of this, God in his wisdom said, 'I will send them prophets and apostles, some of whom they will kill and others they will persecute.' ⁵⁰Therefore this generation will be held responsible for the blood of all the prophets that has been shed since the beginning of the world, ⁵¹from the blood of Abel to the blood of Zechariah, who was killed between the altar and the sanctuary. Yes, I tell you, this generation will be held responsible for it all.

⁵²"Woe to you experts in the law, because you have taken away the key to knowledge. You yourselves have not entered, and you have hindered those who were entering."

⁵³When Jesus left there, the Pharisees and the teachers of the law began to oppose him fiercely and to besiege him with questions, ⁵⁴waiting to catch him in something he might say.

THIS PASSAGE CONTAINS Jesus' most direct rebuke of the Pharisees and scribes, a significant portion of the Jewish religious leadership.[1] The difference between Jesus and them has become a chasm, and this exchange deepens their resolve to remove him. The Pharisees and scribes were not the majority on the ruling council of Judaism (the Sadducees were), but they did have great influence there. While the Sadducees basically followed the Torah (Genesis to Deuteronomy), the Pharisees developed an extensive tradition of oral law, applying it to every area of life; this factor made them the strictest of the Jewish religious sects. Though small in number (estimated to be over 6,000 at this time), as a lay movement they represented one of the more powerful influences on Judaism.[2] The scribes were scholars who tried to determine what following the law meant. They were respected by most Jews.

The setting of this section is a meal, where many significant discussions occur in Luke (cf. 5:29; 7:36; 10:38; 14:1; 22:1; 24:42). The catalyst is Jesus' failure to wash his hands in preparation for eating. Jewish practice often noted this action in the Old Testament and followed it, though it was not included in God's law (Gen. 18:4; Judg. 19:21; cf. Mark 7:1–5).[3] Jesus knows what his host is thinking, so he addresses all of the Pharisees about the question. He begins with a fourfold rebuke. The first is a general rebuke, and the last three consist of specific woes.

The general complaint is that the Pharisees clean the outside of the cup and dish, but inside there is the filth of extortion and greed. In the language of 11:33–36, they are dark inside; they have not taken in light. In mentioning "greed," Jesus seems to have in mind the leadership's use of resources (Matt. 23:16–22; Luke 20:45–47), while moral integrity is the

---

1. This text has a conceptual parallel in Matthew 23. Most regard Luke to have relocated that event here. Against that conclusion stand the distinct setting, the lack of overlap in vocabulary between the two texts, and the order of the woes. What we have are distinct but conceptually parallel sayings.

2. Josephus, *Antiquities* 17.2.4 § 42; 18.1.3–5 §§ 12–22. For this portrait of the Pharisees, see E. P. Sanders, *The Historical Figure of Jesus* (London: Penguin, 1993), 44–46.

3. *Mishnah, Yadim* 1; Josephus, *Jewish Wars* 2.8.5 § 129; R. Booth, *Jesus and the Laws of Purity: Tradition History and Legal History in Mark 7* (JSNTSS 13; Sheffield: JSOT Press, 1987), 119–50, 194–203.

issue in the reference to "wickedness" (Gk. *poneria*). His rebuke sounds like the prophets (Isa. 1:10–17; 58:4–8; Amos 5:21–24; Micah 6:6–8), whose call for integrity in relating to those around them serves the basis for Jesus' rebuke. He is committed to challenging these people who claim to represent God and his ways.

Jesus raises a question. Did not God create both the inside and the outside? The Greek particle *ouk* that begins this sentence indicates that a positive answer is anticipated. That is, God is concerned with both spheres. In fact, the inside is especially of concern to him. That is why he calls them "foolish people" even before he raises the question.

Using a metaphor and a common custom of giving alms to the poor, Jesus calls on them to give alms to what is inside.[4] This figure means that a person should give energy to the care of the heart, like a person who might perform the venerated act of offering alms to the poor. That is, one should be sensitive both to God and to others. Alms was an honorable religious act, so this attention to the inner life is honorable as well. In doing so, the inner life will be clean.

Jesus then offers three rebukes. The first treats tithing, even of the smallest herbs, as the Old Testament calls for (Deut. 14:22–27; 26:12–15), while ignoring justice and love. The complaint is like that in verses 39–41. They should be sensitive both to tithing and to their character.

But hypocrisy is not the only problem. There also is the issue of pride. They love the front seats in the synagogue and the special greetings they receive on the road. Such privileged attention leads to an elitist mentality rather than to the commitment to serve. In fact, Jesus describes them as being like death for others, since they are like an unmarked grave over which people walk without knowing. They are the conductors of spiritual uncleanness, because they do not model real spirituality. Such leadership is destructive, so Jesus pulls no punches in condemning it.

Someone at the table comes to the Pharisees' defense. A scribe notes that if Jesus insists on condemning the Pharisees, he must include the scribes also. This man has nerve, but at least he is honest, unlike others who keep their opinions to themselves.

So Jesus issues three more rebukes, this time with the scribes in view.[5] The first rebuke can be understood in one of two ways. One view argues it may

---

4. On the Jewish view and high regard for alms, see Sirach 7:10 and Tobit 12:8–9. My reading of this text disagrees with the NIV translation. It reads the text more literally as referring to giving what is inside the dish to the poor, but this does not make sense in this context. It is better to see a rhetorical figure here.

5. On scribes, see Luke 5:17–26.

refer to outright hypocrisy, where the leadership requires of others what they will not do themselves. In other texts, Jesus complains about oaths others take, while the Pharisees excuse themselves by how they make the oath (Matt. 23:16–22). The second views see a more subtle form of hypocrisy, where they offer no aid or loving support to help those who have great burdens to bear.[6] For example, the Sabbath controversies show how the Sabbath law restrictions prevented works of compassion on such days (Luke 13:10–17). Since the tradition seems fairly clear that the leaders took their rules seriously, it seems that the complaint is about showing lack of compassion to others as the burdens of the rules are pursued. So Jesus complains that they call on others to bear the weight of tradition on their back, but do nothing to help them carry the load. In effect, Jesus calls on them to be more considerate and compassionate.

The condemnation becomes even stronger when a historical tie to the past is made with a twist. Jesus notes their forefathers' building of tombs for the prophets. He argues, using a rhetorical picture, that they approve of what their fathers did. The best prophet was a dead prophet! They are like their ancestors, who not only built the tombs, but helped to put the prophets there by denying their message! They killed the prophets, and the scribes honor the tombs they created. Jesus is confident that the pattern will continue with another set of prophets and apostles (cf. Jer. 7:25).

John the Baptist already revealed the potential for the pattern to emerge, and God knows they will persecute the messengers to come. So they will be held responsible both for their actions and for the actions of all who have rejected God since the days of Abel.[7] Since Jesus is the one who reverses all sin, to deny him means culpability for the presence of all sin. Luke highlights once again the crucial choice that Jesus creates. It is a terrible thing to be a generation responsible for creating an environment of rejection around Jesus. As 19:41–44 indicates, judgment of the nation is the first major consequence.

In the strongest remark of all, Jesus condemns the scribes for being the exact opposite of what they think. They believe they possess the key of knowledge.[8] But in fact, they are an obstacle to truth. Not only do they not enter through the door, but they stop others from getting in. There can be no greater rebuke for teachers of religion. This charge is like the unmarked grave charge of verse 44.

---

6. K. Weiss, "φορτίον," *TDNT*, 9:85.

7. Who this Zechariah is, is not clear. It is either the martyr mentioned in 2 Chronicles 24:20–25 or the minor prophet Zechariah. Of the two, the former is slightly more likely.

8. On the image of the key of knowledge, see H. F. Weiss, "Φαρισαῖος," *TDNT*, 9:48.

These woes are a devastating condemnation of pride and self-assurance in the pursuit of piety. The neglected heart has become a blind and hard heart. The obsessive pursuit of what is right can result in some serious wrong. The reaction is immediate. The scribes and Pharisees begin to "lie in wait" for Jesus, or, as the NIV says, "besiege him." They hope to catch him in some major error (their final effort in this regard will come in 20:1–40). If they can trap him, maybe Rome can get rid of him. The woes Jesus pronounces do not lead to repentance, but to hardness of heart.

THE PHARISEES LIVED lives of legalism and hypocrisy as they tried to walk with God. At the same time, they were neglecting what was taking place around them and missing what God had sent to them. Though they believed deeply in what they tried to teach, zeal and sincerity were not enough. Jesus wanted them to be clean of greed and wickedness and be filled with justice and the love of God.

Though these woes were directed against the Pharisees, a religious group that no longer exists, the spiritual errors of their walk are still with us today. The issues Jesus raises here are dangers that those of a conservative theological bent always face. In pursuit of truth and the way of God, far too many people conduct their zeal for righteousness by making sure that every "i" is dotted and every "t" crossed, and by watching over others to make sure they are acting properly. On the other hand, these same people have often lost sensitivity to God's call for justice. God wants us to care about those whose plight is less fortunate than our own (Rom. 12:16). We must let God define truth through his Word and not allow our own preferences and traditions to dictate our actions.

A note should also be made about Jesus' tone and manner of approach in his ministry. He was open and frank in his response to the Pharisees. He issued his rebuke in public, after having spent considerable time with this group. He had no hidden agenda and did not engage in behind-the-scenes criticism of the Pharisees—unlike his opposition, who tended to talk behind his back and plotted secretly his demise. Jesus was honest about where he stood and where he thought they stood, and he gave them numerous opportunities to change.

Why was Jesus so hard on this religious group? Though the text does not tell us, their claim to represent God and then be an obstacle to him made these opponents dangerous to the spiritual well-being of others. A sinner who knows he or she is such is not a hypocrite. What you see is what you get. But a religious person who does the opposite of what he or she says is not only a liar, but is also often a cause for others becoming closed to God. Our claims to represent God and his ways must reflect the compassion and service Christ calls for here. So Jesus takes their religious hypocrisy seriously, even if it comes from well-meaning people. That reality also is a bridge into our era.

THIS TEXT IS about religious hypocrisy and legalism and how God condemns it. I have been in groups that could have been cousins to the Pharisees. The environment is stifling. One gets the feeling that everyone is watching everyone else and knows what he or she is doing. Their goal is to catch them at some sin so they can let them know it, all in the name of mutual accountability—an accountability where the right to criticize is a given but the right to be criticized is rejected. Just as the Pharisees checked to see if Jesus washed his hands according to custom, so such people check on a whole series of forbidden or required activities to see if a person is right with God. A legalistic person feels he or she has the right to be everyone's spiritual keeper, using a list of requirements that is not scriptural. Legalism usually blocks the true knowledge of God, so that people are damaged, not edified. That is what makes it so insidious.

Legalism can manifest itself in various ways. (1) Frequently legalists refuse to speak directly to those whose behavior bothers them. The Pharisees disagree here about what Jesus is doing, but they discuss it only privately, in their own inner circle.

(2) Legalists major in minors and ignore the major relational requirements God asks of his followers. Jesus' major complaint is that in keeping such close tabs on what is on the outside, the inner heart is ignored, and along with that, justice and God's love. Jesus is not decrying tithing or watching out for one's spiritual walk. What he does condemn is a pretense of being so self-focused on spiritual matters that one ignores the condition of the heart and fails to notice those who are truly hurting.

(3) The close association of pride with this condition is no accident. Pride tends to make us into nonlisteners. We can speak, but we cannot hear. We think no one has anything to tell us. If so, we are slipping into a legalistic, prideful mind-set, which is death to genuine spirituality. We should criticize only with the attitude that we too are tempted and might fall into sin (cf. Gal. 6:1).

(4) A legalist is often quick to criticize but slow to help. In making sure others know their spiritual responsibilities, they often are the last in line to encourage others in the pursuit of those goals. The absence of relational

commitment is a symptom of a deeper problem. If there was one thing Jesus' ministry shows us, it is a commitment to people.

One of my students once told me about his days at his college, a school he now regards as teeming with legalism. They had a student demerit system for everything. Students received demerits for walking on the grass. At night, boys and girls were required to walk at least three feet apart on campus. Dating on the weekend required that the couple stay within the town's city limits. A certain number of demerits led to a letter to the pastor, then a second level to pastor and parents, and then finally to expulsion. In other words, three strikes and you were out! One student apologizing to a professor for a prank pulled in class asked for forgiveness but received a lecture that he would never amount to anything and never be a success in ministry. The professor refused to talk with him after the confession. Something is wrong when grace is elevated as the central message of God's Word and little grace is evidenced in actual practice. While these rules may have been well motivated, many of the students suffered great emotional damage. It is difficult to appreciate grace and forgiveness while living the Christian life with such a scorecard environment. Legalism is like carbon dioxide suffocation; it kills slowly and sometimes very subtly.

In contrast to the characteristics of legalism, Jesus is a model of how to pursue righteousness. He encourages those who feel out of touch with God so that they can know him. Though he points out sin, he also points the way to righteousness, simply noting the consequences of a failure to respond. Spirituality is not demanded; it is offered, though he makes clear the accountability one undertakes by failing to respond. In our battle with our culture, which often thinks little of spiritual discipline, honesty, integrity, and justice, the church can learn from Jesus' model of forthright but gentle persuasion.

Finally, Jesus' pronouncement of woes means that everyone, including those who claim an association with God, are accountable for their choices. Our culture loves to claim the right to choose. But such "rights" do not end the ethical discussion. One must also embrace the responsibility that comes with the choice. Jesus' condemnation of those who seek to exercise control in an overbearing way does not mean that people have license before God to do what they wish without impunity. Jesus' warning to the Pharisees is a warning to all. So choose wisely.

Luke 12:1–12

MEANWHILE, WHEN A crowd of many thousands had gathered, so that they were trampling on one another, Jesus began to speak first to his disciples, saying: "Be on your guard against the yeast of the Pharisees, which is hypocrisy. ²There is nothing concealed that will not be disclosed, or hidden that will not be made known. ³What you have said in the dark will be heard in the daylight, and what you have whispered in the ear in the inner rooms will be proclaimed from the roofs.

⁴"I tell you, my friends, do not be afraid of those who kill the body and after that can do no more. ⁵But I will show you whom you should fear: Fear him who, after the killing of the body, has power to throw you into hell. Yes, I tell you, fear him. ⁶Are not five sparrows sold for two pennies? Yet not one of them is forgotten by God. ⁷Indeed, the very hairs of your head are all numbered. Don't be afraid; you are worth more than many sparrows.

⁸"I tell you, whoever acknowledges me before men, the Son of Man will also acknowledge him before the angels of God. ⁹But he who disowns me before men will be disowned before the angels of God. ¹⁰And everyone who speaks a word against the Son of Man will be forgiven, but anyone who blasphemes against the Holy Spirit will not be forgiven.

¹¹ "When you are brought before synagogues, rulers and authorities, do not worry about how you will defend yourselves or what you will say, ¹²for the Holy Spirit will teach you at that time what you should say."

IN 12:1–48, JESUS calls people to discipleship. This includes fearing God rather than human beings (vv. 1–12), being careful with resources (vv. 13–21), trusting God (vv. 22–34), and being faithful in our stewardship (vv. 35–48). The disciple must look to God and pursue one's calling with an undistracted eye. Knowing God means we have nothing to fear, so we can walk confidently with him.

Jesus turns his attention to the disciples in 12:1–12, as they deal with the huge crowds pressing around them.[1] People are almost walking on top of each other. Their press raises an issue that becomes a temptation to the disciples: hypocrisy. An effort to maintain popularity easily leads to hypocrisy. Jesus warns them not to follow the example of the Pharisees, whose record Luke has just noted (11:37–52). He calls them to be on guard against "the yeast of the Pharisees." Yeast refers to their teaching and its hypocrisy, which can permeate in a community like the substance people put in bread.

To enhance the warning, Jesus emphasizes that everything will be disclosed before God in the coming day of judgment (Rom. 2:15; 1 Cor. 4:5), when our lives will be evaluated. Nothing will be concealed. The reference to "inner rooms" in verse 3 describes the innermost location in the house. God's omniscience penetrates every locale and every thought. Even what is whispered will be known. On that coming day, disciples will have their stewardship of God's gifts and opportunities examined, and they will be rewarded accordingly (1 Cor. 3:10–17), though forgiveness and eternal life come only through drawing on the forgiveness Christ provides. Those who do not know the Lord will have their actions condemned (Rev. 20:11–15; 21:27; 22:15).

A being who knows all our secrets should be feared. Therefore, Jesus declares, we should fear the One who has the power to place us in hell, not someone who can merely kill the body. The latter means only the end of this life, while the former means permanent separation from God. As Jesus asked in 9:25, what good is it to gain the whole world and lose one's soul?[2] Jesus discusses the issue of whom to fear because the world's rejection for identifying with him is a real prospect—so real that some may back off from coming to him. But to fear the multitude and to turn away from God is to make the wrong choice.

On the other hand, the fear of God and his presence can also bring incredible comfort. Our Lord is aware of the needs of those who belong to him, just as he is aware of and cares for birds that are sold for a few small, cheap coins. God knows even minute details like the number of hairs on our head. Someone who knows us so well will certainly care for us. So in fear-

---

1. The parallels to this text are scattered in their location in the other Gospels, raising the possibility that what is present are sayings that Jesus taught on various occasions: Luke 12:1–2 is like Matthew 16:5–6 and Mark 8:14–15. Luke 12:3–9 has a potential parallel in Matthew 10:26–33. Luke 12:10 is like Matthew 12:31–32 and Mark 3:28–30. Luke 12:11–12 has conceptual parallels in Matthew 10:19–20; Mark 13:11; and Luke 21:14–15.

2. The Jews had a similar understanding. 4 Maccabees 13:14–15 reads, "Let us not fear him who thinks he kills; for a great struggle and peril of the soul awaits in eternal torment those who transgress the ordinance of God."

ing God, we have nothing to fear from anyone else, for we are worth more than the sparrows.

This message about fearing God is reinforced in remarks about Jesus as the Son of Man (vv. 8–9). To acknowledge this being is to be acknowledged by God; to disown him is to face disownment later. This juxtaposition of fearing God with the Son of Man again shows the close connection between his ministry and God's call. Virtually every passage in this Jerusalem journey section highlights the importance and consequences of choosing to believe in Jesus.

Verse 10 is one of the most enigmatic in Luke. The sin of denying the Son of Man can be forgiven, but to the person who blasphemes the Spirit there will be no forgiveness. There are four choices as plausible definitions for this blasphemy: claiming that Jesus has come from Satan (11:14–20), renouncing Jesus because of persecution (that is, apostasy), rejecting the preaching of the apostles, or persistently rejecting the message of the gospel. The final choice is the most likely, since it fits the warning about being thrown into hell and the warnings in Acts about what is at stake for rejecting the apostles' message (Acts 3:22–26; 13:38–41). Speaking a word against the Son of Man refers to a specific act of rejection, while rejecting the testimony of the Spirit refers to a permanent rejection of that message of salvation. The best example of this principle is Saul, who stood at Stephen's execution in Acts 7, but who later came to faith and thus received forgiveness for his previous acts against preaching about Jesus. He had spoken against the Son of Man, but ended up not rejecting the Spirit's call to believe in Jesus. This decision about the testimony the Spirit gives is the key issue for Jesus.

This connection is reinforced in verses 11–12. There is nothing to fear in persecution, because the Holy Spirit will teach his people what to say before the synagogues, rulers, and authorities. Their message will be his message. If they reject them, they reject Jesus, but he will serve as the source of strength and wisdom for his people. Thus, by fearing God, disciples have nothing to fear from people.

THIS PASSAGE ASKS fundamental questions about our identity. Will we fear God or the masses? Does our affirmation come from above or from our neighbors? Some Christians in choosing for God will inevitably face rejection from others. Jesus anticipates this as he speaks of his disciples' being brought before the synagogues and rulers. In such pressure moments, they will be tempted to court popularity and thus perhaps be hypocritical. Jesus' call to guard against such "hypocrisy" (v. 1) is a warning to us not to court numbers as we face rejection. The theology that undergirds these remarks—the omniscience of God and the support of his Spirit—also stands as a constant that informs this text and all our lives.

This text addresses our accountability before God. We must fear him, which in this setting means to respect his authority as judge and his knowledge of us. We sometimes like to think that we have moments of privacy when no one sees what we do or knows what we think. That may be true with reference to people, but this is not true of God. He sees in the inner room, even when the lights are out and when no one else can see. Respect for his knowledge and our accountability to him means we will conduct our lives like an open book, where we have nothing to hide.

If we are righteous before God, we have nothing to fear from him. As 1 John 3:1–3 suggests, those who live in light of the hope of the return of God, knowing that he knows everything, will purify themselves with the hope of his return and the responsibility it puts on us to be faithful. If we do fail, we remember the grace of God and the forgiveness Christ offers us rather than fall into a hopeless despair. The availability of forgiveness is part of what makes grace so amazing and God's love so divine. Hymns like "Amazing Grace" and "Love So Divine" underscore the beauty of the true richness of God's forgiveness. We fear God without being afraid of him when we rest in his grace, draw on its resources, and pursue righteousness through the enablement he so graciously gives.

The fundamental choice to hear the Spirit's testimony and fear God is also a theme that spans the ages. The Spirit inside of us leads us into drawing on his enablement in the difficult moments when we are confronted by those hostile to our faith. We need to be prepared both to respond when challenged (1 Peter 3:15) and to draw on the encouragement and instruction God provides within our communities.

We should also rest in the knowledge that God is there with us as we face opposition. Numerous testimonies have come from the former Eastern block of believers who stood firm, even in the face of death or torture, to testify to their faith in God. Sometimes others were drawn to Jesus through their strength.[3] There is little in this passage that does not enter into our era, except the express form of persecution that the first generation of disciples faced, which occurs today only in some places around the world.

---

3. Chuck Colson, *The Body* (Waco, Tex.: Word, 1992) is full of accounts from such contexts. He describes people who drew on what God provided through his Spirit. Suggestions for how we can be prepared come in Bob Briner, *Roaring Lambs: A Gentle Plan to Radically Change Your World* (Grand Rapids: Zondervan, 1993). A classic account of the options Christians have is found in John Bunyan, *The Pilgrim's Progress* (New York: Penguin, 1965; originally published in 1678 and 1684).

The rejection the early Christians faced tended to come from the Jewish circles in which they grew up; today's rejection comes from a much wider array of sources and often takes a more subtle form, where physical life may not be challenged but ostracism may occur.

But what must the church do to stand effectively in this era? Charles Colson and Bob Briner both have helpful observations as to how to fear God before other human beings. Colson notes about the church's need to be prophetic:

> When Christianity was made the official religion of Rome in the fourth century, the church became socially and politically acceptable. People with halfhearted faith flocked to churches that could no longer disciple them. Soon the word "Christian" became meaningless. And when the empire that sanctioned it collapsed, the church nearly went down too.
>
> In the Middle Ages, the unholy alliance of church and state resulted in bloody crusades and scandalous inquisitions. And in our own day, one of the most inglorious examples can be found in the church's failure to stand solidly against Hitler in Germany during the 1930s.
>
> The church must stand apart from the state. Independence from a culture is what gives the church its reforming capacity and enables it to point society toward the truth. The church must be free to address issues biblically across the spectrum and to speak prophetically, regardless of who is in power.
>
> Ironically, political flirtations and dalliances have threatened the church's independence in the West even more than the direct oppression of the Communists in the East.[4]

Briner states the hope of the church's testimony this way, using the image of roaring lambs:

> It's time for lambs to roar.
>
> What I am calling for is a radically different way of thinking about our world. Instead of running from it, we need to rush into it. And instead of just hanging around the fringes of our culture, we need to be right smack dab in the middle of it.
>
> Why not believe that one day the most critically acclaimed director in Hollywood could be an active Christian layman in his church? Why not hope that a Pulitzer Prize for investigative reporting could go to a Christian journalist on staff at a major daily newspaper? Is it

---

4. Colson, *The Body,* 239.

really too much of a stretch to think that a major exhibit at the Museum of Modern Art could feature the works of an artist on staff at one of our fine Christian colleges? Am I out of my mind to suggest that your son or daughter could be the principle [*sic*] dancer for the Joffrey Ballet Company, leading a weekly Bible study for other dancers in what was once considered a profession that was morally bankrupt?[5]

The best way to testimony is through credible engagement from within our vocational call.

WE ALL HAVE moments of truth—the time where we must put our soul where our mouth is and stand up and be counted. To be a Christian, we often must face people who do not understand us, who reject the principles we live for, or who may even be hostile to our beliefs about our God. Sometimes in having the opportunity to share him we must risk the possibility of being rejected. Our values may cause us to do things or not do things that produce a negative response to us. All of this can come with the territory of identifying with Jesus.

When I worked with Young Life in college, we often posed the question this way: If you were on trial for being a Christian, would there be evidence to convict you? Do people know by how you live (not just by what you say) that you are allied to him? The foundational attitude that enables such a testimony to emerge is to fear and serve God. Jesus calls for such a basic attitude in the face of a world that often reacts negatively to Christians.

In a sense, Jesus does not call for action here, but for an attitude. There is little to do but much to sense about ourselves in relationship to God and his care. We are accountable to him for how we respond to situations and pressures that come as a result of our walk with him. We should trust that he cares for us and believe that he will supply the Spirit's strength when needed. To fear him means to respect his presence, to trust in his care, and not to worry about how others react to us. It means not going along with popular opinion, for the majority may not always be right. With this recognition, we can respond with inner strength and dependence to situations that emerge where our faith is challenged.

Another application relates to the serious nature of the choice of rejecting the testimony of the Spirit about Jesus—a point Luke has been making in these last few chapters. The unforgivable sin is rejecting what God has

---

5. Briner, *Roaring Lambs*, 31.

offered in the forgiveness present in Jesus. There can be no "it makes no difference" approach to Jesus' question. Our culture may say there are many routes to God, but Jesus does not provide that option.

The "no escape" conclusion of this passage indicates just how seriously Jesus took the prospect of final judgment. God can throw someone into hell. This doctrine is among the more controversial teachings of the Christian faith. Some have argued that God does not punish eternally. Rather, those who fall into judgment are destroyed, and all texts on eternal destruction are metaphors for the destruction of the soul.[6] But texts like Revelation 20:10–15 and 22:15 suggest that the unrighteous continue to exist outside the presence of God, having discovered that he exists and that it is too late. In what are surely the most tragic texts of the Bible, these passages teach that to reject God and to come into judgment is one of the most despairing experiences possible. For after the judgment, a person knows for certain that there is a God and that they have forever missed the chance to know him. What a horrid feeling it must be to discover God exists, that Jesus is the answer, and then to know, after seeing God face to face, that the opportunity for blessing has been missed. That is why the teaching about judgment is so important, and that is why it is so crucial to share Jesus with those who need to know him.

---

6. This position is called *annihilationism*. It is particularly prominent in Britain, where I first encountered it. For a examination of this view, see Clark H. Pinnock, "The Conditional View," in *Four Views on Hell*, ed. William Crockett (Grand Rapids: Zondervan, 1992), 135–66.

Luke 12:13–21

SOMEONE IN THE crowd said to him, "Teacher, tell my brother to divide the inheritance with me."

[14]Jesus replied, "Man, who appointed me a judge or an arbiter between you?" [15]Then he said to them, "Watch out! Be on your guard against all kinds of greed; a man's life does not consist in the abundance of his possessions."

[16]And he told them this parable: "The ground of a certain rich man produced a good crop. [17]He thought to himself, 'What shall I do? I have no place to store my crops.'

[18]"Then he said, 'This is what I'll do. I will tear down my barns and build bigger ones, and there I will store all my grain and my goods. [19]And I'll say to myself, "You have plenty of good things laid up for many years. Take life easy; eat, drink and be merry." '

[20]"But God said to him, 'You fool! This very night your life will be demanded from you. Then who will get what you have prepared for yourself?'

[21]"This is how it will be with anyone who stores up things for himself but is not rich toward God."

Original Meaning

A MAJOR OBSTACLE to one's spiritual life, especially in the midst of persecution, can be the misuse of resources. Jesus already noted possessions as a threat to spirituality in the parable of the soils (8:4–15), and he will return to the topic in the parables of 16:1–13, 19–31; 18:18–30 (also 12:24–34; 14:12–33). The possessions and comfort pursued by this rich fool lead him to neglect the pursuit of God, so that he poorly uses the resources he has received.

The occasion for the present discussion is a complaint by one brother against another to give him a share of his inheritance. Jesus is being treated like a rabbi here, since he is asked to become an arbiter on this family squabble[1]—except that the request is not really to arbitrate, but to be an advocate for the petitioner against his brother. This may well be a clue to why Jesus

---

1. Ellis, *The Gospel of Luke*, 177.

responds as he does. He refuses to be drawn into choosing sides, preferring instead to raise a question about greed, which can cut through relationships, especially family relationships, like a dagger. This parable is unique to Luke.

Before he goes into the parable, Jesus issues a warning to everyone, not just the brother, against all forms of greed. This message occurs frequently in the New Testament (Rom. 1:29; 2 Cor. 9:5; Col. 3:5; Eph. 4:19; 5:3; 2 Peter 2:3, 14). The Greek present imperative in "be on your guard" calls for constant vigilance against greed, since life does not consist in the abundance of possessions.

The main issue in this parable is not wealth. Rather, it is one's attitude to obtaining wealth. The man in the story happens to have a fruitful harvest, and he must decide what to do with the overflow. He did not acquire his harvest immorally; he simply had a good year. Prudently, he decides to build in order to store what has been provided. His error comes how he views what has become his. Five times in verses 17–19 he speaks of what "I" will do, as if he owns it all. Moreover, he speaks about "my" fruit, "my" barn, "my" goods, and "my" soul. He will not share his abundance, but keep it for his own private use. His goal is to ease back and withdraw from life. He will "eat, drink and be merry." He feels no concern or responsibility for anyone else. The essence of greed is keeping what resources God brings your way for yourself.

Jesus then notes that God will require the man's life that very night.[2] God raises the rhetorical question: "Who will get what you have prepared for yourself?"[3] The answer, of course, is that the man who thought he was set for the future will not get the fortune! This is the ultimate "you can't take it with you" parable. Jesus calls the man a "fool" (v. 20), an Old Testament term that describes someone who either acts without God or acts without wisdom in a self-destructive way (Ps. 14:1; 53:1). His approach to his stumbling on wealth is to become self-centered and therefore self-destructive.[4] He uses his resources in a way that displeases God.

Jesus concludes that this is how it will be for any who pile up treasures for themselves but are not rich toward God. Richness towards God means

---

2. The reference to "they will require of you" in the Greek of v. 20 (NIV: "your life is demanded from you") is either a Semitic indirect reference to God (Prov. 9:11b) or a reference to the angelic execution of the task. Either way heaven has issued a call and the man's life is at an end.

3. The parable is similar to remarks in Sirach 11:18–19. A second Jewish text where the conclusion is similar but the assumption is that the wealth has been collected immorally is *1 Enoch* 97:8–10. See G. Nicklesburg, "Riches, the Rich, and God's Judgment in 1 Enoch 92–105 and the Gospel According to Luke," *NTS* 25 (1978–79): 324–44.

4. W. Pilgrim, *Good News to the Poor*, 112.

responding to life and blessing in a way that he desires, in a way that honors him—through service and compassion (Eph. 4:28). The conclusion condemns greed as the attitude that piles up stuff simply for one's own use.

JESUS AGAIN TREATS fundamental attitudes of the disciple here. The issue of possessions and its relationship to the spiritual life is as real today as it was in Jesus' day, though it may well be a more pronounced word for our era. In many Western cultures, there are so many resources available that the tension may be more acute for people today than it was then. It does not, after all, take a megamillionaire to be rich by the world's standards. It is fair to say that many Westerners are wealthy, not only by present-day world standards, but also by the standards that apply across the centuries.

Our wealth opens up choices for us that allow us to pursue our own interests in a variety of ways. Such pursuits can easily keep us from using resources in a way most honoring to God. Note that Jesus is not condemning wealth as such, but its use. How do we use what God has given us? Do we seek to pile up treasure for ourselves? Is generosity our habit? Or does compassion take a back seat to our personal desires? The questions raised here are timeless. The fact that greed is a vice in the New Testament makes Jesus' teaching here one of significant ethical import.

Another subtle issue is raised here. We tend to hoard our possessions because we are convinced that this life is all there is; at least, that is the view our culture feeds us. A familiar old cultural proverb is "eat, drink, and be merry, for tomorrow you may die." The contemporary equivalent is the commercial jingle, "You only go around once in the life, so grab for all the gusto you can get." There is no accountability, no sense of a future with God, or no sense of honoring values that he has set forth in this now-or-never approach. Jesus' statement, "This very night your life will be demanded from you," challenges our culture's worldview much like an Old Testament prophet. The point of the passage calls for us to reflect about how we make the choices we do, as well as about the perspective that informs those choices.

The proper use of our resources raises important questions. Do we provide for our family responsibly? Do we save for college for our children? Do we prepare for retirement? The rich fool's error was his desire to provide only for himself. Jesus does not condemn the use of our resources for the benefit of family and for others. While we need not always provide the "best" or most expensive item, we should not ignore making wise and responsible provisions for our children. The fundamental test for the use of resources is whether they become tools of service that benefit others and enable them to be in a position to serve God better. Note that Romans 12:8 actually lists contributing to the needs of others as one of God's gifts to the church.

THIS TEXT CALLS for self-examination. How do I feel about what God has given to me? Is it mine? Am I a steward of what has come my way? Am I generous? Do I take the things God has given to me and store them up for my own purposes? Do I seek to grab what others have? Both the wise use of resources and the absence of greed are addressed here, since one attitude is the cause of the other.

The implications of this text extend beyond simply what we do with what we have. How we relate to others and what we leave for them is also in view. Even in the Old Testament the corners of the fields were left for those in need (Deut. 24:19–22)—a principle the rich fool ignored in his storing up goods just for his own use. We must ask ourselves about the most basic resources of the earth: Is it right for us in some parts of the world to consume the vast amounts of food and other resources when others have little of any access to such benefits?

A test of our heart is how we give. Are we generous or are we hoarders? This is a test that we have to engage in privately before the Lord. No one can tell someone else exactly how to answer such questions, for there is no magic percentage that is to be reached. The Old Testament standard of a tithe (10 percent) might be too low for what we are capable of doing (2 Cor. 8–9). But the issue of our potential generosity can and should be raised as a matter for spiritual reflection. That is the function this parable performs.

My wife and I annually discuss what our tax returns often reveal, namely, that we could probably afford to give more to others and to the Lord. As a result, we often look for additional people in the Lord's work to support. Though we still have a long way to go, we try to expand our giving each year. Sometimes we have delayed or decided against getting something new because it was not necessary. That choice often frees us up to use our resources more generously. We should all perhaps ask ourselves similar questions.

As I write, I am personally facing the opportunity to give to two major building projects from organizations to which I belong. A crucial question for me in the next few years will be how I will contribute to these necessary efforts. Will I simply figure what my percentage will be to make it happen, and give no more? Or will I contribute generously, perhaps enabling someone else to benefit because my gift picked up the share that they were unable to give? When it comes to using our resources, these are the kinds of questions we must honestly ask ourselves. We must also remember that how we used our wealth is one of the aspects of stewardship that God will examine one day. That prospect should lead us to reflect on how we use what God gives us.

Luke 12:22–34

THEN JESUS SAID TO his disciples: "Therefore I tell you, do not worry about your life, what you will eat; or about your body, what you will wear. 23Life is more than food, and the body more than clothes. 24Consider the ravens: They do not sow or reap, they have no storeroom or barn; yet God feeds them. And how much more valuable you are than birds! 25Who of you by worrying can add a single hour to his life? 26Since you cannot do this very little thing, why do you worry about the rest?

27"Consider how the lilies grow. They do not labor or spin. Yet I tell you, not even Solomon in all his splendor was dressed like one of these. 28If that is how God clothes the grass of the field, which is here today, and tomorrow is thrown into the fire, how much more will he clothe you, O you of little faith! 29And do not set your heart on what you will eat or drink; do not worry about it. 30For the pagan world runs after all such things, and your Father knows that you need them. 31But seek his kingdom, and these things will be given to you as well.

32"Do not be afraid, little flock, for your Father has been pleased to give you the kingdom. 33Sell your possessions and give to the poor. Provide purses for yourselves that will not wear out, a treasure in heaven that will not be exhausted, where no thief comes near and no moth destroys. 34For where your treasure is, there your heart will be also."

Original Meaning

THE ONE WHO fears God and builds up treasure for him has nothing to fear. Jesus therefore underlines the importance of trusting God. The illustrations he uses here draw on creation. Ravens, lilies, and grass have much to teach us. Jesus closes with a short note about generosity in verses 33–34. If we can trust God to care for us, then we can be generous, unlike the rich fool of verses 16–21.[1]

---

1. The parallels to this passage come from Matthew's Sermon on the Mount: Matthew 6:25–34 for Luke 12:24–32 and Matthew 6:19–21 for Luke 12:33–34.

Jesus begins with a call not to worry. The Greek present imperative used here implies that we should be constantly free of anxiety. We are subject to God's care, so we should rest in his hands. The issue in this passage concerns the basics of "life" (v. 22): food, health, and clothing. We should not be excessively distracted about our physical circumstances, for food and clothes are but the wrapping paper around which true life revolves.

The first example Jesus gives involves an unclean creature, ravens (Lev. 11:15; Deut. 14:14). This choice is significant, since ravens were among the lower rank of living creatures.[2] In their coming and going, God is aware of their needs. They do not plant or store grain; yet God feeds them. If he cares for them, how much more will he care for us! Not only is life more than food or clothes, but God is also more concerned about people as the objects of his care than for the rest of the creation.

From this illustration Jesus takes up some practical considerations about anxiety. What does worry contribute? Does it add any length to one's life?[3] If not, then why worry about the things of life? Some things in our world accomplish nothing. Anxiety, though perhaps a natural response to sensing events that are beyond our control, is one such profitless activity.

Examine beautiful flowers like the lilies—a second example from nature. There is no labor in their existence; they simply do what they are created to do. Yet they represent the height of beauty and aesthetic fashion, even more beautiful than Solomon with all of his wealth (2 Chron. 9:13–21). Who can dress themselves as God has dressed them? Even the grass, which lives for a short period and then is cast into fire, is cared for and clothed by God.[4] If God cares for them, he will care for human beings.

Worry casts doubt on God's care. So Jesus addresses them as people "of little faith" (v. 28). The essence of trust is to recognize that God will take care of what is in his hands. Thus, there is no need to worry about food and clothing. This approach to life is different than "the pagan world," those who go through life without awareness of God's presence. They scurry after physical concerns, but the Father knows what his disciples need. Jesus' shift to mentioning the "Father" adds an image of family and concern to his remarks. Every good father watches over his children.

---

2. Fitzmyer, *Luke X–XXIV*, 978.

3. In Greek the reference is to adding a cubit to one's life. Some debate whether Jesus is referring here to length of time or to one's height. The second example is a bit more ridiculous, which would add an emotive note to the remark. The point either way is that worrying does not change such realities. It serves no positive purpose.

4. Grass is a standard figure for that which is transitory (Job 8:12; Pss. 37:2; 90:5–6; 102:12; Isa. 37:27; 40:6–8).

Jesus calls for a single issue to be a disciple's major concern: God's kingdom (v. 31). God will care for the rest. To "seek [God's] kingdom" means to live as his representatives. As members of his household and the citizens of his community, we are to conduct ourselves in the best interests of home and country. We must represent him and reflect his righteousness in a world unconcerned about knowing God. That is the constant call of the disciple, as the Greek present imperative "seek" indicates.

There is nothing to fear in this task, since God desires to give this kingdom to his sheep. The pastoral image in verse 32 is informative, since sheep can be among the more skittish of creatures and tend to be frightened easily. Jesus casts God as a caring great shepherd who cares for his own and gives them what they need in order to do what he has called them to do (Ps. 23).

If we do not need to worry about the provisions of life, then we can be generous with what God has given us. So Jesus calls for selling possessions and being generous by giving to the poor. Such generosity God honors; he gives us "treasure in heaven." Such treasure involves God's commendation and reward for service that pleases him. For that treasure no security guard is needed, since no thief or moth can get to it.

Being generous reveals more than merely supplying aid to others. Where our treasure is, there our heart will be as well. In other words, how we use our resources communicates our values. If we invest in earthly possessions, we show we care about things. If we invest and care for people, we radiate our love for others. God's kingdom is about people. That is where our investments of time and resources should be, especially with those who have needs to be met.

There is another fundamental reason for this exhortation. A life attached to possessions becomes a stumbling block, because it leads to high anxiety. Jesus indicates that one way in which disciples can be different in their testimony is to reflect that people and needs have priority over possessions and ownership. Acts 2 and 4 and the example of Barnabas at the end of Acts 4 show that the early church reflected such values. The ethics of an absence of anxiety is also an ethics that is aimed at relating to people through generosity, because we are confident of God's care.

Bridging Contexts

WHAT JESUS CALLS for in this text is countercultural in terms of values and orientation for the modern world. For most people living is defined by what they can gather for themselves to make life comfortable and secure. Whether we think of the home as a nest or a castle, our desire to build a safe world of privacy is one of the most fundamental values our culture espouses. Consider these messages from our culture: "You deserve a break today"; "You have earned it." They articulate a philosophy that we are entitled to such things as kings or queens of our own mountains.

How frustrating it is for many that life often reveals we cannot control its affairs and circumstances. That is beyond our call in God's world. Those who do meet with some success and achieve a certain level of comfort in life find themselves in the position of the rich fool of 12:13–21; it is a short-lived reality. The pursuit of materialistic goals and heaping up treasures on earth results in emptying life of what God has designed as one of his most precious gifts: the honor of serving those around us. The conflict between Jesus' call and the call of our culture may be why, though we respond with understanding about his remarks on worry, we tend to resist what he says about the use of our resources.

The combination, however, is both intentional and timeless. God wants saints who trust his care and rest in his hand, doing what he has called them to do rather than pursuing agendas and emotions that are counterproductive. The nest God gives us is designed to be a base of operation, a haven of service for him. This is what we should concern ourselves about, not our food or clothing. God will care for us, so we need not worry about how he will provide for us.

We would do well to recall that Jesus is speaking this to an audience that is predominantly poor or humble in social status. Jesus' teaching often targets the poor (cf. 4:16–18). Most of his audience were people who labored from day to day for one day's wage. If he can say such things to those of humble means, how much more are they true for those of us whose daily needs come with more consistency. The sensitivity called for here reminds us that when we spot people with needs, we should strive to meet them. Many organizations in the Christian community that provide basic needs for the poor are often seen as not doing true ministry, but nothing is further from the truth. God often shows his love for sinners by how his saints reach out in love to meet their needs. The means of care for those who go hungry are often those who have something to give.

HOW DOES ONE apply a call not to worry and to be generous? The issues that lead to application reach deep into the human psyche. We all want to feel secure. We like being in control, but we are fooling ourselves if we think we have life by the throat. Doctor's offices and hospitals are filled with people who are emotional wrecks because they have failed to control their world and become lost in emotional space. My father-in-law was a practicing doctor, and I remember how often his visits to patients were related not to their being physically sick, but being emotionally at sea.

The first step in wisdom is to know better. We ought to leave ourselves in the Father's tender loving care. He can direct us to use our gifts and abilities, and we must trust him to provide for us as we work to serve him. That is why before Jesus addresses our pursuing the kingdom, he addresses the need for trust. Human attempts to attain security can come from a variety of sources. We can attempt to create a safe environment for our lives. We can try to create a world where we control others. We can seek the accolades of peers to give ourselves worth. We can withdraw so that we are safe in our own little world. We can seek to be different, so we are noticed and affirmed as present, whether positively or negatively—a route the teenager makes into a vocation! Each of these attempts is really an evasion of the need to seek identity in the one source who can give it, the tender care of God.

Jesus pleads for his disciples to observe nature and to understand that God is in the business of caring for needs, and that by doing so, he models how we are to care for others. The world fights and worries about territory, power, and turf control, while God feeds the ravens, clothes the lilies, and gives splendor to the grass. He longs for disciples whose identity is so secure in God that they graciously and generously pursue kingdom values, honoring him by living with integrity and serving others around them, regardless of the cost. The God who gave his Son to show the way promises his care as we walk the same path. He knows what we need and understands what the call requires.

A major obstacle to pursuing God's call, however, is to think that we need to get security in other areas of our lives before we can be freed up to serve as he wishes. In the process we short-circuit what God calls us to do and get distracted with personal security issues. Sometimes we can be most effective when God has us in a place where our reliance on him is a necessity and is obvious to all around us. The spiritual life as Jesus sees it is not a life of comfort, but of risk, exposure, weakness, and vulnerability. He wants us to venture out in waters where the course has not been charted out clearly, simply relying on him to give us the opportunity to do what we have been created to do (2 Cor. 1). Thus, without trust it is impossible to please God or serve him effectively. The call of God will never take us to a place where the grace of God cannot sustain us.

The generosity this text calls for has often been questioned. Are we really called to sell all our possessions? Jesus' point is that we must give up viewing what we call ours, as if it were a private possession to be hoarded. When Zacchaeus in Luke 19:8 offered to sell half of what he had and give it to the poor, Jesus commended him without qualification. What Zacchaeus did is take the step of faith that says, "My resources are not mine, but yours. Show me how to use them for your glory, O God." That was the prayer of a disciple who sought to apply what Jesus teaches here. Beyond the prayer are the moments of truth, when we take our resources and give them up or put them to use so that others can benefit from their use.

Yet such a prayer can be a rationalization if it is not uttered with an inner sense of being willing to carry through on its request. Zacchaeus not only made a statement of his intentions; he acted on it. Seeking God's kingdom through proper orientation to God means that the use of what he provides is not restricted to our own selfish interests. We see ourselves as part of a community to be served and loved. For such a commitment, God promises to meet our real needs—those that develop our character—as well as to reward our generosity with his affirmation, both now and in the age to come.

Luke 12:35–48

BE DRESSED READY for service and keep your lamps burning, ³⁶like men waiting for their master to return from a wedding banquet, so that when he comes and knocks they can immediately open the door for him. ³⁷It will be good for those servants whose master finds them watching when he comes. I tell you the truth, he will dress himself to serve, will have them recline at the table and will come and wait on them. ³⁸It will be good for those servants whose master finds them ready, even if he comes in the second or third watch of the night. ³⁹But understand this: If the owner of the house had known at what hour the thief was coming, he would not have let his house be broken into. ⁴⁰You also must be ready, because the Son of Man will come at an hour when you do not expect him."

⁴¹Peter asked, "Lord, are you telling this parable to us, or to everyone?"

⁴²The Lord answered, "Who then is the faithful and wise manager, whom the master puts in charge of his servants to give them their food allowance at the proper time? ⁴³It will be good for that servant whom the master finds doing so when he returns. ⁴⁴I tell you the truth, he will put him in charge of all his possessions. ⁴⁵But suppose the servant says to himself, 'My master is taking a long time in coming,' and he then begins to beat the menservants and maidservants and to eat and drink and get drunk. ⁴⁶The master of that servant will come on a day when he does not expect him and at an hour he is not aware of. He will cut him to pieces and assign him a place with the unbelievers.

⁴⁷"That servant who knows his master's will and does not get ready or does not do what his master wants will be beaten with many blows. ⁴⁸But the one who does not know and does things deserving punishment will be beaten with few blows. From everyone who has been given much, much will be demanded; and from the one who has been entrusted with much, much more will be asked.

To fear God (cf. 12:4–5) means being prepared to serve, so Jesus turns his attention to faithful service. Part of the treasure we store up in heaven (12:33–34) comes through such service. As we serve, we also know we will be accountable to the Lord when he returns. Eschatology (teaching about the future) in the Bible exists not so much to inform us of the details of the future as to prepare us to serve God faithfully today. This unit comes in three parts: the basic exhortation and beatitude (vv. 35–38), the picture of the knowing when the thief comes (vv. 39–40), and the parable of the unfaithful servant (vv. 41–48).[1]

Disciples should prepare for the Lord's return by living in a way that honors him when he comes to assess our walk with him. An ancient way of calling for that preparation was to "gird up your loins" (NIV: "be dressed ready for service"). The Greek perfect imperative implies a constant state of readiness, a readiness that once taken up, is to remain in place. The Old Testament provides the background of the image (Ex. 12:10; 1 Kings 18:46; 2 Kings 4:29; Isa. 59:17).

A second way to make the same call is to exhort disciples to "keep your lamps burning." That is, they must be on the constant watch, even in the midst of the darkness of the night.[2] This exhortation shares the same imperative as the previous image, so this preparation is constant as well.

A third image completes the initial exhortation. Disciples should be like servants not knowing exactly when the master will come home from a wedding.[3] They should be ready to open the door when he arrives. A contemporary image would be like a baby-sitter waiting for parents to return home to reclaim care for their house. The master who returns is looking for one thing from a servant—that he is ready to hand over the house, having faithfully watched over it.

As always, Jesus' images carry a twist. Here the twist is that the master, on finding the house well cared for, turns around and serves the servants. This is the blessing he holds out to them. The NIV's phrase "it will be good for them" (v. 37) speaks of the blessing faithful servants will receive. In other words, blessing awaits those whom the master finds ready and waiting at his return, even if he comes in the middle of the night, that is, at a

---

1. This parable has a conceptual parallel in Matthew 24:42–51. Much of the rest of the passage is unique to Luke. We call the parable conceptually parallel because of the distinct settings in which they appear.

2. W. Michaelis, "λύχνος," *TDNT*, 4:326.

3. In an ancient wedding the celebration could go on for a week, so the return was not always predictable.

time (the second or third watch [9 P.M.–3 A.M.]) when others might not be ready.

Jesus then uses the picture of the thief to illustrate his point. If people knew when a burglar would try to enter their house, they would be prepared and take measures to protect it.[4] So also believers must be constantly ready, since the Son of Man (i.e., Jesus) will come at a time when they do not expect. The reality of the return in the face of the uncertainty of its timing demands vigilance. Accountability to the Lord is a major New Testament theme (1 Cor. 3:10–15; 4:1–5; 1 Tim. 4:12–16; 2 Peter 2:1–2, 13). Grace does not end accountability. Rather, the goal of grace is to create a people who are faithful and zealous in their service for God (Titus 2:11–14). God cares what we do with his gifts, and at Jesus' return, he will honor those who are faithful and discipline those who are not.

Peter understands the drift of Jesus' remarks and asks if the Lord is only speaking to the leaders like the Twelve or to everyone. Jesus answers with yet another parable, defining the faithful servant. He tells of a servant who is responsible for giving the other servants their allowance of food while the master is away on business. When he returns, blessing (NIV: "it will be good") comes to that servant who does his job well; he will be promoted to serve in a higher capacity.

If Jesus had ended the parable here, he would have simply illustrated faithfulness. But the rest of the parable opens other responses by those called to serve. What if the servant decides that the master will be gone for a long time? Instead of caring for the servants and giving them their rations, therefore, he does the opposite, beating and abusing them as well as selfishly indulging in all kinds of excess consumption. What will the master do when he returns unexpectedly? He will punish that servant.

To understand how serious this possibility is, we must look at verses 46–48 and compare the three punishments. (1) The servant who is outright disobedient, doing the opposite of what is commanded, will be dismembered, and the Lord will assign him a place with unbelievers. Some translations water down the phrase "cut him to pieces," but the NIV preserves its true force. The picture here is of outright rejection. (2) Someone who knows what his master wants and who simply fails to obey that command will be severely disciplined; he will receive many blows. The picture here is of a disciplinary judgment. (3) But for the servant who fails to obey because he does not know what he must obey, he will be beaten with a few blows. Jesus pictures an accountability here that varies, depending on what one does and

---

4. The image of the thief as a picture of the return is frequent (1 Thess. 5:2, 4; 2 Peter 3:10; Rev. 3:3; 16:15).

what one knows. The picture here is also of a disciplinary judgment, but less severe. The gradation of the judgments shows that accountability before the Lord does express itself with variation at the Lord's judgment.

Jesus closes by saying that to whom much is given much is demanded, and those entrusted with much will be asked much. That is, those who receive grace have received much, so they are asked to be faithful to the responsibilities their new-found relationship gives to them. The gifts of God must be used responsibly in service. Jesus does not answer Peter's question of verse 41 directly because his main principle is the kind of service we give, not sorting out who is responsible to give it. Answering in this way shows that all have a call to serve others in the body well during the time of Jesus' absence. To be a member of his community is to have responsibility in it; this is especially true of the leadership. In the Western church, where resources of instruction and communication are readily available, most of us have access to much, making us responsible for much. But such an observation anticipates how we bridge into the present.

Bridging
Contexts

JESUS' TEACHING HERE combines two fundamental New Testament themes: his return and the call for a faithful stewardship. The internal dynamics of the parable help us delimit the subject more specifically, in that the faithfulness has to do particularly with how those in the church serve others who are associated with the household of faith, broadly understood. Thus a primary audience for the passage are those who are given specific responsibilities and ministries in the community. Teaching, pastoring, missionary service, evangelism, serving the youth in the church, and a whole host of ministries come into view.

On the other hand, the possibility of a wider application to all who are called to serve in God's house exists because the remarks about faithfulness and the principle of serving one another in a way that preserves and builds up the community reflect values all disciples should possess. In sum, the application is for clergy and laypeople, with faithfulness required of all.

The theme of the Lord's return is also relevant to us, for we still await his coming. Since we do not know exactly when it will be, we must remain watchful and faithful. In fact, this is especially the case as more time passes, since the passing of the years might make one complacent about the prospect of the Lord's coming.

A final theme bridging the contexts is the nature of the accountability in view here. The most difficult issue is the intended result for the slave who is "dismembered." If we can figure that out, then the meaning of the other two examples in verses 47–48 also becomes clearer. Three options exist for verse 46. (1) Some argue that because the servant is a member of the house, this assumes that he is a believer, so that the punishment cannot be a loss of salvation, given the security of the believer as taught in Scripture. Rather, the punishment means that though he remains in the house, he is regarded as unfaithful and unworthy to receive any reward from the Lord for his service. This option is questionable, for it appears to makes salvation by faith but rewards by works. It also suffers from the problem of underinterpreting the reference to dismemberment in verse 46.

(2) Another option shares the premise that a believer is in view, but argues that the punishment is such that the person is ultimately rejected. This approach does not accept the security of the believer and thus argues that his judgment is exclusion from the community on the basis of his disobedience. Such a position runs counter to those texts that assure the believer that their position in the Lord is grounded in the certainty of his work in them (cf. Rom. 8:28–30, 38–39 ; Phil. 1:6). In the end, this view implies a salvation that is ultimately by works.

(3) The best option argues that the people here are associated with the household of faith and even have responsibilities in it, but their description says nothing about their spiritual condition. The dismembered servant, then, describes someone associated with the church whose attitude shows no faith and no relationship to the master in any positive sense. He does not lose what he has; rather he shows he never had a proper relationship to begin with. His very attitude toward the master reflects a disregard that can hardly be equated with trust. His punishment is his ultimate exclusion from the community (the same as that reserved for "unbelievers"). This interpretation rejects the idea that a believer's position in the Lord can be lost. One person who fits this description is Judas, one of the Twelve who walked with Jesus and participated in his household with responsibility, yet was "a devil" (John 6:70–71). Another passage like this one conceptually is 1 Corinthians 3:14–18, where some are blessed at the Lord's return; others are saved "as one escaping through the flames" (cf. Luke 12:47–48 here), and others are destroyed for attempting to destroy God's temple.[5]

---

5. The literary sequence of 1 Corinthians 3 is key to understanding it. Each punishment moves down the scale. Since those who are saved as through fire (v. 15) barely make it, the next step down must be a description of those who in the end are out (vv. 16–17). Theologically we would say that although they were associated with the church and appeared to be members of Christ, in fact, they never were. You cannot lose what you never really had. The parallel of Corinthians is important, because it shows the variety of categories people can fall into.

ONE MAJOR APPLICATION is to live in such a way as to honor the Lord and be ready for his return, which can come at any moment. When that happens, our Lord will assess how we have walked with him, especially in the community of faith. The issue most in view as a basis of his evaluation in this text is how we serve others in the community. Do we build up or destroy the saints? Jesus places a paramount value on how the members of the community relate to each other because in the pressure of ministering in the world, it is crucial to maintain unity. That is why he prayed for unity before going to the cross (John 17) and why books like Ephesians (4:1–16) emphasize it so highly. The nature of differences among most believers is nothing compared to the differences they have with the world. So Jesus calls for faithfulness, especially in how we care for one another while the master is away.

Perhaps there is no more sensitive topic for many communities than the tension between seeking unity and the concern for truth and purity in doctrine. Often when believers beat one another up, as is alluded to in this parable, it is over disputes about what we believe. Most of us are aware of vehement disagreements on topics such as the Lord's return, the permanence of spiritual gifts, lordship salvation versus an emphasis on grace, modes of baptism, Calvinism versus Arminianism, etc.

I recently read a document concerned with a dispute within a given theological tradition that affirmed the theological effort to reach for unity, but was concerned that conformity with Scripture be maintained. It affirmed a level of separationism from groups it otherwise acknowledged as Christian. Their commitment to Scripture was laudable and necessary, but we must remember that many of our traditional commitments also involve judgments about the interpretation of Scripture. Here is where humility is called for and wisdom must be exercised. For what may appear clear to me as a scriptural teaching may not be clear to others in the church. They may regard another teaching as more central or another view as more accurate. A claim to possess the certain leading of the Spirit on either side precludes interaction. In such cases it is important to distinguish central convictions from those that are debatable and to respond accordingly.

The central truths of the faith are things about which we must have firm conviction. These truths can be hard to identify in the midst of the many areas of theology and interpretation. If I may hazard a guess at the key themes, they are the authority of all Scripture, the Trinity, the deity and humanity of Christ, the unique work of Christ, the need for faith in Jesus to save from sin, the effective presence of the Spirit as the transforming agent of God in the believer's life, the blessings of grace for the believer, the importance of the church as God's community, the value of baptism and the Lord's table as rites Jesus asked believers to participate in, the reality of the Lord's return, the reality of judgment and eternal punishment for those who do not know God, the centrality of prayer and worship for the health of the believer, the importance of ethical integrity, and the call to evangelism. These are themes we must hold to as central.

But within each of these areas are subthemes open for discussion. As we relate to one another, we must be careful to distinguish the fundamental areas from the proper areas for discussion. Certainly the subthemes contain some key teaching and ideas. The church must pay attention to them, but never in such a way that lower level disputes cut us off from a oneness that Christ said we all possess.

I have recently participated in a decade-long group discussion where people of differing traditions with a long history of tension and hostility have come together with an agreement to talk about doctrine and to respect each other as we talk about our differences. The experience has been refreshing for all of us. Not only have we understood the issues better, but we have also learned to be fair to each other in discussing those differences. We have been able to be more honest about where we make our judgments and why we differ, yet without losing our respect for one another as brothers and sisters in Christ. The result has been growth and deeper understanding for all, even though we still disagree about many details. We have learned how to discuss without being destructive or disagreeable. One of the things the Lord wants most is that his followers treat each other with care, even as they serve the truth.

The Lord wants faithfulness, especially at the level of our interrelationships. Note the issues Jesus discussed with his disciples just before he went to the cross: the call to love one another (John 13:34–35; 15:9–17), the importance of service over position (Luke 22:24–30). His last prayer before the cross was for the body's unity (John 17). Of course, being a manager of God's house and having a stewardship means managing well, not just in terms of relationships, but also in handling resources or making good judgments about the priorities involved in the use of resources.

We will be held accountable to the Lord at his return. This concept is frightening only if we have something to fear because we are unfaithful. With his return comes the hope of casting off our sinful humanity for a glorified and purified existence forever with God. These texts exhort us to live like what we shall become. If we live righteously, we will have nothing to fear when the Lord returns.

Not everything in this passage warns of judgment. Is there a more amazing promise in Scripture than that the Master will serve the faithful at the table? Thus, at the heart of the Lord's return is a reminder of where our relationship with God should take us, namely, to make us more like him. In all the speculation about when and how he might come, we should perhaps pay more attention to who we will be when he comes.

So we serve and wait expectantly, not knowing exactly when he may return. This uncertainty has a warning with it. Though Scripture tells us to keep watching and be ready, it compares Jesus' return to a thief in the night. We cannot know exactly when he will return, and we should be suspicious of anyone who dates Jesus' return. Instead, we should concentrate on being faithful the whole time he is gone and look forward to the day when the master appears.

Luke 12:49–13:9

I HAVE COME to bring fire on the earth, and how I wish it were already kindled! ⁵⁰But I have a baptism to undergo, and how distressed I am until it is completed! ⁵¹Do you think I came to bring peace on earth? No, I tell you, but division. ⁵²From now on there will be five in one family divided against each other, three against two and two against three. ⁵³They will be divided, father against son and son against father, mother against daughter and daughter against mother, mother-in-law against daughter-in-law and daughter-in-law against mother-in-law."

⁵⁴He said to the crowd: "When you see a cloud rising in the west, immediately you say, 'It's going to rain,' and it does. ⁵⁵And when the south wind blows, you say, 'It's going to be hot,' and it is. ⁵⁶Hypocrites! You know how to interpret the appearance of the earth and the sky. How is it that you don't know how to interpret this present time?

⁵⁷"Why don't you judge for yourselves what is right? ⁵⁸As you are going with your adversary to the magistrate, try hard to be reconciled to him on the way, or he may drag you off to the judge, and the judge turn you over to the officer, and the officer throw you into prison. ⁵⁹I tell you, you will not get out until you have paid the last penny. "

¹³:¹ Now there were some present at that time who told Jesus about the Galileans whose blood Pilate had mixed with their sacrifices. ²Jesus answered, "Do you think that these Galileans were worse sinners than all the other Galileans because they suffered this way? ³I tell you, no! But unless you repent, you too will all perish. ⁴Or those eighteen who died when the tower in Siloam fell on them—do you think they were more guilty than all the others living in Jerusalem? ⁵I tell you, no! But unless you repent, you too will all perish."

⁶Then he told this parable: "A man had a fig tree, planted in his vineyard, and he went to look for fruit on it, but did not find any. ⁷So he said to the man who took care of the vineyard, 'For three years now I've been coming to look for fruit on this fig tree and haven't found any. Cut it down! Why should it use up the soil?'

362

⁸"'Sir,' the man replied, 'leave it alone for one more year, and I'll dig around it and fertilize it. ⁹If it bears fruit next year, fine! If not, then cut it down.'"

IN LUKE 12:49–14:24, Jesus is calling on his audience to note the nature of the time—a time when God is making divisions among people, a time when people should be able to see what God is doing through Jesus, and a time when Israel had better respond before becoming nationally culpable for rejecting God's messenger. That this generation of the nation is on shaky ground becomes clear in the warnings of 13:6–9, 31–35, and later in 19:41–44. The kingdom is approaching and the narrow door remains open, but failure to respond means that Israel will meet with a judgment that will leave her desolate. God's people must also develop an attitude of service to others around them, especially those who are not as able to help themselves. After this section, Jesus' attention will shift almost exclusively to his disciples, for Israel will have missed the warning he issues here.

Luke 12:49–59 has three subunits: the cause of division (vv. 49–53), the call to consider the signs of the times (vv. 54–56), and the call to settle one's accounts (vv. 57–59).[1] The sequence is important. Jesus' ministry forces choices and divides families. In considering such choices, one should examine the evidence that indicates that God has indeed sent Jesus, just as one reads the skies for the weather. And one should remember that if anyone becomes indebted to God, then he or she will have to settle accounts, so the choice is an important one. Jesus is beginning his final appeal to the nation of Israel to repent. In 13:31–35 he warns what will happen if they fail to respond. As with all of Luke 12, the issue is responding to God and to the One he sent, the Son of Man.

Jesus begins noting that he has come "to bring fire on the earth" and wishes it were already kindled. Jesus' "I have come" statements are designed to summarize his ministry. The image of fire can refer to judgment (3:9) or to the Spirit (3:16). The Old Testament image of fire describes the purifying message of the prophets (Jer. 5:14; 23:29). Jesus' message reveals the judging and purging work that his ministry represents: to provide the way for people to make decisions about where they stand and to offer them the

---

1. The parallels to this text are also conceptual, as with many passages in this chapter. Luke 12:49–53 is like Matthew 10:34–36 and Mark 10:38. Luke 12:54–56 is tied to Matthew 16:2–3. Luke 12:57–59 is like Matthew 5:25–26. But the differences in setting and in vocabulary between these texts means they are not true parallel descriptions of the same event.

opportunity to be healed (5:31–32). But before he can exercise such judgment and authority, he must undergo his own baptism, so he is limited in what he can do until then. "Baptism" is a reference to his approaching death. As later texts make clear, Jesus will engage in a great cleansing act, where he will identify with the sins of humanity and provide a basis for both saving and condemning by his experiencing God's judgment in their place (John 3:16–21; Rom. 5:12–6:6). In the judgment he experiences, he provides the opportunity for others to be spared.[2]

Jesus knows that he forces choices, so he does not bring peace "but division." The rejection he will suffer is only a portion of the tension introduced by his presence. Families will be divided as some opt for him and others choose against him. Every combination possible gets mentioned: father and sons, mothers and daughters, in-laws against in-laws. The choices are real, and people will go different ways. No one should be surprised that in forcing choices, division of opinion will emerge.

But there is guidance for the decision. Jesus calls on the crowd to reflect on their skills of discernment. Living in Palestine, they can decipher the weather by checking the wind and the clouds. If clouds come from the west and the Mediterranean, they know rain is coming. If wind comes from the southwest (NIV "south") off of the desert, they know it will be hot—so hot that the grass wilts (James 1:11; cf. Isa. 49:10). They can read and anticipate the weather just by looking around. Yet they are unable to discern the nature of current events that surround Jesus. They do not assess his miraculous work or his message of deliverance rightly. Word and deed are ignored. In calling them "hypocrites," Jesus is trying to shock them into reflection, as if to say: "How can you miss all that is going on around you in my ministry?" Their poor judgment leaves them at great risk.

So Jesus calls on the people to reflect on "what is right," to assess their condition appropriately (vv. 57–59). The example he uses comes from everyday life, from a legal dispute, where apparently the subject is debt to another. The magistrate is like a sheriff in charge of a debtor's prison.[3] As you head to the judge, it is better to settle and be reconciled than to let judgment occur. The court may find you guilty, and then you will be locked up in prison until the full debt is paid.

This illustration is often taken to refer to personal relationships, since that is how Matthew 5:25–26 uses the image. But in Luke's context of warning, the remark makes more sense as a reference to a debt before God. Jesus

---

2. A. Oepke, "βάπτω," *TDNT*, 1:535–36; Job 9:28; 32:35; Ps. 18:4; Jonah 2:3–6. The texts show the association of water with judgment.

3. K. Rengstorf, "ὑπερέτης," *TDNT*, 8:539; C. Mauer, "πράκτωρ," *TDNT*, 6:642.

---

is urging us to settle our accounts with God, or else the prospect of judgment remains. There will be no release until every last dime of the debt is paid. The background of the image is painful, since in debtor prisons inmates were beaten in order to encourage someone to step forward to make the payment.[4] The central idea, however, is not that one can get out of hell, but that one will be held accountable for every sin one commits.

In a passage unique to Luke, the author turns his attention to issues related to the nation of Israel and its citizens (13:1–9). That the nation is in view is suggested by the image of the fruitless fig tree (vv. 6–9). This allusion does not mean that every Jew rejected Jesus, for many did respond to him, but it does argue that the bulk of the nation, especially her religious leaders, did so, thus leaving the nation vulnerable to God's judgment (19:41–44; 20:9–19). These texts also show the importance of deciding that Jesus has been sent from God.

The first incident (vv. 1–5) examines the issue of judgment, especially as tied to tragic events. Jesus argues that judgment will come on all if they do not repent. The second incident involves a parable (vv. 6–9), which tells Israel that she has a short time to respond before facing a national judgment.

In the discussion of the two tragedies in verses 1–5, the question emerges whether a worse level of sin causes a person to suffer a special judgment, either in being the victim in a series of events or in being the victim of a natural catastrophe.[5] The temple massacre of the Galileans whose blood Pilate mixed with Jewish sacrifices raised the question whether God was exercising a special act of judgment against them. The collapse of a tower at Siloam that killed eighteen was a natural catastrophe—one of those things that just happens. But here the question also becomes, "Did God judge them for excessive sin?"[6] In both cases the question is the same: Is God giving back to people what they deserved?

Jesus responds by changing the import of the question. The reason such events are so tragic is that they expose our mortality. Death exists in a fallen world, and nothing exposes our mortality more than when death comes suddenly and unexpectedly, cutting short a life that had the potential to be much fuller. Jesus argues that what should be contemplated is not the cutting

---

4. S. Safrai and M. Stern, *The Jewish People in the First Century* (Philadelphia: Fortress, 1974), 1:554–55, discuss private law and torts.

5. The two events referred to here are not known outside their mention here. Though several candidates have been suggested for these events from Josephus, none really fits; Fitzmyer, *Luke X-XXIV*, 1006–7.

6. The term for "sinner" is an interesting one in v. 4, since it describes people who were more indebted than others. The comparison of sin to debt is common, as the Lord's Prayer indicates; F. Hauck, "ὀφείλω," *TDNT*, 5:561–63.

short of these particular lives, but the fact that life terminates. This raises an even more basic question, what comes after that? How does one prevent the end from being the ultimate end? Jesus has taken a question about mortality and made it a question about the possibility of eternal punishment, which Scripture later calls the "second death" (Rev. 20:11–15). So he urges the people to repent, without which all will perish—only in a death that is more than a mere loss of mortality. His point is that with death comes a decisive encounter with God, one that does deal with sin. Whether one is a little sinner or a big one, repentance now is the only way to survive that coming encounter.

Now some may question whether Jesus is really alluding to ultimate judgment and death, but it is suggested by four points. (1) The previous passage (12:57–59) has raised the issue of clearing accounts with God, which looks at repentance for forgiveness of sin. (2) The following passage (13:6–9) looks at the judgment of the nation and alludes to losing fundamental access to God's blessing. (3) If Jesus is referring merely to physical death because of failure to repent, then he answers the question about the tragedies affirmatively and notes somewhat insignificantly that physical death is in the cards for his audience in the future. (4) To see physical death as Jesus' point is decidedly misleading, since they will all die physically eventually anyway. So it seems Jesus' point is to challenge the audience to think about deeper issues, not to give a roundabout answer to their question about these tragedies.

Jesus deflects the question about the degree of sin because it distracts from the real question, the presence of sin, no matter what its form. Often we compare sinners so that we may excuse ourselves as not being as bad as others. Jesus wants no such escape from responsibility here. So he centers his thoughts on the most visible question. That is why he cites no specifics about sin in this passage.

The call to repent is a fundamental theme in Luke (3:8; 5:31–32; 15:1–32; 18:9–14; 24:47). Jesus has in mind that change of direction that comes from a change of orientation after hearing God's messenger. Before one repents, one is not concerned about being related rightly to God. With repentance comes a change of mind that effects a change of direction, since one's orientation of life is directed in faith to God. That is why the Old Testament concept of repentance uses a term that describes "turning."

This section of Luke alternates between individual exhortation (vv. 1–5) and national warning (vv. 6–9). The two are related, because the response of the individuals will determine what the nation's response in this generation is like (e.g., 11:29–32, 50–51). The closing parable, therefore, discusses the nation, using a variation on a standard figure about Israel—a vineyard or a tree garden (cf. Ps. 80:9–19; Isa. 5:1–7). Jesus may be alluding specifically to Micah 7:1, where God looks for grapes and figs in the garden of the nation but cannot find any. The fig tree should have borne fruit by the third year, but it has failed. The owner has given plenty of opportunity for the tree to be productive and has exercised a lot of care into getting it to be fruitful.[7] So the failure to yield fruit is both disappointing and costly. The owner therefore commands the fig tree be cut down, but the caretaker of the grounds asks him to relent and give the tree a little more time. If in a year the fig tree is not productive, then it can be cut down.

The image describes the unfruitful state of the nation of Israel, for reasons Luke has made clear in chapters 9–12, and indicates that the time for the nation to respond is limited. The parable also pictures God's patience. He will give the nation a short time yet before exercising judgment. But the shortness of the time also highlights the importance of making a decision quickly before it is too late. The nation has failed by and large to respond. In other words, while some in Israel are responding, most are not. Luke seems to hold the Jewish leadership most responsible, though he is not beyond giving Rome some responsibility (Acts 4:24–27). The judgment came on Israel in A.D. 70 (Luke 21:5–7), but as Paul indicates in Romans 11:12, 14, 26–27, it will not be a permanent judgment, because God is gracious and will bring the broken branches back into the plant.

Bridging Contexts

BASIC SCRIPTURAL THEMES are present in this text: the reality that Jesus brings division, even in families; the call to see the evidence God leaves to show Jesus is God's chosen one; and the call to make sure one's spiritual debt to God is paid. One should draw on the opportunity Jesus provides to come into God's family and receive forgiveness.

The decision to trust Jesus can still divide families. Particularly sensitive today are decisions by Jews to come to Jesus. According to messianic Jewish ministries, many Jewish children are ostracized from families and treated as if they no longer exist. Converts from Islam or from certain Asian faiths face a similar isolation. So Jesus' ministry still purges and makes distinctions within humankind, but now in a wider variety of contexts. When this happens, the church needs to rally around those who have "lost family" because they have believed. God calls us to surround them with a new host of brothers and sisters (cf. 18:29–30).

---

7. G. Stählin, "ἐκκόπτω," *TDNT*, 3:859.

Reading the signs of the times (12:54–56) might take on a different form today from Jesus' day. We do not have the benefit of his miraculous ministry, so the evidence of God's work through him is left in the testimony of Scripture, in the evidence of transformed lives, and in the ministry of the church at large. The very existence of the church, emerging from next to nothing and growing through twenty centuries, is a testimony to God's work. In all corners of the earth Jesus is active, sometimes in places far distant from the original new community.

Yet the way into the church is no different now from what it was then. We all have a debt of sin before God that someone must pay (Rom. 3:9–31). Either Jesus does it in our stead by his sacrifice on the cross, or we will pay every last cent before God, resulting in a debt we can never totally extinguish. That is why Jesus warns so strongly about the need for repentance in 13:1–9.

The topic of 13:1–5 is a general one about the nature of mortality and the culpability of sin. Since we are all sinners, we all need to turn to God for forgiveness (Rom. 3:20–26). What really kills permanently is not death in this life but the "second death" that sin produces. So the call of Jesus to repent is timeless, whether the call is issued to a covenant nation like Israel or to individuals who need to enter into a relationship of grace and forgiveness with God.

Another important idea in this text is that we cannot always determine why some tragic twists of fate occur. It is cruel to assume that a personal tragedy has happened because of sin in someone's life (see also John 9).

The parable of 13:6–9 is context specific. It refers to Israel as the fig tree. The interaction of judgment and the idea of a short time to decide is related to its national status. On reflection, however, the principle of the possibility of judgment for one who never repents can be applied individually, since that is the point of verses 1–5. We must beware not to let our condition before God slide unattended throughout our lives (cf. Rom. 1:18–32).

Finally, the parable raises the question about how displeased God is with lack of fruit in our lives. Though the judgment in view here is unique to Israel, God's displeasure with any who ignore or waste the resources he provides is a principle that exhorts all of us to be fruitful. Those who know his grace and are secure in it should respond gratefully with a life of fruitfulness (Eph. 2:8–10; Titus 2:11–14). We have come to him with a heart that recognizes our need of his grace, and having now experienced his mercy, our story should be different from that of this unfruitful fig tree (Rom. 12:1–2).

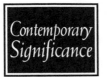

THE CONTEMPORARY PORTRAIT of Jesus is skewed. Our culture tends to see him as a man who did not engage in confrontation or talk about judgment.[8] He came as the ultimate peacemaker, who sought peace at any cost. He never challenged anyone other than to call for love and tolerance. As a teacher of wisdom and a teller of parables, Jesus did not force people into hard choices; or if he did, it had nothing to do with his own person, only with the need for Israel to reform ethically. Scot McKnight, in criticizing the Jesus Seminar in their view of Jesus, notes the inadequate options modern studies offer: Jesus the sage, Jesus the religious genius, or Jesus the social revolutionary. They are all inadequate portraits of the one who comes to bring us to God. McKnight summarizes his view well:

> While it is perhaps inappropriate to offer sweeping criticisms of scholars whose work I respect and from whom I have learned a great deal, I must say that the above treatments of Jesus are unfair in that each presentation limits the evidence of the Gospels to a handful of sayings or events and builds an entire picture of Jesus primarily from one strand of the Gospel tradition. Yes, Jesus was a wise sage and a deeply religious man, and his teachings were undoubtedly more socially revolutionary than many evangelicals imagine; each of these portraits says something truthful about Jesus. At a bare minimum, they need to be combined for a fuller presentation.
>
> My fundamental disagreement with each of them is that *such a Jesus would never have been crucified, would never have drawn the fire that he did, would never have commanded the following that he did, and would never have created a movement that still shakes the world.* A Jesus who went around saying wise and witty things would not have been threatening enough to have been crucified during Passover when he was surrounded by hundreds who liked him. A Jesus who was a religious genius who helped people in their relationship with God and was kind, compassionate, and gentle would not have been crucified either. A social revolutionary would have been crucified (and this partly explains Jesus' death, in my view),

---

8. For example, one of the reasons the Jesus Seminar believes that certain portions of Jesus' words in the Gospels are not rooted in his actual teaching is because he did not, in their view, teach judgment. That was something they argue was added by the early church to the portrait of Jesus. This is an example of creating Jesus in an image that makes him more palatable. For an example of such an explanation, see R. Funk and R. Hoover, *The Five Gospels: What Did Jesus Really Say?* (New York: Macmillan, 1993), 332–35. For a critical assessment of the Seminar's claims, see M. Wilkins and J. P. Moreland, ed., *Jesus Under Fire: Modern Scholarship Reinvents the Historical Jesus* (Grand Rapids: Zondervan, 1995).

but it is doubtful that such a revolutionary would have given birth to a church that was hardly a movement of social revolution. And if in the process of surviving, this movement had to shave off the socially revolutionary bits of Jesus, it is amazing that they decided to connect themselves, even root themselves, into a person who was a social revolutionary at heart. No, these pictures of Jesus will not do.[9]

This section of Luke challenges the contemporary portrait of Jesus. Jesus sees himself here as a figure who brings division. He forces choices, not only about how life is lived, but also about how he fit into God's plan. Simply put, Jesus is the way into a relationship with God. In a sense Jesus' ministry confronted people, not harshly but directly, but by calling them to account before God. His call is not to bring peace at any price, but to sort through humanity in order to draw some to him, while others turn away. He was and is the Great Divider. His ministry burns consciences, and our reaction to him determines the nature of his judgment.

This text calls each reader to consider where he or she stands before God and to consider all the evidence God has left as indicators for that decision, namely, the activity of Jesus' ministry as well as the ultimate sign anticipated by a text like this, the resurrection. The Jesus of popular culture does not force such choices, but we may not manipulate the biblical Jesus into our own image. The Gospels are clear that many reacted against him because he challenged them in a threatening way with his prophetic call.

Another application of this passage is that if one is in a debt before God (debt being a figure for sin; cf. 11:4), then settling that debt is of prime importance. It is important to clear the books with God. It is a wise thing to assess one's debt correctly and have it paid it off before the case is closed.

Much of 12:49—59 raises the issue of judgment and accountability before God. Yet all too often we try to package Jesus for our culture today as if sin were a minor topic on his agenda. This is not only the work of skeptical scholars like those noted above, it is also found in the way we preach Jesus in evangelism. For all the value of seeker-sensitive approaches, if as a result of trying to market Jesus churches soften the message at this point, then they distort the gospel and do not preach the Jesus who offers renewal of life. To remove accountability to God for sin is to remove one of the realities that make grace so powerful. In the effort to make the gospel palatable, we risk emasculating it of its most precious truth, that God has paid the debt for our failure and has washed it white as snow. Ironically in trying to exalt God's love by ignoring sin, we remove the most powerful evidence of its presence.

---

9. Scot McKnight, "Who Is Jesus? An Introduction to Jesus Studies," in *Jesus Under Fire*, 61—62.

Luke 13:1–5 underscores the importance of considering our status before God. We must repent and turn to him, or we will perish. In the context of this Gospel, such turning involves responding to Jesus and his teaching (6:47–49). Repentance is not an emotion or a mere mental assent to a proposition. It is a reorientation to a new life. To repent is not merely to regret things we have done or to apologize for them or to recognize a wrong has been committed. To repent is to agree that a change of direction is required, and then to respond accordingly. That is why John the Baptist speaks of producing the fruit of repentance (3:8). That is also why Paul could speak of repentance and the good works they produce in the same breath (Acts 26:20). Those who repent of their sin receive the gift of life.

Luke 13:6–9 shows that God is patient, but there does come a time when it is too late to repent. Those who anticipate a kind of deathbed repentance so they can "enjoy" life until the end usually do not care to repent when the end comes. Those who think the old wine is good do not try new wine. To repent means seeing that life lived outside of God and Christ is not life as God meant it. We must respond to God before it is too late or before we become accustomed to sinful ways.

This message has an implication. Often in sharing the gospel we give ourselves a sense that there is much time for people to decide. In a sense that can be true, for God is patient and does delay his judgment. But in a sense it can lull us to sleep. As we share Jesus, we can get complacent. Although ultimately the Spirit causes people to respond to Jesus, if we take a laid-back attitude, we will not be as sensitive to opportunities to share as we could be. Note how the caretaker kept trying to fertilize the fig tree. We too should try to keep feeding those who need to hear the gospel with the seed of truth.

Luke 13:10–17

ON A SABBATH Jesus was teaching in one of the synagogues, [11]and a woman was there who had been
crippled by a spirit for eighteen years. She was bent
over and could not straighten up at all. [12]When Jesus saw her,
he called her forward and said to her, "Woman, you are set
free from your infirmity." [13]Then he put his hands on her, and
immediately she straightened up and praised God.

[14]Indignant because Jesus had healed on the Sabbath, the
synagogue ruler said to the people, "There are six days for
work. So come and be healed on those days, not on the Sabbath."

[15]The Lord answered him, "You hypocrites! Doesn't each of
you on the Sabbath untie his ox or donkey from the stall and
lead it out to give it water? [16]Then should not this woman, a
daughter of Abraham, whom Satan has kept bound for eighteen long years, be set free on the Sabbath day from what
bound her?"

[17]When he said this, all his opponents were humiliated, but
the people were delighted with all the wonderful things he
was doing.

JESUS HAS FREQUENTLY called the people to
repent. In a miracle only Luke narrates, we discover whether the Jewish religious leadership
(e.g., the Pharisees and synagogue rulers) have
responded to this call. Have any of them taken a closer look at him and recognized their accountability in refusing his message? This event is a "mirror
miracle," because it repeats activity earlier in the book (4:31–44; 5:12–26;
6:6–11) and allows us to see in the replay whether anything is different in
terms of response to Jesus. The rebuke in verse 15 shows nothing has
changed, so new warnings will surface in 13:22–35.

A second major theme in this text is the portrayal of a battle with Satan,
the source of this woman's bondage. Luke's remarks here reflect back on the
imagery of release in 4:16–30, indicating that release has a crucial spiritual
dimension in the cosmic struggle between Satan and Jesus.[1] Just as 10:18

---

1. R. Tannehill, *The Narrative Unity of Luke-Acts*, 1:65.

and 11:14–23 tie Jesus' work to this cosmic conflict, so this text highlights the battle, showing the diminishing authority of Satan. As a result, Jesus' ministry reveals God's compassion.

This is the first miracle since 11:14 and is one of the last Luke records. The miracle in 14:1–6 will show the reaction here is not a fluke, but is part of a pattern of response. So the event has a defining importance in the Gospel's story about the reaction to Jesus.

Jesus is in a synagogue. Among the people is a woman who has suffered for eighteen years from the presence of a spirit that caused her to be weak and bent over (presumably her physical situation involved either some type of bone degeneration or muscular paralysis). Since Luke does speak of disease by itself when he wishes, there is obviously more than a medical problem here. The mention of the length of her suffering underscores the seriousness of her condition. In this culture, being a woman and suffering from such a malady makes her an outsider on two counts.[2] Jesus notices her and immediately tells her that she is "set free from [her] infirmity." He lays hands on her, and she straightens up immediately. Luke loves to note instant healing (4:39; 5:25; 8:44, 47, 55; 18:43). This would have been cause for immediate rejoicing except for one fact: It was the Sabbath.

The synagogue leader argues that the healing could have waited. Jesus has violated laws of working on the Sabbath (Ex. 20:9–10; Deut. 5:12–14). It is crucial to see what his work consists of in order to appreciate the complaint. Jewish tradition was particular about Sabbath labor. In the *Mishnah*, the book of Jewish tradition from the late second century, we are given a list of thirty-nine activities prohibited for the Sabbath (*Shabbat* 7:2). Other texts outline the limits for how one handles cattle on the Sabbath (*Shabbat*

---

2. S. Safrai, "The Synagogue," in *The Jewish People in the First Century: Historical Geography, Political History, Social, Cultural and Religious Life and Institutions*, ed. S. Safrai and M. Stern (Compendia Rerum Iudaicarum ad Novum Testamentum; Assen: Van Gorcum, 1974), 2:919–20, discusses the role of women in the synagogue. Luke loves to discuss women. He has forty-two passages with motifs related to women. Three are shared with all the Gospels, nine with the Synoptics, five with Matthew, two with Mark. That leaves twenty-three specifically Lucan passages; T. Seim, *The Double Message: Patterns of Gender in Luke & Acts* (Nashville: Abingdon, 1994). On the position of women in the culture, they were generally not counted when it came to worship, since only men counted for a quorum in the synagogue formal service (Mishnah, *Megillah* 4:3). Generally they were left to work in the home (ibid., 118–24). Women might attend synagogue, but how active they were is debated. Mishnah, *Megillah* 4 does not mention women in discussing reading Scripture in the service (cf. Babylonian Talmud, *Megillah* 23a, which is clearer in stating the point). For a more active view of women's role in the synagogue, including claims of leadership roles, see M. D. Hamm, "The Freeing of the Bent Woman and the Restoration of Israel: Luke 13.10–17 as Narrative Theology," *JSNT* 31 (1987): 23–44.

15:1–2; 5:1–4; *'Erubin* 2:14). The rules are specific, though it is not clear precisely which rule Jesus has violated. All he has done is to address the woman and touch her.

Jesus responds sternly, addressing those who agree with the synagogue ruler as "hypocrites." He cites an example of their own practice by raising a question that in Greek expects a positive reply. Do they not lead their donkey or ox to water on the Sabbath? The *'Erubin* and *Shabbat* texts noted above discuss an example much like this, indicating that such practices did occur. The only limit was the length of travel a person was permitted on the Sabbath (at Qumran, the limit was 2000 cubits [about 3000 feet]), but leading cattle to water was permitted.[3] If people show so much compassion to animals on the Sabbath, how much more compassion should a human receive!

Jesus drives the point home. Should not this woman, bound by Satan for eighteen years, be set free on the Sabbath? What more appropriate day for this to happen to a daughter of Abraham, a daughter of promise? What more appropriate day to defeat Satan and release people from his bonds than the day of rest when God is to be contemplated? Here is a day to remember God and celebrate the goodness of his healing grace. The connection of this language to the remarks of 4:16–30 is obvious. Jesus is exercising his ministry of deliverance and release. He is Lord of the Sabbath (6:5). Yet Jesus' approach to the issue is the exact opposite of the Jewish leadership's view.

The reaction is instantaneous. The leadership stands humiliated, while the crowd is delighted with what Jesus has done. In the cosmic battle over the woman, a ministry of compassion has emerged. Those who wish to apply the rules improperly stand rebuked. Legalism stands condemned.

THE MAJOR ISSUE in this text is not the debate over Sabbath activity, but what stands behind it. Sabbath practice was not a highlighted issue in the early church (Rom. 14:5), since different believers did different things on the Sabbath; but the call to have compassion was important.[4] The text emphasizes that it is appropriate to be compassionate all the time, and it is Jesus' compassion that causes the crowds to rejoice. The synagogue leader, however, is so bound up on his rules that he cannot rejoice in the blessing of deliverance that has taken place.

---

3. *Damascus Document* 11:5–7 notes the Qumran community's practice.

4. Romans 14:5 suggests that Jews and Gentiles may have handled this issue differently, but it is not a matter of law in the New Testament. Rather, the different practices are a matter of mutual tolerance.

Another timeless issue is the debate about Jesus' authority bound up in this event. If Jesus has the authority to heal and God endorses that authority on the Sabbath by giving him power to effect this healing, then what does that say about Jesus? In the Jewish view, God would not endorse a violation of his Sabbath law, so where does the power come from to reverse the condition of the woman that Satan is responsible for? That source cannot be Satan, since he is responsible for the woman's condition; thus, the healing must be divine (11:14–23). God is at work through Jesus, so the entire event reinforces the authority of Jesus, furthering the claim Luke makes for his right to call for a response to Jesus.

We also see illustrated in the passage the depth of hardheartedness. Jesus has repeatedly warned the Jewish leadership and his generation about the risk of rejecting him. He continues to reinforce his claim, but many keep on challenging what he does. They even stretch the "nonlabor law" on the Sabbath to try to discredit him. But in the healing God casts a vote for the challenged teacher. The healing shows whose side God is on. The issue of choosing Jesus in light of who he is and what he does is of paramount importance in any era.

A worldview issue also surfaces here. Westerners tend not to consider the possibility that some conditions are not just physical, but carry a hostile spiritual dimension. We treat sickness as merely that. We tend to treat violence in people as merely that. Though hard to ascertain, the possibility of spiritual dimensions in certain situations should make us more sensitive to prayer for these conditions, so that spiritual resources can be brought to bear (James 5:14–15).

I will never forget talking with one of my students who worked in the state penitentiary for years. He reported account after account of inmates who engaged in demonic activity. Even the unbelievers among the guards sensed that something paranormal was involved in the attitude of those inmates. One prisoner, for example, nicknamed "the meanest man in Texas," could bounce back immediately from the harshest of blows with a night stick and keep attacking others. Others even wore tattoos proclaiming their allegiance to the devil. These examples may be more extreme than this woman's illness, but they show how real these forces can be in the lives of people. So we should access divine aid, especially when we are not certain of the source of such conditions.

When it comes to the demonic, no one has spoken more eloquently that C. S. Lewis in *The Screwtape Letters*.[5] The whole book is worth reading and

---

5. C. S. Lewis, *The Screwtape Letters* (New York: Macmillan, 1961). The following citations are from pp. 3, 20, and 32 respectively.

reflecting on, especially in an era that has seen an increase in interest in Satan. Here are a few key citations:

> There are two equal and opposite errors into which our race can fall about the devils. One is to disbelieve in their existence. The other is to believe, and feel an excessive and unhealthy interest in them. They themselves are equally pleased by both errors, and hail a materialist or a magician with the same delight.
>
> [Screwtape to his devil assistant]: It is funny how mortals always picture us [devils] as putting things into their minds: in reality our best work in done by keeping things out.
>
> [Screwtape to his devil assistant]: Our policy, for the moment, is to conceal ourselves.

What Lewis understands so well and pictures so powerfully is that the devil either wants us to be consumed with his presence and power or else conclude he is not there at all. A healing like this tells us to be aware but not afraid, for God is more powerful than anything such hostile forces can throw at us.

AS WITH MANY texts in the last few chapters, this one also calls for a response to Jesus. The leaders' failure to respond reveals just how stubborn unbelief can be, even in the face of widespread testimony and evidence. They represent the stubborn unbelief that can be found in many places. We have made this point enough in other texts, so we will not develop it further here.

The image of salvation as release from Satan's clutches is the major positive picture in this text. Jesus has come to free us from the prison of Satan's grip. The woman has been shackled by a physical condition, but Satan's presence is also manifest in this situation.[6] He can damage both physically and emotionally, causing us to depend on substances or behaviors that are compulsive and destructive. Whether the challenge is being "bent over" and "brought low" by alcohol, drugs, sex, or some other debilitating situation, Jesus' deliverance is designed to free us up to relate to him in a way that enables us to shed the limitations Satan sometimes chains us with.

As John 9 shows, not every illness or debilitation is tied to Satan; but when he strikes, we need to be assured that in God we can face and overcome whatever comes, regardless of the physical outcome. Such conditions may

---

6. The issue of physical healing for today is also discussed in our comments on 4:31–44.

be reversed suddenly or over time, or transcended in the life to come; but the picture of physical deliverance here serves notice that deliverance is possible through Jesus. The establishing of a relationship with God and the access to the power of God's presence in his Spirit empower us with resources to renew our lives. Any time is appropriate for such a move towards restoration. It is what Jesus' ministry—and the church's ministry today—are all about.

Finally, we must be careful not to let our pursuit of religious practices according to our preferred custom outweigh our responsibility to be compassionate. Many churches have battled over the role of music or other elements of church practice that are not issues of spiritual significance. We must not allow the tyranny of comfort in practice or even the tyranny of keeping to some type of predetermined schedule prevent us from being sensitive to others around us.

THEN JESUS ASKED, "WHAT is the kingdom of God like? What shall I compare it to? ¹⁹It is like a mustard seed, which a man took and planted in his garden. It grew and became a tree, and the birds of the air perched in its branches."

²⁰Again he asked, "What shall I compare the kingdom of God to? ²¹It is like yeast that a woman took and mixed into a large amount of flour until it worked all through the dough."

²²Then Jesus went through the towns and villages, teaching as he made his way to Jerusalem. ²³Someone asked him, "Lord, are only a few people going to be saved?"

He said to them, ²⁴"Make every effort to enter through the narrow door, because many, I tell you, will try to enter and will not be able to. ²⁵Once the owner of the house gets up and closes the door, you will stand outside knocking and pleading, 'Sir, open the door for us.'

"But he will answer, 'I don't know you or where you come from.'

²⁶"Then you will say, 'We ate and drank with you, and you taught in our streets.'

²⁷"But he will reply, 'I don't know you or where you come from. Away from me, all you evildoers!'

²⁸"There will be weeping there, and gnashing of teeth, when you see Abraham, Isaac and Jacob and all the prophets in the kingdom of God, but you yourselves thrown out. ²⁹People will come from east and west and north and south, and will take their places at the feast in the kingdom of God. ³⁰Indeed there are those who are last who will be first, and first who will be last."

³¹At that time some Pharisees came to Jesus and said to him, "Leave this place and go somewhere else. Herod wants to kill you."

³²He replied, "Go tell that fox, 'I will drive out demons and heal people today and tomorrow, and on the third day I will reach my goal.' ³³In any case, I must keep going today and tomorrow and the next day—for surely no prophet can die outside Jerusalem!

34"O Jerusalem, Jerusalem, you who kill the prophets and stone those sent to you, how often I have longed to gather your children together, as a hen gathers her chicks under her wings, but you were not willing! 35Look, your house is left to you desolate. I tell you, you will not see me again until you say, 'Blessed is he who comes in the name of the Lord.'"

Original Meaning

JESUS NOW TURNS to a brief discussion of the kingdom he brings. Since his miracles testify to his authority, what exactly does his rule look like? His remarks are important in light of a Jewish expectation that the kingdom would come all at once and with great power. The parable of the mustard seed (vv. 18–19) and the parable of the yeast (vv. 20–21) make fundamentally the same point, that the kingdom starts out small but will eventually cover the whole earth.[1] Jesus compares the kingdom to a mustard seed that is sown in a garden and becomes a tree where birds can reside in its branches.[2] The image of a tree that shades the birds comes from Ezekiel 17:22–24, where the great, promised Son of David is a source of deliverance to his people. The image also contrasts with Daniel 4:10–12, where the great tree of Nebuchadnezzar ends up as a stump. The growth of the tree in the parable is portrayed as inevitable and amazing. What the Jews expected to come all at once will grow gradually into greatness.

The parable of the yeast is similar. Here the point is the permeation of the presence of the kingdom. Jesus picks a huge amount of flour for the illustration: three seah (almost fifty pounds). A pinch of yeast eventually permeates the entire loaf. This too is inevitable. What starts out as an insignificant movement will cover the whole earth in the end.

Jesus tells these parables to call for trust. He is building the kingdom, and people should trust God that it will come, even though the movement

---

1. The parallels to this passage are Matthew 13:31–33 and Mark 4:30–32. In those Gospels the remarks are part of a kingdom parables discourse. Here the parables stand alone, but this is teaching Jesus would have repeated on a regular basis.

2. The type of tree in view here is debated. Is it *Salvadora Persica*, which could grow to twenty-five feet? Or is it a *Sinapis Nigra*, which grows to ten feet? For the discussion, see C.-H. Hunzinger, "σίναπι," *TDNT*, 7:288–89. The text is not clear enough to decide. The point is not the specific tree, but the contrast between a small seed and a shady tree. In fact, the story has a twist, since mustard seeds do not normally become trees. In other words, the growth viewed here is unusual, supernatural.

starts out looking so insignificant. God's plan is advancing; his kingdom will come.[3] Nothing will stop its coming in fullness.

The parable in 13:22–30, though filled with conceptual parallels elsewhere in the Gospels, is unique to Luke.[4] It serves as a warning to Israel. Since the kingdom is coming, people should respond now, before the door closes. Many of those originally invited, descendants of those to whom the original promise came, will miss the blessing if they do not respond. There is nothing more tragic than being close to God's blessing and then missing out.

Jesus is heading toward Jerusalem.[5] Someone asks him if only few are going to be saved. Perhaps he senses that Jesus' rebukes of Israel mean that salvation will not be as automatic or as based on genealogy as some had thought. The Jews expected that the faithful in the nation would experience God's blessing, and faithfulness was considered a given for most born in the nation.[6] Jesus' reply makes it clear that this man's suspicion is correct.

Jesus exhorts his audience to "make every effort to enter through the narrow door." The verb "make every effort" (*agonizesthe*) speaks of laboring to get in. This implies that there is a specific route by which to enter; that is why Jesus mentions a *narrow* door and sets forth what it is.[7] Those who fail to enter by that door, even though they desire to get in, will not succeed. Once the door is shut, it will be too late. For individuals, the door shuts at death— if not before, because of the hardness of one's heart.

---

3. For a more complete treatment of the theme of the kingdom, see earlier discussion in 9:27, 58–62; 10:8; and 11:14–23. As we noted there, the kingdom is not just the church, but is in the process of realization, which involves the church now and a rule of Jesus to come. It is debated whether that future rule is in the new heaven and new earth alone (amillennialism/postmillennialism) or includes a thousand-year earthly reign from Israel (premillennialism). I prefer a premillennial reading of Scripture in light of texts like Acts 3:14–26; Romans 11:13–32; Revelation 20:1–6. Even recognizing the symbolic nature of Revelation, the portrait of Revelation 20 supports an intermediate kingdom before the establishment of the new heaven and new earth (Rev. 21–22). Such a kingdom, according to Acts 3, completes the promises laid out in the Old Testament, that include Jesus' ruling from Jerusalem. Regardless of this issue, what the parable makes clear is that the program of Jesus' rule starts with the planting of this tree, an event that began with his ministry as he worked to form a new community of the faithful.

4. The conceptual parallels are Matthew 7:13–14, 22–23; 8:11–12; 19:30; 25:10–12. They treat one theme or another of the various themes present in this parable.

5. This is one of several Lucan Jerusalem travel notes in this section: 9:51; 17:11; 18:31; 19:28; and (conceptually) 13:31–34; 19:44.

6. See *Mishnah, Sanhedrin* 10:1; 2 *Esdras* 7:47; 9:15. The idea that few are saved was not unusual for Judaism; the issue was who the few were (see 2 *Esdras* 8:1, 3).

7. G. Bertram, "στενός," *TDNT*, 7:605–6 (cf. John 10:7).

The banquet image looks at the time after Jesus returns, when those who trust in him are gathered to share in the celebration of salvation. There are no post facto opportunities. Those who seek to enter late will be told by the Lord that he does not know where they are from, and they will be denied access. In other words, entry comes through the means Jesus provides or not at all.

The appeal to enter into the banquet late is based on the fact of having seen Jesus, eaten with him, and heard him teach (v. 26). But the reply is emphatic. The doorkeeper (who represents Jesus) will reply that he does not know them and will tell them to depart as "evildoers." Outward contact with Jesus counts for nothing; what he desires is an inward response.

The end result is "weeping" and "gnashing of teeth,"[8] a sense of pain and frustration at having missed the moment. Though their birth made them excellent candidates, they did not respond and have missed the blessing. What is especially painful is seeing the fathers of the faith—Abraham, Isaac, Jacob, and all the prophets—but not being able to sit at the table with them. Many will come from every direction to feast with them, but some who have had the greatest opportunity will miss the blessing. This alludes to a shift in fate for those in Israel and those in the nations, so that the last become first and the first become last (v. 30). This final theme of the parable is common in the Gospels (Matt. 19:30; 20:16; Mark 10:31). The effect of Jesus' remarks has altered the theoretical nature of the original question to a practical level. The question, "Will the saved be few?" has become, "Will the saved be you?"

In 13:31–35 Jesus warns the nation by mentioning the city that represents her, Jerusalem. In a style reminiscent of the prophets, he argues that judgment for her is inevitable.[9] Jesus has issued multiple warnings that have gone unheeded, so now God will discipline his chosen people. The punishment will last until the nation, considered as a whole, recognizes God's representative. Many in Israel did hear Jesus and respond to him, but the vast majority, including many of those responsible for the nation, did not. The principle

---

8. K. Rengstorf, "βρυγμός," *TDNT*, 1:642; "κλαυθμός," *TDNT*, 3:726. In Judaism the phrase was reserved to describe the ungodly.

9. Luke 13:31–32 has no parallels, while verses 33–35 are similar to Matthew 23:37–39. The different settings suggest these are conceptual parallels as opposed to being the same event. Luke's placement of this detail here, whether a separate event or a mere topical arrangement, sets the tone for the transition to follow in this journey section. From this point on, Jesus spends more time teaching his disciples about facing rejection and prepares them for the hard road of discipleship. Those notes come with the black cloud of Israel's approaching rejection already prophetically presented. Jesus' message here is repeated in 19:41–44, where the city's destruction is predicted as evidence of the judgment that will come on this generation of the nation (cf. 11:29–32).

here is not unlike the one in Kings and Chronicles, where the fate of the nation is patterned after the king's righteousness.

Verse 31 opens with the Pharisees warning Jesus that Herod is seeking to kill him. The remark is significant, because it shows that Jesus has caught the attention of the leadership. It may also provide a way for the Pharisees to rid themselves of Jesus without doing anything that places culpability at their feet. The threat of Herod's executing Jesus could eliminate the nuisance of Jesus' call for repentance if he flees to save his life. While their statement looks like one of concern, it is really expedient.[10] They have been consistently portrayed as doubting and challenging Jesus, so to have them now looking out for his welfare is totally out of character.

Jesus replies by stating that he will complete his mission. Nothing will stop him. So they are to tell "that fox," that is, the one who wants to destroy Jesus,[11] that he will continue to exorcise demons, heal people, and then complete his task. He must go this way, since a prophet cannot perish outside of Jerusalem. Death is not to be avoided, but is the pivot point in his ministry. Jesus' presentation of himself as a "prophet" underscores his function as the revealer of God's will. Just as God at the Transfiguration told the disciples to "listen to him," now he asserts his prophetic mission to Israel. In rejecting him they are rejecting the call of God through him.

Then comes Jesus' lament. The emotion and pain of his declaration is noted from the start with the double address to the city, like David's cry over Absalom (2 Sam. 18:33). Jesus' pain comes from realizing the privilege of Jerusalem's position as representative of the nation in contrast to the history of her response in killing and stoning the prophets. Jesus speaks in the first person for God, as is typical of a prophet, and explains how he has longed to care for and protect Jerusalem as a hen cares for her chicks (Deut. 32:11; Ruth 2:12; Ps. 17:8; Isa. 31:5). Is there be a more tender image than this? However, the chicks did not want to stay in the nest, an allusion perhaps to the nations' lack of desire to be gathered again before him in the protective care of his salvation.

The result is the isolation and freedom from God's will that those in Israel desired when they refused to enter into his tender care. One of the tragedies of rejecting God's will is that people get what they ask for, including the dire consequences. Their house will be left desolate. The image of the des-

---

10. J. Darr, *On Character Building: The Reader and the Rhetoric of Characterization in Luke-Acts,* 105–6, 127–46, has an incisive examination of the character of Herod and of the Pharisees in Luke's Gospel.

11. For the meaning of "fox" as "destroyer" rather than indicating cunning, see Darr, *On Character Building,* 140–41. The background to this image is Nehemiah 3:35; Song of Songs 2:15; Lamentations 5:17–18.

olate house recalls the painful era of exile (Jer. 12:7; 22:5). The nation and its citizens face abandonment to their own weak devices. Such desolation will remain until a large majority in the nation recognize the blessedness of the one "who comes in the name of the Lord"—words taken from Psalm 118:26 (cf. Luke 3:15–16; 7:18, 22). In this psalm, the people at the temple recognized the king and his entourage as they sought to enter the temple. Until Jesus garners such acceptance, the nation is at risk. They must recognize Jesus as the figure the Baptist announced and the one whom God has been attesting to through his works. The word "until" suggests that though this judgment is serious, it is not forever.[12] If the nation of Israel turns, God will again take them under his wings.

This event is a major turning point in the Gospel, for Jesus will now concentrate on teaching his disciples rather than addressing the nation. They have made their decision and sealed their fate.

Bridging Contexts

THE NATURE OF kingdom growth is an important theme. Jesus describes how the rule of God through him will manifest itself from its small inception to its grand consummation. Though it has already begun (11:20), the kingdom and its promises extend into the future and look to the day when peace through the presence of the king will be complete.

As Matthew 13 indicates, this growth is part of the "mystery" about the kingdom, fresh revelation that makes clear how the presence of his rule will proceed. God is expressing his authority and distributing the benefits of life through the community he is forming. Though only a few gathered around Jesus in the first century, today we see a large and overarching community of Christ's followers. Yet even the church today is only a part of what is still to come.

Combining the imagery of the mustard seed with the imagery of the yeast presents a picture of the penetration and expansive presence of God's rule on earth. Jesus emphasizes how the presence of God's authority among his people becomes more extended as his Spirit moves to draw more people into his saving care. The crucial point about growth is not numbers in the church or power in the culture, but a declaration about the protective presence of a caring God.

---

12. Luke 21:24 and Acts 3 also suggest a future for Israel, since in Acts 3 the rest of what is promised in the Old Testament will occur at Jesus' return (vv. 18–21); see Tannehill, *The Narrative Unity of Luke-Acts*, 155–56.

To reflect on the image as one of God's presence among the growing community of the saved means that texts like these should not be misapplied into thinking that the church brings in the kingdom. The kingdom is bigger than the church and is directed by God as a place where "birds can nest." It emphasizes the care of God in providing salvation and a place of righteousness and peace. The final manifestation of the kingdom requires the Lord's return, an event whose timing is a sovereign secret. Yet since the days of Constantine the church has struggled with her identity by thinking a text like this is a call to exercise increasing power. The way of discipleship, however, is the way of service and sacrifice. The church is not called to the sword or to power but to service (Mark 10:35–45). Whenever the church has confused these two, it has had disastrous results. God will bring a transformation into our world at the time of Christ's return. Until then we must minister in faithful service to the believing community and to society at large as a testimony to the love and care of God. We can do so with the confidence that God's plan will advance no matter what we face.[13]

The parable of 13:22–30 has a specific context in mind—the danger that those in Israel will miss the blessing they have been awaiting for centuries. In a directly applicable sense, Jesus addresses the Jews, the descendants of the patriarchs. So this text most directly continues to address Jews, asking them to consider whether they are open to entering through the "narrow door" Jesus provides.

But in principle, the text suggests other applications. One can be so close to the promise of God and yet miss it. This can manifest itself in a variety of ways. People in the church can assume that because they have been born into an attending family, they are in and will automatically receive God's blessing. Like Jews who thought it was mostly a matter of heredity and cultural heritage, some call themselves Christian, not because of any faith commitment, but because of a family connection, a denominational affiliation, or cultural contact with Christianity, a contact that may express itself by attendance at church twice a year (at Christmas and Easter).

While in Scotland, I attended the local church in my village of eight hundred people. Sunday attendance was usually about thirty-five people, most over the age of fifty and several of whom were Americans. But twice a year the church held communion service. In that church a person had to attend

---

13. The cultural mandate of the church is not primarily the reconstruction of society and culture but the proclamation of the gospel and the reformation of the community of God as an example that can be pointed to as a place where healthy, restored, and reconciled relationships can be seen. Often when the church takes on society with too much zeal, the church loses focus on how it is to be a community of character and virtue; see S. Hauweras, *A Peaceable Kingdom* (London: SCM, 1984).

one of these services to keep their name on the church roll. Those weeks had triple services, as almost everyone in town showed up. This kind of cultural commitment to the church is not a relationship with Jesus. It is a tragically erroneous assumption to think that a mere formal connection to him means that one will celebrate with him in the end.

More subtle still is to assume that because a culture is "Christian," all born into that culture have an automatic relationship to God. Being personally proximate to the hope of the gospel does not put you in. Entry through "the narrow door" means responding personally to Jesus. The danger of getting close but not responding is that you end up outside the table of fellowship forever. Thus, this passage crosses the ages, either directly by addressing Jews or indirectly by addressing any who are close to God's promise without being in. Association with a church or having relatives who attend church is not enough. God does not save us through our activity, through heredity, or by proxy.

What allows this general principle to be made is the reality of the judgment to come and the basis on which such judgment will be made. The central issue is *knowing* Jesus, not just having casual contact with him. To know Jesus means to trust him to deliver us, to open up a life that interacts with him as a part of day-to-day living. Those who only have mere contact with the believing community must be encouraged to see if they know him and have experienced forgiveness through faith in the living Christ.

Luke 13:31–35 deal with events that have already taken place. The ministry of Jesus met its key turning point in the cross as Jesus accepted his fate on behalf of humanity. He did just what he said he would do, with all the courage and resolve it took to die a suffering, martyr's death. He did not back off his call simply because it was dangerous. In turn, the nation met its fate of desolation in the destruction of Jerusalem in A.D. 70. They still await deliverance and their Messiah, having suffered much in the interim. The realization of what Jesus says here indicates the trustworthiness of God's promises and the certainty of his plan. The rest of what he promises—a day of glory that includes the descendants of the patriarchs—will also come to pass.

THE PROGRAM OF God's kingdom gives us hope. His plan does not proceed by accident but by design. It is comforting to know that the kingdom can be pictured as a place of repose, for it offers rest to those who share in it (Matt. 11:28–30; Heb. 3–4). We must not be fooled by the seeming obscurity of the origins of this community, since God is behind its growth.

Describing the kingdom this way should result in a greater trust of God's direction. What he presents is a community that offers protection until its task is done. Some argue the church, as a part of the kingdom program, is an irrelevant or unimportant institution; yet to God it is a most precious community, where he is actively providing his presence and care (Eph. 1:23). The resources of world power may be located in other quarters today, even given the size to which the church has grown. But when the time comes, God will reveal the commitment he has to the fullness of the kingdom's promise and to its people as he exercises his authority over all the earth through the extension of its presence in the era to come. Those who know Jesus are a part of its history, heritage, and growth.

In the meantime, the kingdom is present in a more "hidden" form today. It does not manifest the fullness of power that it will possess one day, nor is its call to any one nation, party, or human institution. Rather, the kingdom is found wherever God's people are found. Its power is revealed in the effective transformation of lives that serve as a testimony to the living God (Rom. 14:17–18). To "manifest" the kingdom's presence is not to build buildings or pass laws, but to honor God with a quality of life that is directed powerfully in the transforming work of his Spirit. If God's people have any priority, it should be the commitment to live, relate, and serve in a way that honors him.

Luke 13:22–30 issues a warning. People should be sure they have responded to the one who brings in the kingdom. It is easy to think we automatically qualify—by birth, by cultural connection, or by heritage. But to Jesus, a relationship with God requires personal appropriation on the path Jesus has set (John 1:12).

This principle is fundamental in a culture that argues that there are many ways to God, as if the road to heaven is a complex interstate highway system, which offers dozens of routes and interchanges. Jesus uses a more focused image, the narrow and soon-to-be-shut door. For Israel as a people, the door was shut in a significant way with her judgment in A.D. 70 (19:41–44). That did not close off all Jews, nor does it mean the door remains shut to that nation forever (see Rom. 11:12, 14–15, 26–27, which argues for a future return of faithfulness for them). Yet it was a turning point in God's plan.

The door remains open individually for everyone. It is an equal-opportunity road, with access to all who will take it; but the route is marked out by God, not by us. Though in our hearts we may want God to take in everyone, that is not what Scripture teaches. He wants people to consciously enter into relationship with him, aware of their sins and shortcomings, their need for God, and the salvation Jesus has achieved for them. To respond to God is to respond to the one he sent to pave the way for life through his death. John's Gospel calls him "the gate for the sheep" (John 10:7). Those who have ears must hear what Scripture says about those who want to experience God's blessing.

Another implication in this text comes from the questioner's theoretical question about everyone else, "Are only a few people going to be saved?" There is nothing wrong with such a question, but often it is asked to turn attention away from oneself. Jesus takes our theoretical questions and personalizes them. As interesting as the question is of whether God will save the lost in far away places, a more fundamental question for all of us to answer is whether we have a relationship to God. Jesus challenges each one of us where we stand with God.

According to 13:31–35, nothing will block God's plan from taking place. Herod thought he could remove God's agent. The Jewish leadership thought they could remove him by making him aware of a threat on his life. Similar efforts at intimidation often appear in our culture today.[14] Listen to how an African-American Yale law professor states the dilemma so well for American culture:

> Contemporary American politics faces few greater dilemmas than deciding how to deal with the resurgence of religious belief. On the one hand, American ideology cherishes religion, as it does all matters of private conscience, which is why we justly celebrate a strong tradition against state interference with private religious choice. At the same time, many political leaders, commentators, scholars, and voters are coming to view any religious element in public moral discourse as a tool of the radical right for reshaping American society. But the effort to banish religion for politics' sake has led us astray: In our sensible zeal to keep religion from dominating our politics, we have created a political and legal culture that presses the religiously faithful to be other than themselves, to act publicly, and sometimes privately as well, as though their faith does not matter to them. . . .
>
> Yet religion matters to people, and matters a lot. Surveys indicate that Americans are far more likely to believe in God and to attend worship services regularly than any other people in the Western world. True, nobody prays on prime-time television unless religion is a part of the plot, but strong majorities of citizens tell pollsters that their religious beliefs are of great importance to them in their daily lives. Even though some popular histories wrongly assert the contrary, the best evidence is that this deep religiosity has always been a facet of the American character and that it has grown consistently through the

---

14. For how this operates in our modern culture, see Stephen Carter, *The Culture of Disbelief* (New York: Basic Books, 1993).

nation's history. And today, to the frustration of many opinion leaders in both the legal and political cultures, religion, as a moral force and perhaps a political one too, is surging. Unfortunately, in our public life, we prefer to pretend it is not.[15]

Efforts to try to thwart the presence of religious truth abound. They range from cries that Christianity is outdated and on the way out to attempts to bully and threaten Christians in Third World countries, where persecution is overt and martyrdom is a real possibility. Whatever results through the social and political process, God's ways will not be thwarted. For the Christian, there is often victory in seeming defeat, a point the church desperately needs to remember in an era where the appearance of victory may only be an apparition. Some of the strongest testimonies we have to God's faithfulness comes from accounts of those who have stood faithful in the midst of persecution—stories that often encourage the saints. With such stories come accounts of people drawn to Christ from among the former persecutors as a result of their watching such a stirring stand for the Lord.

We often treat the battles in our society as life and death matters, where we must win from the standpoint of appearance or "all is lost for righteousness' sake." But Jesus' death has already brought the way to life, regardless of the specific environment we are asked to function in. Victory is ours no matter what happens in the world. The point is important, not as an excuse to withdraw from engagement in society, but to encourage the engagement with the right perspective on what victory is. Victory comes in faithfully representing him, not in winning the argument or vote. Jesus' own life is the model here. No level of intimidation or rejection could keep him from completing his appointed rounds.

Another application that emerges from this passage involves the Jews. Though most of Israelite descent stand at a distance from God's activity in Christ at the moment, the nation has not been removed permanently from the hope of finding blessing in Christ. When they acknowledge Jesus as the one whom God sent, their house will no longer be desolate. In their recovery will stand a monument to God's faithfulness, which will have stretched out over several millennia. Luke does not address when this will happen, but the "until" of verse 35 suggests the day will come (cf. also Acts 3:18–22; Rom. 11:12–32).[16]

---

15. Ibid., 3–4.

16. Such a view of Israel's future is not limited to dispensational teaching; see the interesting work by the Reformed New Testament scholar, David Holwerda, *Jesus & Israel: One Covenant or Two* (Grand Rapids: Eerdmans, 1995).

Finally, Christ's compassion should be noted. His is not the heart of a figure who loves and desires revenge. Israel's error is painful, and Jesus suffers as he issues his warning. Judgment is not relished, but its reality must still be declared. Here is a heart that is worthy of emulation as we stand in the midst of a sometimes hostile world.

Luke 14:1–24

O NE SABBATH, WHEN Jesus went to eat in the house of a prominent Pharisee, he was being carefully watched. [2]There in front of him was a man suffering from dropsy. [3]Jesus asked the Pharisees and experts in the law, "Is it lawful to heal on the Sabbath or not?" [4]But they remained silent. So taking hold of the man, he healed him and sent him away.

[5]Then he asked them, "If one of you has a son or an ox that falls into a well on the Sabbath day, will you not immediately pull him out?" [6]And they had nothing to say.

[7]When he noticed how the guests picked the places of honor at the table, he told them this parable: [8]"When someone invites you to a wedding feast, do not take the place of honor, for a person more distinguished than you may have been invited. [9]If so, the host who invited both of you will come and say to you, 'Give this man your seat.' Then, humiliated, you will have to take the least important place. [10]But when you are invited, take the lowest place, so that when your host comes, he will say to you, 'Friend, move up to a better place.' Then you will be honored in the presence of all your fellow guests. [11] For everyone who exalts himself will be humbled, and he who humbles himself will be exalted."

[12]Then Jesus said to his host, "When you give a luncheon or dinner, do not invite your friends, your brothers or relatives, or your rich neighbors; if you do, they may invite you back and so you will be repaid. [13]But when you give a banquet, invite the poor, the crippled, the lame, the blind, [14]and you will be blessed. Although they cannot repay you, you will be repaid at the resurrection of the righteous."

[15]When one of those at the table with him heard this, he said to Jesus, "Blessed is the man who will eat at the feast in the kingdom of God."

[16]Jesus replied: "A certain man was preparing a great banquet and invited many guests. [17]At the time of the banquet he sent his servant to tell those who had been invited, 'Come, for everything is now ready.'

¹⁸"But they all alike began to make excuses. The first said, 'I have just bought a field, and I must go and see it. Please excuse me.'

¹⁹"Another said, 'I have just bought five yoke of oxen, and I'm on my way to try them out. Please excuse me.'

²⁰"Still another said, 'I just got married, so I can't come.'

²¹"The servant came back and reported this to his master. Then the owner of the house became angry and ordered his servant, 'Go out quickly into the streets and alleys of the town and bring in the poor, the crippled, the blind and the lame.'

²²"'Sir,' the servant said, 'what you ordered has been done, but there is still room.'

²³"Then the master told his servant, 'Go out to the roads and country lanes and make them come in, so that my house will be full. ²⁴I tell you, not one of those men who were invited will get a taste of my banquet.'"

LUKE RETURNS TO a meal scene, which will extend to verse 24.[1] The meal comes in three segments: a healing (vv. 1–6), a discourse on humility (vv. 7–14), and a closing parable (vv. 15–24). The miracle, unique to Luke, occurs on the Sabbath and completes the mirroring that also came in the miracle of 13:10–17. It is one of several Sabbath incidents Luke narrates (4:16–38; 6:1–5, 6–11; 13:10–17). The repetition puts these religious leaders on notice. What will they do with the evidence of God's power Jesus provides through these healings? By the end of this account, they are silent. Yet they will not believe, since they are filled with blindness and hardheartedness.

A healing (vv. 1–6). As Jesus enters the house for the meal, the Pharisees have their eye on him (cf. 11:53–54; 20:20).[2] A man suffering from dropsy is there, a condition of retaining bodily fluids. Many see the condition as a result of God's judgment.[3] So Jesus takes the initiative and asks the Pharisees and scribes if it is lawful to heal such a person on the Sabbath. They remain silent. Jesus then takes the man's hand, heals him, and sends him on his way.

---

1. Such meal scenes in Greco-Roman culture would have been called *symposia*, where a figure of wisdom shares his knowledge with others. Luke has several: 5:29; 7:36; 10:38; 11:37; 22:14; 24:30, 41.

2. Riesenfeld, "παρατηρέω," *TDNT*, 8:147.

3. Both the Talmud and texts from the Greek culture indicate this suspicion (see van der Loos, *The Miracles of Jesus*, 506).

He defends his action by noting that if they had a son or ox in the ditch, they would pull him out (cf. 13:10–17). In other words, it is appropriate to show compassion on the Sabbath (or any other day!).

The repetition of these "mirror" miracles and the discussion of the appropriateness of compassion may grate on the patience of Luke's readers. But Luke is trying to show that, even after all these demonstrations of power and compassion, the leaders do not get the message. Sin is blinding, and a hard heart is tough to break (11:29–36, 47–52). Despite numerous opportunities, the leadership fails to see what God is doing.

A discourse on humility (vv. 7–14). Jesus then pursues other related issues (vv. 7–14). This passage, also unique to Luke, highlights the importance of genuine humility. The imagery recalls Proverbs 25:6–7, where the author writes that it is better for the host to call someone up than to assert oneself to try to get his attention. Humility means not reflecting social snobbery, not exalting oneself, and not thinking only of one's own gain. God honors those who have friends on both ends of the social ladder.

This parable is a poignant story of genuinely relating in a needy world. Jesus tells it because the guests at the Pharisee's table are trying to find places of honor. At an ancient meal, the table was usually in the shape of a U, and the host sat at the base. The seats of honor were located next to him. Often the most honored guests arrived the latest.[4]

Jesus pictures a gathering where many prominent people are invited, such as a wedding feast or some other special feast,[5] and he discusses the fundamental question about how to approach being honored. In the background are the issues of God's relationship to us and of the nature of our standing before him. Before God and in light of who he is, no one stands exalted; but if the Lord exalts anyone for services well rendered or attitudes well held, then that is indeed an honor. Luke 14:11 makes this connection clear by noting that exaltation by God, not self-exaltation, is where honor resides, and that God is committed to exalting the humble. Nonetheless, the exhortation itself concerns affairs in this life. The connection to God's response in verse 11 only highlights the fact that the exhortation also applies to divine relationships.

According to Jesus, you should not seek a seat of honor, for a more distinguished person may arrive who gets your seat. Then the host will ask you to move, and you will have to move to the least important seat. That move

---

4. Marshall, *Commentary on Luke*, 581.

5. The Greek term *gamos*, used here, can refer to a wedding feast or a more general feast (Est. 2:18; 9:22). See Fitzmyer, *The Gospel According to Luke XX-XXIV*, 1046.

will come with a sense of shame, because you will have assumed more honor for yourself than others acknowledge. The mention of shame is important, because in ancient Near-Eastern culture, honor and shame were key issues of a person's identity, worth, and character.

If you are a wise person, Jesus says, you will take the least important place, so when the host comes and sees you in a seat that is not worthy, he will beckon you up to a better place. Then, instead of shame, glory (*doxa;* NIV "honor")—that is, approval and commendation—will result. Such honor God will also give in the age to come. The principle of the passage is clearly stated in verse 11—God will exalt those who humble themselves. The kingdom is his gift. Though he owes his blessing and divine acceptance to no one, he makes the way to divine favor open to all. Paul shows how Jesus is the greatest example of this truth (Phil. 2:5–11). On the other hand, those who exalt themselves will be humbled by God. The passive verbs in this verse suggest that the humbling and exaltation come in terms of God's assessment. How we treat others impacts how God treats us.[6]

Jesus expands the call in verses 12–14 as he introduces another topic. Beyond worrying about what seats we get as guests at a table, there is the question of whom we seek to serve as guests. Jesus calls us to serve those who cannot repay our kindness. We should not invite friends, relatives, or rich neighbors, for the repayment comes in the fact they will invite us back. Jesus' point is that loving and hosting those who love you and are your friends is not inherently morally commendable. One expects that to be the case. Rather, we should invite "the poor, the crippled, the lame, the blind."[7] The best hospitality is that which is given, not exchanged. Then divine commendation will come. Though those invited cannot repay, God will reward such care in the resurrection to come (1 Cor. 4:5). Again, the promise of reward is expressed in the passive voice ("will be blessed"), which means that God gives the response. He commends those who reach out to the needy and minister to them, often in quiet ministries that no one ever sees. True righteousness does not look for a payback but is offered free of charge, graciously, just as God in Christ has forgiven us free of charge (Eph. 4:32; 5:2).

A closing parable (vv. 15–24). This final portion of the meal scene (vv. 15–25) serves as a summary of all Jesus has warned the nation about in these last few chapters. A remark from one of the guests about the blessedness of those who sit at the banquet table in the kingdom leads Jesus to tell

---

6. The concept is similar to being forgiven (passive voice) by God because we forgive others (Luke 11:4; Eph. 4:30–32).

7. The second group in this list are the severely maimed in contrast to the third group, which is a general term for the lame.

another parable.[8] The remark probably is designed to remove some of the tension Jesus' remarks and actions have created. Its force is, "Despite our differences, won't it be nice for all of us to experience the blessing of sitting in fellowship before God when he reasserts his rule fully?"[9] Jesus challenges some of the assumptions in that remark. Those who appear to be in line for such blessing run the risk of not making it to the table at all. The points made here build on 11:37–54 and 13:6–9, 31–35.

Jesus tell the story of a man who is planning a great banquet at his home. This is a major affair, which includes an initial invitation and an ancient form of RSVP. When the time for the party comes, the owner sends out servants to announce the beginning of the meal (cf. Est. 5:8; 6:14; *Lamentations Rabbah* 4:2). To opt out of the meal at this point is rude.

At this moment the story gets interesting. Three of the invitees, who have previously accepted, opt out of coming. Each has what he considers a good excuse. One wants to check out a recently bought field, a post-purchase inspection that will seal the deal. This reason sounds similar to the reason one might use to be excluded from participating in Israel's wars (Deut. 20:5–7).[10] The second excuse involves the purchase of five oxen. Recently purchased livestock also need to be inspected. The purchase suggests that the man is wealthy, holding two to five times the amount of land of an average landowner.[11] Of course, the man could make this inspection after the meal, but his desire to consummate the deal and his priorities compel him to absent himself. The third excuse is a commitment to a recent marriage—the Old Testament sometimes allowed newlyweds to beg off certain vital responsibilities (Deut. 20:7; 24:5). Since the banquet probably includes just the men, this third invitee opts out because his new bride cannot attend.

The servant tells the master about the last-second cancellations. The host is in a dilemma. Does he postpone the party to a better time, even though the food is out and ready? Or does he go ahead? Rather than waste what has been prepared, the party will go on as scheduled. So the servant goes out and invites the poor, maimed, blind, and lame—groups already mentioned in 14:13 (also 1:52–53; 6:20–23; 7:22–23). God will invite all kinds of people to the table, including those usually excluded (cf. Lev. 21:17–23). Kingdom tables must be filled.

---

8. This passage is often considered a parallel to Matthew 22:1–14, but it is only conceptually similar, as the differences are too great to establish identity. See Blomberg, *Interpreting the Parables*, 237–39, for a list of differences.

9. The reference to the kingdom alludes to the Jewish expectation of God's rule and blessing in the future, when Israel will have a central role in God's plan. See Psalm 22:26; Isaiah 25:6; *1 Enoch* 62:14, 25:5; *Baruch* 29:8; cf. Behm, "ἐσθίω," *TDNT*, 2:691.

10. L. T. Johnson, *The Gospel of Luke*, 229.

11. J. Jeremias, *The Parables of Jesus* (London: SCM, 1972), 176–77.

With the first round of secondary invitations, the room begins to fill with people, but there is still room for more. So the host sends his servant out to the edges of the city, to the highways and hedges.[12] There he must urge others to come to the banquet. These folks will not know the host, even secondhand, so they will need encouragement to come. The master intends to have a fully attended party.

Here is the crux of the parable. The original invitees represent Israel. Although the nation as the originally invited is not responding, the time for the arrival of the kingdom has come, and the initial celebration of its blessings will go ahead. Others previously thought excluded from the celebration will get invitations. These people represent the spread of God's blessing beyond the bounds of the needy of Israel. In all likelihood, the inclusion of Gentiles is alluded to here (Isa. 49:6). Israel, though first in line, is missing her present chance to sit at the table. The first have indeed become last.

Bridging Contexts

THOUGH SABBATH ISSUES are no longer with us, the importance of compassion is. Jesus models a ministry that is ready to meet needs at any moment. Excuses for failing to show compassion, even those that might look pious, are not excuses at all. The sheer repetition of these themes shows how Luke worked to make this point. At the same time, the lesson of the powerful force of sin to blind someone to human needs is an attitude that still resides in humanity today. To hear God one must open the mind to seeing things his way.

Luke 14:7–14 treats two key themes: humility and generosity. Both attitudes are important to the development of Christian character, and both reflect commitments to be giving in life. We are to give rather than look how to receive. But these attitudes also run counter to the expectations our culture tends to instill in us. Our culture loves to tell us to go for what is ours by right and to "go for the gold." We love to cater to the rich and famous, the powerful, the movers and shakers. It is prestigious to minister to these circles. These ministries are not inherently wrong, but they should be pursued in a way that reflects God, who "does not show favoritism" (Rom. 2:11). The rich and the poor (James 2:5), the master and the slave (cf. Eph. 6:9), are all alike in his sight (cf. Gal. 3:28). The attitudes inherited from our culture subtly destroy the ability of people to minister compassionately to anyone.

---

12. On this part of the terrain, see W. Michaelis, "ὁδός," *TDNT*, 5:68. Highways are the main roads running out into the country, whereas hedges are the enclosures that surround vineyards or other fruit gardens outside the city.

Another attitude that derives from our culture is that certain conditions in someone else's life are that person's problems. For example, people are poor because they are lazy. Such an attitude does not breed compassion to help such people, who may have grown up without any familial support, training, or reinforcement in life. All our "back to the family" emphasis in Christian circles today, as good as it is, must come to grips with the reality that some have never had a family to go back to! A genuine humility is a guard against a personally destructive and blinding perspective that ignores such people.

The benefit of thinking outwardly is that it helps to build community. Jesus exhorts against pride because it makes community impossible to build. In the selfless outreach that takes place in true Christian ministry, a goodwill can be built that allows ministry to deepen and advance in its effectiveness. People who know we care are also more likely to hear when hard things need to be said.

Our highlighting of Israel in the parable of 14:15–24 addresses concerns about position and timing in God's plan. This feature of the parable is unique to its setting in Jesus' time, in that the Jews were the first in line to receive God's invitation to his kingdom banquet, but they were refusing it. But one should not overlook the result for anyone who refuses Jesus' invitation to join in the benefits he offers. When he issues an invitation to sit at the table of divine welcome and forgiveness, one should take it. No claims of proximity to Jesus will help if we have not personally come to the table. To refuse means in the end missing the celebration altogether.

The beneficiaries of Israel's refusal are the many others—the Gentiles—who now are invited to the party. This list of "late invitees" opens up the parable into the timeless future, for such groups are still being invited and are coming to the banquet. The kingdom will be made up of people from a wider spectrum of background than many originally conceived. Israel's refusal became an opportunity for God to show his grace to the world (Rom. 11). To come to the table means to embrace the offer of salvation Jesus makes. We should come with humility and gratitude, for many of us are "late invitees." A later parable, building on earlier remarks, will speak further of the vineyard going to others as a result of national refusal (20:9–19).

Contemporary Significance

THE THEMES OF this passage recall the applications of other Sabbath healing texts. The major lessons deal with the willingness to show compassion and with how sin can blind one to the activity of God. The Jewish leadership failed to see what Jesus was doing because they had a fixed expectation of God's rules and methods of operation. They failed to appreciate the scope of those laws. They had elevated into an absolute prohibition what God had intended as a positive expression of celebration and worship. The Sabbath became a day of exclusion for them, so that compassion was limited in how it could be expressed. God was showing through Jesus that he desired compassion, even on his day.

This type of legalistic view, where laws are pressed beyond their scope to create a stifling environment, we already noted in 11:37–54. The Pharisees were not ready for any surprises. They wanted to define the limits of God's work. We sometimes risk missing what God is doing because we think we know how he will act. Those who wish to see God at work must be careful not to dictate to him. He acts as he wills, and he has revealed aspects of his will to us; but that does not mean that he cannot sovereignly choose to manifest his grace in new ways not yet revealed to us. God will accomplish his plan, but we can be sure that it may come in surprising ways.

That Luke 14:7–14 offers a call to humility is obvious. But actually developing a humble spirit and living in light of it is difficult, because it goes so against our own tendency to desire strokes of affirmation. It is difficult not to seek the honored role, to voluntarily move down a few seats, to let others bring credit to our work, or to pay attention to those who may not be able to give back. Do we ignore "unimportant" people? The service we give, when offered without cost, becomes a badge of honor that God sees.

It is also difficult to praise a colleague when we want to blow our own horn. Jesus does not speak against all honor here. There is an appropriate time to receive "glory" from others and from God, but such glory should emerge spontaneously and naturally. We need to ask ourselves: Do we seek attention? Do we act sensitively only to those who can repay us with kindness or status?

A good litmus test of a community is to see how many activities it engages in that are outwardly directed as opposed to being self-serving. Selfishness can surface not just individually but corporately. It can be instructive to examine programs in the church or in the budget and ask how many activities are used on our own interest versus how many represent genuine giving. Our personal use of time and resources can be assessed similarly.

In our church we recently as a board of elders realized that we had neglected missions as we turned more inward to deal with issues related to our numerical growth as a community. A self-study revealed that in our early years we were actually giving more to outside concerns. The result was a fresh commitment to raise more money for missions, both local and international, even in the midst of trying to raise funds for a building program. Our premise was that if we were not committed to ministry that reflected genuine giving, how could we expect God to honor our growth? Would not an outward emphasis be healthy for us and for those who were coming our way?

I know of individuals who have volunteered to tutor inner city kids with no payback other than knowing they are meeting an important need. I know of a family that has regularly made their home a "temporary" foster home, so that a child would not be aborted and might have an opportunity at life as a new permanent home is found for them. Here care is given to those who cannot pay us back. Those who benefit from God's grace should know what it is to receive and be givers in turn. They understand that we give not to get, but out of gratitude because God has given us so much. That is the kind of attitude and ministry Jesus calls for here.

The parable of 14:15–24 is a painfully tragic description of opportunity missed. Many in the nation of Israel missed entering into blessing when the time came because they failed to see the importance of the invitation that came their way. But the opportunity to share in God's celebration is still being extended today. Whether the invitation is one that comes to an original invitee (a Jew) or to others in the city or to those on the city's edge, the point is that an opportunity to sit and share in the blessings of God is being offered. We must respond to the invitation. Nothing in life should get in the way of responding to what God is doing through Jesus.

We must be careful not to presume that God will eventually bless us, either because he is not judging us right now or because we can repent at the last minute. I have known people who, upon hearing about grace, say, "I'll wait until just before I die. That way I can live as I want now." Such a response often surfaced with my Young Life work among high school and college-age kids. That remark ignores one important fact: Scripture warns that the longer we refuse the offer, the more likely we will have a hardness of heart that becomes callous to any word from God. There are many excuses people give for not responding to the gospel. In college it was, "That will cramp my style." Later in life it is, "I do not need a crutch." These responses are attempts to gain freedom from accountability and responsibility before God. They are, if I may be blunt, a form of self-idolatry. It places God in the position of waiting on us. This type of pride is precisely why God's choosing of and sensitivity to the poor, lame, and blind is so important a Lucan theme (4:16–19; 7:22–23). It reveals how God values the humble and needy. Those who know their need and position before God are the ones he will bring to himself (18:9–14; cf. 1 Cor. 1:26–31).

Furthermore, God is not caught by surprise when some reject him. The celebration of blessing goes on without the original invitees, and by God's grace others are invited to the table. The important question is not when we are invited to the table, but that we come when invited. God graciously continues to call people to the banquet. If some refuse, others will be found. The loss is not God's, but those who miss the party.

Central to the imagery of this parable is the assumption that Jesus is the one issuing the invitation. Blessing is not a function of mere devotion or zeal; it must be accompanied with knowledge of and response to God's Chosen One. Failure to note this reality is what made the Jews' rejection as represented by the early invitees so tragic (see Rom. 10:1—4). They thought that heritage alone and being a part of God's chosen people alone were enough. Jesus replies that it is not enough to be among the originally invited. Those invited must choose to attend. If they do not, they will not get a chance to sit at the table of blessing. What a tragedy to hear the invitation to blessing and yet miss it when the time comes.

Luke 14:25–35

L ARGE CROWDS WERE traveling with Jesus, and turning to them he said: ²⁶"If anyone comes to me and does not hate his father and mother, his wife and children, his brothers and sisters—yes, even his own life—he cannot be my disciple. ²⁷And anyone who does not carry his cross and follow me cannot be my disciple.

²⁸"Suppose one of you wants to build a tower. Will he not first sit down and estimate the cost to see if he has enough money to complete it? ²⁹For if he lays the foundation and is not able to finish it, everyone who sees it will ridicule him, ³⁰saying, 'This fellow began to build and was not able to finish.'

³¹"Or suppose a king is about to go to war against another king. Will he not first sit down and consider whether he is able with ten thousand men to oppose the one coming against him with twenty thousand? ³²If he is not able, he will send a delegation while the other is still a long way off and will ask for terms of peace. ³³In the same way, any of you who does not give up everything he has cannot be my disciple.

³⁴"Salt is good, but if it loses its saltiness, how can it be made salty again? ³⁵It is fit neither for the soil nor for the manure pile; it is thrown out.

"He who has ears to hear, let him hear."

THIS SIXTH UNIT of Luke's journey section (9:51–19:44) contains only one passage—the call to consider what discipleship means. This unit stands near the center of the journey to Jerusalem and summarizes the shift in emphasis from confrontation with the Jewish leadership to preparing the disciples for his departure. Discipleship is not easy, but our accountability to God and the rigor of the task require that we understand the commitment required to walk successfully as his disciples.

Jesus' attention turns here to his followers, asking them to assess what discipleship requires.¹ He wants them to be aware of what is required to

---

1. This text is unique to Luke, though parts of it sound like Matthew 10:37–38; the concluding two verses are conceptually similar to Matthew 5:13 and Mark 9:49–50.

walk the full route with him. His main point is that successful discipleship requires Jesus to be a priority in life. We must therefore count the cost of following him if we are going to finish the walk. His will and the direction he leads are the lodestones of our lives. We must present our lives to him and reflect values that honor God.

Jesus makes these remarks to the multitude, unlike earlier remarks in 9:18–27, 57–62, where only disciples were present. He has no desire to hide his requirements from those who want to follow him, as if he wants to get our decision first and then tell us the rest of the story. Jesus makes it clear to everyone just how much following him requires. He must be first, and they must be ready to identify with him and his suffering. That may mean ostracism by some of the Jews rejecting him, or it may mean isolation and persecution. Discipleship is a tough road to walk. To trust him is to embrace him as the answer to the journey of salvation, including the rough patches that come with discipleship.

Jesus gets right to the point. If anyone wants to follow him, he must hate father, mother, wife, children, brothers, sisters, and even his or her own life. The background for this remark and its rhetorical force are crucial to understanding it correctly. The meaning of "hate" carries a comparative force here.[2] The idea is not that we should hate our family or lives, but that in comparison to Jesus, if we are forced to choose, the winner in that choice must be Jesus. He is to be loved more than anyone else (cf. a similar concept in Matt. 6:24). Moreover, in a first century context, to decide for Jesus for some did mean deciding against family (Luke 12:49–53). Those who loved family more would not even consider Jesus. Those who loved their own lives more also would not consider Jesus, since trusting him might eventually mean martyrdom. Thus Jesus' remarks come in the context of what conversion may require. People should understand the cost.

To get his point across clearly, Jesus uses two illustrations. One is of a man who builds a watchtower over his land or over a city.[3] Such an undertaking is expensive, and he must be sure such a project is affordable. Thus, it is best to estimate the cost before starting to build. How sad to start construction and not have the money to finish. All of us probably know building projects that started but did not get finished for lack of funds. What a waste to have half a building! Jesus drives the point home by picturing passers-by ridiculing the lack of closure on the project. In other words, moving toward successful discipleship takes reflection; it is not an automatic exercise. There is

---

2. J. Denny, "The Word 'Hate' in Luke 14:26," *ExpTim* 21 (1909–10): 41. The idiom is known in Greek (see Epictetus 3.3.5). See also O. Michel, "μισέω," *TDNT*, 4:690–91.

3. On such towers, see J. Jeremias, *The Parables of Jesus*, 196, n. 19.

no positive testimony in a walk with God that is abandoned because the cost has not been properly assessed. Rather, it is tragic.

The second parable pictures a king assessing his strength in preparation for war. As I write, Haiti has just negotiated for peace rather than face an invasion from the United States, which illustrates this passage. What king goes to war outmanned? Does he not first sit down and consider whether his ten thousand can beat his opponent's twenty thousand? If he realizes he cannot win, he will send a delegation and negotiate peace. Similarly, says Jesus, those who want to be his disciples must make such an assessment. A person must negotiate peace with God. He or she has two options. (1) One can go one's own way, with the result being taking a stand against God. (2) One can take a wiser approach by suing for terms of peace with God, on the Lord's gracious terms. This second option means giving God his due and then following him. God desires disciples fully aligned with him. The giving up of "everything" means recognizing that God has claim on all areas of our lives. Part of discipleship is learning from God what he desires in these areas. No one can know at the start of the walk everything involved, but one can enter the journey with an understanding that God has access to all that we are.

Jesus issues a final warning in the picture of salt. Salt is of value and useful as long as it continues to be salty. In this part of the world, such salt could maintain its potency for up to fifteen years.[4] Whether used as a type of seasoning or as a catalyst for a fire, it was only useful when it was salty. If it ceased to function as salt, it was thrown away. The remark notes that God can dispense with disciples who do not complete their call. This means that discipline, even as severe as taking one's life,[5] can come from God. That is why he calls us to hear what he says. Discipleship takes dedication and focus, and God is concerned how his disciples walk. Different eras involve different walks, since not everyone is called to suffer as many Christians did in the early centuries. But those differences do not alter the need to walk as faithful disciples. Jesus wants everyone on the journey to bring to it an understanding of what it requires and to resolve to stay on the path every step of the way.

THE MAJOR DIFFERENCE between the context of this passage and the consideration of the text's function today is that Jesus' remarks come in a period that marks the start of Christianity rather than the current period, when many people live in a post-Christian culture.

---

4. F Hauck, "ἅλας," *TDNT*, 1:229.

5. An example of this kind of judgment is 1 Corinthians 11:30, where some believers died in Paul's judgment for taking the Lord's Supper in an inappropriate manner.

The problem of choosing for Jesus was harder to make then than now, though it is more difficult now than it was in the "Christian" culture that predominated in the Western world fifty to two hundred and fifty years ago. In Jesus' time and in the early generations after him, to decide for Jesus usually meant facing rejection, ridicule, and tension. No one decided to embrace him casually. Today, many people assume they are Christian simply because they live in a culture grounded in Judeo-Christian roots. Though some may be hostile toward believers, this does not occur in many, more tolerant contexts of our modern world.

On the other hand, there are other parts of the world where a choice for Jesus means isolation. Those who come to Jesus out of a strong Jewish heritage, out of a Muslim cultural context, or in those parts of Asia where ancestral worship reigns risk rejection from the outset. So the cultural force of the call of this text will manifest itself differently, depending on the locale of the application.

Of course, the call of this text is the same: Discipleship requires that Jesus be given primary allegiance. The Lord wants to have priority in every area of life. Discerning how this works itself out in life takes interaction with God's Word, prayer, involvement in a healthy community that encourages our walk, and listening to God through all the means he makes available to his disciples. That aspect of the call is timeless.

Difficulties in applying the text come in contexts where a detached association with Jesus is possible. How does this passage look at such people? Remember first that it addresses the reality of discipleship as a long journey. People grow in their understanding and application of what giving Jesus a primary role in their lives means. Most of us, if we are honest, know that God is constantly claiming more of our lives for himself. We continue to discover fresh areas of our lives that need attention as we apply ourselves to the areas he has already addressed. We never completely arrive as disciples; we are always on the road with God. Unfortunately, we can be slow in relinquishing control to him.

Yet Jesus is not teaching that we must be perfect in order to be saved. Salvation is by grace, and the gifts he gives us are the resources that make possible and enable us to be what he calls us to be. We do not fix our faults so that we may earn his favor; instead, we turn to him so that he can begin the work of renovation he wishes to work in our lives. In a real sense, a disciple (i.e., a learner[6]) is a person under constant renovation. I often joke with my classes that if there is any doubt renovation is needed, all I need to do is ask their spouse or roommate! A good disciple recognizes that renovation is

---

6. On the disciple as learner, see K. H. Rengstorf, "μαθητής," *TDNT*, 4:419–21.

never done. He or she also recognizes that sometimes renovation means tearing down before building up something fresh and new. The rebuilding that God does is not always easy or pleasant, but like the goal of renovation, what emerges is much better than what was there at the start. The hope of such transformation is what makes discipleship worth the journey.

THE FUNDAMENTAL QUESTION about discipleship is to consider its relationship to faith. For Jesus it is clear that discipleship takes reflection and focus. That is why only cross-bearers can be disciples. If we cannot walk the path of rejection Jesus walked, then we are not ready for the journey of faith Jesus calls believers to take. Sometimes discipleship is portrayed as a distinct phase from saving faith, but Jesus rejects such a distinction. Though faith and discipleship are separable conceptually, the ideas are inseparably linked since one trusts Jesus by an act of faith and then walks with him in trust. Jesus calls us into a relationship, not just a decision. As a learner, a disciple enters into relationship with Jesus and joins a lifetime journey of learning. Paul called that journey the "obedience that comes from faith," a lifestyle that he expected from those whom he evangelized (Rom. 1:5; cf. Acts 26:20). Grace brings a relationship with God as a gift, but included is the journey of walking by God's grace.

Another application of this text requires serious self-reflection. Do I yield to the Lord in every area of my life—my possessions, my family, even my own life? Do I really trust him to care for me? Or do I have to help him along by seizing control or by being careful that I avoid some of the tension that inevitably comes into the process when one takes a position of representing Jesus to a needy world? These are hard questions, because it can be easy to say we have given over all, when we have only given over what we are comfortable handing over to him.

Part of the problem in counting the cost is that often we do not know ahead of time what the real cost will be. For example, a person may decide to go into full-time ministry, and that decision may mean that their families will have to live on less than if they had brought the same level of education and skill to a more secular pursuit. That sacrifice can be understood as loving Jesus over family—though one hopes that churches will work to make sure their ministers are meaningfully cared for.

Sometimes a decision for Jesus means refusing to offer support to a family member for a decision that may be immoral in God's eyes. Taking that stand may be painful but necessary. It may mean refusing to endorse a relationship before God that has been conducted in a way that dishonors him.

It may mean telling a brother, sister, relative, or friend engaged in adultery, in a painful act of confrontive love, that God is not pleased with his or her actions. It may mean discussing destructive behavior at the risk of never speaking to that person again. It may be perceived as loving God over family or friends, when ironically it means loving both!

Sometimes people do not understand why ministers will not marry people in the church in certain circumstances. Sometimes it is a choice to be loyal to Jesus and represent him faithfully in a dark world rather than turn a blind eye to immorality. To marry a couple who have openly lived together before marriage is to pretend that God is disinterested in our moral lives, a dangerous signal in a world full of temptation. The policy in our church for such situations is, stressing God's willingness to forgive, to ask people to live separately until marriage, in order to reaffirm their understanding of God's moral standards. Such a policy has become necessary because living together is now commonplace, and some people, after coming to the Lord, decide they want to honor God in their lives by getting married. We wish to encourage their desire to walk with God and put their relationship on fresh, morally healthy terms, without suggesting that what they have done has put their spiritual walk beyond recovery.

Sometimes being honest means testifying about a crime when everyone in the office will argue that you are a slimy tattletale. The pursuit of faithfulness in the midst of a workplace where honesty is a relative value determined by the end in view can be hard. To choose to be in step with God and out of step with office partners can be a painful path to walk.

The choices of discipleship are not always easy. To follow Jesus and share his cross may mean that neighbors and friends do not always understand why we do what we do. Sometimes they will not support us and may even do things that hurt. Our understanding of what counting the cost means is only theoretical until we are put in such circumstances. But those who have contemplated counting the cost will be ready when the moment comes. They must rely on God and turn to him for wisdom if and when a time comes to choose God over family, self, or possessions. Those who wish to follow Jesus should give attention to who has priority, even when they are just considering starting the journey with him.

Luke 15:1–10

NOW THE TAX collectors and "sinners" were all gathering around to hear him. ²But the Pharisees and the
teachers of the law muttered, "This man welcomes
sinners and eats with them."

³Then Jesus told them this parable: ⁴"Suppose one of you
has a hundred sheep and loses one of them. Does he not leave
the ninety-nine in the open country and go after the lost
sheep until he finds it? ⁵And when he finds it, he joyfully puts
it on his shoulders ⁶and goes home. Then he calls his friends
and neighbors together and says, 'Rejoice with me; I have
found my lost sheep.' ⁷I tell you that in the same way there
will be more rejoicing in heaven over one sinner who repents
than over ninety-nine righteous persons who do not need to
repent.

⁸"Or suppose a woman has ten silver coins and loses one.
Does she not light a lamp, sweep the house and search carefully until she finds it? ⁹And when she finds it, she calls her
friends and neighbors together and says, 'Rejoice with me; I
have found my lost coin.' ¹⁰In the same way, I tell you, there is
rejoicing in the presence of the angels of God over one sinner
who repents."

IN A SERIES of three parables in Luke 15, Jesus
defends his involvement with the lost. This unit
can be separated into two parts: two short parables (vv. 1–10) and a longer one (vv. 11–32).
Our Lord explains how heaven rejoices at the arrival of one lost sinner back
into the house of God. This hope drives Jesus to pursue the lost, to look for
them as one would a lost sheep or coin. The parables also explain why Jesus
urges those alongside the prodigals to receive them with open arms in hope,
rather than with doubt, jealousy, or bitterness. God calls us to pursue the lost.
The hope of the parables is that in seeking the lost we will find some and lead
them back to him.

God is committed to finding the lost, as this chapter explains. Jesus deals
with the contrast between this divine attitude and the temptation among
many believers to ignore the lost. Jesus once again chooses the scribes and

Pharisees as the foil for his comparison. They cannot believe that he is spending so much time receiving sinners and eating with them. Such table fellowship represents an absence of the separation they think righteousness demands. Jesus argues, however, that the call of God demands time be spent seeking the lost.[1]

Verses 3—10 consist of two parables: the lost sheep (vv. 3—7) and the lost coin (vv. 8—10). These two set up the more developed parable of the forgiving father (vv. 11—32). The links between the passages are the themes of "lost" and "found" and "rejoice" (vv. 6, 9, 24, 32).[2] Luke consistently raises the issue of associating with sinners (5:29—32; 7:36—50; 19:1—10). All these texts drive toward Jesus' commission statement in 19:10.

Anyone who has ever searched for something lost knows how maddening it is to look for it and not find it. That frustration underlies this text. Jesus' first story fits the agrarian and pastoral setting of Palestine. A shepherd counting a hundred sheep comes up one short. The flock belongs to an owner of modest means (the average flock ran anywhere from twenty to two hundred head).[3] It is possible that the owner and the shepherd are the same person, since there is no watchman to help him.

The shepherd goes to look for the lost animal. We are not told if he leaves the rest of his flock with neighbors, though that is likely in the natural understanding of the situation, for he would hardly put the ninety-nine at risk for one sheep. On the other hand, sometimes parables are intentionally surprising, and the twist may be a part of the drama. If so, then Jesus is saying that finding the one is so important that he is willing to take such a risk. The hunt is successful when he finds the lost animal, not shred to bits by some wild animal, but alive and well. The shepherd rejoices at finding his valuable sheep.

The note of joy fits the cultural context, since such animals had commercial value. But Jesus' point is not a self-serving one about recovery of lost property, but a comparison of the effort the shepherd makes to recover the lost sheep with his own effort at evangelism. The imagery looks to the Old Testament and to God's tender care of us (Isa. 40:11; 49:22).[4] The model of God's care should be our model in relating to the lost.

The recovery of the lost sheep leads to shared joy. The shepherd calls his friends and neighbors to celebrate the recovery of his animal. Here is a picture of God's heart and joy at the turning of one sinner back to him. "In the

---

1. This passage is unique to Luke, though Matthew 18:12—13 is conceptually parallel to the parable of the lost sheep.

2. Stein, *Luke*, 400.

3. J. Jeremias, *The Parables of Jesus*, 133.

4. H. Preisker and S. Schultz, "πρόβατον," *TDNT*, 6:690.

same way," says Jesus, "there will be more rejoicing in heaven over one sinner who repents than over ninety-nine righteous who do not need to repent."[5] Jesus searches for sinners because heaven rejoices at their recovery.

The second image is similar. This time a woman hunts for a lost coin. The "silver coin" that is in view here is equal to a denarius or a day's wage for an average worker. It is a modest sum. Her search takes time and effort. She lights a lamp, sweeps the room, and searches carefully until she finds the coin. When she does, she is as excited as the shepherd was. She also calls her neighbors to celebrate with her. Again, this is a picture of heaven's joy at a sinner's repentance.

These parables are among the simplest stories of Jesus, communicating both truth and emotion. God wants servants who understand his heart to restore sinners. In both cases, the search takes work. In both cases what is searched for seems, on the surface, to be a modest object. In fact, the search becomes a priority. Yet in both cases, the recovery of what was lost leads to rejoicing with others. This imagery underscores God's desire for disciples to share the goal of winning the lost back to him. Note that the focus is on the joy at the recovery of a sinner, not on the fact that Jesus is the only one to do it. That is why the parable begins, "Suppose one of you. . . ." By telling the story this way, the listener is brought into the story as the shepherd. Jesus is training other disciples after him to do as he has been doing.

Bridging Contexts

THE ATTITUDE EXPRESSED here is fundamental to the church's accomplishing its mission. God does not want believers to isolate themselves from the world to such a degree that they never relate to the lost. Jesus was constantly out among people, especially people who did not know God. Though some grumbled that he had the wrong associations, Jesus knew why he was building such relationships. He knew that something might develop to influence a person who did not know God to consider him more seriously. People like Matthew or Zacchaeus were discovered this way.

Another feature that bridges the centuries is Jesus' implicit rebuke of the approach of the Pharisees. They kept their distance from sinners and refused to accept a spiritual leader who seemed to love and associate with them.

---

5. The rhetoric about the ninety-nine righteous looks like 5:31–32 in tone. It is a way of saying how much God loves a turnaround in a person's life. The comparison with those "not needing to repent" shows that it is a priority that the shepherd leaves those already in God's forgiving care to find more lost sheep.

Jesus challenges their attitude—not only in his ministry but especially in his death for the lost, which restores sinners to relationship with God. At the heart of the gospel is God's reaching out to the sinner and making provision for their forgiveness.

It is easy to dismiss as insignificant the variety of people whom our culture has cast aside or views with contempt. People who suffer from debilitating diseases like AIDS or people on welfare (often viewed as leeches on society) are modern equivalents to the tax collectors and sinners of Jesus' world. Jesus pursued these very people with such vigor that the religious community of the first century questioned his character. But these parables explain why this pursuit meant so much to him. He knew that rescue was possible, and love compelled him to rescue the perishing. If Jesus' attitude and perspective possesses such a theology of lost persons, so should ours. We are called to action, because we appreciate just how much heaven wants us to search for those who are lost.

THIS PASSAGE SAYS much about the heart of God in engaging those who are not interested in him. He cares enough for them to go looking for them, even when they have stayed away consciously. We should be like raiders in search of great treasure, only the treasure we seek are the lost souls of vulnerable sheep. The search is not always easy, but the joy at the end makes the effort worth the cost.

Believers should be engaging the lost in meaningful relationships. Often in the church, however, I see the opposite. We withdraw from the multitudes for fear of compromising our testimony. As a result, there is no one around to testify to! Evangelism requires time and energy, like the shepherd's and woman's search, in order to capture the lost. Some searches even take years, but our Lord calls us to get out among people and build the relationships that allow us to draw others to God.

In our fast-moving and busy culture, developing such relationships can be hard. The best opportunities come from work, school contacts, and neighbors. In each case opportunities exist that can lead to deeper relationships. One member of our church had a creative idea to meet unbelievers. He and his wife home-schooled their children and also were active in the church, a combination that made finding, much less pursuing, the lost difficult. They decided to have a "Who Are Those Guys?" party. They invited their neighbors over for ice cream and a cookout. Whoever wanted to come and meet the people they lived next to but rarely got to know could do so. They now hold the get-togethers periodically in order to build relationships with the people God has placed them next to. That type of initiative is good example of how to apply this text about searching for the lost.

Lunches at work provide another opportunity. Over a period of weeks, months, or even years, we can build relationships where we communicate in a caring way that we are praying for fellow employees. There are numerous possibilities for evangelistic contact, once we commit ourselves to look for opportunities. Jesus calls us to be on the lookout for the lost, just as he was, and to be prepared to take the initiative in helping them find their way home to God.

Luke 15:11-32

JESUS CONTINUED: "THERE was a man who had two sons. [12]The younger one said to his father, 'Father, give me my share of the estate.' So he divided his property between them.

[13]"Not long after that, the younger son got together all he had, set off for a distant country and there squandered his wealth in wild living. [14]After he had spent everything, there was a severe famine in that whole country, and he began to be in need. [15]So he went and hired himself out to a citizen of that country, who sent him to his fields to feed pigs. [16]He longed to fill his stomach with the pods that the pigs were eating, but no one gave him anything.

[17]"When he came to his senses, he said, 'How many of my father's hired men have food to spare, and here I am starving to death! [18]I will set out and go back to my father and say to him: Father, I have sinned against heaven and against you. [19]I am no longer worthy to be called your son; make me like one of your hired men.' [20]So he got up and went to his father.

"But while he was still a long way off, his father saw him and was filled with compassion for him; he ran to his son, threw his arms around him and kissed him.

[21]"The son said to him, 'Father, I have sinned against heaven and against you. I am no longer worthy to be called your son.'

[22]"But the father said to his servants, 'Quick! Bring the best robe and put it on him. Put a ring on his finger and sandals on his feet. [23]Bring the fattened calf and kill it. Let's have a feast and celebrate. [24]For this son of mine was dead and is alive again; he was lost and is found.' So they began to celebrate.

[25]"Meanwhile, the older son was in the field. When he came near the house, he heard music and dancing. [26]So he called one of the servants and asked him what was going on. [27]'Your brother has come,' he replied, 'and your father has killed the fattened calf because he has him back safe and sound.'

[28]"The older brother became angry and refused to go in. So his father went out and pleaded with him. [29]But he answered

his father, 'Look! All these years I've been slaving for you and never disobeyed your orders. Yet you never gave me even a young goat so I could celebrate with my friends. ³⁰But when this son of yours who has squandered your property with prostitutes comes home, you kill the fattened calf for him!'

³¹"'My son,' the father said, 'you are always with me, and everything I have is yours. ³²But we had to celebrate and be glad, because this brother of yours was dead and is alive again; he was lost and is found.'"

THIS THIRD PARABLE in Luke 15 is by far the most detailed. It is unique to Luke and highlights God's willingness to receive sinners. It also discusses the older brother, which treats how people should respond to one who repents. The negative foil is the grumbling of the Pharisees and scribes that opened the chapter (15:1–2). This parable is often called "The Prodigal Son," but it is really about different reactions to the prodigal. The key reaction is that of the father, who is excited to receive his son back. Thus a better name for the parable is "The Forgiving Father." A sub-theme is the reaction of the older brother, so that one can subtitle the parable with the addendum: "and the Begrudging Brother."

The parable is almost allegorical, since each member in the story contributes significantly to its meaning. The father pictures God the Father in heaven. The prodigal pictures the sinner who repents. The older son pictures the attitude of the Pharisees in not desiring sinners to turn to God.[1] Jesus is defending his right to associate with sinners for the sake of the gospel. In fact, the gospel is for sinners, and his mission fits his message.

The parable begins when a younger son asks for his portion of his father's estate (in Greek this is called the portion of his father's being [i.e., "life holdings"]). As the younger son, he would have received one third (Deut. 21:17). Interestingly, Judaism had advice about this kind of a request. Sirach 33:19–23 begins with the statement: "To son or wife, to brother or friend, give no power over yourself while you live; and give not your goods to another so as to have to ask for them again." To distribute the estate too soon was to risk having to fall into another's care. Nevertheless, the father in the parable grants the request. This detail pictures a father who is letting a sinner go his own way.[2]

---

1. R. Tannehill, *The Narrative Unity of Luke-Acts*, 1:171.
2. Schrenk, "πατήρ," *TDNT*, 5:983–84.

What was feared takes place. The son squanders his fortune in a distant land. Throwing away his inheritance, he lives and plays hard. But a famine when his money runs out presents a predicament. He needs to eat. This pictures the dire circumstances that sin produces.

So the son acts prudently and gets a job feeding pigs. This detail is significant, since in Judaism a pig was an unclean animal (Lev. 11:7; Deut. 14:8). This job is thus a dishonorable one. And he is still hungry, longing to eat what the pigs have for a meal.[3] With no one to help him, he is living a tragedy.

Then he recognizes things have to change. He decides that he will be better off as a slave of his father than working on the edge of the earth alone. He comes "to his senses." How foolish to starve when his father's slaves live better than he does. So he resolves to confess to his father and ask for status as a slave. He has sinned against heaven and his father, and he knows he should admit it. Here Jesus pictures the humility of one who comes and places his spiritual welfare in God's hands, demanding nothing but his grace. He will rest in the father's mercy.

The son heads home. But the father does not wait for him to walk up to the house. Rather, he runs out to embrace him. This part of the story is a cultural surprise.[4] Normally a father waits to be addressed by the son and to receive some indication of respect before responding. But God's compassion is exceptional. The father is so full of joy that he drapes himself around his lost son's neck and welcomes him back with hugs and kisses of affection.

The son is not deterred. He begins to confess, but does not even get through his response before the father makes it clear that full restoration awaits him. The son is received back into the family with full honor and privileges, as if nothing has happened. He gets the best robe, a family ring, and sandals, and there is a big celebration. The feast declares that the lost son has been found. Here is God's joy at a sinner returning to him (cf. 15:7, 10).

The older brother, unaware of what has occurred, returns from a hard day's work and hears the music. He asks a servant what is going on and hears about his brother's return and the celebration. He is angry and refuses to go in. He wants nothing to do with his lost and wayward brother, even though he has returned. In fact, he registers his complaint, noting that in all his years of faithful service not once has his father thrown a party and slain even a goat to celebrate. In a classic presentation of sibling tension, the older brother asks about justice and fairness in the father's house. The force of the remark is

---

3. In later Judaism an expression arose about how dire circumstances could bring a change of perspective: "When the Israelites are reduced to carob pods, then they will repent" (*Leviticus Rabbah* 35 [123c], a rabbinic anthology of interpretations on Leviticus).

4. Blomberg, *Interpreting the Parables*, 176.

almost that this loyalty is owed to him by the father. To drive the point home, the older brother notes that "this son of yours" (note: not "my brother"!) has squandered property and lived with prostitutes.

The father responds without defensiveness, noting that the older son already has access to what is the father's. Given that the older son represents the Pharisees, this detail suggests that the full rights of sonship are the older son's as well, if he asks for them. But the celebration for the sibling ("this brother of yours"!) is necessary, since he is back from the dead. A sinner found is a cause to celebrate.

The story ends here. The parable pictures reversal through the details of space. The son who was out of the house is now very much in, while the older son sits on the outside. The story ends with a point to ponder, in that we do not know how the older son responds to the father.

THE PARABLE IS open-ended. It calls on Luke's readers to reflect on what they would do if they were in the older brother's sandals. Would we accept the sinner home and celebrate, or would we be too worried about ourselves to share in the joy of the return? The parable obviously implies that we should respond as the father calls the older son to do. We should pursue sinners and welcome them with joy when they return home.

This passage is certainly about God's attitude and activity toward sinners and the way others respond to them. God's attitude is seen in the longing father, who longs to embrace the departing son and keep him as a member of his family, though he will not force him to stay home. When the son asks to go, he lets him walk out the door and go his own direction. Yet the father's response on his return makes it clear that he was thinking about the departed son all along. His quick embrace shows his love for the son was constant and the pain of his departure real. His forgiveness is total and immediate. There are no grudges; the past pain has been washed away in the waves of joy at the son's return. The discussion of the father with the older son shows he is ready to defend the return, urging others associated with him in the house to give an equally warm welcome.

This parable is preeminently about God the Father, revealing his character as compassionate and forgiving. But God seeks a relationship that is consciously entered into by his children. The older brother has been around the father but does not really know him well. The younger brother approaches the father humbly and discovers just how full of grace the father is. It is no wonder that we sing hymns like "Amazing Grace" when we contemplate texts like this that illustrate the depth of God's grace. Those who come to him with contrite hearts can know that God runs to greet us and wrap his arms around us to welcome us home.

In its original setting the parable clearly has the Pharisees in view in the older brother. They stand close to God, at least in an apparent way, and appear to have an inside track to his blessing. Everything God has in terms of promise is available to them, for "everything I have is yours." Yet they are really on the outside, for they never choose to embrace it by acknowledging God's goodness in terms of the forgiveness Jesus offers to all. The picture of the older brother still has value today in depicting how those who perceive themselves as close to God should respond to the lost. The parable invites us to consider the Pharisees' attitude and reject their sense of alienation at the prodigal's return.

The text also warns us through the older brother that activity for God by itself or proximity to him is not the same as knowing him through a relationship grounded in a conscious, humble turning to him. The older brother sees God more as a taskmaster who uses his services rather than as a gracious Father. When we come to God on the basis of his grace, humbly recognizing our need for him rather than trying to earn his favor, we find the arms of God ready to welcome us in celebration. We risk missing the joy of relationship with God when we turn him into a scorekeeper.[5]

In addition, the attitude of the prodigal on returning home is a snapshot of the essence of repentance. The previous two parables expressed the joy of heaven at one who repents; this parable pictures that repentance. As the prodigal approaches his father, he relies totally on his mercy, completely humble and recognizing that the only right he has is the appeal for his father's help. That is the essence of what it means to turn to God. As 5:31–32 says, Christ comes to call sinners to repentance. What awaits the penitent who turn to Jesus is a great physician who heals them spiritually and a Father who cannot wait to fully celebrate the return home.

THE ATTITUDE OF God is at the center of the parable. We can be assured that God approaches sinners who turn to him with open arms. Even more, God goes on the active search for sinners, taking the initiative with them, for he came "to seek and to save what was lost" (19:10). He rejoices to bring us into his family, and he celebrates our turning to him.

---

5. For a development of the practical side of a grace walk with God, see Charles Swindoll, *The Grace Awakening* (Dallas: Word, 1990).

Those with especially sensitive consciences about whether they are saved should be careful not to doubt God and his gracious desire to welcome us. I remember a believing friend of mine who always doubted his salvation. I always told him that the fact his conscience was so sensitive was itself a sign that he loved God and that God loved him. Yet there was always the struggle of whether God had really embraced him. Finally, I raised the issue of the nature of faith. Faith is trusting in the presence and care of God, that he is the rewarder of those who seek him (Heb. 11:6). This is the central issue of the parable. Do we believe that God embraces those who turn to him? This text calls us to see that he does and then to rest in the encouragement that such love and grace generates.

Another major application of this text involves how people respond to the lost. The parable justifies Jesus' involvement with sinners and urges us to rejoice when we see someone come into the Christian community. Jesus wants a community filled with people who can forgive and restore those who turn to God. He is displeased with any who are disgruntled and sit sulking on the outside.

As a pastor I sometimes see people in situations where they know they have sinned in a big way (though Scripture teaches us not to think of sins as big and little!). When they return, one of the hardest things is to regain people's trust that they are trying to walk with God again. When someone with a infamous past life comes to Jesus or a believer who falls into serious sin returns, it is important that they be restored, in order to reestablish the connection that makes for support in the walk to come.

I remember one incident involving a church member, who upon returning was deeply hurt by the lack of trust others showed over the return. That reaction can be natural, but that does not make it right. Do we want to invest ourselves in supporting a person who let us down in the past? To be safe, we keep our distance and put the person to the test. But such skepticism can also be damaging, showing a lack of faith in a person struggling to get back on his or her feet. Our response should be like the father's. We should welcome the person who turns back with open arms. If there is subsequent failure, we can deal with that then. In the meantime it is important to say, "Welcome home! You belong!" After all, we have been accepted into the family ourselves only by God's grace and by the sacrifice of his Son Jesus. There is no reason to offer higher standards than God's to others who seek to walk with him.

Luke 16:1-13

JESUS TOLD HIS disciples: "There was a rich man whose manager was accused of wasting his possessions. [2]So he called him in and asked him, 'What is this I hear about you? Give an account of your management, because you cannot be manager any longer.'

[3]"The manager said to himself, 'What shall I do now? My master is taking away my job. I'm not strong enough to dig, and I'm ashamed to beg—[4]I know what I'll do so that, when I lose my job here, people will welcome me into their houses.'

[5]"So he called in each one of his master's debtors. He asked the first, 'How much do you owe my master?'

[6]"'Eight hundred gallons of olive oil,' he replied.

"The manager told him, 'Take your bill, sit down quickly, and make it four hundred.'

[7]"Then he asked the second, 'And how much do you owe?'

"'A thousand bushels of wheat,' he replied.

"He told him, 'Take your bill and make it eight hundred.'

[8]"The master commended the dishonest manager because he had acted shrewdly. For the people of this world are more shrewd in dealing with their own kind than are the people of the light. [9]I tell you, use worldly wealth to gain friends for yourselves, so that when it is gone, you will be welcomed into eternal dwellings.

[10]"Whoever can be trusted with very little can also be trusted with much, and whoever is dishonest with very little will also be dishonest with much. [11]So if you have not been trustworthy in handling worldly wealth, who will trust you with true riches? [12]And if you have not been trustworthy with someone else's property, who will give you property of your own?

[13]"No servant can serve two masters. Either he will hate the one and love the other, or he will be devoted to the one and despise the other. You cannot serve both God and Money."

Original Meaning

THIS NEXT PART of Luke's journey section (16:1–31) can be divided into three parts, each focusing on the need for disciples to be wise and generous with the resources God has given them. The parable of the unjust manager calls for faithfulness and wisdom in handling money, followed by a series of exhortations that develop points emerging from it (16:1–13). A shorter unit rebukes the attitude of the Pharisees and declares the arrival of a new era, which, though new, does not change the ethical standards God requires (16:14–18). Finally, the parable of the rich man and Lazarus emphasizes the ethical call God has made to be generous in meeting human needs (16:19–31). Christ's followers, unlike the Pharisees, should not be lovers of money. Recognition of the accountability God holds his disciples to has ethical and lifestyle implications, even down to the use of resources.

Luke 16:1–8 contains probably the most difficult parable in Luke.[1] It clearly teaches about the use of money and the responsibility attached to its presence, but how precisely is that point made? Two options stand out.[2] (1) The manager was dishonest in reducing the bills of the master's creditors but was thinking ahead; so Jesus commends his crafty, forward-looking use of resources. (2) The manager may have been dishonest earlier, but in reducing the bills, he is simply cutting out some of his own hefty commission in hope of goodwill later.[3] If so, Jesus commends him for his creative use of foresight that provides for his care later.

---

1. The parable is unique to Luke, though verse 13 is conceptually similar to Matthew 6:24. In addition, Luke 16:10–12 has some points of conceptual overlap with Matthew 25:20–30 and Luke 19:17–26.

2. D. J. Ireland, *Stewardship and the Kingdom of God: An Historical, Exegetical and Contextual Study of the Parable of the Unjust Steward in Luke 16:1–13* (Leiden: E. J. Brill, 1992), 5–47, notes the various attempts to explain this passage in the history of its interpretation. He notes six prominent options in that discussion, of which we discuss the two most significant alternatives. There also is some discussion of where the parable ends. Does it end at vv. 7, 8a, 8b, or 9? We prefer to see the parable go to v. 8a, with everything after it being the various applications Jesus makes from the parable.

3. For discussion of this later option, see Fitzmyer, *The Gospel According to Luke X–XXIV*, 1098. On the cultural background here, see Fitzmyer, "The Story of the Dishonest Manager (Luke 16:1–13)," *TS* 25 (1964): 23–42, and J. D. M. Derrett, *Law in the New Testament* (London: Darton, Longman, & Todd, 1970), 48–77. Fitzmyer and Derrett explain the background slightly differently. Derrett argues the manager simply removed the interest from the debt (Ex. 22:24; Lev. 23:36–37; Deut. 15:7–8; 23:20–21). Fitzmyer, *The Gospel According to Luke X–XXIV*, 1097–98, argues that what was removed was the manager's commission. Either of these explanations is possible, though a variation in the rate of commission depending on the item in view might be more natural than a variation in the rate of interest.

The choice between the options is one of those cases where the interpretive decision is difficult. Either option can be correct. Jesus may be using a negative example of an unethical action to make the point about the use of resources in a negative way. But I prefer the option that argues the manager acted with foresight in this situation by cutting himself out of the bill short term, so that people he knows will have compassion on him later. Thus Jesus' point is not built on an example of dishonesty. It illustrates precisely Jesus' point, namely, to use the resources God gives us wisely and generously. My exposition takes this approach, but note that if the other option is adopted, the point made by the passage is fundamentally the same, though the route taken to get there is a little different.

The account begins with a rich man who has a manager in charge of administering his affairs. He apparently serves as a bill collector. Some bring charges against him that he has wasted the master's resources. Interestingly, Luke uses the same term here as he did to describe the prodigal's squandering in 15:13. The connection shows the negative emotive force of the term. The manager has not been an effective manager. The master apparently believes the charges and orders the manager to account for his stewardship in a type of audit. With the audit will come the loss of his position.

Facing a future on the streets, the fired manager contemplates his options. He does not want to work as a daily laborer, for he is not strong enough, and it will also be embarrassing for someone who used to collect the bills from such men to become their temporary hired hand. The alternative, begging, is not particularly attractive either. Contemplating his options, he develops a plan whose goal is simply to ingratiate himself to his master's debtors so that they will help him. He is a prudent planner. Having lost the protection of his former master, he looks for help elsewhere.

The manager takes inventory, one at a time. In each case, he lowers the creditor's bill. The parable gives two examples (both agricultural in character, fitting the Palestinian setting and economy). The first bill involves a hundred baths of olive oil (more than eight hundred gallons). The oil would have cost one thousand denarii, or a little over three years' salary for an average wage earner. The man who has the debt is not an average wage earner, but the debt can still be appreciated as a significant one. By eliminating the manager's commission, the debt is reduced by half. Needless to say, this deflationary trend would not have been resisted! The second example concerns a thousand bushels of wheat, representing the yield of about a hundred acres and costing 2,500–3,000 denarii, anywhere from just over eight to nine and a half years' wage.[4] This bill is reduced to slightly over eight hundred

---

4. There is some dispute about how to count this measure in the ancient texts. We have opted for the larger measure above. If more modest standards are applied, then one hun-

bushels. Again, the manager sacrifices his commission. The reduction is significant and would be met with much appreciation.

Jesus is ready to make the point. He notes that the master commends "the dishonest manager." He has prepared the soil for his future care by what he has done. Such foresight is worthy of appreciation.[5] The manager has acted in light of what the future may bring, and he is ready for it now.

In this first of several applications, Jesus notes that the "people of this world are more shrewd . . . than are the people of the light." That is, people in the world give more thought to their physical well-being than the righteous do to their spiritual well-being. He develops the point by a specific example in verse 9. Wealth of this world should be used generously to gain friends, so that when the resources are gone, that disciple will be welcomed into eternal dwellings. Monetary resources, which possess a power to distort values, should be put to generous and serving use, so that heaven will be pleased to accept the one who has been generous. God honors those who are generous. When the end comes and no more money is available, the one who has seen into the future and acted prudently will have handled the resources and stewardship God has given wisely. Zacchaeus is a positive example of this (19:1–10).

In addition, those who can be trusted with little can also be trusted with much, just as those who are dishonest with little will be dishonest in much. Who can entrust people with significant things of real value if they cannot handle worldly wealth? The question probes values. Are our resources put to selfish or generous use? If one cannot manage what is given as part of a stewardship, who will give us what is truly our own? Jesus drives for a character in his disciples that reflects God's integrity, generosity, and grace.

The decisive point is then made. A person in this world is faced with a fundamental choice of allegiance. No servant can serve two masters. The moment will come when the servant must choose which one gets the service. At that time one will be loved, the other hated; devotion will be offered to one, while the other will be despised. One cannot serve both God and Money. If the resources we receive are a stewardship from God to be used

---

dred measures would be much smaller, equaling one tenth of the total or the wage for an average worker for 8 to 9.5 months. For these variations, see Marshall, *Commentary on Luke,* 619. Either way the amount is significant and so is the reduction.

5. I opt for the commission view because I find it implausible that the master would commend the dishonest manager if he continued to cheat him in the last round of pricing. Jesus' parables usually have an element of internal coherence to them, even when there are twists in the story. So the master's commending the manager for continued dishonesty looks unlikely. The manager is called "dishonest" because of his earlier actions, not his more recent ones.

in service to him and to others, then to serve God is to give our resources to meet the needs of those around us. Some day God will evaluate our use of resources, whether we have handled them in a way that anticipates his desires and values; if we have, his commendation will follow. Just as the unrighteous manager was prudent in considering what the future required, so we must be prudent in considering how God desires us to handle his resources.

Bridging Contexts

THE PARABLE TREATS fundamental attitudes in how we handle resources. Jesus makes it clear here that money and the other material resources we possess are not ours, to be used in whatever we please. Rather, they have been placed into our care in order to meet the needs of those around us. What Jesus says here is similar to what Paul says in Ephesians 4:28. We earn resources in order to help the needy and to share with them.

This understanding of resources runs counter to the values of our culture, which instills in us the idea that what we have earned is ours and that we can use it as we want. Jesus makes the point that what we have is entrusted to us, and God watches how we use it. This perspective transcends the ideological debates about which economic system is endorsed by Scripture. It asks us to reflect on what God does when he gives us our resources and encourages us to consider how to direct their use.

The timeless value Jesus wishes for his disciples has to do with service, generosity, and people. Resources ought not be counted and hoarded but planted for a harvest of generosity that serves others and meets their real needs. The stewardship of money is not an end but a means, where others can see acts of caring from those who say God cares. Since greed and selfishness have a deep home in the human heart, the message of this text not only bridges the contexts, it explodes in them.

A good example is the declaration in verse 13 that one cannot have two masters. Do we serve God or our resources and the pursuit of them? For many, this is the most fundamental question in life. The pursuit of wealth can cause us to ignore God, undervalue family, walk over people, use them, act unethically, and engage a host of other destructive actions. This is why some biblical texts call greed idolatry (Eph. 5:3). To pursue wealth and the status that often comes with it means to worship creation, not the Creator. This is why Jesus says a person must know who he or she will serve, for when a choice has to be made, a person cannot serve both. Everything here calls on us to choose God.

LUKE HIGHLIGHTS THE role of money throughout his Gospel. This parable, especially the applications at the end, argues that the use of
resources is a litmus test of spiritual stewardship.
This is a dangerous area to discuss. On the one hand, the church has to be
careful in handling money (and in asking for it), so that it does not succumb
to the seductive power of money to distort our values. God wants us to make
our decisions for the right reasons and not to make culturally popular choices
just so that resources and big givers may be retained. In addition, the church
must be careful not to talk about money so much that what it preaches on
this issue seems as if it is the topic that determines spiritual success. Perhaps
the most obvious example of excess here is the way some television ministries
function with an omnipresent request for funds. Watching these programs
sometimes leaves the impression that spirituality is defined by what someone gives to the church. That error is as old as indulgences and the other
excesses that helped to produce the Reformation.

It might seem odd to highlight an application that starts with how the
church appeals for money, since the exhortation of the passage is an appeal
to individuals. But how can individuals learn to use resources and give wisely
if the church is guilty of exploitation in how it obtains what God makes
available? Modeling of values in the use of resources should be most evident
in the body Christ formed to serve those who need to know God, his grace,
and his love. The stewardship responsibility of church leaders is an important aspect of modeling spirituality.

Another tragedy in the area of giving is that the use of resources in meeting needs has almost become ideologically identified with something foreign
to church values. In condemning programs that do not help people get off
of welfare, we have thrown out the baby with the bath water. We should support programs that help people care for themselves, but too many people see
giving to those who suffer in our society as evidence of a commitment to
some distorted social agenda. Yet centuries ago, pious Christians were the
ones committed to a witness reflective of biblical values, leading efforts to
meet the needs of widows, orphans, and the other poor who needed evidence
that God cared about them.

The Old and New Testament have much to say about how people in
need should be seen and cared for (see Matt. 25:31–46; James 2:14–16).
The point is significant, because one of the ways we evidence God's care is
by concretely showing our love through the use of resources. Consider how
quickly we give to relief and aid to a natural disaster overseas through a missionary's appeal, yet how quickly a similar and equally valid appeal from

neighbors within our own cities may get rebuffed because it is viewed as politically motivated.

If the call of Jesus is to be generous with resources, we should be on the lookout for opportunities to give. Most Westerners are wealthy and blessed by the world's standards. So many of our resources are poured out in all kinds of endeavors that feed ourselves in one way or another. This text challenges us to ask how can we give generously to meet needs around us. How conscious are we that what we own is not really owned by us but has been loaned from the Lord, who wishes to see how faithfully we handle his resources to serve those in need? Jesus will soon reinforce such questions in 16:19–31, where he raises the question of how a poor, needy man, Lazarus, was treated by a rich man.

Opportunities to honor faithfully the call of this passage exist everywhere. One cannot meet every good cause in the world, nor can one fund every valid ministry. God's call to be generous means that one will be on watch for valid ministries and needs. Some of that giving may be directed to local churches and ministries. But just giving to the local church may narrow our vision too much. We should also contribute to the work of agencies by laboring in areas of need, whether it be feeding the poor, working with agencies that promote education in areas where family support for education is not present, or dealing with unwed mothers in need or the elderly.

Other opportunities may be to underwrite institutions that educate our church leaders. Churches that do not support the seminaries that supply their pulpits should consider their stewardship of the ministry God has made available to them. Parachurch organizations engage in the crucial work of evangelism in corners of our culture that the local church does not touch. Missionary needs are also great, especially those where men and women from foreign countries need support to conduct their ministries effectively in their own country. Sometimes it is financially more efficient to give to nationals to train for ministry in their own culture than to underwrite the cultural transfer of an American into a foreign land. Nationals can usually serve in the same ministry for substantially less than the Americans who are sent over. The variety of options is almost overwhelming, but a text like this calls us to use our resources in ways that contribute to effective ministry. We must say to a needy world, "We care for you, and so does our God."

The question also presses at the level of values. Do I work to obtain a certain salary? Or do I serve because of the call and merits of the ministry God gives to me, whether they be in professional ministry or in a secular pursuit? Is the key issue in my work how much I make or how I can serve and do so faithfully? Subtly even those who do not make megamillions can be distracted from serving because of preoccupation with how much they bring in.

We must be responsible with how much we make in order to care for those we are responsible for, but how often are our choices dictated by wants rather than by needs? The treasures we most need to pursue are those that cause God to be pleased.

Luke 16:14–18

THE PHARISEES, WHO LOVED money, heard all this and were sneering at Jesus. [15]He said to them, "You are the ones who justify yourselves in the eyes of men, but God knows your hearts. What is highly valued among men is detestable in God's sight.

[16] "The Law and the Prophets were proclaimed until John. Since that time, the good news of the kingdom of God is being preached, and everyone is forcing his way into it. [17]It is easier for heaven and earth to disappear than for the least stroke of a pen to drop out of the Law.

[18]"Anyone who divorces his wife and marries another woman commits adultery, and the man who marries a divorced woman commits adultery."

Original Meaning

THIS SHORT UNIT in Luke 16 is difficult to put together. It stands between two passages that clearly address the topic of money, but the connection seems obscure. However, it is introduced by a remark that the Pharisees, "who loved money," scoff at Jesus' comments, making a connection explicit. That is, Jesus' remarks about money raise the issue of his authority, since the presence of the kingdom raises the question of the source and allegiances of one's values.[1] The kingdom exposes divided loyalties, for one serves either God or Money (vv. 10–13). Idolatries are revealed by its presence, and God hates them (vv. 14–15). A key to such values is total integrity, which is why the example of the divorce pledge gets noted in verse 18. The hinge is verses 16–17, where the arrival of the kingdom is linked to the preaching of Jesus. He has the right to call on people to examine how they use their resources and to reflect on the nature of their walk with God in terms of integrity.

If this description of this unit's argument is correct, then the Pharisees' scoffing indicates that they do not understand the values that Jesus insists are reflective of his kingdom. Their love for money has put them out of touch with his message. So Jesus directly mentions where they stand before God. They may justify themselves before people, but God knows their hearts.

---

1. Tiede, *Luke*, 285–88.

What they value highly, God detests. Jesus can hardly use a stronger word than what the NIV translates as "detestable."[2] On the continuum that measure values, God and the Pharisees are on opposite ends.

Our knowledge of God-endorsed values comes from both Old and New Testaments. "The Law and the Prophets were proclaimed until John," but now a new era has come—the good news of the kingdom. Jesus brings its message, and its presence means the initiation of the time of fulfillment. In addition, he reveals the ethical standards God desires. But those standards do not represent the destruction of the values reflected in the Law, since it is easier for the creation to pass away than for the least stroke of the Law to be altered. Jesus is arguing that what he brings represents the *fulfillment* of the promise and *hope* of the Law, to bring righteousness to God's people.

The text makes another point. God's plan divides into two periods: Law and Prophets, and kingdom. The boundary line is John the Baptist's ministry. The call of Jesus is the beginning of the realization of promise. Now the kingdom is being proclaimed.

The last part of verse 16 is disputed. The NIV translates the verse, "Everyone is forcing his way into it"—a reading that suggests acceptance of the gospel that is more widespread than Scripture portrays. The word "is forcing" (*biazetai*) can be read differently, however, since the form is a middle-passive voice. We prefer to read a passive here and translate it: "Everyone is urged insistently to enter in." With this reading, the emphasis is on the preached word, which is what Jesus gives here.[3] He highlights that his call and the call of those who follow him is to preach the word of the kingdom.

Jesus closes with a note about divorce to illustrate that the ethical call of the kingdom is rooted in an integrity that matches the integrity of the period of the Law and the Prophets. If anyone makes a commitment before God in marriage and then divorces, this represents adultery, not only because it is an act of unfaithfulness but also because it is a violation of the original vow made before God. The point of this passage is not to discuss possible grounds for divorce, as Matthew 5:31–32 and 1 Corinthians 7:14–16 do, but simply to illustrate the importance of personal commitments made in the new era. The commitment to marry is a commitment to stay married. To break that commitment and remarry is to commit adultery. That is how serious the commitment of our word is to be in our relationships.

---

2. The Greek term can be translated "abomination." See Foerster, "βδελύσσομαι, κτλ.," *TDNT*, 1:600.

3. For the full lexical defense of this interpretation, see J. B. Cortes and F. M. Gatti, "On the Meaning of Luke 16:16," *JBL* 106 (1987): 247–59.

Bridging Contexts

THE DESCRIPTION OF the two-part division of God's plan over time is a timeless breakdown of how promise became fulfillment through Jesus. We call this today the Old Testament era and the New Testament era, but it is important to remember that this is one promise being realized in two phases: the period of the church and the period that follows Jesus' return. The roots of New Testament fulfillment begin with God's promise to Abraham (cf. Gal. 3).[4] As a result, certain practices are no longer required, such as sacrifices for sin (Heb. 8–10). In addition, the new era brings fresh elements to the promise, as Gentiles are graciously included in God's community more directly than before (Rom. 9–11; Eph. 2:11–22).

These changes we now take for granted, but they were revolutionary at the time. What clearly carries over from our reading of the Old Testament is the reflection of its ethical values of commitment to holiness and meeting the needs of others, so that we live in a way that does not take advantage of others. Even in areas of worship, though we do not bring lambs to the altar, we are called to give a sacrifice of faith that honors and gives thanks to God (Rom. 12:1–2). The Old Testament is filled with instruction that is profitable for the Christian (2 Tim. 3:16–17).

Another fundamental truth expressed in this text is the warning that God does not necessarily value what we value. Engaging in rhetorical overstatement, Jesus speaks of God's detesting what we value. In mind here is our tendency to be attracted to material things and to pursue status in a way that abuses others. The specific application of this idea is discussed elsewhere in Luke (e.g., 12:22–34; 16:1–13, 19–31). Luke hammers away at this theme,

---

4. For discussions of this theme from a Reformed and a dispensational perspective that are close to each other in highlighting how the eras of promise and fulfillment are connected, see (for the Reformed) O. Palmer Robertson, *The Christ of the Covenants* (Phillipsburg, N.J.: Presbyterian & Reformed, 1980); (for a dispensational approach) C. Blaising and D. Bock, *Progressive Dispensationalism* (Wheaton: Victor Books, 1993). It is important to recall that aspects of these promises still await fulfillment at the time of Jesus' return. What the period to come looks like is discussed among Christians. Some see Jesus returning to set up the eternal state (amillennialism and postmillennialism), while others agree there is an intermediate earthly kingdom before the eternal state (premillennialism). Most of the discussion turns on how Revelation 20 is read. What most agree on is that the fulfillment starts with Jesus' ministry and that Jesus' activity in the end will be comprehsnsive. For more discussion, see Luke 21:5–38. This passage also alludes to the complex issue of the Law's relationship to the Christian, a topic that continues to spawn new books. Among three of the most helpful are G. Bahnsen, W. Kaiser, Jr., D. Moo, W. Strickland, W. VanGemeren, *The Law, the Gospel, and the Modern Christian: Five Views* (Grand Rapids: Zondervan, 1993); T. Schreiner, *The Law and Its Fulfillment* (Grand Rapids: Baker, 1993); F. Thielman, *Paul and the Law* (Downers Grove, Ill.: InterVarsity Press, 1994).

possibly because Theophilus comes from a socially high background, so that if his ministry is to be effective, his handling of resources and his social status will need special sensitivity. The use of money in our world takes special spiritual strength, since our culture so ingrains us with expectations that are high and self-focused. Developing generosity means denying the self, which is one of the most fundamental of spiritual virtues.[5]

There is a juxtaposition of continuity and discontinuity in what Jesus says here about God's promise. On the one hand, a shift of era has taken place. No longer do we reside in the period of the Law and the Prophets. On the other hand, what Jesus brings represents fulfillment of all the Law stood for, in that he has provided a permanent forgiveness and a means of enablement in the Spirit, so that we may walk in a way that leads to holiness (2 Cor. 3–4).

This juxtaposition is important because theological systems risk ignoring one side of this equation. Some, highlighting the newness of the new era, emphasize the discontinuity and thus tend to dismiss significance of portions of the Gospels or the Old Testament for today, especially those portions relating to ethics and values. Others highlight continuity and emphasize that little, if anything, is really different in the new era of realization. The approach to many issues on which the Old Testament had specific legal instruction has been impacted and altered in form by what Jesus did, so that appealing directly to the Old Testament is not always appropriate. For example, the appeal to maintain the distinction between clean and unclean food, which some Christian works argue for because of health considerations, is really a misuse of the declaration Mark cites that Jesus declared all food clean (see Mark 7:1–20; Acts 10). One of the merits of Luke's text here is its declaration that what Jesus brings is both a new era and a realization of the promises of old.

The short text on divorce and adultery becomes significant in an age where divorce abounds. God's standards do not change, but the need for the church to minister wisely in a context where many come from broken homes becomes greater in a culture where marriages are not holding together. The emphasis on families and on keeping them together is a good preventive approach. We need to encourage couples and instruct them before they get to a stage where they desire divorce. We must remind people that the romantic notions attached to marriage today are not the fundamental keys to a marriage that honors God. Marriage is not held together by feelings;

---

5. Two thought-provoking works on this topic are: R. Sider, *Rich Christians in a Hungry World* (Dallas: Word, 1990), and J. Schneider, *Godly Materialism* (Downers Grove, Ill.: Inter-Varsity, 1994).

cultural expectations for marriage often idealize it so greatly that we are set up for disappointment and an emotional roller coaster when we discover our mate is not perfect and that marriage takes work. At the base of a good marriage is a commitment to God and to each other, to honor each other and him by following through on promises. That means working together and learning to live graciously with one another, as well as being forgiving to each other. The short remark on divorce highlights that one's ethical commitments are still to be maintained in the new era.

Support also needs to be offered for those who have made the choice to split up. Such couples need to see that divorce is not something God desired and that there may be issues in their lives that contributed to the demise of their marriage. On the other hand, though divorce is sin, it is not an unpardonable sin. Divorce does sometimes occur, and after it happens, the process of restoration must begin. The penalty for divorce may mean certain functions in the church (like eldership) may not be an option for ministry (1 Tim. 3:2), since the church is called to model its values in its leadership; but that does not mean that a remarriage disqualifies one from other types of ministry. Those who have remarried can and should be restored in the church to reflect a new commitment to faithfulness.

This text is but one of several on the theme of marriage and divorce, so this text does not decide the entire issue. It functions rather as an illustration of a truth about integrity, a more modest goal than to treat fully the divorce and remarriage question. One must work with other texts to come to a biblical understanding of the issue.[6]

JESUS HAS THE right to preach the kingdom and to speak with authority. The basic application to this small unit is to respond with obedience to the kingdom demand for ethical integrity, whether it be in how we deal with our resources or how we approach our marriages. The values of the Pharisees, with their love of wealth, are not values endorsed by God. One's word before God in an issue like marriage should be one's word. To honor God means to be faithful to him in all areas of life.

---

6. For a good survey and interaction over the various approaches to this question in the church, see H. Wayne House, ed., *Divorce and Remarriage: Four Views* (Downers Grove, Ill.: InterVarsity, 1990). Two other key works are W. Heth and G. Wenham, *Jesus and Divorce: The Problem with the Evangelical Consensus* (Nashville: Nelson, 1984), and C. Keener, *And Marries Another* (Peabody, Mass.: Hendricksen, 1991). Heth and Wenham argue for no remarriage after divorce, while Keener opts for the right to remarry.

The message of the kingdom is a message about the beginning of fulfill-ment. Believers are urged to encourage others passionately to enter into its blessings. That is why others are urged insistently to enter in (v. 16b), not in a sense of coercion, but with a pleading that says, "Be reconciled to God" (cf. 2 Cor. 5:20–21). As ambassadors we represent Jesus not just in terms of our preached call to respond to the gospel, but also in the character and val-ues he calls his church to have.

The new era Jesus inaugurated is now nearly two thousand years old, but the dynamics that run it are as fresh as they were at the beginning. The key to the kingdom Jesus brings is the total forgiveness he offers and the Spirit he provides for us until the day he completes what has been promised. The Christian community should be a place where transformation and growth are evident. God has brought us into relationship with him in order to remake us into his image. That is why it is so amazing to see Christian communities where change is viewed negatively.

The essence of the founding of the community is that its dynamic will change us. We must think through how to make this fundamental dynamic of the Christian walk remain vibrant in the midst of pursuing a walk of integrity that is not controlled by values formed by our world. This does not mean that we are so separate in style that we cannot relate to the lost. It does mean that we know the difference between tradition we have made into law and that which God asks of us, so that neutral matters of form are not seen as constitutional-like issues that cannot be changed.

Luke 16:19–31

THERE WAS A rich man who was dressed in purple and
fine linen and lived in luxury every day. ²⁰At his gate
was laid a beggar named Lazarus, covered with sores
²¹and longing to eat what fell from the rich man's table. Even
the dogs came and licked his sores.

²²"The time came when the beggar died and the angels car-
ried him to Abraham's side. The rich man also died and was
buried. ²³In hell, where he was in torment, he looked up and
saw Abraham far away, with Lazarus by his side. ²⁴So he called
to him, 'Father Abraham, have pity on me and send Lazarus to
dip the tip of his finger in water and cool my tongue, because
I am in agony in this fire.'

²⁵"But Abraham replied, 'Son, remember that in your life-
time you received your good things, while Lazarus received
bad things, but now he is comforted here and you are in
agony. ²⁶And besides all this, between us and you a great
chasm has been fixed, so that those who want to go from here
to you cannot, nor can anyone cross over from there to us.'

²⁷"He answered, 'Then I beg you, father, send Lazarus to
my father's house, ²⁸for I have five brothers. Let him warn
them, so that they will not also come to this place of torment.'

²⁹"Abraham replied, 'They have Moses and the Prophets;
let them listen to them.'

³⁰"'No, father Abraham,' he said, 'but if someone from the
dead goes to them, they will repent.'

³¹"He said to him, 'If they do not listen to Moses and the
Prophets, they will not be convinced even if someone rises
from the dead.'"

THIS PARABLE IS unique to Luke and is the only
one to name any of its characters. The naming of
the poor man as Lazarus and the failure to name
the rich man personalizes the level of concern
for the poor man, while making clear that the rich man is a representative figure. God cares for each poor person and is fully aware of their plight. The
rich man could be any rich individual.

An important feature often discussed about this passage is whether it truly is a parable. Some avoid identifying it as a parable for fear that it removes the precision about the teaching on the afterlife, since a parable is more pictorial and representative than a real story. However, the fundamental theological affirmations about the afterlife—for example, that once one receives his or her judgment, one cannot alter that position for eternity—are true regardless of the genre classification.

The story does differ from other parables in not being about a repeatable everyday situation, but rather is a specific story. In this sense it is like the parable of the good Samaritan. Still, the account does not recount a historical interchange between a specific rich man and a specific Lazarus, but pictures it. The details of the discussion in the afterlife, including the rich man's ability to engage Abraham in discussion, are apocalyptic-like features in the account that show its rhetorical, parabolic, and symbolic character. Yet realities about accountability before God are portrayed.

The account comes in three parts: the situation before death (vv. 19–21), the situation in the afterlife (vv. 22–23), and comments about that situation (vv. 24–31). In addition, the third part comes in two portions: the discussion of getting Lazarus's help and the attempt to warn the rich man's brothers. The warnings show what God looks for in a person during this life and how fixed one's position is after death. Two themes dominate: the idea of divine evaluation in the afterlife and the hardness of heart that cannot be overcome even by resurrection. But just as important to the parable is what God evaluates. Our service to others shows something about our loyalty to God.

The first portion of the account contrasts the condition of the rich man with that of Lazarus. The man is very wealthy. He lives in a home with a gate and wears clothes made with purple dye, one of the touches of luxury in that era.[1] He dresses in fine linen, a description of the quality of his undergarments.[2] Lazarus, a man with nothing, lies at his gate, begging, full of sores, longing to get the crumbs from the rich man's table, and having his sores licked by the wild dogs on the streets. This licking is significant, since it makes Lazarus ceremonially unclean.[3] His situation is as tragic as the rich man's is sumptuous.

---

1. Kistemaker, *The Parables of Jesus*, 236–37.

2. Fitzmyer, *The Gospel According to Luke X–XXIV*, 1131.

3. On the use of wild dogs as a negative image, see Michel, "κύων," *TDNT*, 3:1103. Some have pressed the detail to argue that the dogs show more compassion than the rich man, but this ignores the Jewish background to this scene, where the act is seen as bringing uncleanness; thus, it is not a positive symbol. The later rabbis would have called Lazarus's life no life at all; see the Talmud, *Batzah* 32b, which states that not having a life meant depending on someone else for food, being ruled by a wife, and having a body full of sores.

But death is the great equalizer, even reverser, since after death the one thing that counts is the human heart. Possessions and status symbols are left behind. What God considers is not written down with numbers and dollar signs. Lazarus dies and is welcomed into divine favor—what the text calls "Abraham's side" (Gk. "Abraham's bosom"). He is in the place of blessing. The rich man dies and is buried, but ends up "in hell" (Gk. *Hades*); in torment, far away from Lazarus, the roles are reversed.[4] Lazarus is in; the rich man is out. The standards of the afterlife are different from those of the appearances of this world.

The rich man looks up and sees Abraham and Lazarus together. He calls to the great patriarch of the Jewish faith and asks for Lazarus to be sent to give him relief from the heat and his agony. Several points are worth noting here. (1) The heat of torment may well depict the intense agony of what it means to be confined to the underworld, knowing that God exists and knowing that one is not in heaven. (2) The rich man knows who Lazarus is. During the time on earth, he knew the poor man was out there, had needs, and even knew his name! (3) The rich man's view of Lazarus has not changed since his death. He still views him as beneath him, as someone who might to be sent to give him relief. This reveals the lack of heart in the rich man.

Abraham must give the reply for eternity. Heaven is not like earth. He points out how the tables were reversed during life on earth: The rich man had all and Lazarus had nothing; the rich man had comfort and Lazarus coped with torment. In this reversed condition, there is one other crucial feature. "A great chasm," an uncrossable gulf, prevents any crossing over from one arena to the other. In effect, Abraham notes that there was a time when the rich man could have done for Lazarus what he is asking that Lazarus do for him now, but he refused to give Lazarus aid. What he measured in the past is being measured to him, only with one crucial difference: The current set-up is permanent.

Understanding that all is lost for him, he intercedes for his five brothers, whose attitude is similar to his own. He pleads for Abraham to send Lazarus to warn them. Abraham's reply here is crucial to understanding what was said both to the rich man earlier and to Luke's readers: "They have Moses and the Prophets; let them listen to them." In other words, if one wants to understand what God asks of his people in terms of caring for others, one need only read the Old Testament. A warning is useless, since the Scripture is clear on what God desires. The texts in view here are passages like Deuteronomy 14:28–29; 15:1–3; 7:12; 22:1–2; 23:19; 24:7; 25:13–14; Isaiah 3:14–15; 5:7–8; 10:1–3; 32:6–7; 58:3, 6–7, 10; Jeremiah 5:26–28; 7:5–6; Ezekiel

---

4. On Hades as the place of the dead, the Greek name for Sheol, see Psalm 86:13; in Judaism, Psalms of Solomon 14:6, 9–10; 15:10.

18:12–18; 33:15; Amos 2:6–8; 5:11–12; 8:4–6; Micah 2:1–2; 3:1–3; 6:10–11; Zechariah 7:9–10; Malachi 3:5. God's Word has made clear what he desires. Our devotion to him is seen in our care for others. Jesus calls this "the great commandment"—love God with your whole being and love your neighbor as yourself (Mark 12:28–34).

There is irony in this reply. What Abraham refuses for the brothers is accomplished for the readers of the parable by warnings issued for them. We hear a person in torment warn us to respond with compassion to those around us. In this parable, the grave speaks so that we might hear.

The rich man persists. He insists with Abraham that if one were sent from the dead to warn them, they will repent. Something spectacular and supernatural will change people's minds. Abraham's reply is also revealing, for it shows the depth of hardheartedness: Even if one rises from the dead, they will still not be convinced! Those reading the parable in the Gospel, knowing the story of Jesus, are aware just how true this remark is. Jesus' resurrection convinced only some that God was working through him. A hard heart produces eyes that do not see the activity of God and ears that do not heed his warnings, much less the revelation he graciously reveals. The parable closes with a dark and tragic note about how humanity often misses the opportunities God makes available to them.

Bridging Contexts

THE PARABLE RAISES key questions about the afterlife. What is hell like? How permanent is it? How should we read the imagery here? It also discusses relational values and what God desires of us. What does he expect of the wealthy? How does he wish us to treat one another, especially in areas where people have needs? How will he evaluate the stewardship of our lives? These features reflect basic ethical commitments God has and desires his people to possess.

I have already argued that this unit is a parable, but that does not mean that it should be read as mere story. It depicts a tragic and serious reality. The coming judgment is permanent for those rejected by God. Eternal torment is in store for those who know that God exists but have failed to respond to him in this life. Christians debate, however, whether to take the afterlife imagery literally (as if Hades is a place of fire) or more metaphorically (as a picture of a place of discomfort and torment). They also debate whether such a condition can be reversed (as the Catholic teaching on purgatory suggests) or is temporary (by arguing that the lost are annihilated).[5]

---

5. The four views noted in the last two sentences are summarized in an interactive format in John Walvoord, William Crockett, Zachary Hayes, and Clark Pinnock in *Four Views*

For all its imagery, this text suggests that suffering in the afterlife is permanent ("a great chasm" that cannot be crossed). Once entered, we cannot escape hell, and the torment there is painful and conscious. I prefer to read the imagery of "fire" in the afterlife as metaphorical of conscious suffering (most fires consume!), though the difference between the metaphorical and the literal views is slight, since both argue that the judgment is real and permanent. These images are among the most tragic and serious warnings in the Bible. Our culture avoids such ideas by denying their truth. That is a fateful gamble to make, for if one is wrong, the consequences are devastating. Refusal to respond exacts a great price.

One troubling aspect of a text like this is that it appears that God's evaluation of our lives is based on works. But this is not the way to understand the text in light of the entirety of Scripture. The ethical call of God reveals what he expects of people. Other portions of Scripture reveal the way God enables us to accomplish this calling and to reflect his will. Enablement is graciously provided by the Spirit to those who trust in him for their spiritual well-being. In other words, what God calls for here is possible because he gives us the resources to have a compassionate and caring heart.

Furthermore, the test of a heart that loves God, which is the most basic ethical command of Scripture, is that it heeds his words. How we relate to God vertically influences how we relate to people horizontally. Thus this parable states the goal in terms of our relationships and their concrete ethical expression on earth. Others texts make clear that such a response is the product of hearts that have been gifted with the blessing of the Spirit through Christ (Acts 4:32–37; 1 Tim. 6:6–18). If we love God, we must respond compassionately to his call to treat others sensitively. For if God judges for such things, those who love him should not do what he judges people for.

THE APPLICATION OF this text reinforces the application of 16:1–13. God calls the rich to share their resources with generosity. The parable is designed to have us reflect on how we respond to people like Lazarus. Though illustrated negatively, the parable is about defining compassion. A compassionate heart sees need and moves to help. Failure to do so is a failure of great ethical proportions. If we find it difficult to help someone in need, then this parable exposes the hard quality in our heart that God desires to soften.

---

on Hell, ed. W. Crockett (Grand Rapids: Zondervan, 1992). The four views are literal, metaphorical, purgatorial, and conditional.

Implications of a text like this touch on lifestyle choices we make and the way we use resources. But it is important to appreciate that aid to those in need is not limited to simply throwing money at people, even though in the short term that may be necessary. There are numerous organizations like World Vision, Samaritan's Purse, STEP, and local food kitchens whose commitment is to aid and educate those in poverty so they can stand on their own. Other institutions in our culture, including some run by governments, need support because they give children a chance to get out of debilitating backgrounds. These organizations usually need personal time donated to meet what is otherwise lacking, for the children with whom they work often lack roots or come from broken families. The people touched by these organizations need a stable environment, where there is emotional support to undertake what can be an arduous road to restoration.

Expressions of compassion in contexts of need is not merely a matter of money, but of true compassion. Had the rich man merely thrown crumbs at Lazarus, that would have been only a first step. Lazarus would have needed much more care to reach restoration. The positive example in Scripture of giving more than mere resources is the example of the good Samaritan, who fully involved himself with the man who fell among the thieves. This text challenges each one of us to ask: "What am I doing?"

The principles called for here are also illustrated in the New Testament letters (e.g., James 2:14–16, which illustrates a living faith). At the level of the local church, one way to test a community's sensitivity to such issues is to ask what ministries the church supports that are targeted to these kinds of needs. Our goal should be something more than an annual Christmas or Thanksgiving drive. God wants continual involvement in the lives of needy people.

The issue of accountability in the end is also an important application to make in terms of forming our values. If God is gracious and calls us to be gracious in turn, then we should respond to his grace by reflecting those attributes. Such a response to him indicates our desire to reflect his character to the world. As Jesus said earlier in this Gospel, disciples are to be merciful, because he is merciful (6:36).

The parable also portrays the stubborn nature of sin. Apparently not even the resurrection is a good enough witness for some. Therefore, we need not be surprised when some do not respond to God's call. The failure to see what God is doing applies not just to failing to see his revelation, but failing to see the evidence he leaves behind that points to his revelation.

Finally, one can point to the parable's underscoring of the sufficiency of all of Scripture. Jesus' parable clearly reveals that God's ethical call is set forth in Moses and the Prophets. They are more important than any miracles God could offer, since it is his voice that speaks. Today we have the benefit of even more revelation. To Moses and the Prophets one can add the Evangelists and the apostles, not to mention Jesus' own teaching. If we are to see what God wills, here is the place to find it. Scripture is worthy not just of our reading and study, but of contemplation as well. Through it we see the heart of God unto salvation.

Luke 17:1–10

J ESUS SAID TO his disciples: "Things that cause people to sin are bound to come, but woe to that person through whom they come. ²It would be better for him to be thrown into the sea with a millstone tied around his neck than for him to cause one of these little ones to sin. ³So watch yourselves.

"If your brother sins, rebuke him, and if he repents, forgive him. ⁴If he sins against you seven times in a day, and seven times comes back to you and says, 'I repent,' forgive him."

⁵The apostles said to the Lord, "Increase our faith!"

⁶He replied, "If you have faith as small as a mustard seed, you can say to this mulberry tree, 'Be uprooted and planted in the sea,' and it will obey you.

⁷"Suppose one of you had a servant plowing or looking after the sheep. Would he say to the servant when he comes in from the field, 'Come along now and sit down to eat'? ⁸Would he not rather say, 'Prepare my supper, get yourself ready and wait on me while I eat and drink; after that you may eat and drink'? ⁹Would he thank the servant because he did what he was told to do? ¹⁰So you also, when you have done everything you were told to do, should say, 'We are unworthy servants; we have only done our duty.'"

THIS SHORT UNIT contains four parts: a warning (vv. 1–3a), instruction (vv. 3b–4), exhortation (vv. 5–6), and a parable about service (vv. 7–10).[1] Each of these parts concerns some aspect of discipleship, a topic Jesus highlights as he draws closer to Jerusalem.

The warning (vv. 1–3a) treats the topic of causing someone to sin. This is inevitable within the Christian community, but woe to the one responsible for being the source of stumbling in the body. The term *skandalon* prob-

---

1. Conceptual parallels exist to these texts. For Luke 17:1–3a, Matthew 18:6–7 is similar. Mark 9:42 is like Luke 17:2. For Luke 17:3–4, similar ideas are present in Matthew 18:15, 21–22. Luke 17:6 is like Matthew 17:20, while Mark 9:28–29 is comparable to Luke 17:5–6. The parable is unique to Luke. The repetition may well indicate that Jesus taught certain ideas in various settings.

ably refers to serious enticement to sin, like actions leading to apostasy.[2] Jesus says the fate of the culprit is worse than if a huge millstone were placed around his neck and he were cast into the sea. In sum, death would be a better fate than to face God's judgment for his crime. That is how seriously Jesus takes causing sin in the body. The members of the body are called the "little ones." They are special objects of God's tender care.

The major responsibility for this warning resides with teachers. So Jesus issues a final warning for his disciples to watch themselves (v. 3a). The present imperative indicates the constancy of attention Jesus' followers should give to their spiritual walk.

But though the warning about sin is serious, equally important is the need to forgive (vv. 3b–4). Sin is to be rebuked, which reveals the community's commitment to righteousness. Yet the sinner's repentance should produce the church's forgiveness. Disciples pursue spirituality in dependence on each other for support. Religion is not a private pursuit, but is a shared family responsibility. It is a supportive environment, not a matter of keeping a constant watch on each other. This is why forgiveness is central.

The possibility of forgiveness raises the question of how often forgiveness should follow repentance. Jesus answers that seven times a day is required— a figurative way of saying that as often as repentance occurs, forgiveness should be given. The sin that needs forgiveness involves the participants ("if he sins *against you*"). This means that accountability for keeping relationships working comes from those involved in the events. Often in such situations, the participants refuse to interact with each other, but Jesus argues that maturity handles such matters directly.

Another key characteristic of discipleship is having faith (vv. 5–6). The issue for Jesus is not the amount of faith, but its presence. The disciples ask for their faith to be increased, but Jesus replies that all that is needed is faith the size of a mustard seed. Such faith is able to take a black mulberry tree with a deep root system and say to it, "Be rooted up and planted in the sea," and it would happen. In other words, a small faith can accomplish amazing things and lead to unusual events.[3]

A final image in the passage is a short parable about service (vv. 7–10). Jesus discusses the life of a slave. Whether he plows or watches sheep, when

---

2. Stählin, "σκάνδαλον," *TDNT*, 7:351, refers to its use as involving sin that leads to defection. The millstone was a heavy upper stone in a grinding mill. The distinction about sin leading to apostasy is important. Jesus has the most destructive situations in mind.

3. A grammatical touch makes the point even stronger. The verb describing the tree's obedience is in the aorist tense, in a contrary-to-fact condition. It suggests that the tree was ready to obey the command. In effect, the remark says, "If you had done this, it would have obeyed you!"

he comes in, the slave will still have to fix dinner for his master and then serve him before he gets to have his own meal.[4] Yet no thanks is offered to the slave, since he is simply doing what is commanded. The service of Jesus' servants works in precisely the same way. Our attitude should be that we have only done our duty. Obedience is not a matter of merit (though God does honor it), but of duty. We do not have the right to pick and choose what to obey.

 EACH OF THE four major parts in this text deal with fundamental relational aspects of our walk with God. The warning about being the cause of sin in the body is a serious remark about the responsibility members share. Jesus knows that sin will come. Nonetheless, one should not be the cause of any stumbling in the body, for God takes the source of sin in the body seriously. The remark here is like the warning of 1 Corinthians 3:17: The one who causes destructive damage to the body is himself destroyed by God.[5] The warning crosses the centuries. God holds the source of such falls totally accountable.

The second topic treats corporate relationships. It, too, concerns mutual accountability in the body. Sin must be rebuked and forgiven. Both parts of the equation are important. The rebuking of sin shows how seriously the community takes the pursuit of righteousness, while forgiveness points to how sincerely the community honors the road to restored relationships. No matter which side of the divide one is on, the goal is to produce a community where the destructive effects of sin are not allowed to eat at the body. As 1 Corinthians 5:7 argues, unchecked sin is like yeast roaming through the community, a virus that grows if unchecked. If forgiveness is not offered, there is no way to restoration after someone turns from sin. The absence of restoration can be as deadly to the life of a community as the presence of sin, since through restoration we can grow beyond our past failures.

Faith also plays a central role in our spiritual lives. We are saved by faith and we walk by faith (Gal. 5:25; Heb. 11). There is no more basic attitude of the spiritual life than to walk with God in trust, which means recognizing what God is capable of doing while accepting what he delivers. Jesus is primarily concerned *that* faith is present; he is not concerned about its size. We must ask God to do the extraordinary or enable us to exercise spiriutal

---

4. The use of the Greek particle *ouchi* in verse 7 indicates that Jesus' question expects a positive reply.

5. For more on the force of 1 Corinthians 3:17, see "Bridging Contexts" section on Luke 12:35–48.

strength, not in a selfish way but for our spiritual welfare (cf. 11:9–13). Faith may mean having the strength to endure rejection. It may mean trusting God for spiritual insight. It may mean asking him for deliverance. It may mean accepting what he has brought into our lives and relying on his grace (1 Cor. 12:7–10). Above all, it means never letting go of the commitment to go where God is taking us. What it does not mean is treating God like a king of a "give me what I want" machine, who simply answers requests we make because we have them. Our spiritual development requires that he be in charge of where we are going.

The last timeless theme of this text is service without strings attached. Sometimes we want to bargain with God, but Jesus instructs us to understand what being a servant of God means. A "servant" (*doulos;* cf. Rom. 1:1) responds to God without question as a matter of duty. This text, however, should not be left by itself when it comes to the theme of service, for God does honor faithful service (see 12:37). The balance is important, because the servant needs to appreciate what his duty is, while God is clear that service well done is honored. God rewards those who serve without thought of reward.

I once heard a message on this text, given by a person in corporate authority, that stressed the duty side of the equation alone. The message communicated was that subordinates should do their job, period. There was no sense of collegiality or no sense that the ministering institution also had responsibility. The point of the balance is that servants should serve dutifully, but the one who is served may not brusquely treat his servants as if they mean nothing (Eph. 6:8). Our heavenly Father does not treat his children that way, and neither should we.

JESUS' WARNING ABOUT being the cause of sin treats the possibility of leading others in the community into serious sin. Such defection can result from serious doctrinal deviation or be caused by dangerous practical advice about sin. The church today is prone to pay too little attention to details of doctrinal teachings in God's revelation, a response that puts the community at risk. Some practical errors emerge because theological errors stand behind them. The spiritual and theological advice we give should be carefully thought through in terms of its faithfulness to maintaining a strong walk with God. No doubt Jesus is anticipating here the battles with false teachers like those Paul warns the Ephesians about in Acts 20:28–30 (cf. also 1 Tim. 4:1–5; 2 Tim. 3:1–9). These warnings deal with a kind of ethical indifference to the presence of sin or to the lack of pursuit of moral values. These admonitions suggest that truth and integrity belong together. God cares about character as well as truth. Both need to be pursued with diligence and tender loving care.

Regarding balancing the pursuit of righteousness with the necessity for restoration, a major applicational test of this balance is whether a community is recognized simply for being a watchdog about sin or has a reputation for compassion that seeks quickly and unconditionally to restore a sinner, even again and again ("seven times in a day"!). It is easy to keep those who have sinned down in the muck of their past failure and constantly remind them of past missteps. Both in our personal and community relationships, this tendency to remind is not a sign of true forgiveness.

Sin must be acknowledged and dealt with. But once confessed, the blood of Jesus is sufficient cleansing to prohibit any additional requirements being added on top. Discipline may require some time to pass before one takes on full responsibilities again, in order to demonstrate that the issues leading to the failure have been dealt with, but the acceptance of someone who sins and repents should not be a matter of debate. Friends should give support and encouragement to those who stood previously rebuked, so that the love of the community for those who seek to honor God is evident.

This passage also requires us to reflect why communities are so slow to forgive. Do they feel they must control restoration? Is it out of a sense of risk about God being taken advantage of? Is God not big enough to take care of himself? Are not people ultimately accountable to him for their response and not us? We should reflect on such questions when we are hesitant to forgive. It is too easy to want to make people pay in full for their failures rather than to create an environment where restoration is possible. We must consider how to make our communities sensitive to sin, but not closed to grace.

When one thinks of the issue of trust, the applications are numerous. Do I trust God that he desires what is best for my spiritual welfare? Do I recognize that sometimes suffering is what is best for spiritual growth? Do I believe he can transform my heart, so I can walk righteously? Do I believe that God will support my efforts to share his goodness with others? Do I trust God to fight for me when I uphold his honor? Can I trust God to reverse a severely damaged relationship? The spheres in which true faith can exercise itself in uprooting trees and planting them in the sea are endless.

Of course, the remarks about uprooting trees and planting them in the sea are figurative for doing amazing things. Faith has a way of opening us up for God's use and presence to work in us. This is more than positive thinking; it is relating to and connecting with God. Sometimes faith requires going in a direction that differs from the direction our culture says we should go. Sometimes it means walking by faith and not by sight (2 Cor. 5:7), trusting in God's care for us. Faith that merely means living life on natural instincts is not faith. No trust is required if we simply cruise through life on the basis of our own expectations. In this passage, Jesus does not call for a magic amount of faith, just its presence. When we lean on him, his strength can carry a long way and will accomplish amazing things.

The major application of this text with respect to service is to avoid getting in a bargaining position with God. In fact, we should not have a reward mentality at all. We should serve God because of who he is and because he is worth serving. If a good slave does his duty for his master faithfully, how much more should God's children, as those loved by him, serve him faithfully? Service, obedience, and duty are not rights we negotiate with God to exercise. They are the natural outgrowth of appreciating his act of grace in saving us, so we might bring honor to him.

The earlier picture in 7:41–43 of forgiven sin as a debt removed helps us to appreciate the attitude reflected here. If someone paid a lifelong debt for me so that I am now freed from its limitations, my gratitude would cause me to honor that person for what he or she had done. Our service for God comes as a duty, because he freed us to have a relationship with him.

Note, however, that though Jesus uses the picture of the slave here, the Scripture also uses the image of adoption to express our position with God. That image is also revealing, because children who love what their parents have provided for them will respond to them with faithfulness. In fact, one can compare the family-adoption image to an orphan rescued and brought to a new home. Expressing appreciation for God's action means being both a faithful child and a faithful servant. Given our past, I have no right to negotiate with God about the conditions of my service. I serve willingly and proudly to honor the privileged position he has obtained for me.

Luke 17:11–19

Now on his way to Jerusalem, Jesus traveled along the border between Samaria and Galilee. [12]As he was going into a village, ten men who had leprosy met him. They stood at a distance [13]and called out in a loud voice, "Jesus, Master, have pity on us!"

[14]When he saw them, he said, "Go, show yourselves to the priests." And as they went, they were cleansed.

[15]One of them, when he saw he was healed, came back, praising God in a loud voice. [16]He threw himself at Jesus' feet and thanked him—and he was a Samaritan.

[17]Jesus asked, "Were not all ten cleansed? Where are the other nine? [18]Was no one found to return and give praise to God except this foreigner?" [19]Then he said to him, "Rise and go; your faith has made you well."

In the next section of the journey portion of Luke's Gospel (17:11–18:8), eschatology becomes a crucial theme. After a miracle that highlights the importance of faith and gratitude (17:11–19), Jesus notes that the kingdom is in their midst (17:20–21). He then details the circumstances that will precede his final return (17:22–37), which will be a frightening time of judgment. In the meantime, disciples should pray for vindication, though Jesus wonders who will keep the faith in the interim (18:1–8). The unit as a whole calls for trust in God's plan and timing. The saints should walk faithfully with him and look expectantly for Christ's return, when he will vindicate them.

Luke begins this miracle story, unique to this Gospel (17:11–19), by drawing our attention again to Jesus' journey.[1] This is the fourth of five miracles in the journey section (11:14; 13:10–13; 14:1–4; 18:35–43). Jesus is now moving east to west along the boundary between Samaria and Galilee. In other words, Luke's journey section is not a straight-line journey, but a journey of fate (note 10:38–42, when Jesus was at Martha's house, located in Bethany near Jerusalem [John 11:18]).

---

1. Though some equate this miracle with Mark 1:40–45, the parallel to that miracle is Luke 5:12–16; thus, the present miracle is unique to this Gospel. Even at the end of his journey, Jesus is still ministering with compassion, despite the growing rejection around him.

The miracle contains a double level of cultural tension, since the main figure is both a leper and a Samaritan. Lepers were culturally isolated (see 5:12–16), and Samaritans were disliked by Jews for their religious defection and for being racial half-breeds (see 9:51–56). The idea of a Samaritan leper receiving God's help was undoubtedly shocking to many, since they had written off people in either category as being beyond help.

As Jesus enters a village, he is approached by ten lepers. The fact that they draw near to him says much, since lepers were expected to isolate themselves from people. What they know about Jesus tells them that he is approachable. Still, they call to him from a distance, honoring the Old Testament command not to mix with other people (Lev. 13:45–46; Num. 5:2–3). As we noted in Luke 5:12–16, leprosy refers to a wide range of conditions, but the possibility of those conditions being contagious meant isolation until the condition cleared.

The lepers ask for mercy (NIV "have pity on us!"). This is a cry for compassion, a request that comes frequently to Jesus (Matt. 9:27; 15:22; 17:15; 20:30–31; Mark 10:47–48; Luke 16:24 [not to Jesus]; 18:38–39). They want to be healed. Given all the conflict that has attended Jesus' ministry, the reader wonders if Jesus' healing will continue. Can grace be manifested in the midst of opposition?

Jesus immediately removes any doubt about his desire to show compassion. Those who come to him receive relief, even from a distance. He tells them to go show themselves to the priest, as the law commands (Lev. 13:19; 14:1–11). One does not go to the priest until he or she has been healed, so Jesus' telling them to go indicates healing will occur. If they believe Jesus, they will obey.[2] As the lepers turn, they are healed. This event pictures God's grace. The healings allow these men to return to a normal life, though subsequent events show that the deliverance is not full forgiveness.

One of the men breaks from the group. Full of praise for God, he falls at Jesus' feet and offers thanksgiving for his cleansing. Luke notes that the man is a Samaritan, which means he comes from racial roots that represent insensitivity to God. Jesus then notes that ten men were healed, but only one ("this foreigner," a word often meaning "pagan" or "heathen")[3] has taken the time to stop and praise God for his work. "Where are the other nine?" Jesus asks. His follow-up remark to the Samaritan is similar to 7:9, where the centurion's faith is commended as being unlike anything found in Israel. In other words, Jesus does two things simultaneously here. He commends the example of gratitude in the Samaritan, and he also shows that response to him is

---

2. Jesus' order is similar to the one given to Naaman, who was told to wash in the Jordan seven times in order to be healed (2 Kings 5:10–15).

3. This is normally a derisive term; see van der Loos, *The Miracles of Jesus*, 500.

possible from those outside the nation. In some cases, those most sensitive to the gospel came from outside the nation.

Jesus then issues a final encouraging commendation. He tells the man that his "faith has made [him] well." Jesus is probably saying that although ten have experienced the blessing of healing, only one has faith and has turned to establish ties with Jesus that indicate the presence of salvation (cf. 7:50; 8:48; 18:48). The deliverance Jesus affirms here is greater than the healing the man has experienced. He had learned everything the miracle can teach him.[4] Faith and salvation again merge.[5]

 THE PORTRAIT OF Jesus' compassion, even in the midst of rejection, is a crucial theme here. Jesus continues to minister to any who reach out to him. None is turned away. When people cry for pity, Jesus offers it. God is not an ogre who hoards his compassion and needs persuading to exercise it. All he asks is that we approach him humbly and on his terms, recognizing that he is ready to help.

Also significant in this story is the example of who is helped. Jesus reaches out to those who are regarded as outsiders. He touches especially those whom others have often given up on. Similarly, our ministry needs to share the scope of audience that Jesus' ministry had.

The notes of faith and gratitude are also responses that span the centuries. The Samaritan knew that God cared and that Jesus had a major role in that response. His turning to Jesus in praise and recognition pictures the link between God's activity and Jesus' work. The gratitude the Samaritan showed represents a fundamental response of faith to God's work. He appreciated his restoration to life and expressed his appreciation toward God and life through what Jesus did. To understand the isolation that sin produces is to understand the freedom that salvation brings.

 EXPRESSING APPRECIATION TO God is an attitude that is growing in the church today, and that is a good thing. When I was in college and seminary, the major feature of worship was teaching. We sang a hymn or two, but the goal of the hour was to give the

---

4. Some argue that a unique declaration of salvation is not in view here; rather, the other nine had an incomplete faith. But it seems the isolated and unique quality of Jesus' remarks to this man indicate the salvation noted here is his.

5. A. Oepke, "ἰάομαι," *TDNT*, 3:211.

preacher as much time as possible. Teaching is still important (cf. 17:1—10), but our hearts need to commune with God and express praise and gratitude to him. Luke is filled with passages where people take the time to thank and praise God.

Praise is important because it reestablishes our relationship with God on its proper terms. We appreciate his activity in our lives. In the communion of praise comes the cleansing of attitudes that life often implants in our hearts. It allows us to recount God's goodness. Restoring the balance between teaching and praise reminds us that God is not only to be understood, he is to be honored as well.

Allowing time for *personal* thanksgiving is also important. Much of the evangelical tradition highlights the quiet time. Such time is important, not only because we study about God through the Word, but we enter into relationship with him. A good quiet time includes moments of quiet reflection, prayer, and praise. We should stop in the midst of life's activities, as the Samaritan did, and give thanks. A healthy proportion of time spent with God, reflecting on his care and goodness, may save us from the bitter pills we tend to swallow because we move so hectically through life.

The reaction of the nine in not returning thanks to Jesus shows how often we tend to take God's gracious actions for granted. I have made it a habit to thank God for his grace virtually every time I pray. I hope this is not merely a formulaic exercise but a way of concretely expressing from the heart gratitude for those many gifts that come from him daily. When the blessings of life are seen as a result of God's grace, it makes us into gentler, more grateful people. Such an attitude prevents us from assessing life in terms of what we are owed, an attitude that can sow seeds of anger and bitterness.

As with many texts, a fundamental picture of salvation is present here. The Samaritan stopped to recognize that God was at work through Jesus. He understood that God's blessing came through his agent. In turning to thank Jesus, he showed how he personally appropriated the blessing Jesus had given him. In return, the Lord gifted him even more—the declaration that faith had made him well. Luke's Gospel has consistently called for decision about Jesus. Here he pictures someone who made the right choice. If we have not chosen him, Luke calls for us to follow in the Samaritan's footsteps.

The fact that the Samaritan is the example warns us against unduly limiting our ministry and whom God might bless through it. Some methods of evangelism today assert that a homogeneous ministry makes for a better community. I am not sure. It makes community easier, but there is something to be said for forging a community out of disparate elements to show just how far and wide God's reconciliation can go (Eph. 3:2—13). We must be careful to model ministry in such a way that the suggestion never exists that God blesses some but not others. Sometimes faith shows up in surprising cross-cultural places; sometimes God crosses social or racial lines to remind us his grace is for all. Our ministries may have a natural audience, but in the midst of such ministries, we must communicate values and attitudes that make it clear that the gospel is for all who trust in Jesus.

Luke 17:20–18:8

✺

ONCE, HAVING BEEN asked by the Pharisees when the kingdom of God would come, Jesus replied, "The kingdom of God does not come with your careful observation, 21nor will people say, 'Here it is,' or 'There it is,' because the kingdom of God is within [among1] you."

22Then he said to his disciples, "The time is coming when you will long to see one of the days of the Son of Man, but you will not see it. 23Men will tell you, 'There he is!' or 'Here he is!' Do not go running off after them. 24For the Son of Man in his day will be like the lightning, which flashes and lights up the sky from one end to the other. 25But first he must suffer many things and be rejected by this generation.

26"Just as it was in the days of Noah, so also will it be in the days of the Son of Man. 27People were eating, drinking, marrying and being given in marriage up to the day Noah entered the ark. Then the flood came and destroyed them all.

28"It was the same in the days of Lot. People were eating and drinking, buying and selling, planting and building. 29But the day Lot left Sodom, fire and sulfur rained down from heaven and destroyed them all.

30"It will be just like this on the day the Son of Man is revealed. 31On that day no one who is on the roof of his house, with his goods inside, should go down to get them. Likewise, no one in the field should go back for anything. 32Remember Lot's wife! 33Whoever tries to keep his life will lose it, and whoever loses his life will preserve it. 34I tell you, on that night two people will be in one bed; one will be taken and the other left. 35Two women will be grinding grain together; one will be taken and the other left.

37"Where, Lord?" they asked.

He replied, "Where there is a dead body, there the vultures will gather."

---

1. We prefer a different translation from the NIV here, because it gives a misimpression about the meaning of this verse. Jesus is addressing Pharisees here, so he is not about to tell them that the kingdom of God is inside of them. Rather, he is speaking about what his presence indicates: "The kingdom of God is among you."

^{18:1}Then Jesus told his disciples a parable to show them that they should always pray and not give up. ²He said: "In a certain town there was a judge who neither feared God nor cared about men. ³And there was a widow in that town who kept coming to him with the plea, 'Grant me justice against my adversary.'

⁴"For some time he refused. But finally he said to himself, 'Even though I don't fear God or care about men, ⁵yet because this widow keeps bothering me, I will see that she gets justice, so that she won't eventually wear me out with her coming!'"

⁶And the Lord said, "Listen to what the unjust judge says. ⁷And will not God bring about justice for his chosen ones, who cry out to him day and night? Will he keep putting them off? ⁸I tell you, he will see that they get justice, and quickly. However, when the Son of Man comes, will he find faith on the earth?"

THE PHARISEES KNOW that Jesus teaches about the coming of the kingdom and that he has presented himself as having a role in its arrival. But they also know that Jesus' ministry does not look like the ministry of the kingdom that they expect. Thus they ask him to explain his teaching about the coming of the kingdom.[2] Such a question should not be surprising, for John the Baptist had asked a similar question for similar reasons (see 7:18–23).

It is possible that the Pharisees not only ask when the kingdom will come, but what signs will accompany its arrival. Jewish expectation held that the kingdom would come as a part of the Day of the Lord and that cosmic signs would welcome its arrival. The kingdom's coming tended to be portrayed in two ways. Some treated its arrival in prophetic terms, which meant that it would come within the normal movement of history. God would raise up a Messiah from the seed of David or from some other origin to deliver the

---

2. The background and parallels to this event are much discussed, since so much of what Jesus says here is conceptually paralleled in Matthew 24 and Mark 13. But the settings are different. Jesus is speaking in Matthew and Mark privately to his disciples during the last week of his ministry. Here he addresses the Pharisees, long before he reaches Jerusalem. Thus, this looks like a unique event that conceptually parallels what Jesus says to his disciples later. Regardless of whether one event was originally in view in Luke's report here or two [my preference], he has decided to split the presentation of events about the future, since other elements do appear in Luke 21.

nation.[3] Others spoke in more apocalyptically oriented imagery about a figure who would come from above with heavenly signs and great power. The Old Testament used both sets of images. Thus, a question about the kingdom's coming was a natural one. If the later history of the Pharisees is any guide, they tended to downplay the more apocalyptic side of this imagery but still anticipated God's powerful deliverance one day in the future. But it is also possible that they held in the earlier period to a more apocalyptic-like expectation, which they abandoned when the Jewish War of A.D. 70 and the Bar Kochba rebellions of 132–35 failed disastrously.

Jesus begins his reply by noting that the kingdom does not come with signs to be observed. This remark is important, because Jesus is challenging the idea that the kingdom's coming is marked with some cosmic display.[4] The Pharisees' expectations need changing. They will not need to point here and there and announce that they have found it, because the kingdom is "in their midst" or "within their reach." Jesus' point is that the kingdom hope is present in his presence. All efforts to try to determine where it might be located are a waste of energy, given its proximity.

Luke 17:21 is one of the key verses in the New Testament about the kingdom. Various meanings for "in your midst" have been proposed. (1) Some, as the NIV translates it, argue that it means "inside of you." But as we noted above in a footnote, Jesus would not address Pharisees with this kind of statement. If there is one place the kingdom is not, according to Jesus, it is inside his opponents!

(2) Others argue that the Greek present tense *erchetai* ("does . . . come," v. 20) is really a futuristic present, a position that is grammatically possible. This view takes the meaning that the kingdom will come in their midst, since so much of what Jesus goes on to say is about the future. The problem with this approach is that there are much clearer ways to make this point, such as using the future tense or even the present tense of *eimi* (Gk. "to be"). In other words, the juxtaposition of present tense with future ideas looks conscious. In addition, to argue for a future understanding puts Jesus in a contradiction. He is saying it does not come with signs, but if a future sense is taken, he goes on to enumerate the signs that signal its arrival! Finally, the term *entos* can mean "in your midst," "in your grasp," or "within your reach," a sense that fits here since Jesus and his message are the sign they need.[5]

---

3. On the variety of messianic expectations in Judaism, see J. Neusner, W. Green, and E. Frerichs, eds., *Judaism and Their Messiahs* (Cambridge: Cambridge Univ. Press, 1987).

4. Riesenfeld, "τέλος," *TDNT*, 8:50.

5. L. T. Johnson, *Luke*, 263; R. Stein, *Luke*, 438. Stein distinguishes between "in your midst" and "in your grasp," preferring the former, though noting either makes good contextual sense.

(3) It is best, therefore, to take verse 21 as teaching that the initial manifestation of the kingdom has come with Jesus' ministry.[6] The Pharisees do not need to look for the kingdom's coming in the sky, because it is already here in him! If they would just consider all the evidence all around them that portrays the presence of God's delivering power, they would not be wondering where to look. As Luke has said in various ways, the time of fulfillment is present in Jesus (4:16–30; 7:22–28; 9:1–6; 10:18; 11:20; 16:16).

Jesus indicates that the expected day of the Son of Man's coming in power is a day they will long for but will not see. That is, the powerful display of that Day is still coming. The days of the authoritative manifestation of the Messiah are not yet here. Even though many are saying, "Here it is," or "There it is," Jesus warns them not to follow such claims. When the Son of Man comes, it will be visible and obvious, like lightning flashing across the sky.[7] One crucial event must precede all of this. Luke uses the Greek term *dei* to highlight the event that must take place according to the divine plan.[8] That central event is the suffering of the Son of Man. Suffering precedes glory for Jesus. Rejection must come before glorious rule can follow.

Jesus compares the nature of the messianic judgment to the flood in the days of Noah (Gen. 7) and to the days of Lot at Sodom and Gomorrah (Gen. 19), two great periods of judgment against humanity. Just as they did then, people will engage in the affairs of life with little attention to God. In that day people will eat, drink, marry, and be given in marriage, just as they did up to the day Noah got into the ark and the Flood came. That was the end; life stopped. Similarly in the days of Lot, there was eating, drinking, buying, selling, planting, and building. But when Lot left Sodom, judgment came, and nothing of the formerly vibrant city was left. Both comparisons picture the absolute finality of God's judgment. The days of the Son of Man will be like those ancient days of judgment. The idea that there is a second chance on the judgment day is a myth as far as the Bible is concerned.

To underscore how total and swift the judgment will be, Jesus notes that people will not have time to grab things out of their houses to take with them as they attempt to flee. Nor can workers in the field go home to recover possessions. There will be no time to look back or retrace steps. That is why Jesus urges the disciples to remember Lot's wife. She looked back and in the process looked for the last time. If the world is not careful, they will not be

---

6. G. Fitzer, "φθάνω, κτλ.," *TDNT*, 9:89, n. 10; K. L. Schmidt, "βασιλεία," *TDNT*, 1:584.

7. A. Oepke, "λάμπω, κτλ.," *TDNT*, 4:25.

8. Other key uses of *dei* include 4:43; 24:7, 26, 44.

prepared for the judgment when it comes, being too tied to the things of earth to hear the voice of God.

Such misplaced allegiance is why Jesus says that the person who seeks to save his or her life will lose it, while those willing to lose their lives will save them. To choose the Lord may mean persecution from the world and putting one's life at risk, but that is better than a soul put at permanent risk (12:1–12). Deciding to honor God may mean some suffering now, but it means eternal glory to come. For Christ's followers this is the crucial point of the passage—we must be faithful until he comes.

So what does the day look like? Two people, whether in bed or grinding grain, will be divided.[9] One will be taken and the other left behind. This picture involves the separation of the righteous from the unrighteous. The examples of Noah and Lot picture those taken into deliverance. God will vindicate and protect his own. Luke 17:37 confirms this approach to the passage, since what is left is left for the vultures to devour.[10] That image is brutally graphic in portraying the total devastation and death that comes from rejecting the way to God. The disciples' question "Where?" (v. 37) asks about the locale of such judgment. Jesus deflects the question by pointing to the mood and reality of what he is saying: The day of the Son of Man will be a day of judgment. When he is done, only vultures will remain for those left in judgment. The warning about the return closes with a field full of carcasses staring at us. The imagery intends to move our soul to reflect about how devastating the end will be for some.

Luke 18:1–8 contains a parable and an application that continue the theme of Jesus' return. The application of the parable in verses 7–8 keeps our focus on the attitude we should have about his return. This section is unique to Luke and is one of the most entertaining of Jesus' parables. It portrays the importance of prayer for God's vindication of the saints. If they minister in a world that will not accept them, how should they handle the injustice of that rejection?

The answer comes in a call to pray persistently without losing heart. It is another way to call for enduring faith. Luke often treats the issue of prayer, protection, and hope (4:25–30; 11:2; 12:5; 22:41). The point is made emphatically when Luke again uses the Greek word *dei* in 18:1, which denotes

---

9. The grinding mill in view here is a handmill that grinds grain for bread. Verse 36, which supplies a third illustration of separation, is not found in the better manuscripts of Luke. But its omission is not significant, since it merely supplies an additional picture of the separation that comes at judgment.

10. The Greek word used in verse 37 can also be translated "eagles," but in this context about judgment and death, the rendering "vultures" is better.

necessity ("should"). It is important to maintain faith in the light of patiently awaiting his return.

What makes this parable so effective are its two characters, with whom it is easy to identify. The widow who needs help represents a person helpless in the society, whose only appeal for justice comes from the authority of the judge. Though we probably think of her as an older women, in the ancient world a widow could be as young as in her thirties. She is seeking justice and appeals to a judge for help. This likely involves some type of vindication involving money. The woman is persistent, a quality Jesus makes exemplary in the story.

The judge does not fear God or respect people. He is a fiercely independent man[11] and represents, in a contrasting manner, the potential for God to respond to the cries for justice from his people. Jesus' argument goes that if a judge, who is no respecter of persons, hears the cry of the widow, how much more will a compassionate God hear the cries of his people!

The fact that the main petitioner in the story is a widow means that the judge does have a cultural and moral obligation to be sensitive to her. She is in an exposed and vulnerable position. God expected the poor to be defended (Ex. 22:21–24; Deut. 24:17–18; Pss. 65:8; 82:2–7; 146:9). The widow makes her appeal again and again. She intends to get the justice she is entitled to receive from her adversary.

For some time the judge does not act, but he eventually relents. Her persistence wears him down. Anyone who has experienced persistence in a request can understand how the judge feels. The woman is "bothering" him constantly (a Greek word meaning that her actions "cause him trouble"). He anticipates being "worn out" by her (a Greek expression that can refer to giving someone a black eye!).[12] He is not worried for his reputation here, since he does not care what others think of him. But he is tired of her persistence, so he will act.

The Lord asks us to "listen to what the unjust judge says," that is, to reflect on his reaction to the persistent requests of the woman, which in turn picture the prayers of the saints. God will vindicate his people who constantly cry out to him. The remark is stated emphatically with a double negative (*ou me*): God will *definitely* vindicate his people. If an unjust judge responds to such pleas, God will certainly respond to such cries from his own chosen ones. As verse 7 makes clear, it is "justice" or vindication that will be delivered (see vv. 3, 5 for the same term). God will judge those who persecute the

---

11. On this description, see Josephus, *Antiquities* 10.5.2 § 283, who used it to describe Jehoiakim.

12. G. Stählin, "χηρα," *TDNT*, 9:450; H.-F. Weiss, "ὑπωπιάζω," *TDNT*, 8:590–91.

righteous. He will not delay, but will vindicate them with "justice, and quickly."

The remark about quick justice has received much attention, since total vindication has not yet come. It can be understood in two ways. (1) Luke desires to emphasize that the return can come at any moment, without specifying when that is. Vindication is the next thing on the divine calendar, and once it comes, in light of the eternity that follows, it will be a quick exercise of justice. (2) The vindication comes in part in the protection that God offers to his own. Even though they suffer, they do not perish, and that is a sign of their vindication. Either meaning is possible here. Perhaps a text like Sirach 35:21–23 gives help in understanding the passage:

> The prayer of the humble pierces the clouds,
> 　　and it will not rest until it reaches its goal;
> it will not desist until the Most High responds
> 　　and does justice for the righteous, and executes judgment.
> Indeed, the Lord will not delay,
> 　　and like a warrior will not be patient
> until he crushes the loins of the unmerciful
> 　　and repays vengeance on the nations;
> until he destroys the multitude of the insolent,
> 　　and breaks the scepters of the unrighteous.

God longs to vindicate the saints, and he will do so. When he does, his justice will be swift and sure, and our suffering will seem short-lived compared to the glory to follow. In the meantime he protects us.

One final thought remains. When total vindication comes, will the Son of Man (i.e., Jesus) find faith on the earth? In other words, will the delay, which is to some degree assumed in the parable, affect the faith of some, since Jesus calls us not to give up (v. 1)? No answer is given to this question, but Jesus calls for faith and prayer to hang in there over the long haul.

Bridging Contexts

CURIOSITY ABOUT WHERE history is headed can be a fascinating topic. It does not take long to see how interested many are in the future. The popularity of astrology and the fascination in figuring out biblical prophecy both testify to the power of trying to determine what the future holds. But this text is serious in claiming that such exercises in the end are speculative enterprises. In fact, Jesus does not give any eschatological text so we can figure out when he will return. The texts exist to exhort us to keep watch, to call us to faithfulness, to indicate that the end will be difficult for many, and to remind us that we are all accountable to the God who will one day manifest his awesome power in judgment. Jesus' only intent is to make clear an end is coming and to reveal its general outline so his saints will stay alert.

When Jesus treats the issue of what the end looks like, he is not trying to entertain us and satisfy our curiosity. That moment will be devastating and traumatic. It will mean decisive judgment delivered. People will be separated. Life will be given to some; death will come to others. Teaching about the end is deadly serious business because of what God will do at that time. The reality of the coming judgment is a reality that awaits humanity. God has not dated the event for us, other than to tell us it will come.

When it does, we will not need to work hard to figure that out. It will be as visible to all as lightning in the sky. The important thing is to be ready and to be on the correct side. The authority of the Son of Man in his return is a good reason to respond to the call of the Son of Man now, before that day arrives. Though Jesus will suffer, he will return. To know the Savior of the cross is to know the glorious promise and hope of vindication at the time of his return. That truth is just as true on this side of the cross as it was before he went to meet his divinely destined fate.

For Luke, the kingdom comes in stages. Some of its blessings come now with Jesus—the offer for forgiveness, the initial defeat of Satan in Jesus' ministry and at the cross, and the provision of the Spirit after his ascension. This expression of kingdom presence manifests itself in the church community that confesses Jesus as the Christ, the anointed King and Son of God. The church now bears a cross, not a sword. We are an instrument of service and faithfulness; one day we will be honored as Christ's bride.

But another phase of kingdom authority is future. So Jesus addresses his disciples about it in verses 22–37. That kingdom phase does come with signs and represents the completion of the kingdom program of God. God will then show his power, the saints will be vindicated, and justice will be accomplished. It will be a period of joy or despair, depending on how one is related to the Lord. In the interim, we are called to lose our lives and to offer ourselves to the Lord's service in ways that honor him. Many go on with life as if the Lord will never return, but we must serve him with an awareness that he may return at any moment, a day that means disaster for those who do not know him.

The longer time goes on until the Lord's return, the more relevant Jesus' parable in 18:1–7 becomes. The parable calls for prayer, persistence, and patience, something that becomes more necessary the longer we wait. At the base of the parable is an attitude about facing injustice as believers. Our call is not to strike back in kind, but to turn to God and rest in the promise he has made to vindicate us. The parable is therefore both an exhortation and a promise, whose point is as valuable now as it was two millennia ago. We must pray and keep looking to God for the vindication he will bring one day.

The second lesson of the parable is that God will bring justice. As Romans 12:19 indicates, he will one day execute vengeance. We tend in our culture to shy away from the God of judgment, but a God of judgment is really a God of accountability. We require such a concept in our everyday lives. What would our streets be like if there were no law and order, no courts and prisons? A God of justice reminds us that we cannot do as we please and be accountable to no one.

Finally, the text issues a call for faithfulness. When the Lord returns, will there be faith on earth (v. 8)? Like 12:35–48, God calls us to be faithful managers in the interim. We should pray in a way that leaves judgment to the Lord and serves him with diligence until he comes.

THE INITIAL PHASE of the kingdom of God calls us to be worthy citizens (Phil. 3:20–21). Peter calls believers "aliens and strangers in the world."[13] We are servants of the Lord, who represent him on this earth; we must not define our lives through earthly or cultural attachments. Hauerwas and Willimon define a "resident alien" this way:

> The church exists today as resident aliens, an adventurous colony in a society of unbelief. As a society of unbelief, Western culture is devoid of a sense of journey, of adventure, because it lacks belief in much more than the cultivation of an ever-shrinking horizon of self-preservation and self-expression.[14]

To experience the divine favor that comes from sharing in the kingdom promises, Jesus tells the Pharisees they must deal with him. It is no different today. In the face of great debate whether Jesus is the only way, the Lord's stress is that the road to blessing and participation in God's presence goes through him.[15] To follow him is to be different.

---

13. S. Hauerwas and W. Willimon, *Resident Aliens: Life in a Christian Colony* (Nashville: Abingdon, 1989), discusses the ethical implications of such a worldview.

14. Ibid., 49.

15. The debate centers around whether Christ is the only way to God. Some, calling for openness to God, argue that we should not restrict God to just saving through Jesus; for a solid critique of this "openness to God" theology, see R. Richard, *The Population of Heaven* (Chicago: Moody, 1994).

No area of theology breeds more speculative attention than the end times. Reactions to this issue span the spectrum. Some give their lives trying to figure out the "signs of the times" and just how close we may be to the end. Elaborate theories about how it will all unwind bring together huge sections of the Scripture into a unified scenario. A few have even set dates for Christ's return or come close to it, a commitment Scripture does not make (Mark 13:32; Acts 1:6–8).[16] Some ministries devote their full attention to such concerns. On the other end are those who view such speculation as a waste of time and energy. God knows how it will turn out, so we just should do what we are called to do in the meantime.

Both approaches are overreactions. It is hard to take the Bible seriously if one ignores its discussion about the end, since a significant portion of the Bible touches on eschatological themes about the promises of God. The only way for us to make sense of life today is to appreciate where the future is going. Scripture outlines that future, not with detailed dates, but with a general outline of what is to come. That outline is designed not to have us prepare charts, but to prepare our hearts. The return of Jesus is serious business, a time when God will be engaged in definitive judgment.

Jesus talks about the end in grim terms and gruesome detail to make clear how serious an issue judgment is for God. Judgment means accountability. In a society that tends to view adults as accountable only to themselves and their own consciences, it is a critical reminder that God does hold us responsible for our actions. That is why Jesus in the parable of Luke 18:1–8 asks if he will find faith on the earth when he returns. Those who recognize their accountability to God will go through life with circumspection. To ignore the end is to risk forgetting accountability.

The world is headed towards an end when many will simply engage in life without concern for God. It will be like the days of Noah and Lot. That many end up spiritually disengaged from God should not surprise us. That does not mean that we should give up in trying to share the gospel with those who are simply traveling through life. Too much is at stake to simply ignore our neighbors. When the Lord returns to exercise judgment, there will be no second chance. For those who are his, the blessed rule of his kingdom will last forever; but for those who miss out, it is an opportunity missed forever. The passage closes with the bleak image of the vultures gathered, not

---

16. For a chronicling of such attempts, see Paul Boyer, *When Time Shall Be No More: Prophecy Belief in Modern American Culture* (Cambridge, Mass.: Belknap, 1992). Among the more famous predictions were those by William Miller in the nineteenth century (1844) and those more recently who suggested that the generation after Israel's return to the land of Palestine in 1948 would see the Lord's return, making 1988 the key date. But such efforts appear almost annually.

because there is joy in the judgment to come, but because the tragedy is all too real. This text screams to every person to choose wisely when it comes to the things of God. There is too much at stake to make an erroneous choice.

Furthermore, every moment until the Lord returns is an opportunity to be God's instrument in changing the destiny of someone who does not yet know him. God is delaying the day of judgment, being patient and allowing time for others to come to him (2 Peter 3:9). Thus the moments that remain should motivate the church to be the vessel through which others come to see and enjoy the grace of God.

The major application of the parable in Luke 18:1–6 is to keep our eyes focused on the hope that is yet to come. We wait for his return with expectation, but in the meantime we have been saved and have been called to be a people zealous to serve God with good works (Titus 2:11–14). Though the struggle of this life is sometimes hard and even unfair to Christians as they seek to honor God in a world that often does not honor God, we must not lose heart. Sometimes the persecution or the rejection can make us wonder if it is worth it. Other times we become frustrated because those unfaithful to God look as if they have everything. But we must remember that such a life is the "full payment" they get for their choice to pursue riches on this earth. There will come a time when that cupboard is bare. So Christ urges us to pray to God that we might draw on his faithfulness for daily strength.

The parable also reveals something significant about prayer. Most prayer meetings I attend take on a predictable character. We pray for one another's needs—usually issues like finances and health. Occasionally a request for the opportunity to share with a friend or a neighbor comes in, along with the obligatory prayer for the leaders of our country and missionaries. The victims of natural or political disaster also get attention.

What is often missing in such meetings are the types of concerns reflected in this parable's call for persistent prayer. We are to pray earnestly for the vindication of our testimony in the world and our eventual full redemption by the hand of God. To use the imagery of the parable, do we as a church community "wear God down" with such a request for vindication? The prayer most like the one called for here in Scripture appears in Acts 4:23–31, where the church asked for enablement to perform what God had called them to do, even in the face of fierce persecution. They desired vindication, that God would show his presence powerfully through their ministry. We should do no less.

Luke 18:9–17

❦

To some who were confident of their own righteousness and looked down on everybody else, Jesus told this parable: ¹⁰"Two men went up to the temple to pray, one a Pharisee and the other a tax collector. ¹¹The Pharisee stood up and prayed about himself: 'God, I thank you that I am not like other men—robbers, evildoers, adulterers—or even like this tax collector. ¹²I fast twice a week and give a tenth of all I get.'

¹³"But the tax collector stood at a distance. He would not even look up to heaven, but beat his breast and said, 'God, have mercy on me, a sinner.'

¹⁴"I tell you that this man, rather than the other, went home justified before God. For everyone who exalts himself will be humbled, and he who humbles himself will be exalted."

¹⁵People were also bringing babies to Jesus to have him touch them. When the disciples saw this, they rebuked them. ¹⁶But Jesus called the children to him and said, "Let the little children come to me, and do not hinder them, for the kingdom of God belongs to such as these. ¹⁷I tell you the truth, anyone who will not receive the kingdom of God like a little child will never enter it."

Original Meaning

The unit of Luke 18:9–30 contains three scenes: the commendation of the tax collector over the Pharisee (vv. 9–14), the picture of childlike faith (vv. 15–17), and the rich ruler's exchange with Jesus (vv. 18–30). In each case, the basic issue is humility or whom will I trust? The tax collector has a humble trust, while the rich man trusts his possessions for his security. In contrast stand the disciples who have left all for Jesus. They receive his commendation as well, and the promise that to those who have faith God gives the richest of blessings, including eternal life.

The parable of the tax collector and Pharisee in 18:9–14 is found only in Luke. It focuses on the type of person God blesses (5:27–32; 7:29–30). What commends a person to God? Is it the qualities that the world emphasizes, like self-sufficiency and social status? This parable is really the parable of the two prayers. In those prayers appear two kinds of hearts, whose contrast is not only seen in the way they make their request, but also in the way they approach God.

The text is explicit about its audience: those "who were confident of their own righteousness and looked down on everybody else." "Were confident" is a perfect participle, a tense that indicates a residing confidence that never wanes. "Looked down" is a strong word, which can also be translated "despised" or "rejected" (23:11; Acts 4:11; Rom. 14:3, 10). It is easy to compare ourselves to people who do not measure up to us, at least in our own eyes! The characters in the scene cannot be more different in origin. The Pharisee is a respected religious leader, while the tax collector is viewed as a leech on society and a traitor for working with Rome.[1] Given it is a time for private prayer, this event may have taken place at any time of the day.

The Pharisee approaches God boldly and begins what looks like a praise psalm: "I thank you, God." In this type of psalm, the petitioner usually thanks God for something God has done or some blessing he has provided. But this Pharisee is grateful for himself, that he is not like other sinners, such as robbers, evildoers, adulterers, or even a tax collector. He honors God by fasting voluntarily twice a week (probably Monday and Thursday) and by tithing. Such a fast included only bread and water. Since it is above and beyond the call of duty, the Pharisee wears it as a badge of achievement that should cause God to give him favor. Tithing means that one-tenth of the Pharisee's earnings went to the Lord.

But this prayer is actually a distortion of the praise psalm, because when the Pharisee is done, his prayer in effect is, "I thank you, God, that I am so great!" In fact, one gets the impression that God should be honored that this "faithful" Pharisee is on his team. Five times in two verses he uses the first person singular pronoun, making himself the major subject of the prayer.[2] He even puts down the tax collector praying beside him, referring to him derisively as "this tax collector."

In contrast, the tax collector does not stand up but approaches God with a sense of distance. He does not look up to heaven, a sign of contrition, but beats his breast, fully aware that he approaches God as a sinner.[3] His prayer is different: "God, have mercy on me, a sinner." There is no self-congratulation. There is no summary of his good deeds. There is no sense that God ought to feel honored or obligated to the petitioner. There is but one recog-

---

1. For the ancient view of tax collectors, see S. Kistemaker, *The Parables of Jesus*, 259.
2. O. Michel, "τελώνης," *TDNT*, 8:105.
3. J. Jeremias, "αἴρω," *TDNT*, 1:185–86; W. Michaelis, "ὀφθαλμός," *TDNT*, 5:377, n. 11; G. Stählin, "τύπτω," *TDNT*, 8:262 n. 18; 264.

nition: his need for God's mercy. His request for mercy uses a Greek word that in the LXX translates the Hebrew word meaning "to cover." Its background and use assume that the petitioner cannot earn forgiveness, so he simply makes an appeal for God's forgiving compassion.[4] He comes to God desiring only to improve his relationship to God.

Jesus' comment closes the passage. He endorses the tax collector's humility. The one justified before God, the one whose prayer is heard, is not that of the religious man with all of his works. The prayer God hears is the call for mercy. Jesus explains why. Those who exalt themselves will be humbled, while the humbled will be lifted up. As I have heard preachers say in a homespun way, "The best way up is down, and the quickest way down is to lift oneself up." This principle rings throughout this Gospel (1:52–53; 6:20–26; 10:29–37, 38–42; 11:37–41; 12:21; 14:11). Bravado and appearance mean nothing. Résumé and social status mean nothing. Self-reliance means nothing. What counts is a heart that appreciates what God can give. The tax collector, therefore, is the one whom Jesus says goes home justified. In seeking God's forgiveness, he receives it.

The short passage in 18:15–17 shows just how subtle humility is, while also exhorting the disciples to have faith.[5] When Jesus is ministering, many seek to have him touch their little children. The disciples are convinced that babies and toddlers are not important and that such desires are a waste of the Lord's time. So they try to stop the parents from coming.

Jesus takes the opposite attitude. He invites the children to come to him, because they are important people. They picture what the kingdom is all about. One must trust God with the simple faith and humility of a dependent child. The kingdom is made up of people who display such qualities. How can his disciples regard these illustrations of kingdom realities as unimportant? The disciples still have much to learn. The way we value people is not how God sees them.

Jesus drives the point home by noting that only those who receive the kingdom like a child enter it. Entrance into the kingdom is a matter of humility that recognizes a need for God. What is commended in children is their inherent dependence, for they bring nothing but themselves to the feet of Jesus.

---

4. F. Büchsel, "ἱλάσκομαι," *TDNT*, 3:315.

5. This passage is paralleled in Matthew 19:16–22 and Mark 10:17–22. This is the first passage with a substantial Marcan parallel since Luke 9:49.

Bridging Contexts

JESUS TREATS THE basic attitudes of humility and pride here (cf. 14:1–12). The values God honors are those whereby we look at ourselves in light of who he is, not through the distortion that comes from comparing ourselves to others. But the attitude of the Pharisee is all too often the rule—that of judging people by sight or simply because of their station in society. This is an unfortunate error, since we often are such poor readers of character. How often does the socially smooth operator turn out to be a moral snake, while simple people turn out to be full of integrity? The text also reveals much about the human heart, for we often approach God himself on the basis of favorably comparing ourselves to others.

The problem of pride is one that rides the centuries. Humility is rare in a society that loves to brag about uniqueness and merit. But merit has a negative side. It can become a manipulative way to invoke a bargaining chip. Rather than approach God on the basis of his mercy and grace, we approach him by appealing to our track record and subtly suggesting he owes us a response. The real danger of pride is that it blinds us to how we really stand before God.

On the other hand, humility takes a sober look at where we stand, never forgetting that the standard of comparison is the character of God himself. We should never lower that bar so that we can easily jump over it. The credit of the tax collector is that he knew where he stood as he approached God. He was not a product of his own achievement, but a result of God's kindness in extending mercy. This way of approaching God alters radically the dynamic of how we see him, ourselves, and others. Understanding ourselves as the objects of mercy breeds compassion. We do not rate ourselves more highly than we ought, nor do we suggest that God is blessed to have us on our side. The privilege is ours to know him. The attitude of humility rests on his grace; pride is an affront to God.

As with so many texts in the journey section, 18:15–17 also treats fundamental values that a disciple should possess. Jesus honors people regardless of their social status. This is the opposite of what we tend to do, since we often are drawn to the powerful (cf. James 2:1–12). In fact, Jesus sees in these little ones a picture of what we are to be like.

Jesus' attitude toward these children suggests that they should be studied and appreciated for qualities God honors. In an era when many children do not have both parents, we are not only robbing them of the support God desires them to have, but often in the process we miss lessons about what our walk with our own father should look like. My children often remind me by their responses how important a good father is, and they make me reflect on how good God is to us. Like the disciples, we often ignore the child rather than embrace him or her and thus miss God's blessing.

THE LESSONS OF 18:9–14 emerge through the contrast of pride to humility. Pride preaches merit; humility pleads for compassion. Pride negotiates as an equal; humility approaches in need. Pride separates by putting down others; humility identifies with others, recognizing we all have the same need. Pride destroys through its alienating self-service; humility opens doors with its power to sympathize with the struggle we share. Pride turns up its nose; humility offers an open and lifted-up hand.

Yet in our assertive society, pride (or at least subtle forms of accomplishment tied to it) often gets the accolades, despite what it does to relationships and character. As I write, there has been a major dispute going on in sports. I live in Dallas, which means the city has a well-known football team, whose goal is to win at all costs. The new head coach, Barry Switzer, asked for and received permission to go see his son play college football on Saturdays, rather than attend the final team meeting the night before the games. The coach explained that his family came ahead of his job. As a father he wanted to show his son how important he was to him. The former head coach, Jimmy Johnson, was a man recognized as a "winner" and criticized his replacement for abandoning the team and risking defeat by distorting team values. For this former coach life was defined by winning, by sacrificing all on the altar of achievement, even wife and family. He already had lost his wife and sons years ago over his pride of achievement to be a winning football coach. But in the game of life, which coach has the distorted and losing values? What is amazing is how many people are blinded into siding with the "winner." Pride means that the task is more important than the people. The objective becomes the obstacle to human relationships. Jesus condemned pride because it is so insidiously destructive.

Humility is harder to discuss because it does not discuss itself. It simply gets out there and serves, often with sacrifice. It does not claim rights; it tries to do what is right. It does not brag about integrity; it displays it. Sometimes it is easy to miss what does not point to itself. But God sees the humble heart and lifts it up in honor. That is Jesus' challenge.

In reflecting on this text, we should ask who compares to the Pharisee today. Pharisees can come in many packages. Many pious folk are proud of their achievements and often identify themselves by talking down to others who "do" less. A parable like this applies to them. People with high visibility roles in our culture are also at risk here. They often are praised and put on a pedestal, and an air of invincibility or infallibility surrounds all that they do and say. Insofar as they feel they can learn little from others, something is wrong.

The contemporaneous tax collector might be an almost unseen deacon in the church, who faithfully and honestly week after week serves and never says a word about what he is doing. He will never be up front in the church, nor will he seek to be. He faithfully walks with God and relies on him. Such people are often unappreciated in the church, but God knows who they are. The tax collector may also be someone who is faithful to his or her spouse, fulfills responsibilities, and yet knows when he or she fails to live in a God-honoring way, the best thing to do is seek forgiveness from a gracious God. They do not wear a badge on their shirt that says "religious." They just try to be faithful to God.

Two points emerge from 18:15–17. (1) This passage calls us to reflect on faith. We should look at a child hanging on its mother's arm and ask, "Do I turn to my Father in heaven like that?" When life slows down long enough for me to look around, what often catches my eye is a child walking by the side of a parent with a small hand stretched up as high as it can go so his or her fragile fingers can lock onto the hand of Mom or Dad. I inevitably see the child's feet walking as fast as they can to keep up with the parent's gait. In that scene is a picture of a child of God. We are to place our hands in his and walk with him at our side, letting him direct our steps. Such humility, trust, and dependence calls on us to seek the face of our heavenly Father and stay close to him as we walk with him.

(2) We should also note the precious nature and importance of children. When I was in seminary, I erred here. I was only interested in the classes that treated adult ministry. Christian youth education courses were required, and I would never have chosen them for myself; they were course hours to be endured. I suspect some people view parenting or even teaching children's church the same way.

How shortsighted that thinking is! Children are among those most open to God. On our faculty are people whose testimonies include how someone took the time to care for them as a child and take them to church, even when their parents did not go. There they met God and began to serve him. There are more years of ministry in front of a child than any other age group. Children are not an inconvenience; they are the future church. In fact, statistics indicate that most people who have a relationship with God establish it before they leave home for college. Children are often most open to God and less impacted by a culture that draws them away from considering God. If Jesus can take them into his arms, so can and should we.

Luke 18:18–30

A CERTAIN RULER asked him, "Good teacher, what must I do to inherit eternal life?"

¹⁹"Why do you call me good?" Jesus answered. "No one is good—except God alone. ²⁰You know the commandments: 'Do not commit adultery, do not murder, do not steal, do not give false testimony, honor your father and mother.'"

²¹"All these I have kept since I was a boy," he said.

²²When Jesus heard this, he said to him, "You still lack one thing. Sell everything you have and give to the poor, and you will have treasure in heaven. Then come, follow me."

²³When he heard this, he became very sad, because he was a man of great wealth. ²⁴Jesus looked at him and said, "How hard it is for the rich to enter the kingdom of God! ²⁵Indeed, it is easier for a camel to go through the eye of a needle than for a rich man to enter the kingdom of God."

²⁶Those who heard this asked, "Who then can be saved?"

²⁷Jesus replied, "What is impossible with men is possible with God."

²⁸Peter said to him, "We have left all we had to follow you!"

²⁹"I tell you the truth," Jesus said to them, "no one who has left home or wife or brothers or parents or children for the sake of the kingdom of God ³⁰will fail to receive many times as much in this age and, in the age to come, eternal life."

Original Meaning

THIS TEXT DRAWS on two common tendencies in Luke: the use of contrast and the discussion of wealth as the basis for a call to faithfulness.[1] Note how often Luke discusses wealth or the associated issue of generosity (3:11; 5:11; 6:23–26, 34–35, 38; 7:5; 8:3, 14; 10:34–35; 11:41; 12:13–21, 33; 14:12–14, 33; 16:9–13, 19–31; 18:22; 19:8).[2] Handling material goods is a major life and spiritual issue.

---

1. This text has parallels in Matthew 19:16–30 and Mark 10:17–31. The Lucan version is closer to Mark in the way it proceeds than Matthew.

2. R. Stein, *Luke*, 459.

Contrasts echo throughout this text. The rich man stands in contrast to the disciples in verses 28–30. Interestingly, we know this man as the rich *young* ruler, but Luke does not relate his age, just his status (Matt. 19:22 tells us he is young). Luke is more interested in the man's attitude than suggesting any kind of immaturity, since the attitude is destructive no matter how old a person is. This rich man also stands in contrast to the blind man who seeks Jesus' healing in 18:35–43. That man, though blind, sees clearly, while the rich man, though possessing eyes, has his vision clouded by his possessions. The rich man is like the Pharisee in 18:9–14, in that he is more concerned with where he stands than in knowing God's grace.

The text begins with the ruler asking Jesus what he must do to inherit eternal life (cf. 10:25). He is probably someone of social status, who is not only wealthy but holds some level of civic power. He wants to know how he can be sure he will be saved when God passes out the gift of life.[3] The ruler addresses Jesus as "Good teacher," perhaps in an attempt to gain a good hearing. But Jesus puts the ruler on notice at the start that he will not be won over with a flattering greeting, warning the man that only God is good. When Jesus exhorts the ruler to go in a difficult direction with his wealth, the teaching is not accepted as good but is rejected with a change of countenance (v. 24).

The issue of goodness raises the question of honoring God. Jesus replies in terms of God's commandments (see Ex. 20:12–16; Deut. 5:16–20), omitting the ones related to God. The Old Testament basis for Jesus' reply is Deuteronomy 30:15–20, which shows that loving God first from the heart means not being drawn away into various expressions of idolatry that the world offers.[4] One of the key dangers of wealth is that possessions come first and people slip down the list. Adultery, murder, stealing, and lying should not to be a part of a believer's walk, while honoring parents should be. Jesus calls for character that is not self-serving and does not take advantage of others.

The ruler replies that he has been obedient to these commands since his youth (probably when he assumed adult responsibility around age thirteen). There is nothing for him to learn or fear. Jesus replies by adding an additional test to see if the man will serve God. Remember that the ruler has just called Jesus a "good teacher." Surely he will respect the challenge of this mentor.

---

3. The expression "to inherit life" has a rich Jewish background. See Psalm 36:9, 11, 18; Daniel 12:2; 2 Maccabees 7:9; 4 Maccabees 15:3; 1 Enoch 37:4; 40:9; 58:3; Psalms of Solomon 3:12.

4. The parallel in Matthew 19:19 cites the command to love one's neighbor, which is seen as a corollary and outgrowth to loving God in light of the Ten Commandments as a whole.

Jesus then calls on the man to sell everything he has and give to the poor; by doing so he will receive treasure in heaven. After that, he must follow Jesus and join him in walking with God (v. 22).

The combination is crucial to understanding the nature of Jesus' reply. Will this man prefer what earth can give him or what heaven offers? This is not a test of works but a probing of his heart, an examination of his fundamental allegiance. Jesus is asking, in effect, "Are you covetous, and is your security in God's call or in your possessions?" Jesus has already taught that one cannot serve God or Money (16:13), so the reply is designed to see which the man prefers.[5] In sum, Jesus wants to know if his faith is in the things of the earth or in the way of God.

The man reacts with sadness. He is wealthy and would have to give up much. Jesus' commentary in verses 24–25 implies that the personal identity of a rich person is so bound up with the things of this earth that it is all but impossible for him to turn everything over to God's care (cf. 6:24; 12:15, 21; 16:9). The remark about the eye of the needle sounds strong. If a camel going through the eye of a needle is impossible, where does that leave the rich for whom entry into the kingdom is even harder?[6]

Jesus' remarks to the rich man have traumatized the disciples. The rich were often seen as the blessed. After all, did not Old Testament teaching on wealth suggest as much (Prov. 6:6–11; 10:4; 28:19)? If the rich cannot get into heaven, who can? Who can be saved (v. 26)? But we should note that the rich are not always portrayed as the recipients of divine blessing in the Old Testament. The prophets often took them to task for not using their resources generously, and blessings did not automatically await them (Amos 6; Micah 6). Jesus' call stands solidly in the Old Testament prophetic tradition.

What human beings cannot do, God is able to do. He must change the human heart and open the way to himself. There are those who are able to do what Jesus asks. God makes it possible. So Peter steps forward and raises the fundamental question. His statement, "We have left all to follow you," in effect is asking whether they have passed the "sell all" test. Have they done what Jesus is asking the ruler to do? Jesus' reply basically responds affirma-

---

5. There is another indication of the rhetorical force of Jesus' request of the rich man. Zacchaeus was a rich man who sold half of his possessions to give to the poor; yet Jesus said of him that salvation had come to his house. This rich man simply turns away, showing that he does not even want to discuss the call with Jesus. His heart is firmly rooted in his material identity.

6. Some have argued that Jesus is alluding to Needle's Eye Gate in Jerusalem here, but this is entirely unlikely, since then there is no figure of speech to interpret. A camel going through a gate was not a difficult assignment; see D. Bock, *Luke* (Downers Grove, Ill.: InterVarsity, 1994), 301.

tively to Peter. Anyone who leaves home, wife, children, or the family for the sake of the kingdom of God will receive much more family in this life, the family of God, and eternal life in the age to come.

The passage ends with the same topic that began it: "eternal life." We must ally ourselves in relationship to Jesus and rest all our welfare on his care. We call this faith—trusting Jesus with our welfare is to enter a new family and to receive the gift of life. Jesus is saying to Peter that he has that gift. God has made possible what would have otherwise been impossible.

THIS TEXT'S EXAMINATION of one's fundamental allegiance is really an exposure of the most subtle forms of idolatry. It is a timeless test of the heart. We must pause and reflect as we read this story, asking why Jesus would make such a challenge. Like a prophet, he probes the heart and raises a question that not only this rich man needs to hear, but all of us as well. This man thought he had a righteous heart, but Jesus' question exposed that he had other gods who offered him more than he thought heaven could give. The call to sell all touched a nerve that exposed this man's lack of allegiance to God and should have led to his turning to God for grace. But he is not interested in laying his priorities out before God.

So what is Jesus' view of wealth? That question requires that we look at several texts, not just this one. This background to the question and the later example of Zacchaeus show that the central issue is not selling everything in order to know God. Salvation does not come through an empty bank account. Rather, what bridges the contexts is the question of where our trust resides. Does it center in our possessions and the security they give? Or does it center in God? Do we recognize that everything we have is part of the stewardship God gives us that is not ours to own? Will we pretend to be righteous, while we hold to other resources as security in the face of God's offer?

Peter, Zacchaeus, and others passed the test, not because they literally sold all (Zacchaeus continued to own resources), but because the direction of God became the central orientation for their lives. They had left all for the sake of the kingdom. Even though in some moments there was gross failure, as in Peter's denials, their hearts were turned in the right direction.

Also central to this passage is the recognition that God changes the human heart. What humans are too self-focused to accomplish on their own, God does by changing the heart. Salvation is an act of his grace; he is able to cause us to see differently. Even the rich can become poor in spirit through his work.

Furthermore, when God directs us, the resources we have are put to use for the needy. Jesus called the rich man to turn his resources over to God so that they could be used to help such people. This type of generosity demonstrates a heart turned toward God. When God is truly sought out, he points us to service for others. Jesus' own ministry is the best example of this.

THIS PASSAGE CHALLENGES us to ask where our fundamental anchors of identity lie. Possessions can be one such root. They can shade our sight from the central values and chain our heart to the wrong point of identity. Few biblical figures are as tragic as this young rich man as he walks away from Jesus' invitation. But others factors, such as achievement, pride, and family, can also reside in the place that should be reserved for God. Anything that excessively anchors us to the earth rather than freeing us as commissioned representatives from God indicates a breakdown in the discipleship process. What is really frightening is how easy it is for all of us to choose earth over heaven. We do not, of course, have to be perfect to be saved, but God's people must recognize just how important trust in him is. Through hearts focused on the Lord, we receive eternal life and come to know him more fully.

The text also suggests we should carefully consider how to use the resources God gives us. Luke 12:13–21 and 16:1–13 have raised this question already, but this passage highlights the direction our resources should go. Meeting the needs of the poor is a concrete expression of compassion. In a world where a few people, relatively speaking, hold the majority of the world's resources, application of this passage is not easy. Needs exist everywhere. The rich who have turned to God should act concretely by performing deeds of ministry and service to those who have genuine needs (cf. discussion on 4:16–30; 14:7–14).

Perhaps the most fundamental application is one that Peter later develops—that Jesus' followers are as "strangers and aliens" on this earth (1 Peter 2:11ff.). When Jesus asks this man to sell all and follow him with the promise of treasure in heaven, he is asking the man to become a citizen of heaven. Such citizenship (Phil. 3:20) means that the things of earth grow strangely dim in light of our glorious and gracious relationship with God. Our resources cease to be ours; they become tools of heaven in order to serve him. Only when we have a sense of detachment from the things of earth can we give our all to God.

Another encouraging feature of this text is that such detachment is possible. Peter asked if they had done it, and Jesus assured them that they had.

It is possible to take one's heart and place its welfare into God's tender loving care. Jesus tried to get the rich man to give such trust, but he could not. Peter and the other disciples, on the other hand, had and thus joined that family of fellow travelers who honor God. In the end, they gain far more than anything they give up.

Finally, the text makes it clear that we gain an entire new family when we come to Jesus. This truth is particularly important in context where many come from fragmented families. The church becomes a place where new "brothers and sisters" provide encouragement, emotional support, and/or other forms of sustenance. We note this especially whenever small groups in churches rally to a family's needs in the midst of a crisis. Through such support, taking the difficult road of discipleship becomes a little easier.

Luke 18:31–43

❦

JESUS TOOK THE Twelve aside and told them, "We are going up to Jerusalem, and everything that is written by the prophets about the Son of Man will be fulfilled. ³²He will be handed over to the Gentiles. They will mock him, insult him, spit on him, flog him and kill him. ³³On the third day he will rise again."

³⁴The disciples did not understand any of this. Its meaning was hidden from them, and they did not know what he was talking about.

³⁵As Jesus approached Jericho, a blind man was sitting by the roadside begging. ³⁶When he heard the crowd going by, he asked what was happening. ³⁷They told him, "Jesus of Nazareth is passing by."

³⁸He called out, "Jesus, Son of David, have mercy on me!"

³⁹Those who led the way rebuked him and told him to be quiet, but he shouted all the more, "Son of David, have mercy on me!"

⁴⁰Jesus stopped and ordered the man to be brought to him. When he came near, Jesus asked him, ⁴¹"What do you want me to do for you?"

"Lord, I want to see," he replied.

⁴²Jesus said to him, "Receive your sight; your faith has healed you." ⁴³ Immediately he received his sight and followed Jesus, praising God. When all the people saw it, they also praised God.

THE END OF Jesus' journey to Jerusalem is drawing near. In the final portion of this journey (18:31–19:44), Jesus is preparing for what lies ahead. So he issues another prediction of his approaching fate (18:31–34). Then he displays his power to heal as the Son of David (18:35–43) and reveals his authority to bestow salvation as he commends the transformation of Zacchaeus (19:1–10). This tax collector illustrates a rich man who comes to faith, underlining the theme that anyone can come to Jesus. Jesus' authority to judge is reinforced in the parable of the ten minas, which issues a call for faithfulness (19:11–27). Jesus approaches the city to great praise, as well as to skepticism from the Jewish leadership (19:28–40). The journey ends on a tragic note: Jesus weeps for the city, which will face judgment for rejecting her Messiah and missing the day of her visitation (19:41–44). Everything about this closing unit shows the authority of Jesus. He is still the issue, even as he nears his death. Removing him changes nothing, since God will vindicate him. Only his base of operation will change.

Luke 18:31–34 presents the sixth direct allusion to Jesus' death in this Gospel (5:35; 9:22, 44–45; 12:49–50; 13:32–33; 17:25).[1] It is also the fourth passage to mention the Son of Man dying (9:22, 44; 17:25). Two elements are unique to Luke here: Jesus' actions as fulfilling what is in the prophets (v. 31) and the disciples' lack of understanding (v. 34). The disciples cannot comprehend how Jesus' death will accomplish God's will. The coming events will clarify their understanding.

Jesus announces that they are heading to Jerusalem to fulfill all that the prophets have written. This note of fulfillment emphasizes that the events about to occur are part of a divine design that must happen (2:39; 12:50; 13:22, 32; 22:37; 24:44–47; Acts 2:23; 13:29). Nothing catches Jesus off guard. Jerusalem has been identified as the city of destiny for some time (Luke 9:22, 31; 13:33–34).

Jesus will be given over to the Gentiles. In the events to come, the opponents will mock, insult, spit on, flog, and then kill him. Luke does not mention here who will give him over; he has already done so in 9:22—the elders, chief priests, and teachers of the law (cf. Matt. 20:18; Mark 10:33). But the story continues. On the third day, he will rise again. After suffering will be glory and vindication.

The disciples do not understand this—at least, not until 24:45, the moment when they finally understand the Scriptures. The mystery of what God was doing in a new way emerges at that time (cf. 10:21; 1 Cor. 2:7; Eph. 3:9; Col. 1:26). Jesus' life fulfills Jewish prophecy, yet it is full of surprises as to how that fulfillment comes. The early church will see that Jesus has fulfilled the hope of the Old Testament, while at the same time declaring new approaches to circumcision, Sabbath, food laws, and sacrifices. How can fulfillment alter such fundamental aspects of Jewish worship? How is it possible for the promised Messiah to die? All of these events are initially incomprehensible, even to those who follow Jesus. It is part of the mystery of the plan they have trouble fathoming.

---

1. The parallels to this passage are Matthew 20:17–19 and Mark 10:32–34. An indirect reference to Jesus' death appears in 2:35, but it is too implicitly stated to be called a clear allusion.

Jesus claims himself to be the means and fulfillment of the promise—inaugurating, reordering, and completing the map of Jewish faith. He is both the end and the completion of all the Law has pointed to. The rejection of this claim by many Jews leads to his death. The approaching death of one honored as the Son of Man is but one of the many surprises we now take for granted in the church. It is often difficult to appreciate just how surprising the road Jesus takes is. But God's subsequent actions will make clear what is currently hidden to his disciples.

Luke 18:35—43 is the fourth and final miracle in Luke's journey section (cf. 13:10—17; 14:1—6; 17:11—19).[2] Miracles have been few in this section, as instruction and conflict have dominated. But this last miracle is significant because it highlights the one who does the healing: Jesus heals as the Son of David. Ironically, while many struggle to see who Jesus is, a blind man has full clarity of vision.

As Jesus travels near Jericho, a blind man is begging by the road and hears the commotion. He asks what is going on. They tell him that "Jesus of Nazareth" is passing by; the blind man has apparently heard about Jesus and knows that he is not just a Nazarean.[3] Everything in his response to Jesus shows that he has heard something about this man and believes he can change his life. It is a moment he may have waited for, but never thought would come. The man calls out to Jesus, "Son of David, have mercy on me." In calling Jesus the "Son of David," the blind man recognizes that Jesus is the Promised One of God. In Judaism, there was a tradition that Solomon as Son of David had the power to heal, exercising great authority over the forces of evil.[4] The blind man wants Jesus to exercise the power he has heard about on his behalf. He trusts his welfare to Jesus as the Son of David.

The popular perception is that this blind man is too insignificant for Jesus to pay any attention to. He should be quiet and leave the teacher alone. But the rebukes solidify the blind man's resolve, and he cries out even louder for

---

2. The parallels to this account are Matthew 20:29—34 and Mark 10:46—52. There are differences in these versions. Matthew and Mark speak of a healing as Jesus leaves Jericho, while Luke appears to have the healing as he enters. Matthew has two blind men healed. Some appeal to two Jerichos to deal with the locale issue, but it may simply be a case of reordering two events in Jericho so that the healing of the blind man can come before the Zacchaeus account to add to the second event's symbolic value. Thus the difference may only be one of literary arrangement and superficial appearance. Matthew's additional blind man is also merely a difference in narrating the details of the event.

3. The Nazarean connection to Jesus appears often in the New Testament (Matt. 2:23; 26:71; John 18:5, 7; 19:19; Acts 2:22; 3:6; 4:10; 6:14; 22:8; 26:9).

4. Josephus, *Antiquities* 8.2.4—5 §§ 42—49. The Davidic tie is frequent in the New Testament: Matthew 9:27; 12:23; 15:22; 20:31—32; 21:9, 15; Mark 10:47—48; 12:35; John 7:42; Acts 2:29—32; Romans 1:3; 2 Timothy 2:8.

mercy. Such cries for mercy to Jesus are common (Matt. 9:27; 15:22; 17:15; 20:31–32; Mark 5:19; 10:47–48). Its roots go back to David's penitential cry in Psalm 51:1 and recall language about God's delivering mercy and loyal love in Luke 1:72. For to a sensitive person, the expression of God's grace is an extension of his mercy, not an act that is owed the recipient.

Jesus hears the cry and asks that the man be brought to him. The crowd is wrong. Jesus is concerned about people like the blind man. The surrounding culture may want to ignore him, but Jesus, despite the blind man's lack of position in the world, wants to respond to his insightful cry for help. God looks on the heart, not a person's social status. Jesus asks the man what he wants, probably to elicit his desire publicly and to draw out his faith in Jesus. The blind man replies he wants to see again. Jesus then grants his request and notes that his faith has delivered him.

This exchange symbolizes much more than the ability to see again. The blind man trusts that by asking the Son of David to provide what his power can deliver, he will be restored. Jesus then not only opens his eyes, he also affirms that the blind man can walk on the road with his eyes on God. His faith has brought deliverance and sight. Those who approach God in confidence that he can make them see are given spiritual sight.

So the blind man begins to follow Jesus and praise God. The people likewise change their tune and praise God. God has worked powerfully again through Jesus. This act represents another indication of the fulfillment Jesus announced in 4:16–18. Access to God has been opened up through faith.

 **Bridging Contexts**

LUKE 18:31–33 IS a descriptive prediction Jesus made to his disciples. What he declares would happen, did in fact take place. And the fog that the disciples have about God's plan eventually clears up, leading them to declare the gospel with boldness.

The text reveals how we are sometimes slow to see what God is doing, because our expectations prevent us from seeing it. No doubt part of the disciples' problem was their expectation of seeing something instant and awesome from Jesus in coming to set up the kingdom. The blind spot of false expectations caused them to pass by the difficult moments of his ministry. We sometimes handle God's promises similarly and create a similar imbalance in expectations. We cling to the "good bits" tenaciously and shy away from the more demanding parts of his call. We prefer the victory to the agony, whereas often God molds and shapes victory through the forging that comes in the difficult part of our walk. Just as the disciples had trouble understanding that glory would follow suffering, we too can be slow to see the same point.

It is important to consider Luke's handling of miracles in 18:35–43. This commentary has argued consistently that the miracles of Jesus are pictures of deeper spiritual realities. No miracle makes that fact as clear as this one. A blind man, living on the side of a road and reduced to begging, confesses Jesus as the promised Messiah, as the one who has the power to restore sight to humanity. Jesus then restores the man's sight. Faith leads to restoration. This text reveals the most basic spiritual truths about seeking and finding one's way on the path with God.

Those who see most clearly are often not those most visible in our society. The blind man stands in marked contrast to the rich ruler of 18:18–24. That man had everything the world offered, but he could not see clearly enough to realize that a trade of earthly things for heavenly treasure was a good deal. The blind man was begging for his earthly sustenance, yet he saw in the darkness of his blindness the light of heavenly promise. The sight that counts is what the heart sees. A faith that sees Jesus possesses insight that the world cannot recognize. That is what Jesus affirms in this healing.

Contemporary Significance

JESUS IS PART of an organized plan to send the promise of hope and salvation to humanity. The prediction in 18:31–33 underscores that the events of God's plan were indeed planned! What Jesus did was not part of a second or backup plan of God because "Plan A" failed. As early as Isaiah 52:13–53:12, God had predicted that his servant would be despised and rejected by his own people and would die. The Bible also promises that the one who was crucified will return to exercise his authority over the earth. Those remaining parts are just as certain to be realized as was the first part of the plan. Thus, God is moving the events of history to realization in their proper time.

The disciples' failure to see God's ways challenges us to ask ourselves whether we miss God's direction in our lives because we do not want to see those parts of his call that ask us to take the hard road. Such questions are answered in the silent moments of private reflection or through interaction with those who know us well. Are we hesitant to step out in faith because we cannot guarantee the results? Do we shy away from certain ministry opportunities God is opening up for us because of fear? Do we hesitate to share the gospel because we do not want to face the possible rejection that might come from being vulnerable about our relationship to God? The road God wants us to travel is not always the most comfortable one.

The basic application in 18:35–43 revolves around the blind man's seeing heart and the boldness with which he embraces Jesus. Here a social outsider, face to face with the opportunity of experiencing Jesus' blessing, comes forward in the midst of public rebuke to embrace Jesus. We ought to reflect trust as this man did, praise God after receiving his grace, and follow Jesus. The switch from begging at the side of the road to journeying along with Jesus pictures the change of direction and status Jesus brings to life. No matter how low our social position has been, when we come to Jesus, we are elevated to the highest possible station in life, the position for which we were created—a relationship with God. The function of the Christian community is to reaffirm this valuation of the believer.

One of the most enjoyable services I attend each year is the Sunday we trade pulpits with a church in the poorer part of Dallas with whom we have developed a relationship. This inner city community visits us with its pastor and choir. What is so refreshing about their visit is the simplicity and clarity of their faith. I learn many things about compassion and kindness worked out by the Spirit from people who have had to minister in a rough and hostile environment. The message is filled with wisdom discovered on the streets. Sometimes I sense we in our middle-class suburban churches have major blind spots whereas these brothers and sisters have 20/20 vision. Different social or personal contexts can lead us to have additional insights into the character of God and of ourselves.

This also explains why a church that is open to involvement at a multiethnic environment can develop a depth of sensitivity that one-dimensional churches lack. Sometimes we think ministry can only go from the haves to the have-nots. This passage reminds us that sometimes those who lack see better than those who have. We must not be too quick to make judgments about what a person can offer to the body of Christ because of what he or she appears to lack.

Of course, the recognition of Jesus as Son of David is the basis of everything pictured in this passage. Luke never stops making the person of Jesus the issue of this Gospel. All the blessings he notes revolve around the choice of deciding who he is. Luke tells the Jesus story gradually, but virtually every passage asks the same question about him. Those who know him already are reassured about him; those who do not know him are called to recognize him. This passage asks the questions in visual terms: Do you see who Jesus is, or are you blind? Blindness becomes sight when one turns to him.

Luke 19:1–10

J ESUS ENTERED JERICHO and was passing through. ²A man was there by the name of Zacchaeus; he was a chief tax collector and was wealthy. ³He wanted to see who Jesus was, but being a short man he could not, because of the crowd. ⁴So he ran ahead and climbed a sycamore-fig tree to see him, since Jesus was coming that way.

⁵When Jesus reached the spot, he looked up and said to him, "Zacchaeus, come down immediately. I must stay at your house today." ⁶So he came down at once and welcomed him gladly.

⁷All the people saw this and began to mutter, "He has gone to be the guest of a 'sinner.'"

⁸But Zacchaeus stood up and said to the Lord, "Look, Lord! Here and now I give half of my possessions to the poor, and if I have cheated anybody out of anything, I will pay back four times the amount."

⁹Jesus said to him, "Today salvation has come to this house, because this man, too, is a son of Abraham. ¹⁰For the Son of Man came to seek and to save what was lost."

LIKE THE BLIND man whom Jesus healed while entering Jericho, the Zacchaeus episode (unique to Luke) portrays response to salvation. Here is a man who is sought and saved by the Son of Man (v. 10).

Zacchaeus is a "chief tax collector," which means he stands at the top of the collection pyramid, taking a cut of commission from those who collected taxes for him.[1] He is therefore a wealthy man, though many consider his wealth ill-gotten. This cultural background is important in appreciating the crowd's reaction to Jesus' encounter with him.

As Jesus moves through Jericho, Zacchaeus longs to see the famous teacher, but his short stature and the crowd prevent him from doing so. But

---

1. O. Michel, "τελώνης," *TDNT*, 8:104–5. On the disdain tax collectors received, see comments on Luke 3:1–20, as well as Mishnah, *Nedarim* 3:4, where they are paired with murderers and robbers.

he is resourceful, so he runs ahead and climbs a sycamore tree, a tree with a short trunk and wide, lateral branches. Jesus breaks the ice by noticing Zacchaeus in the tree. He stops and tells him to come down out of the tree, because he "must" (*dei*) stay at his house today. Jesus' stay with the tax collector is a necessity because it pictures what his ministry is all about—to lead to God those whom others have given up on, to call those who, like the tax collector Levi, need to repent (5:31–32). His mission is to reclaim the prodigals (ch. 15) and justify the humble (18:9–14).

Zacchaeus welcomes Jesus gladly. One who has simply sought to get a glimpse of the teacher now gets to meet him face to face. His development of intimacy with Jesus underscores how one who approaches God on the Lord's terms gets more than he or she may have expected.

The reaction to Jesus' choice for a host does not meet with popular approval. The religious leaders judge that Jesus has chosen to be "the guest of a 'sinner,'" and they "begin to mutter" (*diegongyzon*, a verb like the one used of the Israelites when they complained about being in the desert after the Exodus [Ex. 16:7; 17:3; Num. 11:1; 14:27–29; cf. also Luke 15:2]).[2] Their complaint is both right and wrong. Zacchaeus is indeed a sinner, as his own remarks will show, but he is not beyond the touch of God or his call. But like the Pharisee who had given up on the sinful woman in Luke 7:36–50, so this crowd has written off Zacchaeus. But Jesus does not write off those who remain open to God. Jesus' visit with Zacchaeus reveals his acceptance of the tax collector. He does not worry about the impression on his testimony this association makes, because his priority is to associate closely enough with the lost that they may come to know the grace of God.

Zacchaeus expresses his appreciation of Jesus' acceptance of him by declaring his intent to be a different man. Because of his new relationship with God, he will do two things: Half of his possessions will now go to the poor, and those he has wronged will receive restitution at four times the amount taken. He is aware of his sin and desires to right the wrongs he has done. Both actions stand out in light of cultural expectations. If later Judaism is any guide, it was considered generous to give away twenty percent of one's possessions.[3] And the restitution Zacchaeus notes is better than the highest standard set by the law (Lev. 5:16; Num. 5:7). He actually penalizes himself with the standard required of rustlers (Ex. 22:1; 2 Sam. 12:6). As Ellis notes, this is the "thank offering of a changed heart."[4] In Zacchaeus's changed heart, love for God expresses itself in love for others.

---

2. K. Rengstorf, "γογγύζω," *TDNT*, 1:728–37.
3. See the Talmud, *Kethuboth* 50a.
4. E. Ellis, *Luke*, 221; O. Michel, "τελώνης," *TDNT*, 8:105 n. 154.

Giving away half of one's possessions, which Jesus commends here, shows that other texts where Jesus calls for people to sell everything (18:22) serve as a rhetorical way of stating that one should see their possessions as under the stewardship of God. What God gives is to be used for others (Eph. 4:28). That Zacchaeus understands this call is demonstrated by his giving alms and his intention to make restitution. Treasure in heaven is more important than hoarding earthly resources. The resources we possess are the Lord's, and he guides us in how we are to use them. As we grow in the Lord, we must place resources into his service rather than into our service (cf. Rom. 12:8). Such giving as Zacchaeus intends is not required by God's law, but does reflects a heart given over to God.

Jesus endorses the response fully, noting that this very day "salvation has come to [Zacchaeus's] house." This statement testifies to a heart changed by the presence of God. The Lord has been reclaiming a formerly lost child. Zacchaeus is truly now a son of Abraham—what Paul calls a child of faith (Rom. 4; Gal. 3). Even more exciting is the explanation of what this tax collector's return represents in verse 10. Jesus as Son of Man has come to seek and to save what was lost. He has taken the initiative to point to Zacchaeus as a man who can know God's acceptance, and the tax collector has embraced the opportunity. As Luke 15:1–10 argues, one suspects heaven fully celebrated his return.

Bridging Contexts

THIS TEXT, AS so many others in this latter section of Luke's journey material, reveals basic attitudes about how God responds to the humble and to those who recognize that the way they have walked is wrong. His commitment to sinners has been affirmed throughout this Gospel (5:31–32; 7:29–35; 15:1–32). This text pictures the initiative Jesus undertakes to reveal this divine commitment. God reaches out to accept the sinner who discovers he or she can turn to God.

Zacchaeus demonstrates how one should respond to the gospel of Jesus. After recognizing his failures, he not only confesses them publicly but seeks to make appropriate restitution for the wrongs he has done. Moreover, he embarks on a new, more giving approach to life. The transformation of his heart in openness toward God expresses itself in openness toward needy people. Such faith is not an intellectual exercise; it is a change of worldview. Jesus enthusiastically commends what takes place here, similar to his comments on the faith of the centurion in 7:1–10 and of the Samaritan in 17:11–17. Zacchaeus is another "outsider" who has turned out to be an "insider" by God's grace.

Furthermore, we are warned by this passage that how our community judges us in our associations is not necessarily how God judges. If Jesus had used the crowd's standard of association, he would never have addressed Zacchaeus. But this episode is one of the most picturesque accounts of the essence of his ministry. The church must become the means for restoring the lost and rejected by seeking them out, not by remaining isolated from them.

THIS PASSAGE SUMMARIZES many key themes Luke has highlighted throughout his Gospel—most notably Jesus' mission to seek and save the lost, a mission that now belongs to the church as his body. One of the errors the pious can make is to separate themselves from the world in such a way that they lose contact with sinners. Usually two factors feed such isolation: (1) a healthy desire not to succumb to standards of living that destroy moral integrity, and (2) a subtle but deadly feeling of superiority, so that we feel we are inherently better than others (much like the attitude of the Jews that Paul condemns in Rom. 2). This second element in the equation can squeeze out our ability to empathize with the sinner's plight. It forgets that our blessing is the result of God's gracious work, not our inherent character.

To want to live a moral life is part of God's call for believers. Along with that is the desire to keep one's distance from morally suspect practices. This principle is a good one. However, it risks being applied so thoroughly that one ceases to associate with unbelievers for fear of what comes with the relationship. It can be difficult to build the relationships on which much evangelism depends.

I remember a story one of my students shared with our class. He and his wife had worked for months to develop a relationship with several unbelievers, to the point where they had to begin discussing God's role in this association. They had finally achieved such a level of trust that several of these families asked them to go along on a weekend outing. As they contemplated going, moral dilemmas set in. What did their friends intend on doing? Where would they go? What kinds of stories would they tell? Here was the chance they had waited for—to spend personal time with people for whom they had been praying! Their fear is as revealing as the desire to serve, but such fear comes with the territory and may even indicate we have already been withdrawing too far from others.

They opted to go, trusting God to exercise their best judgment and knowing that issues of language, taste in stories, and activities might require tact and judgment. After all, how can one expect someone to reflect standards that they may have never been taught? Their goal was to reflect their own commitments while consolidating their friendship with these families. This student and his wife are like many in the church who, in their commitment to seek the lost, do something profound and challenging by simply loving their neighbor (Rom. 13:8–10)! They were willing to risk a moment or two of discomfort for the sake of getting to know those who needed Christ. They have seen many come to Christ, because they have remained open to truly befriending the lost. When Jesus asked to stay at Zacchaeus's house, he potentially took on such a challenge. His initiative was honored with a response.

Those of us who did not grow up in the church often are brought to the Lord, as I was, by such friendships. A Christian roommate who modeled Christ in the midst of my desire to enjoy my freshmen year at college was primarily responsible for leading me to the Lord. I had heard the gospel for years but was resistant, deflecting the efforts to consider what was in my soul with all the intellectual diversions our culture can raise. But this roommate, though he could not answer my questions, cared for me as a friend and modeled Jesus' love in the process. That willingness to spend time, talk, and sometimes just hang out together provided far more answers than my whole list of questions. Many believers can offer this difference to their friends if they pursue such relationships with sincerity while trusting the Lord. Such is the initiative we must take to seek the lost. We must not give up on those whose hearts God may get a hold of through the testimony our love might communicate.

Another key application in this passage comes in the portrait of faith. Faith transforms people. They see the world and God differently after exercising it. That does not mean that Christians are perfect. The church is not full of perfect people, but forgiven people. The difference is crucial.

A transformed faith responds to wronging others differently than our instincts do. Our instincts tell us not to admit our wrongs and to cover up any signs of weakness. When I was growing up, such an attitude was romanticized into a saying that came from the popular novel, *Love Story*: "Love means never having to say you are sorry." As sweet as this sounds, it avoids a fundamental issue in relationships, namely, the honesty to bring the integrity of admitting error. Marriages are severely damaged by an unwillingness to admit wrong; so are a host of other relationships, either personal or professional.

One of the most painful things we can do in a relationship is to commit a wrong and then pretend it never happened or did not do any damage. Such blindness builds up resentment and eats away at the relationship. Admitting wrong, asking for forgiveness, and trying to make restitution are like a spring shower that can open up the possibility of a fresh start. That is why Zacchaeus's desire to make restitution meets Jesus' commendation—not as a requirement for the tax collector's salvation, but as an indication that his heart recognized that a wrong needed acknowledging and fixing. Here attitude and resources combined to show how clearly Zacchaeus recognized his wrong. If there was any doubt Zacchaeus meant what he said, his pocketbook spoke volumes.

Zacchaeus also pictures an honesty and vulnerability about sin that reveal the inherent beauty of the gospel in being able to deal with sin and failure. The Christian faith is the ultimate "recovery" movement, because what is recovered is the fundamental relationship with God that allows recovery in other areas to take place. That "recovery" is what Zacchaeus's remarks so vividly reveal. The church needs to highlight such testimony. Some of the most moving services in the church are those where sinners tell how God "recovered" them from lostness and brought them back into his fold. As they exposed their sin before God, he brought them back into relationship with him and with others.

We do too little of sharing our testimony in our communities as an act that can bind us together. A church made up of "perfect" people who cannot confess sin does not give evidence of the gospel's transforming power. To know him is to not slip into the delusion we are something apart from him. The Reformation called this principle "being justified while being a sinner." That is, God saves me to make me different and enables me to walk with him; without the provision he gives us, we go nowhere. This requires a lifelong walk of faith and dependence on him. We are a new creation, but in him we are under continual renewal. The moment we forget our continual need for renewal, we slip into the self-delusion of being spiritually independent. Nothing is more devastating for the Christian walk than forgiven sinners who think they can live like saints on automatic pilot. Independence is not the essence of faith; humility and dependence are.

Luke 19:11–27

W HILE THEY WERE listening to this, he went on to tell them a parable, because he was near Jerusalem and the people thought that the kingdom of God was going to appear at once. ¹²He said: "A man of noble birth went to a distant country to have himself appointed king and then to return. ¹³So he called ten of his servants and gave them ten minas. 'Put this money to work,' he said, 'until I come back.'

¹⁴"But his subjects hated him and sent a delegation after him to say, 'We don't want this man to be our king.'

¹⁵"He was made king, however, and returned home. Then he sent for the servants to whom he had given the money, in order to find out what they had gained with it.

¹⁶"The first one came and said, 'Sir, your mina has earned ten more.'

¹⁷"'Well done, my good servant!' his master replied. 'Because you have been trustworthy in a very small matter, take charge of ten cities.'

¹⁸"The second came and said, 'Sir, your mina has earned five more.'

¹⁹"His master answered, 'You take charge of five cities.'

²⁰"Then another servant came and said, 'Sir, here is your mina; I have kept it laid away in a piece of cloth. ²¹I was afraid of you, because you are a hard man. You take out what you did not put in and reap what you did not sow.'

²²"His master replied, 'I will judge you by your own words, you wicked servant! You knew, did you, that I am a hard man, taking out what I did not put in, and reaping what I did not sow? ²³Why then didn't you put my money on deposit, so that when I came back, I could have collected it with interest?'

²⁴"Then he said to those standing by, 'Take his mina away from him and give it to the one who has ten minas.'

²⁵"'Sir,' they said, 'he already has ten!'

²⁶"He replied, 'I tell you that to everyone who has, more will be given, but as for the one who has nothing, even what he has will be taken away. ²⁷But those enemies of mine who did not want me to be king over them—bring them here and kill them in front of me.'"

THIS IS THE final parable in Luke's record of Jesus' final journey to Jerusalem.[1] Its themes are Jesus' authority in judgment and the faithfulness of his disciples, important topics in light of his coming departure and eventual return. What relationship will people have with Jesus? What accountability will they possess in light of his absence and return? What will happen to the nation that rejects him?

Luke is clear about why Jesus tells the parable. As he is drawing near to Jerusalem, expectation rises that the kingdom will be decisively brought in, that it will "appear at once" (v. 11). This expectation of the kingdom's nearness means, in Luke, the complete display of kingdom authority. Jesus must inform his disciples that the full expression of kingdom authority will not come until his return, and he must explain what he expects of them in the interim.

This parable has a historical background. Both Herod in 40 B.C. and Archelaus in 4 B.C. went to Rome to receive ruling authority from the emperor. In the case of Archelaus, who was not popular, there was a public outcry not to grant him the position. Rome responded by giving him a less comprehensive mandate—an ethnarchy, not a kingship.[2] Part of the captivating interest in this story for Jesus' original audience was its parallelism to these well-known ancient events.[3]

A man of noble birth goes to a far country "to have himself appointed king and then to return." The Greek expression literally refers to his "receiving a kingdom"—a remark that pictures Jesus' reception of the kingdom after the vindication of his upcoming resurrection and ascension. While gone, the nobleman's interests need to be administered. So he calls ten servants and gives each of them a mina (equivalent to one hundred drachmas or about one hundred days of an average working wage).[4] The servants are to see what they can do with these resources until the master returns. The servants represent anyone following Jesus.

---

1. There is a conceptually similar parable in Matthew 25:14–30. For example, Matthew has talents, while Luke has minas. There is an explicit group that rejects in Luke 19:14, which Matthew does not mention, a detail that also explains why Luke 19:27 is unparalleled. Luke portrays the parable as involving a king, while Matthew's version is decidedly less regal. These differences suggest that this may be a parable that Jesus told more than once with some variation in detail. A similar metaphor appears in Mark 13:34–35.

2. Josephus, *Antiquities* 14.14. 1–4 §§ 370–85.

3. C. Blomberg, *Interpreting the Parables*, 217–20.

4. The NIV's "three month's wage" (footnote) slightly underestimates the value, assuming a six-day work week.

In addition to servants are subjects who hate the ruler and do not want him as king. They send a delegation to those making the selection to inform them of their complaint. This pictures the rejection of Jesus by Israel.

Despite their complaint, the nobleman receives the kingship. Returning home, he asks for an accounting by his servants. Have they used the resources in a way that benefited him? Though ten were given resources, the story is kept compact by relating the situation of only three servants.[5] The first one has taken the one mina and made ten more from it, an impressive gain. So the master commends him for his trustworthiness and puts him in charge of ten cities. A second servant has also done well, earning five more minas. His trustworthiness, though not as elaborately praised as the first servant's, earns him five cities.

The main exchange takes place between the master and the third servant. The parable's pace slows down at this point, because this is a central concern Jesus wants to raise. The third servant simply returns the mina, having hid it in a cloth, and explains why. He is afraid of the master, knowing him to be a hard man, who takes what he does not work for and reaps what he does not sow. The third servant has no sense of loyalty to his master. Why should he honor him with his labor? This rhetorical detail about the servant's attitude is important, because it shows that although he is associated with the master, there is nothing that indicates any trust of the master. This servant is a disciple of sorts, but there is no meaningful relationship within that connection.

The master's reaction to the servant is strong and clear. This wicked servant will be condemned on his own testimony. If he did not want to work for the master, he could have at least put the money in a bank, where it would have gained interest! If he really knew the master as a hard man, then surely he should have been wise enough to take some action. Interestingly, the master's response to the other servants showed him to be anything but a hard taskmaster, since he has rewarded the other servants with more responsibility. This wicked servant does not really know the character of his master. The master's remarks in verse 22 are not his confession that he is a hard taskmaster, but a condemnation of the third servant's failure to follow through on how he viewed the master. Verse 23 shows the third servants's attitude should have led to a different response. Thus, there is irony in the master's

---

5. This difference in detail has led some to suggest two parables are combined here, but the difference may be nothing more than telling the story as concisely as possible. On two parables combined here, see Nolland, *Luke 18:35–19:53* (Dallas: Word, 1993), 910–11. For a careful discussion leaning to one parable in the entire tradition history, see Marshall, *Commentary on Luke*, 700–702. He is uncertain whether two parables were combined into the one parable that he sees behind both Matthew and Luke (see his n. 402).

remarks. He is measuring the servant by the servant's own standards, a measure he fails to live up to.

Thus, the master orders that the mina be taken away from the third servant, who ends up with nothing, and be given to the servant who made ten minas. The crowd protests, noting that the first servant already has enough. The note is important, because it indicates that the servants do not lose the additional money they have earned. It remains theirs to administrate, in order to continue their stewardship.

Jesus then makes the application. The one who has gets more, but the one who has nothing loses even what he has. Jesus applies a mathematical warning to the third slave. Nothing from nothing leaves nothing. The one who has no trust in God' goodness, even though he or she has a "connection" to God, has no relationship with God and ends up with nothing from him in the end. Such a servant loses even what he thinks he had. The key to understanding the plight and identity of this third servant comes in verse 22: He is "a wicked servant," who is not among the blessed in the end, for he does not know the master (like the picture in 12:46).[6] The third servant represents all those tied to the community who neither trust nor know the goodness of the master Jesus. Perhaps a figure like Judas is in view here. Mere association with the community counts for nothing; what counts is personal relationship to Jesus.

Jesus deals with one more group in the parable—the subjects who did not want the nobleman to be king. These enemies are slain. This represents the fate of those who reject Jesus outright. They are judged and excluded from blessing, no matter how close to him they have previously been. This detail represents the irreversibility and severity of the final judgment.

Bridging Contexts

THIS PARABLE HAS two major themes: Jesus' authority and the accountability of all to him. This makes the parable a call to faithfulness. Its treats both Israel's rejection of Jesus and the accountability of any who associate with him. That is, because the period covered in the parable extends to the time of his return, it addresses us as well.

---

6. The alternative to this reading of the text is to see the third slave as one who loses salvation or as one who receives no reward but still belongs to the community. The problem with the first view is that it underestimates the New Testament teaching about the permanent effect of regeneration (John 6:37), while the second ignores the decidedly negative imagery of v. 22. The negative imagery here is reinforced by the parallel to the third servant in Matthew 25:30. There the servant is worthless, is confined to *outer* darkness, and experiences "weeping and gnashing of teeth." This is not someone just on the edge of the kingdom of light; rather, he is subjected to the deepest recesses of darkness.

Everyone is accountable to Jesus in one way or another. Those who associate with him are responsible for a ministry of service. Those who reject him are accountable for not recognizing who he was and is. Much of the parable is spent with the third servant, who depicts a hybrid, someone who has become associated with the community Jesus founded but who never really trusts Jesus as a source of grace. Such people, though they appear as members of the community, have never walked through the door of faith that responds to grace, providing a genuine entrance into the community. They end up on the outside, with nothing.

This parable also emphasizes the graciousness of Jesus in rewarding faithfulness. The first and second servants receive the warm commendation of the master for their faithful service. Not only do they keep what they have earned, but they receive the opportunity for additional service as well. The concept that God graciously and generously honors faithfulness crosses the time frame between the parable and our reading of it today.

WE ARE ALL accountable to God for how we conduct our journey through his world. One day he will render judgment. This concept is not popular in some circles today, but it is a biblical concept. God will require each person to render an account of their walk in his creation and will vindicate his saints.

As our culture grows more independent from God, many claim they are not his subjects, or they try to create God in their image and form him in the frame of their expectations. They argue that each person's destiny is his or her own business. One of the key expressions that used to float around in popular culture was "to your own self be true." There is a good use of this expression when it refers to integrity, but it often means that one can and should be led by one's own self-interests. In this understanding is a great danger, for accountability is not a matter of self-determination. We are not the standard by which life is measured. In all the talk about becoming accountable today, one key note is missing: We are already accountable to God. Our lives last a short span in this world, and that visit is subject to examination by One who is the source of life and breath.

This parable also emphasizes that God has given kingship to Jesus. He undertook that rule when he rose to the side of the Father after his death (see Acts 10:42–43; 17:31). His kingship includes judgment. Scripture consistently presents the judgment of God through his Son Jesus as an inevitable stop in the journey of each life. An illustration may help drive the point home. If I am arrested, I do not have the right to pick my judge or even the country in which I am tried. This principle was illustrated vividly in the famous "caning" case from Singapore during the early 1990s. An American was charged with defacing personal property and had to face the state's legal punishment for the crime. No matter how much protest was made of whether such a punishment was cruel, no one doubted the right of a nation to follow its own rules of governing. It is a good reminder that standards of judgment are set by the judge! So also, this parable declares God's right to hold us accountable in his creation and to evaluate our stewardship as he wills.

The third servant also represents a strong warning. Connection to a Christian community is not what makes a Christian, even if that person has stewardship responsibilities in that community. A Christian is a person who has a relationship of trust with Jesus. The Christian knows, because he or she has responded to the gospel, that God is gracious to those who turn to him for forgiveness. Service to him and other people is the response of a changed and grateful heart that has embraced what it means to be forgiven. The first and second servants have understood the call to respond to the nobleman, while the third servant doubted the master's character in slanderous ways. This parable calls on us to examine whether our perceived relationship to God is purely formal or real.

The parable suggests on the surface that the third servant lacks fruit in his life, but there is really a more basic complaint. He is condemned on the basis of his own words, that is, on the basis of his own heart attitude to God, for he sees the master as a hard, unjust taskmaster. Behind his lack of fruit is a lack of recognition of God's grace. That absence of faith is what Jesus condemns here, for it is that heart attitude that prevents this servant from pursuing the master's call. Membership in a church is not a union card to heaven; knowing and embracing God's grace is.

A positive note in the story is the recognition that Jesus will reward the faithfulness of those who walk with him. The provision of additional responsibility to the first and second servants shows that God sees and commends faithfulness. The judgment is a time of blessing to those who have walked with God, and we have nothing to fear if we have been faithful stewards. Our lives are an open book to God anyway, so we should live as those who know that God rewards those who seek him (Heb. 11:6). For those who are faithful, the judgment is a time for affirmation. God has given us abilities and resources (minas) through which to serve the church, increasing the benefits that come to the body through our applying these gifts. Jesus exhorts us here to apply ourselves fully to the task, so that in the day of his assessment, our stewardship may be an occasion for rejoicing (1 Cor. 4:5).

What do these rewards look like and what do they involve? It is hard to be sure what is meant. Those who see a millennial period argue that there are stewardship responsibilities in that kingdom era and that the degree of our faithfulness now determines what our responsibilities will be then. Those who see us moving directly into the eternal state see this parable as representing our role in the judgment alone. There are not many texts that explain this issue in detail. One of the most suggestive is 1 Corinthians 6:2–3, where Paul writes that believers will share in judging the world and angels at the end. We will all equally receive salvation and share in God's rule, but apparently our responsibilities will vary. As to what that means precisely, the rule of exposition should be the less speculation, the better.

Luke 19:28-44

❦

AFTER JESUS HAD said this, he went on ahead, going up to Jerusalem. ²⁹As he approached Bethphage and Bethany at the hill called the Mount of Olives, he sent two of his disciples, saying to them, ³⁰"Go to the village ahead of you, and as you enter it, you will find a colt tied there, which no one has ever ridden. Untie it and bring it here. ³¹If anyone asks you, 'Why are you untying it?' tell him, 'The Lord needs it.'"

³²Those who were sent ahead went and found it just as he had told them. ³³As they were untying the colt, its owners asked them, "Why are you untying the colt?"

³⁴They replied, "The Lord needs it."

³⁵They brought it to Jesus, threw their cloaks on the colt and put Jesus on it. ³⁶As he went along, people spread their cloaks on the road.

³⁷When he came near the place where the road goes down the Mount of Olives, the whole crowd of disciples began joyfully to praise God in loud voices for all the miracles they had seen:

³⁸"Blessed is the king who comes in the name of the Lord!"
"Peace in heaven and glory in the highest!"

³⁹Some of the Pharisees in the crowd said to Jesus, "Teacher, rebuke your disciples!"

⁴⁰"I tell you," he replied, "if they keep quiet, the stones will cry out."

⁴¹As he approached Jerusalem and saw the city, he wept over it ⁴²and said, "If you, even you, had only known on this day what would bring you peace—but now it is hidden from your eyes. ⁴³The days will come upon you when your enemies will build an embankment against you and encircle you and hem you in on every side. ⁴⁴They will dash you to the ground, you and the children within your walls. They will not leave one stone on another, because you did not recognize the time of God's coming to you."

THIS PASSAGE, KNOWN as the Triumphal Entry, is a complex event.[1] Not everyone is thrilled that Jesus enters Jerusalem riding the back of a donkey. In addition, the use of a "Solomonic-like," humble regal entrance blunts concerns that Jesus is a threat to Rome, since he neither seizes power nor gives any indication that he is a king of power. The contrast between Jesus' entrance and that of Roman leaders is culturally obvious.[2] In sum, Jesus' entry is a major statement about God's plan and the nature of his kingship. It is a message some rejoice in, others do not understand, and still others emphatically reject.

As Jesus approaches Jerusalem, he begins to direct events. Near Bethphage and Bethany at the Mount of Olives, some two miles east of Jerusalem, he tells his disciples to procure an animal for entry into the capital. Luke describes the animal only as a previously unridden colt; the gospel tradition specifies the colt as a donkey (Matt. 21:2; cf. Zech. 9:9).[3] The disciples must untie the animal, and if anyone asks what they are doing, they are simply to say that the Lord needs it. The cultural background for this response is the *angaria*, where a dignitary could procure use of property for personal reasons. This right extended to people like rabbis. So the request is not unusual.[4]

The disciples do just as Jesus has instructed them, and everything happens as he said it would. This sense of knowing the future adds to the mood of the passage. The events about to happen in Jerusalem are not surprises for him. He knows exactly what he is riding into. In effect, Jesus is directing the sequence of events that leads to his death.

The role of the animal becomes clear as Jesus nears the capital. The disciples throw their cloaks on the colt and put Jesus on it. As he proceeds, people spread their cloaks in front of him as well, much as a red carpet functions today. The description uses language from several Old Testament passages. The image of Jesus on the colt recalls Zechariah 9:9 and the ride of the humble, peace-making Messiah. Placing garments on the animal and on the ground recalls Jehu's regal accession in 2 Kings 9:13. The journey as a whole is like Solomon's procession to Gihon in 1 Kings 1:38–39. But while

---

1. The parallels to this entry are Matthew 21:1–11; Mark 11:1–11; and John 12:12–19. These accounts are told with a great deal of similarity, thought the discussion with the Pharisees in Luke 19:39–40 is unique to Luke.

2. B. Kinman, "The 'Atriumphal' Entry (Luke 19:28–48)," unpublished Ph.D. dissertation (University of Cambridge, 1993).

3. O. Michel, "πῶλος," *TDNT*, 6:959–61.

4. J. D. M. Derrett, "Law in the New Testament: The Palm Sunday Colt," *NovT* 13 (1971): 243–49.

the background is regal, the ride on a humble animal denotes not a Messiah of raw power, but of humility and service.

Luke lacks any mention of palm branches, possibly because this imagery is decidedly Jewish and complex. Normally one expected the waving of branches at the Feast of Tabernacles, but this is the Passover. Tabernacles looked forward to the end times, while Passover pictured both the sacrifice for the forgiveness of sins and the final deliverance. This combination is instructive, for Jesus brings both.

Luke stays focused on the person of Jesus. As Jesus passes the Mount of Olives, the disciples start to praise God for the miracles Jesus has performed. The mention of this mountain (another detail unique to Luke) adds to the messianic feel of the event, since it is the predicted locale of the Messiah's appearance (Zech. 14:4–5). Luke's explicit mention of disciples as the source of praise is important, because they form the catalyst for the praise from the crowds the other Gospels note. This detail explains how a few days later the same crowd can urge that Jesus be crucified. Their praise of Jesus is luke-warm and follows the lead of other, more sincere followers. The popular masses are always fluctuating in their understanding of Jesus.

The disciples praise of God is also praise of Jesus. They proclaim the hope of Psalm 118:26, where blessing falls on the king who comes in the name of the Lord. The reference to "the king" is not in the original psalm, though it probably depicts a king as he leads people in the temple for worship. In that psalm the king is greeted by the priests at the temple, with the recognition that he comes to worship and serve God. The psalm was also sung in Judaism as part of the praise celebration in association with the Passover meal, so it was well known and full of end-time import.[5] The disciples, by echoing the words of the psalm, declare that Jesus is the sent king who comes with authority given by God. They are also filled with joy as they note the presence of peace and glory in heaven (cf. 2:10–14). For disciples, this is a great moment. For the crowds, as the parallels tell us, this is a time to join in.

The reference to the one "who comes" (v. 38) also recalls earlier Lucan references (3:15–17; 7:19–23; 13:35).[6] Luke has therefore left two sets of clues as to who Jesus is. One appeals to Old Testament background, while the other treats the events of Jesus' ministry (especially the miracles). Each explains the other. Jesus is the Promised One whom John the Baptist mentioned; he also is the one who comes in the name of the Lord, whom Jesus predicted would be slain in Jerusalem (13:31–35).

---

5. D. Bock, *Proclamation From Prophecy and Pattern*, 122.
6. E. Ellis, *Luke*, 225.

But the vote is not unanimous. The Pharisees come and ask Jesus to reject the claim and rebuke his disciples. The regal claims are offensive to them.[7] Jesus' reply makes clear how appropriate the remarks are: If the disciples do not speak, creation will. This remark is important, for creation speaks when an injustice needs to be avenged (see Gen. 4:10; Hab. 2:11; James 5:4). It also contains an inherent rebuke, in that inanimate creation knows more about what is taking place than they do. The situation cannot be more tragic, as the tears of Jesus will soon show.

As Jesus approaches the city, we get a glimpse of his heart.[8] Like Isaiah and Jeremiah (Isa. 29:1–4; Jer. 6:6–21), he declares pending judgment for the nation. Rejection of the divinely selected king will cost greatly. The prediction of national judgment shows just how much God believes in Jesus and how seriously the decision about him should be taken. As the parable of the fig tree warned (13:6–9), Israel has run out of time. Her house is desolate, and she will face severe judgment until she acknowledges him (13:31–35). Luke is not specific here, but he still holds out hope for the nation, since Acts 3:18–22 looks to the day when Old Testament promises are completed as already proclaimed. Those remaining promises give a major role to Israel in the end.

Luke 19:41 shows the last leg of Jesus' journey to Jerusalem (9:51–19:44). He is approaching the city. Despite the fanfare, the entry is not a pleasant one for him. He knows what lies ahead and that the pain he will suffer will not be limited to himself. The nation has made a frightful choice, with dire consequences for itself. The people, considered as a community, have missed the day of messianic visitation (1:68–69, 78–79; 7:16; 19:44 ["God's coming" is literally "God's visitation"; cf. Acts 15:14]). Though some individuals have responded, the nation as a whole has not. Luke 19:42 describes the day as one that "would bring you peace" (cf. 1:79; 2:14; 7:50; 8:48; 10:5–6; 19:38; Acts 10:36).[9] A major opportunity has been missed. If they had known it, they could have experienced blessing.[10] But now, something more dire lies ahead.

What Jesus predicts is the "curse" for covenant unfaithfulness (Ps. 137:9; Isa. 29:1–4; Jer. 6:6–21; 8:18–22; Nah. 3:10). The roots of his prediction go back to Deuteronomy 28–32, where God warned that such unfaithfulness

---

7. Some, like Danker, *Jesus and the New Age,* 313, argue that the Pharisees fear Roman reprisal, but the interaction of Jesus with the Pharisees suggests that this is not the whole story, though it may be an element in their concern. They do not even regard Jesus as a prophet (7:39), so regal claims for him are certainly exaggerated in their view. Their complaint in this passage is about what is being claimed for Jesus, not what they fear as a result.

8. This passage is unique to Luke's Gospel. Its presence shows Luke's concern to discuss the fate of Jerusalem and, as a result, that of the nation.

9. W. Foerster, "εἰρήνη," *TDNT,* 2:413.

10. Luke expresses this point in verse 42 in a "contrary to fact" (second class) Greek conditional clause. They did not know what kind of day it was.

would lead to his judgment through other nations. Through Assyria and Babylon Israel already experienced such judgment. They are continuing to miss the moment of truth, and they are now responsible for their decision.

Josephus describes these judgments in great detail (*Jewish Wars* 5.11–12 §§ 446–572; 6.1–10 §§ 1–442). In A.D. 70, Titus of Rome overran the city. The final act was a great siege, the essence of which Jesus summarizes here. Anyone who knows how Rome took large cities can describe what Jesus does here. His prophetic insight is his understanding of what their rejection of the Messiah will cost them.

Jesus' reference to "the days will come" indicates a prophetic oracle (1 Sam. 2:31; 2 Kings 20:17; Isa. 36:9; Jer. 7:32–34; 32:38; 33:14; 49:2; Zech. 14:1). Here it is an oracle of doom. An embankment will be built around the city, and the people will be encircled and hemmed in. When the enemy finally enters the city, everyone will be slaughtered and there will be total destruction. This is exactly what Titus brought. So thorough was his destruction that even the great temple fell. Jesus knows what he is talking about. The decision to reject Jesus is a fundamental violation of covenant trust.

THESE EVENTS, AS with most events linked to Jesus' time in Jerusalem, point to the central events that reveal his mission and procure salvation for humanity. Designed by God, they show how Jesus is the hub of God's plan. How one views these events determines how one relates to God's plan. Even though they are now nearly two thousand years old, they are set forth like recent events that call the reader to assess what God has done through Jesus. These events issue a call for decision anew in each generation.

But the timeliness of the account does not stop there. The various reactions to Jesus in this passage reflect the range of responses to the question of who Jesus is. The two most prominent responses come from the disciples and the Jewish leadership—views that cannot be more opposed. The disciples regard Jesus as the Promised King through whom God has been working with great power, as evidenced by the miracles. In him is peace and glory, the presence of the gracious authority from heaven. The leadership, on the other hand, sees the claims as exaggerated, even as something Jesus should not accept (v. 39). Luke's readers of every age are asked in effect to choose sides. Jesus' appeal to creation shows how fundamental the claims of the disciples are. Even creation knows they are true. The whole narrative structure of the passage challenges us to ask ourselves where we place Jesus: Is he the humble king of peace and glory or not?

The combination of a regal entry on a beast of burden is an important bridge in understanding the portrait of Jesus' career. He is a humble king for now, as he faces the cross and as the church lives in light of his example. A day will come, however, when he will be the glorious Son of Man on the clouds, ruling with great power and fully exercising it (Rev. 19:11–21). At that time Jesus will hold a scepter and sword. The difference is important, for the church has sometimes tried to see herself as an alternative government in the world, a type of national force that should actively overthrow God's enemies.

History has shown this to be a tragic mistake. Whether the Crusades, the Spanish Inquisition, parts of the Reformation (including the Civil War in England), or more recent attempts to confuse the church with national government, the road of the church exercising political power, in contrast to moral persuasion, has been a cul-de-sac. Romans 13:1–7 recognizes that secular governments have a role for good and for judgment, even though they lack a covenant relationship with God (Paul's exhortation addresses a Roman context, hardly a model of morality). Society certainly runs better when it is conducted on a high moral plane, and in democracies like those in the Western world, we should share in the public square. But we should not confuse the church with government, or vice versa. To transform humanity, a change in the heart is needed. That is not the business of government, nor can it be achieved by laws, rather, it is a part of the church's prophetic call and the work of God's Spirit.

The predictions of unique judgment on Jerusalem in 19:41–44 points to a one-time event in the history of the nation of Israel for missing the day of her visitation. Israel will be isolated from her promise until she turns back to embracing the promise as it stands now in Jesus. Romans 11:12–32 looks to a day when the natural branches will again be grafted into the vine of divine promise. The implication of this is that even an event as amazing as the reestablishment of the nation of Israel in 1948 is not necessarily a fulfillment of Scripture in preparation for the end. It is possible that displacement from the land like that of the earlier eras of exile could come again, as unfortunate as that result would be. Fulfillment begins when Israel turns back to God.

Another corollary emerges from the reality that resulted from this judgment, namely, the inclusion of the Gentiles into God's family (Rom. 11:11–16). God's blessing in Christ, though it includes his covenant commitment to Israel, now incorporates Gentiles into blessing through the work of Abraham's seed to bless all the nations (Gal. 3–4). There is no Jew or Greek in Christ. This means that while Israel retains blessings of promise, those blessings in terms of salvation are no longer unique to her. Her failure has led to the gracious inclusion of others. But Paul anticipates a day when the fullness of Gentiles will come in, to be followed by a renewal of faith in Israel as they embrace the One they previously rejected (Rom. 11:25–27). At that time, promises made to Israel long ago, including the prospect of peace within her homeland, will come.

The events of A.D. 70 for the nation, as 21:5–37 will show, picture an even more significant judgment to come. While Jesus' remarks here are unique to its Israelite setting, a principle about decision and judgment emerges here. Though the exact expression of judgment may differ in detail, a decision against God's Chosen One, Jesus, does leave one exposed to God's judgment. One is free to reject Jesus; but one is also responsible to pay the consequences for that choice. In addition, the picture of judgment for covenant unfaithfulness remains a divine principle (see the warnings to Gentiles in Rom. 11:17–21). Such judgment as applied to individuals rather than corporate groups takes the form of discipline rather than outright rejection, but God holds us accountable for how we respond to him (e.g., 1 Cor. 11:27–32).

Judgment is not a pleasant subject. But two aspects of Jesus' reaction are important in thinking about this difficult topic. (1) Judgment brings Jesus pain. He weeps for Jerusalem as he thinks about her suffering. The coming rejection is painful for him, just as Israel's rejection was painful for Paul (Rom. 9:1–4). The nation is turning down an opportunity to be reconciled to God. Jesus, like a prophet of old, warns them of the opportunity, though he does not compel them to come into such blessing. The choice is theirs to make. This scene of weeping shows their tragic choice. It also reveals how we should see the judgment to come. It is real, inevitable, painful, and tragic— something to shed tears over. (2) The reality of such judgment should motivate us to reach out to those who do not know Christ. Everything about Jesus' ministry pushes in the direction of making the hope known, of doing the things that make for peace (cf. Eph. 2:11–22).

THIS PORTRAIT OF the Messiah and how he went about making his claims has much to say about how the community portrays him. In praising him as the one who comes in God's name, there is also the reminder that this Messiah came in humility. For the most part, he did not go around declaring who he was. He let others proclaim it and preferred to let his actions reveal his identity. Jesus incarnates his evangelism with a humility of service that is represented even in the way he as king enters Jerusalem. With actions and symbols, he shows how God cares for those around him. When he mentions faith and forgiveness, it is in contexts where concrete response displays the presence of what is proclaimed. Like her Messiah, the church needs to be a community, not just of testimony and words, but of presence and service among those whom it seeks to reach. The touch of God's presence reveals his mercy. Proclaiming and revealing Jesus are more than a matter for the head.

The wedding of life to theology is important because God has revealed his attributes in a similar way. His character is not revealed in a set of philosophical propositions. It comes through what he is doing in people's lives. To see God in the midst of our activities is fundamental to a Christian worldview. To proclaim Jesus is to testify to him as active in our world and lives. Like these disciples who proclaimed Jesus here as the Promised King on the basis of his miracles (cf. 18:35–42), so we proclaim him most effectively when we wed our knowledge of him to his direct involvement in our lives. This assumes, of course, that we live a life of faith attuned to seeing him and recognizing him.

We can expect a variety of reactions to Jesus. There is no need to force a positive response, for that is God's work. When Jesus is confronted by the Jewish leadership (vv. 39–40), he does not beg or cajole them into a response. He consistently lays out before them their responsibility in making the choice. His appeal to creation here notes that if no one speaks up for Jesus, an injustice before God has taken place. In other words, to fail to recognize him for who he is places one on the side of injustice with all the "rights and privileges" that come with making that choice (cf. also 19:45–20:8). The church's message to a culture that does not believe that God speaks truth (or that he does so in many voices) is to call that culture to consider the responsibility they undertake if they are wrong. It is a tragic, even permanent, mistake to misjudge what God has revealed.

Two applications from verses 41–44 are evident. (1) God has left a trail of evidence that he controls the affairs of humanity. Certain events, such as the collapse of Israel in A.D. 70, are explicitly marked out as reflecting his judgment. That collapse is not the end of her story, as Acts 3:14–26 and Romans 11 make clear, but this event shows that God's fingerprints are manifest in certain events.

(2) The importance of making a wise decision about Jesus is a constant theme in this Gospel. Acceptance of him leads to great blessing, while rejection leads to great pain. We should contemplate the consequences of rejecting God's offer of grace in Jesus. God desires our allegiance. When we refuse to give it, we become responsible for that choice. A time will come when we will have to own up to our decision. Making the right decision determines the character of that meeting.

Luke 19:45–20:8

THEN HE ENTERED the temple area and began driving out those who were selling. ⁴⁶"It is written," he said to them, "'My house will be a house of prayer'; but you have made it 'a den of robbers.'"

⁴⁷Every day he was teaching at the temple. But the chief priests, the teachers of the law and the leaders among the people were trying to kill him. ⁴⁸Yet they could not find any way to do it, because all the people hung on his words.

²⁰:¹One day as he was teaching the people in the temple courts and preaching the gospel, the chief priests and the teachers of the law, together with the elders, came up to him. ²"Tell us by what authority you are doing these things," they said. "Who gave you this authority?"

³He replied, "I will also ask you a question. Tell me, ⁴John's baptism—was it from heaven, or from men?"

⁵They discussed it among themselves and said, "If we say, 'From heaven,' he will ask, 'Why didn't you believe him?' ⁶But if we say, 'From men,' all the people will stone us, because they are persuaded that John was a prophet."

⁷So they answered, "We don't know where it was from."

⁸Jesus said, "Neither will I tell you by what authority I am doing these things."

Original Meaning

THE FINAL SECTION of Luke's Gospel (19:45–24:53) presents the "passion" of Jesus, the events leading to his death and resurrection. The emphasis in this account is on Jesus' innocence of the charges for which he is executed. Inexplicably, except for the hardness of the human heart, he goes to the cross. He suffers as a righteous sufferer. In fact, he even helps get himself there, since at his trial, when the Jews are having a difficult time convicting him, he utters words that lead to his condemnation.

Before the trial a series of controversies occurs that indicates just how far apart Jesus and the Jewish leadership are. His cleansing of the temple indicates how great the gap is between the worship Jesus calls for and what goes on in the temple. Jesus again predicts the fall of Jerusalem and uses it to picture what the events of his return will be like. Though Jesus is an innocent man sent to his death, he also is the vindicated one, who will return through God's power.

The resurrection is the first step of that vindication. It takes the disciples by surprise, even though Jesus predicted it. Through it and the appearances that accompany it, Jesus explains God's plan and prepares his disciples for the era that takes place while he is at God's right hand. Jesus manifests his presence through his Spirit. Drawing on that resource, they can take the gospel to the world.

The first subunit of this concluding section (19:45—21:4) covers a wide array of controversies. Who initiates the controversy keeps switching. Jesus cleanses the temple (19:45—48), tells the parable of the tenants (20:9—19), and asks about the identity of the Messiah (20:41—44). The Jews ask about the source of Jesus' authority (20:1—8), the issues of taxes to Rome (20:20—26), and the doctrine of resurrection (20:27—40). The subunit closes with Jesus' warning to the people not to be like the leadership; he then lifts up a poor widow as an example of spirituality (20:45—21:4). These events, underscoring how the two opposing factions became so opposed, continue the tension already detailed in chapters 9—13.

In 19:45, Luke shows that once Jesus is in the city of Jerusalem, he wastes no time communicating his feelings about certain religious activities there.[1] The background to this event is central to understanding what takes place here. In the temple precinct, items necessary for sacrifices were sold: animals, wine, oil, salt, and doves (John 2:14; *Mishnah, Seqalim* 1:3; 2:4).[2] In addition money was changed from Roman currency to the required Hebrew shekels in accordance with the law (Ex. 30:11—14). This exchange had a built-in surcharge, some of which probably went to the high priest's family. In Jesus' view, the temple has become an excessively commercial enterprise, not a place of worship and prayer. Jesus' action goes on to raise the issue of the source and nature of his authority, since the temple is the most sacred site in Judaism.[3]

---

1. The parallels to this text are Matthew 21:12—13 and Mark 11:15—19. Many also regard John 2:13—17 as a parallel, which is possible, assuming a literary rearrangement for emphasis by either the Synoptic writers or John. But the differences in the account, like the different Old Testament texts cited, and their differing placement make it more likely in my judgment that John is not narrating the same event, so that two cleansings took place in Jesus' ministry. If one event is in view, then John is likely to have moved the account forward to anticipate the issue of conflict and Jesus' comparing his resurrection to temple restoration.

2. V. Eppstein, "The Historicity of the Gospel Account of the Cleansing of the Temple," *ZNW* 55 (1964): 42—58, notes that some of these innovations may have just been put within the temple courts.

3. B. Witherington, *The Christology of Jesus*, 107—16.

Luke tells the story of the temple cleansing succinctly. Jesus drives out the merchants and quotes a composite Old Testament citation. The first part of verse 46 (the temple as "a house of prayer") comes from Isaiah 56:7—a text that calls for justice and acknowledges the way to God is open to all, including foreigners and eunuchs, if they are faithful to God's law. The second part comes from Jeremiah 7:11, which declares that God's people have made the temple "a den of robbers." Jeremiah calls the nation to repent of their misdeeds, warning them of judgment if they refuse to do so. With the support of the prophets behind him, Jesus condemns the desecration of the temple's holy function.

Is the act messianic as well as prophetic? Little within the event itself is a reflection of messianic function.[4] But its temporal juxtaposition to the Triumphal Entry means that this import cannot be far away. The one who entered the city to praise from Psalm 118 now cleanses the temple. The Messiah was supposed to bring wisdom and light to his people, so any activity related to the integrity of worship is certainly included.

Jesus' action strengthens the resolve of the leadership to deal with him (6:11; 11:53–54). He cannot be allowed to dictate how worship will be conducted at the temple and thus blatantly challenge priestly practices. His actions would undoubtedly be regarded as blasphemous if they did not come from someone with prophetic authority, which is why the issue of Jesus' authority is the next question raised (20:1–8). As Jesus shows up at the temple daily, the Jews plan to destroy him.[5] But his popularity makes them hesitant. How can they do it when people are hanging on his very words? That is why they try to trip him up into saying something inappropriate.

Luke 20:1–8 returns to the central issue of the Gospel. Where does Jesus' authority come from?[6] This dispute is a serious one, since Jesus' right to question worship at the temple is directly related to the source of his power. He has had no formal training and is a thorough outsider. So what gives him the right to tell the priests how to run a temple that they have been in charge of for centuries? What right does he have to make great religious claims?

---

4. If a messianic allusion to an Old Testament text exists, Malachi 3:1 is a candidate, but the problem with that text is its obscurity and the lack of a connection to this tradition. Is "the messenger of the covenant" in Malachi equal to the "messenger, who will prepare the way"? If so, then is that messenger not John? Moreover, is the Lord's coming to the temple a reference to Jesus or to the Lord's eventual powerful manifestation on his return? The following verses in Malachi suggest the latter sense.

5. The Greek reads they planned to "destroy" him, which the NIV simplifies to "kill."

6. The parallels to this text are Matthew 21:23–27 and Mark 11:27–33. In this account the texts are similar, except that Luke lacks reference to the withering of the fig tree. Luke is zeroing in on the Jesus issue.

Such concerns motivate the priests and teachers of the law to probe Jesus as he teaches in the temple courts and shares the gospel. Their question comes in two forms. By what authority does Jesus do these things, and who has given it to him? The reference to "these things" (v. 2) tells us that the action at the temple is only one thing that bothers the leadership.

Jesus responds with his own question. He asks them to assess John the Baptist's ministry. The question is brilliant because John's roots were as obscure as those of Jesus. Like Jesus, he had no formal training. He too preached repentance for all, yet the people acknowledged his ministry. What would the Jewish leadership say about a ministry like his? Sometimes a pointed question deserves a pointed question in return. The answer is significant because it links the two ministries together and the public has already made a judgment about John. The principle by which the leadership is judging Jesus—namely, he has no official priestly credentials—will also result in the rejection of John's ministry, but John has already been accepted by the people as a prophet. Jesus has put them in a corner.

The character of the leadership emerges in their deliberations among themselves. The issue they discuss is not the truth, but appearances. To confess John's ministry as possessing roots in heaven will expose their own lack of response. That answer is an embarrassment. However, to answer that it is from men rejects popular opinion, and they will face the wrath of the people for claiming an acknowledged prophet is not one after all. Everything about the reply is concerned with how it "will play in Peoria."

The Jews decide to take a safe route and punt, claiming they do not know. The refusal to take a position leaves the door open for Jesus to refuse to commit himself, not because he does not wish to make a claim, but because the answer is obvious and need not be debated. They refused to recognize John, and now they are maintaining their distance from Jesus. Yet throughout his ministry Jesus has given plenty of evidence about the source of his authority (see 5:24; 11:20). The time for debate is past. The leadership has made their decision, and they should own up to it. Their failure to do so is the narration's indictment on their action.

Bridging Contexts

THIS CLEANSING OF the temple took place at an institution of God that no longer exists. But a principle about worship surfaces in Jesus' remarks that is still valid, even if the temple is no longer with us. Worship is a sacred trust, where commerce and hypocrisy have no place. The irony of this scene is that the priests' concern for the temple and their authority over it lead them to contemplate destroying Jesus, the true temple (John 2:19–22). The sin of excessive religious commercialism has become compounded into contemplating murder. The mixed citation in verse 46 emphasizes that the sacred places of God are places of worship, not commerce. In addition, the worship God desires is linked intimately to the condition of the human heart (see John 4:24).

Another point to bear in mind is that sin usually does not take place in isolation. One sin tends to result in more sin. This tendency of sin to multiply like a cancerous cell is why turning from sin is so important. It prevents the disease from spreading to even more damaging proportions.

The fundamental issue in 20:1–8 is the source of Jesus' authority. The linkage between John the Baptist and Jesus, as well as the evidence of Jesus' own ministry, provides Luke's answer. Beginning with 1:15–2:52, a significant number of texts in Luke raise this authority question because it is so central to everything he does to reassure Theophilus about who Jesus is. Important questions need lots of testimony, and Jesus' ministry has supplied it, despite the hesitation of the chief priests and Jewish elders to admit it.

Also significant in this section is how rejection manifests itself. There is something fundamentally evasive about the Jewish leadership's dealings with Jesus' question. They do not want to answer it honestly and directly. This portrait of politics and public relations adds to the narrative portrait of how subtly sin works. The leadership's continual sitting on the fence has an air of careful assessment, but their response to Jesus reveals the falseness of such assessments. Failure to embrace God's way may manifest itself in this type of innocent-looking evasion, but it may be a response that is not as innocent as it looks.

In fact, there is a power play and manipulation in this text that reveals how sin often operates not overtly but covertly. The leadership's behind-the-scenes dialogue to justify lack of public declaration is too often the case in our relationships. Honestly declaring where we stand and why is stifled by concern for how others may view us. The Christian faith is not committed to gaining the most votes, running a popularity contest, or finishing high in the polls. We must take a hard and honest stand for truth, even if it is not popular. Maneuvering to protect constituencies, as the Pharisees do here, is a sign of spiritual weakness that can kill a ministry or personal credibility. If we keep our eyes on the votes of our culture, God's truth and being honest about it usually suffer. Being truthful does not mean being callous, but it does mean we should show enough honesty to make clear where we stand and why.

OUR CULTURE MAY be right about certain expressions of the Christian faith when it accuses us of being too commercial. When money and prospering through the faith become more central than the worship of God, a distortion like that which occurred at the temple has taken place. It is hard to watch certain television ministries and not sense that money is more central than worship or ministry. When one attends church to facilitate meaningful business contacts, this distorted principle is also at work. What is most tragic is that resources from many well-meaning people may be going to sources that are less responsible than many organizations engaged in more authentic forms of ministry.

Often the lifestyles of the ministers who benefit from these resources are a clue as to how responsible the stewardship of God's money is in such organizations. If a ministry refuses to be audited or to open its books for scrutiny, then its integrity may well be suspect. Neutral organizations like the Evangelical Council for Financial Accountability audit and verify the integrity of a ministry's financial practices. One should check to see if a ministry has such financial oversight and accountability before giving. Note how Paul expected that the money he was collecting for Jerusalem would be carried in such a way that more than one person knew about it (1 Cor. 16:3).

In our church we have recently assessed how we use our worship space as a venue for selling tickets for church functions and other items related to church activities. Though many well-meaning groups want to sell tickets to various fund-raisers or other events, we as a community have decided to move such sales away from the sanctuary as a way of honoring texts like Luke 19:45–46. Though less convenient, keeping the business of worship as the only business for the sanctuary seems the best way to keep a worshiping heart focused on meeting God.

We noted above how sin has a tendency to beget more sin. In Luke 19, concern for excessive commercial interests grows into a desire to eliminate Jesus. No doubt the leadership would have pled in their resistance to Jesus that they were merely trying to prevent someone from coming in and creating havoc at the temple. They may well have argued that law and order is not only the affair of governments; worship also needs oversight. But failure to engage in serious self-examination led to further sin. It is like the lie a spouse may tell to cover an affair. More damage follows as the marriage is eventually destroyed by compounding acts of sin against a vow originally made before God. Sins, like lies, tend to travel in packs and devour like wolves. Untreated, sin becomes a thoroughly destructive force.

As to the fundamental issue of Jesus' authority and where it resides, does he have the right to do what he has done here? If so, we must take the warning here to heart. As Jesus nears the cross, we must reflect whether the official opposition to Jesus is appropriate. Preaching the arrival of God's promise and cleansing the temple are acts that either are sanctioned by God or are wrong. Jesus is not just a good man here. The kind of benign respect our culture pays him is not a possible category that the Bible leaves open. He does not allow fence-sitting. He should either be embraced as Savior and Lord or opposed. If John the Baptist pointed to him as the Coming One, then Jesus is the Promised One of God.

Note Jesus' hesitation to answer his enemies. Sometimes when ample opportunity has been given to respond, there no longer remains any need to keep answering what is essentially the same question. Jesus has answered numerous times in word and action the question the Jewish leadership raises. In our lives, this translates into a recognition that when we have shared Jesus with someone over a long period, there comes a time when answers may no longer be appropriate. Instead, we should urge the person to reflect on what has already been revealed. In some contexts, the only appropriate response to repeated inquiries is continued love, not more words.

The negative character lesson of the Jewish leaders' deliberations has been noted above. But do we do the same things? Do we hesitate to speak up for our association with Jesus in contexts where it might not be popular? Do we use evasive tactics to hide previous actions that we now know were wrong? Do we tell people in public debate we are searching for truth, when our mind is already made up? Are we manipulative like the leaders here? Jesus urges us elsewhere that our "yes" should be "yes," and "no" should be "no" (Matt. 5:37). Any other action undercuts integrity and trust.

HE WENT ON to tell the people this parable: "A man planted a vineyard, rented it to some farmers and went away for a long time. ¹⁰At harvest time he sent a servant to the tenants so they would give him some of the fruit of the vineyard. But the tenants beat him and sent him away empty-handed. ¹¹He sent another servant, but that one also they beat and treated shamefully and sent away empty-handed. ¹²He sent still a third, and they wounded him and threw him out.

¹³"Then the owner of the vineyard said, 'What shall I do? I will send my son, whom I love; perhaps they will respect him.'

¹⁴"But when the tenants saw him, they talked the matter over. 'This is the heir,' they said. 'Let's kill him, and the inheritance will be ours.' ¹⁵So they threw him out of the vineyard and killed him.

"What then will the owner of the vineyard do to them? ¹⁶He will come and kill those tenants and give the vineyard to others."

When the people heard this, they said, "May this never be!"

¹⁷Jesus looked directly at them and asked, "Then what is the meaning of that which is written:

"'The stone the builders rejected
has become the cornerstone'?

¹⁸Everyone who falls on that stone will be broken to pieces, but he on whom it falls will be crushed."

¹⁹The teachers of the law and the chief priests looked for a way to arrest him immediately, because they knew he had spoken this parable against them. But they were afraid of the people.

Original Meaning

THIS SIGNIFICANT PARABLE summarizes the history of God's activity with Israel.¹ Its placement here provides the answer for the questions of the origin of Jesus' authority raised in 20:1–8. He is the only Son, sent from God. Relying on basic Old Testament themes and alter-

---

1. The parallels to this passage are Matthew 21:33–44 and Mark 12:1–11. The variations in details indicate how this parable circulated and was summarized in various versions.

ing them, Jesus warns the nation about their perilous position. The image of the vineyard echoes Isaiah 5:1–7, where Israel is the vineyard. In Jesus' parable the imagery is more complex. The vineyard is probably "the promise," while the tenants refers to Israel, especially as represented by the leadership.[2]

The other Old Testament image in the passage comes from Psalm 118:22, a psalm that already appeared in Luke 13:35 and 19:38. Here the point is that the rejected stone has become the stone God has exalted (see also Acts 4:11; 1 Peter 2:7). Jesus confidently states through the Old Testament quotation that rejecting him will not result in his defeat, though it will negatively impact the nation.[3]

The picture in this parable is a common one. It was not unusual in Palestine, as in many parts of the world today, for land to be owned by one person and farmed by others. When a man plants a vineyard and rents it out to tenants, he expects to collect proceeds from the profit on the crops. Even if his absence is long, he expects the land to remain profitable.

When harvest time comes, the owner sends servants to collect the proceeds from the vineyard. The first one is sent away after being beaten. A second servant is also beaten and treated shamefully. A third is wounded. All the owner's efforts to collect his share are rebuffed with impunity. The detail portrays the persistent unfaithfulness of the nation in their lack of response to the prophets. The Old Testament is full of such failure (1 Kings 18:13; 22:24–27; 2 Kings 6:31; 21:16; 2 Chron. 24:19–22; 36:15–16; Neh. 9:26; Jer. 37:15; 44:4). As Luke 13:6–9 notes, the nation has no fruit to give God.

For example, in Matthew the interaction with the servants is summarized briefly, while Mark has an escalating severity in the way the servants are treated. Luke is less severe still, with the first servant sent away empty-handed, while the second is beaten and the third wounded. Only Jesus is slain. Luke also shortens the citation of Psalm 118, leaving out verse 23, and reverses the order of the slaying of the son, casting him out of the vineyard before slaying him.

2. For a different opinion, with the vineyard as Israel and the tenants as the leadership, see Blomberg, *Interpreting the Parables*, 248 n. 100. I see this parable operating much like Romans 11, where the olive tree contains Israel as natural branches, but is really a reference to the promise. I prefer a reference to all Israel, for Luke's view is that as the leadership goes, so goes the response of the nation. A parable like this and the judgment it predicts show why the nation is responsible as a whole for their reaction to Jesus' messianic visit (cf. 19:41–44). Thus, though the leadership is primarily in view (v. 19), the implications of the parable treat the nation's role. The "others" to whom the tending goes in verse 16 are the Gentiles.

3. The theme of national disobedience leading to divine discipline reflects texts like Jeremiah 7:21–28, which in turn are built the warnings of Deuteronomy 28. The themes raised here reappear with Stephen's speech in Acts 7.

The owner decides to send "my son, whom I love." This expression may well be a way of describing him as an only son, since the tenants expect his death to lead to their being given the land. The owner assumes the tenants will treat him with respect. But when they see the son arrive, they see an opportunity. Barring any breach of relationship, it was not unusual for land to pass to tenants if no heirs existed.[4] But the logic of these tenants is skewed: "If we kill the heir, we will become the heirs!" How will killing the heir reap benefits for them? How twisted sinful thinking can be. Blindness can see strange things in the dark. The allusion here is to their approaching execution of Jesus, which is the parable's key point. Jesus knows exactly what they are about, even though it makes no logical sense.

Jesus asks the people how the owner will respond to the execution of the son. The pattern of previous behavior made finding the culprit for the crime easy. The owner will come, kill the tenants, and lease the land to others. This alludes to the coming involvement of the nations in the promise, as Acts shows, though it also includes a reference to the Twelve, who form the base of the new community Jesus is forming. The crowd gets the point about the shift in who gets to tend the vineyard and exclaims, "May this never be!" Surely Israel and her leadership could never be guilty of such reckless disobedience.

Jesus cites Scripture and a popular proverb to drive home his point. Psalm 118 teaches that the righteous one rejected by others is exalted by God as the key figure. This text is probably about the king who leads the procession into the temple. Old Testament Jews would have thought of their king in these terms, and Jews contemporary to Jesus would expect the nations to be in the place of blessing. The rejectors would have been the nations. Jesus turns the image upside down, noting that now the king is rejected by his own people (cf. Isa. 53). If God then exalts the stone into the key foundational role, it is risky business to stand opposed to the foundation.[5] Everyone who falls on the stone is broken, and those on whom the stone falls are crushed. This proverbial remark is much like the later Jewish Midrash on Esther 3:6: "If the stone falls on the pot, alas for the pot; if the pot falls on the stone, alas for the pot!" Either way it is a problem to oppose the precious stone whom God has exalted—his Son Jesus.

Opposition to Jesus grows more intense, for they know Jesus is challenging them, just as he did earlier at the temple. He accuses them of being

---

4. J. Jeremias, *The Parables of Jesus*, 75 n. 99.

5. Both Psalm 118 and this text refer to Jesus as a foundation of the building (cf. 1 Cor. 3:10; Eph. 2:20), not as a capstone. See R. McKelvey, *The New Temple* (Oxford: Oxford Univ. Press, 1969), 195–204. We accept the NIV footnote translation here.

in the exact opposite place of where they see themselves. They want to arrest him, but the people remain an obstacle. Jesus is still too popular with them. He will have to be discredited first. So to this effort they turn their attention.

Bridging Contexts

THE PARABLE OF the tenants explains why God has broadened the scope of his blessing. Israel no longer sits at the center of blessing because she has persistently and stubbornly rejected any attempt by God to lead her into righteousness. They have asked to do without God's way, so that is what they get.

The major features of this parable revolve around the basic role of Israel in God's plan. The promise, now that the nation is set aside, is placed in the care of "others," that is, the Gentiles. The commentary on this passage is Romans 11, where Paul uses a similar imagery of a vine to discuss where God's plan is headed. His discussion differs, however, in looking to the future of the nation, not to its involvement with Jesus. That is, Paul picks up where Jesus' image leaves off. He makes the point that though the original branches (Israel) have been cut out, they can and will be grafted in again in the future (Rom. 11:12, 14–15, 26–27, 29–32). In other words, a day is coming when Israel will again have a major role in God's plan. In the meantime, the grafted-in branches of Gentiles must serve faithfully, for if God can cut off unfaithful original branches, he can do the same with unfaithful grafted-in branches. Proximity to blessing is not a cause for pride but for humility.

This historical overview is focused on Israel. Still, these events contain a warning to the church, similar to Paul's exposition in Romans 11. Furthermore, this parable indicates that what was about to happen to Jesus as God's Son was no surprise. History operates within the boundaries God sets. And God's plan was marching forward, even though it looked as if it were not moving. Everything about Israel's response suggests that it would undercut that plan. However, it did not. Resurrection and God's power to bring life meant that others would be found who would respond to God's saving message.

Finally, this passage warns us about not presuming on God's promise. In effect, the tenants thought that the vineyard was theirs forever, but they were mistaken. God came to the vineyard looking for produce, and all he got was hostility and grief. Presuming on God brings judgment (see 19:41–44). Those who are in the vineyard must build up the body and honor God with the fruit he seeks.

THOUGH THIS TEXT seems harsh in portraying God's casting aside of Israel for a time, it is important to look at how patient and long-suffering God was. He had sent numerous servants to his people, and finally he sent his Son. They had been given every opportunity to respond. But their blindness had become stronger and stronger as their hostility continued. That is often the way sin works. Once present, it becomes more deeply ingrained (Rom. 1:18–32). God's judgment is not capricious; it is rather the culmination of a long process. He rejects people only after a long effort to try and gain a response from them. Jesus wept as he entered Jerusalem because judgment is not what God desires to bring on humankind (2 Peter 3:9). Judgment comes only because we fail to respond to God's compassion.

The text again highlights the centrality of Jesus. He is the cornerstone, and to oppose him is to face rejection by God. That stone breaks those who remain opposed to him. The message is clear in various places in this Gospel that opposing Jesus means facing rejection from God. It also shows that nothing will frustrate his plan. As the center of that plan, Jesus through the resurrection becomes the base of a new community, a fresh temple where God's presence dwells. In fact, the Spirit in us is what gives this new living temple its life (1 Cor. 3:17–18). That temple is sacred to God and functions under his protection. If anyone attacks it, as the Jewish leadership did the Son, and does not repent, judgment will fall on them. God seeks honor from the community in whom he lives, as well as from those who refuse to give it. One day all will acknowledge him. It is better to do so willingly now than to be forced to acknowledge him later.

Luke 20:20–26

KEEPING A CLOSE watch on him, they sent spies, who pretended to be honest. They hoped to catch Jesus in something he said so that they might hand him over to the power and authority of the governor. ²¹So the spies questioned him: "Teacher, we know that you speak and teach what is right, and that you do not show partiality but teach the way of God in accordance with the truth. ²²Is it right for us to pay taxes to Caesar or not?"

²³He saw through their duplicity and said to them, ²⁴"Show me a denarius. Whose portrait and inscription are on it?"

²⁵"Caesar's," they replied.

He said to them, "Then give to Caesar what is Caesar's, and to God what is God's."

²⁶They were unable to trap him in what he had said there in public. And astonished by his answer, they became silent.

Original Meaning

THE JEWISH LEADERSHIP now tries to trip up Jesus on political grounds.[1] The issue is the Roman "poll tax." This unpopular tax represented one of the most decisive examples of Rome's sovereignty over Israel.[2] The plot thickens by the way Luke describes the setting. The leadership has sent spies into Jesus' midst, their assignment being to watch Jesus like a hawk. They hypocritically present themselves as "honest," but they are looking for anything Jesus might say to allow them to hand him over to the governor on a political charge. The result would be in their best interest. In Roman custody, Jesus could be subject to the death penalty for treason, thus sparing the leadership of any direct blame for his death. In addition, Rome would appreciate the Jews' looking out for Rome's interests.

These infiltrators have a brilliant plan. They ask Jesus: "Is it right to pay taxes to Caesar or not?" If Jesus supports Rome, his allegiance to Israel will be questioned. If he sides with the Jews, then Rome can be called. Their initial praise of him as one who teaches "what is right" (v. 21) only highlights

---

1. The parallels to this passage are Matthew 22:15–22 and Mark 12:13–17.
2. On the Jewish view of this tax, see Josephus, *Antiquities* 2.8.1 §§ 117–18; 7.8.1 §§ 253–58; 18.1.1. §§ 1–10.

their hypocrisy. Everything they do represents a rejection of Jesus. They no more think that he teaches the way of God and the way of truth than they believe that Rome is the height of righteous piety.

The question is posed in either/or terms. But Jesus is aware of their craftiness (NIV "duplicity"),[3] calls for a coin, and asks who is responsible for its inscription. This coin, a denarius, would have read, "Tiberius Caesar, Augustus son of the divine Augustus." Roman sovereignty was minted all over it. The Jews were carrying such coins in their pockets, proof that they already lived under Rome's sovereignty and accepted it by participating in its commerce. God had ordained such government and their current power over Israel (cf. Rom. 13:1–7).

Jesus' reply is brief: "Then give to Caesar what is Caesar's, and to God what is God's." He turns the question into a both/and. Government has the right to exist and function, but its presence does not destroy one's allegiance to God (Rom. 13:1–7; 1 Peter 2:13–17). Jesus is not a political revolutionary who rails against Rome, nor is he an ardent nationalist. No one can charge him with political subversion. He does not step into the trap set for him, and the leadership recognizes their effort has failed. They can only be silent in the face of his reply.

Bridging Contexts

THIS TEXT IS the closest to a political statement Jesus makes. It is not a comprehensive one, but it does reveal much about how he dealt with (or de-emphasized!) issues of state. In many ways Jesus' handling of this question shows that he is not interested in the political agenda of changing Rome. He is not a zealot. He is more interested that Israel be a people who honor the God they claim to know than being concerned with their relationship to Rome.

A basic principle about church and state is also in view here. Governments, even a pagan government like Rome, have the right to exist and to expect its citizens to participate in contributing to its functions. Supporting such a government, including taxes, does not violate one's commitment to God.

But Jesus is after something far more fundamental and comprehensive than dealing with a specific government. He desires to call out a people from Israel (after his death, from the nations) who will walk with God and witness to him before a world across national lines. Jesus will not issue an attack on Rome. In fact, his earlier entry into Jerusalem (19:28–40) showed

---

3. The term for craftiness really refers to trickery, O. Bauernfiend, "πανουργία," *TDNT*, 5:726.

that he came humbly as a king who represented peace and the hope of directing a people into righteousness. What he seeks to build transcends national lines. That is partly why he can urge that taxes be paid to a government that was pagan. Jesus' work involves spiritual transformation and the establishment of a distinct colony of God in the midst of Israel and the nations. There he hopes to manifest God's presence, showing others how people should live in community before him (Eph. 1:22–23; 1 Peter 2:13–17). This distinction is essential as we contemplate how the church should function in the world.

 HOW SHOULD THE church view government? Does God desire a Christian nation? And what does that phrase mean? If we mean that God desires the structures of society to relate to people in a way that honors God and humanity, then the answer is surely yes. God holds nations, even those who are not in covenant relationship with him, accountable for how they treat people. But if we mean that God has a special contract of blessing with any given nation, the answer is no, since only Israel had a special relationship with God. Today, in the place where God is especially at work, the church transcends any national boundaries (Phil. 3:20–21).

The church today risks looking for God's nation in the wrong place. That Christian nation is not in a political capital like Washington, London, Berlin, Tokyo, Guatemala City, Lagos, Sao Paul, or Moscow. That nation is the community Jesus has formed to be the world's light, a citizenship whose roots are in heaven (Phil. 3:20–21) and whose call is to reach out to people in every nation and tribe to be a part of this community. To render to God what is God's is to give to God faithful service on behalf of his kingdom in the midst of the nations. The Bible does not call the church to side with any particular nation or political ideology, but to conduct its mission before all people, since every nation needs God.

What does this imply about political activity? Christians have the right to be full citizens in any country, even the duty to do so. The church has the right to contend in the public marketplace for those values that make for a healthy community. John the Baptist himself challenged Herod on his lifestyle by raising the issue of his accountability to God. But the church is not in the business of wielding secular power or the sword. Its experiment with that approach in the time of Constantine and in the medieval church must be regarded a dismal failure. Even efforts like those at Geneva during the Reformation obtained only mixed results. When people who do not wish to belong to the church are coerced to be a part of it, the church is impacted negatively. God himself lets people refuse to be a part of his community and then holds them responsible for the choice.

We are called to serve, to display righteousness and personal integrity in the midst of a world that is slow to acknowledge the presence of sin and moral accountability. One should be able to point to the church and say, "Here is a place where healthy relationships and genuine, even multiethnic, community can be found." In the world we should support causes that reflect a sense of moral justice that is not wedded to any particular ideology. In fact, one can argue that in order to do the work of testifying to God's grace, every institution should be examined by God's high standards. The political motto of the church is to love God and one's neighbor. The application of that credo can take so many forms that it is limited only by the church's imagination and energy. The church has much work and reflection to do in this area. Our capital is found at the right hand of God.

The debate about Christ and culture is old, and various approaches have been taken to the issue. In 1951 H. Richard Niebuhr wrote his famous *Christ and Culture*, in which he considered five different options to this question in the history of the church: "Christ against culture," "Christ of culture" (he is the author of culture), "Christ above culture" (he transcends it), "Christ and culture in paradox," and "Christ the transformer of culture."[4] One option is missing: the church as the model of a reconstituted culture. The last option argues that the retooling of culture is something God does in the end.

Though we can seek it, the church's call is not to reform culture, because reformation cannot take place by changing structures alone; hearts must be changed. The dynamic for that kind of structural and internal change exists in the church community, which serves as light—a place to which people should be able to point as one that operates differently from the world. The church should be able to show the world what healthy relationships look like, how the needs of the poor can be met with compassion, what absence of racism looks like, how people can engage in business with integrity, how reconciliation takes place when people have failed one another, and so forth.

What does this perspective mean for our involvement in politics? Many of us in the Western world live in participatory democracies, so we have the right to be fully engaged in the obligations that come with being citizens. We have the right to participate in the public square, and we should.[5] As Richard Neuhaus has pointed out, a naked public square is not desirable:

---

4. H. Richard Niebuhr, *Christ and Culture* (New York: Harper and Row, 1951).

5. For a solid work on religious public discourse, see Richard Neuhaus, *The Naked Public Square* (Grand Rapids: Eerdmans, 1984). A periodical devoted to such concerns is called *First Things*.

The naked public square is, as Murray suggests, an "impossible" project. That, however, does not deter people from attempting it. In the minds of some secularists the naked public square is a desirable goal. They subscribe to the dogma of the secular Enlightenment that, as people become more enlightened (educated), religion will wither away; or, if it does not wither away, it can be safely sealed off from public consideration, reduced to a private eccentricity. Our argument is that the naked public square is not desirable, even if it were possible. It is not desirable in the view of believers because they are inescapably entangled in the belief that the morals truths of religion have a universal and public validity. The Ten Commandments, to take an obvious example, have a normative status. They are not, as it has been said, Ten Suggestions or Ten Significant Moral Insights to be more or less appreciated according to one's subjective disposition. Even if one is not a believer, the divorce of public business from the moral vitalities of the society is not desirable if one is committed to the democratic idea. In addition to not being desirable, however, we have argued that the naked public square is not possible. It is an illusion, for the public square cannot and does not remain naked. When particularist religious values and the institutions that bear them are excluded, the inescapable need to make public moral judgments will result in an elite construction of a normative morality from sources and principles not democratically recognized by society.[6]

But we must be careful to let religion operate in its own sphere. It should not be coerced, but participation should come through conviction. On the other hand, our debate in the public square must be sensitive to make arguments grounded in what is the "common good" for our society. Here a case for public morality can be made, because what is moral is healthy for humanity (that is why God gave instructions on it). But confusion of political ideology and religion or ideology and civil religion should be avoided.[7] God has no philosophy of government that matches any of our political party's agendas. One could make the case that the record of each party is mixed from a biblical standpoint and that the moral quality of a party's position depends on what point of policy or what issue is in view. The church as an alternative to the culture must stay above culture in its critique of how government or any other institution does business. Government exists to protect the people, administer law and order, collect taxes, and serve the

---

6. Ibid., 86.

7. Highly recommended here is Os Guinness, *The American Hour* (New York: Macmillan, 1992), esp. 147–61, 371–93.

common good as a principle of justice (Rom. 13:1–7); the church exists to nurture hearts and souls.

These questions become more difficult when one gets specific. What about abortion? This is an issue of public morality. It is an inherently religious and philosophical discussion in a culture that does not know how to have such discussions. That is why the discussion is so culturally painful. It is like teaching a married couple how to communicate, when both sides have no clue how to listen to their partner. As I write, ABC's *Nightline* has just had a feature on abortion. Their statistic is that 2 to 3 percent of women of reproductive age had an abortion last year. We should, of course, encourage the protection of human life, but we must also be prepared to put in place structures that support the children if abortion were to be made illegal. We cannot argue passionately for the preservation of life, only to abandon that concern once the child is born. That means that arguments of financial expediency may cut against what is morally required. Some argue for abortion by stressing how much it costs for unwanted children to come into the world—both emotionally and economically. Those who argue against it may need to be prepared to bear the moral and social costs of making a moral choice. The road of righteousness is not always the easiest one. The choice to abort is often an expedient choice, while the choice to raise a child costs a lot of money. As we make the case, we will need to offer ourselves as good neighbors, willing to help on the follow-through of a choice to bear a child, especially in contexts where emotional and financial support is lacking.

What about prayer in school? Here is a delicate question. I am all for prayer and teaching the value of prayer to God, but how will we pray in a multicultural environment? We cannot argue, I believe, that we are a monoreligious community, for we are not. I prefer a public square where the issue of religious belief is treated openly and directly, as a matter of public interest and information. But we must exercise sensitivity, as Paul did on the Areopagus in Athens (Acts 17:16–34). I have been asked to pray at civil functions where I was aware of the scope of the nationalities and religions present. How do we function in this context? Are we like Daniel, faithful to our God in our own conduct and worship, yet discretely but truthfully generic in broader contexts? The prayers I have offered in such contexts have majored on God's role in creating us and on our responsibility in humbly seeking his face. Our culture needs to reflect on the value of religious questions in general before it can ever focus on specific religious questions with care and concern. The best prayers in our multireligious contexts are those that allow the individual time for personal prayer. Otherwise, battles will ensue over who gets to write the prayers the class prays. What is rendered unto God should be rendered sincerely, not by coercion.

Luke 20:27–40

S OME OF THE Sadducees, who say there is no resurrection, came to Jesus with a question. ²⁸"Teacher," they said, "Moses wrote for us that if a man's brother dies and leaves a wife but no children, the man must marry the widow and have children for his brother. ²⁹Now there were seven brothers. The first one married a woman and died childless. ³⁰The second ³¹and then the third married her, and in the same way the seven died, leaving no children. ³²Finally, the woman died too. ³³Now then, at the resurrection whose wife will she be, since the seven were married to her?"

³⁴Jesus replied, "The people of this age marry and are given in marriage. ³⁵But those who are considered worthy of taking part in that age and in the resurrection from the dead will neither marry nor be given in marriage, ³⁶and they can no longer die; for they are like the angels. They are God's children, since they are children of the resurrection. ³⁷But in the account of the bush, even Moses showed that the dead rise, for he calls the Lord 'the God of Abraham, and the God of Isaac, and the God of Jacob.' ³⁸He is not the God of the dead, but of the living, for to him all are alive."

³⁹Some of the teachers of the law responded, "Well said, teacher!" ⁴⁰And no one dared to ask him any more questions.

Original Meaning

THE NEXT NEW angle in challenging Jesus is a theological one.[1] The protagonists are the Sadducees.[2] They raise the issue of the resurrection, which finds them on the opposite side of the Pharisees, for the Sadducees did not believe in resurrection. As a priestly aristocrat movement, they accepted the first five books of the Old Testament as carrying supreme authority and disliked the oral tradition of the Pharisees. They tended to be rationalistic and were by and large wealthy.[3] Yet

---

1. The parallels to this passage are Matthew 22:22–33 and Mark 12:18–27.

2. This is Jesus' only encounter with the Sadducees in Luke. For background on them, see Josephus, *Jewish Wars* 2.8.14 §§ 163–65; *Antiquities* 18.1.4 § 16.

3. R. Meyer, "Σαδδουκαῖος," *TDNT*, 7:35–54.

despite their differences, when it came to Jesus, they joined the Pharisees in trying to bring him down.

The Sadducees had a standard question they liked to pose on the resurrection to try to show how ludicrous it was. Drawing on levirate marriage (Gen. 38:8; Deut. 25:5; Ruth 4:1–12) and assuming that a man was to be a husband of one wife in heaven, they constructed a "Whose wife will she be?" dilemma.[4] The questioners begin by noting the levirate custom and then walk Jesus through the story. Each of seven marriages of a particular woman ends childless (the absence of a child triggers the levirate process). The story has a touch of humor, since one gets the feeling that it is death to marry this woman! Finally the woman dies. The question now emerges, "At the resurrection, whose wife will she be?" After all, there are seven candidates. The Sadducees do not really want an answer, for they are convinced that the dilemma shows the lack of logic in a resurrection. They also assume that the afterlife is like this life.

The question is a crucial one for several reasons. (1) Some Jews did believe in a resurrection. (2) Jesus has predicted his own resurrection to the disciples. (3) Resurrection is at the center of what became the Christian hope. So for all the humor in the query, the question must be seriously addressed.

Jesus replies at two levels. (1) He notes that the afterlife is not like this life, in that there will be no marriage in the era to come. Since people will live forever, there will be no need for marriage and producing progeny to replenish the earth. Relationships will operate on a different plane in heaven.[5] People will become like angels, who do not eat or marry (cf. 1 Enoch 15:6; 51:4; 104:4–6; Wisdom 5:5, 15–16).[6] Those worthy of resurrection, the children of God, will be children of resurrection.

(2) As a more subtle point, Jesus implies that not everyone will be resurrected. He speaks of those "considered worthy of taking part in that age." Therefore, some risk being excluded from that era.[7] This second point does not relate to the question, but raises the issue of who gets to receive the resurrection to everlasting life.

To solidify his argument, Jesus makes one final point from the Pentateuch, the one section of Scripture the Sadducees trust. Jesus notes how God said to Moses that the Lord is the God of Abraham, Isaac, and Jacob (see Ex. 3:2–6). God is the God of the living, not the dead. So if God *is* still God to the patriarchs as he speaks to Moses, long after their deaths, they must be

---

4. Some note similar themes in Tobit 3:8; 6:9–12; 7:12–13.

5. E. Schweizer, "υἱός," *TDNT*, 8:347–49, 355.

6. Jesus is actually making a second dig here, for the Sadducees did not believe in angels!

7. Some in Judaism also held to this distinction (1 Enoch 91:10; 92:3; 103:3–4).

alive or present somehow in the midst of God.[8] God is the God of promise for these patriarchs. For them to share in the realization of the promise, they must live to see it.

In other words, Jesus' reply takes two forms. The Sadducean marriage dilemma misunderstands the afterlife, since marriage does not occur there. Thus, the problem the Sadducees pose is a pseudo-problem. And Scripture does teach resurrection in the Torah in how it mentions the patriarchs. If God makes promises to them and the afterlife is known (cf. also "Abraham's side" in 16:22), then resurrection seems an appropriate deduction. This is a fundamental doctrine of hope.

The reaction to Jesus' answer is instant. Some, no doubt of the Pharisees, like his defense of resurrection. Jesus also silences his opponents, so that they do not want to ask him any more questions. On his own ministry's authority, on politics, and now on theology, his enemies have been soundly rebuffed. This entire encounter makes a basic point: Jesus knows more about God's will and where he is going than his opponents. He may be outnumberred a few thousand to one, but he can be trusted to teach the way of God.

ALTHOUGH THIS CONTROVERSY deals with a unique problem as far as the Sadducees were concerned, the topic it treats is a fundamental one: Will people be raised from the dead? The resurrection is a central teaching of the Christian faith because on it hangs three central issues: accountability before God, judgment, and eternal life. Without a resurrection, death would be the end, our accountability to God would be limited at best to this life, and judgment and eternal life would become meaningless concepts. The most eloquent defense of resurrection as a central Christian truth surfaces in 1 Corinthians 15, where Paul talks about how Jesus' resurrection is the proof for our own future resurrection. It has often been said that death is the great equalizer, since we all must die. Yet resurrection is the great opportunity, since we all have a chance to enter into eternal life.

As for a second bridge into our era, we often think that ancient people were unsophisticated, gullible, and nonempirical, believing in gods and spirits at every turn. But some in the ancient world were skeptical of spiritual teaching, just as moderns are. The Sadducees were "modern" people in an

---

8. The text is not explicit here, and neither is the general Jewish teaching on the life to come. Usually the resurrection is associated with the last days, so that the patriarchs would be understood to be awaiting resurrection at the end while existing with the righteous in Sheol (see 1 Enoch 22).

ancient time, questioning both the existence of angels and the resurrection. They were committed materialists, dedicated to pursuing life on this earth. In a sense, they speak for a common attitude today.

One major difference between this passage and our era adds to the shock of Jesus' answer for us. In the ancient world, marriages were arranged and were often a business issue in order to associate families. That is still true in some parts of our world today. But in the West, with our notions of romantic love, individual choice, and dating practices, marriage has become more personalized. That means that some of the basic reasons for marriage, such as providing a home where children can be raised and nourished, have a less visible priority to more relational concerns. This is not to say that marital love did not exist in biblical times (see Song of Songs and Eph. 5:22–33). But the romantic aspects of love have a more central role in our modern perception. Thus, when Jesus speaks of the end of marriage in heaven, it almost comes as a shock to our ears.

But we must remember that the quality and purity of relationships will extend far beyond what marriage provides today. Sin will no longer cloud our relationships, and the quality of personal interaction in a world will be directed fully by the presence of God. The absence of evil and the presence of God make marriage as a supportive and protective institution superfluous. For those who hesitate at this remark because their marriage has been good, just remember, heaven will be even better.

THE TWO BASIC applications of this passage revolve around the reality of resurrection and the resulting accountability we have to God. These applications emerge when we assess the slogan of a particular advertisement years ago that summarizes twentieth-century popular philosophy: "You only go around once in life, so grab for all the gusto you can get." This saying, theologically, is an example of a mixed bag.

That you only go around once in life is good theology. Belief in reincarnation creates a certain absence of responsibility, for if I do not do well in this life, I can recover in the next one. Life is not like elementary school, where a person can repeat a grade if failure occurs. The Bible knows nothing of return visits in new forms of existence. So the proper response to that reality is vastly different than the view of the advertisers. Rather than grabbing for all the gusto one can, the uniqueness of our journey means that we should pay careful attention to our one chance to walk with God. We should live as we have been created to live. The reality of resurrection and the prospect of being "considered worthy of taking part" in it means we should be careful what we believe and how we respond. Jesus is challenging the Sadducees to realize that there is more to that life than what exists on this side of death. You only go around once in life, so grab for all of God's goodness you can get.

Regarding the resurrection, we do not just go to heaven when we are raised from the dead; we are transformed (1 Cor. 15:35—58). Life after the resurrection takes place in a transformed community, where sin no longer exists. We live in a world so full of sin, including our own, that it is hard to appreciate how wonderful such an existence will be. Yet God assures us that he will make us like himself. It is not just where we are going that makes the hope so great, but who we will be when we get there.

Luke 20:41–44

❧

THEN JESUS SAID TO them, "How is it that they say the Christ is the Son of David? 42David himself declares in the Book of Psalms:

"'The Lord said to my Lord:
"Sit at my right hand
43 until I make your enemies
a footstool for your feet."'

44David calls him 'Lord.' How then can he be his son?"

Original Meaning

THE FINAL CONTROVERSY is raised by Jesus.[1] It, too, is a theological quiz, treating the subject of the Messiah and raising consciousness about his identity. One favorite identification of the Messiah among the Jews was to mark him as "the Son of David" (Pss. Sol. 17–18). Jesus wants to test that identification, not as wrong, but as incomplete. He uses a rhetorical argument like that used by later rabbis, where two conflicting ideas are placed next to one another, not to deny either but to relate them to each other.[2] At the center of the discussion is Psalm 110:1, the most popular Old Testament text used by Jesus and the early church (Acts 2:30–36; 7:55–56; 13:33–39; 1 Cor. 15:22–28; Eph. 1:19–23; Heb. 1:3–14; 5–7).

This psalm is a regal promise psalm that articulates the hope of what Israel's ideal king will be. The language of the "right hand" declares the king's close relationship to God as his vicegerent. It suggests someone acting with authority in proximity to someone else (Pss. 16:8; 45:9; 109:31; 110:5; Isa. 63:12). Views like those expressed in the psalm explain why the king's palace was located to the right of the temple and why the throne on which Solomon sat was called "the throne of the kingdom of the LORD" or "the throne of the LORD" (1 Chron. 28:5; 29:23).[3] Jesus notes that David is the speaker of the promise. So the psalm presents the promise made to his descendants in the hope that the line will be characterized by such rule. Of course, that expec-

---

1. The parallels to this passage are Matthew 22:41–46 and Mark 12:35–37. The accounts are similar.

2. D. Daube, *The New Testament and Rabbinic Judaism* (London: Athlone, 1956), 158–63.

3. For details on the possible historical background of this psalm, see H. Bateman, "Psalm 110:1 and the New Testament," *BibSac* 149 (1992): 438–53.

tation is most heightened when Messiah is seen as the subject, for he will be everything the Davidic kingship should be and more.[4]

The hub of the issue Jesus raises comes in the question of verse 44. If David is the speaker of this psalm and addresses the regal, messianic figure as his "Lord," how can the title "son of David" be the best title for Messiah? The cultural assumption in the question is the respect accorded a patriarch in that society. A father normally did not bow to a son. So the dilemma in the question is why David shows this figure such total respect and submits to him if he is his son rather than his ancestor.

The text ends here with no answer. The question is posed for reflection. That is precisely how Luke uses it. The issue of Jesus' identity will be the central point of debate as he goes to the cross. What emerges from the image of being seated at God's right hand is that Jesus is both Lord and Christ (cf. 22:69; Acts 2:22–36). He is the Son of David, but more fundamental to his role as Son of David is his role as Lord. The title "Lord" expresses the sovereignty he possesses as God's promised regal agent. If, therefore, David showed such respect to the promised King, should not the Jewish leadership? Though Jesus does not identify himself as the Messiah, it is implied in all that has been taking place. He is beginning to supply the answer to the question asked in Luke 20:2, "By what authority are you doing these things?" It is by God's authority, an authority David recognized when he called the promised descendant "my Lord."

THIS TEXT PRESENTS a theological question that probes the identity of God's Chosen One. The text used, Psalm 110, is a text that describes kings, especially the king who would be the example of all. As each king ascended to Israel's throne, the people hoped that maybe this one would be all that the promised line should be. The Old Testament books of Kings and Chronicles detail how no king matched up even to David, much less exceeded him. Nonetheless, the hope remained. Jesus claims that this kingship will have the submission of even David.

The later events that complete the meaning of the psalm clearly show why David sees such authority in this promised line. The ascended Jesus is now at God's right hand, bringing every enemy into submission. Together with

---

4. Rabbinic interpretation of Psalm 110 tended to apply it either to Abraham or to the Messiah (see Midrash on Ps. 110). Jesus makes nothing of the footstool image here, since he is interested solely in the question of this figure's position. But the psalm looks forward to the day when all of Jesus' opponents are totally subjected to him, not only in position but in reality as well (1 Cor. 15:20–28).

God, he wields authority to redeem humanity. He is "Lord" because the Son rules with the Father. The reality of the psalm's promise is clearer today after the resurrection than it was when Jesus raised the question. Now Jesus is at God's right hand, ruling in his position of authority.

The issue of the Lordship of the Messiah is a crucial one, because this title suggests the sovereignty that Jesus shares with the Father. God has set up Jesus as viceregent so that divine blessings are mediated through the Son (Acts 2:30–36; Eph. 4:7–16). When Scripture speaks of Jesus' Lordship, this key role in grace is highlighted, for he has authority over salvation and its blessings. Thus the title suggests deity, but it also describes his function as a minster of grace that Jesus has in the midst of this authority.[5]

 THIS TEXT FUNCTIONS as yet another call for reflection and decision about Jesus. As one who is both Son of David and his Lord, he should be honored with an allegiance worthy of a king. In those forms of Western culture where kings no longer function as genuine sovereigns, it is hard to appreciate the force of such texts. The image of a regal figure installed and worthy of honor is lost in a world of elected leaders. But Jesus' presence in heaven at the side of his Father enables him to dispense divine blessings (Acts 2:30–36). It also enables him to be appointed "as judge of the living and the dead" (Acts 10:42; 17:31). His rule does not emerge through congregational committee, nor does he serve at the whim of humanity. His commission comes from a higher call and functions at a permanent plane.

In Jesus' position as Lord, we see how powerful our Savior is and what his position entitles him to in the future. Here is the One whom God invests with authority to give us all the blessings of grace. He is the One before whom all enemies will submit. In light of his great power and position, we should be fully responsive to him. If we opt to ignore him, we are turning our backs on divine authority. Thus, the recognition that the Messiah is Lord calls us to humility in our walk with him. Our responsibility to him is greater than to any other being, and we stand before him not as peers but as servants. That is why Paul often begins his letters by describing himself as "a servant of Christ Jesus" (cf. Rom. 1:1). He knows who his Lord is and that he ought to respond faithfully to him.

---

5. D. Bock, "Jesus as Lord in Acts and in the Gospel Message," *BibSac* 143 (1986): 146–54.

Luke 20:45–21:4

WHILE ALL THE people were listening, Jesus said to his disciples, ⁴⁶"Beware of the teachers of the law. They like to walk around in flowing robes and love to be greeted in the marketplaces and have the most important seats in the synagogues and the places of honor at banquets. ⁴⁷They devour widows' houses and for a show make lengthy prayers. Such men will be punished most severely."

²¹·¹As he looked up, Jesus saw the rich putting their gifts into the temple treasury. ²He also saw a poor widow put in two very small copper coins. ³"I tell you the truth," he said, "this poor widow has put in more than all the others. ⁴All these people gave their gifts out of their wealth; but she out of her poverty put in all she had to live on."

Original Meaning

JESUS ISSUES A final warning about the Jewish leadership to his disciples.[1] He is willing to say publicly what he thinks privately. He warns of the pride of the teachers of the law, revealed in their long robes and the special greetings in the marketplace, not to mention the seats they get in the synagogues and at feasts (11:43; 14:7–14).[2] Pride leads further to an elevation of the self that ends up seeing others (such as widows) as inferior and capable of being used as pawns. Jesus desires a ministry that speaks on its own terms, where credit comes because it is earned, not because honor is coopted by practices undertaken to underline one's importance.

Jesus condemns the misuse of widows' funds. A widow represented the most vulnerable in society, whom the pious were supposed to serve. So Jesus is making a serious charge.[3] Apparently in managing a widow's affairs, the teachers of the law took a large cut for themselves. Their pretentious long prayers for others in the face of such inconsideration made matters worse.

---

1. The parallel to this text is Mark 12:38–40. The remarks are conceptually similar to parts of Matthew 23:1–36 and Luke 11:37–54. The presence of this remark in Luke may indicate he is aware of the longer condemnation Matthew describes.

2. On these special salutations, see Windisch, "ἀσπάζομαι," *TDNT*, 1:498. Descriptions of these robes are found in Josephus, *Antiquities* 3.7.1 § 151; 11.4.2 § 80.

3. Examples of such care appear in Luke 7:12 and Acts 6.

God wants mercy, not just religious exercise (Hos. 6:6). A greater condemnation is headed their way, for they claim to lead the people and to be examples of God's will, but their callousness shows through.

Luke 21:1–4 shifts to a different type of response to God. In contrast to the Pharisees and the rich who shower gifts into the treasury, a poor widow comes with two copper coins.[4] Contributions for running the temple were placed in trumpet-shaped receptacles, thirteen of which were located in the court of women.[5] An officer oversaw the collection and often counted what had been given. These coins were the smallest ones made—each worth 1/100 of a denarius (about five minutes of labor at minimum wage). The woman here is not looking for credit, but for how she can humbly serve God.

But God does not see things as we do. He does not count; he weighs. Jesus calls this widow's gift the greatest gift of those that his disciples have been observing. What others give comes out of their excess, and they will hardly miss what they toss in for the temple. But this woman is giving out of her poverty. She gives what little she has, even though she needs it to live on. Jesus calls that real giving.

THE TYPES OF actions mentioned about the Jewish leadership in 20:46–47 raise basic issues of how the leaders in the church relate to others. Such people should not see their positions as an excuse to exercise power or as a means to enhance personal worth. Leaders should do everything they can to point people to Jesus and deflect attention from themselves. The danger is a real one, since we usually shower respect on those who minister to us. What takes place is a subtle elevation of the self above others, which then runs the risk of leading leaders to take advantage of those they are called to serve.

In fact, sometimes what accompanies a leader and his corporate-like authority is not subtle at all. Nothing is more dangerous than a leader who keeps authority tightly in his grip, directs the ministry fully in his direction, and takes no criticism in the process. Jesus wants his disciples to be leaders of a different kind. So he warns them about a visible negative example in their midst.

---

4. The parallel to this text is Mark 12:41–44.

5. Nehemiah 12:44; Josephus, *Jewish Wars* 5.5.2 § 200; 6.5.2 § 282; *Antiquities* 19.6.1 § 294; 1 Maccabees 14:49; 2 Maccabees 3:6, 24, 28, 40. Such offerings were freewill gifts to the temple.

This text, therefore, calls us to examine our hearts. Wrestling with pride can be difficult, especially for those who are high achievers. Everything they do rewards them for their hard work and their exercise of effort and talent. Instead of seeing the abilities they have, especially in ministry, as being the faithful exercise of stewardship from God, they take personal credit for them. But if what they have has been received from God, there is no room for boasting and self-exaltation. If Jesus is Lord (vv. 41–44), there is no place for pride. Those who boast should boast in the Lord (1 Cor. 1:31).

Jesus turns his attention in 21:1–4 to a contrastive image. Rather than discussing people looking for praise, he considers someone who is a consummate giver. How does one measure giving? The point of this story is that true giving is directed toward God. Jesus highlights two types of giving, both of which are appreciated, yet one speaks far more than the other. Giving out of abundance is appreciated, but it costs little. Giving out of life means that basic things may be given up in order to honor God. One's prioritization in giving shows where one's emphasis lies. That is why Jesus praises the widow here. Her attitude and action serve as an example of how believers should live.

Jesus turns the tables of evaluation here. We tend to appreciate the amount of a gift, not necessarily the sacrifice that went into the giving. As in other Lucan texts, the example comes from a person on the fringe of society, a poor woman who would have been a nonperson culturally. Yet God sees her gift as among the most significant. His evaluation of resources differs greatly from our way of reading giving. A seemingly poor gift can actually be rich in what it costs and represents.

Contemporary Significance

"PRIDE GOES BEFORE destruction" (Prov. 16:18). What is subtle about pride is that it develops at such unconscious levels in the mind that it is often unnoticed by the person who has it. But it does emerge in the way others are treated. Proud leaders manifest a condescending attitude toward others, which is reinforced by the way our culture honors them. Though Scripture expects respect for leaders, that courtesy should not be abused into thinking that leaders are somehow a "cut above" others.

I remember a story one of our staff members told me about a seminary professor. This part of the seminary was located off-site, which meant that the logistics of opening and closing the building for students was particularly tricky. The professors who flew in often had to leave immediately after class to catch their planes home, so that someone else had to lock up. In an effort to solve the problem, a professor on location was asked to lock up, since he was there at the same time as the visiting professors. This professor replied: "That is janitorial work, and I am a department chair." The answer was clearly intended as a refusal, but it said far more about his heart than he realized.

Distressed, the staff person called another chairman to ask if the request had been unreasonable. He replied, "I do that stuff all the time. Whatever I can do to help, I will do." This is service leadership—a mind-set that is unaware of titles. The more special we make ourselves, the less special God becomes. Unfortunately, others often see it clearly, and the damage is not only to God, because of the presence of hypocrisy, but also to those who are blind to their love of the limelight. Just before Jesus takes the worst seat possible in his suffering on the cross, he exhorts his disciples that the service he expects is a "not-for-profit" operation, nor is it a matter where exemptions exist.

In order for giving like the widow of 21:1–4 to take place, we must give consciously and with planning. First Corinthians 16:1–4 speaks of setting aside at the first of the week what we plan to give. What we give to God deserves priority. He should not receive our leftovers. As is all too common, the leftovers mysteriously shrink in size to take care of things that are not necessities. On the other hand, giving to God that is set aside from the first inevitably limits what we use for ourselves. It develops not only a healthy recognition that our resources belong first of all to God, but it can also lead us to be more disciplined with what is left for us after we give.

Another important point about giving surfaces here. No one is too poor to give. The issue is not the amount but participation. In one sense, this woman's gift would not have been missed had she kept her two copper coins to live on. But what would have been missed was her sense of participation in the community where God was being honored. Had she walked by the temple and kept the coins, she would have been the loser. On the other hand, by contributing her two coins, she communicated an appreciation and trust for God that few others experienced. Jesus' remark memorializes her courageous act and urges us to do the same.

It has been said that baby boomers and baby busters are poor givers. If this is true, then it is a sad day for the church. Many worthy projects at Christian organizations sit on the drawing board because the church does not have the funds needed for ministry. At the same time, the Christian entertainment business is growing into a mega-dollars industry. The church needs more givers like this woman, who desire to see ministry advance and in doing so give from the heart. We should evaluate needs and respond to them as we are able. Sometimes a minimal gift takes a maximum sacrifice, while for others the minimum might not really be much of a gift at all.

Second Corinthians 8–9 has much to say about how we give. God loves cheerful givers—people who give as they are led by God. Believers should institute personal structured programs where they agree to up their giving until it reaches a level that they feel God has led them to. I know families who make a commitment before God to increase their giving a certain amount or percentage every year, so that as they make giving a part of their structured plan, they have a sense of involvement in ministry and a feeling that God is leading them. Usually their heart follows where their dollar goes in the Lord's service. To those who do give and at great cost, this text reminds us that God sees what we are doing.

Luke 21:5–38

S OME OF HIS disciples were remarking about how the temple was adorned with beautiful stones and with gifts dedicated to God. But Jesus said, ⁶"As for what you see here, the time will come when not one stone will be left on another; every one of them will be thrown down."

⁷"Teacher," they asked, "when will these things happen? And what will be the sign that they are about to take place?"

⁸He replied: "Watch out that you are not deceived. For many will come in my name, claiming, 'I am he,' and, 'The time is near.' Do not follow them. ⁹When you hear of wars and revolutions, do not be frightened. These things must happen first, but the end will not come right away."

¹⁰Then he said to them: "Nation will rise against nation, and kingdom against kingdom. ¹¹There will be great earthquakes, famines and pestilences in various places, and fearful events and great signs from heaven.

¹²"But before all this, they will lay hands on you and persecute you. They will deliver you to synagogues and prisons, and you will be brought before kings and governors, and all on account of my name. ¹³This will result in your being witnesses to them. ¹⁴But make up your mind not to worry beforehand how you will defend yourselves. ¹⁵For I will give you words and wisdom that none of your adversaries will be able to resist or contradict. ¹⁶You will be betrayed even by parents, brothers, relatives and friends, and they will put some of you to death. ¹⁷All men will hate you because of me. ¹⁸But not a hair of your head will perish. ¹⁹By standing firm you will gain life.

²⁰"When you see Jerusalem being surrounded by armies, you will know that its desolation is near. ²¹Then let those who are in Judea flee to the mountains, let those in the city get out, and let those in the country not enter the city. ²²For this is the time of punishment in fulfillment of all that has been written. ²³How dreadful it will be in those days for pregnant women and nursing mothers! There will be great distress in the land and wrath against this people. ²⁴They will fall by the sword and will be taken as prisoners to all the nations.

Jerusalem will be trampled on by the Gentiles until the times of the Gentiles are fulfilled.

²⁵"There will be signs in the sun, moon and stars. On the earth, nations will be in anguish and perplexity at the roaring and tossing of the sea. ²⁶Men will faint from terror, apprehensive of what is coming on the world, for the heavenly bodies will be shaken. ²⁷At that time they will see the Son of Man coming in a cloud with power and great glory. ²⁸When these things begin to take place, stand up and lift up your heads, because your redemption is drawing near."

²⁹He told them this parable: "Look at the fig tree and all the trees. ³⁰When they sprout leaves, you can see for yourselves and know that summer is near. ³¹Even so, when you see these things happening, you know that the kingdom of God is near.

³²"I tell you the truth, this generation will certainly not pass away until all these things have happened. ³³Heaven and earth will pass away, but my words will never pass away.

³⁴"Be careful, or your hearts will be weighed down with dissipation, drunkenness and the anxieties of life, and that day will close on you unexpectedly like a trap. ³⁵For it will come upon all those who live on the face of the whole earth. ³⁶Be always on the watch, and pray that you may be able to escape all that is about to happen, and that you may be able to stand before the Son of Man."

³⁷Each day Jesus was teaching at the temple, and each evening he went out to spend the night on the hill called the Mount of Olives, ³⁷and all the people came early in the morning to hear him at the temple.

Original Meaning

LUKE 21:5–38 IS Luke's version of Jesus' Olivet Discourse (cf. Matt. 24–25; Mark 13). His version focuses more on the destruction of Jerusalem (the third such prediction in this Gospel; cf. 13:31–35; 19:41–44). A remark about the temple's grandeur causes Jesus to begin this discussion. The nation is headed for hard times. Her rejection of Jesus will be painful and costly.

The discourse is prophetic in character, since in speaking about Jerusalem and her destruction in the short term, a pattern of events emerges like the events associated with the return of the Son of Man at the end of time. A prophet could speak about the short-term fulfillment, or the long-term, or both at the same time in different portions of the same speech, since the events mirror one another. In the Synoptics, Mark tells the account with the greatest ambiguity in the time references. Matthew focuses on the long-term realization, while Luke highlights the short-term event. Because of the "mirror" nature of the events described, each perspective is a good summation of Jesus' teaching.

Jesus here treats many themes that connect to the Old Testament hope of the Day of the Lord. The picture of one who comes on the clouds looks back to Son of Man imagery in Daniel 7:13–14. While prophetic remarks dominate Luke 21:7–24, apocalyptic elements appear in verses 25–28. What is the difference between these two? *Prophetic promise* frames itself in terms of everyday history where God works through agents already present, while *apocalyptic* speaks explicitly of God's breaking into history in a marvelous way. When the nation of Israel comes at risk in the end, God will step in through the Son of Man to deliver his people. In the meantime, the disciples will face persecution and Israel will be overrun. Though Jesus does not say so explicitly, the predicted events begin with persecution in the early church and end with the Lord's return, a time frame we now know represents centuries.

The discourse begins in verse 5 with an observation about one of the great structures of the ancient world, the temple in Jerusalem. Jesus and his disciples have just been at the temple, watching the widow make her offering (21:1–4). Luke does not separate the scene as a distinct discourse, as Matthew and Mark do. Some of the disciples comment on the temple's beauty, especially its noble stones and the ornaments that made it such a unique edifice.

When one looks at a powerful nation, it is easy to think that it will exist forever. Most people at the height of the Roman empire would have found it difficult to imagine that it would one day be relegated to the pages of history. Other institutions also take on this air of indestructibility, one of them being the temple. In Jesus' day, it was in the midst of a grand rebuilding program. Starting about 20 B.C., it continued until A.D. 63–64. So when Jesus spoke in A.D. 33, the program was well underway.[1] Certainly a building so grand would have a long life. After all, it was decorated by gifts from many

---

1. The date of Jesus' crucifixion is debated as either A.D. 30 or 33. The former date is more popular, but I believe the latter is more likely. For the arguments, see H. Hoehner, *Chronological Aspects of the Life of Jesus* (Grand Rapids: Zondervan, 1977), 95–114.

of the surrounding nations and was a building that had received notice around the Roman world.[2]

Jesus notes immediately that the building will not be permanent. "The time will come when not one stone will be left on another." With these words he predict the destruction of Jerusalem in A.D. 70, for the only way the temple can be leveled is if the city comes under severe attack.[3] The phrase "the time will come" (lit., "the days will come") uses the same phraseology Jeremiah did when he made a major announcement about the nation's fall (Jer. 7:1–14; 22:5; 27:6; 52:12–13). Jesus' remark is devastating, since the temple was the heart and soul of Israel's worship. How could God allow the sacred locale of worship to be reduced to rubble after so much effort had gone into restoring it? Therefore, the disciples ask, "When will these things happen?"

Three points about Jesus' extended answer need attention. (1) It is important to see how Luke lays out the chronology since his account is more specific than the other Synoptics. A careful look at verses 8–9, 11–12 shows that Jesus answers the question by working at points in the discourse backwards in time. He starts with the time of the end and then goes back to the time he is speaking. It is like playing a video tape in reverse, with the events of verses 12–19 looking to events that come before Jerusalem's fall in verses 20–28, but only after explaining what the period all the way to the end is like in verses 7–11. The two key phrases in the sequence are: "but the end will not come right away" (v. 9b), and "but before all of this [i.e., the end]" (v. 12a). His answer begins with a warning not to be deceived (v. 8) and with an assurance that the end is not yet (v. 9). So verse 12 speaks of events that take place before the things he mentions in verses 8–11. At verse 20, the fall of Jerusalem is central. The tape moves forward now. Then the thing that will happen at the very end of history begins in verse 24.

(2) As noted already, the events tied to Jerusalem's fall mirror events that bring the Son of Man's return. In other words, the discourse discusses the character of an entire period from the time of Jesus' remarks through the destruction of Jerusalem and into the period of the Lord's return. His first warning is that messianic pretenders will abound. Thus, his followers should not be deceived. Jesus has already told them in 17:22–25 that his return will be visible to all. So, although it will come like a thief, its arrival will be obvious. If anyone claims to be the promised Messiah and argues that the time is near, such pretenders should not be followed.[4]

---

2. Josephus, *Jewish Wars* 1.21. 1 § 401; 5.5. 1–6 §§ 184–227; *Antiquities* 15.11.1–7 §§ 380–425; Tacitus, *History* 5.8.1. He described it as a "snow clad mountain looming over the city."

3. Danker, *Jesus and the New Age*, 330.

4. On the phrase "the time" (v. 8) as a technical term for the end, see Delling, "καιρός," *TDNT*, 3:461.

(3) The presence of wars and rumors of wars should not startle them either. Great calamities, like those that engulfed Jerusalem in A.D. 66–70, should not take them by surprise. Such events must (*dei*) happen first. Nations will rise against nations, and natural calamities will be widespread: earthquakes, famines, pestilence, along with other fearful events and great heavenly signs. This imagery has rich Old Testament roots: Isaiah 5:13–14; 13:6–16; 19:2; Jeremiah 4:13–22; 14:12; 21:6–7; Ezekiel 14:21; Haggai 2:6–7; Zechariah 14:4.[5]

But even before the claims of messianic pretenders and the cosmic chaos comes the persecution of God's people. This actually starts almost immediately after the crucifixion, and large portions of Acts can be read as initial fulfillments of this prophecy. Enemies will lay hands on them, persecute them, and confine them to prisons.[6] Some of this persecution will come from Judaism, for the disciples will have to give a defense in the synagogues. There will be even opportunity to testify before kings and governors (e.g., Paul, who testified before Herod Agrippa, Felix, Festus, and even Caesar). The persecution is religiously directed, since it all takes place "on account of my name." One reason this discourse is so important for the disciples to hear is because Jesus wants them to understand that before the end arrives, believers will experience rough times.

Through these opportunities, the disciples will be "witnesses" for Jesus (v. 13). The theme of the witness is a major one in Acts, beginning with Jesus' instruction and promise of the Holy Spirit in Acts 1:8. There is hardly a role more important for the disciple than that of witness. Sometimes the most effective witnessing takes place in the crucible of pressure about one's faith. In such moments faith is seen as a central, serious, and even exceptional aspect of a person's life. These disciples will have the chance to step up to the public microphone and testify to him.

In contrast to Mark 13:10, Luke remains focused on what is going to happen soon as the gospel goes out to the Jewish community. Such opportunity for testimony requires resolve, because of the uncertainty that results from being under such pressure. Jesus therefore tells the disciples not to worry about how they will undertake their defense. Luke 12:11–12 already made

---

5. The Synoptic summaries of this discourse show variation here. Only famines and earthquakes are mentioned in all three accounts. Mark 13:8 calls all of this the beginning of birth pains, a phrase that signals the beginning of the final drama; Luke lacks this phrase. The difference is not a sign of disagreement but of emphasizing different ends of the mirror images of the paired set of events. For both writers, everything from this time on is a part of the unfolding divine plan of the end, a view also shared by Paul (Rom. 8:18–25, esp. v. 22). Luke mentions similar signs again in verse 25 to show they also appear at the end.

6. For the idiom "laying hands on you" in this sense, see 1 Samuel 21:6.

such a promise, but the fact that Jesus repeats it shows how important a commitment God makes to anyone who will testify to him. Here Jesus says he will give them the words to say, while in Luke 12 it was the Spirit. The difference indicates how closely together Jesus and the Spirit work. He is the one who sends the Spirit, who in turn enables us to stand for him (John 16:5–15; Acts 1:8; 2:30–36). Jesus will give them answers to silence their opponents (see Acts 4–5; 7; 24–26).

Some betrayal will come from within families (cf. 12:49–52). Parents, brothers, relatives, and friends will be involved in the persecution. Some may even be martyred for their faith. Deciding for Jesus can be serious business.

Jesus goes on to give a word about ultimate protection (v. 18; cf. 12:1–5). Though death may come (v. 16), not a hair on any believer's head will perish.[7] When it comes to life that counts, eternal life (18:28–30), believers can know God will welcome them. There is "no way" they will be harmed ultimately; that is why they can face suffering in the short term (see Acts 7:55–60 for proof). God will protect his disciples. To stand with Jesus is to have salvation.

At verse 20 Luke again diverges from Matthew and Mark. He does not mention that the tribulation period is the most intense ever to fall on humanity, nor does he say that these days of suffering will be cut short. But he does mention "the time of the Gentiles" (v. 24) and "its [Jerusalem's] desolation" (v. 20; the other Gospels specifically mention the abomination of desolation at the temple). In other words, Luke is interested primarily in the short-term destruction of the capital and only indirectly in the end-time event.[8]

Luke 21:20–22 reviews predictions already made in 19:43–44. Jerusalem will be surrounded by armies, so its desolation is near. Jesus expects the temple to fall when the city falls. This in part answers the disciples' question about when the temple will be left in ruins. The image of desolation alludes to the terrible destruction that will come with this invasion. Josephus tells us that a million Jews were killed and nearly a hundred thousand taken captive. Though some argue the numbers are high (Josephus is noted for exaggerating), they do indicate how devastating this invasion was.[9] The judgment was horrific; children were even cooked for food.[10]

---

7. This idea is expressed most affirmatively, using the Greek emphatic *ou me* (i.e., "surely not be harmed").

8. Some have argued that the difference is evidence that Luke wrote after the fall of A.D. 70, but that position is not necessary. Everything described here fits with a divine judgment for covenant unfaithfulness. so there is no need to appeal to a *post facto* reading of this text. The distinct time frames can be addressed by different writers because one event pictures the other.

9. Josephus, *Jewish Wars* 5–7. See especially 6.5.1 §§ 271–73; 6.9.3 § 420; 7.5.3 § 118; 7.5.6 § 154.

10. Josephus, *Jewish Wars* 6.3.4 §§ 201–11.

Jerusalem should be avoided at all costs during this time. Those in Judea should flee to the mountains, while those in the city should try to get out. No one should enter Jerusalem. The appeal to the Danielic language of "desolation" is important (Dan. 9:27; 11:31; 12:1). As already quoted, Matthew 24:15 and Mark 13:14 allude to the passage where the desecration of the temple is specifically in view. Luke appeals to the term as a general reference to judgment (Luke 21:20).[11]

All these events take place "in fulfillment of all that has been written" (v. 22). There are no surprises in God's plan. Israel's being overrun and the temple's being destroyed do not indicate anything amiss in the plan. What the NIV calls "the time of punishment" is called in Greek, "the days of vengeance." Unfaithfulness is something God does not ignore.

Two types of people are especially vulnerable at this time: pregnant women and nursing mothers. To have little ones or to be on the verge of having a baby will mean great stress. Distress and wrath will be on all sides (19:44; 23:29).[12] Israel will be on the wrong side of God's judgment. These women and children will fall to the sword, as often happens in an all-out siege. "They will fall by the sword" (cf. Isa. 3:25; 13:15; 65:12; Jer. 16:4) or "be taken as prisoners," a sign of total defeat. Jesus sounds like the prophets of old here. Jeremiah predicted and recorded similar images in announcing the earlier fall of the nation into Babylonian captivity.[13] Jesus' audience would recognize the type of destruction in view; Israel had experienced it before in her history.

Jerusalem will become a trampled city. Gentiles will have a role in the city until "the times of the Gentiles" are done. This phrase, which marks out an era, suggests that a time will again come when Israel will be prominent in God's plan. This point is debated among Christians, since many hold that with Jesus' return comes the new heavens and new earth. This position argues either that there is no thousand-year reign with Jesus' return (amillennialism) or that the church is the kingdom today and as such fulfills millennial promises (postmillennialism). But others argue that Jesus' return will begin a thousand-year earthly rule (premillennialism)[14] and include a central role for Israel in that rule.

---

11. This would be odd if the text were a post facto update of the prophecy, since the most horrendous thing that happened in the war from a Jewish point of view was the temple's destruction. By referring it to Jerusalem in general rather than the temple, the passage testifies to its authenticity, for it does not update details in Jesus' speech.

12. W. Grundmann, "ἀναγκάζω," *TDNT*, 1:346.

13. L. T. Johnson, *The Gospel of Luke*, 323 (see Jer. 7:14—26, 30—34; 16:1—9; 17:27; 19:10—15; Mic. 3:12; Zeph. 1:4—13. The early church made much of the fulfillment of this prediction; see Justin Martyr, *Dialogue with Trypho* 16, 92, 110, 115; Tertullian, *Against the Jews* 13.

14. For a presentation of amillennialism, see A. Hoekema, *The Bible and the Future* (Grand

Part of this debate turns on how one takes Revelation 20:1–6. After a return by Jesus (Rev. 19) comes a specific period of rule, marked off by resurrections on each end and distinguished from the new heaven and new earth in Revelation 21–22. Even recognizing the symbolic character of apocalyptic in Revelation, one must interpret the symbolism and referents with some consistency. Revelation 20 seems to foresee an intermediate kingdom before the remaking of the creation in the end—a point for premillennialism. Premillennialists argue that at the end of the time of the Gentiles, a new era of restored prominence for Israel emerges (cf. Acts 3:16–22; Rom. 11:26). Nothing Jesus said in the forty days he spent with the disciples after the resurrection disabused them of the notion that Israel still had a future (cf. Acts 1:6). I believe a premillennial reading of these texts makes the most coherent sense of the Bible's teaching on eschatology, but it should be noted that this discourse does not get into any of these details.

When "the times of the Gentiles are fulfilled," then God's promised plan will move toward completion, a plan Jesus launched in his earthly ministry. So at verse 25, Jesus addresses "the end" that begins with his return. Accompanying that return will be great cosmic signs; for this reason one will not have to search to find it. This imagery is standard Old Testament description of the end of human history.[15] The disturbances will be so great as to bring great distress and anguish. One need only picture the trauma that comes at a major catastrophe and multiply it many times to get a feel for what is described here. When the earth becomes an unstable environment and the heavens give evidence of instability, it will be a frightening time.

At such a moment of insecurity, the Son of Man will appear riding on the clouds (see Dan. 7:13). The Son of Man is a human figure who is given divine-like authority, a supranatural figure who rides the clouds like God (Ex. 14:20; 34:5; Num. 10:34; Pss. 19:1; 104:3).[16] His identity in Daniel is debated, but it is best to see him as a representative of the saints whose presence means their vindication. The return of such a figure in great power and glory will put a stop to the chaos of the end, a chaos like the destruction that Jerusalem will undergo. The Son of Man's presence—that is, Jesus' return—

Rapids: Eerdmans, 1979). For a presentation of premillennialism, see D. K. Campbell and J. L. Townsend, *A Case for Premillennialism: A New Consensus* (Chicago: Moody, 1992).

15. K. H. Rengstorf, "σημεῖον," *TDNT*, 7:232. Even the use of this imagery in Acts 2:19–20 looks to the end and not back at the crucifixion; see D. Bock, *Proclamation from Prophecy and Pattern*, on Acts 2 for a defense of a partial fulfillment looking to the future in this portion of the Acts text.

16. The term "supranatural" is conscious. This Danielic figure is mysterious in the way he mixes supernatural and natural qualities. He is a man in contrast to the animals of the vision, yet like God, he rides the clouds. In the New Testament, the mystery is removed in the explicit teaching about incarnation.

will mean that vindication has come near. Saints present at that time can lift their heads, for their redemption is near. In place of the fear (vv. 25–26) comes hope.

As bad as the fall of Jerusalem is, it is not the end of the story. The Son of Man's return means that God's people will see victory. That is why the disciples should keep watch. To see these things is to know redemption and God's kingdom, his powerfully manifested presence in rule and judgment, is near.

To drive home the point Jesus tells a short parable. He notes how one can tell the time of year by noting the condition of a fig tree. When it sprouts leaves, one an knows summer is near. So also, Jesus says, when one sees these things happening, one knows that the kingdom is drawing near. Jerusalem's fall represents evidence that God's plan is moving forward. All that is left on the divine calendar after its collapse is the completion of the plan. The resumption of a variety of cosmic signs will indicate the end is really near. So the parable says, in effect, to keep one's eyes open for what God is doing.

Jesus then notes that "this generation will certainly not pass away until all these things have happened." This is one of the most difficult verses in Luke. "This generation" appears to set a specific time frame for these events, all of which did not take place in the lifetime of the disciples. It seems clear that whatever "generation" means, it did not refer to the generation of Jesus' time or that of Luke's readers. Some do argue, however, that Jesus is referring here only to the events of A.D. 70, in which case "generation" could mean the generation of the disciples. But this leaves another problem—that of "all these things," not just the start of them. Note that the Son of Man did not return visibly at that time. So the meaning of "this generation" cannot be a reference to the time of the disciples or Luke.

Though some argue Jesus got this detail of timing wrong, more likely he had another meaning of "generation" in mind. (1) Some argue that this word refers to a race, the Jews, though this meaning is unprecedented. (2) Another option argues for a reference to "the generation of humanity" as a whole or to the evil generation of humankind. In other words, the end will come before humanity is destroyed. Such a view is possible, though it seems a little unusual to give the phrase this force. (3) Still others argue that "generation" is not a term of time but of quality. That is, Jesus is saying that "this generation of the righteous" will not pass away. Again, this view is possible, though it too represents an unusual reading of the word "generation." (4) The view preferred here is that the "generation" that sees all these things refers to the generation present in verse 25. In other words, those who see the beginning of the end in the cosmic signs will see the arrival of the decisive era in the Son of Man's return. Once the events of the final act commence, they will take place rather quickly.[17]

Jesus is so certain that what he is saying is true that he argues that creation will pass away, but not his words (v. 33). The discourse is designed to inform and encourage faithfulness. To do so, what he declares about vindication must take place. Jesus' disciples can count on that fact.

Jesus then continues to warn the disciples to be sure that the day does not take them unaware like a trap. That means that "dissipation, drunkenness, and the anxieties of life" should be avoided. Their hearts should not be weighed down in light of their eventual redemption. What Paul calls the "blessed hope" of our redemption by God is something that should encourage us to live wisely before God, with a degree of detachment from the events of life that often do weigh us down (Titus 2:11–14).

When the Lord does come back, everyone will be faced with the reality of his return and his powerful presence. Some will be ready for it, while others will be surprised. Jesus calls his disciples to "be always on the watch" in looking for his return. This is a present imperative, meaning that our attentiveness should be ongoing. We must pray in order to escape what lies ahead, both short term in Jerusalem and long term in the end (Jerusalem is mostly in view up to v. 19; the end is the major topic after v. 23). The ultimate goal is to "stand before the Son of Man" (cf. 12:8–12). All those who identify with the Son of Man will stand in that day.

Luke ends this section by noting that Jesus taught at the temple each day and slept at the Mount of Olives at night. Every morning the people gathered to hear him, and he had a great opportunity to teach and preach the hope of promise. But this was stopped short by the events Luke now turns to narrate. There is nothing ahead of Jesus now but the cross.

Bridging Contexts

IN THINKING THROUGH how this text addresses our era, several questions need attention. In the original meaning section we tried to delineate carefully how this text addressed both short-term and long-term issues.[18] The issues of persecution and false messianic claims

---

17. For all the options noted here, see R. Maddox, *The Purpose of Luke-Acts* (Edinburgh: T. & T. Clark, 1982), 111–15. The problem with the preferred view is verse 28, which appears to tell the disciples to watch and know certain things are near; but this verse may be referring back to the temple issue that started the discussion and guarantees what is said about the end.

18. For another survey of issues tied to Christian view of the Lord's return, as well as the options taken, see S. Grenz, *The Millennial Maze* (Downers Grove, Ill.: InterVarsity, 1992).

span the centuries. They remain as possibilities for the saints as long as the final vindication has not yet arrived. Only one main feature has changed: The Jewish character of the persecution of Christians is for the most part no longer with us. Opposition to the gospel comes from variety of corners, but being brought before synagogues is not one of them. Only those who come from Jewish roots might see something like this in terms of rejection. With that exception, as a "typological" or "pattern" text, this passage addresses the entire period from the time Jesus spoke until he returns. His followers live in a world where he is not physically present and where rejection and suffering may well come with the decision to believe.

Jesus' discourse here serves to reassure believers that God is advancing his plan. The events of A.D. 70 show, as we look back at them, that God was, and still is, directing the affairs of the human race. Those events include calls to faithfulness and warnings about judgment. The severe character of the judgment reveals how serious God is about sin and unfaithfulness. As painful as the fall of Jerusalem was, it is nothing compared to the judgment to come. This feature gives this text its theological power. Our culture tends to minimize the authority of God to punish unrighteousness. Yet that theme is one of the more important notes raised in this passage.

When it comes to God's predicting the future, our culture has a love-hate relationship. On the one hand, the popularity of astrology and other strategies of reading the future show how entranced people are with the prospect of things being fated. On the other hand, many view detailed predictions of doom with some skepticism. They question whether Jesus made any such predictions, since they limit him to a role as a religious teacher of wisdom. If Jesus is a prophet, it is not because he predicts but because he convicts and calls us to love. This is a one-sided view of him. This text is significant because it shows how Jesus testified to a coming judgment and a future vindication of the saints. His life and death are much more than a moral legacy. He will return to judge, and that judgment is serious business.

Regardless of differences of detail in the Christians' view of the end, it is important to affirm what most Christians agree about on the question. Grenz says it well this way (p. 215):

> The eternal reign of God has dawned, is dawning and will one day dawn in its consummated fullness. The God who has reconciled us to himself through Christ will one day bring us into full participation in the grand eschatological community of his divine reign. This is the vision that should inspire us in this in-between era to seek to be a kingdom people now and to proclaim now in word and deed the good news of the coming eternal reign of God.
>
> Corporate eschatology, with its vision of God's glorious program for history, confronts the church with a grave question: Will we as the church be motivated by the vision of God's ultimate future to be about the Lord's business in the present era until Christ comes in glory and splendor?

The promise of final vindication comes with an important corollary. The church is not called to enforce dominion on those around it; rather, we as a community will suffer as Christ did, until he returns. To forget we bear a cross and not a sword in this era is to abandon a basic aspect of our calling: to proclaim, reflect, and serve Jesus. Only in the end will we be rescued from pain and rejection. Theologies that promote the triumph of the church outside the return of Jesus forget where the source of vindication resides. He is the one who brings the victory, not we. Those who are not prepared to stand as witnesses before the world, which does not understand him, do not understand the call God gives to his church.

One final feature is important to note about the teaching on the end times. It is specific enough to keep us watching, but general enough that we should never succumb to the tendency to predict exactly when Jesus will appear. God wants us to watch diligently, but such a watch does not mean he desires the church to figure out exactly when he will return. When the disciples posed such a specific question to Jesus in Acts 1:6, he answered by telling them to mind their own business and live out their calling faithfully in the power of the Spirit. It was not for them to know "the times or dates." We know he is coming back for us, and we should keep watching with anticipation. In the meantime, there is plenty of work for the church to do.

THIS PASSAGE TELLS us something about God, about Jesus, about Israel, and about ourselves (both unbelievers and believers). We will consider the applications for each one of these.

(1) Twila Paris wrote a popular song whose title beautifully proclaims "God Is in Control." This is an important message in an era with so much human chaos. To that biblical message should go the addendum that his timing is his own. Sometimes we get impatient with God's control and timing. Like the psalmists, we complain that God does not hear the cries of his people and that evil seems to be victorious. Jesus in this discourse asserts God does control the direction of history. He calls us to be patient and to use our time in presenting the gospel of God's grace to others.

This text also reveals the righteousness of God. When he judges, his judgment will be comprehensive. No defense lawyer will sit at the celestial table to argue the merits of our case on the basis of our own righteousness. The only righteousness that will triumph is that of Christ. Thus, a decision to be without God and go one's own way means missing the opportunity for eternal salvation that God has so graciously provided through Jesus.

(2) We have already noted that this text reveals a side of the prophetic

Jesus we tend to underestimate. On the other hand, it is all too easy, as church history teaches us, to get excessively enthralled with predicting the end. Eschatology is but one topic of theology. It is an important one because it sets a perspective for current events and reminds us that the present and past are not all there is to life. But neither should we become so preoccupied with the future that we lose sight of our calling in the present. Jesus taught about the end, but he did not major in it. He longed to lead people into a healthy relationship to God in the here and now. We must constantly watch, but only in a way that serves God honorably so that Jesus' return is a reason to rejoice without shrinking back. We must live ethically in this world. According to the apostle John, contemplating Christ's return purifies us (1 John 3:3).

(3) The lesson for Israel is a call to reflection. Why did she lose her precious temple centuries ago? With love and tears (cf. 19:41—44), the church proclaims that she missed her time of visitation. In doing so, she became an example to herself and to all of the painful price of turning away from God's call. It is hard to read these constant declarations of Israel's fate and not feel a deep sense of sadness for a great moment missed. Yet her national story is no different than the story of anyone who chooses not to respond to the call of God's grace.

In her persecution of God's children, Israel paved the way for her own judgment in A.D. 70. Jesus teaches that the measure by which one measures will be the measure received in judgment. The standard held true for the nation, but the lesson was not for her alone.

(4) Anyone reading the details of this discourse or the book of Revelation knows how graphic and horrifying the end-time judgment is. These sections cause us to ponder where we stand before God. I cannot count the number of seminary students I have had whose testimonies have roots in considering their mortality and accountability before a God who will judge the unrighteous. Many first became open to the possibility of a relationship with God by contemplating what life without him might mean. Our world often downplays such accountability, as if no judgment will ever occur. But God has provided through Jesus the means whereby we can gain forgiveness for any wrongs we have done. We cannot provide for our own salvation. The road of proclaiming one's own self-righteousness was the road the Jewish leadership had taken, and this text makes it plain where Israel ended up. The warning to us is not to make the same mistake.

(5) Finally, what does this text say to believers? We must keep watch, stand fast, and trust God's timing with the reassurance that one day our deliverance will surely come. Events may be painful, for even our families may oppose us and hostility can reach the limit. Whether we think of Stephen in

Acts 7 or Jim Elliott in South America, commitment to Jesus throughout the centuries has occasionally led to intense opposition and even to the sacrifice of the most basic of gifts, that of life. Christ's followers need to have resolve to endure, a resolve that grows in the face of the assurance that God will indeed do what he has promised. He will vindicate his children. Thus, we must continue to walk with trust. Trust means continuing to hope in what we cannot see (Heb. 11:1). Yet even though we cannot see it, we can see Jesus, the author and defender of our faith, who promises that one day he will return for us in great power and glory. So looking to him, we serve and wait with great expectations.

Luke 22:1-6

NOW THE FEAST OF UNLEAVENED Bread, called the Passover, was approaching, ²and the chief priests and the teachers of the law were looking for some way to get rid of Jesus, for they were afraid of the people. ³Then Satan entered Judas, called Iscariot, one of the Twelve. ⁴And Judas went to the chief priests and the officers of the temple guard and discussed with them how he might betray Jesus. ⁵They were delighted and agreed to give him money. ⁶He consented, and watched for an opportunity to hand Jesus over to them when no crowd was present.

Original Meaning

THE EVENTS IN 22:1-38 leading to Jesus' arrest provide his final opportunity to share with his disciples before his departure. This final meal functions much like his last will and testament. After noting Judas's plan to betray him (22:1-6), Luke goes on to record Jesus' plans to celebrate the Passover one last time with his disciples (22:7-13). At the meal, Jesus observes the Last Supper (22:14-20), a meal that becomes the basis of the Lord's Supper (1 Cor. 11:17-34). The final discourse treats a wide array of subjects: betrayal, greatness in humility, appointment to authority, prediction of denials, and warnings about rejection (Luke 22:21-38). Jesus spent most of the journey to Jerusalem preparing his disciples for his coming absence. The time has come to face the cross. The disciples will need to conduct their faith walk in light of his departure. The moment of truth for all has come.

The Jewish leadership has been powerless to do anything about Jesus because of his popularity. All of that changes when Judas, one of the Twelve, steps forward.[1] What they cannot generate on their own becomes possible through this disciple. The irony in most of the events surrounding Jesus' arrest, trial, and crucifixion is that those who appear to be in control are not. They happen only because Jesus allows them to proceed. As will become clear, Jesus is fully aware of what Judas is doing (22:22-23).

The crucifixion took place during one of the most sacred parts of the Jewish year, the Feasts of Passover and Unleavened Bread, which followed each other on the calendar. These festivals commemorated the sparing of

---

1. The parallels to this text are Matthew 26:1-16 and Mark 14:1-11.

Israel's firstborn and their release from captivity in Egypt (Passover, Nisan 14–15; Unleavened Bread, Nisan 15–21).[2] The entire celebration recalled how Israel was "passed over" by the angel of death and redeemed (Ex. 12). Israel recalled her salvation and God's grace.

During this time, "the chief priests and teachers of the law" were trying to find a way to remove Jesus. Their search was a constant one, for Luke uses the imperfect tense (*ezetoun*) to describe their attempts to find a way to seize Jesus. The juxtaposition of the holiday with the plotting is intentional by Luke. What the feast day celebrates, forgiveness and salvation, Jesus will actually perform. At the time Israel is recalling her deliverance, the leadership is conspiring to rob Jesus of his very life. The text is ironic in its contrast. But the people are flocking to him. So there is currently no good way to get him without causing major turmoil.

But the opportunity for an inside job removes all of those obstacles. For the first time since Luke 4:1–13, Satan is named as an active player in the drama. He enters Judas. What this means is not entirely clear. Is this possession? Most think that is too strong a description. What it suggests at a minimum is satanic direction and influence. The remark does show that Jesus' mission has cosmic dimensions; even the forces of evil have a view about him and desire his removal.

So Judas goes to the leadership to discuss how he might hand Jesus over to them. Both the chief priests and the temple guards take part in these deliberations. Judas gets the equivalent of cabinet-like attention. The chief priests' presence shows that the decision is being made at the highest levels. The guard is present because they will have to carry out the arrest. So thrilled is the leadership that they give Judas a fee for his action. The amount is not noted here, though Matthew 26:15 tells us it is thirty pieces of silver, a small price to pay to regain control of the Jewish religious mind.

It is hard to appreciate just how great a break this offer is for the Jewish leaders. Now they can figure out Jesus' private whereabouts, and they have in-house testimony against him. Anyone who challenges their efforts at restraint will have to face the reaction of Judas, an insider, who knows how Jesus works. No wonder they are so open to Judas and pleased about the situation. They can distance themselves from the action as they look out for the larger public interest.

All that is needed is to find an appropriate time to arrest the teacher. It must be a time when crowds are not present. Judas will determine that time. Sinister forces are behind Jesus' death.

---

2. The two holidays came so close to one another that Unleavened Bread could refer to the entire week. See J. Jeremias, "πάσχα," *TDNT* 5:898–904; Josephus, *Antiquities* 14.2.1 § 21; *Jewish Wars* 2.1.3 § 10; 3.105 § 249.

THE UNIQUE EVENTS of the Passion communicate their message not so much through the events themselves as in the examples of the types of people who share in them. In studying narrative, scholars often speak of archetypal figures. The lessons come through characters in the account who represent certain types of people or realities in the world. Such figures are spotted by noting how developed their character is within the story and by considering the fundamental characteristics they possess in their role. In the case of the Gospels, reactions to Jesus are types of response to him from which we can learn. Such analogies especially apply when reading the Passion accounts, since they record reactions that lead to clear decisions for and against Jesus. As we move through these chapters in Luke, we will point out these archetypal figures.

We do not have chief priests and scribes residing around a temple today. But these characters depict the reactions of people who stand adamantly opposed to Jesus. Judas is the example of an "insider" who really is not an insider at all. In a subversive manner, he plots against the one whom he claims to know as the one who brings God's promise. He reminds us that not everyone closely tied to Jesus really knows him. According to John 6:70, Judas is tied to the devil.

WE SEE VIVIDLY how Jesus was rejected and betrayed. The actions of his enemies are a graph of how sin does its work. In the background stands the presence and influence of Satan. The event reminds us that people can be led by forces that pull them in destructive directions (cf. Eph. 2:1–3). All the plotting and intrigue show how much effort and deceit went into the destructive plan to get Jesus. The hypocrisy of celebrating the Exodus and plotting Jesus' death adds to the pathos of it all.

What is so tragic is that if we stop and analyze the role of sin in our own lives, we see the same types of behavior and choices. One sin often leads to more sin in the effort either to set it up or to cover it up. The deceptive nature of sin hatches plots in dark places and attempts to do its work in secret or highly private locales. It credo is, "I can do this, if no one or only a few select people see."

In addition, the mood of betrayal is fundamental to the character of all types of sin. In fact, sin is fundamentally a betrayal, not just of God, but of others who are injured by it. It even betrays the sinner as the destruction it brings does its damaging work. This passage is not just a lesson in history, but a study of human nature at its worst, revealing the form sin takes as it compounds itself in action. How often, for example, has a man or woman engaged in an affair without considering its devastating effect on their families, especially the children? What do such actions say about the integrity of our vows made before God? Sin usually does not limit its effect to a small sphere; it has a ripple effect that encompasses many others.

Another lesson in the pattern of rejection from the leadership and Judas is the tendency of sin to make someone else the sinner. Sin tends subtly to create a layer of insulation in a form of rationalization that works as a protective shield against the sinful action, a type of cover-up that can place blame elsewhere—such as the leadership's buffer that gets created through Judas. Such a diabolical barrier is built when a man who is cheating on his wife maintains that her coldness forced him to look elsewhere for tender nurture. Such a shield surfaces when children fight and blame the other child's bad behavior for the right to strike back in kind.

This event also discloses the fact that Jesus is of concern to cosmic, evil forces. Satan attempts to do everything he can stop God's plan of salvation from advancing. The narrative underscores this point by revealing that there are forces at work beyond Judas. One should also remain sensitive to the fact that this diabolical opposition is not yet finished. If Satan opposed Jesus here, he will oppose the church. Defection from within is one of the most effective means he has to bring discredit on the church. The strategy is an old one, stretching all the way back to Adam and Eve, where Satan led Eve into sin as a way of getting to Adam. Faithfulness to God's will prevent Satan from getting such a foothold.

The reality of defection is another lesson in this text. Judas represents the "disciple" who is no disciple at all. For years, the eleven accepted him as a full member of their community. This event reveals where his heart really was. This reality reminds us that church membership and association alone are not the marks of salvation. Faith saves, but only a faith that does not turn its back decisively on Jesus. A believer may deny Jesus, as Peter does, but a believer will never engage in the full-scale defection that Judas does. There is a difference between a lack of nerve and a conscious decision of the heart to reject Jesus after having had contact with him. Judas represents the latter category.

There is no salvation for one who does not trust Jesus to the end. The defection of a Judas-like figure, once undertaken, is permanent, but real faith keeps faith. Pastorally, it is not always easy to spot the difference between a period of coldness and outright rejection. This is an attitude that cannot be read from the outside; it is a matter of inward conviction. But complete rejection usually does not wrestle with a deep sense of guilt or hesitation about the change of direction undertaken. People whose hearts grow cold are disengaged for a time and uninterested, but this falls short of callousness. A period of coldness can even last some time, but it is not accompanied with an outright denial of connection to Jesus. Romans 8:16 speaks about the Spirit's giving believers a sense of sonship to God, something total rejection indicates is not present. As the entire passion narrative shows, our world is filled with a kalidescope of reactions to Jesus.

Luke 22:7–20

THEN CAME THE day of Unleavened Bread on which the Passover lamb had to be sacrificed. ⁸Jesus sent Peter and John, saying, "Go and make preparations for us to eat the Passover."

⁹"Where do you want us to prepare for it?" they asked.

¹⁰He replied, "As you enter the city, a man carrying a jar of water will meet you. Follow him to the house that he enters, ¹¹and say to the owner of the house, 'The Teacher asks: Where is the guest room, where I may eat the Passover with my disciples?' ¹²He will show you a large upper room, all furnished. Make preparations there."

¹³They left and found things just as Jesus had told them. So they prepared the Passover.

¹⁴When the hour came, Jesus and his apostles reclined at the table. ¹⁵And he said to them, "I have eagerly desired to eat this Passover with you before I suffer. ¹⁶For I tell you, I will not eat it again until it finds fulfillment in the kingdom of God."

¹⁷After taking the cup, he gave thanks and said, "Take this and divide it among you. ¹⁸For I tell you I will not drink again of the fruit of the vine until the kingdom of God comes."

¹⁹And he took bread, gave thanks and broke it, and gave it to them, saying, "This is my body given for you; do this in remembrance of me."

²⁰In the same way, after the supper he took the cup, saying, "This cup is the new covenant in my blood, which is poured out for you."

Original Meaning

NOW JESUS TAKES control of events.[1] He sends his disciples to prepare to celebrate the festal meal of the Passover at a house that is ready to host them. Note how Jesus continues to celebrate the festivals of the Jewish faith right until the end. Nothing about his piety in worshiping God can be challenged.

Peter and John go to find the place Jesus designates—one group of thousands looking for a place in Jerusalem to hold the meal. Peter and John must

---

1. The parallels to this event are Matthew 26:17–19 and Mark 14:12–16.

not only obtain a locale, but also secure the lamb for the sacrifice and pick up the bitter herbs and unleavened bread that are part of the meal.[2]

What is unusual about this instruction is the detail that comes with it. Jesus tells them to look for a man carrying a water jar, who will lead them to a house. They must ask the owner where the "guest room" is where the Teacher can hold the Passover meal. The owner will show them a large, upper room, already furnished,[3] probably with reclining couches. The details given may reflect that some type of prearrangement is in place, since Matthew 26:18 suggests that the host knows who this "Teacher" is. The mood of this text is like events in the Old Testament, where divine direction and provision are at work (1 Sam. 10:2–8). The disciples go and find things just as Jesus has told them (v. 13). What he says can be trusted. Peter and John prepare the Passover, proving themselves faithful.

Luke 22:14–20 describes one of the most famous moments in Jesus' ministry.[4] It occurs during the fifth of seven meal scenes in Luke (5:29–32; 7:36–50; 9:12–17; 10:38–42; 11:37–54; 14:1–24; 24:28–32; 24:36–42). Such intimate events are the context for much of Jesus' teaching, which can be characterized as "table talk." The meal is also known as the Last Supper, and it forms the basis of the Lord's Supper. The background of the meal is likely a Passover meal, though others express uncertainty about this conclusion.[5]

The disciples honor the traditional commitment to hold the feast in the city (2 Chron. 35:18). The meal serves as the occasion of Jesus' last testament. Greeks would recognize the scene as a *symposium*, where a teacher of wisdom shares his thoughts with his followers; but a Jewish background in terms of a farewell scene also exist. The two forms are not contradictory to each other; they merely highlight different themes. The hour comes for Jesus to

---

2. Stein, *Luke*, 538. Later custom was summarized in the Talmud (*Pesahim* 64a–65b).

3. G. Stählin, "ξένος," *TDNT*, 5:19 n. 136.

4. The parallels to this text are Matthew 26:20, 26–29 and Mark 14:17, 22–25. First Corinthians 11:23–26 also alludes to this event in a form similar to Luke.

5. The debate here is complex. Stein, *Luke*, 539–40, argues that the problem is not solved. L. T. Johnson, *The Gospel of Luke*, 341, argues that one of the Evangelists, either the Synoptics or John, has made an error and that we cannot know first-century Passover custom, given the lateness of our Jewish sources. But the case for a Passover meal can be made. See D. A. Carson, "Matthew," in *EBC* (Grand Rapids: Zondervan, 1984), 8:531–32; I. H. Marshall, *Last Supper and Lord's Supper* (Exeter: Paternoster, 1981), 30–75; J. Jeremias, *The Eucharistic Words of Jesus* (London: SCM, 1966), 15–84. Carson explains how there need not be an error here, while Marshall and Jeremias defend the presence of a Passover meal. The Mishnaic tractate *Pesahim* describes Passover customs. This was a sufficiently old and conservative liturgical tradition, so that the Mishnaic form likely reflects long-time practice, even though it dates from the second century A.D. If a Passover meal is present, it is likely that the portion of the meal the Synoptics depict is associated with the main portion of the meal and the third cup of wine (out of four).

recline at the table and share this final meal with his disciples. He notes how he has "eagerly desired" (a Semitic expression indicating great emotion) to celebrate this meal before he suffers. The mention of approaching suffering adds pathos to what follows.

Jesus will not celebrate this meal until "it finds fulfillment in the kingdom of God." Jesus has in mind here the fulfillment of the kingdom in the consummation. At that time a meal like the Passover will celebrate the completion of the promise. Jesus longs for that moment, but until then, this is the last such celebration he will engage in.

Luke alone notes two cups, the first of which appears in verse 17. The Jewish Passover meal came in four courses. This remark probably alludes to the first or second cup, since Jesus' remarks about sacrifice in a later cup (v. 20) fit best with the third portion of the meal. Jesus again announces that he will not taste of the fruit of the vine until the banquet celebration when the consummated kingdom arrives (v. 18). The disciples become aware that the end of Jesus' ministry with them is near. This will be the last moment of sustained shared fellowship with him for some time. The remarks with the bread and the cup indicate this.

But his death means far more than the end of his ministry.[6] The "bread" Jesus takes is a part of the third course of the meal, eaten along with the lamb and bitter herbs. Jesus makes a fresh symbol out of the bread in light of his death. He takes it, gives thanks, breaks it, and passes it around the table. "This is my body given for you; do this in remembrance of me." In that moment the Jewish meal becomes christianized, a memorial act in memory and proclamation of Jesus' death (1 Cor. 11:23–26). The bread symbolizes the broken body of Jesus offered on behalf of his community.

The call to "remember" is Jewish, which the nation did annually in the Passover as they looked back at the Exodus. Such recalling solidifies a community's identity by taking them back to their roots, to events that forged who they have now become. It gives them a chance, as one body, to reaffirm what God has done for them. The sacrifice he offers and the symbolism in which they share recalls the Hebrew concept of *zikron*, where something is to cling to the memory (Ex. 2:24; 12:14; 13:9; Lev. 24:7; Num. 5:15; 10:9–10; Ps. 20:3; Ezek. 21:23).[7] This meal is like a new start.

---

6. There is a textual question that influences how the text is read from this point. Luke 22:19b–20 are not in some manuscripts and Latin versions. Textual critics often prefer the shorter reading on the premise that scribes add to clarify and generally do not remove clear wording from the text. So some have argued Luke did not include these verses. But it is more likely that they are a part of Luke, especially since they are included in some of the major Greek manuscript witnesses (e.g., א, B, P⁷⁵, and texts of the Byzantine family).

7. O. Michel, "μνεία," *TDNT*, 4:678; "μνημονεύω," 4:682.

Thanksgiving to God for the bread is also thanksgiving for the offering that clears the way for a relationship to God. Exactly how Jesus' body is offered for them is not specified here. Acts 20:28 suggests how Luke saw this, while Romans 3:21–31; 5:6–8; and 1 Corinthians 10:16 show how Paul viewed it. In Acts Luke uses the imagery of purchasing, the securing of a relationship with God through the shedding of innocent blood as a payment for sin. The connection with the Passover at this meal also suggests the image of a substitutionary sacrifice, imagery Paul makes use of. The Passover was a time when judgment came to the Egyptians in the death of their firstborn, but Israel's firstborn were "passed over" and spared the judgment because blood of a lamb was placed on the lintel of the door at their homes. Jesus now becomes the symbol of such protection.

Jesus goes on to refer to the cup as "the new covenant in my blood." The reference to blood looks at Jesus' coming sacrifice as that which inaugurates the covenantal provision that the disciples will benefit from as a result of Jesus' death. The new covenant is a major theme in the New Testament (Jer. 31:31; Matt. 26:28; 2 Cor. 3–4; Heb. 8–10). In it are the promise of forgiveness of sins and the enabling power of God's Spirit, expressed as the law written on the heart—a theme the 2 Corinthians passage develops in detail. Jesus' blood shed for them clears the way for the distribution of the blessings of this covenant (Luke 24:49; Acts 1:8; 2:14–39; Heb. 8–10) and opens up a new era of God's blessing.

In sum, the meal and its memorialization commemorates and declares Jesus' sacrificial death. To share in this meal in the future is to affirm the relationship established by what Jesus is about to do. The meal affirms an intimate oneness between Jesus and those who identify with his death.

Bridging Contexts

THE MOOD OF the passage is the key bridge. Everything about this event reflects the calmness of Jesus and the control of God present in the activity. Jesus directs all the activity, knowing how each detail will fall into place. Though the Passover meal is being celebrated, in another sense the Passover Lamb is preparing to offer himself after this one last meal with his disciples. Nothing catches him by surprise. The disciples faithfully follow the instructions of their teacher. He, in turn, leads by example, trusting that the Father will lead him to complete his course.

Two attitudes are central: God's sovereignty and Jesus' faithfulness displayed in the face of it. Jesus walks into Jerusalem, fully aware of what is about to take place and that God has brought him here to meet his departure. He meets his call with a total commitment to walk in God's way. We often face situations where God's sovereignty calls us to walk a path where he is clearly leading, though the outcome, unlike this situation in Jesus' life, may be unclear. Anyone who has faced the prospect of relocation understands what it is like to ask the Lord to show his direction, so that the ministry God desires can take place. The direction is usually not as clear for us as it was for Jesus. But God calls us to seek his face and direction in the midst of the questions, so that he makes his will known through forces often outside our control. We can follow his lead as Jesus does here.

The importance of celebration and remembrance, even of table fellowship in the church, is often underestimated, especially in traditions where the word is paramount and liturgy is de-emphasized. However, something significant is in view here. The disciples as a community are about to share a meal whose roots are centuries old. They gather together to reflect on what God has done and is about to do. Sometimes the complaint goes up that meeting together for a meal is not real fellowship, but when a group meets together to share God's goodness and activity, then something spiritual and bonding does take place. Part of the reason Jesus commanded this meal to be observed after his departure is that it connects us anew with him and reaffirms our connection to each other (1 Cor. 10:16).

This final meal sets the basis for the Lord's table as celebrated in the church. The major difference between this meal and those that follow is that where the Last Supper is prospective, anticipating Jesus' sacrifice, the meal the church celebrates is retrospective, looking back to that death. First Corinthians 11:26 gives a type of timeless quality to the meal: It looks back to the Lord's death and looks forward to his return. The celebration of the meal links our present relationship with Christ with the past and future presence of Jesus. Since it is his supper, we reflect on his death for us at Calvary and his return for us in glory. In one moment, the great events of salvation are chained together in solemn celebration. Eternity touches time, and we are the beneficiaries of a rare moment of fellowship. Thus this meal establishes an important link in the church's worship of her Lord. There is no more fundamental reminder of God's grace than to recall how our relationship to God was procured.

Also fundamental in the teaching of this text are the short notes about how Jesus' death was for us, that is, for our benefit. Luke does not explain in detail why Jesus died for us; that emphasis appears later in the New Testament (Rom. 3:21–31; 1 Peter 2:21–25; Rev. 4–5). Luke prefers to focus on who Jesus is and how he has the power to bring victory. But this text and Acts 20:28 show that he is aware that a divine transaction took place on the cross. What we could not do for ourselves, God did for us through his Son. Giving a life in order that many might gain life is the consummate act of God's love. This is the message of the Lord's Supper that calls us to remember this unique moment in history.

This supper is a major moment of fellowship that the Lord had with his disciples before departing. It also is a meal he wants repeatedly celebrated as a reminder of what he accomplished on the cross. With it comes an attitude of expectation about his return. This meal with all it signifies was never meant to be just another aspect of the worship service. As one of the few designated rites in the church, its special place has always been marked out.

This is especially the case given the dual affirmation of the meal: We proclaim both the Lord's death and our community oneness with fellow celebrants at the table. This combination was designed to drive us to act in a way that affirms what we share so fundamentally through Jesus' death. That reminder is a healthy one, even as we recall what this meal is all about. The church is not ours, but his. Our life is not ours, but his. Our relationship to one another is not an accident, but a product of great design and cost. That theological reality should cause us to relate to each other with great sensitivity.

JESUS IS DEDICATED to the way and will of God. Facing betrayal and death, he calmly leads his disciples into the celebration of God's goodness in salvation. Though he will soon go to the cross and experience rejection, he leads his disciples in worship and reminds them of their call to follow in his steps. There is something almost eerie about his calm in this event. The juxtaposition of mood may say something about the nature of trust. Jesus rests in the knowledge that God cares for him. There will be moments in which tensions and anxieties are expressed to God through prayer, but at the base there is a sense of God's being in control and of Jesus' awareness of what is going on.

All of this is reassuring to those who read Luke's account. God's control even in the midst of dire circumstances is important to recall as we face the painful circumstances of our own lives. Though our modern difficult circumstances may not involve martyrdom, there are moments where we or others face desperate circumstances. We may struggle with God's activity in our lives or we may have a breakdown in major relationships. Perhaps we are suffering from health problems that cause us to turn more fervently to God. The way in which Jesus faced the ultimate end of his ministry is not unlike coming to grips with the hard curves that often throw trauma into our lives. Granted the example is Jesus, but his trust and calm in the face of what is ahead reveals a deep trust in the direction God leads.

As Jesus takes this journey, he will look to God and respond with an absence of defensiveness. All of that can be done because he understands God's care for him in the midst of the turmoil about him. Though he will share the trauma of his heart in prayer at Gethsemane, in all other situations he reflects calmly God's presence in the midst of what was going on. Through prayer and supplication, Jesus lets his requests be made known to God, and God's peace serves to guard him. At the base of his assurance stands the God who is represented in the meal he is sharing with his disciples, a God who provides for the deliverance that really counts when all else seems awry.

In a real way, the application of this text about the Last Supper meets us in the celebration of the meal that emerges from this solemn moment. It is perhaps a great tragedy in the church that this meal often gets relegated to a minor role in the church's worship. Many observances of the Lord's table are relegated to a quick addition to a service, observed once a quarter or even less. This supper was never designed to be a "tacked on" element of worship. Though we are not told how often to observe it, there can be no doubt that the call to engage in this meal as an act of remembrance was designed to bring believers together regularly to share as a unified body in the reflection and proclamation it represents. One can make a strong case for observing the meal more often than once or twice a year. John Calvin made the same complaint centuries ago:

> What we have so far said of the Sacrament abundantly shows that it was not ordained to be received only once a year—and that, too, perfunctorily, as now is the usual custom. Rather, it was ordained to be frequently used among all Christians in order that they might frequently return in memory to the Christ's Passion, by such remembrance to sustain and strengthen their faith, and urge themselves to sing thanksgiving to God and to proclaim his goodness; finally, by it to nourish mutual love, and among themselves give witness to this love, and discern its bond in the unity of Christ's body. For as often as we partake of the symbol of the Lord's body, as a token given and received, we reciprocally bind ourselves to all the duties of love in order that none of us may permit anything that can harm our brother, or overlook anything that can help him, where necessity demands and ability suffices.[8]

In the Lord's Supper, we acknowledge the presence of our Lord, his death, and his coming again. Sharing in the elements together, we affirm our oneness before him and our submission to him, and we recall how we came to

---

8. John Calvin, *Institutes*, 4.17.44.

receive such grace. The benefit of such reflection, done carefully, is that we are refocused on that which unites us in faith and on the central truths that make the church different from any other organization. By taking part in this meal, we make a public statement more powerful than uttering a creed. For in the partaking is the recognition that our very sustenance and life comes from him.

The table becomes an act that sustains our unity by drawing around the One who made us his body. In it are brought together sacrifice and promise, as he becomes the Lamb who brings the new covenant (cf. 1 Cor. 5:7). God's presence and enablement are within us through the Spirit. Jesus left so that another helper could come (John 14–16). That exchange is also represented in the table. Our call is to respond to what that sacrifice made possible.

Jesus' sacrifice reminds us that our response to him should be the sacrifice of a life honoring to him and drawing on the resources the new covenant (Rom. 8:1–17; 12:1–2). The spiritual service of worship involves more than sharing in the elements of his death, for his death means a new life for us. So the ultimate application of sharing at his table is to serve him faithfully with the new life he obtains for us. We should therefore celebrate with the unleavened bread of sincerity and truth and shed malice and wickedness (1 Cor 5:7–8). The ultimate commemoration of the Lord's table is a righteous life. If new life comes through his death, new life is what should be manifested in response.

Luke 22:21–38

𝕎

BUT THE HAND of him who is going to betray me is with mine on the table. ²²The Son of Man will go as it has been decreed, but woe to that man who betrays him." ²³They began to question among themselves which of them it might be who would do this.

²⁴Also a dispute arose among them as to which of them was considered to be greatest. ²⁵Jesus said to them, "The kings of the Gentiles lord it over them; and those who exercise authority over them call themselves Benefactors. ²⁶But you are not to be like that. Instead, the greatest among you should be like the youngest, and the one who rules like the one who serves. ²⁷For who is greater, the one who is at the table or the one who serves? Is it not the one who is at the table? But I am among you as one who serves. ²⁸You are those who have stood by me in my trials. ²⁹And I confer on you a kingdom, just as my Father conferred one on me, ³⁰so that you may eat and drink at my table in my kingdom and sit on thrones, judging the twelve tribes of Israel.

³¹"Simon, Simon, Satan has asked to sift you as wheat. ³²But I have prayed for you, Simon, that your faith may not fail. And when you have turned back, strengthen your brothers."

³³But he replied, "Lord, I am ready to go with you to prison and to death."

³⁴Jesus answered, "I tell you, Peter, before the rooster crows today, you will deny three times that you know me."

³⁵Then Jesus asked them, "When I sent you without purse, bag or sandals, did you lack anything?"

"Nothing," they answered.

³⁶He said to them, "But now if you have a purse, take it, and also a bag; and if you don't have a sword, sell your cloak and buy one. ³⁷It is written: 'And he was numbered with the transgressors'; and I tell you that this must be fulfilled in me. Yes, what is written about me is reaching its fulfillment."

³⁸The disciples said, "See, Lord, here are two swords."

"That is enough," he replied.

Original
Meaning

THE DISCOURSE THAT follows Jesus' sacred meal with his disciples consists of five units: prediction of betrayal, discussion of greatness, mention of authority over Israel, prediction of Peter's denials, and discussion of swords.[1] How the disciples should handle power, authority, and rejection marks them out as different kind of people, though it will take them some time to learn the message. This material forms a type of farewell meal where a leader indicates the key principles he wishes to see in the community he is leaving.[2] These final words of Jesus stand in contrast to his post-resurrection discussion, which form his initial words for the new era of relationship in light of his exaltation.

Jesus notes with the sharing of the meal that the hand of the betrayer is at the table. He is fully aware of what is taking place, and he goes to his death willingly. This course has been decreed for the Son of Man. But "woe" (i.e., judgment) awaits the one through whom Jesus is betrayed. The remark catches the disciples by surprise. One person at the table undoubtedly knows what is meant; his surprise may well be that Jesus knows his heart. It is hard to imagine what Judas must have felt when Jesus reveals his awareness of the betrayal. As the disciples discuss who this person might be, the message that Jesus is soon going to his death is sinking in.

Ironically, as Jesus faces his death and Judas engages in betrayal, the disciples worry about their status before Jesus. Which one of them is the greatest? In fact, the text notes that some contention exists on this question.[3] They are concerned with their role in any future kingdom Jesus brings in. Power, not service, dominates their thinking.[4]

---

1. The unit distinct to Luke is the sword discussion in 22:35–38. Parallels to the betrayal and the prediction of the denials are Matthew 26:21–25, 30–35 and Mark 14:18–21, 26–31. The discussion of greatness and authority over Israel is like Mark 10:41–45 and Matthew 20:24–28 and 19:28. These earlier settings in the other Gospels suggest the repetition of a theme, not the same event. The appearance of these five units together stresses that Jesus' community, to function in a context of rejection, will need humility, dependence, and a sense of self-identity that looks out for one another.

2. R. Stein, *Luke*, 545–46. Such farewell addresses usually involved a meal, warnings and instructions, prayer, and some type of appointment of leadership. Some have connected this section with the Greek *symposium*, but a Jewish background also exists, stretching back to Jacob's farewell in Genesis 49 and Moses' farewell in Deuteronomy 31 (cf. also *The Testament of the Twelve Patriarchs*).

3. On the term contention (*philoneikia*), see its adjectival form in 1 Corinthians 11:16; 2 Maccabees 4:4; 4 Maccabees 1:26; 8:26.

4. The parallels in Matthew 20:24–28 and Mark 10:41–45 may indicate that this was an ongoing in-house discussion, much like what can take place within many businesses.

The dispute is significant because it impacts the unity of the community. Jesus' reply is like his remarks in the other Synoptics. Disciples are to be different from the world in the way they exercise their roles. Kings and rulers wield power and "lord it over" the people.[5] They are regarded as "Benefactors," those to whom the people are beholding. That is not the type of leadership Jesus calls for. The disciple-leader is to function like young people who serve their elders.[6] Ruling in Jesus' dictionary means service, not power. Elitism and debate about status are out.

To drive the point home, Jesus offers an illustration. Who is greater in the eyes of the world—the one who is served at the table or the servant who delivers the meal? In the world, it is better to be the master. But then why has Jesus been among them "as one who serves"? By noting the character of his own ministry, Jesus sets forth a contrast that is the new example. Better to be a servant than to be served. The term *ho diakonon* ("one who serves") describes Jesus' work in their midst. His leadership means meeting needs and bringing relief to others. If the foot-washing incident of John 13 also stands in the background, then Jesus has made this point both verbally and in action.

Jesus is not uninterested in their status question. He just does not want them to compare themselves to each other. He is aware that these disciples have faithfully "stood by" (*diamemenekotes*) him through thick and thin. The Greek perfect tense in this participle suggests their abiding with Jesus over time.[7] Their constancy is noted and rewarded. The eleven will receive what Judas misses.

God the Father has assigned Jesus a kingdom, so Jesus appoints his disciples to a role in it. Two benefits emerge from the appointment: They will sit at the banquet table when the victory is gained, and they will sit on thrones judging the twelve tribes of Israel.[8] This marking out of authority over the twelve tribes shows that Jesus is forming a new community from his disciples. Their authority is not only for this era, but for the one to come as well. These disciples have a central and unique role in God's plan. Jesus' remark makes one more thing clear: Although he is headed for his death and Israel will send him there, his rule will never come to an end. At some future day he will judge all humanity, and the disciples receive authority now to help Jesus exercise that rule at a later time.

---

5. This verb (*katakyrieuo*) is merely the term *lord* (*kyrios*) put in verbal form, showing that authority and power are the issue.

6. H. W. Beyer, "διακονέω," *TDNT*, 2:84–86; G. Bertram, "εὐεργετέω, κτλ.," *TDNT*, 2:655; F. Büchsel, "ἡγέομαι," *TDNT*, 2:907–8.

7. E. Ellis, *The Gospel of Luke*, 256.

8. On the throne imagery, see Marshall, *Commentary on Luke*, 818; Tiede, *Luke*, 387. Note also 1 Corinthians 6:2; *1 Enoch* 62.

But not everything is rosy. The cosmic struggle goes on. Jesus singles out Peter for special attention, because Satan has zeroed in on this central disciple, asking to take him through the sieve. Like wheat separated from chaff, Satan wishes to check out what Peter is really made of (cf. Satan's effort against Job). But Peter does not face this alone. At his side stands Jesus, who intercedes for him and for his faith. That does not mean success in the middle of the test is guaranteed, for Jesus goes on to note that when Peter has "turned back," he will be called on to strengthen the people. This implies there will be a temporary failure. In the restoration, the ultimate success of Jesus' intercession emerges, showing how even after a disappointment, his work can lead to recovery.

Peter seems to get the point, for he declares his total allegiance to Jesus. He feels he is willing to go to prison and even to death with Jesus (v. 33). Peter obviously comprehends by this time that death awaits Jesus, and he is confident Jesus need not face it alone. But Jesus knows Peter better than Peter does. He predicts that before the cock crows in the hours just before dawn, Peter will have denied Jesus three times. Despite all the instruction and the benefits Jesus has graciously given his disciples, they still have much to learn about depending on him. They are weak without Jesus.

The pressure on Peter shows how things are changing, so Jesus must prepare them to face future realities. Earlier, when Jesus sent them out and asked them to depend on being supplied with the necessities of life, they lacked nothing (9:1–6; 10:1–24). God provided for them through people. But now it will be necessary to take a purse, a bag, and even a sword. They are now going to minister in a world that may well be hostile to them. What takes place fulfills Isaiah 53:12. Jesus will be reckoned among criminals ("transgressors"), and, by implication, so will those who identify with him. These things must (*dei*) take place. The citation from the Servant Song is important. Luke does not cite the portion of Isaiah 53 that deals with Jesus' suffering, but with how others will wrongly view him. The opposition of the nation is predicted. The disciples must be prepared for what lies ahead and understand that ministry takes place in a context of opposition.

As becomes evident in 22:49–51, the disciples misunderstand his rhetorical remarks about defending themselves in the face of opposition. They think that Jesus wants them to take a sword inventory to get ready for battle, and they note they have two swords (*macharai;* i.e., battle swords). But the sword inventory they really need is an inner one. Jesus thus makes a dismissive remark: "That is enough." This phrase closes the discussion. The disciples still do not understand what their responsibility is. In the next few hours, they will find out.

Bridging Contexts

EACH TOPIC IN this section shows some connection to our age. Although Judas's betrayal is unique, he portrays the person who, although close to Jesus and ministering for him, eventually rejects him. There are people today who reflect his attitude. From every external measure, Judas looked like a faithful believer and disciple, but he was, in fact, "a devil" (John 6:70–71). Eventually his lack of faith surfaced in his outright act of betrayal. Sometimes we too see people with a long history of association with the church who eventually turn their backs on it. Exposure and service for Jesus do not necessarily mean we know him. Those who truly know our Lord do not abandon him and reject him. The type of categorical renunciation of Jesus Judas manifested is what made his action distinct and more heinous than Peter's denials. It revealed where his heart was all along.

The discussion of humility and greatness touches on the topic of service among Jesus' disciples, especially those who function in roles of leadership. Real leadership does not concern itself with status or rank, but with service. Jesus' own ministry indicates how central this perspective was in his thinking. He ministered to the poor, the rejected of society, the sick, those of different race and gender, children, or anyone who had a need. Position and status meant nothing to him. The church still needs such service and such an attitude today.

The disciples' appointment to twelve thrones results from their unique role in Jesus' ministry. Of course, Judas is already excluded from what is in view here, having opted for another allegiance. But that Jesus honors those who identify with him and that blessing results from this association are abiding principles in this text. Though what Jesus gives the Twelve here is unique, he will give all his servants praise one day for the faithful works they perform (1 Cor. 3:12–14; 4:5).

Peter's denials are also significant in instructing us about how we fail and how we can recover from failure. On the surface, his actions look much like what Judas did, but with crucial differences. Judas took active action against Jesus; Peter sought only to distance himself publicly from Jesus. Judas had a failure of heart; Peter had a failure of nerve and was visibly hurt by his failure. These differences are instructive, for Jesus intends to restore Peter, while Judas becomes a painfully remembered, condemned, and pathetic figure in Acts 1:15–20. Those close to Jesus can hurt him; they can fail under pressure. Any who are confident they can survive on their own strength are often standing on the edge of a fall (1 Cor. 10:12). Peter's denials remind us that we can all fall. But the fact that Jesus lays the groundwork for Peter's restoration even before he falls indicates God's compassion for us when we turn back to him. It takes great love to forgive and restore.

Jesus' final remarks about taking one's own provisions, including a sword, show just how serious the world's reaction may be to believers. They will now have to fend for themselves. It is important not to miss the rhetorical character of these remarks. The disciples take the comment about the sword literally—one of the disciples will even wield his sword at Jesus' arrest, a reaction Jesus rebukes. But the Lord has in mind here a toughness and focus of attitude that do not need accolades or the world's acceptance and care. Disciples serve as aliens in a strange land (1 Peter 2:11), as citizens of heaven (Phil. 3:20–21). They will need to draw together to support one another, while not expecting support from those who do not share their devotion to the Lord.

STARTING WITH ACTS 20:29, Scripture warns about wolves who come from among the Christian community to ravage the church. Many other New Testament texts likewise warn about those who will lead the church astray. A figure like Judas shows just how close to the Lord such people can get. The possibility of defection from within is a difficult topic to address. The community is to be a place of trust, where believers affirm one another. The last thing churches need are heresy hunters who take it upon themselves to sniff out the least suspicion of error. Such an environment communicates mistrust and often sees danger where it does not reside.

Yet the New Testament does not take such a clandestine approach to the possibility of defection. Rather, it issues warnings for people to remain faithful to God and to his Word. It also warns those who attempt to bring down the church that God will deal with them (1 Cor. 3:17–18; Titus 3:9–11; 2 John 9–10). These texts suggest that people who do not maintain the central truths of the faith should not be heeded. Professions of faith and association with the church are not in and of themselves signs of true faith. Faith does, of course, save, and such faith continues to believe, as the saying "Once saved, always saved" implies. God is, after all, thoroughly committed to those who genuinely trust him.

But there is a corollary that goes with such a statement: "Once trusting, always trusting." That is, those who trust Jesus with a faith that saves always have the sense that they are children of God and do not let that faith go into outright denial (Rom. 8:15). The Spirit who indwells us gives us a sense that we are his children, even in those moments of doubt that can fill our thoughts.

Judas is the negative example who makes the positive point. There came a day when he said that Jesus was not the answer. His statement revealed where his heart had always been, though no one knew it up to the moment of his defection (cf. 1 John 2:19). His case warns us not to overestimate ourselves but to stay closely allied to Jesus. The message of this passage is, "Cling to Jesus, and do not be surprised if some people do walk away from him."

Jesus has had much to say in this Gospel about humility and service. Verses 24–27 show just how different Jesus' thinking is from the world's. In the world, the leader gets all the perks and receives service. He wields power and authority with a recognition that his rank gives him the right to direct and coerce into action. Jesus' approach to leadership is the exact opposite. Leadership is not attaining a rank that allows one to exercise authority with one's own interests in mind. Leadership is a responsibility and a trust to exercise one's skills and energies to serve those who are led.

Our culture witnesses many battles that revolve around power. The Bible, however, does not deal in power politics. People in positions of authority are stewards who look to God to meet their needs and who serve him according to their calling. In the last few years, a movement has emerged to call men to be the "heads" of their homes. What is significant about the headship passage in Ephesians 5:22–33 is that it says nothing about the exercise of power. Rather, the passage exhorts husbands to mirror Christ, who gave his body for his bride and calls on them to nourish and cherish their partners. Headship and leadership are not positions that call for the raw exercise of power, but a sensitive display of compassion, care, and service. Pastoral leadership is no different. The nurturing of communities through prayer, counseling, instruction, compassion, and other forms of service is not a matter of wielding power but of sharing spiritual resources and energy in a way that leads by example. Real leadership serves, even when no one is looking. God exalts those who humble themselves, even as they lead by serving.

The example of Peter warns us that we can easily turn our backs on Jesus when we are under pressure. His failure was short-lived because he learned from the experience and found reassurance in the Lord's restoration in John 21. When we meet Peter again in Acts, he was able to stand and testify to Jesus. He made one significant decision that represented a reversal of where he had been: He no longer cared whether others accepted him. That does not mean he set about becoming a Christian bull in the china shop of the world, creating reaction and offense wherever he could. But it does mean that restored to the opportunity to share and proclaim Jesus, he renewed his commitment to be faithful. The disappointment of Peter's denials needs to be balanced with the lessons of the rest of his life. Sometimes we can see complete restoration from a severe fall. Of course, a key part of the difference in Peter is the provision of the Spirit he receives at Pentecost that explains his boldness in Acts. The resources Peter had are the same we have today. Through the Spirit, transformation and restoration are possible.

I suspect that all of us understand Peter. We have all had times when we had a chance to identify with Jesus but remained silent or denied him because we did not know what reaction might set in. We have failed in standing up for Jesus. But like Peter, we also can learn from our failures and grow. And like Peter, Jesus calls us back to strengthen his people and to serve them.

Jesus heads to his death, having armed his disciples with an awareness of the opposition they face. The situation is no different today. Christians are often "out of their element" in the world, at least if they are functioning in a Christian manner. Fending for themselves means drawing on the unity the church is to have in the Lord. Many denominations and Christian groups obscure the basic unity we possess, even though our allegiance to Jesus should bring us together and cause us to fend for each other. Magnifying our differences, which are often tiny in comparison to our differences with the world, we end up spending our energy wielding swords on each other, rather than facing the more fundamental conflict that exists in the world. The church is called to a rescue mission, but it is hard to perform when the tactical squads spend all their time sniping at each other.

Some, of course, think our differences are significant. Perhaps some are, but we should never forget they are minor "in-house" discussions compared to the battles we face in the world. Far too many Christian groups do not work together today because they are divided on issues that are not central to the faith. We can and should have "in-house" discussions, but not in a way that leaves our mission at risk.

The last part of this discourse warns us that a battle lies ahead. The church has been wrestling with the spiritual forces of darkness for centuries (Eph. 6:10–18). But wars are never won when allies are divided. All our energy and resources should go into making sure we have the provisions to carry out our mission. We can continue to talk about the most effective strategies, but to accomplish our call we must respect those we recognize are on our side and keep the real enemy in our sights. The disciples needed such unity when they launched the church through the Spirit's enabling in Acts. We need to regain such unity to continue her task effectively today.

In contrast to this tendency to fight in-house, Jesus urges preparation and a recognition that we as a community must provide for ourselves. This means the church cannot expect the world to come to its defense. Rather, we must stand together. The defense called for here manifested itself in Acts as the community looked out for, prayed for, and protected figures like Peter and Paul. Our opposition must not be a militant or violent one, a reaction

Jesus specifically disapproves of in verses 50–51. But it is a form of defensive engagement where the community stands up for its own, offering them protection or caring for them, even if they are called to send them along to a location where they may be at risk. We must work with each other and support each other as the gospel is shared in the world.

Luke 22:39–46

J ESUS WENT OUT as usual to the Mount of Olives, and his
disciples followed him. ⁴⁰On reaching the place, he said to
them, "Pray that you will not fall into temptation." ⁴¹He
withdrew about a stone's throw beyond them, knelt down and
prayed, ⁴²"Father, if you are willing, take this cup from me; yet
not my will, but yours be done." ⁴³An angel from heaven
appeared to him and strengthened him. ⁴⁴And being in
anguish, he prayed more earnestly, and his sweat was like
drops of blood falling to the ground.

⁴⁵When he rose from prayer and went back to the disciples,
he found them asleep, exhausted from sorrow. ⁴⁶"Why are you
sleeping?" he asked them. "Get up and pray so that you will
not fall into temptation."

Original Meaning

LUKE 22:39–23:56 DETAILS the final road of Jesus
to his death. From his prayer in Gethsemane,
where his trust in God is affirmed, to the burial
in Joseph of Arimathea's tomb, this section details
how an innocent man came to die for others. What the Jewish leadership
could not do was to get testimony to convict Jesus. So Jesus supplies the
words that bring about his death. Ironically, he dies for speaking the truth.

At trials before Pilate and Herod, Jesus is declared to have done nothing
worthy of death, yet they send him to the cross. Some actively seek his
death, while others stand by and let it occur. In his place a criminal is released
in an exercise of ironic logic that pictures what Jesus' death is about: an innocent person dying in place of someone who has sinned. On the cross, Jesus
is mocked with taunts to save himself and others. Ironically, he does just
that with the criminal who asks to be in his kingdom. His death, unjust as it
is, appears on the surface to be a defeat. But because of who he is, Jesus turns
it into victory, not just for himself but for all who embrace what he achieved
on a lone piece of wood one Palestinian afternoon.

In 22:39–46 Jesus turns from addressing his disciples to praying to the
Father.[1] His honesty in his prayer shows the depth and quality of his rela-

---

1. The parallels to this passage are Matthew 26:36–46 and Mark 14:32–42. The Lucan
version is the shortest of the three accounts, but he alone notes Jesus' distance from the disciples as "a stone's throw," the angelic aid, and Jesus' sweating drops like blood. It is debated

tionship with the Father. This is a significant moment, for he turns to God just before his arrest. In the prayer itself we see both Jesus' agony and his desire to follow God's will, even if it means his life. The disciples underestimate the severity of this moment, for they fall asleep. What they need is not rest but a renewed turning to God, lest they plunge into failure.

Jesus takes his customary evening trip to the Mount of Olives, and the disciples accompany him (22:37). Before he himself prays, he tells them to pray so as to not fall into temptation. One almost has the sense that he is exemplifying what he calls for from them. As the moment of his sacrifice approaches, all his emotional distress will be laid before the Father on an altar of prayer. If the discourse here is any indication, the temptation the disciples will have is the possibility of denying him (cf. 22:31–32). Prayer is important, since it brings us into communion with God and allows us to draw on his presence with us. Jesus' command to "pray," written in a Greek present imperative, in this context may suggest an ongoing commitment to pray as opposed to a single moment of prayer. Temptation is avoided only by continued dependence on God (11:4).

Jesus prays "about a stone's throw" from the disciples, a distance of several yards (Gen. 21:16). The text literally says he "pulled away" from his disciples, a remark that adds a touch of emotion to the story. He kneels down and intercedes, asking if there might be some other way to accomplish what lies ahead. The request is couched in the fundamental commitment Jesus has to doing God's will, "Father, if you are willing. . . ." The thought in Greek is abbreviated at this point, another indication of intense emotion.[2] Jesus' main request is, "Take this cup from me." Such a request for a change in God's will is not unprecedented (Ex. 32:10–14; 2 Sam. 15:25–26; 2 Kings 20:1–6). Jesus wants the cup of wrath to be passed from him, but only if there is another way.[3] So he adds, "Yet not my will, but yours be done." Jesus has bracketed his request on each end to a commitment to do God's will.

---

whether verses 43–44 are a part of Luke; we accept them as authentic, given its presence in early manuscripts like ℵ and D (see Marshall, *Commentary on Luke*, 831–32). Those who argue for omission base their conclusion that it is the shorter reading, that the lack of emotion in the text fits Luke, and that the text looks too instructive in character to be original. But does the shorter text rule apply when a whole verse is in view? The addition includes a reference to prayer that is very Lucan. In addition, the text may have been removed because it argues for angelic strengthening, which makes Jesus look too human. The dispute is important, because these verses indicate just how human Jesus' reaction was as he turned to face his death.

2. G. Schrenk, "βούλομαι," *TDNT*, 1:633.

3. On "cup" as a figure for wrath, see Psalm 11:6; 75:7–8; Isaiah 51:17, 19, 22; Jeremiah 25:15–16; 49:12; 51:57; Zechariah 12:12; C. Cranfield, "The Cup Metaphor in Mark xiv.36 and Parallels," *ExpTim* 59 (1947–48): 137–38.

An angel appears to strengthen him (cf. Matt. 4:11, which makes a similar statement about the aftermath of the temptation account). The importance of the angelic appearance is that the strengthening from above shows heaven's willingness to stand beside Jesus as he faces his calling.

The intensity of the emotion increases as Jesus prays more fervently and sweats drops like blood (the text uses the Greek term *agonia* to describe Jesus' intense "anguish"). Jesus is laying his burdens before God as he faces the prospect of rejection and death. Here is a very human portrait of Jesus, facing his death with a range of emotions. Luke's portrait of Jesus does not hide behind his deity. He presents a Jesus who can identify with our weaknesses and traumas (Heb. 4:15).

Finally, Jesus gets up and returns to his disciples, finding them "exhausted from sorrow" and asleep. They have begun to understand that rejection for Jesus lies just ahead, and it has wiped them out emotionally. Jesus asks them why they are sleeping at this crucial moment and again calls them to pray that they will not fall into temptation. The only way they will be ready for what is ahead is if they prepare for it as he has. Faithfulness is grounded in being in touch with God.

THIS TEXT BOTH reveals something about Jesus' character and provides an example for how we can face the great trials of life God sends our way. In these verses we see a man dependent on God and committed to doing his will. We see an individual who faces trial by turning to God. We see a person who reveals his intense emotions to God in prayer. In contrast, the disciples have only their exhaustion and emotional pain. Even as Jesus exhorts them to pray, all they can do is sleep. Everything about Jesus' approach models how one should face the tension of trial.

Jesus is not spared the trial, but what is supplied is the strength to face it. Though he does not hesitate to ask if another way can be found, he affirms his resolve to go the way God wants. Heaven responds not by granting Jesus his request for another way, but by giving him the strength to face what God has called him to do. This union of submission to divine call and divine strength supplied is at the heart of the passage.

THIS PASSAGE REVEALS at least two exemplary points about the character of Jesus as he faces the trial of the cross. (1) Jesus takes both his pain and his need to God in prayer. His custom of communing with God is not altered by the unique events that descend on him. Often when we are the busiest, we neglect to take the time to go to God with our needs. Trials often force us to our knees, but frequently the hectic pace of life keeps us on the run and inhibits us from praying. That is not the case for Jesus. His pattern reminds us that prayer is important, even in the most frantic of times. And his prayer is not a matter of merely checking in; it is full of honesty, emotion, and pain. Real prayer takes work. Too often we bow our head, close our eyes, and let our minds wander, rather then laboring in prayer.

(2) Jesus manifests honesty and humility in prayer. He sincerely desires that God will not make him go through what lies ahead and honestly shares that, yet he is even more committed to being in God's will. The prayer, though different from the laments in Psalms, is similar in that those petitioners also took their innermost feelings and pain to God. The private confrontation that takes place in prayer often produces the solace we need to take our next steps holding God's hand. Moreover, prayer is not a haphazard exercise. Jesus prays with his entire being as he seeks God out in the midst of his situation. He even sweats drops like blood. Jesus can walk with God because he regularly seeks God.

The disciples are a stunning lesson in contrast, for they sleep rather than pray, as Jesus asked them to do. We often take a Scarlett O'Hara approach to our problems—"I'll think about that tomorrow." This type of procrastination argues that time or fate itself will settle such matters. Maybe it reflects a view that prayer really accomplishes little. But in moments of tension and strain, there are issues to get out on the table before God, as Jesus does here. We as his disciples must not regard prayer time at our meetings and functions as a formal preamble to the event, but part of the work of ministry itself, where a genuine transaction of relationship takes place between us and God.

As committed to God as Jesus is, heaven is just as committed to him. The remark about angelic strength should reassure us that as we turn to him, he will strengthen us. Other texts are clear about how God provides "the way out" for us if, as we face temptation, we recognize our need for him (1 Cor. 10:12–13).

Luke 22:47–53

W HILE HE WAS still speaking a crowd came up, and the man who was called Judas, one of the Twelve, was leading them. He approached Jesus to kiss him, [48]but Jesus asked him, "Judas, are you betraying the Son of Man with a kiss?"

[49]When Jesus' followers saw what was going to happen, they said, "Lord, should we strike with our swords?" [50]And one of them struck the servant of the high priest, cutting off his right ear.

[51]But Jesus answered, "No more of this!" And he touched the man's ear and healed him.

[52]Then Jesus said to the chief priests, the officers of the temple guard, and the elders, who had come for him, "Am I leading a rebellion, that you have come with swords and clubs? [53]Every day I was with you in the temple courts, and you did not lay a hand on me. But this is your hour—when darkness reigns."

Original Meaning

JESUS' ARREST MEANS he will experience the cup.[1] He submits to God's will and will not allow any attempt to fight his way out of this situation. The healing of the arresting servant's ear is the last miracle of Jesus' ministry recorded in Luke. Ironically but poignantly, Jesus heals to the very end; even his enemies are beneficiaries. The time for darkness has come as Jesus complains about the manner of his arrest. They are treating him like a rebel, a sad fate for a Savior.

The betrayal comes as a crowd approaches and Judas comes forward to give Jesus a kiss. The text notes that Judas is one of the Twelve, thus underscoring how far his rejection has penetrated. The kiss, a sign of affection, has become a sign of defection. The warping of this act of intimacy is noted in Jesus' question, "Are you betraying the Son of Man with a kiss?"[2]

---

1. The parallels to this text are Matthew 26:47–56; Mark 14:43–52; John 18:2–11. Luke has three unique points: the healing of the ear, a remark to Judas (v. 48), and the remark to the disciple who wields the sword (v. 49).

2. On misused kisses, see Genesis 27:46–47; 2 Samuel 15:5; 20:9; Proverbs 7:13; 27:6.

The disciples recall Jesus' remarks about swords. Not understanding what the moment requires and that God has called Jesus to walk this course, they ask Jesus if they should fight. One of them (Peter, according to John 18:10), does not wait for the reply. He strikes at the servant of the high priest, severing his right ear.

Jesus puts a stop to the action. He wants no struggle at his arrest. He will submit to God's call and to the Jewish leadership's desire to arrest him. They will be held accountable to God for their actions. Then he picks up the severed ear and heals the servant. We do not know what effect this may have had on the audience, but it does not stop them from carrying out their duty. Everything about the arrest is told in a way that indicates how amazing it is that anyone seeks to arrest Jesus.

Jesus adds one more note. He questions the chief priests, the officers of the temple guard, and the elders whether they really needed to come as if to arrest someone "leading a rebellion." The Greek word *lestes* refers to a robber or highway bandit (cf. 10:30, 36). The word can also be used of revolutionaries, but it need not carry that meaning here.[3] Jesus complains that they act as if he is a common criminal, whereas he has been with them daily in the temple, and they did not arrest him then. He knows that they left him alone because of the people. There is only one explanation for what is happening: "This is your hour," and that of "the authority of darkness" (lit.). Satan's attempt to stop Jesus is underway. Though a valiant effort, it will be stopped short—not by preventing Jesus' death, but through resurrection. Ironically, the cross will accomplish the exact opposite of what the darkness wishes. Such is the mystery of God's ways. Though the Jewish leadership seems to be in control, God and his agent are really in control.

JUDAS REVEALS THE character of sin carried out. He betrays his master with a kiss, so that sin's actions are the exact opposite of what the kiss symbolized. Such deception and hypocrisy often lie at the base of sin.

Jesus teaches us here about the character of his ministry. He is not into a power battle that involves the sword. He will indeed judge one day, but that time is yet to come. These events provide examples to us for facing circumstances often more mundane than those Jesus and Judas participate in here.

---

3. Josephus, *Antiquities* 2.13 2–3 §§ 253–54. It was not used of a revolutionary during Jesus' life, so such a technical use is probably not intended here. See R. Brown, *The Death of Messiah* (Garden City, N.Y.: Doubleday, 1994), 687.

Do we panic and try to seize total control, often by a misuse of force or power?

Paramount in the text is the sense of emotion it should generate in the reader. Do we sense the irony of Jesus' performing a healing as his enemies arrest him? Do we sense the fundamental injustice of the arrest and the fact that Jesus is seriously misread by his opponents? Which side do we take as he is led away? Even as the text presents the facts of the passage, there is something revealing about the world's lack of understanding and appreciation for who Jesus is. Such errors of judgment about him prevail today as well. Often we are misread, because he is misread.

JUDAS REVEALS THE hurtful and distorted view of relationship that sin sometimes produces. In his decision to betray Jesus *with a kiss* is the essence of a deceptive quality that is often part of sin. Jesus' question to Judas about betraying the Son of Man (i.e., Jesus) with a kiss brings the deceptive irony to the surface. Did Judas hope his act of betrayal would be covered up as the arrest took place? Or did he know he would be identified as the betrayer? We do not know what was in his mind. Yet the action he performed was the exact opposite of the affection and respect he was supposedly displaying.

That sin tries to cover its tracks is not at all unusual. One can think of stories of men who shower their wives with flowers and gifts while seeing another woman on the side. Or one can think of examples where people pilfer funds designated for the needy as they work for relief organizations. Such actions show how hard sin works to disguise itself.

In contrast stands Jesus. As his enemies arrest him and approach him as a dangerous criminal, he gives testimony to the threat by stopping his disciples from fighting back and by healing the high priest's servant. The irony and the picture are a cameo of the gospel. Jesus ministers to sinners in need. What Judas and the high priest's crowd represent is what Jesus came to minister to. How amazing that such hardness of heart and blindness see Jesus perform such a gracious act and then turn around to arrest him! Everything Jesus does indicates that he is not who they think he is. In essence, Luke is asking those reflecting on his Gospel to think through which side they identify with.

When Luke calls the moment of Jesus' arrest a time "when darkness reigns," he is noting that though his death has been ordained, it is not just (Acts 2:22–24). To reject Jesus and his claims is to side with those who arrest him, since their premise is that Jesus is not who he claims to be. Thus, as this Passion account proceeds, the constant question is, "Which side represents God?" Luke asks the reader to ponder the question and respond not just with an intellectual choice, but with a decision to embrace the forgiveness and blessing Jesus offers those who recognize him through faith.

There is something in Jesus' response and absence of violence that communicates a sense of confidence in God's sovereignty. He renounces the use of force. Defense comes through the injustice of his suffering, not through the sword. A day is coming when Jesus will do battle (see Rev. 19), but we do not need to take up the sword for Jesus now. Our call is to share the Word, love our neighbor, and work for the unity of the saints. The early church in Acts never took up arms against its opponents. It should not be like David Koresh in defending itself with bulwarks and guns. There is a subtle strength in facing persecution as Jesus did, passively resting in the active defense of his God. The power of such a defense can be seen in our own time with those who have taken a similar approach to ethical issues in the public square. That is why many texts in Luke speak about the Spirit's supplying words for us as we defend ourselves (Luke 12:11; 21:13–15). That reality also shows itself in the numerous trial scenes in Acts. The church today has all the resources to be as bold for Jesus as the early church was.

Luke 22:54-71

❦

THEN SEIZING HIM, they led him away and took him into the house of the high priest. Peter followed at a distance. ⁵⁵But when they had kindled a fire in the middle of the courtyard and had sat down together, Peter sat down with them. ⁵⁶A servant girl saw him seated there in the firelight. She looked closely at him and said, "This man was with him."

⁵⁷But he denied it. "Woman, I don't know him," he said.

⁵⁸A little later someone else saw him and said, "You also are one of them."

"Man, I am not!" Peter replied.

⁵⁹About an hour later another asserted, "Certainly this fellow was with him, for he is a Galilean."

⁶⁰Peter replied, "Man, I don't know what you're talking about!" Just as he was speaking, the rooster crowed. ⁶¹The Lord turned and looked straight at Peter. Then Peter remembered the word the Lord had spoken to him: "Before the rooster crows today, you will disown me three times." ⁶²And he went outside and wept bitterly.

⁶³The men who were guarding Jesus began mocking and beating him. ⁶⁴They blindfolded him and demanded, "Prophesy! Who hit you?" ⁶⁵And they said many other insulting things to him.

⁶⁶At daybreak the council of the elders of the people, both the chief priests and teachers of the law, met together, and Jesus was led before them. ⁶⁷"If you are the Christ," they said, "tell us."

Jesus answered, "If I tell you, you will not believe me, ⁶⁸and if I asked you, you would not answer. ⁶⁹But from now on, the Son of Man will be seated at the right hand of the mighty God."

⁷⁰They all asked, "Are you then the Son of God?"

He replied, "You are right in saying I am."

⁷¹Then they said, "Why do we need any more testimony? We have heard it from his own lips."

THIS ACCOUNT COMES in three parts: Peter's denials (22:54–62), the mocking of Jesus (22:63–65), and the trial of Jesus (22:66–71).[1] This section shows the wide array of reactions to Jesus, traces the public failure of one prominent disciple, and outlines the discussion that leads the Jews to recommend to the Romans that Jesus be crucified. Since Rome alone had authority to execute, a charge had to be found that would be worrisome to Rome. Luke 23:2 shows the result.

After his arrest, Jesus is brought to the house of the high priest. Since "High Priest" is a title that stays with a person for life, even those not currently serving, it is not clear if Annas or Caiaphas is meant in verse 54.[2] John 18:13 refers to Annas, while 18:24 speaks of Jesus being bound and sent to Caiaphas (Matt. 26:57 also refers to Caiaphas). Neither do we know if there is a brief meeting with Annas before more official proceedings begin with Caiaphas. Complicating the discussion further is the fact that Annas and Caiaphas may have lived in different wings of the same house. Thus, making a clear decision about the number of trials is difficult. It seems clear that what starts in the evening concludes early in the morning, whether it is one long meeting or has up to three separate smaller ones.[3]

Peter has trailed at some distance and ends up sitting down by a fire in the courtyard area of the location where Jesus is being held. It is a cool mid-spring evening. Most large homes had open courtyards. The servants of this particular house are gathered there; the events of the evening have stirred them. One of the maidservants recognizes Peter as one of Jesus' followers and says so: "This man was with him." But Peter denies that he even knows Jesus. The text never tells us why Peter engages in these denials, but the uncertainty

---

1. The parallels to this passage are Matthew 26:57–75; Mark 14:53–72; John 18:15–18, 25–26. Luke has no discussion of the temple charge, probably because it ended up being irrelevant. He also places Peter's denials together and has the mocking in an earlier location. The tradition of the mockings seems to have existed in various forms. The details of who challenged Peter differ, as well as how many times the rooster crowed (Mark has the rooster crow twice during Peter's three denials, while Matthew and Luke speak only of one crowing). Perhaps different traditions had differing degrees of specificity, while the differences in those who speak to Peter shows how engaged those present were in trying to determine if he was a disciple.

2. This title works like our title Governor or President.

3. Matthew and Mark relate an evening trial, while Luke has the conclusion in the morning. Perhaps Luke's absence of a temple discussion is caused by the fact he narrates only the concluding meeting of the early morning. What is less clear is whether the interrogation of Jesus that the Synoptics relate is part of the same point of inquiry. It is possible Matthew and Mark discuss an earlier exchange, which the morning session simply confirms. John 18 also seems to suggest some short encounters took place.

and danger of the moment offer plausible explanation. The disciples have failed to pray in preparation for this moment, and Peter's confidence, so strong in the privacy and safety of a meal, has wilted. His denial sounds like the Jewish ban formulas of what the synagogue said to a Jew they dismissed: "We no longer know you."[4]

Sometime later, someone else repeats the claim. "You are also one of them."[5] Peter replies instantly, "Man, I am not!" The words of Jesus in 22:34 are coming to pass. Peter's denial here is not only of knowing Jesus, but of any association with his fellow disciples.

The last denial follows about an hour later. Peter has been hanging in there, though by a thread. A third person becomes insistent: "Certainly, this fellow was with him, for he is a Galilean." Peter's accent identifies him as a man from the northern region of Israel, and he responds, "Man, I don't know what you are talking about." He claims they have the wrong person. The disciple who said he was ready to go to prison and even die for Jesus denies for a third time any connection to Jesus. The "rock man" (which is the meaning of Peter's name) has been crushed to pieces by the pressure.

With the third denial, the rooster crows, just as Jesus predicted. In an additional touch of drama, the Lord looks at Peter, an act that indicates he knows what Peter has just done. Whether Jesus is being moved from one place to another at that time, can glance through a window, or is outside for a moment is not clear. The Lord's glance leads Peter to recall the prediction of a threefold denial. It is too much. He departs, weeping bitterly. His heart knows what he has done. The pain of his action expresses his real allegiance, a connection his lips cannot utter. Peter has experienced a major failure of nerve. The Lord's word, as always, has come true. He knew Peter better than Peter did.

Meanwhile the soldiers—in all likelihood, the temple guards who arrested Jesus—are having a grand time with him, mocking him mercilessly. The game appears to be some type of version of Blind Man's Bluff, though three ancient games might fit the description.[6] In addition, they beat him. In their mocking, they identify him as a "prophet," the most popular conception of Jesus. But the Jewish leadership needs a stronger charge than that to get Jesus before the court of Rome. Rome worried about would-be kings, not prophets. The soldiers continue to "insult" Jesus (v. 65). Luke tells the story with a sense of pain, using the Greek word from which we get our word "blasphemy."

---

4. D. Catchpole, *The Trial of Jesus* (Leiden: Brill, 1971), 273.

5. Luke refers to another here, while Mark 14:69 attributes the charge to the same girl. John 18:25 says that "they" raise the issue, so apparently Peter is a topic of the servants' discussion.

6. For details, see R. Brown, *The Death of Messiah*, 575.

At daybreak, the "council" (probably the Sanhedrin, composed of leading Jews) meets with Jesus. Collective responsibility for this action will make it more persuasive when Rome is eventually called to respond. The account of the trial has several irregularities, if the Mishnaic tractate *Sanhedrin* is any guide of more ancient practice.[7] Here are a few of the procedures that are at variance with the rules in the Mishnah. (1) The proceedings did not take place at the temple. (2) Jesus is allowed no defense. (3) Jesus does not blaspheme in the technical sense of the term by using the divine name (*San.* 7:5). (4) The verdict comes on the same day as the trial, when two days were required for capital crimes. (5) Jesus is being tried on a feast day, normally prohibited. (6) Contradictory testimony is supposed to exonerate the defendant (*San.* 5:2; this point applies more to the temple discussion in Matthew and Mark). (7) The high priest is not supposed to issue the pronouncement of guilt. Exceptions to some of these procedures might be allowed in certain situations, but the mass of them indicates just how quickly (and illegally?) the trial proceeds.

With chief priests and teachers of the law gathered together, Jesus is examined. Luke narrates only the central question. "If you are the Christ, tell us." This question is designed to get a political charge against Jesus so that they can claim Jesus is a revolutionary, an alternative king to Caesar. It also focuses on the key title of the early portion of the Gospel (1:32, 35; 2:11, 26; 3:15; 9:20; 20:41). In the question is probably rooted the Jewish expectation of a great political deliverer (cf. Pss. Sol. 17—18). If Jesus accepts this title, then his own words can be presented against him. Jesus' reply is like his reaction in Luke 20:1—8: "If I tell you, you will not believe me." He subtly raises the question whether they really want to have a fair trial here, or if their minds are already made up.

Jesus then goes on to make one of the most significant statements in this Gospel: "From now on, the Son of Man will be seated at the right hand of the mighty God." He makes three claims here, if we remember that he has called himself the "Son of Man" throughout this Gospel and that Son of Man refers to the supranatural figure of Daniel who receives authority from the Ancient of Days and rides the clouds like God (Dan. 7:13—14). (1) Jesus predicts that he will eventually be seated at God's right hand in heaven, an allusion to his approaching resurrection-ascension. (2) He claims to have authority from God, an authority he will exercise from this moment on. (3) He has authority over them. This may be their trial, but he is the one who will ultimately judge. Jesus answers their question indirectly, but his reply is actually more than they may have anticipated.

---

7. The Mishnah was written down about A.D. 170, so we cannot be sure all the practices of the first century matched these standards.

His interrogators follow up the claim with an additional question. "Are you then the Son of God?" Note how Luke is weaving titles together here: Christ, Son of Man, and Son of God. Jesus replies to the Son of God question with (NIV), "You are right in saying that I am." This is the implication of the Greek's more elliptical, "You say that I am." The audience takes it positively (see also Mark 14:62). They have their man. "Why do we need anymore testimony? We have heard it from his own lips."

The nature of Jesus' remarks is significant on two levels. (1) He supplies the testimony that brings about his conviction. What the leadership has been unable to do, namely, to get convicting testimony against Jesus, the Lord brings against himself. In essence, Jesus is the witness the leadership sought and sends himself to the cross. Jesus, of course, spoke as he did because his claim is true.

(2) The nature of Jesus' blasphemy (cf. Mark 14:64) has always been a subject of debate. Was it a claim to be God? Was it the claim to be Messiah? Was it the claim to sit at God's side in heaven? Just what did Jesus say that was so condemning in Jewish eyes? The key remark appears to be his claim to be Son of God (i.e., the Messiah), not merely in a regal sense, but *as it is tied to the claim of being the Danielic Son of Man.* Jesus in effect is claiming the right to go directly into God's presence and be seated with him in heaven. To Jewish ears this is highly offensive—worse than claiming the right to walk in and permanently reside in the "Holy of Holies" at the temple, since the temple represented God's presence in heaven. Jews fought wars over attempts to profane the temple. Thus, the leadership sees the remarks as blasphemous, even as Matthew and Mark indicate when they mention the priests' rending of garments.[8] In a real sense, Jesus sends himself to the cross because he is faithful to his identity in the midst of an audience that rejects his claims. He makes no effort to save his life by denying who he is. So the Sanhedrin sends him on to trial before the Roman governor.

Bridging Contexts

THE PASSION ACCOUNT functions as both history and narrative. Its major concern is to summarize Jesus' initial trial, but it also documents the failure of Peter, predicted by Jesus. The account informs us both of the trials and of the shocking treatment Jesus receives as

---

8. For details, see D. Bock, "The Son of Man and the Debate Over Jesus' 'Blasphemy,'" in *Jesus of Nazareth, Lord and Christ,* ed. J. B. Green and M. Turner (Grand Rapids: Eerdmans, 1994), 181–91. This article also treats many of the historical objections critics make about the trial.

his trial approaches. The major feature of the Jewish trial is that Jesus' claim about himself is what sends him to his death. He is the issue, not only of this scene but of the entire Gospel. Luke wants his readers to reflect on who Jesus is. His claims force a decision. A neutral position is a position that rejects him.

On the narrative level, each of the characters reveals something. (1) The failure of Peter stands in stark contrast to the nerve of Jesus. This disciple fails because peer pressure of the world and the threat of death are too great for him to bear. (2) The soldiers show how some in the world do not take Jesus seriously. For them religion is a game, and this leader is a joke to be played with. Their mockery and belittling of Jesus reveal a spirit that is not unusual in our world. (3) The Jewish leaders are more civil than the soldiers, but their view of Jesus is just as negative. He is someone whose presence and visibility need to be removed. He is a nuisance, not a king or Savior.

Jesus' defense leads to his rejection. He testifies to his position boldly, but he does not defend himself in terms of challenging the verdict as wrong. The injustice he bears here is tragic. In Acts, vigorous defense of the right to preach Jesus will continue. Upon arrest, the disciples do plead innocence and speak forth their testimony. Yet they serve out their arrests until judgment is made or supernatural forces release them. So the example of Jesus' boldness carries over into the early church.

Finally, Jesus is standing before his accusers and facing a fate he has been predicting (13:31–35). He does not lose nerve. Like a sheep going silently before its shearers and like a lamb headed for the slaughter, he faces death so others may have life. How ironic that the trial of Jesus is really our trial, for what we think of it reveals what we think of him. He is really the judge. In a theological sense Jesus is on trial for us. He stands where we ought to be standing. Without our sin he would not have been there. This is one of the most timeless messages in the Bible. And in Jesus' resurrection, he assumes a place at the right hand of the Father, so that his claims are vindicated. The judged becomes the judge and calls on us to issue a verdict about this trial, where he took our place. We all face the simple question: How will we respond to the Son of Man, who is now seated at the right hand of the Father?

THE APPLICATIONS OF this text come at various levels. (1) The account is designed to be appreciated as a historical summary of how Jesus got to the cross. Many in our world today question the Bible even on this level. But Christianity is a historically grounded faith. Without a cross, the Christian faith is reduced to a mere form of moral suasion, of no more value than many other religious ethical systems or forms of psychology that seek to make us stronger people. Throughout this Gospel we have seen Jesus make himself the issue; reducing Christianity to moral teaching eliminates the unique person of the Christ from Christianity. Without him and what he accomplished in his death and resurrection, there is not much sense to the faith. Thus, the issue of the trial is the issue of Jesus' identity. Luke wants us to ponder whose side are we on. If we side with Jesus, we are recognizing his claim to sit at God's side as judge and Savior. If any king deserves honor, it is the one who sits at God's side.

(2) Note the varied character of rejection in this passage. The soldiers and the Jewish leadership represent two distinct forms of rejection, though at their base they are similar. (a) The soldiers take Jesus frivolously. We all have met people who have no time for religion and love to mock its existence. What is so tragic about such mocking is that what they treat as frivolous is deadly serious. Sin blinds people from properly perceiving what is significant. Those who mock the faith are often those who could use it the most. Pretending to be above it, they reveal their need for it. This text shows us that we should not be surprised at the existence of such responses.

(b) The leadership reveals another side of rejection—of a more civil but staged character. Though often giving the appearance of fairness, there is a sense in which the jury is stacked in its soul. A hard heart is a tough nut to crack. That is why evangelism in the end must be a supernatural undertaking. We cannot go where the change needs to occur. That is, we cannot enter the heart as the Spirit can. As we will see at the end of this episode, some do listen, either at the trial or before it. Joseph of Arimathea, for example, has an open heart. What the opposition cannot see, he sees (23:50–51). We do not always know how our testimony will strike those who are opposed to us. Sometimes the Spirit uses our lives and words to melt a hard heart.

(3) The lesson of Peter is tragic. Here is a man who thinks he will stand up for Jesus, but he is not as ready for battle as he thinks. It is hard to overestimate the pressure Peter faced here. It shows that without total reliance on God, circumstances can cause even the most intimate of Jesus' followers to crumble. The disappointment of his fall is great. His failure is so painful that it leaves him in tears. Many of us can identify with his plight because we have been there too. Though it is probably not with as high a set of stakes, we know what it like not to stand up for Jesus. What is encouraging about Peter's story is that he learns from his failure. Only a few chapters down the road in Acts, we see this same man risking everything to tell about the forgiveness he has found in Jesus. If anyone appreciates what forgiveness and restoration mean, it is Peter.

In fact, the entire story of Peter underscores an important principle about the Christian walk. The goal of the church is not to shoot its wounded to death, but to restore them. One could argue that Peter's denials should have disqualified him from any leadership position. But Jesus has already set the stage for Peter's recovery when he noted that after Peter turned, he should strengthen the people (22:32). With a recognition of wrongdoing and a return to the Lord, forgiveness must follow. Though Peter's failure is great, his victory comes through his restoration, a restoration made possible because Jesus is ultimately about forgiveness.

(4) Finally, Jesus prepares to bear his cross, something Peter has failed to do. He testifies boldly to his identity, even at the prospective cost of his life. In doing so, he becomes an example of a bold witness for the gospel. Several figures in Acts will take the same risk, and many saints since have done likewise, as the classic work *Foxe's Book of Martyrs* documents.

Luke 23:1–12

THEN THE WHOLE assembly rose and led him off to
Pilate. ²And they began to accuse him, saying, "We
have found this man subverting our nation. He
opposes payment of taxes to Caesar and claims to be Christ, a
king."

³So Pilate asked Jesus, "Are you the king of the Jews?"

"Yes, it is as you say," Jesus replied.

⁴Then Pilate announced to the chief priests and the crowd,
"I find no basis for a charge against this man."

⁵But they insisted, "He stirs up the people all over Judea by
his teaching. He started in Galilee and has come all the way
here."

⁶On hearing this, Pilate asked if the man was a Galilean.
⁷When he learned that Jesus was under Herod's jurisdiction,
he sent him to Herod, who was also in Jerusalem at that time.

⁸When Herod saw Jesus, he was greatly pleased, because
for a long time he had been wanting to see him. From what he
had heard about him, he hoped to see him perform some miracle. ⁹He plied him with many questions, but Jesus gave him no
answer. ¹⁰The chief priests and the teachers of the law were
standing there, vehemently accusing him. ¹¹Then Herod and
his soldiers ridiculed and mocked him. Dressing him in an ele-
gant robe, they sent him back to Pilate. ¹²That day Herod and
Pilate became friends—before this they had been enemies.

Original Meaning

AFTER THE SANHEDRIN meeting, Luke narrates
three more trials that lead to Jesus' crucifixion:
two meetings with Pilate (a private and a public
one) and a meeting with a curious Herod. The
first meeting with Pilate represents the Jewish attempt to get Roman help
in the execution of Jesus.¹ Roman authority was required when the death
penalty was involved.² Pilate's examination is fascinating because despite

---

1. The parallels are Matthew 27:2, 11–14; Mark 15:1b–5; John 18:29–38. The meeting with Herod is unique to Luke, while Luke 23:11 is like Mark 15:16–20.

2. Josephus, *Jewish Wars* 2.8.1 § 117.

his judgment that Jesus is innocent, the process continues. In effect, the governor stands aside and lets others make the decision for him. This is a form of nondecision.

After the Jewish trial (22:66–71), the entourage heads for Pilate. No doubt the meeting is quickly arranged. The heart of the case is a threefold accusation: (1) Jesus subverts the nation; (2) he opposes payment of taxes to Caesar; and (3) he claims to be Christ, a king. For Pilate the most dangerous charges are the second and third, though the first charge may suggest Jesus is a source of public unrest. It may be the first charge is general, while the second two are more specific.

(1) The first charge may actually be that Jesus "perverts" the practices of the nation (the Greek word *diastrepho* can mean "to subvert" or "to pervert"),[3] though subversion is more likely the political charge intended here. It naturally leads into the other two complaints. An internal religious dispute is of no interest to Pilate, so more concrete political charges are needed. (2) Since Pilate is responsible to keep the peace and collect taxes, the taxation charges challenge his ability to do his job faithfully. This second charge is blatantly false, as readers of Luke recognize from 20:20–26. (3) The third charge is, on the surface, substantial, since if Jesus were a revolutionary, he would need to be watched by Rome. But Jesus is not seditious, as Pilate will sense.

The third charge is the one Pilate pursues (see John 18:33–38 for a longer exchange on this charge). He simply asks, "Are you the King of the Jews?" Like his reply to the Jewish query earlier in 22:70, Jesus responds with an expression in Greek that reads literally, "You have said so." This is a mild affirmative. Jesus is saying yes, but not quite in the sense Pilate intends.[4] It is not clear here what leads to Pilate's decision, but he concludes there is "no basis for a charge" against Jesus. He has done nothing worthy of death. Pilate views Jesus as a "harmless enthusiast."[5] This should have been the end of the matter.

Yet the leadership continues to press Pilate, noting that Jesus has stirred up the people from Galilee to Judea. They adamantly insist that he is dangerous. In effect they are saying, "It would be dereliction of your duty to let him go, Pilate!" On hearing mention of Galilee, Pilate thinks up a brilliant solution. He will send Jesus to the Jewish political leader, Herod, since he has authority over that region. Now any decision Pilate makes will have Herod's

---

3. "διαστρέφω," BAGD, 189.

4. Blass, DeBrunner, Funk, *A Greek Grammar of the New Testament and other Early Christian Literature* (Chicago: Univ. of Chicago Press, 1961), sec. 441.4.

5. Plummer, *The Gospel According to St. Luke*, 521.

consultation, and Pilate will be protected either way. Political courtesy and passing the buck are both possible here.[6]

Herod is excited about meeting Jesus. He has heard about him and wants to see the Galilean perform miracles. But he is disappointed by Jesus' lack of response. Not only are there no miracles; there is no reply. Pilate, of course, has stated Jesus' innocence, so why should Jesus continue to answer questions (cf. also Isa. 53:7)? But the Jews "vehemently" press their case (v. 10); they are the catalysts in these events. The roles of Pilate and Herod are more passive, but contribute enough to the situation that they share blame (see Acts 4:24–28).

In the face of Jesus' silence, Herod and others react with more mocking. They dress Jesus in some type of regal clothing (whether white or purple is debated)[7] and make fun of the "king," who in their view possesses so little power. Then they send him back to Pilate. Pilate's plan works, for from that day he and Herod are friends. This suggests an A.D. 33 date for the crucifixion, since relations between the two did improve after Tiberius Caesar's key anti-Semitic aid (and Pilate's boss), Sejanus, passed away shortly before this time.[8]

WE ANALYZE THE text at both a historical and a narrative level. At the level of history, these events indicate that two sets of political leaders, after examining Jesus, find him innocent (vv. 4, 15). Yet amazingly the trials continue. These details indicate that Jesus will die an innocent martyr's death. He is righteous, even though he suffers on the cross. This is an indictment of Roman and Jewish justice, for both share in Jesus' death. Responsibility for sending Jesus to the cross is expanding. Soon rejection will touch the crowds. More and more of humanity becomes responsible for his death.

We also see a variety of attitudes contributing to Jesus' fate in the narrative. Neither Pilate nor Herod regard him as guilty. Pilate is more serious and professional than Herod (who allowed the soldiers to mock Jesus). Neither shows any malice toward him, though they do not defend him either. Their indifference reflects how many treat Jesus, as a curiosity or a side show. These

---

6. Pilate had developed a record of insensitivity to the Jews by placing Roman shields in Herod's palace, an insult to the Jews (see Philo, *Legation ad Gaium* 38.299–305). This may be political expediency here to reverse his recent reputation.

7. Oepke, "λάμπω, κτλ.," *TDNT*, 4:17; Danker, *Jesus and the New Age*, 366. There is no way to decide.

8. On Sejanus's fall, see Dio Cassius, LVIII, 4.1–11.7. That death may have freed Pilate up to pursue a more "Jewish friendly" policy, as he reflects here.

types of responses to Jesus add to the collection of reaction we have seen of Jesus. The Jewish leadership continues to press for action against Jesus, even though some of their charges are false. Luke solidifies the portrait we have noted earlier regarding Jesus and his trial.

 THAT SOME MISUNDERSTAND and misrepresent Jesus is not unusual. The portrait of the leadership's charges against him shows how some reject him so thoroughly that they even misrepresent what he is about, though that misrepresentation does contain a small dose of truth. They are right that Jesus is a king, but they fail to appreciate that role other than to see it as a threat. When people are hostile to Jesus, they fail to understand him. If they do perceive his key claims, they reject them out of hand.

The rejection of Pilate and Herod is more subtle. They do not react against Jesus. Their position is virtually a neutral one. He is not guilty, but neither is he to be believed. This type of approach to Jesus reckons him with a little respect, but does not respond to him as he deserves. Pilate and Herod's failure to act on their awareness of Jesus' innocence is a form of cowardice. Once again Luke indirectly calls on the reader to choose sides. He outlines a variety of responses to Jesus, but any failure to embrace him, whether through active rejection, passive neglect, or frivolous reaction, is not commendable.

When we engage in sharing Jesus, we can expect a wide array of responses to him. Some will be decidedly hostile, while others will be more disinterested, just as in the trial scene. But both constitute rejection. Evangelism often requires patience. At the same time, it is important to remember that even in the midst of rejection, the initial reaction may be no clue to the eventual response. Who would have predicted Saul would become an ardent follower of Jesus? Yet others may never change their minds. Our primary responsibility before the Lord is to continue to share him.

We may never know if the seed we plant today will sprout years later. For example, many stories have surfaced from Eastern Europe about how the faithful testimony of believers in the midst of persecution led unbelievers to the Lord. One of our Russian students tells of how an eight-year-old girl was being watched by the KGB mind police, and a new, young agent was assigned to watch her. Her faith was so refreshing that she led him to the Lord! On the other hand, there may come a time when words become superfluous. All that has been said is on the record, and there is no need to say more. As Jesus went silent as the trial continued, so we sometimes may have to say in effect, "I have said it all; there is nothing more to add." The process ultimately has to be left in God's hands.

Luke 23:13–25

PILATE CALLED TOGETHER the chief priests, the rulers and the people, [14]and said to them, "You brought me this man as one who was inciting the people to rebellion. I have examined him in your presence and have found no basis for your charges against him. [15]Neither has Herod, for he sent him back to us; as you can see, he has done nothing to deserve death. [16]Therefore, I will punish him and then release him."

[18]With one voice they cried out, "Away with this man! Release Barabbas to us!" [19](Barabbas had been thrown into prison for an insurrection in the city, and for murder.)

[20]Wanting to release Jesus, Pilate appealed to them again. [21]But they kept shouting, "Crucify him! Crucify him!"

[22]For the third time he spoke to them: "Why? What crime has this man committed? I have found in him no grounds for the death penalty. Therefore I will have him punished and then release him."

[23]But with loud shouts they insistently demanded that he be crucified, and their shouts prevailed. [24]So Pilate decided to grant their demand. [25]He released the man who had been thrown into prison for insurrection and murder, the one they asked for, and surrendered Jesus to their will.

Original Meaning

THIS PUBLIC TRIAL of Jesus has all the elements of a Roman trial,[1] with its set stages of arrest, charges, examination, verdict (with support for guilt or acquittal), and judicial warning.[2] What makes this trial so unusual is that two verdicts of innocence have already been rendered, but Jesus still remains on trial in Roman hands. Something unusual is taking place here. Destiny has its hands on Jesus.

This final scene cannot be more open. Gathered together are the chief priests, the rulers, and the people. A representation of the entire nation in her capital assembles to issue a judgment on Jesus. Though the authority for that verdict resides with Pilate, he negotiates Jesus' fate. The fact that the

1. Parallels to this second, more public trial before Pilate are Matthew 27:15–26 and Mark 15:6–15.
2. J. Neyrey, *The Passion According to Luke* (New York: Paulist, 1985), 81.

people share in this discussion is a dramatic reversal for them, for Jesus' popularity with them was a major factor in the leadership's more clandestine approach to Jesus' arrest (22:2).

Pilate makes his clearest statement yet on how he sees the matter. He restates the charge in the exact form it was given to him in verse 2: Jesus is "inciting the people to rebellion."[3] That is, he is subverting the public peace. Pilate examines the charge openly, in the presence of the leadership. The mention of this public trial is important. There is no private meeting, no back room deals. Everything is done in the open. Pilate concludes that "he has done nothing to deserve death,"[4] the same verdict Herod reached. Two witnesses have assessed the truth (Deut. 19:15). It sounds like Jesus' release is coming.

But Pilate knows he has a political hot potato. So he compromises by offering to "punish"[5] (i.e., flog) Jesus and release him. This chastisement generally involved a whip with metal tips tied to it. Pilate hopes that a little innocent blood, displayed through a gruesome whipping, will satisfy the leadership.[6]

This judgment receives a public reaction, but not the one Pilate wants. "With one voice" they cry out, "Away with this man! Release Barabbas to us!" The response must surely have caught him off guard, for Barabbas was incarcerated for leading an uprising and for murder. He has committed more heinous crimes than the claims made about Jesus. The leadership and people desire the release of a clearly more dangerous man than Jesus.

Pilate knows something is not right, so he addresses them again, hoping to release Jesus. Pilate wants justice but is hesitant to act in the face of widespread public opposition. He is not the first, nor the last, public official to keep his eye on opinion polls! Like a tennis match where volleys are exchanged back and forth, the crowd smashes away Pilate's proposal. They insist on crucifixion. Only Jesus' death will satisfy them. They want to be rid of him.

Crucifixion was a particularly gruesome way to die.[7] Roman citizens could not be executed in this manner. This form of death was designed to deter

---

3. The Greek verb used here is different from v. 2, but is a synonym.

4. Pilate uses the verb *anakrino* to discuss his examination, the formal Greek term for a legal investigation that is conducted to reach a verdict (Acts 4:9; 12:19).

5. Bertram, "παιδεύω," *TDNT*, 5:621; Marshall, *Commentary on Luke*, 859.

6. The best manuscripts of Luke lack verse 17, which refers to Pilate's custom of releasing a man to the nation at this feast. Older manuscripts (‭א‬, B, and p[75]) lack this verse, so it probably was not originally in Luke.

7. M. Hengel, *Crucifixion in the Ancient World and the Folly of the Message of the Cross* (Philadelphia: Fortress, 1977); C. Schneider, "σταυρός," *TDNT*, 7:573–811; n. 15 on p. 573 summarizes non-Jewish views.

criminals. That is why the executions were public. Treason and evading due process were the normal grounds for such a death. It was preceded by a severe flogging that caused bleeding to speed the onset of death. After the flogging, four steps were involved. (1) The criminal carried the crossbeam to the place of execution. (2) He was either nailed or tied to the crossbeam as it lay on the ground. (3) The beam was then raised and fastened to the upright pole. (4) A tablet specifying the crime was nailed to the cross for all to see. The crowd wants Jesus not just to die, but to experience this most gruesome form of execution. He is counted among the worst of criminals (Isa. 53:12; Luke 22:37).

Pilate tries valiantly to get Jesus released. A third time he asks the crowd what evil Jesus has done. The judge has almost taken up the role of the defense attorney, while the crowd is becoming judge and jury. Luke details the procedure because he wishes to highlight that justice is not sentencing Jesus. Something more sinister is at work.

Pilate insists that nothing worthy of death has been done, and he repeats his earlier verdict to chastise and release Jesus. This agitates the crowd even more, and the voices get louder. Pilate has moved from a private hearing to a near riot on a feast day when the city is full of people. Finally he relents and decides "to grant their demand." Barabbas is released, while Jesus is surrendered to the will of the people. It is not justice that sends Jesus to the cross, but a mass of humanity.

Bridging
Contexts

LIKE THE OTHER Passion passages, this one also functions at the level of history and narrative, though theology is also pictured here. Historically, the trial of Jesus appears as a struggle by a Roman magistrate to administer a dangerous political situation. Given the choice between justice and a mass uprising, the Galilean teacher is a sacrificial lamb who does not deserve the punishment meted out. Standing alone, he is expendable. Jesus dies as an innocent, with many people responsible for his death.

At a narrative level, we again see various reactions to Jesus, running from an insistent hostility to an effort to remain as noncommittal as possible. The leadership has gained the support of the masses. Together they drive for Jesus' removal. In contrast, Pilate tries to keep his distance, not wanting to say that Jesus is totally right, but not agreeing that he is worthy of the hostility directed against him. In the end, the greater passion wins out. All of these events are unique, and yet they do pattern a plethora of responses to the claims of Christ.

More significant is the theology built into the picture. The exchange of Barabbas for Jesus testifies to two things. (1) As Pilate's own reaction shows, there is something incredulous about the preference for Barabbas. Here the blindness and logical character of sin are at work. Given the option between a teacher of righteousness and a murderous criminal, the crowd chooses the latter. It shows the kind of passion religious belief can generate and the kind of hostility that it can produce in people. Words are more dangerous than a blade, the soul more important than life. In one sense, the judgment, as irrational as it seems at the surface, is appropriate, for if Jesus is wrong about his claims, he is a very dangerous figure. On the other hand, if he is right (and innocent!), then there can be no worse judgment. The line between truth and falsehood is often the thin thread of a correct perception.

(2) A theological message is wrapped up in the exchange. Romans 5:5–8 summarizes Jesus' death as the just for the unjust. He dies (literally) in an unjust person's place. Though the sin we commit may not be murder, nonetheless Jesus suffers on the cross for our sin. That message resounding from the cross is timeless. Barabbas represents the position we are all in as a result of Jesus' death: We are able to live because he died. In the midst of all the injustice, the grace of God shines through. The message of the cross is that Jesus overcomes evil and injustice, even while in the midst of it. That is the miracle built into God's plan for the ages.

THE PASSION IS narrated for our reflection. As we read or hear it, the text calls for us to make decisions about the various reactions to Jesus. Those judgments are not about the events as history, since that is assumed by the text. The judgments are more subtle and substantive. Who in the narrative represents the truth? Who is acting with justice and fidelity? Which case has the merit?

The leadership in its hostility looks too insistent to be in the right. They have fabricated charges and rejected a solution that would spare an innocent life. They have pressed for execution. Luke leads the reader to see that there was something criminal in Jesus' death, and it was not him. The drivenness that sends Jesus to the cross is a hardheartedness that often comes with a rejection of him.

The fickle people also represent something not quite right. Days before, some hailed Jesus as a king (19:38). Now, however, a murderer is better than him. In just a few days, everything has changed. The people reflect a shallowness of conviction and an ability to be swayed that warns against a superficial approach to these issues. Religious reflection is everybody's business, but to pursue it from a distance means being subject to shifts that are more emotionally driven than thought through. With the lack of sincere reflection comes a wild emotional swing on questions of ultimate significance. This is not unlike today, where the range of emotion expended on such questions can run wildly from indifference to intense passion.

One of the things that used to fascinate me about Madelyne Murray O'Hare was her passion about her atheism. She was so irritated about Christianity that she could not contain her resentment any time she spoke. On the other hand, others table such discussions from their lives. One must realize that the world is full of religious opinion, but the amount of investigation standing behind those opinions, as well as the passion given to it, varies greatly.

Pilate represents a figure caught on the other end of the popular wave. Here is a man who tests the wind more than assesses the truth of Jesus' claim. He knows in his heart some degree of truth about the situation, but does not stand up to his responsibility. Our world contains a host of claims about Jesus. Some include the misrepresentations of Jesus, as the leadership makes before Pilate, with suggestions that Evangelists and apostles distorted the true portrait of Jesus. Such claims often leave others bewildered and confused, much like Pilate is here. The best way to respond to Jesus' religious claims is to read them for oneself in Scripture. Often the most effective tool for preventing the kind of indecision Pilate has is to examine the claims directly and to cease listening to the distorting voices of doubters. The denial of testimony given by Jesus and those who walked with him leave Pilate in a dilemma he solves by opening up the deliberations in the hope that sense might spare Jesus.

The world often passes off major religious decisions as Pilate did. An easy approach is to take a popular vote and accede to the majority. Or better yet, let each one do what he or she pleases and have no solid public dialogue about any of it. Pilate senses that a simple public airing and vote are not the right approach, but proceeds anyway. He hopes that giving the public the poor choice of Barabbas versus Jesus will solve his dilemma. But in the end, public acceptance for Pilate is too important to him for him to make a correct decision based on principles of justice. Religious issues need to be thought through, not simply reacted to, as if a Gallup poll can decide religious truth. How many other Pilates might there be in our world?

Regarding Barabbas, we never hear from him, but in a real sense, he is the story that explains Jesus. Those who know what Jesus accomplished on the cross realize that Barabbas's story is our story. Jesus freed us by his death, just as Barabbas was freed. One who saves a life is owed a life. The Christian walk is a statement of gratitude to the one who has taken our place. He did not complain as he bore the cross for the murderer and for us. He uttered no words of protest about injustice as he hung on Calvary for us. There was only intercession for those enemies who failed to understand what they had really done. There was only forgiveness for another criminal, hanging next to Jesus, who came to his senses as he contemplated what remained of his life. Those who have been rescued from the penalty of sin understand that in Barabbas's freedom is a portrait of their escape from death through the gracious work of Jesus.

Luke 23:26–49

AS THEY LED him away, they seized Simon from Cyrene, who was on his way in from the country, and put the cross on him and made him carry it behind Jesus. ²⁷A large number of people followed him, including women who mourned and wailed for him. ²⁸Jesus turned and said to them, "Daughters of Jerusalem, do not weep for me; weep for yourselves and for your children. ²⁹For the time will come when you will say, 'Blessed are the barren women, the wombs that never bore and the breasts that never nursed!' ³⁰Then

> "'they will say to the mountains, "Fall on us!"
> and to the hills, "Cover us!" '

³¹For if men do these things when the tree is green, what will happen when it is dry?"

³²Two other men, both criminals, were also led out with him to be executed. ³³When they came to the place called the Skull, there they crucified him, along with the criminals—one on his right, the other on his left. ³⁴Jesus said, "Father, forgive them, for they do not know what they are doing." And they divided up his clothes by casting lots.

³⁵The people stood watching, and the rulers even sneered at him. They said, "He saved others; let him save himself if he is the Christ of God, the Chosen One."

³⁶The soldiers also came up and mocked him. They offered him wine vinegar ³⁷and said, "If you are the king of the Jews, save yourself."

³⁸There was a written notice above him, which read: THIS IS THE KING OF THE JEWS.

³⁹One of the criminals who hung there hurled insults at him: "Aren't you the Christ? Save yourself and us!"

⁴⁰But the other criminal rebuked him. "Don't you fear God," he said, "since you are under the same sentence? ⁴¹We are punished justly, for we are getting what our deeds deserve. But this man has done nothing wrong."

⁴²Then he said, "Jesus, remember me when you come into your kingdom."

⁴³Jesus answered him, "I tell you the truth, today you will be with me in paradise."

⁴⁴It was now about the sixth hour, and darkness came over the whole land until the ninth hour, ⁴⁵for the sun stopped shining. And the curtain of the temple was torn in two. ⁴⁶Jesus called out with a loud voice, "Father, into your hands I commit my spirit." When he had said this, he breathed his last.

⁴⁷The centurion, seeing what had happened, praised God and said, "Surely this was a righteous man." ⁴⁸When all the people who had gathered to witness this sight saw what took place, they beat their breasts and went away. ⁴⁹But all those who knew him, including the women who had followed him from Galilee, stood at a distance, watching these things.

Original Meaning

LUKE DEVELOPS THE story of Jesus' crucifixion by telling it through its interaction with a variety of observers.[1] As has been his custom, we see the Passion through many eyes and in varying perspectives.

Jesus goes to his death after a long day and night of emotion. Without sleep and after a scourging, he needs help in bearing the cross. Simon from Cyrene is drafted to carry the cross. He has come a long distance to Jerusalem, since Cyrene is located in what is now Tripoli. It is hard to be sure why Simon is mentioned. Of course this part of the story functions as a historical note, but is there more? There is no hint that he is a follower of Jesus. But this section does emphasize that Jesus' going to the cross is not a private affair. It involves others because of what he is accomplishing there. As he goes to the cross, another person, just like us, shares in his journey there.

Behind Jesus is a host of people. The crowds that urged his execution have stayed on to see it carried out. With them is a group of women, wailing in mourning. Are they sympathetic or simply perfunctory mourners who accompany a person about to die? Jesus seems to treat them on sincere terms, and the narrative puts them in a sympathetic light.[2]

---

1. The parallels to this passage are Matthew 27:31b–56; Mark 15:20b–41; John 19:16b–37. Unique to Luke is the section on the mourning women. The parallels have some differences between them. Two of the more prominent are that different psalms are cited as the narrative proceeds and that the reactions of the criminals as they hang on the cross are in marked contrast. As for this Gospel, only Luke uses Psalm 31 and only he tells the story of the believing criminal.

2. Marshall, *Commentary on Luke*, 863.

Jesus responds to their sense of remorse by redirecting their attention to a more serious issue. He urges them not to weep for him. Painful as his death will be, he knows that he will be taken care of, since his vindication in resurrection is only hours away. The real issue moves beyond what Jesus will suffer to what his death means for those who reject him. His remark in the midst of his trauma indicates his selflessness, for he is concerned about others. The women should weep for the nation and her children, for judgment is surely coming on the nation (see 13:34–35).

Jesus then exercises a prophetic role on his road to the cross. Hard days lie ahead for the nation (cf. 19:41–44), in which "barren women" will be blessed. Here is a reversal of the normal Jewish view that blessing comes from a fruitful womb. That is because the judgment to come on the nation will be harsh. Men, women, and children will be at risk, for that was the nature of war in the ancient world. Victory involved the total destruction of the opponent. Rome will therefore show no mercy. People in Jerusalem will be crushed because of their failure to recognize what they are doing.

Jesus turns his attention to the lesson of Hosea 10:8. The days of judgment will be so painful that people will long to die, to have creation (represented by the mountains and hills) come down on them (cf. Rev. 6:16, where this Hosea verse portrays the terror of judgment in the end time). How painful it is to be the object of God's wrath.

Jesus finishes his remarks with a final rhetorical question, whose force is debated. The NIV has, "If men do these things when the tree is green, what will happen when it is dry?"[3] This translation interprets that ambiguous "men" (lit., "they") as a reference either to the Jews or to humankind. However, it is difficult to see how this subject carries through both halves of the saying. The key to the saying is the contrast between what is done to a green, healthy tree and what becomes of dry, dead wood on a dead tree. "They" may well be an oblique reference to God, as in Luke 12:20.[4] If this kind of fate befalls someone like Jesus, just imagine what kind of fate is ahead for the dry wood responsible for his death! This is Jesus' last lament in Luke over the nation.

Jesus is not executed alone. Two others join him, described as "criminals." Just as Jesus has predicted, he is reckoned among "the transgressors" (Isa. 53:12; Luke 22:37). His word comes to pass.

---

3. The image of dry trees being consumed is from Isaiah 10:16–19 and Ezekiel 20:47.

4. Literally, Luke 12:20 reads, "they will demand your soul from you." See Danker, *Jesus and the New Age*, 372. If this option is not right, the best option is the view that sees Jesus as saying, "If the Jews treated me so for coming to deliver them, then how will they be treated for destroying me." Against this view is that the implicit subject shifts in the first half of the saying to the second from "Jews" to "God." This option and the one preferred do carry, however, the same essential force.

The locale of the crucifixion is a place called "the Skull." In Aramaic, the name is "Golgotha"; in Latin, *calvaria*, which is why we refer to this site as Calvary. The hill where executions take place protrudes out of the ground like a skull.[5] Jesus' cross is situated between the two criminals. This is revealing, since in the debate between the criminals one of them will soon confess him and be saved. Jesus is the bridge by which the unrighteous can become the righteous.

As he awaits his death, Jesus turns again to the Father in prayer,[6] asking that the actions of his enemies be forgiven. He speaks of their ignorance in slaying him. His point is that they have not really comprehended what they are doing. By praying for his enemies, Jesus has fulfilled an ethical standard he himself noted in 6:29, 35, to pray for one's enemies. Jesus evidences his love and compassion here and models his own instructions on discipleship.

The soldiers at the cross are simply biding their time until the execution is complete. They divide up his clothes among them by casting lots. This remark alludes to Psalm 22:18, which is a psalm about the suffering righteous and how they are treated. Another part of the Psalm shows up in Jesus' cry from the cross about being forsaken by God (Ps. 22:1; Matt. 27:46; Mark 15:34). These connections describe the type of suffering Jesus undergoes. He is hanging on the cross as an innocent man, willingly dying for those who do not understand his death and who mock it.

This execution fits the pattern of public crucifixion known in the ancient world. The people "watch" what is taking place, and the leaders "sneer" (v. 35; both verbs appear in Ps. 22:7). Their taunts are ironic. "He saved others; let him save himself if he is the Christ of God, the Chosen One." This taunt may draw on Jewish tradition that believes God helps the righteous.[7] Their sarcasm shows just how much confidence and passion there is in Jesus' enemies. They are comfortable with his execution. The ultimate irony, however, is that God will actually perform their request in Jesus' resurrection.

The soldiers add to the mocking. They offer him *oxos*, a dry "wine vinegar" that was used among the poor. Their taunt is for Jesus to save himself if he is the king,[8] which shows that compassion is not their real motive. At

---

5. Fitzmyer, *The Gospel According to Luke X—XXIV*, 1503.

6. Though some dispute that the prayer in verse 34 is a part of Luke, we believe it should be included. Some good manuscripts (p[75], B, and D) do omit it, but its presence in ℵ and some internal grounds argue for it. Most notably is the parallel to Acts 7:60. Luke loves parallelism between Jesus and the church, which is lost if the verse is omitted. See Marshall, *Commentary on Luke*, 867—68.

7. See Wisdom of Solomon 2:17—22.

8. The remark is expressed as a first class Greek condition, but it does not indicate the speakers believe the kingship claim is true. The form just adds to the picture of the irony

this point Luke records the notice of the crime: "THIS IS THE KING OF THE JEWS." He consistently shows how it is Jesus as the Christ who goes to the cross.

The scene turns back to the criminals. One of them joins the taunting by hurling "insults" (a phrase that alludes to blaspheming). Everyone feels free to be a part of putting Jesus down. Like the leaders, he calls on Jesus to deliver himself if he is the Christ. In addition, he should save them too. But the other criminal speaks up and rebukes the first criminal by asking, "Don't you fear God?" As if to say, "What gives you the right to rebuke Jesus as if you are superior?" He stresses that their sentence is just, since they are getting what they deserve. In contrast, Jesus is innocent. Pilate, Herod, and now a criminal have confessed Jesus' innocence even as he moves toward death.

The criminal turns to make a request of Jesus. He has already shown that he sees Jesus as someone different. Now he asks Jesus to remember him when he comes into his kingdom. This criminal accepts the claim Jesus is a king, and he wants to share in his coming rule and to be among the righteous in the judgment. This criminal gives the first of many positive responses to the cross.

Jesus' reply indicates that an answer to his request will come sooner than the criminal hopes. Even this very day, they will be together "in paradise," a word that refers to the place of the righteous. The solemnity of this reply is indicated by the introductory phrase, "I tell you the truth. . . ." Jesus is saving people even as he hangs on the cross. Those who think the taunts will not come to pass are missing what is taking place.

At the sixth hour, or midday, it becomes dark for three hours. Now even the heavens testify to the nature of the hour. In the Old Testament darkness often indicates judgment (Joel 2:10; Amos 8:9; Zeph. 1:15). God is signaling his presence. The sun is nowhere to be found. The real hour of darkness has come (Luke 22:53).

Another sign then adds to the moment. The curtain at the temple is torn in two. It is debated which curtain is meant—either the curtain at the Holy of Holies or the curtain at the temple court. More important is what this act indicates. (1) A time of judgment has come and the temple is included in that judgment. Since the temple is the center of Judaism's religion, this is a significant judgment for the nation. (2) The tearing of the curtain also suggests an opening of the way to God. The curtain shielded access to God. By ripping it open, restricted access no longer exists. Later, the author of Hebrews mentions that the need for sacrifice has ended because of Jesus' death (Heb. 8–10).[9]

---

of the sarcasm by presenting it so vividly. Of course, what is presented here is a translation of a taunt that was probably not given in Greek.

9. E. Ellis, *The Gospel of Luke*, 270.

With the cosmic signs comes Jesus' death. His final words come from Psalm 31:5, reflecting the trust that he has in the Father: "Into your hands I commit my spirit." Jesus trusts the Lord to care for him. This psalm describes a righteous sufferer, just as Jesus is. What happens from this point on is up to God. He will have to give his testimony about Jesus by what he does in the next few days.

A centurion now offers praise to God. Like the criminal earlier, he also has some insight into the event, which serves as the final commentary Luke supplies for the whole event. He declares that Jesus is surely *dikaios*. This Greek term is ambiguous. Does it mean "innocent" or "righteous" (either is possible)? In one sense, the difference does not matter, since an innocent Jesus is a righteous Jesus. But in a context that has emphasized Jesus' innocence, a final testimony to that innocence makes more sense. The centurion thus becomes a second witness to affirm Jesus' legal innocence as he is dying (Deut. 19:15), and the fourth person in Luke 23 to do so. Luke will later emphasize Jesus' innocence in Acts (3:14; 7:52; 13:28; 22:14).[10]

The crowds also react. They depart, beating their breasts. The cosmic signs may have given them pause. Imagine slaying the Chosen One of God and realizing that the mistake has been made when it is too late to reverse it! Such mourning may have prepared the way for the openness Peter meets with in his speech in Acts 2, since these events became well known (see especially Acts 2:37).

The disciples see things from a distance. Among them is a group of women who have been with Jesus from the start of his ministry in Galilee. The one thing this death has is numerous witnesses. Luke has noted many different groups who share in what has just taken place. He has also noted the variety of perspectives about the event. Which one is true? The closing words of the centurion leave no doubt.

Bridging Contexts

AS WITH THE previous events of the Passion, the text works at historical, narrative, and theological levels. All three levels help bridge the gap to our present age.

The *historical* level presents the events of the cross in a summary fashion. Luke's version gives us a glimpse at a wide array of reactions, ranging from conversion to hostility. He notes how certain events took place in ways that recall the testimony of Scriptures about how the righteous suffer. Jesus suffers as an innocent figure, but by divine design. One of the great ironies here is the taunting to save himself and others, which he is actually performing as

---

10. J. Neyrey, *The Passion According to Luke*, 100.

the taunts take place. The most perceptive people at the scene are a criminal and a centurion, whose attitudes most closely parallel that of Luke.

The *narrative* level works with various representative characters. There is even some interaction between the groupings, such as the interaction that takes place between Jesus and the women. The women, reacting at a normal human level, are convinced that Jesus' death is a tragedy for him. That is why they weep. Yet Jesus' remarks make it clear that the real tragedy is to misjudge who he is. The nation is headed to judgment for their rejection of him. Thus the meaning of the cross is not what it seems on the surface. While it appears to be the end for Jesus, Golgotha is really the locale of a fateful decision by the nation. What is true of the nation is also true for an individual's decision about Jesus. When rejection comes, accountability to God for that rejection follows.

Jesus' compassion is also significant in that it reveals his heart as he dies. God desires in the cross to show his love for lost humanity (John 3:16). Jesus models that heart by his intercession for his enemies (v. 34). An indication of the success of that intercession comes in the conversion of someone like Saul in Acts 9. Some unbelievers come to see God's love through what emerges at the cross.

The taunting by the Jewish leadership and the passersby shows how hostile and blind rejection of Jesus can be. Such blindness leads to the execution of an innocent servant of God. The gloating over Jesus' death shows just how empty of compassion some of Jesus' opponents have become. Their misjudgment about him is a crucial error. What they think is impossible for Jesus to achieve on the cross is precisely what he is accomplishing.

The "meeting of the sides" is summarized in the exchange between the two criminals crucified with Jesus. One is convinced that Jesus has nothing to offer; the other asks him to exercise his authority as a king in order to assure him a place among the saved. This second criminal gives as eloquent and succinct a testimony to Jesus as Scripture offers anywhere. Jesus guarantees the confessing criminal a place among the righteous. This man has gone from guilty to gifted by his coming to Jesus. His faith has moved him to think afresh about Jesus and led him into a defense of the one crucified unjustly.

The narrative also notes the testimony of God through the signs in the heaven. The fact that Jesus had to die is a dark moment in history. Sin is a dark reality in our world. But alongside the darkness is the opening up of access to God. The ripping of the temple curtain shows that no barrier exists between God and humanity that cannot be removed by turning to God through Jesus. The heavens normally give only a silent witness to God (Ps. 19:1–6), but when it speaks as here, we should ponder what is said.

At a *theological* level, the cross requires full commentary. In a sense, one can argue that the entire New Testament is a commentary on the cross. Whether one looks at Romans 3:21–31 or Hebrews 8–10 or considers the testimony tied to rites like baptism and the Lord's Supper, the cross functions as a commentary for each generation. Of all the ironies of the cross that bridge the centuries, none is greater than the idea that eternal life for human beings springs out of Jesus' death. By offering up his Son, God is able to make sons and daughters of all who respond to this work. Therefore, we must believe what God has done through Christ at the cross and respond to it with a life that honors God (Rom. 12:1–2).

Theologically, the cross provides the atonement that forgives sin. Jesus offers himself here in service to others. He prays for the forgiveness of his enemies and accepts one of the criminals into his kingdom. He represents us as he unjustly bears the penalty for our sin in his love. The most important consideration we can give to the cross is to embrace its meaning with a responsive heart that is filled with the forgiveness, love, and humility Jesus so eloquently displays here. The only action that does the cross of Christ justice is to welcome its work with an all-embracing faith.

Melanchthon, Luther's main colleague, states our response to the work of Jesus this way:[11]

> Therefore, we are justified when, put to death by the law, we are made alive again by the word of grace promised in Christ; the gospel forgives our sins, and we cling to Christ in faith, not doubting in the least that the righteousness of Christ is our righteousness, that the satisfaction Christ wrought is our expiation, and that the resurrection of Christ is ours. In a word, we do not doubt at all that our sins have been forgiven and that God now favors us and wills our good. Nothing, therefore, of our works, however good they may seem or be, constitutes our righteousness. But FAITH alone in the mercy and grace of God in Jesus Christ is our RIGHTEOUSNESS.

The Reformer then cites Romans 1:17; 3:22; 4:5; and Genesis 15:6. Because of Christ, the Christian can say, "It is well with my soul."

THE APPLICATIONS OF this text build off issues raised in the previous section. Again, as with all the Passion material, the most fundamental application deals with the decisions made about Jesus and the nature of his work on the cross. Luke has told the narrative in such

---

11. Melanchthon, *Loci Communes*, as cited in W. Pauck, ed., *Melanchthon and Bucer* (LCC 19; Philadelphia: Westminster, 1969), 88–89.

a way as to persuade the reader of the case for Jesus. The different issues the cross raises can only be summarized, because the issue of the cross is in many ways the issue of the New Testament.[12]

The New Testament uses many images to describe what the cross is and how we should see it. It is a ransom (Mark 10:45; 1 Tim. 2:6), a payment for the debt of sin. It is a substitution—Jesus offers himself in our place (cf. the meaning of Barabbas in the previous section; see also Luke 22:18–20; John 6:51–52; Rom. 8:3; 2 Cor. 5:21; cf. Isa. 53:10). It is a propitiation, satisfying the justice of God by dealing with sin (Rom. 3:25). It represents the "lifting up of Jesus," and through it Satan is overthrown (John 3:14–15; 8:28; 12:31–32; 18:32). It is the means by which the church is purchased (Acts 20:28). It is the sacrifice that ends all other sacrifices for sin (Heb. 8–10). It is the precursor to the Lord's being lifted up and seated at God's side (Acts 2:16–39; Heb. 1:3). It is the basis on which God sets apart his children as a holy community (1 Peter 1:2, 18–25; 2:1–11). On the cross Jesus became a curse for us, a mediator of our guilt before God (Gal. 3:13, 19–20). There reconciliation takes place between God and humanity, as well as between Jew and Gentile (Rom. 5:8–11; 2 Cor. 5:20–21; Eph. 2:11–22; Col. 1:21–22; 2:11–15). So God can now justify us, that is, declare us righteous before him (Rom. 3:21–31).

This listing has a matter-of-factness about it that obscures just how amazing and comprehensive this work of Jesus is. Each of the texts above is rich in imaging only one aspect of the complex work of the cross. Numerous hymns also attempt to express what all of this means. Great songs written in honor of the cross, such as "Amazing Grace," "On the Old Rugged Cross," "And Can It Be," and "Love So Excelling, So Divine," lead us to reflect on just what God has done through Jesus. In fact, the cross probably should not be so much discussed theologically as meditated over and pondered. I sometimes wonder if a Good Friday service should not allow for a long period of silence and prayer before the Lord, where each person can reflect quietly on just what the cross means to him or her. Silence is usually not popular in our culture. But the cross is an event that should be absorbed, not just described.

The call, then, is simply to trust Christ for all the benefits that come from recognizing that he has taken our place on the cross. The applications fall into two classes, depending on whether a person comes to this decision for the first time or is already living his or her life out in the recognition that, in the words of that great hymn, "Jesus Paid It All."

The cross is at its heart the offer of God's gracious forgiveness to those

---

12. For a thorough treatment of this theme, see L. Morris, *The Cross in the New Testament* (Grand Rapids: Eerdmans, 1965).

who embrace it. To embrace the cross means to renounce our own works as the basis of our salvation. Our relationship with God comes through trusting in Jesus and in his finished work. "My sin, not in part but the whole" has been wiped away by the forgiveness Jesus provides. The cross offers an opportunity of a new life, lived with a clean slate before God. That offer comes by God's grace, with nothing for us to earn. If we accept his grace, God begins a new walk with us. Our spiritual well-being rests solidly and securely in the hands of a caring heavenly Father.

For those who have made that decision, the cross reminds us where it all started. My relationship with God is a response of gratitude for all he has done to bring me to himself. Grace calls us to live in a way that honors God by reflecting the new life he has provided for us (Rom. 6—8; Titus 2:11—14).

Reconciliation with God not only transforms my relationship with God, but also alters the way I relate to others. As Ephesians 2 stresses, barriers are removed between people of different ethnic origins through the cross. Imagine the effect of a testimony where people of different ethnic origins are able to function together harmoniously. In a real sense, the ultimate application of the cross involves relating to others on a different basis, because we now operate in the world as forgiven people who know where and how they fit in the creation. The cross becomes the ground of all Luke's passages of discipleship (9:51—19:44). Another way to say this is that at the center of God's plan stands Jesus, and at the center of Jesus' work stand the cross and resurrection.

One final application is important here. The cross is described through appeal to a variety of Psalms that point to Jesus' suffering as a righteous innocent. He is an example of someone offering everything to show his love for his neighbor, even when the neighbor is unjust to him. God sees Jesus' suffering and promises to vindicate him, with the first indication being that Jesus' prayer for forgiveness (v. 34) receives an initial answer in the saved criminal (v. 43). Jesus thus shows how the person who walks with God should reach out to the lost. The least we can do is to proclaim to everyone the forgiveness that he died to provide.

I alluded to the hymn "Jesus Paid It All" above. There is no better commentary on the application of the cross than the message of its chorus:

Jesus paid it all,
　　All to him I owe;
Sin had left a crimson stain—
　　He washed it white as snow.

Luke 23:50–56

NOW THERE WAS a man named Joseph, a member of the Council, a good and upright man, ⁵¹who had not consented to their decision and action. He came from the Judean town of Arimathea and he was waiting for the kingdom of God. ⁵²Going to Pilate, he asked for Jesus' body. ⁵³Then he took it down, wrapped it in linen cloth and placed it in a tomb cut in the rock, one in which no one had yet been laid. ⁵⁴It was Preparation Day, and the Sabbath was about to begin.

⁵⁵The women who had come with Jesus from Galilee followed Joseph and saw the tomb and how his body was laid in it. ⁵⁶Then they went home and prepared spices and perfumes. But they rested on the Sabbath in obedience to the commandment.

Original Meaning

THIS PASSAGE CENTERS around two sets of characters: Joseph of Arimathea and some women from Galilee.¹ Some people remain concerned about Jesus even after his death. That the women are careful to observe the Sabbath, showing their Jewish piety, suggests that not all Jews reject Jesus. Some righteous Jews do embrace him.

While many in Israel "fall" before Jesus, some also "rise" (2:34). Joseph belongs to this second group. He is a good and righteous man. In fact, he was against the decision of the council to execute Jesus. He is a "remnant" saint in the New Testament's view,² and is awaiting the kingdom of God. He may have been a believer in Jesus, or at least was open to him.

Joseph asks for Jesus' body to fulfill Deuteronomy 21:22–23. He does not think it appropriate that Jesus should be buried in a pauper's grave. He takes possession of the body, brings it down from the cross, and wraps it in linen (*sindon*)—probably a fine cloth, This is not the shroud of Turin that has caused much recent speculation. Joseph places the body in a previously

---

1. The parallels to this passage are Matthew 27:57–61 and Mark 15:42–46. One detail Luke alone notes is that these women are from Galilee.

2. Tiede, *Luke*, 26, speaks of his being placed among the faithful. The exact location of Arimathea is unknown. One suggested location is about five miles north of Jerusalem, while another is ten miles northeast of Lydda.

unused tomb hewed out of rock. The tomb was probably tunneled out of the side of a rock, having a small door-like entrance of perhaps a yard in height. Such tombs were present just north of the city. Jesus receives an honorable burial.

Luke notes it is "Preparation Day," the day before the Sabbath. Thus, it is about sunset on Friday. On this day everything for the Sabbath had to be prepared. Joseph quickly finishes the task before sunset, since the Sabbath began at that time. His action does not take place privately, for some women observe him as he lays Jesus in the tomb. They apparently never left the scene of the cross (cf. v. 49). The fact that these women are from Galilee indicates that they have been disciples for some time and know Jesus well. They will not make a mistake as to whether and where Joseph has taken Jesus.

As the women prepare for the Sabbath, they also prepare spices and perfumes, a custom common for Jews, since they did not embalm. The spices and perfumes were placed on the body to reduce the stench and decomposition.[3] These women fully intend to return to the tomb. They want to continue to honor the Lord. There is no indication they expect a resurrection that involves Jesus' body.

THIS ACCOUNT SIMPLY narrates how Jesus was buried and that the burial was witnessed by outsiders. It operates basically at a historical level. There is no development of character at a narrative level. The text does reveal a couple of examples of deep concern shown for Jesus. The people here want Jesus to have an honorable burial and be appropriately cared for. Their concern is admirable.

One other important detail emerges. The resurrection was not an anticipated event. Jesus receives the normal treatment a dead person received. He was definitely laid to rest, and the preparation of spices shows that the women expect him to remain there. The resurrection catches everyone by surprise.

It is not unusual for God to be active in our midst and even to tell us about what he is doing, but we miss the point. We can get so locked into a routine of how things normally take place that we risk missing what God is

---

3. W. Michaelis, "μύρον," *TDNT*, 4:801; "σμύρνα," 7:458. Mark's account has the women purchase spices first thing on Sunday. The difference could reflect the fact that the women purchased more spices on that day; or perhaps Matthew and Luke have engaged in literary compression.

doing out of the ordinary. A text like this reminds us to keep our eyes open and to look carefully for God's promises, which might show up in surprising ways.

THIS PARAGRAPH IS a transition paragraph to the resurrection, noting the respect that some accorded Jesus after his death. One feature yields an important application in our skeptical age. One of the charges some make today is that the resurrection was an event created by the early church, in order to allow Jesus' memory and teaching to continue. If that were the case, the Evangelists have certainly found an unusual way to describe the preparation for it. The testimony of Gospels is that the resurrection caught the disciples by surprise. When Jesus died, they figured he had departed. Even though Jesus prophesied his resurrection, it did not sink in. If the resurrection were a fabrication, would its creators portray the disciples as being so much at a loss to understand what Jesus was predicting? It is more incredible to believe in a fabricated resurrection, for which some of Jesus' followers even died, than it is to take the possibility of resurrection seriously. The implications of this contrast lead directly to a decision for the resurrection and to Jesus' claims about who he is.

Luke 24:1-12

O N THE FIRST day of the week, very early in the morning, the women took the spices they had prepared and went to the tomb. ²They found the stone rolled away from the tomb, ³but when they entered, they did not find the body of the Lord Jesus. ⁴While they were wondering about this, suddenly two men in clothes that gleamed like lightning stood beside them. ⁵In their fright the women bowed down with their faces to the ground, but the men said to them, "Why do you look for the living among the dead? ⁶He is not here; he has risen! Remember how he told you, while he was still with you in Galilee: ⁷'The Son of Man must be delivered into the hands of sinful men, be crucified and on the third day be raised again.'" ⁸Then they remembered his words.

⁹When they came back from the tomb, they told all these things to the Eleven and to all the others. ¹⁰It was Mary Magdalene, Joanna, Mary the mother of James, and the others with them who told this to the apostles. ¹¹But they did not believe the women, because their words seemed to them like nonsense. ¹²Peter, however, got up and ran to the tomb. Bending over, he saw the strips of linen lying by themselves, and he went away, wondering to himself what had happened.

Original Meaning

THE FINAL PORTION of Luke's Gospel (chapter 24) comes in three parts: Jesus' appearance to the women (vv. 1–12), the Emmaus road experience (vv. 13–35), and Jesus' appearance to the disciples (vv. 36–43), together with his final instructions and farewell at the time of his ascension (vv. 44–53). This unit is full of discovery, surprise, and wonder. The resurrection consistently catches the disciples off guard, and they have a difficult time adjusting to the reality that Jesus is alive again. Yet Jesus' remarks drive home the point that Scripture predicted these events would take place. God keeps his word, even when it involves things that seem impossible.

The cross was not the end of Jesus' story, for it is followed by a resurrection that signifies a new beginning. The empty tomb and Jesus' resurrection fulfills some of his promises made in Galilee, but that realization hits the disciples with surprise and shock.[1] In fact, the early moments of discovery show that they have to overcome a strong sense of doubt about the events. Their reaction makes them look as "modern," "skeptical," and "sophisticated" as any contemporary person. It takes repeated appearances to convince the disciples that Jesus has been raised. They are just as unprepared for this event as we would have been. What emerges from the surprise is the additional discovery that God's plan has not been derailed. The resurrection was not created by the church; rather, the church was created by the resurrection.

At the break of dawn on the day after the Sabbath, certain women journey to the tomb with their spices to anoint Jesus' body, fully expecting to find it in the tomb. The women want to get there as soon as they can. The first hint that something unusual has taken place is the rolled away stone at the foot of the tomb. Such stones were large and heavy, placed in a channel cut out in front of the tomb.[2] The women enter the tomb only to find "the body of the Lord" missing. Note that the predominant title for Jesus in this chapter is "Lord," the name that, through Jesus' resurrection, reveals his Lordship and points to his exaltation and vindication by God (Acts 2:14–39; Rom. 10:9).[3]

Needless to say, this leaves the women "wondering about" what has happened and what they should do next (v. 4). At this point "two men" appear. Their clothes gleam like lightning, suggesting that the term "men" is a euphemism for "angels" (cf. 24:23, where Luke calls them "angels"). They appear to function as two witnesses (Deut. 19:15). The women know that they are in the presence of some type of supernatural beings, so they bow before them in respect.

The "men" speak to them by asking a simple question: "Why do you look for the living among the dead?" In other words, Jesus is alive. The tomb could not hold him. "He is not here; he has risen [lit., has been raised]!" The verb used in "has risen" is an aorist passive and implies that God is responsible for Jesus' return to life. God has intervened, just as Jesus promised.

---

1. The parallels to this text are Matthew 28:1–10; Mark 16:1–8; John 20:1–18. The major differences appear between John's account and the Synoptics. John tells his own story, about how he discovered the resurrection first and then goes back to Mary's account. This view is defended in detail in my forthcoming book, *Luke 9:51–24:53* (Grand Rapids: Baker), in the section discussing Luke 24:1–12. For other explanations on how the differences are resolved, see J. Wenham, *The Easter Enigma: The Resurrection Accounts in Conflict?* (Grand Rapids: Zondervan, 1984), and G. Osborne, *The Resurrection Narratives: A Redactional Study* (Grand Rapids: Baker, 1984), 149 n. 2.

2. For ancient descriptions of such stones, see Josephus, *Jewish Wars* 5.12.2 § 507; 5.3.2 § 108.

3. Luke is the only Gospel writer to call Jesus "Lord" in his narrative asides. This title is one Luke regards as one of the best summary descriptions of who Jesus is.

"Remember how he told you, while he was still with you in Galilee: 'The Son of Man must be delivered into the hands of sinful men, be crucified and on the third day be raised again'" (cf. 9:22, 44; 13:3; 17:25; 18:32–33; 22:37).[4] This remark is both a call to remember and a rebuke. God often says things we fail to understand because we have trouble accepting them. But when God speaks, we must listen not according to the categories we are used to, but with hearts that recognize who is speaking the promise.

The remark in verses 6–7 is important for another reason. The reference to the necessity of the Son of Man going through these events emphasizes divine design. These things *must* happen. Eighteen times Luke uses the Greek word *dei* to indicate the carrying out of God's plan—a plan promised in Scripture and worked out in Jesus' life.[5] That plan had three steps: betrayal, crucifixion, and resurrection. Two of these reappear in 24:43–47 with a fourth step, preaching to the nations. The angels' remark leads the women to recall Jesus' remarks. God's words are indeed coming to pass. If we want to find the fulfillment of God's promises, we must look to Jesus.

The women journey back to where the disciples and others are gathered and tell their story. Luke then identifies three of them, though he notes that others were with them. Mary Magdalene and Joanna were mentioned in the Galilean group who ministered to Jesus (8:2–3). The reference to "Mary of James" (lit.) is unclear, since it can refer to a mother, wife, or sister. Most equate it to Mark 15:40 and 16:1, that is, to the mother of James the younger and Joses. Beyond this we know little about her.

Despite these numerous female witnesses, their story is not viewed as credible. Not only is it hard to accept, but culturally such a story from women would be viewed with suspicion. One of the main proofs that the resurrection story is credible is realization that the first-century church would never have created a story whose main first witnesses were women. Luke is clear just how skeptical the first audience is that hears about the resurrection. They dismiss the women's account as "nonsense" (or "idle talk"). Maybe Jesus will return one day in the general future resurrection, but an instant, bodily resurrection—that is unbelievable. The first skeptics Jesus faces are his disciples.

But Peter knows better than to doubt the Lord's word. During his denials, he has learned that the Lord knows better than we perceive. So he runs to the tomb, bends down to glance in it, and sees the grave clothes present and the body absent. He leaves the tomb "wondering to himself what had

---

4. The last prediction did not take place in Galilee, but in Jerusalem.

5. Many argue that this is one of the major theological themes in Luke-Acts. See D. Bock, "Luke-Acts," in *A Biblical Theology of the New Testament*, ed. R. Zuck and D. Bock (Chicago: Moody, 1994), 87–100.

happened." Scholars debate whether the Greek word for "wondering" (*thau-mazo*, also translated "marveling") implies faith in Peter at this point. Most say it does not, arguing that 24:24, 34 suggest a later appearance to Peter that convinces him. Osborne seems to be more on target when he says that Peter experiences the "first steps of faith" here.[6] Using a word short of full faith, Luke adds to the drama by having Peter ponder what is going on. The empty tomb raises initial questions that the apostle senses means that something unusual is going on and that God is in it. He may not understand fully, but Peter has learned that Jesus says what he means. Luke's initial resurrection account closes, therefore, with a series of questions about what has happened and about how the disciples will become convinced that Jesus has been raised. The first steps are here, while the full conviction comes in the following accounts.

Bridging Contexts

THERE IS ONE feature about this account that differs little from the modern world: its skepticism about resurrection. What is often lost in the familiarity of this account is the attitude of the disciples. They are usually characterized as open to miracles. But on this occasion they have to be persuaded. The women are more responsive to what God has done than most of the gathered group of disciples. This note is important, because resurrection is a central hope of Christian faith (1 Cor. 15), but the church did not come to believe it easily. The initial "show me" attitude of the disciples fits well with the modern spirit.

Another perennial concern of humanity is the question of what happens after death. It is human nature to want to know about things beyond our experience. Today there is much discussion about "near death" experiences and even about the possibility of reincarnation. I find it amazing that those who question the possibility of resurrection can be so sure of reincarnation. This passage gives us true insight into the issue of life after death. The reality of Jesus' resurrection forms the basis for contemplating our own resurrection. Death is not the end, and we will one day have to stand before our Creator and give an account for our stewardship in this life. Since the Bible teaches resurrection rather than reincarnation, the question we personally face is what will happen to us on that Judgment Day.

A third bridge into our era is the issue of God's plan and his word. All of Luke 24 emphasizes that plan and God's bringing to pass what he has promised. It reintroduces a theme already raised in chapters 1–2. The fact that

6. G. Osborne, *The Resurrection Narratives*, 114.

this theme brackets the Gospel shows how central it is to everything Luke teaches. In a real sense, the key to Luke's reassuring Theophilus is bound up in God's Word being true (1:4). When the angels remind the women of Jesus' promise, they are asserting that God will do what he says he will do. The resurrection of Jesus points to such a hope for us as well (1 Cor. 15:20–28).

ONE APPLICATION OF this text that is not so obvious keys off of the difficulty the disciples have in accepting the women's testimony about resurrection. Perhaps we should be less surprised when people initially stumble over the resurrection. After all, the disciples hurdle it only after much persuasion. We should therefore exercise patience as we share this hope with others. Imagine what Jesus must have felt like when he shared the hope of resurrection during his ministry and all he got back was strange looks. One can only wonder what the women felt as they shared their story. But the Bible is real as it tells its story. The doubt of the disciples is set forth with crystal clarity. Their slowness to believe is not exemplary, but it is instructive. Resurrection is a doctrine that is hard to believe. For that reason the Spirit needs to work in hearts as the gospel is shared.

We have already noted how important the idea is that God keeps his promises. The resurrection is one of the greatest of God's promises. According to the Christian hope, God gives everlasting life to his children in a world that he will remake and renew (cf. Rev. 21–22). If such a world is to come and if God keeps his promises, then preparing for it is one of the most basic tasks of life. The life to come is, of course, of much longer duration than life here and now. Thus, preparing for it is more important than any short-term issues we face today. Visionary thinking, so popular today, is designed to consider the long-term picture. There is nothing more visionary than thinking about our long-term relationship to God. Our allegiance should be to the citizenship that flows into the future.

The Christian hope for a new world is important, because in it is bound up the idea that one day justice will be done in the creation. According to Romans 8:17–39, creation groans for its redemption alongside the redemption of God's children. With vindication comes justice. Without justice in the future, injustice in the past remains. In light of that certain future, then, we live as foreigners on this earth and have a citizenship that represents a stewardship from God (Phil. 3:20–21).

In sum, resurrection changes everything. Luke wants us to ponder the "so what" of Jesus' resurrection—that Jesus is alive and offers forgiveness, so that I can have the new relationship with God through him. For believers, resurrection is a reminder that new life is a gift from God that calls us to a walk of gratitude. To those who do not know him, Scripture calls them to embrace what the resurrection means.

This unit leaves us with a picture of Peter peeking into the tomb and seeing the empty grave clothes. Those empty clothes, as well as the empty tomb, raise the question of what happened to Jesus. Luke will answer that question in this chapter, but there is another question we must answer. If the empty clothes picture the fact that death is not the end but a transition, then what will happen to us when we experience our own resurrection? As the biblical alternative to both reincarnation and no resurrection, we must realize we are accountable to God for what we do in life. There are no reruns, nor is there one life and then nothing. Each one of us should therefore wrestle with the reality of standing before God.

We should not ignore Luke's shift to the name "Lord" here. Jesus is the one with authority, divine authority, over salvation. As Lord of all, the gospel must go out to all. One of Luke's great burdens is to show that God's plan is revealed to the person who understands just who and how great Jesus is. As Lord he is worthy to be trusted, worshiped, and followed. No one is more worthy of praise. In light of his majesty and position, we should all be willing subjects, resting in his care and direction.

Luke 24:13–35

NOW THAT SAME day two of them were going to a village called Emmaus, about seven miles from Jerusalem. [14]They were talking with each other about everything that had happened. [15]As they talked and discussed these things with each other, Jesus himself came up and walked along with them; [16]but they were kept from recognizing him.

[17]He asked them, "What are you discussing together as you walk along?"

They stood still, their faces downcast. [18]One of them, named Cleopas, asked him, "Are you only a visitor to Jerusalem and do not know the things that have happened there in these days?"

[19]"What things?" he asked.

"About Jesus of Nazareth," they replied. "He was a prophet, powerful in word and deed before God and all the people. [20] The chief priests and our rulers handed him over to be sentenced to death, and they crucified him; [21]but we had hoped that he was the one who was going to redeem Israel. And what is more, it is the third day since all this took place. [22]In addition, some of our women amazed us. They went to the tomb early this morning [23]but didn't find his body. They came and told us that they had seen a vision of angels, who said he was alive. [24]Then some of our companions went to the tomb and found it just as the women had said, but him they did not see."

[25]He said to them, "How foolish you are, and how slow of heart to believe all that the prophets have spoken! [26]Did not the Christ have to suffer these things and then enter his glory?" [27]And beginning with Moses and all the Prophets, he explained to them what was said in all the Scriptures concerning himself.

[28]As they approached the village to which they were going, Jesus acted as if he were going farther. [29]But they urged him strongly, "Stay with us, for it is nearly evening; the day is almost over." So he went in to stay with them.

³⁰When he was at the table with them, he took bread, gave thanks, broke it and began to give it to them. ³¹Then their eyes were opened and they recognized him, and he disappeared from their sight. ³²They asked each other, "Were not our hearts burning within us while he talked with us on the road and opened the Scriptures to us?"

³³They got up and returned at once to Jerusalem. There they found the Eleven and those with them, assembled together ³⁴and saying, "It is true! The Lord has risen and has appeared to Simon." ³⁵Then the two told what had happened on the way, and how Jesus was recognized by them when he broke the bread.

THE ENCOUNTER BETWEEN Jesus and the two disciples on the road to Emmaus is one of the most vivid resurrection appearances. The account is unique to Luke and contains key themes of the Gospel: the importance of the promise of the Word, the status of Jesus as prophet, and his messianic role. The passage closes with another instance of table fellowship. Disclosure by Jesus occurs in the context of intimacy with him.

The passage starts with another journey. Two men are traveling to Emmaus, a village whose exact location is unknown. The one usually chosen, known in other ancient sources, is twenty miles from Jerusalem.[1] These disciples apparently are heading home after a traumatic weekend.

They find themselves discussing what has taken place. Verses 19b–24 give a glimpse of the issues they are working through. The discussion seems to have been intense, since the word used (*syzetein*) suggests strong debate (cf. its use in Luke 22:23; Acts 6:9; 9:29).[2] Perhaps they are disputing the meaning of the empty tomb. Jesus approaches them as they talk, though they cannot tell it is him. Their eyes are "kept from recognizing him." Jesus' first

---

1. Luke refers to sixty stadia. A stadia is 607 feet or a touch over 200 yards. So 60 stadia is 6.8 miles. A few manuscripts speak of a 160 stadia, which would be 18.4 miles. This reading, though poorly attested, is why some argue that Emmaus is Ammaous, a locale mentioned in 1 Maccabees 3:40, 57; 4:3. Plummer's suggestion of el-Qubeibeh (El Kubelbeh) is the right distance, but is unattested as a first-century locale (*The Gospel According to St. Luke*, 551–52). See also Fitzmyer, *The Gospel According to Luke X–XXIV*, 1561–62. Josephus mentions an Ammaous some 30 stadia from Jerusalem, which would make the measure of 60 stadia a round-trip figure (*Jewish Wars* 7.7.6 § 217).

2. J. Schneider, "συζητέω," *TDNT*, 7:747.

postresurrection appearance in Luke is both normal and mysterious at the same time. He has a normal human appearance, but is different enough that he is not initially recognized. This description adds to the drama and the mystery of resurrection.

Jesus asks them about their discussion. That question brings them to a halt, and their demeanor changes. What they left behind in Jerusalem is painful to recall, for hope departed with Jesus' death. One of the two, Cleopas, is amazed. With irony he asks, "Are you the only one who travels in Jerusalem and does not know the things that happened in it in these days?"[3] Of course, Jesus knows exactly what has happened, since it happened to him! Part of the narrative delight in the story is that the reader knows the secret the characters do not. No one could have missed what took place, at least if they were circulating among the pilgrim crowds. Nonetheless, Jesus asks, "What things?"

The disciples answer immediately, "About Jesus of Nazareth," and note his prophetic work as one "powerful in word and deed before God and all the people." Luke's readers, if they recall much of Luke 4–18, can identify with this description (4:16–30; 7:16, 22–23, 39; 9:9, 18; 13:31–35; Acts 3:14–26; 10:38–39). They note how the chief priests and rulers handed him over for death by crucifixion. The disciples themselves thought Jesus was more than a prophet and hoped he would be the one to redeem Israel. That was the hope that they saw nailed to a cross in the capital.

But there is more to tell. Three days later, some of the women among the disciples stunned the group.[4] They went to the tomb only to find it empty. They also reported angels telling them that Jesus was alive. Other companions (an allusion to Peter and others) went to the tomb and found it empty, just as the women reported, but Jesus was nowhere to be seen. How ironic the report is in light of Cleopas's audience! The two disciples are baffled by what has taken place. The last thing they expect is a resurrection.

Jesus then launches into a rebuke, whose rationale becomes clearer as events move on. He calls them "foolish" and "slow of heart to believe." For Luke's readers, this is a call to believe and not slip into the fog that these two disciples are currently in. They must believe all that the prophets have spoken, a brief way of referring to the messianic promises of the ancient Scriptures—what Christians call the Old Testament and Jews call the *Tanach*. Luke spends much of Luke-Acts noting specific Old Testament texts about these promises. The career that Scripture outlines for the Messiah is suffering, then glory. This sequence is necessary, since God designed it. Luke again

---

3. This rendering differs slightly from the NIV, but is more precise.

4. The word for "amazed" appears frequently in Luke-Acts for catching someone off guard (Luke 2:47; 8:56; Acts 8:9, 11).

uses *dei* to make the point about the divine design. These things "have to" be, since they are part of God's effort to restore relationship with humanity.

Jesus then begins to explain these promises to the two travelers, working from Moses through the Prophets. These promises concern him, though they do not yet know who is speaking to them. The Emmaus discussion underscores the point that the traumatic events surrounding Jesus are part of God's plan of deliverance. What they have seen is not the end of hope, but its beginning.

As the three near their stop at the village, it appears as if Jesus will journey on. But the two men persuade him to stay with them, since the day is nearly over. As Jesus reclines at the table with them, he shares a meal. In a setting with a pastoral feel and a picture like that of the Last Supper, he takes the bread, gives thanks, breaks it, and gives it to them. In the rush of the narrative up to this point, there is something calming about this scene. Suddenly, their eyes are opened. They see that it is Jesus. They have been spending time with the one they were discussing! But as soon as they recognize him, he is gone.

Cleopas and his friend acknowledge how amazing their walk and talk have been. "Were not our hearts burning within us while he talked with us on the road and opened the Scriptures to us?" Had not God been at work through Jesus' words to help them see what God was all about in the suffering and the glory of Jesus? Was it not the promise of God that they have just experienced? Their reaction communicates no real surprise in light of what has taken place on the road. Now it all makes sense.

It is late, but what they have seen cannot wait to be reported until tomorrow. They must tell the others about Jesus' appearance to them. So they return at once to Jerusalem. There the Eleven and the others are still gathered and quite excited. Before the two from Emmaus can get their story out, the report of the truth of the women's story fills the room. "It is true! The Lord has risen and has appeared to Simon." The Emmaus disciples then tell what has just happened to them on the road and how Jesus revealed himself to them at the table. Jesus is starting to show up everywhere. Despair becomes delight as the truth about Jesus' resurrection begins to sink in.

Bridging Contexts

THE MAJOR SUBJECT of this passage is the same as the previous one, the resurrection. But the discussion has deepened. The previous passage simply announced the empty tomb and the reality of the resurrection. This text involves an appearance of a physically raised Jesus.

Now we no longer merely have a claim to resurrection, but a manifestation of the result. Such experiences pushed the disciples from the category of skeptic to persuaded.

Perhaps the major challenge of this text in our modern world is the believability of such an event. It is important to note that those to whom Jesus appears seem as empirical about the possibility of a dead person reappearing alive again as any modern person. The announcement of an empty tomb was not enough to convince them. Only visible evidence that Jesus has been raised will prove convincing. The reaction of Cleopas and his friend, hesitant to embrace the resurrection, even to the point of being subject to a rebuke by Jesus, helps prove that what is related here really happened. After all, would the church create stories that make Jesus' followers lack faith? Here are two disciples who felt that the cross meant the end of the hope Jesus brought. Only Jesus himself, appearing in his restored existence, can change their minds. In every sense of the term, Jesus is the author of resurrection faith.

A second element of the passage reflects another key theme that spans the centuries between the text and the present. This passage highlights the trustworthiness of God's Word as expressed in promise. Jesus contends that the twofold division of suffering followed by glory is the messianic portrait of the Old Testament. This is a fresh understanding of the Jewish Scriptures.

We know that the Jewish faith, rooted in the promise to Abraham, pondered how to put the Old Testament revelation together when it came to how God would finally deliver his people and bring his rule back to earth. There were passages of hope that the end would produce a great prophet, a great king, a great figure who received authority from God, a servant figure who would proclaim God's hope and yet suffer, and a salvation where God would be present in the life of the community with an intimacy that meant the law written on the heart. All these strands of prophecy contended with each other in Judaism, along with various priestly images. The Jews struggled to determine how many end-time figures there might be and what their relationship to each other would be. Into this world Jesus stepped.

In the Gospels and in Acts, Jesus claimed that the Old Testament promise was unified in him. He was the prophet like Moses, the Son of David, the Suffering Servant, the Messiah, and the Son of Man all wrapped together in one person. His career involved both suffering and triumph. The bridge between the two stages was the resurrection. This is why Jesus claimed to be teaching what the whole Scriptures taught. Only this understanding of who he was made sense of the various strands of promise in the Scriptures. When Luke 24 describes Jesus as prophet and Messiah, it underscores how the promise only makes sense when it is combined with Jesus. This is the central interpretive claim Christianity makes about God's promises and their relationship to Jesus.

Though this passage only gives a general reference to the promises in the Law and the Prophets, the specific texts in view have been noted throughout Luke. Consider Isaiah 40 and its promise of a forerunner (Luke 3:4–6), Isaiah 61 and its proclamation and realization of deliverance (Luke 4:18–19), Psalm 118 and its call to receive one who comes in the Lord's name (Luke 13:35) and its warning that the rejected stone will be exalted (Luke 19:38), Psalm 110 and its promise of a shared rule with God and an exaltation to come (Luke 20:42–43), and Daniel 7 and its picture of the Son of Man coming on the clouds (Luke 21:27).

Many texts not mentioned here will surface later in Acts: for example, Joel 2 and its promise of the Spirit (Acts 2:17–21), references about God's promise to Abraham (Acts 3:25), the declaration of Psalm 16 and a hope for messianic rescue (Acts 2:25–28; 13:35), and Isaiah 55 and the promises to David now available in this new era (Acts 13:34). No doubt the church learned about such texts from Jesus himself during the time of his ministry and in the period just after his resurrection.[5] This central claim of the faith about fulfillment serves as a guide to understanding God's plan.

Furthermore, it is no accident that Jesus is revealed as he sits having table fellowship with the two disciples. The table was the place for fellowship in the ancient world. Here family and friends gathered to share time with each other. Luke has underscored the importance of meal scenes throughout his Gospel. The table was a place where Jesus was heard and where his presence came across most intimately. This fact suggests that Jesus reveals himself in the midst of the basic moments of life. He is at home in the midst of our everyday activity.

This theme will emerge in the next scene as well. When Jesus appears in verses 41–43, he will again sit with his disciples at the table. The imagery is replayed in the church in the Eucharist, which affirms the Lord's presence. Yes, he is raised and serving alongside the Father. As we partake of that meal, we look for the day of his return to sit at the final banquet table in full celebration of his salvation.

---

5. On the use of the Old Testament by the New, see D. Bock, "Use of the Old Testament in the New," *Foundations for Biblical Interpretation*, ed. D. Dockery, K. Mathews, and R. Sloan (Nashville: Broadman & Holman, 1994), 97–114, and the collection of essays in *The Right Doctrine from the Wrong Texts?* ed. G. Beale (Grand Rapids: Baker, 1994).

THE MOST BASIC application of this section, as with all of the resurrection accounts, is to reassure us that Jesus has arisen and is alive. Such reassurance should deepen our faith each time God's work for us is affirmed. Acts 2 will develop what grows out of the resurrection by noting that Jesus now sits at the right hand of God (cf. 5:31; Rom. 1:3-4), where he rules along with the Father (Ps. 110:1; Dan. 7:13-14), intercedes for us (Rom. 8:34; 1 John 2:2), and mediates the blessings that God gives his children. Hebrews 5-10 refers to a ministry according to the order of Melchizedek, a king-priesthood where Jesus mediates blessings to his own in such a way that sacrifices are no longer necessary.[6] Thus the resurrection serves as the basis for our being able to receive the many blessings of grace that God gives his children (cf. 1 Peter 1:3-6), notably, forgiveness of sins, the Holy Spirit, and eternal life. First Corinthians 15 explains exactly how the resurrection achieves this hope by calling Jesus' resurrection the "firstfruits" (v. 20), with more resurrections (ours!) to come.

The two disciples were not the only ones to whom Jesus appeared. This point is significant, because the resurrection is witnessed by many different believers. First Corinthians 15:5-8 gives a short list of Jesus' appearances. The multiple reports in this passage indicate how widespread the testimony became. As already noted, the author of resurrection hope is Jesus himself.

The declaration of Jesus at the right hand of God found its way into the oldest creeds of the church (e.g., the Apostles' Creed). This is not an abstract declaration. Central realities of the Christian life are bound up in this affirmation. Jesus' place at the right hand of God means that he possesses authority over all those forces that stand opposed to humanity, both in this age and in the age to come (see Eph. 1:19-23). Such authority stands behind his ability to give us new birth (Eph. 2:1-10).

This aspect of resurrection hope is important, since we often feel that our sin or the devil is more powerful than we are. Yet in the context of Jesus' power obtained through his resurrection, we have access to the one who enables us to overcome whatever obstacles Satan places in our path. The call of disciples is to follow the leading of the Lord and to draw on the spiritual resources he makes available to us. One could well argue that the letters of the New Testament, besides being commentary on the cross, are

---

6. It is important to appreciate this king-priestly work as one that involves both offices simultaneously. Hebrews 7 makes clear that both authority and intercession are in view here. Attempts to split the imagery into priest now and king later are guilty of dividing the person of Christ in ways the church challenged centuries ago when fighting Nestorianism. Hebrews 1 is clear that his kingship exists now alongside his priestly function.

commentary on the resurrection, since everything that we have in Christ ultimately is only possible through the resurrection.

In fact, there is a combination at work in this Lukan passage that reflects two key features of the Christian reality. The resurrection and the Word of God combine to illustrate the reality of the realization of God's promise. At the one end stands the Word revealed and moving towards realization. As revelation of God, it is to be embraced and believed, something the disciples were slow to grasp. This is why the church has always emphasized that people be taught the Word, for here is found the way and wisdom of God. On the other end stands the raised Jesus, exercising the many prerogatives the Word attributes to him in fulfillment of God's promises. Some of those promises still remain to be fulfilled. When the Lord returns, he will finish what he has started (cf. Acts 3:21). So the resurrection is a bridge into new life and the first step of glory that leads to the consummation of his promise.

There is perhaps no better commentary on this passage than Hebrews 1:1–4. God has spoken to us in his Son, who, as heir of all things, has sat down at the right hand of the Father, having made purification for sins and become superior to the angels, reflecting in the process the name, nature, and role of Son. There is no greater privilege than knowing the Son of God. He is known only through the recognition that God raised him from the dead to become the centerpiece of his promise and plan.

Luke 24:36–53

W HILE THEY WERE still talking about this, Jesus himself stood among them and said to them, "Peace be
with you."

37They were startled and frightened, thinking they saw a
ghost. 38He said to them, "Why are you troubled, and why do
doubts rise in your minds? 39Look at my hands and my feet. It
is I myself! Touch me and see; a ghost does not have flesh and
bones, as you see I have."

40When he had said this, he showed them his hands and
feet. 41And while they still did not believe it because of joy
and amazement, he asked them, "Do you have anything here
to eat?" 42They gave him a piece of broiled fish, 43and he took
it and ate it in their presence.

44He said to them, "This is what I told you while I was still
with you: Everything must be fulfilled that is written about me
in the Law of Moses, the Prophets and the Psalms."

45Then he opened their minds so they could understand
the Scriptures. 46He told them, "This is what is written: The
Christ will suffer and rise from the dead on the third day,
47and repentance and forgiveness of sins will be preached in
his name to all nations, beginning at Jerusalem. 48You are witnesses of these things. 49I am going to send you what my
Father has promised; but stay in the city until you have been
clothed with power from on high."

50When he had led them out to the vicinity of Bethany, he
lifted up his hands and blessed them. 51While he was blessing
them, he left them and was taken up into heaven. 52Then they
worshiped him and returned to Jerusalem with great joy.
53And they stayed continually at the temple, praising God.

Original Meaning

THE THIRD RESURRECTION passage in Luke adds to
the author's portrait of the resurrection's significance in a variety of ways.[1] Luke 24:1–12 highlighted the empty tomb; 24:13–35 presented an
appearance by Jesus and stressed how Scripture prophesied the resurrection.

---

1. This account is unique to Luke, though it has a few points of contact with John
20:19–23.

The present passage reveals Jesus' post-resurrection commission to his disciples to go to all nations. It also gives further evidence, through his partaking of a meal and his invitation to the disciples to touch him, that his appearance is no mere apparition. Any Gnostic-like ideas that Jesus merely appeared to have a raised body are ruled out by this text. Thus it has both instructional and apologetic value.

The scene is an extension of the previous passage, where the reporting over Jesus' various appearances continues. The momentum of his appearances is stacking up, as one meeting follows another in rapid succession. As the disciples are sharing reports, Jesus himself stands among them and gives a beatitude that sums up his ministry in triumph, "Peace be with you." It is a greeting of comfort. God's blessing is invoked on their behalf, as the resurrection means the end of anxiety about Jesus' well-being and the continuation of God's plan (cf. Luke 2:14; Acts 10:36). The group is frightened by his appearance, since they think Jesus is a "spirit" (NIV "ghost"). They still have trouble getting used to the idea that he is risen and is appearing to his disciples.

Jesus asks the group why they are frightened (NIV "troubled") and why they have doubts in their hearts. The "heart" is the place for reflection in the ancient world, much like we use the term "mind" (which explains the NIV term here). Jesus' remarks suggest some are still doubting even after the appearances. So he invites them to look at and touch his hands and feet, where the evidence of his crucifixion remains.[2] As directly as he can say it, Jesus notes that a "spirit" (NIV "ghost") does not have flesh and bones as they see here. In other words, the resurrection possesses a physical element. As 1 Corinthians 15:35–49 argues, the resurrection body is both the same as and different from the physical body, retaining aspects of physicality while existing in a glorified condition. Jesus does everything he can to reassure his disciples that he is truly alive.

As he shows the disciples his hands and feet, they still struggle to believe it all. The remark about not believing may well be a rhetorical understatement indicating they can hardly believe it, since they are also filled with joy and amazement—attitudes that would not be present if they did not think that this was Jesus. They are almost paralyzed by the awareness that Jesus is really risen from the dead.

To drive the point home even further, Jesus asks for something to eat. Broiled fish is available, so he takes some and eats it. The meal indicates that Jesus is not a phantom, but has real being. Once again he reveals himself at a table as fellowship takes place over a meal.

---

2. It is this text and John 20:25 that suggest Jesus was nailed to a cross; see J. Schneider, "σταυρός," *TDNT*, 7:574–75.

Jesus now explains what has taken place. How can he be here like this? What have the cross and resurrection meant? "This is what I told you while I was still with you." He reminds them that he predicted what has taken place (9:22, 44; 17:25; 18:31–33; 22:37). A crucified and raised Messiah is not an adjustment in God's plan; this road was in the design all along (see v. 25). In fact, everything written about Jesus "in the Law of Moses, the Prophets and the Psalms" must be fulfilled.[3] Again the *dei* ("must") of divine design is mentioned. The disciples are experiencing what Scripture promised and what the saints of old longed to see (10:23–24; 1 Peter 1:10–12).

Jesus then instructs in the Scriptures. Note that the church has developed its understanding of the Old Testament from Jesus. His instruction regarding basic elements of divine promise is summarized by three verbs: "suffer," "rise," and "be preached" (all infinitives in Greek). Jesus' death and resurrection lead to an evangelistic commission for the disciples. All three of these stages are reflected in the Old Testament. The Christ, the Messiah, was to suffer (e.g., Pss. 22; 69; Isa. 52:13–53:12) and to be raised (e.g., Pss. 16:8–10; 110:1), and the disciples must now engage in preaching to the nations "repentance and forgiveness of sins," starting from Jerusalem (Luke sees texts like Isa. 40:3–5 and Amos 9:15 as fitting into this promise). Both the desired response ("repentance") and its effect ("forgiveness") are noted here.

Repentance as rooted in the Old Testament is an important concept, since the Hebrew concept of repentance involves a "turning." That is, to repent is to change direction from allegiance to idols to serving the living and true God (cf. 1 Thess. 1:9–10). This change of perspective embraces Jesus and produces the forgiveness he offers. This message of salvation extends to all the nations, though the disciples will take ten chapters of Acts before they see that "the nations" means more than Diaspora Jews. They must preach to every tribe and nation—a fact we take for granted today, but was revolutionary at the time, since religions had a stronger ethnic character to them.

The disciples have served as witnesses of the events surrounding Jesus. They saw him hang on the cross and have now seen his resurrected body. Their calling is to share that what they know has taken place according to the Scriptures (1 Cor. 15:1–5). Jesus will send them out, but not before he has equipped them. To this end he will send to them the Spirit from his Father, in an event described as being "clothed with power from on high" (see Acts 1:8; 2:1–11). The allusion here is to Joel's promise of the Spirit in the end time and to Jeremiah's promise of the coming of the Spirit as part of the

---

3. Moses, the Prophets, and the Psalms refer to the three mains parts of the Hebrew Bible. On fulfillment as a theme in Luke, see G. Delling, "πληρόω," *TDNT*, 6:295–96; G. Schrenk, "γράφω," 1:748.

new covenant. The Spirit is the one who enables us to witness and testify to Jesus effectively (Luke 12:11–12). As God's plan moves ahead, the disciples are a major part of its advance. But until the Spirit comes, they must remain in Jerusalem.

This Gospel closes with Jesus' taking the disciples out to Bethany, lifting up his hands, blessing them, and departing into heaven. The ascension is summarized here and detailed in Acts 1:9–11, linking Luke and Acts together.[4] Jesus blesses the disciples as he departs to continue his work from God's side. What follows for them are worship and joy. They return to the temple, where Luke's story began with Zechariah, in order to praise God for all that has take place. Luke never forgets that the heart of a believer's walk involves responding to God with joy.

Bridging Contexts

MOST OF THE issues related to bridging contexts have been taken up in the previous passages on resurrection. The resurrection is built on the realization of God's promise, which in turn reassures us about the rest of his promises. But three points remain. (1) Jesus takes this appearance as the occasion to issue a commission to the church to take the gospel to the world. Here is the type of open-ended commission whose outworking never stops. We are witnesses, however, in a different sense than these original disciples. They testified to what they saw, whereas we bear witness to their testimony and to our experience of the resurrected Jesus.

(2) The response to the gospel in terms of worship is another fundamental feature of this text. We tend to think of worship merely in terms of the offer of praise, but at its base worship involves a renewed attitude and openness toward God. The worship present in this text is not only offering praise to God, but also obeying what Jesus has commanded (vv. 49, 52). The transformation that comes with response to the gospel should refresh and renew our hearts so that we not only thank God with our lips but with our actions. The Gospel of Luke closes with disciples ready to obey the call of Jesus, and to do so with joy. Acts 4 shows them still doing so, and we should still emulate that thrill of mission today.

(3) The key to accomplishing that commission is the enabling work of God's Spirit. By his leading and power the message goes out, and rejection can be faced boldly (Acts 4:24–32). A quick look at Acts 2 shows how Peter himself is transformed from the timid figure of denial and failed nerve at

---

4. For a defense of this reading and linkage, see M. Parsons, *The Departure of Jesus in Luke-Acts*, (Sheffield: Sheffield Academic Press, 1987), 193–94, 196.

Jesus' trial to a preacher with fearless enthusiasm before an immense crowd at Pentecost. The contrast evidences the Spirit's transforming power at work.

THE COMMISSION IN Luke 24 calls us as a community to take the gospel to all nations. But how can we do that effectively? Each generation must begin that message and frame its basic content of forgiveness and relationship to God in terms the particular culture can comprehend. This type of bridging is important to effective communication of the gospel. Often someone within a given culture does a better job of communicating to an audience than someone outside the culture. They understand the culture's outworking and its metaphors so they can speak in a way people will appreciate.

In communicating cross-culturally, those able to relate the gospel well to the pictures of the culture are the most effective in making the gospel clear and relevant. I know that whenever I travel outside the United States, I always feel a little at a loss in terms of illustrations and communication, because many of the pictures I use in Texas are not appreciated or understood in Tübingen or Guatemala City. That does not mean I cannot share the gospel, but it does mean that I must often spend time asking about the host culture, its values, its heroes, the games they like to play, and other such elements of everyday life. I watch closely so that the message can be personalized in terms of the life people live.

Such variety in communication and sensitivity to a variety of audiences is reflected in the New Testament. Jesus communicated with examples from Palestinian agriculture because he was in a largely agrarian environment. But the speeches of Acts betray an approach to Gentiles that is different from the approach to Jews. Paul, for example, cited Greek poets or used terms of the Greek culture. This is not because the gospel itself differs for the Gentiles, but because different cultures require different images and techniques. Speeches to Jews could appeal to a long history of God's people and their hope of his promise. Speeches to Gentiles had to address God as the Creator or as a judge who establishes a new relationship with humanity. Metaphors about church appealed to body imagery, for the political imagery of the Greeks spoke of the city like an organism. As the church continues to take the gospel to the world, we must think through how to communicate its truth through pictures familiar to our audience.

This includes using illustrations in youth work that plug into their world— for example, sports or athletics. To be effective with business people requires speaking in their language. My church has developed an illustration control group for me, since I tend to love sports illustrations. Some women in our community have taken it upon themselves, whenever I teach a Bible study, to volunteer a "culturally equivalent" illustration when my communication gets one-sided in terms of gender. The move is a healthy reminder to me to think in terms of my total audience.

What all of this means is that prepackaged approaches to the gospel, though helpful to get us started being comfortable in sharing our faith, should not become our only means of sharing.[5] The Bible is full of rich metaphors for the faith. We should appreciate the variety of such terms as we share the gospel. As long as we call a person to embrace the grace of God in faith and not to trust in his or her own deeds for salvation, we are preaching the gospel. We can speak of *repenting* when considering where we start from at conversion. We can speak of *turning* to describe the change of direction that comes from embracing God. We can speak of *faith* in Christ to highlight the object of our hope. We can speak of *receiving him* to emphasize the personal appropriation of faith that is more than mental assent. We can speak of *coming to him* to describe the act from Jesus' perspective. We can talk of *confessing him* as an expression of how faith verbalizes its presence. All these terms highlight the saving act of faith where people embrace Jesus with a trust that he will forgive them by his grace and bring them into relationship with him.

Another issue raised by this text is Jesus' resurrection, because its presence proves that there is an afterlife (cf. 1 Cor. 15). This new life has a consciousness of reality, even though its form differs from life now. The bodily nature of the resurrection shows the continuity between who we are and what we will be. Death is not an end, but a transition. The critical question is, a transition into what? Will a person enter into eternal life or into a second, more permanent death? The choice for life involves a choice for Jesus. This entire Gospel has been about that choice and its benefits. Some of what I have said in these sections has repeated this theme over and over, but that is because Luke wants to make this point again and again.

It is a privilege to be witnesses to Jesus. In the technical sense, of course, a *witness* is someone who has seen the raised Jesus and knows about his earthly ministry. That is only true of those in the first century. In a secondary sense, however, we also know of the Lord's work in our lives and can share that testimony with others as we share the gospel that the disciples entrusted to the church. There is no greater commission or higher calling than to help others find the way to experience God's presence.

---

5. For details on this variety and this debate, see D. Bock, "Jesus as Lord in Acts and the Gospel Message," *BibSac* 143 (1986): 146–54.

Recently I was asked what I would do if I were witnessing and the people to whom I was speaking said they already had a relationship with God (because they had a church membership or some other external reason), but they did not know Jesus. How would I respond? Three points emerged in the ensuing discussion. (1) It is best to begin with careful listening. Christians are often quick to speak but slow to listen. In hearing a person share his or her spiritual journey, we get insight into his or her portrait of God and what that person expects of religious experience. Sometimes by listening to someone's struggle in the pursuit or nonpursuit of God, we can discern how to address him or her. (2) We can probe how confident an individual is of his or her relationship with God. Sometimes an opening for the gospel emerges in an expression of uncertainty (cf. Paul in Acts 17:23). (3) We can share the positive nature of our own experience, starting from when we were introduced to Jesus as the unique way to God.

I often hear people say they are afraid to witness because they are not sure what to say theologically. They do not feel capable of debating with their lost friends, or they do not always want to. But we do not need to learn a rash of theological terms or a ream of apologetics in order to be witnesses; we simply need to tell our story. An effective addition to many church services might be a weekly testimony, moderated by the pastor to prevent people from rambling or being afraid of saying something wrong. In this sharing of God's involvement in our lives, we get practice in verbalizing our testimony and hearing how God works in a variety of ways. God becomes visibly present to others. In order to share Christ effectively with those outside the church, it usually requires time to build relationships with them. That way, we get close enough to them for our testimony to have credibility. Our commission from God is an honor to participate in.

Lest we get too nervous about evangelism, let's remember that we do not share Jesus by ourselves. Jesus has provided his Spirit, who indwells us to help us make sense of our testimony. The disciples waited for the Spirit in order to be empowered and enabled to share with conviction. To see how effective the Spirit can be, we need only contrast the Peter of the three denials with the Peter of the speeches of Acts. The greatest obstacle to our own evangelism is our fear of others' reactions and of our own capability. But the Spirit works to help us share Jesus, while our fear of reactions is really an expression of uncertainty about resting in God's acceptance of us.

Luke's Gospel concludes with what can be called an open ending. The disciples return to await the enablement God will give so they can share Jesus with a needy world. Luke will follow this up with the account of the early history of the church as the disciples fulfill the commission God called them to have. Yet even at the end of Acts, the account of this commission is not over. Around the world the testimony to Jesus Christ goes out one message at a time. It can be shared by a missionary, by a preacher or evangelist, by a wife with a neighbor, by a business person with a colleague, by a teenager with a friend, by a father or mother with a precious son or daughter, or even by a child with a beloved parent or grandparent.

Witnessing can come in moments of joy or despair or even at death's door. The sharing can take place in English, Spanish, German, French, Russian, Korean, Chinese, Japanese, Swahili, or a whole host of other languages. Just contemplating the task and the process is testimony to the power of Jesus' resurrection to ring across the centuries with its message of hope and forgiveness. What other movement has been able to span the centuries and the variety of cultures that the Christian movement has touched? Where else can people of a wide variety of national backgrounds be woven together in a rich fellowship? Part of the gospel's power is surely seen in the success of the commission that was launched from the original apostles. What other movement began so obscurely and ended so comprehensively? God has surely been at work in the movement that began with an announcement at the temple and a birth at Bethlehem.

We have an opportunity to share in that march of faith throughout history. God is at work in it all, fulfilling what he promised centuries ago in some ancient Jewish writings. He is as present in our own sharing as he was in the commission Jesus issued to a small group of mostly Galilean followers in the first century. The march of faith moves one era at a time, one person at a time, one testimony at a time. Centuries ago, Luke wrote to reassure Theophilus that he belonged in that honored line of march. Fortunately for us, God made sure that Theophilus was not the only one to be reassured about his grace through Jesus.

Scripture Index